CORPORATE ORDERING

Corporate Ordering explains how modern corporations navigate social conflict when law is incomplete, politics are polarized, and shareholders disagree about corporate purpose. Drawing on original case studies from ridesharing, climate sustainability, and artificial intelligence companies, the book reveals the internal governance systems corporations use to set standards, justify decisions, and monitor their impact. Moving beyond the familiar debates between shareholder primacy and stakeholder capitalism, the book offers a clear framework for understanding how corporate power actually operates in practice. Written for scholars, practitioners, policymakers, and informed general readers, it provides a timely guide to corporate governance in a world where business decisions increasingly function as social policy.

Stavros Gadinis is the George R. Johnson Professor of Law at the University of California, Berkeley School of Law, where he also serves as Faculty Director of the Berkeley Center for Law and Business.

Corporate Ordering

HOW CORPORATIONS NAVIGATE SOCIAL CONFLICT

STAVROS GADINIS
University of California, Berkeley

CAMBRIDGE
UNIVERSITY PRESS

CAMBRIDGE
UNIVERSITY PRESS

Shaftesbury Road, Cambridge CB2 8EA, United Kingdom

One Liberty Plaza, 20th Floor, New York, NY 10006, USA

477 Williamstown Road, Port Melbourne, VIC 3207, Australia

314–321, 3rd Floor, Plot 3, Splendor Forum, Jasola District Centre, New Delhi – 110025, India

Cambridge University Press is part of Cambridge University Press & Assessment, a department of the University of Cambridge.

We share the University's mission to contribute to society through the pursuit of education, learning and research at the highest international levels of excellence.

www.cambridge.org
Information on this title: www.cambridge.org/9781009873734
DOI: 10.1017/9781009873741

When citing this work, please include a reference to the DOI 10.1017/9781009873741

First published 2026

Cover image: Crowd image: Katerina Sisperova / iStock / Getty Images Plus
Cityscape image: AF-studio / DigitalVision Vectors / Getty Images

A catalogue record for this publication is available from the British Library

A Cataloging-in-Publication data record for this book is available from the Library of Congress

ISBN 978-1-009-87375-8 Hardback
ISBN 978-1-009-87373-4 Paperback

For Katerina, Athena, and Thomas

In memory of my father, Thomas S. Gadinis

Contents

Acknowledgments *page* ix

Introduction 1

1 The Social Impact Challenge 19

2 Governance Gap 55

3 Corporate Ordering for Social Conflicts 95

4 Why Not Regulate? 129

5 Corporate Ordering: Past and Present 160

6 Safety in the Rideshare Industry 191

7 A Corporate Framework for Sustainability 224

8 How to Govern AI? 257

9 A New Fiduciary Standard 299

Conclusion: Reason and Authority 319

Notes 333

Index 411

Acknowledgments

The genesis of this book owes much to an impromptu two-hour conversation on a rainy afternoon in Oxford. Sitting in John Armour's office, we talked about what the emerging heterogeneity of shareholder preferences might mean for the foundations of corporate law. We found ourselves asking how corporate leadership could forge ahead in a world in which the nominal owners of the firm no longer agree on the direction of the enterprise. That conversation captured a broader tension I had been encountering across my work, one that did not fit neatly within existing paradigms.

For most of my academic career, my work moved along two lines. One examined regulation, including competition among regulators, soft law, cross-national influence, standards, enforcement, and regulatory independence. The other focused on corporate governance, including compliance decisions, risk management systems, disclosure regimes, and internal organizational processes. Legal scholarship typically treats these domains as distinct, one governed by public law and public authority and the other by private initiative.

This book grew out of a deepening sense that this division was incomplete. Although scholars have long noted the porous boundary between regulation and corporate governance, corporations continued to appear primarily as objects of regulation rather than as actors that shape rules, standards, and expectations across entire domains. Over time, it became increasingly clear that corporations understand their own influence and have developed internal governance frameworks to confront challenges familiar to any rule maker or rule keeper, public or private.

This book emerged from conversations across several communities that do not always share a common vocabulary. Scholars of regulation and administrative law helped me think more clearly about institutional design, enforcement, and the conditions under which authority takes hold. Corporate law and governance scholars sharpened my sense of how firms make decisions, build compliance systems, and translate legal risk into organizational practice. Work on transnational governance and standards supplied a set of tools for understanding how norms move across jurisdictions and gain force outside conventional public law channels. A fourth community shaped the project in a different way. Through my work as Faculty

Director of the Berkeley Center for Law and Business, I had the privilege of sustained engagement with practitioners who think about these problems with urgency and realism. Taken together, those conversations repeatedly reminded me that the interests, constraints, and trade-offs facing corporations, their management teams, and their lawyers are often more complex than the stylized accounts that dominate the scholarly debate.

Several people played an outsized role in shaping the core ideas and structure of this book. Bobby Bartlett encouraged me to trust practitioners and to write a book they would recognize and engage with, even when doing so meant departing from familiar corporate law paradigms. John Armour persuaded me that reimagining how corporations respond to the growing heterogeneity of shareholder preferences was not only viable but also worth pursuing as a central theoretical project. Amelia Miazad was a constant co-adventurer as we explored how corporations confront social challenges amid a rapidly evolving legal and regulatory landscape. Chris Havasy trained my thinking in political theory, helping me connect contemporary developments to foundational questions about lawmaking and institutional authority. Sharon Jacobs brought discipline and coherence to the project, pushing me to impose a common structure on the case studies so that the unity of the theory would remain visible across diverse subject matters. Howell Jackson, who shaped my thinking early on as my dissertation mentor, urged me to include a historical chapter, reminding me that the role this book describes is not new but one that corporations have played before.

Bobby Bartlett, Ofer Eldar, Dorothy Lund, Chris Havasy, and Amelia Miazad read early drafts of the theory chapters and helped me reframe the argument at a formative stage. Earlier versions of the project benefited from comments and discussion in workshops and conferences where individual chapters were read and debated. I am grateful to Afra Afsharipour, Adam Badawi, Brian Feinstein, Jill Fisch, Brian Galle, George Georgiev, Jeffrey Gordon, Jon Gould, Sarah Haan, Sharon Jacobs, Elizabeth Pollman, Gabe Rauterberg, and David Zaring for engaging with early drafts and pushing the argument in directions I would not have reached on my own. Their questions, disagreements, and collective thinking shaped the project in ways both large and small.

Portions of this book, and earlier versions of its arguments, were presented at workshops and conferences where I benefited from thoughtful engagement and critique. My thanks go to audiences at Wharton, Berkeley, the University of Minnesota, the University of Athens, Greece, and the 2023 Annual Meeting of the Association of American Law Schools for their questions and comments, which helped refine the project at key stages.

I am also deeply grateful to the Berkeley Center for Law and Business, which provided an institutional home for many of the conversations that shaped this book. In particular, I thank Angeli Patel, Executive Director of the Center, and the staff members Delia Violante, Lenique Frazier, and Kuhu Mathur for their support in organizing workshops and for curating a community of academics, legal practitioners, and industry representatives. Without that sustained institutional effort and the conversations it enabled, this book would not have been possible.

My gratitude extends to Silvia Fregoni, the Berkeley Center for Law and Business Research Fellow, for her invaluable assistance with coordination and task management throughout the life of this project. I also thank my research assistants, Peter Coe, Tim Zhao, Yunfei Qiang, Alexandra Sasse, Mahwish Moazzam, Arman Ramezani, Isabel Barney, and James Bonnano, for their careful work on background research, source collection, and fact checking, which supported both the theoretical framework and the case studies.

Several chapters of this book draw on interviews and conversations with practitioners who generously shared their time and experience. For the rideshare case study, I am grateful to Tony West, Kristin Sverchek, and Kate Sampson. For the sustainability case study, I thank Suz MacCormack and Ryan Hart. For the chapter on artificial intelligence, my thanks go to Che Chang, Tom Lue, Jonathan Palmer, and Daniel Kluttz. Their candor and willingness to engage made these case studies possible. The interpretations and conclusions drawn from these conversations are mine alone.

I am grateful to Matt Gallaway at Cambridge University Press for supporting this project and bringing it to publication. My thanks also go to two anonymous peer reviewers whose careful reading and thoughtful comments strengthened the manuscript.

Above all, I thank my wife, Katerina Linos, for her constant encouragement and for her patience through countless dinner conversations about corporations and democracy. I am also grateful to my daughter, Athena Gadini, and my son, Thomas Gadinis, for their joy, curiosity, and perspective, which grounded this project in ways no scholarship ever could.

Introduction

In late 2023, Meta's content moderation teams faced an impossible decision. As conflict erupted in Israel and Gaza, millions of posts flooded the platform: videos of violence, claims and counterclaims about atrocities, calls for solidarity, expressions of grief and rage. Engineers and policy specialists worked around the clock to decide what content to remove, what to label, what to amplify, what to suppress.[1] These decisions were presented as technical implementations of "community standards" and algorithmic optimization. But they were simultaneously governance decisions about acceptable speech, affecting hundreds of millions of people across vastly different cultural and political contexts.[2]

The choices Meta faced could not be neatly categorized as either business decisions or social interventions.[3] The platform could prioritize free expression to maintain its value proposition as an open forum, or prioritize safety to protect vulnerable users and maintain advertiser relationships. It could apply uniform global standards or adapt to regional sensitivities. It could optimize for user engagement or minimize social conflict. Each choice reflected not just technical judgments but fundamental value commitments about speech, safety, and the platform's role in democratic discourse. More importantly, Meta's shareholders offered no consensus.[4] Some institutional investors demanded aggressive content moderation to protect brand value and reduce regulatory risk.[5] Others viewed heavy-handed moderation as political censorship that would alienate users and invite government intervention.[6] Civil libertarian funds argued that platform health depended on minimal restrictions.[7] Tech employees, many holding substantial stock, pressed for stronger protections for vulnerable communities. Each position could be defended as serving shareholder value, but they prescribed incompatible operational choices.

Six months later, on December 4, 2024, Brian Thompson, CEO of UnitedHealthcare, was murdered outside a Manhattan hotel.[8] The killing sparked an outpouring of public fury not primarily at the murderer, but at the healthcare system Thompson represented.[9] Social media filled with stories of denied claims, delayed treatments, and financial devastation. At the center of the controversy was UnitedHealthcare's sophisticated algorithmic claims processing system.

The company had developed automated protocols to review millions of claims efficiently: standardized medical necessity criteria, automated flags for expensive treatments, decision algorithms that could process requests in seconds rather than days. This system was designed as an operational efficiency tool. UnitedHealthcare could not manually review every claim while maintaining competitive pricing and processing speed. But the same system that enabled business efficiency simultaneously functioned as healthcare governance, determining which patients received care, which treatments were covered, and which physicians' decisions were honored.

The nature of this decision defies simple categorization. The algorithm integrates business logic concerning cost containment, risk management, and competitive positioning with medical judgments about appropriate care, clinical necessity, and acceptable trade-offs between expense and outcomes. UnitedHealthcare's shareholders reflected this complexity.[10] Traditional healthcare investors viewed aggressive claims review as essential cost discipline and fiduciary responsibility. Risk-focused institutional investors saw high denial rates as reputational and regulatory exposure that threatened long-term profitability. ESG investors framed denial rates through a patient welfare lens, arguing that companies ignoring stakeholder concerns lose their social license to operate. Public pension funds faced competing pressures from beneficiaries who were simultaneously investors seeking returns and healthcare consumers seeking coverage. Each group could articulate a business case for their preferred approach. None could claim exclusive correctness.

What links these two examples is not an exceptional crisis or unusual strain. It is the fact that business decisions now routinely operate as social policy at scale. For decades, corporate governance operated on a foundational assumption that business decisions and social considerations occupied distinct spheres manageable through separate processes. Companies made operational choices to maximize efficiency and profitability, while social outcomes such as environmental impacts, labor conditions, and community effects were treated as externalities to be addressed through government regulation or separate corporate social responsibility programs.[11] Managers focused on organizing production, optimizing operations, and delivering returns to shareholders, while governments and civil society addressed broader social challenges through specialized institutions. This division of labor seemed both rational and efficient.

This traditional boundary now seems uncharacteristically porous. Corporate decisions that appear purely operational generate intense social and political controversy with remarkable consistency. Content moderation algorithms, claims processing protocols, supply chain management systems, and workplace monitoring technologies all provoke sustained public debate. The business press chronicles this transformation daily, but the underlying dynamic remains poorly understood. The conventional response treats these controversies as anomalies: temporary disruptions caused by polarized politics, social media amplification, or activist overreach.

From this perspective, companies should simply maintain clearer boundaries, focus on core business operations, and avoid unnecessary social entanglements.[12]

This response fundamentally misdiagnoses the problem. These incidents are not aberrations but inevitable consequences of how modern corporations operate. The very mechanisms that enable extraordinary corporate efficiency have inadvertently dissolved the boundaries that once contained corporate influence within traditional commercial spheres. When Meta's engagement optimization shapes global discourse, when UnitedHealthcare's algorithms determine healthcare access for millions, when Amazon's warehouse protocols establish working conditions across entire industries, these companies are not straying from their business focus. They are executing it with ever greater precision. The social consequences are not unfortunate externalities but predictable outcomes of systems designed to maximize efficiency at scale.

I.1 WHAT THIS BOOK IS ABOUT

This book argues that corporations have developed an entirely new governance framework to navigate this terrain. When operational decisions function simultaneously as business strategy and social policy, traditional decision-making processes simply collapse. Companies cannot defer to shareholder primacy when shareholders hold incompatible views. They cannot balance stakeholder interests when those interests conflict and the law provides no weighting principle. They cannot avoid politics when nearly every significant choice can be characterized as political.

Leading corporations have responded by creating what this book calls corporate ordering: systematic processes for making choices that are often rule-like in character, affect millions of people, and require justification that assertions of business necessity cannot provide. This is not corporate social responsibility rebranded.[13] It concerns key business decisions typically central to the company's business model. It is governance infrastructure built from consultation mechanisms for setting standards, disclosure practices that discipline executive decisions, and independent monitoring systems that verify implementation.

This book documents how corporate ordering actually operates in practice. Chapters 1 and 2 explore the challenge of interlocking business and social considerations, as well as the lack of corporate law guidance. Chapter 3 articulates the theoretical framework in detail, showing how companies use specialized governance tools across three interconnected domains to translate abstract disagreements into concrete operational choices. Chapters 6–8 trace this process across three substantive areas with radically different characteristics: ridesharing safety, climate sustainability, and artificial intelligence governance. The demonstration that the same governance infrastructure works across fundamentally different domains reveals that corporate ordering responds to universal functions rather than domain-specific characteristics. Chapter 9 proposes legal reforms that would make corporate ordering not merely voluntary best practice but a requirement of fiduciary duty.

Understanding why corporate ordering has become necessary requires examining the condition that most clearly reveals the inadequacy of traditional frameworks: the fragmentation of shareholder preferences into irreconcilable camps. The assumption that shareholders speak with one voice, or that their interests can be aggregated into a single mandate to maximize value, has collapsed under the weight of actual investor diversity. What was once healthy pluralism about tactics and timeframes has become fundamental conflict about the entire corporate mission.

I.1.1 *The Turmoil of Heterogeneous Shareholder Preferences*

The landscape of modern capital markets has fractured into competing camps with irreconcilable visions of corporate success. This is not a temporary phenomenon driven by political polarization that will subside. It reflects fundamental transformations in how capital is managed, how investors understand their choices, and how global markets operate across radically different regulatory and cultural environments.

On one side, values-driven institutional investors have emerged as a powerful force. The Norwegian Sovereign Wealth Fund manages $1.7 trillion with explicit ethical guidelines excluding weapons, tobacco, environmental damage, and human rights violations.[14] Major public pension funds such as CalPERS, impact funds, and ESG-focused asset managers now control over $30 trillion globally.[15] These investors view climate risk as financial risk requiring mitigation, social license to operate as a business asset requiring cultivation, and stakeholder welfare as affecting long-term sustainability. They demand that Meta improve content moderation even if changes reduce engagement, that healthcare companies provide transparency about denial rates even if disclosure increases costs, and that AI companies conduct extensive safety testing even when delays risk competitive disadvantage.

On the other side, an increasingly organized anti-ESG movement has emerged with comparable conviction and growing political power.[16] State pension funds from Texas, Florida, West Virginia, and Louisiana have enacted policies divesting from financial institutions that restrict fossil fuel financing or incorporate climate considerations.[17] These funds, managing over $500 billion collectively, argue that ESG considerations harm returns and represent political activism rather than prudent investment. Republican state treasurers have organized to pressure financial institutions, threatening to withdraw billions in state deposits from banks considering climate risk in lending decisions.[18] Major financial institutions including BlackRock have moderated climate commitments in response to this pressure.[19]

The conflict extends beyond rhetoric into legal battles, political campaigns, and proxy fights over corporate direction. Republican attorneys general investigate asset managers for ESG practices they claim violate antitrust law.[20] Democratic attorneys general counter with investigations of fossil fuel companies for climate deception.[21] Proxy votes on climate resolutions have become flashpoints, with management caught between investors demanding aggressive action and investors threatening to oppose directors who support climate commitments.[22]

This turmoil extends globally, creating divergent regulatory paths that complicate decisions for any company operating internationally. The European Union has adopted mandatory sustainability reporting, climate disclosure rules, and supply chain due diligence obligations that effectively require ESG integration.[23] Meanwhile, regulatory developments in the United States have stalled or reversed. The SEC abandoned proposed climate disclosure rules.[24] Federal agencies under Republican leadership signal hostility to ESG integration. State-level fragmentation has accelerated, with blue states mandating sustainability disclosure and red states prohibiting climate considerations in pension investment.[25] Companies operating globally must navigate EU requirements demanding climate integration while facing U.S. state laws prohibiting the same practices.

This heterogeneity makes shareholder primacy incoherent and unworkable as a decision-making framework. Boards cannot be maximizing shareholder value when shareholders disagree fundamentally about what value means. The Norwegian fund wants Meta to prioritize user welfare; the Texas pension fund opposes content moderation as political censorship. Both claim to represent shareholder value. The principle itself becomes indeterminate. This heterogeneity is not temporary but reflects permanent features of modern capital markets: global capital flows, diverse investor types, values integration into investment strategies, and decisions involving trade-offs between considerations that financial analysis alone cannot resolve.

I.1.2 *Why Traditional Responses Fail*

For all its current force, the challenge of navigating social dimensions in business decisions is not new. It is not the first time that corporations faced choices where operational efficiency, stakeholder welfare, and social impacts intersect. But for decades, corporate law offered decision-making frameworks that most constituencies could accept. Today, those same frameworks prove inadequate, not because they were poorly designed but because the conditions that made them functional no longer appear justified.

The shareholder primacy doctrine provided the dominant framework, declaring that corporations should maximize profits for shareholders provided they do not violate the law.[26] This principle, most forcefully articulated in Milton Friedman's famous 1970 essay, offered both moral clarity and operational guidance.[27] The law, reflecting democratic choices about mandatory social protections, established floors below which corporate conduct could not fall. Within those legal constraints, managers enjoyed broad discretion to pursue profit maximization. If society wanted corporations to address particular social concerns, the appropriate mechanism was legislation or regulation establishing new requirements, not managerial discretion to pursue social objectives at shareholder expense.

But if one thing has become clear since the 1970s, it is that legislators and regulators typically find themselves at least one step behind companies, if not several miles. Companies face decisions about content moderation, AI safety protocols, and algorithmic bias years before legal frameworks exist. Even when law provides general standards such as nondiscrimination or reasonable care, operationalizing these principles into concrete technical choices requires judgments that law alone cannot resolve. The principle of maximizing profits within legal constraints provides no guidance when shareholders disagree about what maximizes profits and when law is silent about constraints.

Stakeholder theory emerged as an alternative, rejecting shareholder exclusivity and embracing corporate responsibility to multiple constituencies, including employees, customers, communities, and the environment.[28] The Business Roundtable's 2019 statement endorsing stakeholder capitalism,[29] benefit corporation statutes, and the ESG investment movement all embody this approach.[30] Stakeholder theory correctly identifies that corporate decisions affect multiple parties and that a narrow focus on shareholder returns alone produces inadequate outcomes.

The framework fails, however, as a decision-making procedure. When stakeholder interests conflict, and they routinely do, stakeholder theory provides no method for balancing competing claims. AI safety decisions affect investors wanting returns, researchers wanting responsible development, users wanting functionality, and society wanting protection from catastrophic risks. How should these interests be weighted? The framework directs boards to consider all of them but offers no principle for determining priorities. Different stakeholders within putative categories have different preferences. Not all users want the same content moderation policies. Not all employees want the same labor practices. Not all community members want the same environmental standards. Stakeholder theory assumes stakeholder interests are knowable and representable, but actual stakeholder populations are heterogeneous and lack clear mechanisms for preference aggregation. The injunction to balance stakeholder interests describes the problem rather than providing a solution.

With neither shareholder nor stakeholder theories offering any concrete guidance, many urge companies to simply stay out of politics and focus on business. This assumes a stable boundary between business and politics that has collapsed. Whether climate risk management constitutes politics or prudential business judgment is itself contested. Whether content moderation represents political censorship or operational necessity divides reasonable observers. In the current environment, nearly any significant operational choice can be characterized as political by some constituency.[31]

These responses share a common failure. They assume conditions that no longer hold: unified shareholder preferences, comprehensive legal guidance, stable boundaries between business and social spheres, and stakeholder interests that can be identified and balanced. The frameworks are not theoretically incoherent. They simply do not map onto the decision-making environment corporations actually face. Corporate ordering responds to actual complexity by developing processes that can navigate heterogeneity, legal uncertainty, and collapsed boundaries. It does not solve the problem by eliminating complexity but by creating institutional capacity to manage it systematically.

I.1.3 *Corporate Ordering as Response*

Corporate ordering arises because companies face decisions that no traditional framework can readily resolve.[32] It is not a moral ambition but a practical response. When shareholders hold incompatible visions, when business and social dimensions are inseparable, and when law offers little guidance, traditional frameworks simply do not work. Companies need decision-making processes that can address complexity rather than assume it away.

The core mechanism of corporate ordering involves translating heterogeneous abstract preferences into concrete operational decisions through structured deliberation. Companies do not attempt to resolve fundamental disagreements or achieve consensus on values. Instead, they operationalize disagreements by engaging them in specific contexts where theoretical positions must yield to practical choices.

Consider the abstract question of whether companies should address climate change. Climate-focused investors answer yes emphatically, viewing climate risk as material financial risk requiring aggressive mitigation.[33] Climate-skeptical investors answer no, viewing climate considerations as political activism that diverts resources and invites regulatory overreach. The abstract debate is irresolvable. The positions reflect different factual beliefs about climate science, different value judgments about intergenerational trade-offs, different assessments of regulatory probability, and different tolerance for long-term systemic risk. No amount of discussion will produce agreement.

Corporate ordering shifts the focus to concrete operational questions. What are the costs and benefits of different emission reduction pathways? Which technologies are available at what price points? What regulatory risks attach to different approaches? How do various strategies affect competitive position relative to rivals pursuing different strategies? What are the implications for different business units? How do physical climate risks affect assets in different geographic locations? These concrete questions allow companies to make operational choices that address some concerns of climate-focused investors by reducing long-term physical risk and regulatory exposure while addressing some concerns of cost-conscious investors by maintaining competitive positioning and demonstrable returns.

In all likelihood, neither group gets everything it wants. Climate-focused investors may view emission targets as insufficiently ambitious. Cost-conscious investors may view any climate expenditure as wasteful. But both can recognize the operational choices as responsive to their concerns within constraints that the other group's preferences create. The deliberative process makes trade-offs visible, connects choices to evidence, and provides reasons that both groups can understand even when they disagree with conclusions.

The artificial intelligence example follows the same pattern. The abstract question of whether AI safety or innovation speed should take priority yields irreconcilable positions. Acceleration advocates view extensive safety protocols as excessive caution that guarantees losing to less cautious competitors and stifles innovation that could benefit millions.[34] Safety advocates view rapid deployment as enabling catastrophic risks and representing irresponsible development that could cause irreversible harm. The theoretical debate goes nowhere.

Corporate ordering engages concrete operational questions. What testing protocols must systems satisfy before deployment? What deployment guardrails limit high-risk applications while enabling beneficial uses? What monitoring systems track performance and identify problems requiring adjustment? What transparency enables external evaluation of safety practices? What revision mechanisms ensure continuous learning from real-world performance? What organizational structures give safety teams genuine authority over launch decisions? These concrete questions allow companies to make specific choices that give partial weight to competing values in operational contexts.

Acceleration advocates may get faster deployment timelines than safety advocates prefer, but they also accept testing requirements and monitoring systems that safety advocates demanded. Safety advocates may get stronger protections for high-risk applications than acceleration advocates prefer, but they also accept deployment schedules and commercial considerations that acceleration advocates insisted upon. The specific operational choices will not satisfy anyone fully, but they engage the underlying concerns in ways that abstract principles cannot.

The distinctive feature of corporate ordering is that it finds a way through the conflict, not by resolving disagreements, but by charting a workable path. The goal is transformation into workable decisions: converting abstract disputes about values into concrete choices about implementation, monitoring, adjustment, and transparency. Incompatible positions find partial expression through specific design features, with each constituency seeing some of its concerns reflected in final outcomes even when no one gets everything they want.

I.1.4 *The New Frontier of Corporate Governance*

The history of corporate governance shows that major reforms were often prompted by widespread crises exposing fundamental inadequacies in how boards oversee corporate conduct.[35] Typically, a wave of crises in multiple companies reveals structural failures, and reformers respond by creating new institutional capacity where existing frameworks proved insufficient.

Board independence emerged from the business collapses and governance scandals of the 1970s. The Penn Central bankruptcy revealed how poor information flow and ineffective oversight left the board unable to challenge management's decisions.[36] Watergate-era revelations of corporate bribery showed directors failing to prevent illegal conduct because they were too closely tied to management to question or constrain it. The underlying problem was structural: boards dominated by insiders could not effectively supervise the managers they were supposed to monitor. The solution was architectural. Outside directors with no management ties, separate committee structures, and enhanced oversight authority boosted institutional capacity for supervision.

Audit committee independence and internal control systems emerged from the accounting scandals and financial frauds of the early 2000s.[37] Enron, WorldCom, and similar collapses revealed that boards lacked systematic information about financial integrity separate from management assurances.[38] They discovered earnings manipulation, off-balance-sheet liabilities, and fraudulent reporting after the fact, when companies collapsed and shareholders lost billions. The solution was again architectural. Sarbanes-Oxley mandated independent audit committees with direct relationships to external auditors, required management certification of internal controls, and established systematic processes for financial monitoring.[39] The reform created information channels and verification mechanisms enabling boards to assess financial integrity independently.

Corporate ordering represents a similar inflection point, responding to a fundamentally different type of crisis. Corporations now face sustained challenges over social impacts where existing governance structures provide inadequate capacity for decision-making. These crises reveal a new deficit: boards and management lack systematic processes for navigating decisions where business operations function simultaneously as social policy, where shareholders hold incompatible preferences about what companies should optimize for, and where stakeholder concerns cannot be dismissed.

The challenge is architecturally parallel to earlier reforms but addresses a different inadequacy. Director independence created monitoring capacity. Audit committee independence created verification capacity. Corporate ordering must create engagement capacity: the ability to listen systematically to diverse constituencies, understand how operational choices function as social policy, and negotiate among competing legitimate concerns that cannot all be satisfied simultaneously.

Corporate ordering provides this architecture by establishing new institutional tools tied to the underlying features of the choice a company may be facing. When companies need to adopt rule-like practices that apply broadly and uniformly, they build consultation structures that reach widely for expert input, incorporate diverse perspectives, and receive systematic feedback before codifying standards. When executives face decisions with far-reaching implications, they utilize disclosure to connect with affected constituencies, inform them about the scope of impacts transparently, and negotiate solutions. When companies review how their operations align with principles they have adopted, they establish monitoring and evaluation teams as independent from management as feasible, supplemented when necessary by external validation and investigation. Together, these governance tools create institutional capacity for understanding social dimensions of business decisions comparable to what board independence created for management oversight and what audit independence created for financial integrity.

This represents the frontier of corporate governance because it recognizes that the realm of board oversight must expand into new terrain. Director and audit independence remain essential, but they were designed to address different challenges. The question now is whether companies can develop governance infrastructure adequate to the social dimensions of their operations with the same systematic rigor they brought to management oversight and financial integrity.

Corporate ordering is the next step in this architectural evolution. It is not a peripheral addition to governance, nor a rhetorical gesture toward social responsibility. It is the systematic extension of corporate deliberation into domains where operational choices function as public governance. The question is no longer whether companies should engage these issues. They already do. The task now is to build the institutional structures that make such engagement disciplined, transparent, and accountable.

The remainder of this book develops this argument systematically, showing how corporate ordering operates in practice, why it has become necessary, and what legal reforms would make deliberative quality not merely voluntary best practice but a requirement of corporate law.

I.1.5 *The Corporate Ordering Architecture*

Conventional corporate governance thinking treats social issues as if they are all alike, addressable under the umbrella of the business judgment rule through general mandates to consider shareholder or stakeholder interests.[40] Corporate ordering begins from the opposite premise. It recognizes that social challenges come in fundamentally different forms, each requiring a distinct type of governance response. Some require setting standards before countless applications arise. Others involve specific high-stakes decisions made under time pressure. Still others require ongoing monitoring to ensure that practice aligns with principle. The tripartite framework of rulemaking, executive decision-making, and review matches institutional tools to these functional challenges, just as earlier governance reforms matched structures to the problems they were designed to solve.

The rulemaking challenge arises when companies must establish standards that will guide innumerable future decisions before those situations materialize.[41] Content moderation policies, AI safety protocols, supply chain requirements, and climate commitments all require foresight: anticipating how standards will operate across varied contexts, what trade-offs they entail, and what consequences they may generate once implementation begins. Addressing this challenge requires consultative mechanisms that prioritize breadth over speed. Multi-stakeholder initiatives, expert consultations, and systematic stakeholder engagement bring in knowledge that generalist managers cannot generate internally.[42] Board committees may ultimately codify the resulting standards, but the critical governance work lies in the processes that surface diverse knowledge before rules are set. These tools expand the epistemic base and reveal friction points early, allowing companies to build standards that can withstand both operational and social scrutiny.

The executive decision-making challenge concerns the innumerable choices that keep companies functioning.[43] Executives make millions of decisions that implement values in specific contexts, ranging from whether to remove a particular piece of content to how to classify a worker or price a service in a new market. Broad consultation for each decision is impossible, yet their aggregate effect constitutes the company's operational reality. To ensure that these decisions reflect adequate consideration of their social dimensions, companies rely on disclosure mechanisms that create accountability through visibility. Public explanations of reasoning, impact assessments, and transparency about trade-offs serve two functions at once. Externally, they enable stakeholders to evaluate whether decisions engaged their concerns. Internally, the prospect of disclosure disciplines deliberation before decisions are made. Executives cannot explain what they have not considered or disclose impacts they have not measured. Transparency thus becomes a governance tool that shapes decision-making in real time.

The review challenge involves verifying that operations align with principles and standards a company has adopted. Standards set in rulemaking and decisions made by executives can drift as circumstances evolve or incentives change. Yet line management has structural incentives to minimize problems, suppress bad news, and avoid escalation. Effective review therefore requires independence from the operational chain of command. Dedicated monitoring teams with separate reporting lines, protected resources, and authority to escalate concerns allow companies to identify gaps between aspiration and practice. When credibility demands it, external auditors, investigators, or expert panels supplement internal monitoring.[44] Systematic review processes ensure that evaluation is ongoing rather than crisis-driven, enabling companies to identify divergence early rather than after harm has occurred.

Together, these three functions and their corresponding mechanisms create institutional capacity for the social dimensions of business decisions. No single mechanism addresses all three functions adequately. Companies need the full architecture to navigate social complexity systematically: consultation to establish sound standards, disclosure to discipline urgent choices, and independent monitoring to verify implementation. This is what makes corporate ordering a governance innovation comparable to earlier reforms rather than merely voluntary best practices. It extends systematic deliberative capacity into domains where business decisions inevitably shape social outcomes and where traditional frameworks provide no adequate procedures.

I.2 HOW THE BOOK PROCEEDS

I.2.1 *Chapter Overview*

The remaining chapters develop this argument through systematic analysis combining theoretical articulation, case studies, and legal reform proposals. Chapters 1 and 2 establish the problem. Chapter 1 identifies structural forces that push corporate choices more squarely into the domain of social concerns. It shows that the drive for efficiency at scale, the forced transparency of the digital age, and the heterogeneity of shareholder preferences affect multiple industries and are permanent features rather than temporary anomalies. Chapter 2 analyzes how corporate law doctrine creates a governance gap. The business judgment rule offers broad discretion but very little guidance when decisions involve social dimensions that cannot be separated from operational choices.[45] Existing rules for monitoring and disclosure do not provide procedures for managing competing preferences or integrating social considerations into deliberation.

Chapter 3 provides full theoretical articulation of corporate ordering. It defines the concept precisely, showing how corporate ordering differs from regulation, contract, and traditional corporate hierarchy. It develops the tripartite framework of corporate rulemaking, executive decision-making, and monitoring in detail, explaining the distinct functions each serves and the specific tools that enable each function. The chapter provides theoretical foundations drawing from legal theory and political philosophy to ground the argument in broader scholarly traditions.

Chapter 4 addresses the most important objection: why not simply regulate rather than relying on corporate ordering? The chapter explains why companies often act before regulation appears and why public regulators frequently adopt templates that companies first develop.[46] It proposes a diagnostic use of the tripartite framework. Strong adherence to the framework shows that self-regulation has real governance capacity. Weak adherence suggests that external intervention is necessary. The chapter examines timing problems, differences across jurisdictions, and the ways public and private authority can reinforce or limit each other.

Chapter 5 draws connections between modern instances of corporate ordering and historical instances of private initiative in lawmaking. The chapter examines two cases where private corporations took the lead in designing regulatory regimes that subsequently became mandatory: the development of driving codes and traffic regulations in the early twentieth century, and the evolution of corporate financial disclosure practices that culminated in the Securities Act of 1933.[47] By examining the governance processes around these rules, the chapter demonstrates how corporations have historically functioned as incubators of law.

Chapters 6–8 provide the main case study evidence, examining ridesharing safety, climate change, and artificial intelligence. These case studies follow a common analytical structure. Each begins by establishing the stakes and demonstrating how business imperatives and social concerns became inseparably intertwined. The chapters then explore the heterogeneity of preferences among shareholders and stakeholders, showing how different actors championed divergent solutions. This diversity of views necessitated the development of corporate ordering, as companies created comprehensive frameworks through deliberative processes involving rule-making, executive implementation, and monitoring functions. Finally, each case examines how regulators and legislators reacted to these private initiatives, revealing a pattern where corporate governance efforts often preceded and shaped subsequent public regulation.

Chapter 6 examines how the rideshare industry confronted public safety concerns that became inseparable from the promise of a new transportation model. The chapter traces how Lyft created an insurance framework that regulators later adopted as the legal structure for rideshare insurance across multiple states.[48] It also follows Uber's creation of a monitoring system that included continuous background checks, identity verification, and public safety reporting.[49] Although regulators initially clashed with Uber over its safety data practices, they eventually accepted its logic due to stakeholder consultation and support.[50] These examples show how practical operational problems and regulatory conflict pushed companies to create systems of rulemaking, executive practice, and monitoring that shaped later public policy.

Chapter 7 shows how climate change pushed companies into a domain where business survival and environmental responsibility became impossible to disentangle. The chapter describes how BP created the first comprehensive system for calculating emissions, which became the seed of the Greenhouse Gas Protocol,[51] and how Salesforce translated the Protocol into internal rules through automated carbon accounting systems and supplier obligations.[52] Regulators later embraced the Protocol's categories and methods, demonstrating how corporate innovations in rulemaking, executive action, and monitoring laid the foundation for emerging public disclosure regimes.

Chapter 8 turns to artificial intelligence, where innovation, commercial imperatives, and societal risk converge so tightly that firms must build governance systems even in the absence of regulatory guidance. Within this contested landscape, the chapter examines in detail how Microsoft and DeepMind constructed sophisticated systems of rulemaking, executive decision-making, and monitoring that operate as internal regulatory regimes.[53] These internal systems now serve as the foundation on which public oversight is being constructed. Rather than designing independent oversight regimes, policymakers in the EU and U.S. states build outward from the procedures companies have already created, formalizing the corporate ordering that first made AI governance possible.

Chapter 9 translates the insights from the case studies into a structured proposal for legal reform. It distills best practices that specify what sophisticated social deliberation looks like across rulemaking, executive action, and oversight, then asks whether these practices should be incorporated into fiduciary duty. The chapter argues that corporate law has historically absorbed new decision-making tools once they became necessary for informed judgment, and that the same logic now applies to social deliberation. Building on this foundation, the chapter formulates a workable fiduciary standard that requires boards to deliberate when credible evidence indicates significant social dimensions, evaluates whether governance structures provide capacity for inquiry and independent oversight, and treats breach as arising only when boards establish no such structures or when their process is cursory. This approach preserves business judgment deference while supplying the procedural discipline needed to make socially consequential discretion visible, reviewable, and accountable.

The Conclusion synthesizes the argument at three levels. Descriptively, it shows corporate ordering as a site of legal formation where regulatory frameworks increasingly originate in corporate deliberation before governments formalize them. Normatively, it argues that deliberative quality provides the best available mechanism for corporate decision-making affecting social outcomes when electoral authorization is unavailable and shareholder preferences are heterogeneous. Methodologically, it calls for legal scholarship that studies corporate governance processes to understand how contemporary societies actually govern themselves rather than treating corporate governance as peripheral to legal analysis.

I.2.2 *Analytical Strategy*

A central methodological choice of this book requires clear explanation. The analysis draws on three case studies that come from environments with almost nothing in common. Ridesharing safety involves transportation networks, local regulation, and platform operations. Climate sustainability involves environmental science, global markets, and energy systems. Artificial intelligence involves software engineering, safety research, and highly technical innovation. These domains differ in their technical foundations, their regulatory histories, their stakeholder communities, and the rhythms of their operational challenges.

The purpose of selecting such disparate contexts is to show that corporate ordering responds to functional pressures rather than to the particular industries or subject-matters. Whenever companies confront irreducible disagreement, business and social dimensions that cannot be separated, and uncertainty that forces them to reason without complete information, they tend to build the same kind of governance infrastructure. This infrastructure consists of rulemaking processes, pathways for executive decisions, and independent monitoring. It appears in every case even though the problems that trigger it look entirely different on the surface.

This methodological choice carries a tradeoff. All three case studies examine situations in which corporate ordering worked. The cases make visible the internal logic of the governance architecture, because the tools can be observed in action.

The book therefore does not include the many examples in which these tools failed to take hold or were never built. The Facebook Oversight Board illustrates the limitations.[54] It lacked the breadth of rulemaking, the authority to shape executive decisions, and the independence needed for credible review. It failed because the necessary architecture was never established.

The focus on successful examples is deliberate. The goal is to reveal the structure of corporate ordering and to identify the minimum conditions for its operation. Failures become understandable once the successes make the underlying architecture visible. The reader can then see missing elements in cases that did not work. The hope is that breadth of domain reveals more about the governance structure than a mixed set of outcomes drawn from a single industry. The tradeoff is real, but the gain is clarity about the architecture itself. This clarity provides the basis for analyzing failure in future work and for diagnosing missing components in real-world settings.

I.3 WHY THIS ARGUMENT MATTERS

The argument advanced in this book matters for everyone who studies, practices, regulates, invests in, or thinks about corporations. It begins by offering a way out of the narrow fight between shareholder primacy and stakeholder theory, a fight that reduces corporate law to questions about whose interests count more and whose incentives appear stronger. This book turns attention back to the field's central question, which is how fiduciary accountability is exercised through real decision-making. It shows that governance is not only a place where internal conflicts are managed, but a setting in which legal frameworks begin to form long before governments act. Once we see governance as a generator of norms rather than a battlefield of preferences, corporate law becomes an inquiry into deliberation, evidence, and institutional design.

This perspective broadens the work of scholars. Corporate law is often portrayed as a distinct domain defined by the conflict between managers and shareholders.[55] It can feel like a different world, animated by financial incentives and transactional expertise that seems far remote from the public sphere or the concerns of ordinary life. Yet, the real work of governance involves scientists and engineers, communities and workers, advocacy groups and global experts. Their participation shapes operational choices that ripple outward to influence environmental regulation, technology policy, labor standards, and speech governance. Recognizing this terrain means recognizing that corporate governance is often the seed from which later regulatory frameworks grow. This does not resolve the democratic gap that accompanies private decision-making.[56] Corporations have no electoral mandate and cannot supply the legitimacy of public institutions. But as long as their choices shape public outcomes, legal scholarship must examine how they reason and what structures discipline their judgment.

The framework also offers business leaders a path through uncertainty. Many significant decisions involve rulemaking, executive choices, and monitoring. The book identifies concrete tools for each of these functions and shows how they enlarge a company's capacity for thoughtful judgment. They do not neutralize economic incentives. They channel those incentives into reasoning that is intelligible and responsive to competing concerns. The scale of these systems varies across firms, yet the underlying functions remain accessible. Even small companies can adopt the habits of consultation, transparency, and independent review in forms suited to their resources. The case studies reveal both what strong systems make possible and what is lost when governance structures appear sturdy but lack authority.

For public officials, the framework provides a more careful way to assess corporate claims. The public often swings between the view that corporations are effective problem solvers and the view that they are driven by interests that make them unreliable stewards of public concerns.[57] Neither picture captures the full reality. The tripartite structure helps regulators distinguish when corporate practices generate knowledge that public institutions can build on and when information is curated in ways that require external checks. It clarifies where oversight is indispensable, where cooperation is possible, and how public and private authority can reinforce one another without blurring their responsibilities.

Investors gain a sharper lens as well. Traditional governance metrics reveal little about how companies deliberate. The tripartite framework directs attention to features that can be observed. Investors can look to whether rulemaking choices were informed by broad outreach and consultation, whether executive decisions are transparent and accurate, and whether monitoring takes place under effective safeguards for independence. These are visible markers of governance quality and provide practical criteria for evaluating how well companies navigate uncertainty.

The book also speaks to those who study political legitimacy. Corporate influence over public life cannot be ignored, yet corporate deliberation cannot substitute for democratic authorization.[58] The argument here does not claim it should. It shows how procedural discipline becomes the best available form of accountability when social outcomes depend on corporate choices that cannot be postponed until regulation arrives. At the same time, process has limits. It cannot guarantee correct outcomes or resolve conflicts rooted in divergent values. These limits mark the boundary where regulation must intervene. Corporate ordering supports democratic governance by creating clarity about what companies can do well and where public authority must take the lead.

If the argument succeeds, several shifts follow. Governance evaluation moves from a search for perfect outcomes to an examination of decision quality. Courts focus on whether companies maintain structures capable of inquiry and independent oversight rather than trying to arbitrate on substantive grounds. Regulators require transparency into how companies reason and how they generate information, recognizing that internal processes can clarify or obscure the truth. Governance reform strengthens the institutional capacity for deliberation rather than empowering particular constituencies or prescribing results that may not be achievable.

The deeper shift concerns how we understand corporations' social standing. Endless fights about whether corporations should prioritize climate action, stakeholder welfare, or shareholder returns reflect enduring disagreements in values. What can be improved is the quality of the decisions themselves. A focus on governance structure acknowledges pluralism and works within it. It replaces the search for a correct priority with a commitment to the institutional conditions that make judgment possible when knowledge is incomplete and preferences diverge. This is the promise of corporate ordering. It is not a cure for democratic deficits.[59] It is a way to understand how corporations exercise power, how that power can be structured responsibly, and how law can guide that structure as corporate decisions continue to shape public life.

I.4 CONCLUSION

The chapters ahead begin from a simple recognition. Corporate choices reach far beyond the boundaries once thought to contain them. Decisions that appear operational from the inside reverberate as public choices on the outside. The traditional vernacular of corporate law no longer captures what companies actually do, or what their choices now mean for the societies that surround them. This book's aim is neither to praise corporations nor to cast them as reluctant sovereigns, but to observe with clarity the simple fact that their internal deliberations shape public life before governments can respond. This reality unsettles the familiar lines between public and private, business and politics, strategy and responsibility. Yet it also opens space for a different way of understanding governance, one anchored less in verdicts about purpose and more in the quality of judgment exercised under conditions of disagreement and uncertainty.

If the modern corporation has become a place where social choices are made in real time, then its internal processes matter far beyond the interests of investors. They become part of a wider institutional landscape in which democratic governments, regulators, courts, and civil society must interpret and respond to private decisions that carry public consequences. Corporate ordering does not resolve the democratic gap that arises when unelected actors influence the shape of public life. But it can illuminate how those actors reason, how they hear the concerns of others, and how their structures can discipline power when no electoral mandate exists. Transparency of process becomes the emerging scaffolding of democratic accountability in a world where social consequences arrive faster than law can respond.

This book approaches that challenge by treating corporate governance as a site of reasoning rather than a vessel for ideology. It follows companies into the spaces where they build standards, weigh risks, confront disagreement, and revise judgments in real time. It examines how consultation, disclosure, and independent review function as tools for navigating conflicts that cannot be resolved through market logic or shareholder consensus. In platform governance, climate, and AI, the first draft of regulatory practice is already being written inside firms. Thus, this book invites scholars, policymakers, and investors to see corporations not only as market actors but also as institutions that generate norms, construct standards, and mediate conflicts in the public sphere.

The task in the pages that follow is therefore forward-looking. It is to map the institutional arrangements that allow corporations to exercise judgment with care when their decisions carry public weight. It is to clarify how public institutions might evaluate these arrangements, draw from them, or counterbalance them. And it is to offer a way of thinking about corporate power that neither glorifies its reach nor obscures its ramifications, but asks what forms of governance are necessary when disagreement is permanent and inaction is not an option.

1

The Social Impact Challenge

Corporate executives increasingly find themselves navigating a puzzle that traditional business frameworks struggle to solve. Target scales back diversity initiatives.[1] Bud Light partnered with a transgender influencer.[2] Tesla releases autopilot safety data. Google employees protest military contracts.[3] Are these business decisions or social interventions? The question itself reveals the inadequacy of conventional categories that have long governed corporate thinking.

For decades, corporate governance operated on a foundational assumption: Business decisions and social considerations occupied distinct spheres that could be managed separately. Companies made operational choices to maximize efficiency and profitability,[4] while social outcomes, such as environmental impacts, labor conditions, or community effects, were treated as externalities to be addressed through external regulation or separate corporate social responsibility programs.[5] This division of labor seemed both rational and efficient. Managers could focus on what they knew best and delivering returns to shareholders while governments, nonprofits, and civil society addressed broader social challenges through their own specialized institutions.

Yet this traditional boundary has eroded significantly. Corporate decisions that appear purely operational, from algorithm design to supply chain management to workplace policies and pricing strategies, now routinely generate intense social and political controversy. Companies find themselves at the center of debates about democratic governance, climate change, inequality, and cultural values, not by choice but seemingly by virtue of their scale and influence in modern economies. The business press chronicles this transformation daily, but the underlying dynamic remains poorly understood.

The conventional response treats these controversies as anomalies or temporary disruptions caused by polarized politics, social media amplification, or activist overreach. From this perspective, the solution involves better crisis management, more sophisticated public relations, or clearer boundaries between business operations and political engagement. Companies should simply focus on their core business while avoiding unnecessary social entanglements.

This chapter argues that such responses fundamentally misdiagnose the problem. These incidents are not aberrations but inevitable consequences of how modern corporations actually operate. The very mechanisms that enable extraordinary corporate efficiency – standardized operations across global markets, comprehensive data collection and monitoring, and complex shareholder relationships – have inadvertently dissolved the boundaries that once contained corporate influence within traditional commercial spheres. When UnitedHealthcare's algorithms deny insurance claims,[6] when Meta's engagement optimization amplifies divisive content,[7] and when Amazon's logistics networks reshape entire urban economies, these companies are not straying from their business focus. They are executing it with ruthless precision. The social consequences are not unfortunate side effects but predictable outcomes of systems designed to maximize efficiency. Attempts to restore traditional boundaries between business and society now conflict with the basic requirements of competitive strategy in the modern economy.

This chapter argues that three interconnected forces have transformed the relationship between business operations and social outcomes in ways that make traditional governance frameworks inadequate:

The drive for efficiency at scale: Modern corporations coordinate millions of employees, serve billions of customers, and manage supply chains spanning dozens of countries. To achieve efficiency at this scale, they rely on uniform standards and comprehensive monitoring systems that inevitably extend corporate influence far beyond traditional commercial relationships.[8] When ride-sharing companies design driver classification policies, when social media platforms establish content moderation rules, or when retailers implement global supply chain standards, they are making business decisions that function as de facto social policy whether intended or not.

Forced transparency in the digital age: The same technologies that enable corporate efficiency also generate unprecedented visibility into corporate operations and social impacts. Companies now possess detailed data about the social consequences of their choices, while stakeholders have acquired powerful tools to monitor corporate behavior and rapidly mobilize responses.[9] Consider when internal Facebook documents revealed that executives knew Instagram worsened teen mental health but continued optimizing for engagement,[10] when Amazon's own data showed its warehouse injury rates were double the industry average,[11] or when Exxon's internal climate research from the 1970s contradicted decades of public climate denial.[12] These revelations demonstrate how corporate monitoring systems create evidence trails that can no longer be contained. This dynamic creates what might be called a "data trap," as companies cannot selectively embrace the efficiency benefits of comprehensive monitoring while avoiding the transparency consequences that make their social impacts visible and contestable.

The heterogeneous preferences of modern shareholders: The traditional assumption that shareholders uniformly seek profit maximization has become untenable in today's complex investment landscape. Institutional investors, impact funds, and global capital providers bring diverse values and expectations that extend far beyond quarterly earnings. Companies must now satisfy investor coalitions with fundamentally different views about how businesses should address climate change, social equity, and stakeholder welfare, each claiming to represent the true path to long-term value creation.

These forces interact in ways that intensify corporate social exposure. The more companies pursue efficiency through global standardization, the more they encounter regional differences in values and regulations that resist uniform treatment. The more extensively they monitor operations to maintain control, the more data they generate about social impacts that become available to organized stakeholder groups. The more they attempt to satisfy diverse shareholder preferences, the more visible these contradictions become to stakeholders equipped with digital tools for real time monitoring and mobilization. Understanding these dynamics requires moving beyond simple dichotomies like business versus society, shareholders versus stakeholders, or efficiency versus equity, toward a more nuanced analysis of how modern corporate operations actually function and why existing governance frameworks prove inadequate for addressing the challenges they create.

The analysis proceeds in three parts, corresponding to the forces identified earlier. Section 1.2 examines how the drive for efficiency at scale has transformed corporate influence through uniform standards, comprehensive monitoring, and stakeholder coordination mechanisms that extend far beyond traditional market relationships. Section 1.3 analyzes how digital technologies have altered the information dynamics between corporations and stakeholders, creating new forms of visibility and accountability that traditional governance structures were not designed to manage. Section 1.4 explores how the diversification of shareholder preferences has complicated corporate decision-making by requiring companies to satisfy investor coalitions with conflicting values and expectations.

This chapter explains why conventional corporate governance approaches, which assume clear boundaries between business decisions and social consequences, increasingly fail to help companies navigate today's complex corporate challenges. By identifying the structural forces that have made corporate social impact unavoidable, we can establish a diagnostic framework for understanding what new governance approaches companies actually need. This foundational analysis then informs Chapter 2's examination of how current corporate law measures against these emerging governance demands.

1.1 AN INCREASINGLY UNTENABLE DISTINCTION: WHY BUSINESS AND SOCIAL FACTORS CANNOT BE SEPARATED

In the past decade, corporate purpose and social responsibility have evolved into exhaustively contentious battlegrounds. While stakeholder capitalism advocates demand that corporations address environmental sustainability and social equity with unwavering commitment, critics vehemently denounce "woke capitalism" as an existential threat to market efficiency and democratic values. The confrontation has deteriorated into an ideological war, spawning state anti-ESG (environmental, social, and governance) laws, bitter battles over corporate diversity initiatives, and incendiary rhetoric in presidential campaigns. Major corporations such as McDonald's, Amazon, and Walmart faced ruthless coordinated boycotts in 2024–25 simply for scaling back diversity programs, while Cracker Barrel's decision to modernize its logo and remove symbols perceived as racially insensitive triggered outrage from traditionalist consumers who condemned it as "woke capitalism," resulting in devastating stock value drops.[13]

The battle lines extend far beyond American borders. International boycott movements erupted across Canada and Europe, systematically targeting American companies over Trump administration policies,[14] while European corporations face mounting pressure from both regulatory frameworks and activist investor campaigns demanding to counteract these policies.[15] In Asia, companies navigate between authoritarian government expectations and international stakeholder demands, creating complex compliance matrices that would have been unimaginable a generation ago.

1.1.1 *Companies Can No Longer Abstain from Social Controversies*

Yet even as this global confrontation intensifies, both sides implicitly acknowledge a crucial reality that their rhetoric often obscures: The era of corporate social abstention, if it ever truly existed, has definitively ended. Some would adamantly argue that corporations should simply refrain from intervening in politics. If companies avoided public statements and grand gestures, they could ostensibly remain above the fray, stay accessible to customers and employees of all persuasions, and maximize profits for shareholders without controversy. This perspective, while superficially appealing, founders on the practical realities of modern business operations.

To start, selecting the optimal path to maximize profits proves far from straightforward in a fragmented stakeholder landscape. Appealing to one consumer demographic might thoroughly infuriate those vehemently opposed to it, as Goya Foods discovered when its Chief Executive Officer (CEO) praised Trump, leading to boycotts from Latino consumers who had comprised a core customer base, while simultaneously generating support from conservative buyers.[16] Moreover, employees who dedicate their talents to companies' missions increasingly demand that corporate choices align precisely with their values. Google's internal upheaval over military contracts[17] and Facebook's employee protests over political advertising policies[18] demonstrate how workforce expectations now directly impact operational decisions. On the other hand, governments and regulators jealously guard their prerogative to set social policy and remain hostile toward companies that appear to challenge their electoral agenda, while simultaneously expecting corporate cooperation in addressing societal challenges from infrastructure development to pandemic response. Modern corporations, with their thousands of employees, vast networks, and enormous public footprint, inevitably find themselves at the epicenter of social disputes not by choice, but by virtue of their operational scale and societal influence.

The integration of social and business considerations proves either impossible or impracticable to avoid without simultaneously crippling corporations' operational flexibility and competitive positioning. For instance, reducing emissions remains inextricably linked to the energy sources manufacturers utilize to power their facilities, a decision that affect everything from supply chain relationships to facility locations to product design. Addressing toxic workplace culture benefits decisively from well-orchestrated supervisory structures that managers can implement, but these same structures influence recruitment, retention, productivity, and innovation capacity. Maintaining user privacy is deeply enmeshed in the fundamental business models of modern social media and technology companies, affecting revenue streams, competitive positioning, and regulatory compliance simultaneously.

In numerous cases, these social implications constitute not peripheral concerns but elements deeply embedded within core business models and operational choices. Consider the stark mathematics of climate impact: A mere fifty-seven companies bear responsibility for 80 percent of global greenhouse gas emissions since 1988, according to the Carbon Disclosure Project.[19] This concentration dramatically transforms climate change from an overwhelming global challenge into a focused problem requiring specific corporate actions by identifiable actors. When Airbnb's disruptive business model fundamentally reshapes urban housing markets, the impact extends far beyond tourism revenue. In cities such as Florence,[20] Barcelona,[21] and parts of New York,[22] short-term rental listings now dramatically outnumber available long-term rentals, irrevocably altering community dynamics, local economic structures, and political relationships.

The interconnection between business strategy and social impact becomes even more apparent in the technology sector, where platform decisions shape democratic discourse, information access, and social cohesion. When Meta's algorithms prioritize engagement, they simultaneously influence political polarization and mental health outcomes.[23] When Amazon's logistics network optimizes delivery efficiency, it reshapes labor markets, urban planning, and small business viability across entire regions.[24] These are not accidental byproducts, but predictable consequences of strategic choices that companies make to achieve competitive advantage.

And yet, while state and federal laws have constructed an elaborate corporate governance edifice to guide managers' decision-making regarding the financial aspects of their choices and rigorously monitor their performance, they have conspicuously ignored the societal dimensions. For corporate law, shaped primarily by Delaware precedents and federal securities regulation, setting the company's position on social issues constitutes merely another decision managers make within their broad business judgment rule protection. Management's fundamental responsibility remains, essentially, to organize production: envision the company's strategic direction, obtain financing to realize this vision, recruit employees capable of executing it, then implement, supervise, and problem-solve. These critical tasks involve countless choices that managers must make in strict accordance with their fiduciary duties, by demonstrating appropriate care while scrupulously avoiding conflicts of interest.

Managers operate under additional constraints as well. They cannot make choices that violate existing law and must establish frameworks that monitor their employees' compliance with an expanding array of regulations from antitrust to data privacy to environmental standards. They must also provide comprehensive public disclosures if their company is subject to securities laws, typically when its shares are listed on a national exchange, though these disclosures focus overwhelmingly on financial materiality rather than social impact. But provided managers do not violate any laws and genuinely believe they are acting to benefit shareholders, they possess broad discretion to explore or completely ignore the social dimensions of their choices in whatever manner they see fit.

This governance framework, designed for an era when social impacts were widely thought as externalities, now appears increasingly inadequate for addressing the realities of modern corporate power and social integration. The persistence of this gap becomes more puzzling when considered alongside the extensive corporate governance reforms implemented since the late 1990s, from Sarbanes–Oxley's financial controls,[25] to Dodd–Frank's risk management requirements.[26] Throughout the last thirty years, policymakers finetuned the mechanics of corporate governance to optimize consideration of financial information but did little to promote thinking about social factors. Understanding why this gap has become so prominent now rather than in the past requires us to consider the fundamental shifts that have made social factors central to corporate operations and competitive positioning.

1.1.2 *Why Now? Three Forces Reshaping Corporate Governance*

Drawing the line between the corporation as an entirely private entity and the corporation as a social actor has surfaced repeatedly in the history of the modern corporation, but today this fundamental question merits a fundamentally different answer. This transformation reflects three powerful, interconnected forces that make traditional governance frameworks inadequate for today's business environment.

First, the unprecedented scale and concentration of modern corporate networks create an imperative drive for efficiency that demands systematic frameworks applicable across vast operations, while simultaneously amplifying the social impact of each policy choice. When ride-sharing companies design driver classification policies[27] or Apple establishes App Store guidelines[28] or Twitter bans President Trump,[29] they are creating frameworks that affect millions of people across dozens of countries, transforming routine business decisions into de facto social policy whether companies intend this outcome or not.

Second, forced transparency in the digital age has fundamentally altered the dynamic between corporations and their stakeholders, making corporate social impact both more visible and more immediately actionable. Modern corporations collect unprecedented amounts of data about their social consequences[30] while stakeholders have acquired powerful new tools to monitor corporate behavior and rapidly mobilize responses, making authentic engagement with social issues a business necessity rather than a voluntary strategy. As they embraced the age of information, companies are realizing that the very data that helped them be more efficient might also reveal aspects of their choices that would have previously remained unknowable. From autopilot safety data useful in determining how near we are to a future without cars,[31] to nanotechnology sensors that help with farming choices but also measure emissions with accuracy,[32] examples of how technology is a double-edge sword abound.

Third, the traditional assumption that all shareholders simply want to maximize profits[33] has become increasingly untenable in today's complex investment landscape. Shareholders now diverge significantly in their views about how companies should achieve profitability, creating complex scenarios where different shareholder factions support radically different visions for a company's future, each claiming to represent the true path to long-term value creation. Corporate leaders must convince groups with very different priors and expectations that they are doing a good job of managing the company.

Understanding why social considerations can no longer be addressed through external regulation alone, but require integration into internal governance structures, begins with examining each of these transformative forces.

1.2 DRIVE FOR EFFICIENCY AT SCALE

The scale and complexity of modern corporations dwarf their predecessors, creating business entities that coordinate millions of employees, serve billions of customers, and orchestrate supply chains spanning dozens of countries. Yet, size alone does not guarantee success. To be efficient at scale, today's corporate giants have relied on uniformity and standardization across their operations, ensured through a comprehensive monitoring architecture. Renegotiating these corporate policies has become extremely difficult for stakeholders. The imperative of uniformity and standardization, the architecture of comprehensive monitoring, and the increasing difficulty stakeholders face in renegotiating corporate policies also amplify corporations' social influence. Their impact extends far beyond traditional commercial relationships, shaping how billions of people work, communicate, consume, and live. Understanding how these mechanisms operate reveals why corporate decisions have become central to addressing society's most pressing challenges, from climate change to democratic governance.

1.2.1 *The Imperative of Uniformity and Standardization: From Internal Hierarchies to External Orchestration*

That corporations aim to increase efficiency by introducing uniform rules of interaction has been clear at least since Ford came up with the production line.[34] In the corporate law tradition, the idea that corporations are hierarchies dates to Ronald Coase, who contrasted the well-oiled corporate production machine to the constant bargains among independent individuals in a free market.[35] In this sense, the power to set rules of interaction is inherent in the concept of the corporation; the ability to organize different inputs into a single production line is corporations' key constitutive feature and their main contribution to economic activity.

Modern corporate hierarchies are far more sophisticated than those that Coase had the opportunity to observe in the early twentieth century. Contemporary corporations have taken this logic to extraordinary lengths. Internal operations now follow detailed organograms that sometimes span multiple pages, ensuring that top executives maintain tight control over sprawling business empires. Production chains have become increasingly standardized, while internal codes of ethics and conduct have expanded dramatically in both size and scope. Communications with consumers follow specific templates designed to create consistent brand experiences across millions of interactions.

The drive for uniformity begins within corporate walls but quickly radiates outward, as it also orchestrates behavior among external stakeholders. Consumers signing standardized contracts with franchises expect identical quality and service whether they visit a store in Manhattan, Mumbai, or Moscow. Suppliers must conform to detailed operational requirements that govern numerous aspects of their production processes, from sustainability standards to delivery schedules. The power of uniformity lies in its ability to remove individual choice and negotiation from countless interactions.[36] Corporations make policy decisions that apply to everyone who engages with their platforms, products, or services, often without knowing the specific identities of those who will be affected. This standardization reduces transaction costs for managers while allowing them to implement solutions at unprecedented scale.[37] However, it also means that corporate policy choices become building blocks of social organization, establishing norms and practices that extend far beyond traditional commercial relationships.

Illustrations of corporate standardization punctuate our daily life, as the examples discussed later show. These examples are especially striking because they have surfaced repeatedly in headlines, public debates, and even congressional hearings. Each case has attracted attention for different reasons, sometimes labor practices, sometimes consumer protection, sometimes environmental responsibility. Yet, when we step back and consider them together, what emerges is not just the diversity of disputes but also the commonality of corporate method. Whether in supply chains, distribution models, or governance frameworks, the approach is one of imposing uniformity across markets and operations. This consistency underlines the powerful effects of standardization: it can create efficiency, predictability, and global reach, but it also shapes how other actors operate and respond.

1.2.1.1 Platform Power and Digital Standardization

Platform companies have pushed conventional corporate orchestration even further, by becoming the architects of digital ecosystems that govern how billions of people communicate, work, and consume information. Apple's App Store operates according to uniform policies that affect over 2 million apps and billions of users worldwide.[38] The company's decision to charge a 30 percent commission and mandate specific payment systems creates a standardized framework that shapes the entire mobile app economy, generating over $85 billion in annual revenue.[39] The Epic Games legal dispute highlighted how these uniform policies can determine the economic viability of entire business models. Epic challenged Apple's requirement that all iOS apps use Apple's payment system and pay the 30 percent commission, arguing that developers should be free to use alternative payment methods and that Apple's policies constituted illegal monopolizations. The case demonstrated how a single company's standardized rules can control market access for thousands of developers and determine whether innovative business models can survive.

Facebook's content moderation policies[40] – or the deliberate absence of such policies in certain areas – establish uniform norms that influence how 2.9 billion monthly active users engage in political discourse and social interaction. The company's decision to maintain relatively permissive standards for political speech while strictly regulating commercial content creates a standardized framework that affects democratic processes worldwide. Facebook allowed political figures to post content that would be removed if shared by ordinary users, such as disputed claims about election integrity or inflammatory rhetoric about immigration.[41] This uniform approach to nonintervention has shaped the digital public square in ways that affect democratic discourse worldwide, from the 2016 U.S. election[42] to Brexit campaigns[43] to political movements in developing countries.[44]

TikTok's global expansion began with a revolutionary approach. A single, highly sophisticated algorithm could transcend cultural boundaries without requiring deep local knowledge. ByteDance's team of Chinese engineers, who lacked extensive understanding of foreign cultures, deployed an algorithm so effective that it could treat international markets as "complete black boxes," quickly learning user preferences through passive personalization[45] and becoming wildly successful across diverse regions from India to the Middle East.[46] However, this algorithmic uniformity, which delivered the same recommendation engine whether users were in Beijing, Berlin, or Brooklyn, eventually triggered significant geopolitical backlash.[47] India imposed the most dramatic response, banning TikTok entirely in June 2020 during heightened border tensions with China, citing data privacy and national security concerns and effectively removing the app from one of its largest markets.[48] The United States followed with sustained pressure culminating in divestiture-or-ban ultimatums,[49] while European regulators launched investigations under GDPR and forced algorithmic modifications through the Digital Services Act.[50]

The gig economy exemplifies how modern corporations use uniformity to reshape entire industries. Companies such as Uber and Lyft did not merely create new transportation services. They established comprehensive frameworks for how drivers, passengers, and regulatory authorities interact within their platforms. These frameworks determine everything from pricing algorithms to safety protocols, creating standardized experiences that can be replicated across millions of rides worldwide.[51] Uber operates in over seventy countries, applying largely uniform policies despite vastly different local transportation regulations and cultural norms.

The controversy surrounding whether gig workers should be classified as independent contractors or employees illustrates how corporate choices about uniform policies can have profound implications for labor law and worker rights. California's Assembly Bill 5 attempted to reclassify gig workers as employees, but companies successfully lobbied for Proposition 22, a constitutional amendment that created a new classification specific to app-based drivers.[52] This uniform policy framework now affects over 1.5 million California workers and serves as a model for other jurisdictions.[53]

1.2.1.2 Retail Transformation through Uniform Networks

Amazon has revolutionized retail through standardized fulfillment processes that enable same-day or next-day delivery for over 150 million Prime members globally. The company's uniform approach to inventory management, pricing algorithms, and customer service creates consistent shopping experiences whether customers purchase books, electronics, or groceries.[54] This standardization extends to Amazon Web Services, which provides identical cloud computing infrastructure to companies ranging from Netflix to the CIA, standardizing how much of the internet operates. Amazon's relentless drive for efficiency and standardization has revolutionized commerce, but it has also sparked controversy with key stakeholders. Its warehouse algorithms and productivity quotas deliver speed but have been criticized for unsafe conditions and union resistance.[55] The promise of rapid delivery boosts convenience but increases environmental costs.

Tesla's direct-to-consumer sales model has challenged traditional automotive distribution by bypassing dealer networks entirely.[56] The company applies uniform pricing and sales processes across markets, eliminating the haggling and regional price variations typical in traditional auto sales. This standardization extends to Tesla's Supercharger network, which provides identical charging experiences across 70,000+ outposts worldwide,[57] creating a uniform infrastructure that supports the company's vehicles regardless of location. For years, critics argued that this infrastructure reinforces lock-in to Tesla's ecosystem while limiting interoperability with competitors, thus harming the objective of increasing EV driving. Ultimately, Tesla yielded to pressure and is gradually opening up its network to other manufacturers.

1.2.1.3 Global Supply Chain Standardization

Multinational corporations have pushed supply chain standardization to unprecedented scales, creating uniform practices that operate across diverse legal and cultural environments. Apple, for instance, enforces identical technical and ethical[58] requirements across its suppliers in China, India, and Vietnam.[59] Standardized specifications ensure that an iPhone assembled in Zhengzhou meets the same quality and safety benchmarks as one produced in Chennai. Yet Apple's drive for consistency has also drawn criticism, as reports of excessive overtime and inadequate worker protections[60] show the tension between global standards and local enforcement realities. Walmart's global procurement system similarly imposes uniform pricing, packaging, and safety requirements on thousands of suppliers from Latin America to Southeast Asia.[61] While this has created efficiencies and elevated food safety standards in places with weaker regulatory regimes,[62] it has also generated controversies around squeezing local producers and homogenizing consumer options.

In the apparel industry, H&M and Zara have standardized auditing and compliance programs across their supplier networks in Bangladesh, Turkey, and Cambodia. These uniform codes of conduct have helped raise awareness of fire and building safety following tragedies like the Rana Plaza collapse.[63] Still, critics argue that audits often fail to detect persistent wage theft or unsafe conditions, showing the limits of top-down uniformity when local power dynamics resist enforcement.

The seafood industry demonstrates both the promise and pitfalls of global standardization. Firms like Thai Union[64] and Nestlé[65] have implemented traceability systems that can track fish from boats in the South China Sea to supermarket shelves in Europe or the United States. While these programs set common antislavery and sustainability standards across fleets, enforcement has been challenged by local corruption and weak maritime oversight, highlighting how global corporate uniformity can both raise expectations and expose enduring governance gaps.

1.2.1.4 Climate Impact through Standardized Practices

Corporate standardization is often discussed in terms of efficiency or branding, but its environmental impact is just as profound. Because a relatively small number of multinational corporations dominate global supply chains, the standards they may adopt shape entire sectors of the world economy. From shipping and steel to fashion and food, standardized practices can amplify climate harms or accelerate solutions. Understanding how these choices play out across industries helps show both the potential and the limits of uniformity as a tool for addressing climate change.

The shipping sector demonstrates how collective standards can deliver immediate global benefits. When the International Maritime Organization imposed a uniform sulfur cap in 2020,[66] every major shipping line shifted fuel and equipment practices simultaneously. Because the entire industry moved in lockstep, sulfur oxide emissions fell by more than three-quarters almost overnight, producing measurable air quality improvements worldwide.[67] Heavy industry is also beginning to move toward standardized climate practices. Cement and steel producers such as LafargeHolcim[68] and ArcelorMittal,[69] which together help drive nearly 15 percent of global CO_2 emissions, are piloting uniform carbon accounting and hydrogen-based steelmaking methods. Given how deeply standardized production methods already are in these sectors, even small changes, once codified across companies, can cascade through global construction supply chains.

The fast fashion industry shows how standardized practices can create both environmental harms and opportunities. Global brands such as H&M and Zara scaled polyester-heavy fabrics worldwide, embedding microplastic pollution into oceans and waterways as a byproduct of everyday laundry.[70] Yet the very uniformity of these practices means the industry could pivot quickly: coordinated commitments to recycled fibers, biodegradable alternatives, and circular design standards would shift billions of garments per year toward lower-impact production. The technology sector illustrates a similar potential. Giants like Apple, Samsung, and Dell already standardize global supply chains for rare earths, batteries, and assembly, but their policies on recycling, repairability, and e-waste recovery remain fragmented. A collective move toward uniform product design for durability and recyclability could dramatically cut the 50 million tons of electronic waste generated each year.[71]

Agriculture and food production underscore how much room for improvement remains. A small number of agribusiness firms, including JBS, Tyson, and Fonterra, dominate global meat and dairy markets, yet they lack uniform methane-reduction standards despite livestock being a major contributor to climate change. A shared approach on feed additives, manure management, and supply chain transparency could meaningfully lower emissions across entire protein markets. Aviation provides another critical case. Airlines account for roughly 2.5 percent of global greenhouse gas emissions,[72] but they have not yet coalesced around uniform adoption of sustainable aviation fuels. Instead, initiatives remain fragmented, with a handful of voluntary offset schemes and pilot projects. Industry-wide commitments to fuel blending, efficiency standards, or carbon reporting would harness the same collective force that made the IMO's sulfur cap so transformative for shipping.

The petrochemicals and plastics industries remain among the largest untapped opportunities for standardized climate action. A small cluster of multinational producers dominate global supply, yet they have resisted coordinated commitments to phase down virgin plastic production or eliminate toxic chemical additives. Their uniform reliance on plastics has made microplastics nearly ubiquitous, from drinking water to human bloodstreams, demonstrating how standardized corporate choices can spread environmental harms. By contrast, coordinated standards for recycled content, biodegradable materials, or extended producer responsibility would deliver rapid improvements at scale. Given the industry's concentration, a uniform shift among a handful of firms could alter the material basis of modern consumer economies.

Taken together, these examples reveal how corporate uniformity functions as a hidden lever of global climate impact. Industries that adopt standardized sustainability measures, such as shipping under the IMO sulfur cap, can deliver rapid and measurable benefits. At the same time, sectors such as aviation, agribusiness, and petrochemicals highlight how much remains undone, where fragmented or voluntary approaches have left vast climate costs unaddressed. The lesson is not simply that corporations should do more, but that the very structures they rely on, such as global supply chains, uniform production processes, and standardized service models, make them uniquely capable of transforming climate outcomes at scale. Harnessing that capacity will determine whether standardization continues to magnify environmental harm or becomes a primary tool for systemic improvement.

1.2.2 *The Architecture of Corporate Monitoring*

1.2.2.1 A Pervasive Monitoring Infrastructure

The drive for uniformity and standardization calls for a robust monitoring system that will carry this operational imperative into practice. Corporate monitoring systems have become both more pervasive and more powerful with advancing technology. Modern corporations track virtually every aspect of their operations with a precision that would have been unimaginable just decades ago. Amazon warehouse workers wear devices that track their movements and productivity down to the second, monitoring everything from walking speed to the time spent on bathroom breaks.[73] The company processes over 5 billion data points daily to optimize its fulfillment operations.

Digital technology has enabled corporations to monitor their supply chains with remarkable granularity. Walmart requires suppliers to use its Food Traceability Initiative, which can trace contaminated products back to their source within seconds rather than the weeks previously required.[74] Individual components can be monitored as they move through complex global manufacturing networks, with companies like Intel tracking microchips through dozens of production stages across multiple countries.[75]

Financial institutions trace transactions as money moves through banking systems from remote jurisdictions, creating comprehensive records of corporate financial flows. JPMorgan Chase processes over $10 trillion in payments daily[76] through monitoring systems that flag suspicious activities in real time. Cryptocurrency transactions, despite their reputation for anonymity, create permanent digital records that corporations and regulators can analyze to trace financial flows with unprecedented precision.

The gig economy has pioneered new forms of performance monitoring that blur traditional boundaries between surveillance and service quality. Customers rate their interactions with drivers, delivery workers, and service providers directly through the apps they use to request services. These ratings become crucial metrics that determine whether workers continue to receive assignments, creating systems of peer surveillance that supplement traditional managerial oversight. This surveillance extends beyond simple performance metrics to encompass behavioral monitoring. Driver-facing cameras in rideshare vehicles record interactions between drivers and passengers, protecting their safety but also creating comprehensive archives of personal conversations. Delivery workers' smartphones become tracking devices that monitor their locations throughout their shifts, creating detailed maps of their movements and rest periods.

1.2.2.2 The Corporate Surveillance Paradox

This extensive monitoring capability creates what might be called a corporate surveillance paradox. On one hand, it enables managers to control minute details of stakeholder experiences, helping companies differentiate themselves from competitors, build brand recognition, and foster customer loyalty. On the other hand, this same technology makes corporate actions more visible to external observers who increasingly expect access to corporate records and explanations for company decisions.

The double-edged nature of corporate monitoring became starkly apparent during various corporate scandals. Travis Kalanick's confrontation with an Uber driver was captured on the vehicle's internal camera system and went viral, contributing to his eventual resignation as CEO.[77] The footage provided undeniable evidence of leadership behavior that contradicted the company's public image. A lapse of judgment can be beamed through social media, going viral in moments. Digital records increasingly enable investigators and journalists to trace decision-making chains with precision, making it more difficult for corporate leaders to maintain plausible deniability when misconduct occurs.

This dynamic becomes even starker in the context of legally mandated compliance systems. Companies operate under countless laws and regulations, with managers and directors bearing a fiduciary duty to ensure compliance, typically interpreted to mean that they cannot knowingly violate the law or ignore red flags, and must establish appropriate supervisory systems. While no supervisory system is foolproof and isolated failures are generally excusable provided they do not indicate systematic problems, advanced corporate monitoring creates a double-edged sword. As monitoring infrastructure becomes sophisticated enough to ensure uniform service quality across all operations, companies find it increasingly difficult to argue that compliance failures were unforeseeable or excusable. The very systems that demonstrate precise operational control undermine claims that misconduct simply slipped through the cracks. In this environment, demands that companies do more to prevent misconduct find increasingly fertile ground.

The #MeToo movement in 2018 offers a great illustration of that double-edged dynamic. Legislators had long put in place strict laws on sexual harassment in the workplace. But for decades, these laws were enforced only sporadically, because monitoring mechanisms were narrowly focused on recording evidence of malfeasance, generally difficult for victims to provide. Then #MeToo took hold, forcing top executives to lose or leave their positions to face their accusers in court and demanding a policymaking response.[78] There was little that Congress could have done, as misconduct prohibitions were firmly in place. But the pressure on companies that had turned a blind eye to executive misconduct for decades became inescapable. Managers and boards quickly realized they would be held accountable if they did not try harder to protect their female employees.

Corporations responded to the #MeToo challenge by installing a number of governance reforms that seek not only to facilitate evidence gathering and bolster independent reporting, but also to improve general attitudes and revolutionize company culture.[79] Many firms strengthened their sexual misconduct monitoring apparatus, which now includes not only behavior strictly criminalized behavior, but a broader set of practices detrimental to vulnerable employees. Reporting and supervisory structures changed to afford greater independence to supervisors and give greater weight to victims. Oversight equipment, like cameras, were installed to deter violations. Women's rights organizations were invited to provide input on measures the companies could undertake to encourage victims to report incidents and better support them in the aftermath. Town hall meetings were held to consult with employees and stakeholders. The resulting governance mechanisms are much more substantial, giving rise to hopes that they can better reflect the changing attitudes and lay the foundations for long-lasting change. Regardless of how successful these reforms turn out to be, they show that enforcement of crimes committed within the corporate domain is extremely hard without the corporate institutions that support it.

The variation in monitoring approaches reflects corporate discretion in determining how laws and social expectations will be implemented. Some companies maintain meticulous records of communications between executives and board members, while others adopt more relaxed documentation standards. These institutional design choices underscore the role of corporations as final links in law enforcement chains and highlight the extent of discretion they possess in determining how legal and social obligations will be applied.

However, the comprehensive nature of corporate surveillance systems also creates new vulnerabilities. The more extensively corporations monitor their operations and stakeholders, the more difficult it becomes for those same stakeholders to challenge corporate policies through traditional mechanisms. This dynamic leads directly to the third crucial aspect of corporate power: the increasing difficulty of renegotiating corporate decisions.

1.2.3 *The Challenge of Renegotiating Standardized Practices*

As corporations have grown larger and more uniform, the ability of stakeholders to renegotiate corporate policies has become increasingly constrained. The classic contract law paradigm assumes that third parties, such as consumers, employees, suppliers, and other stakeholders, freely choose whether to enter relationships with companies and voluntarily accept the terms those companies set. However, this theoretical framework inadequately describes the reality of choice in contemporary markets. Albert Hirschman's exit-voice framework[80] provides a useful lens for understanding these constraints. Stakeholders dissatisfied with corporate policies can theoretically express their displeasure either by voicing concerns directly to the company or by exiting the relationship and seeking alternatives. However, both options face significant practical limitations that have intensified as corporate concentration has increased and standardization has become more pervasive.

1.2.3.1 The Limits of Consumer Exit Options

Exit options vary among different stakeholder groups but are constrained for most. Even in competitive markets, consumer law has documented numerous ways companies introduce terms beneficial to themselves and detrimental to consumers, creating fundamental imbalances in bargaining power. Amazon Prime's 150 million subscribers face significant switching costs when considering alternatives, given the integration of shipping benefits, streaming services, and cloud storage that would be difficult to replicate elsewhere.

Many large corporations operate in markets where their products have become so deeply integrated into daily life that meaningful exit, while technically possible, becomes prohibitively costly and complex for average consumers. Google processes over 8.5 billion searches daily,[81] while its Android operating system runs on over 70 percent of smartphones worldwide.[82] Users seeking to avoid Google's data collection practices face a daunting web of interconnected services, from search and email to mapping and cloud storage, that have become essential infrastructure for modern life. Successfully disentangling from this ecosystem requires substantial time investment to research alternatives, migrate years of data, learn new interfaces, and navigate compatibility issues with friends, colleagues, and employers who remain within the dominant platform. These switching costs, likely to measure in dozens of hours of effort, potential service disruptions, and social friction, effectively place genuine choice beyond the practical reach of most consumers, regardless of their privacy preferences.

Consumer boycotts, while ubiquitous and sometimes generating significant attention, rarely produce lasting change. The #DeleteUber campaign following revelations about the company's workplace culture and political associations led to approximately 500,000 account deletions.[83] However, Uber's user base continued growing, reaching 131 million monthly active users by 2022.[84] Similarly, Facebook faced calls for deletion following the Cambridge Analytica scandal,[85] but the platform's user base remained largely stable at nearly 3 billion monthly active users.

Similar patterns emerge across industries where consumers face environmental concerns, though the barriers vary in nature and severity. In some sectors, sustainable alternatives exist but demand significant financial tradeoffs: sustainable clothing costs 2–3 times more than fast fashion, requiring consumers to choose between environmental values and budget constraints, while locally sourced, organic food often costs 40–70 percent more and requires shopping at multiple locations and meal planning around seasonal availability.[86] Other sectors present structural barriers that transcend individual choice: going car-free in car-dependent suburbs requires fundamental changes to housing, employment, and lifestyle that may be impossible for many families, while installing home solar panels involves significant upfront costs and complex permitting processes. In still other cases, meaningful alternatives simply do not exist at the consumer level. For example, air travelers have no practical choice regarding jet fuel composition, as airlines universally rely on fossil fuels regardless of passenger preferences, and consumers cannot opt out of the carbon-intensive shipping networks that deliver virtually all goods to stores. These varying switching costs, from budget premiums to structural impossibilities to complete absence of alternatives, effectively place environmentally conscious choices beyond the practical reach of many consumers across different sectors, regardless of their sustainability values.

1.2.3.2 Employee Constraints and Labor Market Realities

Employee exit costs are typically even higher than those faced by consumers. For most workers, employment in large corporate environments offers income security, benefits packages, and career advancement opportunities that are difficult to replicate elsewhere. Amazon employs over 1.5 million people worldwide, making it the second-largest private employer in the United States.[87] Workers seeking to leave face not just income loss but the challenge of finding comparable opportunities in their local job markets. Even in highly competitive markets like Silicon Valley, where talent recruitment is a top priority, employees often find themselves locked into incentive schemes that promise large payouts only after years of service with the same company. Google's equity compensation packages typically vest over four years, creating golden handcuffs that make departure financially painful. Stock options and restricted stock units tie employee wealth directly to company performance, aligning interests but also creating exit barriers.

The geographic concentration of certain industries further limits employee mobility. Seattle's technology sector is dominated by Amazon and Microsoft, meaning that employees seeking to leave one company often find limited alternatives without relocating. Detroit's automotive industry presents similar constraints, with the major automakers creating local labor markets where exit options are structurally limited.

Specialized skills development within large corporations can create what economists call human capital lock-in. Workers who develop expertise in proprietary systems or company-specific processes find their skills less transferable to other employers. Amazon's internal logistics systems, Google's advertising platforms, and Facebook's content moderation processes require specialized knowledge that may not be valuable outside these specific corporate contexts.

1.2.3.3 Other Stakeholder Constraints

Stakeholders with peripheral involvement in corporate operations face even more challenging exit scenarios. State and local governments must balance public interest protection against the risk of driving away businesses and jobs, while also managing the political expectations of electoral coalitions. When Amazon announced its search for a second headquarters, over 200 cities competed with increasingly generous incentive packages,[88] demonstrating how jurisdictions face pressure to accommodate corporate demands rather than impose their own requirements.

New York City's initial agreement to provide Amazon with $3 billion in tax incentives for its HQ2 project[89] illustrates these dynamics. Despite significant public opposition, city leaders argued that the economic benefits justified the concessions. When community resistance ultimately led Amazon to withdraw from the project, the incident highlighted both the limits of corporate power and the costs communities face when opposing corporate decisions.

Communities cannot easily relocate when corporate decisions affect their local environments or economic opportunities. Coal mining communities in West Virginia face limited alternatives as energy companies transition to cleaner fuel sources. The closure of automotive plants in Michigan created lasting economic disruption for communities built around these facilities,[90] demonstrating how corporate decisions can reshape entire regions with limited recourse for affected populations.

The impact of corporate activity on issues such as climate change, inequality, or global development is often inescapable, making exit functionally impossible. The airline industry's contribution of 2.5 percent of global carbon emissions affects everyone regardless of individual flying decisions. Agricultural corporations' practices influence food prices and environmental conditions worldwide, creating impacts that transcend individual consumer choices.

1.2.3.4 Industry-Wide Standardization as a Constraint

Even when stakeholders are willing to bear the costs of leaving one company, finding alternatives that perform better on social dimensions often depends on industry-wide trends that have been shaped by the standardization processes described earlier. The airline industry's uniform reliance on fossil fuels means that environmentally conscious travelers have limited options for significantly reducing their carbon footprint. Business travelers flying from New York to Los Angeles face essentially identical environmental impacts whether they choose American Airlines, Delta, or United.

Employee benefits packages may vary somewhat among employers, but they tend to be comparable within industries and skill levels. Technology companies generally offer similar health insurance, retirement contributions, and parental leave policies, limiting workers' ability to find significantly better alternatives. Working conditions in global supply chains typically reflect local jurisdictional standards rather than individual company choices, meaning that consumers cannot easily find products manufactured under substantially different labor conditions.

1.2.3.5 The Inadequacy of Voice Mechanisms

With exit options severely constrained, voice mechanisms become critically important, but corporate law provides limited formal channels for non-shareholder stakeholders to influence management decisions. The primary direct mechanism for affecting corporate conduct operates through shareholder voting, where shareholders can submit proposals demanding specific social or environmental practices and threaten to replace directors if management refuses to comply.

As a tool, shareholder activism on social issues has important limitations. Proxy season typically sees fewer than 500 proposals submitted across all public companies, while corporations make thousands of policy decisions annually that affect stakeholders. Only the most salient issues can capture activist attention, and campaigns typically focus on a few companies at a time while addressing concerns at high levels of generality. Moreover, proxy campaigns require extraordinary coordination to overcome collective action problems and regulatory hurdles. Some institutional shareholders are combining forces by creating alliances that target issues of concern, like Climate Action 100 plus.[91] However, large asset managers, such as BlackRock, Vanguard, and State Street, who initially championed social issues, are becoming increasingly reluctant to openly challenge management on these terms.

In recent years, shareholder activism on social issues has crystallized into a contested battleground. Perhaps the most celebrated example is Engine No. 1's 2021 successful campaign to place three directors on ExxonMobil's board despite owning only 0.02 percent of the company.[92] The investment firm argued that ExxonMobil needed to diversify its energy portfolio to remain competitive, ultimately convincing institutional investors controlling over 60 percent of shares. After this early success, proponents advanced hundreds of climate, human capital, and political spending resolutions, but average support levels declined. Major institutional investors, such as Vanguard, openly withheld support, while proxy advisors significantly curtailed their recommendations in favor of these measures.

In parallel, corporate boards have witnessed a marked increase in anti-ESG and anti-DEI proposals,[93] often advanced by conservative activists. These resolutions, typically calling for the rollback of diversity programs or the abandonment of climate commitments, have grown from a marginal presence to constituting a substantial share of filed proposals. Yet, they remain almost uniformly unsuccessful at the ballot box, rarely attracting more than one or two percent of shareholder votes. Their persistence underscores the use of the proxy process as a symbolic forum for cultural contestation rather than as a mechanism of corporate reform.

Taken together, these trends illustrate how the proxy arena has become a site of ideological struggle, with environmental and social proposals reflecting both progressive demands for accountability and conservative resistance to perceived overreach. The dynamic has heightened the visibility of social debates, but its real-world impact corporate practices remains contested. Rather, it highlights the limits of shareholder proposals as instruments of structural change, functioning less as binding directives and more as markers of shifting political fault lines within corporate governance.

1.2.3.6 Alternative Forms of Stakeholder Voice

With traditional exit and voice mechanisms increasingly unavailable, other stakeholders often resort to protest tactics to express disagreement with corporate decisions. Employee activism has become increasingly common, particularly in the technology sector where skilled workers have more leverage. Google employees organized walkouts involving over 20,000 workers[94] to protest the company's handling of sexual harassment allegations[95] and its plans to launch a censored search engine in China.[96]

Netflix employees staged walkouts to protest the company's decision to continue streaming Dave Chappelle's comedy special despite complaints about transphobic content.[97] Amazon warehouse workers in Bessemer, Alabama, attempted to unionize in response to working conditions, though the effort ultimately failed.[98] These actions demonstrate both the potential for employee voice and its limitations within existing corporate structures.

Similarly, local citizens and nongovernmental organizations can mobilize media attention to generate negative headlines about corporate practices, hoping to damage company images and anger consumers. The proliferation of smartphones and social media has provided stakeholders with new tools for documenting and protesting corporate behavior. United Airlines' forcible removal of passenger David Dao was filmed by other passengers and viewed millions of times,[99] leading to policy changes and congressional hearings.

Uber CEO Travis Kalanick's argument with driver Fawzi Kamel was recorded and widely circulated, contributing to Kalanick's eventual resignation.[100] These incidents demonstrate how digital surveillance can work in multiple directions, providing stakeholders with tools to monitor and document corporate behavior.

Government authorities can utilize their regulatory and permitting powers to pressure corporations into reconsidering controversial decisions. California's Assembly

Bill 5 attempted to reclassify gig workers as employees, leading to extensive lobbying and ultimately Proposition 22, which created new worker classifications.[101] The legislative process demonstrates both government's potential power over corporate behavior and the resources corporations can deploy to influence regulatory outcomes. Florida's conflict with Disney over the company's opposition to the "Don't Say Gay" legislation resulted in threats to dissolve Disney's special tax district for Walt Disney World.[102] However, implementing such threats proved more complex than initially anticipated, requiring extensive legislative action and potentially creating significant costs for local taxpayers.

Beyond these dramatic confrontations, broader stakeholder unease with corporate social policies manifests in various forms. Employees increasingly consider companies' workplace policies, social profiles, and community contributions when choosing where to work. In innovation-driven economies that depend heavily on talent attraction and retention, these considerations may matter more than in previous industrial eras. Google's decision to end its involvement in Project Maven, a Pentagon artificial intelligence project, followed sustained employee pressure and concerns about military applications of AI technology.[103] The company's employees successfully argued that such work conflicted with Google's mission and values, demonstrating how talent concerns can influence corporate policy even without formal voice mechanisms.

Consumer and government perceptions of corporations develop gradually through extended observation of company behavior rather than forming instantly based on recent developments. Ben & Jerry's long-standing activism on social issues has created consumer expectations that the company will take positions on political matters, leading to conflicts with parent company Unilever over statements about Israeli settlements in occupied territories.[104]

Nongovernmental organizations and academic researchers monitor corporate practices over extended periods, creating long-term assessments that influence public opinion and policy discussions. Organizations such as Corporate Accountability International and Oxfam publish regular reports on corporate behavior that shape media coverage and regulatory discussions, providing indirect mechanisms for stakeholder voice.

1.2.4 *The Social Impact of the Drive for Efficiency at Scale*

The drive for efficiency at scale manifests through three interconnected mechanisms that have fundamentally transformed corporate influence. First, the imperative of uniformity and standardization enables corporations to orchestrate behavior across millions of stakeholders, transforming individual interactions into vast networks of coordinated activity that span continents and cultures. Second, the architecture of comprehensive monitoring allows corporations to monitor and coordinate these standardized interactions with relentless precision, creating systems of oversight that penetrate every corner of global commerce and daily life. Third, the increasing difficulty of renegotiating corporate policies means that once these uniform standards are established and monitored, stakeholders find themselves locked into relationships where corporate preferences become inescapable realities.

None of these elements is entirely new. Since their inception, corporations have sought efficiency through standardization, have needed monitoring systems, and have benefitted from bargaining advantages over individual stakeholders. Compared to their predecessors, however, modern corporations have managed to take these strategies into new heights. The same mechanisms that drive extraordinary efficiency in production and service delivery have also made corporate decisions the invisible architecture underlying how modern societies function. This dynamic is further reinforced by the arrival of the information age, from which corporations were well-positioned to benefit, as Section 1.3 illustrates.

1.3 CORPORATIONS IN THE AGE OF INFORMATION

In an era where social media and digital tools have become ubiquitous, the corporate world finds itself navigating uncharted waters. The rise of these technologies has fundamentally altered the relationship between companies and their stakeholders, because it facilitates the flow of information and provides new tools for monitoring and mobilization. Thus, it alters the calculus on two core concerns for corporate law: informational asymmetries between management, shareholders, and stakeholders, and collective action problems.

The justification for the current corporate governance model conventionally relies on information advantages and tries to correct for informational gaps and biases. For example, shareholders are thought to lack information about the operation of the company and face collective action problems in monitoring management. Stakeholders are presumed to face difficulties in assessing the impact of the company's business and mobilize to influence its direction. Against these two groups, managers are widely expected to possess far superior information, and hence are awarded wide discretion unless they face conflicts of interest. But digital tools are offering managers, shareholders, and stakeholders access to new information, thus complicating interactions among them. While companies are better placed to gather more information about even minute aspects of their operation, they are also more likely to face heightened scrutiny. Moreover, shareholders and stakeholders can obtain, process, and share information more readily and coordinate better against managers.

The paragraphs below argue that the detailed recording of company choices and the abundance of information about company activity in the public domain, coupled with ubiquitous access to collective platforms, has provided shareholders and stakeholders with new insights and tools.

1.3.1 *Companies Gather and Control Information about Their Social Impact*

As companies increasingly rely on big data to finetune their business model, they are finding themselves in possession of information about critical social implications of their choices. Big data is invaluable for companies as it enables them to gain comprehensive insights into consumer trends, inform strategic decisions and product development, and shape marketing campaigns.[105] Additionally, big data helps optimize operational efficiencies by identifying areas for cost reduction and process improvement. It also enhances customer service by predicting needs and personalizing interactions. But as companies leverage big data to increase their profitability, they are gathering huge pools of information about the consequences of their actions, allowing impacted stakeholders to draw connections to specific management choices. Once companies collect the relevant information, they seem disingenuous if they act on it when it suits them and disregard it when it does not. Claims of ignorance and plausible deniability are harder to sustain, while disparaging views of corporate managers are ringing true.

The loop connecting management choices to harmful societal impacts is particularly clear in the controversy around social media and youth. In February 2024, a critical public hearing titled "Big Tech and the Online Child Sexual Exploitation Crisis" was convened before the Senate Judiciary Committee.[106] During this hearing, tech CEOs testified about the alarming effects of social media on youth. Parents shared devastating stories of children who had committed suicide, developed eating disorders, or been sexually exploited through social media platforms.[107] Research presented indicated that frequent social media use by teens is linked to poor mental health and well-being. Social media companies collect detailed user information to tailor content, increase user engagement, and maximize advertising revenue. However, this practice often leads to the recommendation of harmful content, particularly to vulnerable youth. Meanwhile, Meta is facing a lawsuit from thirty-three states accusing it of designing features intended to addict children to its platforms.[108] Revelations from internal communications showed that in 2021, Mark Zuckerberg, Meta's CEO, had dismissed requests to strengthen child safety efforts and support staff.[109] This incident exemplifies how companies' effort to collect information for valid business purposes can also include data about their negative social impact and leave a paper trail leading back to specific management choices.

Congressional hearings and regulatory action against the titans of Silicon Valley often focus on misuse of information they collect. From the Cambridge Analytica scandal of 2018, which saw the personal data of 87 million Facebook users improperly obtained and weaponized for political gain,[110] to the ongoing concerns over the spread of misinformation and extremist content on social media platforms, the executives of companies such as Facebook, Google, and Twitter have been called to account for their role in shaping the digital landscape that now dominates our lives. Meanwhile, the debate over Section 230 and the limits of free speech on social media has pitted Democrats, concerned about the spread of violent extremism and election interference, against Republicans, who claim that conservative voices are being unfairly censored. Through it all, the specter of foreign influence looms large, with the revelations that China may have access to the data of millions of TikTok users[111] adding yet another layer of complexity to an already fraught situation.

Even though social media is an obvious illustration, corporate data collection efforts are ubiquitous and often revelatory about the social implications of companies' choices. From smart home devices that listen in on our conversations to facial recognition systems that track our every move, we are increasingly living in a world where our most personal information is being harvested and monetized. Often, companies know us better than we know ourselves. In a particularly insidious example, Target's algorithms managed to predict a high schooler's pregnancy and send to her father coupons timed to specific stages of pregnancy, even though she herself did not know she was pregnant![112] Even though she did not buy any pregnancy-related or baby-geared merchandise, she bought items from a basket of twenty-five goods that, according to Target's data analysis, were more often bought together by pregnant individuals. Similarly, the FTC brought an enforcement action against Flo, a period tracking app, that shared sensitive information with advertisers.[113] This same information, some fear, could be used to prosecute women who seek abortions in states where the procedure is now illegal. When 23andMe, the DNA analytics company, fell victim to a security breach, it was quickly revealed that the hacker leaked information on Jewish users, offering to sell data about "wealthy families serving Zionism."[114]

Employee performance monitoring is another area where digital tools have become more prevalent, providing companies with an unprecedented wealth of information. Conventional productivity tracking tools, like app and computer usage, digital time logs, email and chat messaging monitoring, are combined with video surveillance, network and device monitoring, and employee engagement tools such as surveys and feedback mechanisms. Just as these tools help companies improve their operational efficiency, they give rise to new concerns about how companies are utilizing this information. Amazon, for example, whose warehouse surveillance tracks how many milliseconds took an employee to scan a second item after scanning the first one,[115] has been the target of regular criticism about the pressure and distrust this system creates. PwC developed a facial recognition tool that can track whether employees working from home are in front of their screens.[116] Uber's notorious "God's View" tool tracked both Uber vehicles and customers who had requested a car, even after they had completed their trip.[117] Dating from just a few years ago, these examples pale in comparison to the capabilities offered by artificial intelligence, who allows companies to train their algorithms based on current employee data.

Interested in discovering what makes their workers more productive, companies are now tracking a vast array of data regarding lifestyle choices within and outside the workplace. Lifesignal sells patches that employees can wear to confirm that they are fit for the workplace – for example, they do not have COVID – but also tracks a lot of additional health-related information. Sleep patterns present a characteristic new frontier. Companies like JPMorgan have used wearable devices to monitor employees' sleep patterns, physical activity, and other health indicators. Google, Apple, and other companies are monitoring sunlight and air quality in office locations in an effort to maintain a healthy indoor environment, but the data can also help illustrate changes in productivity. When the employer is in charge of assigning, not simply projects and tasks, but also sleep and sunlight, their impact over workers' mental health is suddenly more directly attributable to their choices.

The information companies collect goes beyond their impact on individuals and often implicates aggregate social issues. For example, Tesla collects Autopilot safety data to better train its technology, but the data are of critical importance for designing a future with self-driving cars. Tesla had initially released the data publicly but took a hiatus in 2022–23, presumably because the data was not so favorable, before restarting the releases in 2024.[118] On the sustainability front, the information that companies gather for manufacturing purposes is extremely valuable in combatting environmental concerns. Plastics pollution provides a helpful example. In the context of monitoring their manufacturing process, many companies either choose plastics as raw materials or note the use of plastics in their supply chain. Collecting and disclosing this information is a critical first step in understanding the extent of plastic pollution and best ways to combat it. CDP, a nonprofit that assists global disclosure for environmental impacts, coordinated disclosures of plastics data from 3,000 companies, including firms such as Unilever, Nestlé, PepsiCo, IKEA, L'Oréal, Colgate-Palmolive, and others.

The wide availability of granular information on production methods raises the stakes for companies even in areas where they had previously worked hard to establish boundaries. For decades, companies have been developing systems to trace human rights violations throughout their supply chain. But current technology has provided companies with the ability to track, for example, the origins of specific items utilized in their products, from valuable ones like diamonds to relatively inexpensive ones like batches of cocoa beans. Under these circumstances, companies are widely presumed to know more about the conditions under which these materials were produced and came into their possession. Moreover, this information is now assumed to be known by their suppliers, creditors, and other collaborators. Banks like ABN Amro have processes for confirming the financing of sustainable jewelry.

Climate measuring is another area revolutionized by technological advances in the last decade. Nanotechnology sensors have developed to detect pollutants and greenhouse gases with greater sensitivity and accuracy.[119] So called "IoT" (Internet-of-Things) devices collect real time data on environmental parameters such as air quality, water quality, and soil moisture. Many of these technologies have been incorporated into "green buildings" who collect information about various measures, including how much sunlight exposure each cubicle gets. Precision agriculture uses GPS, IoT, and AI to achieve goals such as improving resource efficiency and reducing waste, thus lowering agriculture's environmental impact. Blockchain technology for supply chains facilitates traceability and more accurate measurement, recording information that would have been inaccessible just a few years ago. These advances, combined with the increased use of big data analytics and AI climate modeling, are allowing measures that are more specific and accurate than in the past. Yet, at the same time, they provide companies with vast amounts of information about the environmental implications of their choices.

This wealth of information that companies collect renders them at once more efficient in their operations and more vulnerable to attacks and criticisms. Even before the advances of the digital era, the public was leery of company information. According to an article published in Science, the oil company Exxon had been amassing internal company memos detailing the rising risk of global warming since at least the 1970s.[120] Not only would Exxon scientists' projections prove to be more accurate than those of the wider scientific community; they also showed that climate change is fast advancing due to human behavior, a claim that the company's PR department continued to doubt in public. More recently, plaintiffs have tried to use data collected by fossil fuel companies to establish their claims. In the BP Deepwater Horizon rig case, plaintiffs pointed to information revealed in a host of internal documents such as employee complaints about pipeline corrosion, reports by contractors, or expert testimony about subpar safety measures like shutoff valves or gas and fire detection sensors.[121] Similarly, in a 2012 case against Chevron, involving water pollution in Ecuador, plaintiffs pointed to warnings from the company's own environmental auditors about potential water pollution.[122]

As the examples earlier illustrate, companies have become vast repositories of information, empowering managers to further their business purposes with the push of a button. Privacy scholars are sounding the alarm over how companies might be abusing this information to the detriment of the individuals it captures. But the implications for corporate governance are more far-reaching. Once companies are utilizing this type of information for their intended purposes, it becomes harder to disregard it when it could be useful for other purposes as well. To illustrate this point, consider the following example. To most people, sharing doorbell camera data to help resolve a crime across the street would seem intuitive, even morally imperative. Following the same logic, information about energy use, typically collected to calculate production costs, could also help inform climate footprint estimates. Similarly, employee productivity data can help shed light on issues about occupational safety or workers' rights.

1.3.2 *Stakeholders Have Access to More Information*

Overbooked flights are a daily occurrence in airline travel. Yet on April 9, 2017, the events unfolding on a United Airlines flight from Chicago to Louisville captured the world's attention.[123] United faced the challenge of accommodating four of its employees who needed to be on the flight to later serve on other routes. After futilely offering compensation for passengers to voluntarily relinquish their seats, the airline resorted to a more drastic measure: involuntarily bumping four passengers. Dr. David Dao, a sixty-nine-year-old physician, was among those chosen.[124] Refusing to abandon his seat, Dr. Dao cited his urgent need to see patients the next day. United's response was to summon airport security. What followed was a scene of chaos and brutality. Officers forcibly dragged Dr. Dao from his seat, his anguished cries echoing through the cabin. The violent removal left him bloodied and battered, suffering a broken nose, a concussion, and the loss of two teeth. Horrified passengers recorded the incident, and the harrowing footage quickly went viral.

As the videos and images spread across social media and news outlets, United faced a relentless torrent of criticism. CEO Oscar Munoz's initial defense of the airline's actions only fanned the flames of public outrage.[125] As the backlash grew, he was forced to issue multiple apologies in a desperate attempt to quell the storm. This was a swift reversal for a CEO who had just been named "Communicator of the Year" by PRWeekly.[126] Two weeks later, United scrapped plans to elevate Munoz to Board Chairman, which would allow him to further consolidate power within the company.

The incident, which came before the #MeToo and BLM movements, illustrates the changed landscape that companies now face and that allowed these protests to balloon into widespread societal phenomena. With the click of a button, a disgruntled customer, employee, or activist can launch a viral campaign that can quickly escalate into a full-blown crisis, attracting widespread attention from the public and media alike. Moreover, companies often find themselves in a position where they cannot dispute the events captured in images or videos shared on social media, even if the context is lacking or misleading. These visual elements can be particularly damaging, as they can be easily shared and manipulated, quickly spiraling out of control and wreaking havoc on corporate reputations. This constant threat of exposure has forced companies to become more transparent and accountable than ever before, as they seek to navigate the complex landscape of stakeholder-controlled media. This shift has democratized information, empowering stakeholders to shape corporate reputations and influence governance in ways that were once unimaginable.

Realizing the power associated with commanding public attention through digital media, employees and customers took advantage of these tools to bring to light a string of corporate scandals that left their mark on corporate law in the twenty-first century. In 2016, complaints from Wells Fargo customers about mysterious fees and accounts they did not open led *L.A. Times* reporters to internal whistleblowers that raised alarms about the aggressive sales culture and pressure to meet unrealistic targets.[127] Ultimately, Wells Fargo employees were found to have created millions of unauthorized bank and credit card accounts in customers' names without their knowledge or consent. In 2017, Susan Fowler, a former Uber engineer, wrote a blog post detailing her experiences of sexual harassment and the company's inadequate response.[128] Following the revelations, an internal investigation and the firing of over twenty employees,[129] including senior executives, failed to quell the storm. CEO Travis Kalanick eventually resigned, giving way to significant changes at Uber's leadership and workplace culture.[130]

But if companies interpreted these public controversies as directives to unreservedly embrace diversity, equity, and inclusion initiatives, backlash soon followed utilizing the same digital media strategies. A notable case is the controversy involving Anheuser-Busch and transgender influencer Dylan Mulvaney in 2023.[131] The beer company faced significant backlash from conservative groups after Mulvaney posted a video featuring personalized Bud Light cans sent by the company to celebrate her "365 Days of Girlhood," marking her first year of transitioning.[132] Critics accused Anheuser-Busch of pandering to "woke" culture, resulting in boycotts and a decline in sales. The controversy had a noticeable impact on Anheuser-Busch's sales and stock prices, illustrating the complexities and risks companies face when engaging in socially and politically charged marketing efforts. Similarly, Disney has faced ongoing criticism for its support of LGBTQ+ rights and inclusive content, with some conservative groups accusing the company of pushing a liberal agenda.[133]

1.3.3 *Digital Platforms Help Address Collective Action Problems*

Besides having better access to information, stakeholders can utilize digital platforms to communicate with each other and provide an organized response to corporate choices of which they disapprove. Consumer boycott campaigns have gained new steam through social media. For example, the #StopHateForProfit campaign urged consumers to boycott Facebook in response to its handling of hate speech and misinformation.[134] Similarly, campaigns against fast fashion brands such as H&M and Zara highlight issues like poor working conditions and environmental degradation.[135] Conversely, conservative activists have also utilized consumer boycotts to express their discontent with companies they perceive as promoting liberal or progressive agendas. Conservative groups called for a boycott of Target due to its policy allowing transgender individuals to use bathrooms that align with their gender identity.[136] Chick-fil-A, initially a subject to a consumer boycott due to its past donations to anti-LGBTQ+ groups, found itself threatened by conservative groups when it took action to reverse those policies.[137]

While social media campaigns aim to drive a specific change through mobilization, other digital tools can be just as effective by aggregating information. Review sites like Yelp, discussion boards like Reddit, and specialized apps like Good On You or Ethical Barcode help bring to consumers information that would otherwise have been difficult to access. Moreover, governments are increasingly utilizing digital platforms in order to facilitate information gathering through the public. For example, the SEC's Office of the Whistleblower has an online platform for reporting securities law violations.[138] Comments on the SEC's proposed rulemaking on mandatory climate disclosure exceeded the unprecedented number of 20,000 letters.[139] Companies themselves are harnessing information from customers, users, and other public interactions in a collective format. For example, many companies concerned about human rights risks have set up grievance mechanisms to channel community complaints. This process has been common across a variety of industries and goals, ranging from BP constructing pipelines in Central Asia to Gap, Inc. seeking to monitor suppliers in Lesotho, to Hewlett-Packard in Mexico.

1.4 SHAREHOLDERS DEVELOP HETEROGENEOUS PREFERENCES

The conventional debates surrounding corporate governance often portray managerial decisions as a stark choice between corporate profit and social good, a tradeoff between shareholder interests and stakeholder welfare. Both advocates and critics embrace this dichotomy, yearning for a simple normative direction that can discipline all corporate action. The prosocial camp believes that empathy for stakeholders will guide benevolent managers toward choices that promote social interests while ensuring sustainable development. Meanwhile, shareholder primacy advocates argue that maximizing profits provides a clear yardstick for CEO decision-making, pushing all other considerations aside.

These traditional frameworks, however, conceal an underlying variety of preferences that is vastly more colorful and fluid than the stark dichotomies suggest. This variety emerges from deep structural changes within the shareholder base. Institutional investors now dominate equity markets, wielding enormous influence while serving as fiduciaries for millions of beneficiaries with diverse values. The rise of social impact investing has moved environmental and social considerations from the margins into mainstream investment strategies representing trillions in assets. Generational pressure from younger investors has redefined corporate responsibility as essential to long-term value creation rather than optional philanthropy. Meanwhile, the globalization of capital has introduced investors from different regions, each bringing distinct cultural perspectives on business's role in society. These converging forces have dismantled the myth of the uniform profit-maximizing shareholder, revealing instead a complex ecosystem of capital providers whose expectations extend far beyond quarterly earnings.

As a result, corporate governance must now navigate not only the traditional tension between shareholders and stakeholders, but also the growing heterogeneity of preferences among shareholders themselves, as investors are increasingly unwilling to delegate choice entirely to management without input regarding their specific priorities and values. This heterogeneity manifests in disagreements that extend far beyond profit optimization. Even when shareholders agree on fundamental values, they often diverge on methods, operationalization, timing, and the resources that should be committed to various initiatives. Some shareholders may prioritize long-term sustainability over short-term returns, while others may emphasize immediate profitability. Some may view certain social initiatives as essential to the company's reputation and future success, while others may see them as unnecessary expenditures.

1.4.1 *The Prevalence of Institutional Investors*

Where individual retail investors once held the majority of corporate shares in a fragmented, dispersed pattern, today's markets are characterized by the concentrated ownership of pension funds, asset managers, insurance companies, and other institutional entities.[140] Rather than a simple change in ownership structure, this shift reflects a fundamental evolution in how capital is allocated, how corporate governance operates, and how investment decisions are made. Understanding the scope and implications of this institutional dominance is essential for grasping the current dynamics of corporate ownership, as these sophisticated investors now wield unprecedented influence over corporate strategy, performance standards, and long-term value creation across global markets.

The rise of "universal owners," that is, highly diversified institutional investors such as public pension funds and large index asset managers, exemplifies this transformation. As Jeffrey Gordon's theory of "systematic stewardship" demonstrates, these institutions cannot escape portfolio-wide risks such as climate change, financial instability, or social unrest, since such risks depress returns across their entire diversified holdings.[141] Their fiduciary mandate to maximize risk-adjusted returns therefore requires engagement on economy-wide externalities, even when such engagement yields no clear benefits at the individual firm level.

This orientation fundamentally distinguishes universal owners from traditional shareholders and creates new dynamics in corporate governance. Where individual shareholders might focus on company-specific performance metrics, universal owners must consider how corporate behavior affects systematic risks that threaten their entire portfolio. This broader perspective naturally leads to more expansive engagement on environmental, social, and governance issues that were once considered peripheral to shareholder interests.

The "Big Three" asset managers, namely BlackRock, Vanguard, and State Street, exemplify this evolution, having stepped into roles as what Dorothy Lund describes as "regulators of last resort."[142] These institutions now routinely impose climate disclosure standards and board diversity requirements across corporate America, wielding influence that extends far beyond traditional shareholder activism. Yet their approach is shaped by "double intermediation," since they must answer not only to retail investors but also to powerful institutional clients like pension funds and corporations selecting funds for 401(k) plans. The institutional landscape itself displays remarkable diversity. Amelia Miazad's research on investor climate alliances reveals how different types of institutional investors collaborate yet maintain distinct priorities.[143] European pension funds and faith-based investors often push for aggressive emissions reductions, while certain U.S. asset managers may retreat when facing partisan backlash. Some funds emphasize cost minimization and limited engagement, while others experiment with active stewardship.

1.4.2 *The Rise of Social Impact Investing*

Impact investing emerged from earlier traditions of ethical and socially responsible investing, which often relied on negative screening, excluding industries such as tobacco or weapons manufacturing from portfolios. The term "impact investing" was formally coined in 2007 at a gathering hosted by the Rockefeller Foundation,[144] marking the beginning of a more intentional approach to "doing good by doing business" with measurable social or environmental benefits alongside financial returns. The 2008 global financial crisis proved to be a pivotal catalyst for impact investing. As traditional financial systems failed, investors began questioning whether markets could be harnessed more effectively to address social and environmental challenges. According to the World Economic Forum, "The financial crisis prompted a reevaluation of the purpose of investment and accelerated interest in approaches that could deliver both financial returns and positive societal outcomes."[145] This crisis of confidence led to the establishment of critical infrastructure, most notably the Global Impact Investing Network founded in 2009, which established common language, measurement frameworks, and research demonstrating the viability of impact investments. The 2015 adoption of the United Nations Sustainable Development Goals provided another transformational moment.

The numerical growth has been extraordinary. According to the Global Impact Investing Network's market sizing, self-identified impact investors managed approximately $228 billion globally in 2017.[146] By 2024, this figure had reached $1.57 trillion USD across 3,900 organizations worldwide, representing a compound annual growth rate of more than 20 percent since 2019,[147] with projections suggesting the market could surpass $2.3 trillion by 2032.[148] At the same time, mainstream investors reoriented their funds toward investments that align with environmental, social and governance goals, with assets managed under these mandates having already reached $30 trillion by 2019.[149] Compared to the roughly $114 trillion in global assets under management,[150] the rate of growth and strategic differentiation they represent are profound.

The rise of social impact investing has been significantly influenced by the emergence of millennial investors as a major force in capital markets. With approximately 72 million individuals in the United States and commanding an estimated $2.5 trillion in annual spending power, millennials represent the largest generation in American history.[151] They stand positioned to inherit approximately $24 trillion from older generations over the coming decades,[152] ensuring their investment preferences will shape markets for years to come. Academic studies suggest that millennials show a greater tendency than previous generations to consider social and environmental factors in their investment decisions, contributing to the growth in sustainable investing. In turn, major asset managers incorporated sustainable approaches into distinct investment products in order to meet demand.

A significant development has been the growing importance of alternative assets in impact investing. While public equity and fixed income instruments initially dominated impact portfolios, investors have increasingly turned to private equity, venture capital, real assets, and private debt to achieve more targeted and measurable impact outcomes. Alternative investments offer unique advantages through their longer investment horizons, direct ownership stakes that allow active influence over company strategies, and access to private markets where many social enterprises operate. According to a 2022 report by Phenix Capital, private market impact investments have shown stronger alignment with specific SDG outcomes compared to public market equivalents.[153]

The scale of impact investing has generated new regulatory challenges, particularly around "greenwashing." The European Union has led global regulatory responses through the Sustainable Finance Disclosure Regulation, EU Taxonomy Regulation, and Corporate Sustainability Reporting Directive. These frameworks are designed to discipline the market, enhance comparability, and combat misleading claims, demonstrating that impact investing has grown so influential that it requires comprehensive legal infrastructure.

The rise of impact investing exemplifies the increasing heterogeneity of shareholder preferences that challenges traditional finance assumptions. Where conventional theory assumed shareholders were unified in pursuing risk-adjusted returns, impact investing reveals divergent motivations ranging from concessionary investors who willingly accept lower returns to achieve social objectives, to market-rate impact investors who insist social value can be achieved without sacrificing financial performance.

1.4.3 *The Globalization of Capital*

As foreign ownership of equities and cross-border capital flows have expanded, firms increasingly confront investors with heterogeneous preferences that reflect distinct regional political economies, regulatory traditions, and cultural norms. In the effort to create convergence, globalization of capital ends up embedding contestation within corporate governance itself. Recent developments under the Trump administration underscore this reality. By embracing an explicitly anti-ESG (environmental, social, and governance) and anti-DEI (diversity, equity, and inclusion) stance, U.S. policy accentuated divergences between American investors and their European and global counterparts. The result has been an intensification of regional preference fragmentation in global capital markets.

The relationship between institutional frameworks and investor preferences has been extensively documented in the comparative corporate governance literature, revealing how deeply embedded regional differences resist homogenization even within integrated global markets. European capital markets have historically prioritized stakeholder welfare and sustainability considerations, supported by codetermination regimes, social market institutions, and increasingly comprehensive EU-level regulation. U.S. investors, by contrast, developed within a framework emphasizing shareholder primacy and financial returns maximization. This preference structure, embraced in Delaware corporate law and reinforced by market-oriented governance practices, has historically allowed environmental and social factors only if considered in the best interests of the company and its shareholders.

Against this backdrop of existing regional variation, the Trump administration pursued a systematic ideological repositioning that explicitly challenged the emerging global consensus around ESG principles, deliberately intensifying rather than resolving the tension between efficiency and regional differentiation. This challenge manifested across multiple policy domains, creating a comprehensive anti-ESG architecture that directly confronted European and international investor expectations.

The Securities and Exchange Commission abandoned enforcement of sustainability disclosure requirements that had been designed to standardize climate risk reporting across global capital markets.[154] This regulatory retreat was accompanied by rhetorical delegitimization: senior administration officials characterized ESG principles as a "Marxist march through corporate culture,"[155] explicitly framing environmental and social governance criteria as ideologically suspect rather than legitimate business considerations.

Parallel initiatives dismantled diversity, equity, and inclusion frameworks across federal operations and influenced corporate behavior through signaling effects. Executive Order 14151 eliminated federal DEI programs and created legal uncertainty that triggered widespread reductions in corporate ESG/DEI disclosure and commitment.[156] The corporate response was immediate and measurable: firms sharply reduced ESG references in annual reports, with companies such as Macquarie eliminating DEI mentions entirely – from twenty-four references in one reporting cycle to zero in the next.[157]

The anti-ESG turn had direct consequences in capital markets. Morningstar reported record outflows of $8.6 billion from global sustainable funds in Q1 2025, the largest in history, with U.S. investors driving the withdrawals.[158] Support for ESG shareholder resolutions also fell dramatically: only 1.4 percent of 279 proposals secured majority approval, and while 81 percent of European managers continued to vote in favor, only 25 percent of U.S. managers did so.[159] This divergence illustrates how globalization of capital institutionalizes conflict. European funds, guided by regulatory mandates such as the EU's Corporate Sustainability Reporting Directive, continued to demand robust disclosure and transition plans. U.S. managers, facing political pressure and legal risk under Trump, withdrew support. At the same time, a new segment of "anti-woke" investment funds, such as 1789 Capital, explicitly sought to profit from rejecting ESG/DEI criteria.[160] Globalization thus exposed corporations to a sharper clash between normatively opposed investor coalitions.

The challenge facing multinational corporations becomes clear when examining how specific firms have attempted to manage these irreconcilable regional differences. Shell's recent evolution illustrates the impossibility of satisfying both efficiency imperatives and fragmented stakeholder expectations simultaneously. Facing intensive European investor pressure for accelerated decarbonization strategies, Shell relocated its corporate headquarters from the Netherlands to the UK while developing climate transition plans that satisfied European regulatory requirements. However, the Trump administration's anti-ESG positioning meant that U.S. investors provided diminished support for such initiatives, forcing Shell to maintain different messaging and strategic emphases across regional markets rather than deploying a single, efficient global strategy.

ExxonMobil's governance conflicts demonstrate how this fragmentation penetrates deep into corporate decision-making structures. The successful 2021 proxy campaign initiated by Engine No. 1 relied heavily on European institutional investors to install climate-focused directors,[161] but the Trump administration's anti-ESG agenda simultaneously emboldened domestic investor coalitions to resist further climate commitments. Rather than achieving governance clarity, ExxonMobil found itself managing internal board tensions between directors supported by different regional investor coalitions with fundamentally opposed expectations.

Unilever's experience reveals how companies with strong sustainability commitments become focal points for these broader conflicts. While the company's comprehensive climate and social responsibility programs attracted strong European investor support, U.S. commentators increasingly criticized Unilever for allegedly prioritizing "woke capitalism" over shareholder returns, forcing the company to develop different strategic narratives for different regional markets rather than maintaining the unified global positioning that operational efficiency would suggest.[162]

1.5 CONCLUSION: THE SOCIAL IMPACT CHALLENGE

Three powerful forces have conspired to make the invisible visible and elevate the persistent tension between social and business considerations from a manageable undercurrent into a central governance challenge that refuses to be ignored. The drive for efficiency at scale has enabled corporations to create uniform standards and monitoring systems that coordinate behavior across millions of stakeholders, transforming routine business decisions into de facto social policy. The information age has fundamentally altered the relationship between corporations and their stakeholders, providing companies with granular data about their social impact while simultaneously empowering stakeholders with new tools to monitor corporate behavior and rapidly mobilize responses. The heterogeneous preferences of modern shareholders have dismantled the myth of uniform profit-maximizing investors, revealing instead a complex ecosystem of institutional investors, impact funds, and global capital providers whose expectations extend far beyond quarterly earnings.

However, the true significance of these forces emerges not from their individual effects, but from their mutually reinforcing interaction. The more corporations pursue efficiency through standardization across global markets, the more they encounter regional differences in values, regulations, and cultural expectations that resist uniform treatment. The more extensively they monitor their operations to maintain control over these vast networks, the more data they generate about social impacts that become available to increasingly sophisticated and organized stakeholder groups. The more they attempt to satisfy diverse shareholder preferences spanning different regions and value systems, the more visible these contradictions become to stakeholders armed with digital tools for real time monitoring and rapid mobilization.

This dynamic creates what might be called a "data trap" for modern corporations. The same technological capabilities that enable extraordinary operational efficiency also make corporate social impacts more visible, more attributable to specific management decisions, and more actionable for organized stakeholder responses. Companies cannot selectively embrace the efficiency benefits of these systems while avoiding their transparency consequences. When Tesla collects autopilot safety data to improve its technology, that same data becomes evidence in debates about autonomous vehicle regulation. When social media platforms optimize engagement algorithms to maximize revenue, those same algorithms become focal points for concerns about democratic discourse and mental health. When global supply chains achieve remarkable coordination through standardized monitoring, those same systems expose labor practices and environmental impacts to unprecedented scrutiny.

The globalization of capital further amplifies these tensions by ensuring that corporate decisions face evaluation by stakeholder groups with fundamentally different values and expectations. European investors demanding aggressive climate action collide with American investors resisting ESG mandates, while multinational corporations find themselves caught between irreconcilable regional expectations. The result is not convergence toward shared standards, but rather the institutionalization of conflict within corporate governance itself.

These interlocking dynamics make clear that corporations cannot indefinitely defer confronting the social dimensions of their business operations. The data trap ensures that corporate social impacts will become increasingly visible and contested, while the heterogeneous preferences of global stakeholders guarantee that any corporate position, including the choice to remain silent, will generate organized opposition from some constituency. Under these conditions, treating social considerations as external to core business strategy becomes untenable. Companies that attempt to maintain traditional boundaries between business decisions and social impacts will find themselves perpetually reactive, managing crisis after crisis as their standardized practices collide with diverse stakeholder expectations and their monitoring systems generate evidence of social consequences they can no longer credibly claim to ignore.

The question, therefore, is not whether corporations should engage with social issues, but how they can do so systematically within existing legal frameworks. This is fundamentally a business challenge that demands governance solutions: how can corporations develop decision-making processes that account for social considerations while maintaining competitive advantage and operational efficiency? What tools does corporate law currently provide for managing conflicts between different stakeholder groups with irreconcilable values? How can boards and management teams make principled choices when shareholders themselves disagree about fundamental social and environmental priorities?

These are governance questions that demand legal analysis. Chapter 2 examines how current corporate law addresses these challenges, revealing the limitations of existing frameworks that were designed for an era when social considerations could be treated as externalities rather than core business concerns.

2

Governance Gap

On a crisp January morning in 2025, Mark Zuckerberg appeared in a carefully staged video to announce one of the most dramatic policy reversals in social media history.[1] Meta, the parent company of Facebook and Instagram, would abandon its army of third-party fact-checkers, dismantle content moderation systems built over nearly a decade, and allow previously banned discussions about immigration and gender identity to flourish on its platforms. The company admitted that "one to two out of every 10" of its daily content removal actions may have been mistakes.[2] In a single announcement, Zuckerberg had transformed the speech landscape for billions of users worldwide, citing a return to Meta's "fundamental commitment to free expression."

Critics immediately denounced the changes as "political pandering" and "going full MAGA,"[3] while free speech advocates celebrated the retreat from what they saw as overreaching censorship.[4] Civil rights groups warned the changes would "harm vulnerable users," particularly LGBTQ+ communities who had already faced content restrictions.[5] Yet for all the fierce debate about the wisdom of Meta's decision, a more fundamental question received little attention: How did Mark Zuckerberg and Meta's board decide? What deliberative process led to this sweeping reversal? What legal standards, if any, governed their consideration of the competing interests of free speech advocates, marginalized communities, advertising revenues, and political pressure?

The answer, it turns out, is remarkably little. Meta's transformation of global discourse, affecting how billions of people communicate about some of the most contentious social issues of our time, was governed by the same loose framework of fiduciary duty and business judgment that might apply to a decision about office real estate or marketing strategy.

Meta's content moderation overhaul represents just one dramatic example of how modern corporations routinely make consequential decisions about social issues with minimal legal guidance. Consider the parallel world of corporate environmental commitments, where equally consequential reversals have unfolded with similar discretion and similarly minimal oversight.[6]

Unilever, the consumer goods giant behind brands such as Dove and Ben & Jerry's, quietly scaled back its ambitious environmental and social goals in response to investor criticism that the company was prioritizing "virtue-signaling" over financial performance.[7] What had once been heralded as industry-leading sustainability commitments were suddenly reframed as distractions from core business objectives.[8] Meanwhile, Nestlé subtly altered its recycling pledge from achieving "100% recyclable or reusable packaging by 2025" to using packaging merely "designed for recycling." This shift may sound technical but potentially affects the environmental impact of countless consumer products.[9]

Perhaps most striking, major technology companies including Google and Microsoft have been accused of underreporting their carbon emissions by up to 662 percent through creative accounting with renewable energy certificates.[10] These companies publicly trumpet their climate leadership while employing accounting practices that critics argue constitute sophisticated greenwashing.[11] Meanwhile, financial institutions such as HSBC[12] and energy giants like Shell face legal challenges for promoting "net-zero" commitments that appear inconsistent with their continued massive investments in fossil fuel projects.[13]

These corporate reversals and revelations raise profound questions about governance. When Unilever's leadership decided to retreat from sustainability commitments that had defined the company's brand strategy, what deliberative process guided their decision? How did they weigh the interests of environmentally conscious consumers against impatient investors? When Google's executives chose to rely on renewable energy certificates that critics call greenwashing, what standards governed their assessment of competing environmental accounting approaches? When Meta's board authorized the abandonment of content moderation systems affecting global political discourse, what framework guided their consideration of free speech principles versus community safety concerns?

The uncomfortable reality is that these decisions, which shape environmental outcomes, political discourse, and social equity for millions of people, are governed by the same broad framework of managerial discretion that applies to routine business operations. Corporate law provides directors and executives with extraordinary authority to determine what considerations will guide their companies toward long-term profitability, whether those considerations involve traditional business metrics or complex social impacts.[14] Yet this same legal architecture offers remarkably little concrete guidance about how to exercise that authority when addressing the multifaceted social challenges that increasingly define corporate responsibility.

This chapter examines the central paradox of contemporary corporate governance: while the law grants managers and boards virtually unlimited discretion to address social issues as they see fit, it provides minimal guidance about how to do so effectively.[15] Directors enjoy broad protection under the business judgment rule when making decisions about climate strategy, content moderation, diversity initiatives, or stakeholder engagement, but they receive little direction about what deliberative processes might help them navigate this complex terrain successfully.[16] The result is a corporate landscape that simultaneously showcases remarkable innovation in social governance and troubling inconsistency in approach and outcomes.

The stakes of this governance gap extend far beyond corporate boardrooms. As the examples earlier illustrate, corporate decisions about social issues now routinely affect political discourse, environmental outcomes, and social equity on a global scale. Yet the legal frameworks governing these decisions were designed for a simpler era when corporate social impact was largely limited to employment, local community relations, and basic regulatory compliance.[17] The evolution of corporate influence has far outpaced the evolution of corporate governance, creating a fundamental mismatch between the social authority that modern corporations wield and the institutional frameworks designed to ensure its responsible exercise.

Understanding this governance paradox requires examining both what corporate law allows and what it requires. The following analysis explores how existing legal doctrines, from the business judgment rule to oversight duties to securities disclosure requirements, apply when corporations engage with social controversies. It investigates the limits of shareholder activism and proxy contests as mechanisms for corporate social accountability. It assesses whether current legal frameworks provide adequate guidance for the complex deliberative processes that effective social governance seems to require.

The central question is not whether corporations should address social issues. Market forces, stakeholder expectations, and competitive dynamics have largely settled that debate. Rather, the question is whether existing governance frameworks provide adequate institutional support for doing so effectively.[18] As the Meta content moderation reversal and the widespread greenwashing scandals demonstrate, the current system's combination of broad discretionary authority and minimal concrete guidance produces outcomes that appear both innovative and arbitrary, principled and reactive, sophisticated and undisciplined.

The challenge ahead is developing governance approaches that can preserve the flexibility and responsiveness that enable corporate innovation in social issues while providing the systematic guidance that can help translate good intentions into effective action. As subsequent chapters will explore, some corporations have begun developing their own voluntary frameworks for social governance, creating elaborate deliberative mechanisms that sometimes exceed the sophistication of traditional regulatory processes. Yet these innovations remain isolated experiments rather than established practice, highlighting both the potential for governance evolution and the current absence of systematic approaches to one of the most important challenges facing modern corporate leadership.

2.1 MANAGERS AND DIRECTORS AS THE ULTIMATE POWERHOLDERS

Delaware law famously declares, "[t]he business and affairs of every corporation … shall be managed by or under the direction of a board of directors…"[19] This provision is critical both for what it explicitly provides and for what it implicitly precludes. It enthrones the board of directors as the default powerholder that wields all decision-making authority within the company. It also allows the board to delegate these powers, provided it continues to supervise their exercise. But this provision also prevents other parties, most notably shareholders, from exercising those powers themselves, even if they control a majority of the company's shares, or their proposal has won a majority of the votes. Even in these cases, it falls on the board, and the executives to whom it has delegated its powers, to implement shareholders' stated will.

By choosing to assign all decision-making authority to the board, Delaware law establishes the hierarchy that is so critical in every organization, with the board of directors at the very top of the corporate pyramid. But boards of directors are collective bodies, typically comprised by well-regarded professionals with many other responsibilities.[20] Thus, most boards choose to delegate their powers to one person, the Chief Executive Officer, or manager.[21] Delaware law places only rare limits to how much power boards may delegate to managers, as it provides only for a few instances where a board decision is strictly required (e.g., to recommend a merger proposal to shareholders).[22] Nor does the law place any formal requirement on the CEO to consult with the board before any specific decision. It is up to the CEO and the board to shape their interactions as they see fit. Boards, of course, can fire the CEO at any point, thus CEOs have incentives to seek input on controversial issues.[23] In practice, most boards are content to convene once a month and receive an update from the CEO, providing feedback and suggestions as necessary.[24] Typically, a subset of the board, the Executive Committee, will meet weekly to get more regular updates. But the goal is to monitor, not to dictate.

At its core, then, this corporate hierarchy operates on a fundamental principle: the critical feature of corporate organization is the delegation of decision-making authority to specialized managers rather than direct control by ownership interests.[25] Corporate law provides the vehicle through which expert professional managers can manage collective pools of resources, bringing specialized expertise and focused attention that dispersed shareholders cannot match. The separation of ownership and control means that even shareholders, who are said to "own" the firm, have virtually no power to control either day-to-day operations or long-term policies.[26] The statutory decision-making model creates a structure "in which the board acts and shareholders, at most, react."[27]

It is in this context that the business judgment rule emerges not merely as a standard of judicial review, but also as a regime so deferential to boards that Stephen Bainbridge characterized it as the doctrine of abstention.[28] By directing courts to refrain from reviewing the substantive merits of business decisions, absent clear evidence of fraud, illegality, or conflicts of interest, the business judgment rule effectively grants directors and managers "unfettered" discretion over virtually all operational matters.[29] The Delaware Supreme Court has expressed this principle clearly, observing that the business judgment rule exists "to protect and promote the full and free exercise of the managerial power granted to Delaware directors."[30]

This broad delegation of authority rests on one fundamental premise. It recognizes that directors and managers possess superior information about the company's operations, competitive environment, and strategic challenges.[31] They are intimately familiar with the company's capabilities, market position, and internal dynamics in ways that outside observers simply cannot be. This informational advantage is not merely incidental; it is structural and enduring, arising from managers' day-to-day involvement in running the business. In contrast, courts, focused as they are on legal principles rather than commercial strategy, are institutionally ill-equipped to evaluate whether a particular business decision was optimal or even reasonable. This creates a zone of discretion within which directors and managers can operate with confidence, knowing that their good faith business judgments will not be subject to judicial second-guessing.[32]

The business judgment rule thus emerges as the primary mechanism ensuring that directors and managers retain ultimate decision-making authority in the corporate hierarchy.[33] They become not merely the default decision-makers, but the final arbiters of corporate strategy and operations, constrained primarily by market forces rather than judicial oversight. Classic cases such as *Kamin v. American Express*[34] and *Shlensky v. Wrigley*[35] illustrate how courts have traditionally applied the business judgment rule deference. In *Shlensky*, the court refused to second-guess the Chicago Cubs' board decision not to install lights at Wrigley Field, despite shareholder arguments that night games would increase revenues. The court treated the business judgment rule as creating "a strong presumption against judicial review of duty-of-care claims," requiring plaintiffs to carry "the very heavy burden of rebutting that presumption." The rule thus keeps courts from reviewing board decisions unless exceptional circumstances warrant judicial intervention.

2.1.1 *Managerial Discretion and Social Conflicts*

When it comes to addressing socially controversial issues, managers and directors operate within the same framework of broad discretionary authority that governs all corporate decision-making.[36] This discretion represents a fundamental recognition that social and business considerations are deeply intertwined and often impossible to meaningfully separate. Rather than attempting to untangle these interconnected elements, courts defer to boards' judgments about how to navigate this complexity, allowing managers to implement their own vision for the company's future as their preferred path to increasing shareholder gains.[37]

This judicial approach acknowledges that socially critical choices are not distinct from business strategy but rather integral components of it. A corporation may choose to pay minimum wage to reduce costs or offer premium salaries to attract top talent; it may donate to community causes to build brand loyalty or distribute those funds as dividends; it may invest in renewable energy for long-term market positioning or focus on immediate cost savings. Each represents a different strategic approach that boards may reasonably believe will maximize shareholder value. The law treats these socially critical choices as investment strategies that may chart alternative courses for the company's future while remaining fundamentally oriented toward corporate success.[38] As Chancellor Chandler observed in *eBay v. Newmark*, "this court will not question rational judgments about how promoting non-stockholder interests … ultimately promote stockholder value."[39] Courts understand that determining the optimal path to profitability requires boards to weigh complex, interwoven factors that resist simple categorization as either "social" or "business" concerns.

The recent *Simeone v. Disney* decision powerfully reinforces this framework.[40] When the Delaware Court of Chancery denied shareholders' Section 220 request for access to Disney's internal records regarding the company's opposition to Florida's "Don't Say Gay Bill," the court emphasized that Delaware law "vests directors with significant discretion to guide corporate strategy – including on social and political issues." Crucially, the court recognized that Disney's CEO was primarily motivated by workforce concerns, as he was seeking to placate employees who strongly opposed the legislation, rather than ideological bias. This rationale exemplifies how decisions that appear socially motivated often serve traditional corporate objectives like talent retention and workplace stability, making any attempt to separate the social from the business elements both artificial and counterproductive.

The court's analysis in *Simeone* illustrates the broader principle that corporate political speech, especially after landmark decisions such as *Citizens United*[41] and *Hobby Lobby*,[42] falls squarely within accepted bounds of corporate authority. Given the inevitable diversity of viewpoints among directors, management, stockholders, and other stakeholders, corporate positions on external policy matters will always involve both risks and opportunities. The board's role is to weigh these competing considerations in good faith and determine what best serves the corporation's interests. This is a determination that courts will protect rather than second-guess.

By treating socially critical issues as inseparable from broader business strategy, corporate law has effectively empowered managers to pursue stakeholder-oriented approaches while simultaneously limiting judicial intervention.[43] This framework recognizes that decisions about corporate social responsibility, political engagement, and stakeholder relations are ordinary business matters that should receive the same deference traditionally accorded to operational and strategic choices. Just as courts refrain from questioning decisions about product development, market expansion, or capital allocation, they similarly defer to board judgments about how social positioning and stakeholder engagement can advance corporate interests.[44]

This legal stance allows managers to experiment with different approaches to social issues, focus selectively on matters most relevant to their particular business context, and adapt their strategies according to their own timeline and priorities. Most importantly, it establishes that boards may reasonably conclude that socially conscious strategies represent the most effective path to long-term value creation.[45] As long as directors believe in good faith that their chosen approach, whether emphasizing social responsibility or focusing on more traditional profit metrics, will benefit the company over time, they fulfill rather than violate their fiduciary duties to shareholders.

2.1.2 *Monitoring of Managerial Discretion: Deliberative Decision-Making*

However desirable from a business standpoint, this broad delegation of authority to expert managers creates a fundamental challenge for corporate law. While providing authority to expert managers is essential for establishing a hierarchy, a critical question remains: how will these managers be held accountable, to whom, and under what conditions? This presents a core tension because any mechanism for ensuring accountability will unavoidably curtail managerial discretion.[46] If managers know their decisions will be scrutinized and potentially overturned, they may become risk-averse or spend excessive time second-guessing themselves rather than acting decisively. Yet without accountability mechanisms, there is no assurance that managers will exercise their authority in the interests of the corporation and its shareholders, rather than pursuing their own agenda.

Starting in the 1980s, a significant shift occurred in how courts and policymakers approached the balance between managerial discretion and accountability.[47] Rather than maintaining broad deference to managerial judgment, legal doctrine began introducing more nuanced limitations on director discretion, particularly when decision-making processes exhibited biases or suffered from informational asymmetries.[48]

This evolution marked a fundamental change in judicial review. Rather than evaluating the merits of business decisions, which would improperly substitute judicial judgment for managerial expertise, courts began focusing on the integrity of the decision-making process itself. This process-oriented approach encompasses several critical elements. First, courts assess whether directors had access to all relevant information necessary for informed decision-making, placing an affirmative burden on boards to demonstrate they actively pursued comprehensive and relevant inputs rather than passively accepting whatever information came their way. Second, courts examine the accuracy and reliability of the information reaching the board, with growing attention to industry best practices that enhance information integrity, such as the use of independent third-party experts who can provide objective verification and specialized knowledge. Third, they evaluate whether the board followed appropriate deliberative procedures, ensuring thorough discussion and consideration of alternatives. This shift toward procedural scrutiny reflects an underlying judicial philosophy: that sound deliberation is the pathway to optimal outcomes, while flawed deliberative processes inevitably compromise decision quality. By focusing on the mechanics of how decisions are made rather than second-guessing their substance, courts can maintain appropriate respect for business judgment while still ensuring directorial accountability.

The watershed moment came with *Smith v. Van Gorkom*, a decision that fundamentally reframed the business judgment rule's application. Importantly, *Van Gorkom* did not represent a wholesale abandonment of deference to business judgment. The Trans Union directors were found liable "not because the court believed that the board's decision to sell the company was a bad decision."[49] Instead, they were held liable for breaching their duty of care because "they reached their decision too hastily, without the right information, and without asking the right questions."

This distinction proved pivotal. *Van Gorkom* established that directors maintain broad discretion to make whatever business choices they prefer, provided they have adequately informed themselves before acting. The court's focus was entirely on the decision-making process. Remarkably, the fact that Trans Union shareholders were to receive a price almost 50 percent above market value did not matter to the court's analysis. The procedural fairness of how the decision was reached eclipsed concerns about substantive fairness of the outcome.

Under *Van Gorkom's* framework, courts must determine "whether the directors have informed themselves 'prior to making a business decision, of all material information reasonably available to them.'"[50] While the gross negligence standard for breach remains high,[51] the focus has shifted definitively toward procedural due care rather than substantive review of business decisions. As the Delaware Supreme Court clarified in *Brehm v. Eisner*, "Courts do not measure, weigh or quantify directors' judgments. We do not even decide if they are reasonable in this context. Due care in the decision-making context is process due care only."[52]

Van Gorkom outlined certain key procedural safeguards to ensure that the board not only understands the terms of the proposed transaction, but can also assess the company's value in the context of its long-term prospects and potential alternatives. A critical component of this process is obtaining a fairness opinion from a qualified, independent financial advisor.[53] These opinions help the board evaluate whether the price offered is fair from a financial perspective and provide an objective basis for decision-making. Without such financial analysis, directors risk acting on incomplete or misleading information, a key failure in *Van Gorkom*.

The emphasis on information extends to the structure and timing of board deliberations. Directors must allow sufficient time to review transaction terms, scrutinize supporting data, and consult with legal and financial experts who can clarify complex aspects of the deal. The board cannot simply rely on management's assurances or rush to judgment; instead, it must seek independent advice and create a documented record that reflects serious engagement with the transaction's implications. When potential conflicts of interest arise, such as when a CEO is personally involved in deal negotiations, the board should consider forming a special committee of independent directors to oversee the process. Ultimately, these procedural requirements are designed to ensure that directors make decisions grounded in accurate, comprehensive, and unbiased information, so that their judgment can be both legally defensible and substantively sound.

Van Gorkom's emphasis on informed decision-making had profound implications for the role of informational intermediaries in corporate governance. The decision highlighted the crucial importance of the mechanisms and institutions that process and deliver information to corporate decision-makers. This requirement led to the growing strength and influence of various informational intermediaries like investment banks, law firms, accounting firms, and other advisors whose role became essential in satisfying the procedural requirements established by *Van Gorkom*.

The Delaware legislature's quick response to *Van Gorkom*, through the enactment of DGCL Section 102(b)(7),[54] demonstrates the ongoing tension between accountability and authority.[55] This provision allows corporations to opt out of monetary liability for duty of care breaches by their directors through charter amendments. However, the underlying principle established by *Van Gorkom*, which requires directors to engage in adequate information-gathering processes, remains intact. This evolution reflects a broader understanding that effective corporate governance depends not merely on who makes decisions, but on how those decisions are made. The procedural focus acknowledges that while courts lack business expertise and should not substitute their judgment for that of directors, they can and should evaluate whether directors have followed appropriate processes for gathering and analyzing information before acting.

2.2 STRENGTHENING THE FOUNDATIONS OF DELIBERATIVE DECISION-MAKING

From the 1990s onward, corporate governance underwent a transformation centered on a critical insight: effective governance requires genuinely deliberative decision-making processes.[56] This evolution reflects a growing recognition that unbiased hierarchies, comprehensive information flows, expert support, thorough deliberation, and transparency are essential for sound corporate oversight. Leading companies adopted innovations emphasizing independence, process quality, and information integrity, voluntarily at first, and later as mandatory requirements arising from law, regulation, and judicial precedent.[57] This transition represented a fundamental reconceptualization of governance as a deliberative function requiring institutional support. At the same time, market pressures and institutional investor activism drove companies to enhance transparency and accountability. These mechanisms created channels through which market scrutiny could function as a disciplinary tool, reinforcing the importance of high-quality deliberative processes.

2.2.1 *Building Infrastructure for Unbiased Decision-Making*

The rise of specialized board committees, particularly audit committees, exemplified this evolution.[58] These bodies served as dedicated deliberative forums with focused expertise in complex oversight areas. Stock exchange listing standards require companies to provide audit committees with a general mandate to oversee risk management efforts in the company.[59] When corporate scandals such as Enron and WorldCom[60] revealed the destructive potential of compromised governance, policymakers looked to these tested innovations for solutions. The Sarbanes-Oxley Act of 2002 (SOX) codified these practices by mandating audit committees comprised entirely of independent directors.[61] This requirement aimed to ensure genuine separation from management influence and functional autonomy for challenging executive decisions when appropriate. By giving audit committees authority over external auditors, SOX positioned these committees as guardians of information integrity, critical to deliberative governance.

2.2.2 *Expert Support and Information Quality*

SOX's creation of the Public Company Accounting Oversight Board (PCAOB) addressed another crucial aspect of deliberative decision-making: the need for reliable, expert-generated information.[62] Rather than relying on inconsistent self-regulation, SOX established uniform standards ensuring boards receive dependable, comparable information regardless of which external advisors they employ. The regulatory framework elevated the role of informational intermediaries, whether external, such as investment banks and accounting firms, or internal control personnel in addressing conflicts of interest. These professionals transformed from operational support to essential participants in governance infrastructure. This change reflected understanding that effective deliberation depends on institutional structures as much as individual competence.

2.2.3 *Thorough Deliberation through Institutional Mechanisms*

SOX's emphasis on process enhancement and capacity building institutionalized thorough, methodical approaches to governance. Regular audit committee meetings, detailed reporting protocols, and documented oversight procedures ensured that all public companies maintained the institutional capacity necessary for sophisticated deliberation.[63] These requirements moved beyond simply exhorting directors to be more diligent; they created systematic mechanisms for ensuring high-quality information flows and unbiased consideration.[64] The focus on documentation and periodic review established accountability mechanisms operating independently of individual director preferences or capabilities. The Act's disclosure requirements and management certification provisions recognized that transparent decision-making serves both internal and external governance needs. Market discipline could function effectively only when investors had access to reliable information about corporate performance and the processes generating that information.

2.2.4 *Delaware's Jurisprudential Evolution: Better Process Leads to Better Outcomes*

Parallel to these regulatory developments, Delaware courts underwent their own evolution toward process-focused jurisprudence. Beginning in the 1980s with cases such as *Weinberger v. UOP*, Delaware courts increasingly emphasized the importance of deliberative processes, but this focus intensified significantly in the 1990s and 2000s.[65]

Delaware courts formalized their review of independent committee processes, recognizing these committees as critical mechanisms for managing conflicts of interest. In cases involving controlling shareholders or management buyouts, the courts increasingly looked to whether decisions were made through genuinely deliberative processes by independent directors with proper authority and resources.[66] The courts' analysis became increasingly sophisticated, examining not just whether committees existed but how they functioned. Did they have genuine negotiating authority? Did they receive adequate information? Were they truly independent in practice, not merely on paper? Were they able to push back against offers or suggestions by managers? This scrutiny reflected judicial understanding that deliberative decision-making requires both structural independence and functional capacity.

The culmination of this jurisprudential evolution came in 2013 with *Kahn v. M&F Worldwide Corp. (MFW)*.[67] This landmark decision established that transactions involving controlling shareholders could receive the deferential business judgment review (rather than the more stringent entire fairness standard) if they implemented specific procedural protections: approval by an independent special committee with meaningful negotiating power and informed approval by a majority of minority shareholders. The MFW doctrine represents judicial recognition that properly structured deliberative processes can substitute for substantive judicial review. By establishing clear procedural requirements, the Delaware Supreme Court created a framework that encouraged thorough, unbiased decision-making while providing courts with objective criteria for evaluating governance quality.

Further reinforcing this process-oriented approach, the Corwin doctrine (established in 2015) held that fully informed, uncoerced stockholder approval could "cleanse" potential breaches of fiduciary duty by directors.[68] This doctrine emphasized transparency and informed deliberation as cornerstone elements of legitimate corporate governance. Together, these judicial developments created powerful incentives for boards to establish robust deliberative processes. The promise of more favorable judicial review motivated companies to implement governance structures that facilitated thorough, independent decision-making with appropriate expert support and transparency.

2.2.5 A *Unified Governance Framework*

The evolution from the 1990s onward represents a coherent response to the fundamental challenge of corporate governance: ensuring that complex organizations make decisions through genuinely deliberative processes. Judicial decisions in Delaware courts, federal regulatory interventions, and legislative actions have progressively reinforced this framework, moving corporate governance from an exclusive reliance on managerial incentives to institutional mechanisms supporting systematic deliberation.

It is important to acknowledge that specific implementations of this framework have faced substantial criticism. Various aspects of SOX, particularly the costly requirement for auditors to attest to internal control quality, have been challenged as imposing excessive burdens relative to their benefits.[69] Similarly, elements of the MFW doctrine and its expansion beyond the freezeout merger context prompted intervention by the Delaware legislature.[70] These criticisms reflect legitimate concerns about balancing governance rigor with operational flexibility and efficiency. My goal here is not to defend SOX or MFW, nor to determine which elements were sound policy and which were excessive. Rather, my purpose is to highlight a broader phenomenon: regardless of debates over specific mechanisms, deliberative decision-making has become the mainstay of modern corporate governance. This ascendance stems from a fundamental recognition that proper deliberative processes help companies reach better decisions by ensuring they have all relevant information at hand and take full advantage of it. The specific institutional arrangements may continue to evolve in response to experience and criticism, but the core insight about the value of structured deliberation in corporate governance appears likely to endure.

2.2.6 *Deliberative Decision-Making and Social Conflicts*

The deliberative governance innovations outlined in Section 2.2.5 established sophisticated frameworks for corporate oversight, but these mechanisms were designed to address specific categories of corporate problems rather than social issues broadly. Some of these mechanisms, such as audit committees mandated by SOX, are primarily concerned with ensuring the accuracy of financial information and preventing accounting fraud.[71] Even as companies may choose to leverage these structures for broader oversight purposes, their primary mission remains focused. For example, many audit committees now consider enterprise risk more generally, but this includes a variety of risks that are not social in nature.[72]

Similarly, other areas of corporate activity are governed by specific laws that create targeted compliance mechanisms. Environmental regulations, employment discrimination statutes, securities disclosure requirements, and consumer protection laws each establish particular procedural obligations and substantive standards.

When corporations must navigate these regulated domains, they operate within established legal frameworks that provide clear guidance about required processes and acceptable outcomes. Section 2.2.7 discusses the implications of these laws for social conflicts in greater depth.

However, socially controversial issues that fall outside these specific regulatory schemes occupy a different legal space entirely. In the absence of particular statutory mandates, these matters are grouped together with other general business issues and are thus subject to the same monitoring framework that governs routine corporate decision-making. This means that when corporations engage with broader social controversies, whether taking positions on political legislation, making charitable contributions to contested causes, or adopting policies that reflect particular social values, directors' obligations are governed by the same fiduciary duty standards that apply to business decisions generally.

Under this framework, the fiduciary duty of directors requires them to exercise appropriate care while acting in good faith and believing that their actions serve the benefit of shareholders. This standard does not prescribe specific procedures for addressing social issues, nor does it establish substantive criteria for evaluating different social positions. Instead, it focuses on the quality of the decision-making process itself. If questions about directors' handling of social issues arise in court, judicial review will examine the typical elements of deliberative process as outlined since *Van Gorkom*: whether the board explored various options, engaged in robust discussion and deliberation, collected input from relevant stakeholders and employees, and demonstrated thoughtful consideration of the corporation's interests.

The *Simeone v. Disney* ruling exemplifies this approach, showing how courts apply general principles of deliberative governance to evaluate corporate engagement with social controversies. The court noted that "far from suggesting wrongdoing, the evidence here indicates that the Board actively engaged in setting the tone for Disney's response to HB 1557." The court emphasized that the board "did not abdicate its duties or allow management's personal views to dictate Disney's response to the legislation.[73] Rather, it held the sort of deliberations that a board should undertake when the corporation's voice is used on matters of social significance."

The court's analysis in Simeone provides a detailed look at Disney's deliberative process regarding the controversial legislation. Disney's approach was not impulsive but rather evolved through several deliberative stages. On March 7, 2022, eleven days after the Florida House passed the legislation,[74] the CEO first circulated an internal memorandum to employees expressing the company's "unwavering commitment to the LGBTQ+ community" while explaining that their "lack of statement" should not be mistaken for "a lack of support."[75] The next day, as the Florida Senate passed the legislation, the Board held a special meeting specifically about "Political Engagement and Communications" in response to the legislation.[76]

On March 9, at the annual stockholder meeting, the CEO acknowledged that "many are upset that we did not speak out against the bill" and explained that the company had been "opposed to the Legislation from the outset, but we chose not to take a public position on it because we thought we could be more effective working from behind the scenes, engaging directly with lawmakers on both sides of the aisle."[77] Only after this series of deliberations and following the governor's signing of the legislation on March 28 did Disney issue its public statement opposing the law.

As CEO Chapek told stockholders, the company's original approach "didn't quite get the job done," acknowledging that Disney faced "widespread backlash from its staff and creative talent" before changing course after the full Board deliberation.[78] The court viewed this back-and-forth, with its internal communications, special board meeting, and evolving public stance, as evidence that the company had thoroughly considered its options before taking a definitive position. This deliberative process, starting with caution, engaging in board-level discussions, recalibrating based on stakeholder reactions, and finally taking a public stance, demonstrated the kind of thoughtful consideration that courts look for when assessing whether directors have fulfilled their fiduciary duties.

2.2.7 *The Gap in Governance Guidance*

This judicial stance has both advantages and limitations. By treating socially critical issues like any other business choice, corporate law has allowed managers to experiment with different approaches, focus on issues relevant to their specific business context, and proceed at their own pace. Without such permissiveness, any shift toward stakeholder-friendly practices would be difficult to achieve.

However, the absence of procedural directives comes with significant costs. Corporations must decide for themselves how to best approach social issues, developing their own methods for assessing and evaluating problems. Importantly, this guidance on deliberation does not limit their discretion, but merely provides a framework within which that discretion can be exercised more effectively. Yet without such guidance, a cascade of problematic outcomes often emerges.

Management biases frequently infiltrate corporate decision-making on social issues when formal procedures are lacking.[79] Executives and board members, often sharing similar backgrounds and perspectives, may develop collective blind spots on critical social concerns.[80] These biases can create echo chambers where certain viewpoints dominate while contrary perspectives remain unexplored. When a homogeneous leadership group confronts complex social issues, they may inadvertently filter information through their shared worldview, leading to decisions that fail to account for diverse perspectives. The Disney case is instructive here. Had the company maintained its initial silence without incorporating employee feedback, it might have made a fundamentally different decision that ignored key stakeholder concerns.

Equally troubling is how impacted stakeholders often find themselves voiceless in corporate deliberations about issues directly affecting them.[81] Without established procedures for stakeholder input, corporations may make consequential decisions without hearing from those who bear the brunt of their impacts. For instance, when companies develop policies affecting racial equity, indigenous rights, or environmental justice, the affected communities, who experience the lived reality of these issues, often have no meaningful avenue to shape the dialogue. Unlike shareholders who have formalized channels for expression through proxy voting and shareholder proposals, other stakeholders typically lack protected mechanisms to ensure their perspectives are considered.

This issue connects to a broader structural concern: the absence of protected channels for stakeholder input.[82] While corporate governance has developed robust systems for shareholder communication through quarterly reports, annual meetings, and investor relations departments, comparable structures for engaging other stakeholders remain underdeveloped or entirely absent.[83] Without institutional pathways for gathering, processing, and incorporating diverse stakeholder perspectives, even well-intentioned corporate leaders may miss critical information. These information gaps become particularly acute when addressing nuanced social issues where lived experience provides essential context that cannot be captured through market research or financial analysis alone.

The cumulative effect of these shortcomings is that corporate decisions on social issues frequently appear undisciplined and arbitrary. When observers cannot discern a coherent deliberative process behind corporate social stances, they may perceive these positions as temperamental reactions to public pressure, manifestations of leadership's personal prejudices, or ill-considered attempts to capture momentary market advantage. This appearance of capriciousness undermines corporate credibility across the political spectrum. Conservatives may see corporations as surrendering to social pressure, while progressives may view their social commitments as mere performative gestures lacking substantive commitment.[84] The resulting reputational damage can alienate consumers, demoralize employees, invite regulatory scrutiny, and ultimately destroy shareholder value.

In essence, while courts have established that deliberation should occur when corporations engage with social issues, they have provided little guidance on the form this deliberation should take. The judicial review remains primarily reactive, assessing whether some deliberation occurred rather than setting standards for effective deliberative processes. This creates a significant gap in corporate governance guidance, leaving companies to navigate complex social issues without clear procedural frameworks.

The challenge moving forward is to develop deliberative governance approaches that can fill this gap and provide substantive guidance for corporate engagement with social issues while maintaining the flexibility that allows corporations to adapt to their specific contexts and stakeholder relationships. Such guidance would not constrain the broad discretion that corporate leaders currently enjoy, but rather enhance their ability to exercise that discretion effectively in an increasingly complex social landscape.

2.3 OVERSIGHT DUTIES

Caremark establishes a foundational principle of corporate law: that a board of directors has a fiduciary duty to monitor the corporation's compliance with legal obligations.[85] This duty is not limited to merely establishing formal systems on paper, but encompasses an ongoing obligation to ensure that such systems are functioning effectively. It requires that directors remain informed and responsive when red flags arise, and that they engage meaningfully with the most significant risks facing the enterprise. In *Stone v. Ritter*, the Delaware Supreme Court clarified that when a board's failure to fulfill these obligations amounts to a knowing disregard of their responsibilities, it constitutes a breach of the duty of loyalty.[86] Courts have described this standard as applying in cases where directors "utterly fail" to implement or oversee a compliance system.

Given that the Caremark doctrine is directed at ensuring corporate legal compliance, a logical question arises: does its scope extend beyond legal risks to include the growing number of social and reputational conflicts confronting corporations today? Can the board's failure to monitor or address public backlash, controversies over labor practices, or political disputes give rise to oversight liability? This question has taken on added significance as companies are increasingly evaluated not only on financial performance but also on their broader social impact.

The Delaware courts have been cautious in answering this question. In Citigroup, the Court of Chancery explicitly drew a line between legal risks, which involve potential violations of law as Caremark requires, and ordinary business risks, which remain outside the doctrine's reach.[87] In that case, shareholders alleged that Citigroup's board failed to monitor exposure to subprime mortgage assets. But the court held that such exposure, while ultimately damaging, reflected a business strategy rather than a legal compliance failure. The directors were not expected to anticipate the collapse of an asset class or alter the company's investment model based on business judgments. Caremark, in short, is not a vehicle for second-guessing corporate strategy.

Many of the conflicts currently generating public debate, such as controversies over product design, workforce diversity, content moderation, or environmental practices, resemble the category of risk identified in Citigroup. They often involve competing views about how a business should operate or what values it should prioritize, rather than clear legal obligations that the board is failing to enforce. As such, they typically fall outside the scope of Caremark, even if they generate reputational harm or shareholder activism.

The boundaries of this doctrine, however, came under renewed scrutiny in *Marchand v. Barnhill*.[88] There, the Delaware Supreme Court allowed a Caremark claim to proceed against the directors of Blue Bell Creameries after a deadly listeria outbreak. The company, whose single product was ice cream, had no board-level protocols for discussing or monitoring food safety. The court found that food safety was not just a regulatory issue but a matter essential to the company's operations.

The board's failure to engage with it at all raised questions about whether directors had fulfilled even the baseline obligations of oversight.

The significance of *Marchand* lies in its articulation of what counts as a "mission critical" risk. A mission critical risk is not simply important or consequential, but it must be so intimately connected to the core business of the company that failing to oversee it raises an inference of bad faith. Examples might include safety protocols at a commercial airline, regulatory compliance in pharmaceutical manufacturing, or anti-money laundering systems in a financial institution. These are areas where the company's ability to operate depends on close, sustained board-level attention.[89]

2.3.1 *Why Climate and Social Risks Are Unlikely to Constitute Mission-Critical Oversight Failures under Marchand*

As discussed in Chapter 1, social issues are increasingly embedded in business decisions across virtually every industry and corporate function. From supply chain management to workforce policies, from product development to community relations, boards cannot make strategic decisions without considering their social dimensions and implications. This integration means that directors must develop frameworks for understanding and addressing social considerations as part of their fundamental governance responsibilities. Market forces and stakeholder expectations have largely settled whether boards should engage with these issues. The remaining challenge is determining what legal standards, if any, govern how boards should approach these complex determinations.

Institutional investors have become particularly vocal in pressing boards to address socially controversial issues because they recognize these factors can materially affect long-term financial performance and investment returns.[90] CalPERS, for example, has actively engaged with portfolio companies on climate risk management, arguing that environmental factors pose significant threats to asset values over time.[91] BlackRock has used its shareholder voting power to push for greater board diversity, contending that diverse leadership teams make better strategic decisions.[92] State pension funds have pressured companies to address human rights practices in their global operations, viewing reputational risks as potential threats to brand value and market position.[93] These investor initiatives reflect a growing consensus that social issues can create both risks and opportunities that directly impact corporate financial performance.

Given this context, an important question emerges: can the mission-critical framework established in *Marchand v. Barnhill* be extended to encompass social considerations, such that boards failing to address them adequately would be violating their fiduciary duties under Delaware's oversight doctrine? While this framework was not originally designed to address social issues in business decision-making, the increasing materiality of such considerations to corporate performance raises the question of whether existing legal doctrines might be adapted or expanded to provide governance standards in this domain.

2.3.2 *The Narrow Parameters of Mission-critical Analysis*

Following *Marchand,* Delaware jurisprudence sought to add clarity to the question of which risks would lead to director liability, not least due to an influx of Caremark claims testing the boundaries of oversight obligations. Through a trilogy of landmark decisions, that is, Blue Bell,[94] Clovis Oncology,[95] and the Boeing litigation,[96] Delaware courts have methodically constructed the architecture of "mission-critical" risk identification, establishing parameters that inadvertently but systematically exclude social and climate governance from the purview of fiduciary liability.

The doctrinal foundation rests upon a stark dichotomy that cuts to the heart of corporate accountability: the fundamental distinction between disregard for public values enshrined in binding legal mandates versus mere abandonment of voluntary corporate pledges.[97] This bifurcation proves determinative in assessing director liability, as courts have consistently demanded that mission-critical risks emerge from the nexus of primary business operations and explicit legal or regulatory obligations. In Blue Bell, food safety constituted mission-critical terrain not merely because avoiding consumer harm makes sound business sense for an ice cream company, but because the legal system recognizes food safety as a fundamental imperative for food manufacturers through comprehensive statutory and regulatory frameworks that permeate every aspect of operations.[98] Similarly, Clovis Oncology's clinical trial protocols and Boeing's aircraft safety standards derived their mission-critical status from the convergence of core business functions with comprehensive regulatory frameworks that brook no deviation.

This jurisprudential architecture renders social and climate risks structurally disadvantaged in achieving mission-critical designation, despite their undeniable strategic importance to modern corporate governance. While these risks may increasingly drive investor expectations and stakeholder engagement, their predominantly voluntary character within existing legal frameworks proves their undoing.[99] Climate commitments and social initiatives, however ambitious or well-intentioned, typically emanate from corporate self-imposition rather than legislative or regulatory mandate. This distinction proves fatal under Delaware's exacting standards, which require systematic and pervasive contempt for fundamental societal values that have been "deliberately crystallized into binding legal mandates by legislative and regulatory authorities."[100]

The doctrinal exclusion deepens when examined through the lens of business judgment versus oversight failure analysis. Social and climate governance decisions inhabit the realm of strategic business judgment, where boards navigate complex tradeoffs among competing priorities and stakeholder interests. Traditional mission-critical analysis involves binary compliance determinations where safety protocols either meet regulatory standards or catastrophically fail. Social considerations, by contrast, resist uniform benchmarks and demand nuanced judgment calls that courts have historically declined to second-guess.[101] The legal system's deference to directorial discretion in business risk management, as distinguished from regulatory compliance oversight, effectively immunizes most social and climate governance from Caremark scrutiny.

This framework reveals the profound limitations of applying traditional fiduciary duty concepts to contemporary governance challenges. While climate risks may pose existential threats to long-term corporate viability and social issues may fundamentally affect corporate reputation and stakeholder relationships, their treatment as strategic business decisions rather than compliance imperatives places them beyond the reach of the mission-critical doctrine.[102] The result is a jurisprudential paradox: while companies struggle to develop principles-based frameworks for addressing fundamental social challenges, the fact that corporate leadership necessarily confronts these issues before policymakers and regulators recognize the need for binding mandates means that *Marchand* will likely remain inapplicable to the very governance innovations that define responsible corporate operation in the twenty-first century.

2.4 SHAREHOLDER PROPOSALS: PRESSURE, CONFLICT, AND THE EVOLUTION OF CORPORATE ACTIVISM

Shareholder proposals occupy a peculiar space in corporate governance. They are powerful enough to command boardroom attention and reshape corporate discourse, yet constrained by law and practice from achieving the transformative change their proponents often seek.[103] Over the past decade, these 500-word missives have evolved from focusing primarily on executive compensation and board structure to addressing climate change, artificial intelligence, and human rights.[104] They have sparked intense political debates, mobilized billions in institutional investment, and forced companies to reconsider fundamental business practices.[105] Yet for all their prominence and apparent influence, shareholder proposals remain what they have always been: mechanisms for pressure and persuasion rather than instruments of corporate control. They function as specific prods that can elevate particular issues to boardroom consideration, but they cannot systematically address the full spectrum of social and environmental challenges that modern corporations face. Understanding both their power and their limitations requires examining how legal structures, investor dynamics, and practical constraints shape what shareholders can accomplish through the proposal process.

2.4.1 *The Legal Framework: Expression without Control*

By charging the board and the CEO with running the company, Delaware law precludes shareholders from having an active role in management.[106] There are specific issues that require a shareholder vote, such as director elections or approvals of statutory mergers.[107] There are even certain issues where a shareholder vote, even if not required, produces a remedial effect, such as when conflicts arise between the corporate interests and managers' personal interests. But besides these issues, shareholders have no say over management decisions, however important they are. Rather, shareholders can bring proposals that suggest possible policy priorities for management, falling short of suggesting that management takes specific action.[108] To mirror this requirement, the federal securities laws regulating the distribution of voting proxies to retail shareholders allow the board to exclude from the meeting shareholder proposals that seek to control managers' hand in running the ordinary business of the company.[109] Moreover, Rule 14a-8 limits shareholder proposals to 500 words, if they wish to take advantage of the company's proxy distribution free of charge, rather than pay millions of dollars to run a proxy campaign.[110] This is a text that gives voice to desires and concerns rather than a mechanism for setting corporate policies. Thus, the law is crafted to preserve management's decision-making authority, while providing an avenue for shareholders to express their concerns.

These structural limitations reveal the inherent constraints of shareholder proposals as a tool for addressing the full spectrum of social issues that arise within corporate operations. Even as social proposals have gained prominence, they represent only the most visible peaks of much larger mountains of corporate social impact. The shareholder proposal process, by its very nature, requires significant mobilization of resources, expertise, and political capital, limiting activists to targeting only the most prominent topics where they can hope to gain meaningful support. This selectivity means that countless social issues affecting corporate stakeholders, from local community impacts to supplier labor conditions to customer data privacy, remain largely outside the scope of shareholder activism, not because they lack importance, but because they lack the visibility and broad appeal necessary to sustain a campaign.

2.4.2 A *Decade of Transformation: From Governance to Social Issues*

Taking advantage of this avenue, shareholder proposals on social matters have been a mainstay of proxy season for decades, winning more prominence in recent years as the ESG tide soared.[111] The past decade has witnessed a remarkable transformation in the landscape of shareholder activism, marked by a dramatic shift from traditional governance and compensation concerns toward environmental and social issues. This evolution reflects broader societal changes, increased awareness of climate risks, and growing investor recognition that environmental and social factors can materially impact long-term financial performance.[112]

The surge in environmental and social proposals has been nothing short of extraordinary. Where governance and compensation topics once dominated the proxy season discourse through the mid 2010s, environmental and social proposals now account for the majority of shareholder initiatives. Climate change proposals, in particular, have become the driving force behind this transformation, with approximately three-quarters of environment-related proposals focusing on climate-related issues, emphasizing alignment with the Paris Agreement and net zero targets.[113] Human capital management proposals have similarly proliferated, covering diversity, inclusion, workplace discrimination, employee benefits, and pay equity, which gained heightened attention during and after the COVID-19 pandemic.[114]

The regulatory environment has played a crucial role in facilitating this shift. Under the Biden administration, the SEC adopted changes that allowed shareholders to put more pressure on managers to act, including requests that companies consider their stance on specific topics by certain timelines. The November 2021 SEC Staff Legal Bulletin provided updated guidance on procedural requirements that made it significantly more difficult for companies to exclude proposals from the ballot, catalyzing a surge in shareholder proposals.[115] This guidance effectively lowered the barriers for environmental and social proposals, enabling activists to push forward initiatives that might previously have been excluded under the ordinary business exception.

However, this regulatory facilitation proved temporary. The Trump administration quickly dialed back these accommodating guidelines, reflecting broader political tensions surrounding ESG investing.[116] This regulatory uncertainty has created an environment where the rules governing shareholder proposals remain in flux, with companies and activists adapting to shifting standards for what constitutes excludable content.

2.4.3 *The Mechanics of Support*

In practice, shareholders have increased the number of social proposals they bring, although securing a win remains elusive. As the anti-ESG backlash fueled opposing shareholder groups, recent proxy seasons have seen the highest number of proposals in years.[117] The emergence of so-called "anti-ESG" proposals represents a significant development in this landscape, making up approximately 11 percent of all requests in recent years. These campaigns, primarily driven by political advocacy groups including the National Center for Public Policy Research and the National Legal and Policy Center, challenge company diversity, equity, and inclusion commitments on grounds of potential reverse discrimination, question climate commitments and their associated costs, scrutinize corporate affiliations and political involvements, and raise concerns about operations in China.[118]

Yet even as passions are running high, support for proposals rarely brings them over the majority line and has recently dropped even further. The trajectory of support levels tells a compelling story of initial enthusiasm followed by more measured evaluation. Environmental proposals experienced an explosion of support in 2021, reaching record levels, with nearly half of voted proposals passing.[119] However, median support levels subsequently plunged dramatically, stabilizing at much lower levels in recent years. Social proposals followed a similar though less pronounced pattern, with support peaking in 2021 before declining in subsequent years.

This decline in support reflects several converging factors. Large-cap companies, which are predominantly the targets of shareholder campaigns, have made significant strides in their disclosures and practices. As companies have enhanced their sustainability programs and improved their environmental and social disclosures, it has become more challenging for proponents to demonstrate significant gaps that warrant investor intervention. The evolution of corporate practices has been remarkable: the vast majority of S&P 500 companies now disclose climate change strategies, have established quantitative greenhouse gas emissions reduction targets, and provide human rights policies and supplier codes of conduct. This progress partially explains why investors are less inclined to support proposals targeting companies that have already made substantial improvements.

Simultaneously, proposals themselves have become more demanding and ambitious. Where earlier climate proposals sought broad transition plans, current requests typically ask companies to establish science-based targets or similar specific commitments.[120] As campaigns address companies with increasingly mature environmental management programs and advanced climate disclosures, proponents find it more difficult to rally broad support from other investors. The bar has been raised on both sides – companies have improved their practices, while activists have elevated their expectations.

The political polarization surrounding ESG issues has further complicated the landscape. Investors have demonstrated little interest in proposals that advocate a political viewpoint without demonstrable economic relevance, regardless of whether those proposals come from progressive or conservative perspectives.[121] Anti-ESG proposals, despite their growing numbers, have consistently received minimal support, with median support levels remaining in the low single digits.[122] These politically motivated campaigns have failed to make a compelling case for the economic impact of their requests, instead focusing on political agendas that fail to resonate with investment-focused shareholders.

This pattern underscores a fundamental truth that has remained constant across decades of shareholder activism: economic relevance remains the most important determining factor for investor support. Proposals that successfully demonstrate economic risk or provide transparency that could inform investment decisions continue to resonate with shareholders, while those that primarily advance political positions without clear financial implications struggle to gain traction.

The most successful shareholder proposals are arguably those that do not make it to a vote because management settles ahead of the vote. The rate of proposal withdrawals, typically signaling some form of settlement between proponents and companies, has fluctuated significantly.[123] During the height of ESG momentum, withdrawals reached record levels as companies proved more willing to engage with environmental and social concerns. However, withdrawal rates have since declined, suggesting that companies and proponents are finding less common ground. This trend may reflect companies' substantial efforts to improve sustainability disclosures and management programs, while proponents' requests increasingly push for more robust disclosure criteria and action plans.

In these settlement scenarios, managers often develop proposals of their own, typically incorporating some elements suggested by shareholders, and reach agreements with proposers. Whether they succeed at the ballot box or through settlement, shareholder proposals provide general direction for management while leaving the ultimate choice of means and implementation to managers. This fundamental limitation, namely that shareholders are legally constrained to offer suggestions rather than mandates, means that even successful proposals function primarily as specific prods rather than comprehensive solutions.[124] The board retains the final word on how, when, and whether to respond to shareholder concerns, and while the exact boundaries of this discretion remain subject to ongoing legal interpretation, there is little doubt that management maintains substantial autonomy in crafting its response.

This discretionary framework becomes particularly significant when considering the breadth of social issues that corporations encounter. Climate change may dominate environmental proposals, but companies simultaneously grapple with biodiversity loss, water scarcity, waste management, and countless other environmental impacts that rarely generate shareholder proposals despite their material significance.[125] Similarly, while human capital management proposals focus on high-profile issues like pay equity and diversity, they cannot address the full complexity of workplace conditions, mental health support, skills development, or the myriad ways that employment practices affect communities and families.

The selectivity inherent in shareholder activism means that proposal topics tend to cluster around issues that combine materiality with broad societal resonance. AI governance proposals have emerged not only because artificial intelligence poses unique corporate challenges compared to other technological disruptions, but also because AI has captured public attention in ways that make shareholder mobilization feasible.[126] Countless other technological and social developments with equally significant corporate implications, from biotechnology ethics to social media algorithms to gig economy labor practices, receive far less attention in shareholder proposals, not due to their lesser importance but because they lack the combination of visibility, urgency, and investor appeal necessary to sustain campaigns.

2.4.4 *The Limits of Shareholder Democracy: Proxy Contests and Board Discretion*

The proxy contest mechanism remains shareholders' most powerful tool for disciplining managers and directors, though its effectiveness varies considerably. When managers are underperforming, shareholders can challenge them by submitting alternative leadership candidates, but collective action problems significantly hamper these challenges in practice.[127] For large public companies, proxy campaigns require presenting alternative visions, hiring investment bankers and lawyers, and conducting costly promotional efforts that can cost tens of millions of dollars. These campaigns provide platforms for assessing management's past performance and future vision rather than input on specific decisions, similar to how voters in political elections express views on leaders as a whole rather than on particular policy positions.

The effort to facilitate minority director elections has been a key focus of corporate governance reforms, culminating in the SEC's adoption of the universal proxy card rule in 2021, designed to streamline options and reduce proxy fight costs.[128] The Exxon case provides a fascinating illustration of both the potential and limitations of this approach. Engine No. 1's successful election of three directors to Exxon's board, criticizing CEO Darren Woods and his sustainable energy transition strategy, was celebrated as a turning point for the fossil fuel industry.[129] Yet two years later, Woods remained CEO and acquired Pioneer, a shale drilling company, for sixty billion dollars – Exxon's largest deal since its merger with Mobil.[130] The deal passed with the support of the three minority directors, reaffirming Exxon's commitment to oil and demonstrating that electing a minority slate does not necessarily produce the outcomes proponents desired.

This example illuminates both the potential and the fundamental limitations of shareholder proposals as instruments of corporate change. Even successful proxy contests may not achieve their intended goals, as minority directors must navigate board dynamics, fiduciary duties, and practical constraints that may limit their ability to implement dramatic strategic changes. The Exxon case demonstrates that while shareholder proposals and director elections provide important mechanisms for expressing investor concerns, they operate within a system designed to preserve management's ultimate decision-making authority.[131] More fundamentally, it reveals how shareholder proposals can address only a fraction of the social and environmental issues that corporations confront, focusing necessarily on the most visible and mobilizable concerns while leaving countless other impacts to management's discretion.

2.4.5 *The Inherent Limitations of Proposal-Based Activism: Specific Prods, Not Comprehensive Solutions*

The evolution of shareholder proposals over the past decade reflects broader tensions between stakeholder capitalism and traditional shareholder primacy, between political activism and economic analysis, and between corporate accountability and management autonomy. Yet this evolution also highlights the inherent limitations of the proposal mechanism as a tool for comprehensive corporate social responsibility. As environmental and social issues have moved from the periphery to the center of corporate governance discussions, the shareholder proposal process has become both more prominent and more contentious, but it has not become more capable of addressing the full spectrum of corporate social impact.

The ESG backlash, while significant in its political intensity, has not fundamentally altered these structural constraints.[132] Rather than eliminating social and environmental issues from corporate agendas, the backlash has prompted a strategic evolution in how the most prominent concerns are presented and discussed. Companies and investors have increasingly moved away from the comprehensive ESG framework and its associated terminology, recognizing that the umbrella label had become politically charged and counterproductive.[133] This shift represents a tactical adaptation rather than a wholesale abandonment of substantive concerns, but it also reinforces the selectivity of shareholder activism by encouraging focus on individual, defensible issues rather than systematic approaches to corporate social impact.[134]

Climate change remains a paramount issue for shareholder proposals, not because of ideological commitment to environmental causes, but because climate risks pose genuine threats to long-term asset values and business continuity that can be clearly articulated and measured.[135] The financial implications of extreme weather events, regulatory changes, and shifting consumer preferences ensure that climate considerations remain central to investment analysis regardless of political rhetoric.[136] Yet even within the climate domain, shareholder proposals can address only the most prominent aspects, such as emissions targets, transition planning, or physical risk disclosure, while leaving numerous other climate-related impacts to management discretion.

Similarly, artificial intelligence has emerged as a dominant concern in shareholder proposals, though it is rarely framed in traditional ESG terms.[137] AI-related proposals address issues such as algorithmic bias, data privacy, workforce displacement, and ethical deployment, which combine social implications with financial and reputational risks. These proposals succeed precisely because they focus on specific, measurable business impacts rather than broad social justice narratives. Yet the emergence of AI as a shareholder proposal topic illustrates the reactive nature of the process: issues become proposal subjects only after they achieve sufficient public prominence and investor concern, meaning that corporate social impacts are addressed through shareholder activism only after they have already become entrenched practices.

Other social issues persist in shareholder proposals but in disaggregated forms, often separated from broader ESG frameworks but addressing related underlying concerns.[138] Proposals targeting supply chain transparency, human rights due diligence, cybersecurity practices, and employee safety continue to appear, but are increasingly presented as operational risk management rather than social responsibility initiatives.[139] This reframing reflects a strategic recognition that investors respond more favorably to concrete business cases than to abstract moral arguments, but it also demonstrates the necessarily limited scope of shareholder activism. Each proposal must make an individual case for attention, meaning that only the most compelling or visible social issues receive shareholder scrutiny.

This transformation indicates that the shareholder proposal process functions as a system of specific prods rather than comprehensive oversight. Social issues did not begin and end with ESG. They are merely finding new vocabulary and frameworks for expression among the subset of concerns that can successfully mobilize shareholder support. The underlying investor recognition that social factors can materially impact financial performance has proven more durable than political controversies surrounding ESG terminology, but this recognition operates within the same structural constraints that limit shareholder proposals to addressing only the most prominent and mobilizable concerns.

This transformation indicates that the shareholder proposal process has proven remarkably adaptable to changing political climates. Rather than being derailed by partisan opposition, it has evolved to emphasize business relevance over ideological positioning.[140] The trends suggest that successful shareholder activism increasingly requires demonstrating clear connections between proposed actions and long-term financial performance, regardless of whether those connections involve environmental, social, or governance factors.[141] The future of shareholder proposals may well depend on participants' ability to navigate competing political pressures while maintaining focus on the economic foundations that ultimately drive investor support, thus separating genuine business concerns from partisan positioning.

2.5 SECURITIES LAWS AND SOCIAL ISSUES: ESSENTIAL TOOLS AND STRUCTURAL LIMITS

Securities disclosure stands as one of the most powerful institutional tools of modern corporate governance, demonstrating remarkable capacity to discipline management, inform stakeholders, and drive meaningful corporate reform.[142] The transparency requirements embedded in securities laws compel companies to develop sophisticated understanding of their own operations while enabling investors to pose informed questions and challenge corporate narratives that might otherwise escape scrutiny.[143] This accountability mechanism operates on two levels. Externally, it enables investors to understand, assess, and appropriately price corporate activities while facilitating meaningful comparisons and productive stakeholder engagement.[144] Internally, it pressures companies to establish rigorous information-gathering systems that provide executives and directors with more accurate operational insights.[145] The disclosure process often unearths details that may dismay some within organizations, as it subjects internal choices to public monitoring and criticism, creating powerful incentives for improved decision-making across decades of regulatory evolution.

While the power of disclosure as a tool is well-established, this analysis in this section turns to a narrower question: whether current federal securities law requirements actually compel or guide companies in addressing social issues, particularly in overcoming the distinctive challenges that such issues present in recent years.

The focus shifts from disclosure as a general accountability mechanism to whether, and how, the existing federal securities regime in the United States drives corporate action on social concerns. The question becomes whether current federal securities laws, as understood, practiced, and enforced today, provide adequate frameworks to ensure that companies address complex social issues requiring accountability beyond traditional investor concerns.

The federal securities regime, which emerged with the adoption of the Securities Act of 1933 and the Securities Exchange Act of 1934, has proved largely successful in ensuring investor protection and market integrity.[146] This success has been achieved, in part, through decades of building elaborate regulatory frameworks and standards that have refined and specified its core directives. Without this evolutionary refinement, core directives alone prove inadequate to achieve comparable results for social accountability, as the paragraphs later show.

2.5.1 *The Materiality Solution: If Social Concerns Matter, Disclose Them*

At the conceptual heart of the federal securities regime lies the doctrine of materiality, which serves as the fundamental criterion for determining disclosure obligations and assigning liability. Despite occupying this central position, materiality exists without statutory definition, having been developed through judicial interpretation over nearly nine decades. The Supreme Court's closest approach to definition came in *TSC Industries v. Northway*, establishing that material information consists of facts whose disclosure "would have been viewed by the reasonable investor as having significantly altered the 'total mix' of information available."[147]

This framework gives rise to what appears to be an elegant solution for social accountability concerns. Skeptics argue that if social issues genuinely matter to companies and investors, the existing materiality standard should capture them automatically. The logic appears straightforward: if companies recognize social concerns as essential aspects of their business decisions, they implicitly acknowledge these issues as potentially material to reasonable investors.[148] Climate risks, supply chain labor practices, cybersecurity vulnerabilities, or community relations challenges that could affect business operations should thus trigger disclosure obligations under existing materiality standards. From this perspective, the materiality doctrine could seamlessly extend to encompass social issues, requiring companies to disclose any information that reasonable investors would incorporate into their valuation models and investment decisions.

This approach suggests that additional regulatory frameworks for social disclosure may be unnecessary, as the existing securities regime already provides mechanisms to capture socially significant information that affects business performance. If social issues are truly material to business success, market forces and existing legal obligations should compel appropriate disclosure without requiring specialized regulatory intervention.

2.5.2 *The Circular Challenge of Materiality Determination*

This apparently elegant solution reveals a fundamental circularity that undermines its practical effectiveness. The challenge emerges when companies attempt to determine what constitutes material information regarding social issues, which requires them to predict the interest a reasonable investor would show in information whose significance may not be immediately apparent or quantifiable.

Unlike traditional financial metrics operating within established accounting frameworks, social issues often resist quantitative analysis within the timeframes that inform securities disclosure.[149] The impact of initiatives addressing workplace safety, community engagement, or supply chain ethics frequently cannot be predicted or measured within quarterly reporting cycles or the two-to-three-year horizons typical of securities projections.[150] Companies implementing enhanced worker protection programs or investing in community development may struggle to demonstrate material financial impact within these conventional timeframes, even when such initiatives address significant social concerns.

Moreover, the social implications of corporate choices may not be readily apparent to decision-makers when initial determinations are made, often requiring stakeholder input or public reaction to reveal their full significance.[151] A company's sourcing decisions may appear financially neutral until social advocacy reveals labor conditions that generate reputational risks and regulatory attention.[152] Technology deployment may seem uncontroversial until privacy concerns emerge that affect consumer confidence and market position.

The circularity deepens when one considers that materiality determinations depend partly on investor demand for information, yet investor demand may itself depend on awareness that can only emerge through disclosure. Companies cannot predict what reasonable investors would consider material regarding social issues without understanding investor priorities, yet investor priorities regarding social issues may remain unclear without the disclosure that would reveal their importance. This creates a persistent information gap where the absence of disclosure perpetuates uncertainty about disclosure obligations.

2.5.3 *The Refuge of Vague Disclosure*

Recognizing these uncertainties, companies often gravitate toward disclosure strategies that minimize legal risk while providing minimal useful information.[153] Securities laws do not prohibit disclosure of immaterial information, and companies may choose to disclose social information voluntarily to demonstrate responsiveness to stakeholder concerns. However, the legal risks associated with specific, measurable claims about social performance create powerful incentives for vague, general statements that cannot be easily challenged later as inaccurate or misleading.[154]

This dynamic produces disclosures that are intentionally euphemistic and carefully crafted to avoid specific commitments or quantifiable claims.[155] Companies describe their "commitment to sustainability" or "dedication to diversity" without providing measurable targets, implementation timelines, or accountability mechanisms. They reference "ongoing efforts" to address social concerns without specifying what those efforts entail or how their effectiveness will be evaluated.

Such vague disclosures serve neither transparency nor accountability objectives. While they may satisfy legal requirements for voluntary disclosure, they provide neither the clarity that investors require for informed decision-making nor the specificity that might drive internal accountability and improvement. These statements create an illusion of transparency that may actually impede genuine social accountability by suggesting responsiveness while avoiding meaningful commitment.

The consequences extend beyond mere ineffectiveness to actively undermine social accountability through what critics term "greenwashing," which consists in signaling verbal commitment to well-regarded environmental values while lacking substantive depth regarding actual implementation or measurable outcomes. Companies may proclaim their dedication to sustainability or environmental stewardship without specifying concrete targets, timelines, or accountability mechanisms that would enable stakeholders to assess genuine progress versus aspirational rhetoric. The phenomenon has expanded beyond environmental concerns to encompass what might be called "washing" across various social domains, such as diversity washing, ethics washing, or stakeholder washing, where organizations deploy similar strategies of symbolic commitment without substantive follow through.[156]

This proliferation of superficial commitments has generated widespread skepticism among investors and consumers who have grown increasingly distrustful of corporate social statements that lack verifiable backing. The erosion of credibility extends beyond individual companies to affect confidence in corporate social responsibility efforts more broadly, creating a credibility gap that undermines even genuine efforts at social accountability when they cannot be readily distinguished from mere public relations exercises.

2.5.4 *A European Experiment: From General Mandate to Specific Requirements*

The inadequacies of general disclosure frameworks for social issues are vividly illustrated by the European Union's experience with the 2014 Non-Financial Reporting Directive.[157] This ambitious regulatory experiment required large European companies to provide disclosures on environmental protection, social responsibility, human rights, anti-corruption, and board diversity, while granting companies substantial discretion in determining specific content and format.

The directive represented a sophisticated attempt to mandate social disclosure while preserving corporate flexibility, requiring companies to describe how social issues related to their business models, their implemented policies and due diligence procedures, principal risks, and performance indicators. However, the absence of specific disclosure requirements or standardized metrics left companies to determine appropriate reporting based on their assessment of stakeholder needs.

The results demonstrated the inadequacy of general mandates without specific guidance. By 2020, 72 percent of report users characterized the information as insufficient.[158] Companies engaged in selective disclosure of favorable information while providing general statements that avoided meaningful accountability. Disclosures lacked comparability even within industries, and investors questioned the reliability of unaudited voluntary information.

Recognizing these failures, the European Union responded with the Corporate Sustainability Reporting Directive, which replaced the flexible approach with detailed, standardized requirements.[159] This regulatory evolution from general mandate to specific requirements illustrates the practical necessity of moving beyond broad disclosure frameworks toward detailed, sector-specific standards for meaningful social accountability.

2.5.5 *The Flexibility Paradox and Its Implications*

Paradoxically, the flexibility of current securities frameworks has enabled considerable experimentation with sustainability reporting and social disclosure. The principle-based nature of materiality determinations has allowed companies to explore various approaches to environmental, social, and governance (ESG) reporting without requiring fundamental statutory changes. This flexibility has facilitated the emergence of numerous voluntary reporting frameworks and has enabled regulatory bodies to propose climate-related disclosure requirements based on evolving understanding of materiality.[160]

This adaptive capacity represents a genuine strength of existing securities frameworks, demonstrating their potential to evolve with changing stakeholder expectations and business realities. The proliferation of sustainability reporting initiatives, the development of industry-specific guidance,[161] and the growing acceptance of environmental and social factors in investment analysis all reflect this regulatory flexibility in action.

However, this same flexibility that enables experimentation has also created space for companies to develop their own approaches to social accountability, often banding together through industry bodies to establish standards and practices that fill gaps left by regulatory frameworks.[162] This organic development of voluntary regimes represents a significant phenomenon in corporate governance, one that merits careful examination on its own terms rather than merely as a stepping stone toward regulatory intervention. Rather than viewing voluntary initiatives primarily through the lens of their limitations relative to mandatory frameworks, this examination calls for understanding how these regimes operate, what they accomplish, and why they have become such important features of contemporary corporate accountability.

2.5.6 *Beyond Current Frameworks*

Current securities laws represent an essential foundation for corporate accountability regarding social issues, providing powerful transparency mechanisms and creating meaningful incentives for corporate attention to stakeholder concerns. The flexibility of existing frameworks has enabled valuable experimentation with social disclosure and has demonstrated the potential for regulatory evolution without fundamental statutory revision. However, federal securities laws as currently constituted cannot adequately address the full spectrum of social accountability challenges facing contemporary corporations. The limitations are not merely technical problems amenable to regulatory reinterpretation but reflect fundamental structural constraints arising from frameworks designed primarily for financial disclosure.

Developing effective approaches to help corporate decision-making on social issues requires far more than disclosure mechanisms alone can provide. Companies must navigate complex questions of issue identification, determining which social concerns warrant attention within their specific operational contexts. They must develop sophisticated understanding of stakeholder impacts, assessing how their activities affect diverse communities, employees, suppliers, and broader social systems. Perhaps most challenging, they must identify and implement appropriate means of addressing identified problems, drawing on expertise that extends well beyond traditional business competencies. Disclosure requirements alone cannot provide guidance or motivation for meaningful corporate responses to these challenges. The question is not whether to abandon disclosure-based approaches but how to build upon their strengths while developing complementary mechanisms that can provide the specificity, standardization, and enforceability that meaningful corporate action on social issues demands.

2.6 CORPORATE PURPOSE AND ESG: THE DEBATE OVER ENDS, NOT MEANS

The examination of corporate governance doctrines in the preceding sections, which cover managerial discretion, deliberative decision-making, oversight duties, shareholder proposals, and securities disclosure, may naturally bring to mind the heated contemporary debate surrounding ESG investing and corporate purpose.[163] Indeed, when discussing how corporations navigate social controversies like Meta's content moderation policies or Disney's response to Florida legislation, it would be reasonable to wonder whether this analysis aligns with or challenges the ESG movement that has dominated corporate governance discourse over the past decade.

The governance challenges examined in this chapter, while clearly related to ESG concerns, reveal a distinct set of institutional problems that persist regardless of where companies position themselves in the ESG debate. These institutional deficiencies cut across ideological lines, affecting companies whether they embrace or reject ESG principles. While ESG proponents and critics engage in fierce battles over whether corporations should prioritize profit maximization[164] versus stakeholder value[165] versus broader social welfare, they largely ignore a more fundamental question: how should corporations make decisions when social considerations inevitably arise, regardless of their ultimate normative commitments? The analysis here reveals that even the most ardent ESG opponents must grapple with social factors in their business decisions, and existing legal frameworks provide them with remarkably little guidance on how to do so effectively.

2.6.1 *The Rise and Fall of ESG: A Movement in Search of Governance*

The ESG movement emerged from multiple converging factors, including the growing influence of institutional investors, generational shifts in values, and increasing recognition that environmental and social factors could materially impact long-term financial performance. The movement gained momentum following the 2008 financial crisis, which had damaged public confidence in market self-regulation and created space for alternative approaches to corporate accountability. Environmental concerns, particularly climate change, provided the initial catalyst, but the framework soon expanded to encompass workplace diversity, supply chain labor practices, data privacy, and corporate political engagement.

Two pivotal moments crystallized ESG's mainstream acceptance. In 2019, the Business Roundtable, a lobbying group comprising the chief executives of major American corporations, issued a statement redefining corporate purpose to serve all stakeholders, not just shareholders.[166] Signed by 181 corporate leaders, including Jamie Dimon of JPMorgan Chase and Tim Cook of Apple, the statement declared that companies should "deliver value to all of them, for the future success of our companies, our communities and our country." This represented a dramatic departure from decades of shareholder primacy orthodoxy and seemed to signal corporate America's embrace of stakeholder capitalism.

Simultaneously, Larry Fink, CEO of BlackRock, the world's largest asset manager with over $10 trillion under management, began using his annual letters to corporate CEOs to champion ESG principles. Fink's 2018 letter declared that "society is demanding that companies, both public and private, serve a social purpose,"[167] while his 2020 letter announced that climate risk had become "investment risk" and that BlackRock would make sustainability "integral to portfolio construction and risk management."[168] Given BlackRock's enormous influence as an institutional investor, Fink's pronouncements carried extraordinary weight in boardrooms worldwide.

The ESG tide appeared unstoppable during its peak years from 2019 to 2021. Institutional investors incorporated ESG criteria into their investment strategies, with assets in sustainable investment funds growing from $3 trillion in 2016 to over $35 trillion by 2020.[169] Corporate sustainability reports became standard practice, with the vast majority of S&P 500 companies publishing detailed disclosures about their environmental impact, diversity initiatives, and stakeholder engagement efforts.[170] The COVID-19 pandemic further accelerated these trends, as companies' responses to employee safety, community support, and supply chain resilience became visible manifestations of their stakeholder commitments.

2.6.2 *The Backlash: Politics, Performance, and Polarization*

The ESG movement's apparent dominance, however, masked growing tensions that would eventually produce a fierce backlash. Critics argued that ESG represented a form of "woke capitalism" that prioritized political activism over fiduciary duty, with corporate executives imposing their personal values on shareholders and society.[171] This criticism gained particular force when companies took public stances on controversial social issues, from voting rights legislation to police reform to LGBTQ+ rights.[172]

The political backlash intensified rapidly after 2021. Republican-controlled states began passing legislation prohibiting their pension funds from considering ESG factors in investment decisions.[173] Texas, Florida, and other conservative states enacted laws requiring state investment managers to prioritize financial returns over environmental or social considerations, with some states creating lists of financial firms deemed to be "boycotting" traditional energy companies.[174] These legislative efforts reflected broader conservative opposition to what critics characterized as the weaponization of corporate power for progressive political ends.

The Securities and Exchange Commission became another battleground, with the Biden administration's proposed climate disclosure rules generating intense opposition from business groups and Republican officials.[175] The proposed rules would have required public companies to disclose detailed information about climate-related risks and greenhouse gas emissions, including Scope 3 emissions from their supply chains and customers.[176] Critics argued that these requirements represented regulatory overreach that would impose enormous compliance costs while providing little genuine value to investors.[177]

The 2024 election of Donald Trump as president marked a decisive turning point. The incoming administration signaled its intention to reverse ESG-related regulations and challenge institutional investors' consideration of environmental and social factors.[178] This political shift coincided with growing investor skepticism about ESG's financial performance, as some studies suggested that ESG-focused funds had underperformed traditional benchmarks during periods of market volatility.[179]

Perhaps most significantly, the institutional investors who had championed ESG began retreating from their previous commitments. BlackRock, facing pressure from both conservative critics and progressive activists who argued the firm was not doing enough, quietly scaled back its climate-focused rhetoric and voting practices.[180] Other major asset managers similarly moderated their positions, recognizing that ESG had become too politically charged to sustain broad institutional support.

The corporate retreat proved equally dramatic. Companies that had embraced diversity, equity, and inclusion (DEI) programs during the social justice movements of 2020 began quietly dismantling these initiatives. High-profile corporate reversals, such as Walmart's decision to remove DEI language from its policies[181] and Disney's scaling back of diversity programming,[182] reflected broader recognition that ESG commitments had become political liabilities rather than competitive advantages.

2.6.3 *Two Distinct Conversations: Purpose versus Process*

This brief history of ESG's rise and fall illuminates why the governance analysis in this chapter addresses fundamentally different questions from the corporate purpose debate. The ESG controversy centers on fundamentally normative questions about what corporations should seek to accomplish: Should they maximize shareholder value, stakeholder welfare, or broader social good? Should they engage with controversial political issues or maintain strict political neutrality? Should they prioritize short-term profits or long-term sustainability?

These normative debates about corporate purpose, that is, the ends of managerial discretion, are distinct from questions about decision-making processes, which focuses on the means through which discretion is exercised. Regardless of whether a board believes in shareholder primacy or stakeholder capitalism, regardless of whether executives embrace or reject ESG principles, they will inevitably encounter business decisions that implicate social considerations. The governance challenge lies not in resolving the philosophical debate about corporate purpose, but in developing effective frameworks for navigating social complexities when they arise.

Consider, for example, a traditional energy company whose leadership explicitly rejects ESG ideology and remains committed to maximizing shareholder returns through fossil fuel development. Even this company must make decisions about worker safety protocols, community relations in areas where it operates, supply chain partnerships, and responses to regulatory changes. These decisions involve social considerations not because the company has embraced stakeholder capitalism, but because social factors inevitably intersect with business operations. The question is not whether the company should consider these factors, since market forces and competitive dynamics often make such consideration unavoidable.

Rather, the question is how the company should structure its decision-making processes to address them effectively.

Similarly, a technology company that proudly champions progressive values and stakeholder engagement still faces complex choices about content moderation, data privacy, algorithmic bias, and workforce policies. The company's commitment to social responsibility does not automatically generate answers to specific operational questions about balancing competing stakeholder interests, measuring social impact, or adapting to changing community expectations. Even the most ESG-committed organization requires sophisticated governance mechanisms to translate good intentions into effective action.

This distinction becomes particularly important when examining the governance innovations that have emerged from leading companies across the ideological spectrum. As subsequent chapters will explore, some of the most sophisticated approaches to social governance have developed within companies that explicitly reject ESG framing but recognize the need for systematic approaches to stakeholder engagement and social risk management. Conversely, some organizations that loudly proclaim their ESG commitments have failed to develop effective governance mechanisms, resulting in reactive, inconsistent, or counterproductive responses to social challenges.

2.6.4 *The Persistence of Social Considerations*

The collapse of ESG as a unifying framework has not eliminated the underlying social considerations that drove its emergence. Climate risks continue to threaten business continuity regardless of corporate executives' views on environmental regulation. Workforce diversity remains a competitive factor in talent acquisition even for companies that have abandoned DEI programming. Supply chain labor practices affect both operational efficiency and reputational risk whether or not companies embrace human rights rhetoric. Cybersecurity and data privacy concerns persist as business imperatives independent of any broader social responsibility agenda.

The political polarization surrounding ESG has, if anything, made effective social governance more challenging rather than less necessary. Companies now must navigate not only the underlying social issues that affect their operations, but also the political sensitivities surrounding how they discuss and address these challenges.[183] The need for sophisticated decision-making frameworks has intensified as companies seek approaches that can address substantive social considerations without triggering political backlash from either side of the ideological spectrum.

This dynamic explains why the governance analysis in this chapter remains relevant across the ESG divide. Whether a company positions itself as a champion of stakeholder capitalism or a defender of shareholder primacy, it requires institutional mechanisms for gathering information about social impacts, engaging with affected stakeholders, evaluating competing priorities, and implementing decisions effectively. The specific substantive choices may differ based on the company's values and market position, but the need for deliberative governance processes transcends ideological boundaries.

2.6.5 *Beyond the Purpose Debate: Governance as Institutional Capability*

The ESG experience demonstrates both the promise and the limitations of focusing primarily on corporate purpose rather than governance process. The movement succeeded in raising awareness about the business relevance of environmental and social factors, driving significant improvements in corporate disclosure and stakeholder engagement. However, its emphasis on normative commitments provided limited guidance on operational questions about how companies should structure their decision-making to address complex social challenges effectively.

The political backlash against ESG has created space for a more pragmatic approach that focuses on governance capability rather than ideological alignment.[184] Companies across the political spectrum are recognizing that they need institutional frameworks for addressing social considerations not because of abstract moral obligations, but because effective social governance has become a core competency for navigating contemporary business environments.

This shift toward process-focused governance represents a return to corporate law's traditional strengths: developing institutional frameworks that enable effective decision-making across diverse organizational contexts. Rather than prescribing specific substantive outcomes, these frameworks emphasize the quality of deliberative processes, the integrity of information systems, and the effectiveness of stakeholder engagement mechanisms. Such approaches can accommodate different normative commitments while ensuring that all companies develop the institutional capacity necessary for responsible decision-making on social issues.

The following chapters will examine how leading companies have begun developing these voluntary governance frameworks, analyzing what makes some approaches more effective than others regardless of their underlying ideological orientation. This analysis suggests that the future of corporate social governance lies not in resolving debates about corporate purpose, but in learning from institutional innovations that help companies exercise their discretionary authority more effectively, irrespective of normative goals that authority may serve.

2.7 CONCLUSION: THE GAP IN CORPORATE GOVERNANCE

The landscape of social governance reveals a fundamental paradox at the heart of contemporary business law. Delaware corporate law and federal securities regulation have created a system that simultaneously empowers corporate boards with extraordinary discretion while providing them with minimal concrete guidance for exercising that discretion on social issues.[185] This framework places directors and managers squarely at the center of decision-making authority, granting them the flexibility to determine what considerations will best serve long-term profitability and shareholder value, including environmental, social, ethical, or otherwise. Yet this same legal architecture offers remarkably little direction on how to approach the complex social challenges that increasingly define modern corporate responsibility.

2.7.1 *The Architecture of Discretion*

Corporate law's commitment to managerial authority is deep and deliberate. The business judgment rule protects directorial decisions from judicial second-guessing, recognizing that managers possess superior information about competitive dynamics, operational challenges, and strategic opportunities. Courts have consistently extended this deference to socially controversial issues, treating decisions about stakeholder engagement, political positioning, and community investment as ordinary business judgments deserving the same protection accorded to product development or capital allocation choices. The *Simeone v. Disney* decision exemplifies this approach, validating corporate political speech as falling within the accepted bounds of directorial authority while requiring only that boards engage in thoughtful deliberation rather than achieve particular substantive outcomes.[186]

This broad delegation of authority reflects sound institutional design. Directors and executives possess intimate knowledge of their companies' capabilities, market positions, and stakeholder relationships that outside observers, especially judges, simply cannot match. The separation of ownership and control ensures that professional managers can pursue long-term value creation strategies without being constrained by the potentially myopic preferences of dispersed shareholders or the limited expertise of judicial oversight.[187] When it comes to social issues, this discretionary framework acknowledges that environmental concerns, workplace policies, and community engagement are not distinct from business strategy but integral components of it.

The procedural evolution following *Van Gorkom* has reinforced this discretionary authority while establishing minimum standards for deliberative decision-making.[188] Courts now focus on whether directors have informed themselves adequately before acting rather than evaluating the merits of their substantive choices. This process-oriented approach preserves managerial autonomy while ensuring that decisions emerge from thoughtful consideration rather than hasty judgment or inadequate information-gathering. The emphasis on deliberative procedures, such as seeking expert advice, allowing sufficient time for consideration, and documenting serious engagement with complex issues, creates a framework within which directorial discretion can be exercised responsibly.

2.7.2 *The Guidance Gap*

Yet for all its sophistication in preserving managerial authority, corporate law provides remarkably little concrete direction for how that authority should be exercised when addressing social issues. The deliberative requirements established since *Van Gorkom* offer general direction but remain silent on the dimensions that define effective social governance. How should the company identify which stakeholder perspectives should be considered? What metrics should guide the assessment of social initiatives? How should boards evaluate the effectiveness of their social strategies over time?

This guidance gap becomes particularly acute when considering the distinctive challenges that social issues present. Unlike traditional business decisions where market feedback provides relatively clear signals about success or failure, social initiatives often produce impacts that are difficult to measure, may not manifest for years, and affect stakeholders who lack formal channels for communicating their experiences to corporate decision-makers. The absence of established frameworks for stakeholder engagement means that even well-intentioned boards may inadvertently exclude crucial perspectives from their deliberations, leading to decisions that fail to account for the lived experiences of those most affected by corporate choices.[189]

The limitations of existing accountability mechanisms compound these challenges. While Caremark establishes oversight duties for legal compliance, its mission-critical framework is proving ill-suited to addressing social issues that typically involve business judgments rather than regulatory violations.[190] Shareholder proposals provide avenues for raising specific concerns but cannot systematically address the full spectrum of social impacts that corporations generate. Securities disclosure requirements offer transparency mechanisms but often produce vague commitments that satisfy legal obligations while avoiding meaningful accountability.

2.7.3 A *Landscape of Innovation and Inconsistency*

The result of this paradoxical framework, which combines broad discretion with lack of concrete guidance, is a corporate landscape characterized by remarkable innovation alongside troubling inconsistency. As the following chapters will explore in detail, some companies have utilized their discretionary authority to construct elaborate policymaking frameworks for addressing social issues, often demonstrating greater sophistication and effectiveness than those developed by government legislators. These corporate innovators have created comprehensive systems for stakeholder engagement, impact assessment, and accountability that rival or exceed the deliberative mechanisms found in traditional regulatory contexts.

Yet as subsequent analysis will reveal, other companies have adopted completely different approaches, ranging from minimalist compliance strategies to ad hoc reactive responses. The problem is not that different companies reach different conclusions about how to address similar social challenges. Such variation is not only permissible but often desirable given the diversity of corporate contexts and stakeholder relationships. Rather, the troubling pattern emerges when companies fail to make any sustained effort at thoughtful consideration, reaching decisions about consequential social issues without investing in the deliberative processes that might produce more effective outcomes. Thus, this variation in corporate approaches represents both the promise and the peril of discretionary governance, demonstrating the potential for innovation while revealing the risks of leaving complex social decisions to whatever decision-making processes companies happen to develop on their own.

2.7.4 *The Need for Evolution*

The current moment calls for recognizing both the strengths and limitations of existing corporate governance frameworks while building upon their foundation to address contemporary challenges more effectively. The discretionary authority that corporate law grants to directors and managers remains essential for enabling responsive, context-sensitive decision-making on complex social issues. Any evolution of governance frameworks must preserve this flexibility while providing the concrete guidance that can help translate good intentions into effective action.

This evolution need not require wholesale reconstruction of existing legal architectures. The procedural innovations that have emerged since *Van Gorkom*, such as the emphasis on expert advice, thorough deliberation, and documentation of decision-making processes, provide templates for developing more sophisticated approaches to social governance. However, meaningful progress requires analyzing decision-making processes themselves, not merely their outcomes. The most successful companies appear to be developing voluntary governance regimes that offer valuable insights for broader application.

The challenge lies in learning from these corporate innovations while extending their insights to create frameworks that can guide broader corporate engagement with stakeholder concerns. Since companies are already creating these voluntary regimes for social governance, we can study their decision-making processes to understand what makes some approaches more effective than others. The path forward requires moving beyond the current binary of either broad discretion or detailed regulation toward more nuanced approaches informed by the experiences of companies that have invested seriously in developing systematic approaches to social issues.

As Chapter 3 will demonstrate, examining how leading companies have constructed their voluntary governance frameworks reveals patterns and principles that could inform broader governance evolution. Corporate law's genius has always resided in its capacity to establish principled frameworks that enable effective governance across diverse organizational contexts.[191] The social challenges of the twenty-first century demand that same institutional creativity, applied to developing governance mechanisms that can help corporations exercise their considerable social influence responsibly while maintaining their capacity for innovation and value creation.

The stakes of this challenge extend far beyond corporate governance itself. As social issues become increasingly central to business strategy and stakeholder expectations, the quality of corporate social governance will significantly influence not only business success but also broader social welfare. The current framework's combination of broad authority and limited guidance has produced both remarkable innovations and troubling gaps in corporate social accountability. The task ahead is to build upon the innovations while addressing the gaps, creating governance frameworks worthy of the social influence that modern corporations wield.

3

Corporate Ordering for Social Conflicts

Chapters 1 and 2 revealed a striking gap in contemporary corporate law. Social considerations arise amidst significant uncertainty in many contexts, from developing sustainable product lines to entering emerging markets with complex governance challenges, and from disrupting traditional industries through new technologies to restructuring supply chains to address labor standards. In these situations, corporate directors and managers face decisions with enormous stakes, competing stakeholder preferences, and intense public scrutiny. Yet they must ultimately decide how to proceed with little or no guidance from corporate law. The uncertainty is compounded by the reality that different shareholders often have sharply divergent views about what constitutes responsible corporate behavior. These high-stakes choices unfold under the watchful eyes of activists, media, and regulators, amplifying the pressure on decision-makers.

Managers' choices will almost certainly be protected by the business judgment rule, so long as they can point to good faith and some evidence of deliberation. The ultimate outcome matters little; the process protection remains robust.[1] True, shareholder activists might stir up controversy at the annual meeting, and disclosure obligations may require awkward admissions in securities filings when an issue grows sufficiently to satisfy materiality thresholds. But ultimately, corporate law offers virtually no guidance on how these momentous decisions should be made. It does not prescribe what processes to follow, what factors to weigh, what deliberative structures to employ, or what standards of analysis to apply. Executives enjoy breathtaking discretion to chart whatever course they deem appropriate, armed with little more than their personal judgment and the comforting knowledge that courts will rarely second-guess their choices.[2]

Some would argue this is not a gap at all, but rather a defining feature of corporate law. On this view, the law deliberately leaves managers free to exercise their judgment as they see fit, positioned at the apex of a corporate hierarchy that is essential for efficient business operations. Chief executives, while not autocrats, serve as singular leaders and ultimate decision-makers, and this concentrated authority enables the swift, decisive action that competitive markets demand.[3] Social considerations, by contrast, embody the messy complexity of democratic society, an amalgamation of diverse viewpoints, competing interests, varied perspectives, and distinct backgrounds. Our political institutions manage this complexity through intricate networks of multiple decision-makers, elaborate checks and balances, and sophisticated institutional interactions. Such democratic complexity, the argument goes, would only come at the cost of the streamlined hierarchy that makes corporate governance effective.[4]

Yet this conception of managerial authority fundamentally mischaracterizes the decision-making processes that corporate law actually envisions and encourages. If we truly embraced managers as quasi-autocratic leaders limited only by external regulation, corporate governance mechanisms would be entirely superfluous. Instead, our governance framework reflects a more sophisticated understanding of managers as informed decision-makers who benefit from, and should be subject to, reasoned processes of information gathering and consultation, overseen by boards of directors and accountable to shareholders.[5]

Consider how corporations approach conventional business challenges. Managers do not make decisions in isolation, nor are they expected to rely solely on their personal judgment. Rather, they engage in elaborate processes of information collection and consultation that span both internal and external sources. They canvass markets to understand customer preferences and competitive dynamics. They commission product research to assess technical feasibility and consumer appeal. They conduct extensive market research to gauge demand and identify optimal positioning strategies. They establish specialized departments dedicated to generating the information necessary for sound decision-making, such as research and development, strategic planning, and government relations. They create board committees with specific expertise to oversee critical functions such as audit, compensation, and risk management.[6]

When major decisions loom, managers routinely seek guidance from networks of specialists: investment bankers for mergers and acquisitions, financial advisors for capital structure decisions, marketing experts for brand positioning, public relations specialists for communications strategy, and management consultants for operational improvements.[7] The consulting industry, epitomized by firms such as McKinsey & Company, has never been perceived as undermining managerial prerogatives, but rather as enhancing executive capabilities. Even entrepreneurial founders in startup environments rely heavily on venture capital partners, who bring experience and market sophistication to navigate business uncertainties.[8] The corporate world has developed sophisticated frameworks governing these information-gathering and advisory relationships, encompassing everything from financing arrangements to gatekeeping functions to credit rating processes.[9]

Crucially, the various steps corporations have developed for traditional business decisions have not remained merely matters of best practice. Over time, they have become embedded in corporate law itself. Courts now expect boards to demonstrate that they have followed appropriate deliberative processes, consulting relevant experts, gathering pertinent information, and utilizing specialized committees when making major business decisions as appropriate.[10] These tools might have begun as market-generated efforts to address a business need, but have since evolved into legally relevant steps boards must fulfill to claim business judgment rule protection, mitigate conflicts of interest, demonstrate their awareness of securities disclosures, or avoid compliance-related liability.[11] Yet as to social issues, no such procedural steps have been established or required. The law remains silent on what constitutes adequate deliberation in this domain.[12]

What this book documents is how companies are already developing and implementing innovative frameworks to enhance their decision-making processes regarding social issues. These developments reflect a growing recognition among corporate leaders that, rather than relying on their own intuitions, the prudent approach involves systematic information gathering and consultation, drawing on stakeholder input, expert analysis, specialized research, and structured deliberation.[13] This represents precisely the same principle that guides sound decision-making in other areas of business operations.

This chapter synthesizes the methods, practices, and approaches that leading corporations have adopted to build effective decision-making processes for navigating complex social issues. From these observed practices, this book develops a new theoretical framework that connects the functions corporations seek to fulfill with the specific methodologies they select, illustrated through concrete examples that demonstrate these frameworks in action. Together, these functions form a framework this book terms "corporate ordering." The following chapters then provide in-depth case studies that showcase how these principles apply across diverse substantive areas: rideshare regulation (Chapter 6), sustainability (Chapter 7), and artificial intelligence governance (Chapter 8). Together, these analyses reveal how systematic approaches to decision-making on social issues can enhance both corporate performance and societal outcomes.

The systematization and theoretical development of corporate ordering is not merely an academic exercise, but an essential tool for protecting shareholder interests. Just as corporations have recognized that informed decision-making in traditional business matters serves shareholders by reducing risks and improving outcomes, the same logic applies to social issues. When companies make social decisions without adequate information gathering and consultation processes, they expose shareholders to reputational risks, regulatory sanctions, consumer backlash, and operational disruptions that could have been anticipated and mitigated through better decision-making frameworks. Performing this function well, by establishing systematic processes for gathering relevant information and engaging appropriate stakeholders before making social decisions, ought to represent a core fiduciary service to shareholders.

This recognition demands that corporate law evolve to acknowledge and support these emerging practices. Yet normative debates about whether corporations should address social issues at all have obscured the more fundamental question of how they should make such decisions when they inevitably do. Chapter 9 will explore at length how these disputes have divided legal theorists and practitioners. Yet this divisiveness has prevented legal scholarship and doctrine from developing the analytical frameworks necessary to evaluate and improve corporate decision-making processes in this domain. The time has come to move beyond these normative impasses and focus on the practical imperative of ensuring that when corporations engage with social issues, as they unavoidably do, they employ processes that serve shareholder interests through informed, systematic decision-making.

3.1 ANALYZING CORPORATE FUNCTIONS UNDER THE DISTINCTION OF POWERS

Conventional wisdom thinks of corporate managers as exercising purely executive power. After all, the person at the top bears the title of Chief Executive Officer, and all corporate authority flows through this single individual under delegation from the same governing body, the board of directors.[14] The organizational chart appears to show a straightforward hierarchy of executive power. When we observe corporate decision-making, it seems to follow familiar patterns of managerial authority: leaders set strategic direction, allocate resources, and respond to operational challenges through a unified chain of command. This intuitive understanding aligns with our conventional view of business management as focusing on executive decisions.

Yet this superficial simplicity obscures a remarkable reality. What appears to be a vertical line to executive authority is actually a complex system performing multiple functions under a single institutional umbrella.[15] All power structures inherently perform three distinct yet interrelated functions: a legislative, an executive, and a judicial one. This analytical framework forms one of the most enduring insights of political theory, tracing its intellectual lineage back to Aristotle. It has of course found its most prominent modern application in constitutional design, where the separation of powers into distinct institutions serves as a cornerstone of democratic governance.[16]

However, the utility of this tripartite distinction extends far beyond the realm of constitutional and administrative law. Indeed, whether examining military commands, university rules, or private clubs, every hierarchy must establish norms (legislative function), implement decisions (executive function), and adjudicate conflicts (judicial function), revealing these three dimensions as fundamental pillars of organized authority itself.[17] When we peer beneath the unified facade of corporate hierarchy, the full spectrum of the three functions readily emerges. Just as any hierarchical body, corporations have also evolved, consciously or not, to perform analogous functions through different mechanisms and with different constituencies in mind.

By applying the tripartite distinction to rulemaking, executive, and monitoring functions onto corporate decision-making, I do not mean to suggest that corporations are akin to states, mini-societies, or bearers of democratic obligations. Such analogies obscure rather than illuminate the unique characteristics of corporate influence. Treating corporations as if they were governments prevents us from understanding the true profile of corporate power, with its distinct strengths and limitations. Corporate influence operates through fundamentally different mechanisms than state power, as it relies on contractual relationships, market positioning, and economic leverage rather than sovereign authority, legal compulsion, and democratic legitimacy. Corporate decisions, while often far-reaching in their effects, lack the formal binding force of law and operate within constraints that differ markedly from those facing governmental actors.[18]

Rather, this approach rests on a fundamentally functional argument. Corporations, by their very nature as hierarchical organizations wielding significant economic and social influence, inevitably make choices that fulfill one or more of these essential governance functions. Thus, they are choosing decision-making tools that best serve the goals of each function. These are the choices that Sections 3.1–3.4 will try to illuminate.

3.1.1 *The Tripartite Distinction as an Analytical Tool for Corporate Functions*

The functional differentiation becomes clear when we examine how corporate decisions actually unfold. Rulemaking functions occur when managers create frameworks of general and uniform applicability. These decisions typically face higher stakeholder heterogeneity because general rules apply across many different circumstances, potentially implicating problems managers may not fully understand or anticipate.[19] The broad scope increases visibility and elevates the perceived importance of the solution, often seen as embodying management's values and predicting future moves. Such decisions benefit from wide consultation processes that engage large numbers of stakeholders, reach out to potential opponents, and provide opportunities for direct participation in decision-making.[20]

Executive functions involve individual decisions with far-reaching implications, ranging from implementing long-term strategic visions, such as building new facilities or launching products, to responding quickly to emerging needs. While stakeholder engagement may be valuable, it can be difficult to organize effectively. These decisions are best served by robust disclosure practices that communicate choices and rationales, notify interested parties, and invite future engagement while building trust through transparency and accountability.[21]

Monitoring functions encompass specialized oversight and investigation of past failures and mistakes. These mechanisms both help managers maintain control over large organizations and constrain managerial behavior through statutory mandates, regulatory obligations, and voluntary commitments. Given well-established incentives for managers to shirk responsibility or cover up misconduct, these functions raise critical concerns about independence, integrity, thoroughness, and access to resources.[22]

The tripartite distinction provides analytical clarity by recognizing that different corporate functions require correspondingly different decision-making processes and governance approaches. This framework serves as an analytical tool rather than a rigid institutional blueprint, illuminating both the inherent bargaining imbalances between corporations and stakeholders and the distinct audiences each type of corporate action is intended to address. While ultimate authority formally resides with boards of directors and chief executives, these actors frequently choose to delegate specific functions to different institutional formations, both within the corporate hierarchy and external to it, that possess specialized capabilities or legitimacy to fulfill these distinct rulemaking, executive, and monitoring roles more effectively than centralized leadership by itself.[23]

This tripartite analysis illuminates the true architecture of corporate power, revealing the complex functional edifice hidden within what appears to be simple business management. Understanding these distinctions is crucial because each function demands different governance approaches, accountability mechanisms, and stakeholder engagement processes. Corporate law's failure to recognize these functional differences leads to governance frameworks that treat fundamentally different types of corporate power as if they were identical, undermining both corporate effectiveness and shareholder accountability.

3.1.2 *Mapping Corporate Functions to Governance Solutions*

The practical application of this framework becomes evident when examining how different corporate functions demand correspondingly different governance approaches. Rather than adopting uniform oversight mechanisms across all business activities, effective corporate governance must recognize that each type of corporate decision-making presents unique challenges, stakeholder relationships, and performance requirements that necessitate tailored supervisory structures.[24] The accompanying table synthesizes these critical relationships, demonstrating that effective corporate governance cannot rely on one-size-fits-all solutions but must instead calibrate its mechanisms to the specific demands of each functional category.

Rulemaking functions, which involve creating frameworks of general and uniform applicability, require governance approaches that can handle high stakeholder heterogeneity and broad visibility. The governance goals center on wide outreach and notice-and-comment processes that engage diverse constituencies who may be affected by general rules applied across varying circumstances. Examples like ride-sharing platform policies or post-#MeToo workplace reforms illustrate how companies must reach beyond typical advisory channels to gather perspectives from stakeholders who may experience different impacts from uniform policies.[25]

TABLE 3.1 *Mapping corporate functions to governance solutions*

Type of power	Application to corporations	Governance goals	Examples
Rulemaking	Creating frameworks of general and uniform applicability	Wide Outreach Notice-and-Comment	Rideshare; Post-#MeToo reforms
Executive	Individual decisions with far-reaching implications	Disclosure Accuracy	Net zero commitments
Review	Specialized oversight Averting conflicts	Independence Investigation	Ethics Committees; Civil Rights Audits

Executive functions, characterized by individual decisions with far-reaching implications, call for governance mechanisms focused on disclosure and accuracy. These decisions, whether strategic implementations like net zero commitments or urgent responses to emerging challenges, benefit from clear communication of choices and rationales rather than extensive prior consultation.[26] The governance priority shifts from broad participation to transparent explanation and reliable follow-through.[27]

Review functions, encompassing specialized oversight and conflict avoidance, demand governance structures that prioritize independence and thorough investigation. Ethics committees, civil rights audits, and similar monitoring mechanisms must demonstrate credibility through structural independence from the decisions they evaluate and the resources necessary to conduct meaningful investigations.[28]

This mapping reveals that corporations seeking to optimize their governance cannot simply adopt generic best practices, but must thoughtfully match their governance tools to the functional demands of different types of decisions. The framework thus serves not as a rigid template but as a diagnostic tool for identifying which governance mechanisms will be most effective for particular corporate choices. The following sections systematically examine how these principles apply across major corporate functional areas, with each section addressing a separate domain of business activity (Table 3.1).

3.2 CORPORATE RULEMAKING

The mere suggestion that corporations are themselves actively engaged rulemakers will raise eyebrows in some quarters. Lobbying by corporate interests has been a long-established concern in modern democracies, where politicians often find themselves dependent on large donations to launch successful electoral campaigns. These sums of money, the fear is, are only handed over in expectation that, once elected, politicians will pass laws that favor corporate perspectives, facilitate business goals, or otherwise offer preferential treatment to their supporters.[29] On the regulatory side, corporations are widely considered well-placed to utilize administrative rulemaking to their benefit, by mustering resources to more effectively comment on policy proposals, submit complaints and requests, and represent themselves in exploratory hearings.[30] Moreover, corporations have organized into industry groups like the Business Roundtable that have successfully pressured governments and taken them to court when necessary.[31] This corporate effectiveness in pushing for favorable legislation is in stark contrast to the nameless interests of the public, which unavoidably take a back seat. So, if we distrust corporate involvement in formal lawmaking by elected officials and their appointed executives, what can we expect when corporations themselves are the rulemakers? Why should we even entertain this idea?

In reality, I will argue here, corporate rulemaking is a routine activity in the market that corporations have undertaken since their inception, but it has become far more systematic and consequential as the drive for efficiency at scale has reshaped corporate operations. As outlined in Chapter 1, modern corporations coordinate millions of employees, serve billions of customers, and orchestrate supply chains spanning dozens of countries. To achieve efficiency at this unprecedented scale, they rely on uniform standards and comprehensive monitoring systems that inevitably extend corporate influence far beyond traditional commercial relationships. The imperative of uniformity and standardization transforms individual business decisions into frameworks of general applicability that function as de facto social policy,[32] whether in Apple's App Store policies affecting millions of apps worldwide, Amazon's fulfillment processes standardized across global operations, or Uber's platform rules governing interactions between drivers and passengers across dozens of countries.

Sometimes, corporations set out terms, conditions, norms, or practices that govern their interaction with their stakeholders and customers on a large scale. While some of these might be dictated or constrained by law or regulation, many of them operate in the private or voluntary domain. They represent management's preferred conditions for doing business or, more generally, for entering into a relationship with the party or parties involved. What makes these corporate choices distinctly rule-like, rather than mere contractual terms, is precisely this drive for standardization across vast operations. When Tesla establishes direct-to-consumer sales policies or when Facebook creates content moderation standards, these decisions must apply uniformly across millions of interactions because individual case-by-case determinations would be prohibitively costly and operationally unworkable.[33] The same mechanisms that enable extraordinary corporate efficiency also make corporate decisions into building blocks of social organization.

3.2.1 *Defining Corporate Rules: Generality and Uniformity*

What makes these corporate choices more like rules, and less like individual contractual terms, is that they apply in a general and uniform manner to a large set of actors. First, these rules exhibit generality, as they are meant to encompass a class or category of people interacting with the company in the same way. Often, the corporation makes the choice without even knowing who the persons subject to it are going to be, because the company does not know the group of consumers or employees or local citizens with which it plans to engage.[34] Sometimes, the corporate choice is not even directed at particular persons, but simply chosen to define a term that is going to be useful to many individuals, such as what a company considers appropriate conduct for someone entering its premises. The generality of these rules is often embedded in the design of the product or service that the company is planning to offer, which is built to be used in specific ways, to accommodate or prioritize specific needs, and to appeal to a large audience.[35]

General rules are important because they apply uniformly, in ways that are identical or under exemptions prescribed in the rule. Uniformity is a key building block of any hierarchy, because it allows managers to administer and coordinate their subordinates. Without uniformity, managers would have to engage in individual determinations, an often impractical task. Instead, managers can reduce transaction costs by reaching a determination once and avoid revisiting it until a problem occurs.[36] However, the decision to adopt a uniform rule also alters calculations for managers. By resolving all arising cases at once, management needs to "get it right," making sure that their choice is, from a substantive perspective, the one that will better serve the corporation over a range of potential cases with slight variations.

But while rules clarify expectations and allow for greater predictability and better planning, they are also more likely to produce noticeable effects, since their results are going to be similar and more easily aggregated.[37] Thus, those impacted are going to understand the implications of the rule, as well as that there are other stakeholders in the same predicament as themselves. Moreover, general and uniform rules can be more easily communicated to third parties outside the corporate hierarchy, like consumers, investors, government authorities, and the media. When management adopts a rule, their choice will now be more visible, as it will affect greater numbers of cases all at once. It will be judged both by the group to which it may be directly addressed, as well as by other groups who may not be affected by it but who regularly interact with management.[38]

Most rules and rulemaking frameworks discussed earlier take the guise of contractual commitments, and companies may seek stakeholders' consent or consider them voluntarily incorporated in employment or other contracts. But these terms constitute contracts in formal nature only. They have not been the result of negotiations with impacted parties, which sometimes neither take part in nor are represented in their drafting. Parties rarely have the opportunity to voice consent or disagreement; at most, stakeholders may be presented with the option to either agree to these terms or reject any relationship with the corporation. Consent is often given in a formulaic manner, with stakeholders signing onto frameworks at moments when considering their implications is impractical.[39]

However, the consequences of violating these rules are not only real, but often quite painful for stakeholders. Stakeholders directly subject to the corporate hierarchy, such as employees or suppliers, may be subject to disciplinary procedures, remuneration reductions, or negative reputational consequences.[40] To parties whose relationship with the corporation is more coincidental, managers can deny cooperation if they fail to conform with its terms, an option that may put smaller subcontractors out of business. When corporations have superior bargaining power compared to stakeholders, the line between consent and coercion begins to blur.[41]

3.2.2 *Corporate Rules in Practice: Application and Examples*

Once we understand corporate rules as key components of corporate hierarchies, it becomes clear that managers have relied on them routinely to organize production, coordinate subordinates, and establish efficient exchanges with third parties. Below are some examples.

3.2.2.1 Production and Quality Control

The cardinal mission of every firm is to organize production. In performing these tasks, managers often make determinations that take the shape of general and uniform rules that encapsulate the firm's approach to whole clusters of decisions.[42] For example, managers may decide that they will only use packaging material that satisfies certain biodegradability requirements, occupy offices that obtain LEED certification, or hire employees with specific threshold qualifications. Each individual choice may have a social dimension, whether helping attain sustainability goals, setting terms that govern entire populations of workers, or impacting other stakeholders more generally.[43] These determinations are replicated in numerous choices around the firm, which aggregates their impact and renders them more noticeable to affected groups or external watchdogs. Particularly when a firm's business scales up, the effort to install a common approach to similar problems takes the shape of uniform and generally applicable rules.[44] By setting corporate policies that employees must follow, the company embraces a rulemaking function that helps coordinate production while solidifying the choices managers make vis-à-vis other stakeholders.

3.2.2.2 Customer Interface

An aspect of production that has gained renewed attention in recent years concerns the customer interface.[45] Besides statutory or regulatory requirements, managers maintain significant leeway in structuring their firm's customer interface.[46] Companies have sought to take advantage of new technologies that allow more direct access to consumer data and preferences, more effective monitoring of consumer conduct, and greater use of social media to target specialized audiences.[47]

These developments have brought new concerns regarding the monetization of consumer data, protection for privacy and free speech, and securing access to markets for disadvantaged groups.[48] Addressing these concerns often requires companies to shape frameworks that their employees can follow in a general and uniform manner, such as establishing protocols for managing the storage and use of consumer data.[49]

The wide availability of product information has also changed the customer interface. In the past, consumer mobilization against corporate misconduct required significant effort, often by dominating national headlines or gaining regulatory attention.[50] Today, both monitoring and mobilization are readily collapsed into smartphone apps, while complex information becomes available at consumers' fingertips. This increase in disclosure requires companies to be more intentional about their choices and monitor public reactions more closely.[51]

3.2.2.3 Organizing the Workplace

In the centuries-old fight between capital and labor, the companies' power to regulate the workplace has traditionally featured as a critical battlefield. Managers have set out rules for structuring the internal line of command, how employees should behave toward each other, and how they should treat third parties. They determine dress codes, what customer requests employees can satisfy, and take possession of employee communications.[52] Managers also play a critical role in defining employees' benefits and privileges beyond government minimums: parental leaves, health care coverage, and pension contributions involve important choices that are critical not only for the employees in question, but for society more generally.[53]

A long literature has examined how these rule-based frameworks reproduce social conventions, structures, hierarchies, and values prevalent outside the firm's boundaries, turning the workplace into a microcosm of society.[54] Gender and race discrimination have been central areas of exploration, along with class origins, LGBTQ+ concerns, political and religious beliefs, immigration status, and other issues. Managers have the power to embrace, strengthen, or disregard these external factors.

In recent years, social movements have embraced the corporation not only as a reflection of society, but as a vehicle for change. Following #MeToo and Black Lives Matter, corporations became preferred terrain for social reformers seeking quick and meaningful progress. Popular accounts present this approach as a solution to political gridlock, but they tend to underestimate the significance of this strategic shift. By choosing to focus on changes within corporations, social movements prioritize the implementation phase, ensuring that reform goals are carried out where they are more likely to matter.[55]

The initial corporate response was swift and comprehensive. Companies established chief diversity officers, implemented bias training programs, revised hiring practices to emphasize diverse candidate pools, and committed billions of dollars to racial equity initiatives.[56] Major corporations from Goldman Sachs to Starbucks adopted policies requiring diverse interview panels, set numerical diversity targets for leadership positions, and tied executive compensation to diversity metrics.[57] These represented systematic changes to corporate rulemaking that affected millions of employees and shaped industry practices across entire sectors.

However, the pendulum has swung dramatically in the opposite direction. Beginning around 2023 and accelerating under the Trump administration's explicit anti-DEI positioning, corporations have systematically retreated from diversity initiatives. Major companies including Meta, Amazon, McDonald's, and Walmart have eliminated diversity, equity, and inclusion programs, removed diversity language from job postings, and disbanded DEI teams.[58] This retreat reflects multiple pressures: the Supreme Court's 2023 decision striking down affirmative action in college admissions created legal uncertainty about corporate diversity programs; Republican state attorneys general launched investigations into corporate DEI practices; and shareholder activists filed lawsuits challenging diversity initiatives as discriminatory against white employees.[59]

The speed and scope of this reversal illustrate the central dynamic of corporate rulemaking. When social pressure mounted following Black Lives Matter protests, corporations rapidly implemented uniform policies affecting millions of workers because the reputational and business costs of inaction seemed prohibitive.[60] When the political and legal environment shifted, these same standardized policies were reversed with equal efficiency across entire corporate hierarchies. Individual employees had little voice in either direction. They experienced both the implementation and elimination of diversity programs as unilateral management decisions that reshaped their workplace environments without meaningful consultation.[61]

This cycle reveals how corporate rulemaking functions as a mechanism of social ordering that extends far beyond traditional commercial relationships. The adoption and subsequent abandonment of DEI policies affected not just hiring and promotion practices, but broader questions about workplace culture, speech norms, and the role of corporations in addressing societal inequities. The uniformity required for operational efficiency means that when corporations make these choices, they do so at scale, either creating or dismantling frameworks that govern the daily experiences of millions of workers and shape social expectations about corporate responsibility.

3.2.2.4 Rules of Disruption

Disruption has become a byword of business innovation in the last twenty years, as new technology has spurred development of new ideas. The gig economy has revolutionized services and upended employment relationships; short-term rentals have reshaped urban areas; smartphones have transformed daily lives; and social media has established new means of communication and news distribution. But when redesigning entire spheres of human activity, corporations come face to face with the societal implications of their success.[62]

Companies typically adopt rules, norms, or practices that seek to bring order and predictability to their business activities, at once confirming the hierarchy they have established and governing the new terrain unfolding under them. Airbnb laid down rules on house parties when some became raucous and even resulted in deaths, and opened up rentals to refugees when housing them became problematic.[63] Gig economy companies like Uber sought to maintain the independent contractor status they claimed was preferred by workers while expanding the offerings available to them. These efforts represent legal ordering because they have general applicability and are impossible for individual workers to negotiate around.[64]

Some companies may choose to stay largely inactive, deflecting the need for further intervention because they fear this may reduce the appeal of their product. Facebook's reticence in instituting frameworks for regulating posts illustrates this stance.[65] But this is no less rulemaking than active intervention: it illustrates the moral priorities of the company and represents its view on the norms that should govern the new interactions it has facilitated.

The legal ordering stakes are much higher for disruptors than for companies in established industries.[66] With the disruption fresh in the public's mind, the normative features of the company's conduct weigh significantly in society's assessment of the company's success. The new world that the company is ushering in has clear winners and losers, who are likely to be vocal about their grievances. Policymakers are lobbied on all sides and try to better reflect public attitude. Lacking precedent for addressing newly emerging challenges, companies and their stakeholders have no other recourse but going to first principles. But rekindling fundamental questions about social welfare benefits or the boundaries of free speech is bound to involve deeply held normative beliefs. When addressing these questions, the company is setting in motion practices that will engulf all its users and leave them with few options.[67]

3.2.3 *Governance Implications of Corporate Rulemaking*

Corporate rulemaking instances unavoidably invoke the intense social impact challenge described in Chapter 1, because they necessarily create highly visible standards that affect multiple constituencies simultaneously. Unlike individual business decisions that may fly under the radar, frameworks of general and uniform applicability, whether governing workplace conduct, supply chain standards, or customer data handling, become focal points for stakeholder attention precisely because of their broad reach and lasting footprint.[68] The stakes are inherently high: these rules will shape the experiences of employees, customers, suppliers, and communities, often for years to come, making them natural targets for organized advocacy and public scrutiny.

Moreover, corporate rulemaking directly confronts the challenge of heterogeneous shareholder preferences.[69] When companies establish frameworks that touch on social issues, from diversity policies to environmental standards to content moderation rules, they must navigate shareholders with fundamentally different values and expectations about corporate strategy.[70] Some investors may prioritize aggressive social action while others resist what they view as mission creep, leaving management to make choices that will inevitably disappoint some constituencies.

Faced with these dynamics, corporations cannot simply pronounce rules through traditional internal processes and expect them to avoid contestation. Instead, they are better off turning to governance mechanisms that can help demonstrate the reasonableness and legitimacy of their choices while managing the inevitable tensions between competing stakeholder demands and shareholder preferences. Section 3.2.3 explores the primary tools that companies are using to resolve these tensions and explains the distinctive contribution that each set of governance mechanisms makes to enhancing both the quality and acceptance of corporate rulemaking.

3.2.3.1 External Input and Validation Mechanisms

Companies increasingly recognize that effective rulemaking requires looking beyond internal expertise and business considerations to incorporate external perspectives and validation. One common approach involves engaging outside experts, such as academics, NGOs, or specialized consultants, who can provide independent perspectives and help evaluate the broader societal implications of particular frameworks.[71] This strategy addresses the inherent limitations of internal decision-making by introducing external validation and subject-matter expertise that companies may lack internally. For instance, when developing environmental standards or human rights policies, companies frequently collaborate with environmental scientists or human rights organizations to ensure their frameworks reflect current best practices and address key concerns.

The value of expert engagement extends beyond mere technical accuracy. External experts can identify blind spots in corporate thinking, challenge assumptions about stakeholder impacts, and provide credibility that enhances the perceived legitimacy of resulting frameworks. However, this approach also presents challenges in expert selection, ensuring genuine independence, and managing potential conflicts between expert recommendations and business imperatives.[72]

Equally important are extensive stakeholder consultation processes, where companies actively seek input from affected groups, organize listening sessions, and create feedback channels that allow stakeholders to shape framework development. These processes recognize that those who will be subject to corporate rules often possess crucial knowledge about potential impacts and implementation challenges that internal teams cannot anticipate.[73] For instance, Starbucks worked with Conservation International to create its Coffee and Farmer Equity (C.A.F.E.) Practices, a comprehensive set of guidelines designed to ensure ethical sourcing and sustainability in its coffee supply chain.[74] This collaboration enabled Starbucks to incorporate stakeholder perspectives and address key environmental and social concerns while developing frameworks that were both practically implementable and responsive to farmer needs.[75]

A third external validation strategy involves working with other companies toward industry-wide or even market-wide standard setting or adopting standards set by well-respected independent bodies. This approach offers several advantages: it spreads the costs of framework development across multiple actors, reduces competitive disadvantages that might result from unilateral action, and enhances the credibility and reach of resulting standards.[76] For example, numerous global corporations, including General Motors, Shell, and BP, collaborated with the World Resources Institute and the World Business Council for Sustainable Development to develop the Greenhouse Gas Protocol, which has become the gold standard for corporate carbon accounting. This collaborative effort established a consistent and reliable methodology for measuring, managing, and reporting greenhouse gas emissions across industries worldwide.[77]

3.2.3.2 Values-Based Internal Process and Implementation

Beyond external input, companies must develop robust internal processes for framework development and implementation. Some companies have found success in articulating foundational principles or value statements that serve as reference points for specific frameworks, providing consistency and clarity about the company's broader commitments and priorities.[78] This approach helps ensure that individual rules connect to broader corporate purposes while providing stakeholders with predictable criteria for evaluating corporate decisions. These foundational frameworks can take various forms, from formal corporate mission statements to detailed ethical codes to comprehensive sustainability commitments.[79]

Equally important are procedural safeguards designed to enhance the quality and accountability of rulemaking processes. These include requirements for impact assessments before adopting new frameworks, mandatory comment periods that allow stakeholder input, regular review cycles that ensure frameworks remain current and effective, and clear documentation of decision-making rationales.[80] Transparency mechanisms play a crucial role in enabling external accountability. Companies increasingly publish detailed accounts of their framework development processes, including summaries of stakeholder input received, explanations of how feedback was incorporated or why it was not adopted, and clear statements of the business and social considerations that influenced final decisions.[81]

Effective governance must also address implementation and enforcement challenges. This includes developing clear metrics for evaluating framework effectiveness, establishing mechanisms for addressing stakeholder complaints or concerns about implementation, and creating processes for updating frameworks based on real world experience. Companies must also consider how to ensure consistent implementation across complex organizational structures, particularly for multinational corporations operating in diverse legal and cultural contexts. This often requires developing training programs, establishing clear accountability structures, and creating feedback loops that can identify implementation problems before they become significant issues.

3.2.3.3 Building Legitimacy through Deliberative Governance

Perhaps the most challenging aspect of corporate rulemaking governance involves managing the inevitable tradeoffs between business considerations and stakeholder interests.[82] No governance process can eliminate these tensions, but effective processes can help ensure that tradeoffs are made deliberately and transparently, with clear justification for the choices involved. This requires companies to develop frameworks for evaluating competing claims, establishing clear criteria for weighing different types of impacts, and creating mechanisms for explaining and justifying difficult decisions to stakeholders. Success often depends on early identification of potential conflicts and proactive engagement with affected parties to explore creative solutions that can address multiple concerns simultaneously.[83]

Companies will need to present their choices as reasonable and justified, in an effort to convince audiences to adopt their products, work for them, or create new frameworks that take them into account. The governance mechanisms described earlier, while operating within the constraints of the corporate hierarchy, help ensure that framework development becomes a more deliberative and inclusive process, even as final authority remains with management. The goal is not just to make better decisions, but to create frameworks whose legitimacy stems from the careful consideration and incorporation of diverse perspectives and expertise.

Companies that invest in robust governance processes for their rulemaking activities often find that the resulting frameworks are more durable, face less resistance from stakeholders, and prove more effective in achieving their intended goals.[84] The additional time and resources required for comprehensive governance processes can be justified by reduced implementation costs, enhanced stakeholder relationships, and improved long-term business outcomes.[85] The challenge for companies is developing governance approaches that are appropriately tailored to the specific characteristics of their rulemaking activities – considering factors such as stakeholder diversity, potential impact magnitude, implementation complexity, and competitive dynamics – while maintaining the efficiency and decision-making authority necessary for effective business operations.

3.3 EXECUTIVE ACTION AND STRATEGIC DECISION-MAKING

While corporate rulemaking establishes general principles and creates systematic frameworks for ongoing operations, executive action encompasses the full range of specific decisions that address particular situations or launch discrete initiatives. These decisions may implement existing rulemaking commitments, but they also include countless business choices made independently of any established framework. Thus, executive decisions represent the critical process of translating management's vision into concrete reality. This creates a fundamental dynamic: rulemaking establishes the architecture of corporate values and processes, while executive decisions represent the moment-by-moment construction work that can either reinforce or undermine that foundation.

This translation from principle to practice presents corporations with their most fundamental credibility challenge: how to convince shareholders and stakeholders that their specific actions genuinely advance their stated goals rather than merely paying lip service to them. The proliferation of terms such as "greenwashing," "DEI washing," "social washing," and "sustainability washing" reflects not just growing skepticism about corporate sincerity, but a sophisticated understanding among stakeholders that the real test of corporate commitments lies not in their articulation but in their implementation through countless individual decisions.[86]

The credibility gap has become a defining challenge of modern corporate governance. Companies routinely make sweeping commitments through their rulemaking processes, adopting policies, publishing frameworks, and establishing principles on environmental sustainability, social justice, traditional values, or stakeholder capitalism. But stakeholders across the political spectrum increasingly judge these commitments not by their comprehensiveness or eloquence, but by whether they translate into consistent executive decisions that sometimes require short-term sacrifices for stated principles.[87] When a company commits to carbon neutrality but then makes acquisition decisions based solely on financial returns, or when a company pledges to avoid "woke politics" but then makes decisions that appear to contradict conservative values, or when a company establishes diversity principles but consistently promotes from networks that exclude underrepresented groups, the gap between stated commitments and executive action becomes a credibility crisis.[88]

The governance challenge lies in creating systems that ensure executive decisions consistently implement and advance the commitments established through rulemaking processes, while building stakeholder confidence that these decisions reflect authentic commitment rather than strategic positioning. This requires sophisticated mechanisms that go beyond traditional corporate governance focused on legal compliance and financial performance, extending into domains of credibility, authenticity, and consistent implementation of stated values through concrete action.

3.3.1 *The Nature and Scope of Executive Corporate Choices*

Executive choices represent decisions to move in specific ways on individualized matters, addressing particular situations through discrete actions rather than systematic policy development. These choices encompass the vast majority of daily corporate decision-making, from routine operational matters to transformative strategic initiatives that reshape entire business models.

The scope of executive choices spans an enormous range of corporate activity. At the operational level, executives make countless decisions about resource allocation, personnel matters, supplier selection, pricing strategies, and facility management. At the strategic level, they decide whether to launch new products, enter new markets, pursue acquisitions, divest business units, or respond to competitive threats. Crisis management requires executives to make rapid decisions about addressing emergencies, controversies, or unexpected market disruptions. What unites all these choices is their specificity to particular circumstances and their implementation of broader corporate direction through concrete action.

Most executive choices proceed without raising significant social concerns or attracting stakeholder attention beyond their immediate business implications. Decisions about inventory management, routine hiring, technology upgrades, or standard supplier agreements typically focus on operational efficiency, cost management, and performance optimization. These choices form the backbone of corporate operations, requiring managerial judgment about business trade-offs without invoking broader questions about corporate values or social responsibility.

Strategic executive choices are more likely to raise issues of social importance, both because of their larger impact on corporate direction and because they often bring underlying social issues to the surface. When companies launch new products, these choices inevitably raise questions about their social and environmental implications. When they enter new markets, particularly in different countries or regions, they confront issues about labor standards, environmental regulations, and community impact. When they pursue acquisitions, they must address how combining operations will affect various stakeholder groups and whether the combined entity will advance or undermine their stated commitments.

Society's attention sometimes turns to issues where corporations play major roles, creating moments when executive choices take on heightened social significance. Catalytic events such as George Floyd's murder in 2020 or awareness campaigns about environmental issues can transform routine corporate decisions into tests of corporate commitment to social values.[89] Similarly, backlash against ESG initiatives or concerns about corporate "woke politics" can create pressure for executives to demonstrate through specific actions whether their companies prioritize business fundamentals over political positioning.[90] These moments create pressure for executives to demonstrate through specific actions whether their companies' stated principles represent authentic commitments or merely strategic positioning.[91]

The corporate response to Russia's invasion of Ukraine illustrates how major events can transform executive choices into statements about corporate values. Many companies decided to withdraw from Russia, representing momentous strategic decisions with immediate implications for employees, business partners, and shareholders.[92] These were discrete, one-time choices that implemented broader commitments to human rights or international law, requiring companies to sacrifice short-term financial interests for stated principles.[93]

In contrast, when companies make statements supporting causes such as gender equality or Black Lives Matter, these proclamations represent attempts to establish ongoing commitments that require implementation through multiple executive decisions over time. Similarly, when companies pledge to avoid political activism or commit to religious freedom principles, these statements demand sustained implementation through operational choices. While withdrawal from Russia represents a discrete, easily observable strategic break, broader social commitments demand sustained substantiation through countless operational choices: hiring decisions, promotion practices, supplier selection, resource allocation, and community engagement initiatives. Each subsequent executive choice becomes an opportunity to either validate or contradict the original commitment, creating ongoing challenges for maintaining credibility and authentic implementation.[94]

3.3.2 *Identifying and Assessing Social Significance: The Challenge of Recognition and Calibration*

Determining which executive choices carry social significance requires sophisticated judgment and contextual awareness that goes beyond the formal characteristics of the decision itself. Even seemingly routine executive choices can acquire social significance when they occur in contexts that reflect broader societal tensions, appear emblematic of corporate culture, or attract attention as examples of systematic corporate behavior. The dismissal of a senior officer following allegations of misconduct, and particularly the terms of their departure, represents an executive choice that might have profound social implications despite appearing routine from a legal perspective. Similarly, decisions about facility locations, supplier relationships, or employment practices can become focal points for stakeholder concerns about corporate values and priorities.[95]

The challenge lies in recognizing that social significance exists along a sliding scale rather than as a binary classification. Some executive choices clearly invoke major social concerns, such as decisions about withdrawing from entire markets for political reasons, or high-profile hiring decisions that send clear signals about corporate values. Other choices operate in a gray area where social implications may be present but less pronounced, such as supplier selection decisions that involve modest differences in labor practices, or facility location choices that have some but not decisive environmental implications. Still other decisions appear entirely routine until external events or stakeholder attention transforms them into social issues.[96]

This sliding scale of social significance has important implications for governance requirements. Executive choices with clear, major social implications demand the most rigorous disclosure, accuracy, and oversight mechanisms. Decisions in the gray area may require more limited governance responses, perhaps enhanced internal consideration of social factors and basic stakeholder communication, but not the full apparatus of third-party verification and comprehensive public reporting.

Routine decisions that seem unlikely to raise social concerns may require little special governance attention until circumstances change their significance. The key governance challenge lies in developing systems that can identify where particular decisions fall on this spectrum and calibrate appropriate responses accordingly.[97]

3.3.3 *Governance Implications of Executive Actions: Disclosure and Accuracy*

The governance of executive decisions in the context of corporate social commitments requires fundamentally different approaches than traditional corporate governance focused primarily on financial performance and legal compliance. While conventional governance mechanisms aim to maximize shareholder value and prevent legal violations, governing executive decisions that implement social commitments demands systems designed to build and maintain stakeholder trust through demonstrated consistency between stated principles and concrete actions.[98]

The central governance challenge stems from the credibility gap that opens between corporate commitments and their implementation. Unlike financial metrics, which provide relatively objective measures of performance, social commitments often involve complex, subjective judgments about whether specific decisions authentically advance stated principles or merely provide cover for business as usual approaches.[99] This complexity creates opportunities for companies to engage in various forms of "washing" – greenwashing, social washing, or diversity washing – where executive decisions are framed as advancing social commitments while actually serving primarily traditional business objectives.[100]

3.3.3.1 Disclosure as the Foundation of Credible Implementation

Robust disclosure mechanisms represent the primary governance tool for addressing the credibility gap in executive decision-making.[101] However, effective disclosure for social commitments requires approaches that go far beyond traditional corporate reporting. Rather than simply announcing decisions, companies must develop disclosure systems that explain decision-making rationales, demonstrate alignment with stated principles, acknowledge trade-offs and conflicts, and provide sufficient detail for shareholders and stakeholders to evaluate authentic commitment versus strategic positioning.[102]

The most credible companies have learned that shareholder trust depends heavily on transparency about decision-making processes and outcomes. Successful companies typically explain not only what decisions they made, but why they made them and how these decisions advance specific stated commitments. When companies with human rights commitments make supplier selection decisions, they often provide detailed disclosure explaining how labor practice considerations factored into the evaluation process alongside cost and quality criteria.[103] Similarly, companies with environmental commitments making supply chain decisions frequently detail how environmental factors influenced selection criteria and final choices. This level of specificity allows stakeholders to evaluate whether social commitments actually influenced decision-making or merely provided post hoc justification for choices made on other grounds.[104]

Companies that have successfully managed shareholder expectations around social commitments typically acknowledge that implementing such commitments often requires difficult trade-offs with other business objectives.[105] Rather than claiming perfect alignment between social goals and business interests, credible companies acknowledge these tensions and explain how they balanced competing priorities. When companies choose suppliers with better labor practices despite higher costs, or reject profitable opportunities that conflict with environmental commitments, transparent discussion of these trade-offs tends to build stakeholder confidence by demonstrating that social commitments influenced decisions even when doing so imposed business costs. This approach helps distinguish companies that integrate social considerations into their core decision-making processes from those that consider them only when they align with other business interests.

Shareholders increasingly demand insight into corporate decision-making processes, not just outcomes, leading companies to provide disclosure that illuminates the internal mechanics of executive choice. Companies responding to this pressure typically explain how they structure decision-making to ensure consideration of social commitments, what internal controls prevent backsliding, and how accountability systems ensure consistent implementation across different business units and decisions.[106] This process-oriented disclosure addresses stakeholder concerns that social commitments might influence only high-profile decisions while leaving routine choices to operate under traditional business logic. Companies that reveal the systematic integration of social considerations into decision-making processes can demonstrate that their commitments represent more than aspirational statements or public relations strategies.[107]

Companies have also learned to connect individual executive decisions to broader implementation strategies, helping stakeholders understand how specific choices fit into larger patterns of commitment implementation. Effective corporate communication typically explains how current decisions advance longer-term goals and what future decisions will be required to maintain progress. This forward-looking dimension of disclosure serves multiple purposes for companies: it demonstrates strategic thinking about commitment implementation, creates accountability for future consistency, and provides shareholders with frameworks for evaluating future decisions. When companies can articulate clear connections between individual executive choices and broader commitment implementation strategies, they provide shareholders with tools for holding management accountable for sustained consistency while building confidence in their authentic long-term commitment.

3.3.3.2 Accurate Measurement as the Cornerstone of Shareholder Demands

While disclosure provides the mechanism for stakeholder evaluation through voluntary sharing of information, accuracy represents the substantive requirement for building trust. Without accurate measurement and correct characterization, even the most comprehensive disclosure becomes merely an exercise in corporate communication that fails to serve stakeholders' evaluation needs. Similarly, extensive but vague disclosures that avoid specific commitments or measurable outcomes provide little value to stakeholders seeking to evaluate authentic implementation of social commitments. Companies that have successfully maintained credibility with shareholders who increasingly scrutinize corporate claims about social commitment implementation have learned that accuracy in this context involves several dimensions beyond simple factual correctness. The voluntary act of disclosure means little if what companies choose to share is mismeasured, mischaracterized, or incomplete in ways that mislead rather than inform stakeholder judgment.[108]

The most successful companies have found that honestly characterizing the role social commitments played in their decision-making processes builds long-term shareholder confidence. When business considerations primarily drive decisions that happen to align with social commitments, credible companies acknowledge this reality rather than overstating the commitment motivation.[109] Conversely, when companies make decisions primarily to advance social goals despite business costs, accurate disclosure that highlights this authentic prioritization tends to reassure shareholders that management is making deliberate trade-offs rather than stumbling into costly decisions. This honest characterization helps shareholders evaluate whether management is strategically integrating social considerations or merely engaging in opportunistic positioning.[110]

Companies that maintain stakeholder trust over time typically provide realistic assessments of whether executive decisions actually advance stated commitments and by how much. Rather than overstating the social benefits of their decisions, successful companies tend to provide measured evaluations that give appropriate credit for genuine progress toward stated goals while avoiding exaggerated claims that might undermine future credibility. This balanced approach helps shareholders distinguish between companies making genuine progress on social commitments and those engaging in superficial gestures designed primarily for public relations value.[111]

Particularly effective companies have learned that acknowledging limitations and setbacks, rather than undermining their credibility, actually strengthens stakeholder confidence in their long-term commitment authenticity.[112] Companies that honestly discuss where executive decisions fall short of stated commitments, where competing priorities prevented ideal implementation, and where unintended consequences undermined intended social benefits tend to build stronger relationships with shareholders who prefer transparency about challenges over misleading optimism.

This transparency signals to investors that management has realistic understanding of implementation difficulties and is likely to address problems systematically rather than ignore them.[113]

Finally, companies responding to shareholder demands for accountability have increasingly turned to quantitative precision wherever possible, recognizing that social commitments often resist easy quantification but that specific, measurable information enhances credibility. Rather than relying on vague claims about "improving diversity" or "reducing environmental impact," companies that maintain strong stakeholder relationships typically provide concrete data about outcomes and progress toward specific targets. This quantitative approach allows shareholders to track progress over time and compare performance across companies, meeting investor demands for measurable accountability in areas that were traditionally considered too subjective for systematic evaluation.[114]

3.3.3.3 Additional Credibility-Enhancing Mechanisms

While disclosure and accuracy represent the primary tools for governing executive decisions that implement social commitments, companies responding to shareholder skepticism have developed several supporting mechanisms that enhance the credibility of their claims. These mechanisms address the fundamental challenge that shareholders face in evaluating corporate self-reporting about social commitment implementation.

Companies seeking to address shareholder concerns about the reliability of their social commitment claims have increasingly turned to third-party verification as a crucial external validation mechanism. Whether through environmental auditors, human rights monitors, or specialized certification bodies, independent verification helps companies address the inherent credibility challenges that corporate self-reporting faces with investors who remain skeptical about management's incentives to overstate progress. However, shareholders have learned that the effectiveness of third-party assurance depends heavily on the independence, expertise, and methodological rigor of verifying organizations, leading to more sophisticated evaluation of verification quality rather than mere acceptance of any external validation.[115]

Building on external verification, companies have found that creating systematic mechanisms for stakeholder input and feedback enhances their credibility with shareholders who understand that stakeholder satisfaction often correlates with long-term business sustainability. These mechanisms might include regular stakeholder advisory panels, community consultation processes for decisions affecting local communities, or employee feedback systems for decisions affecting workplace culture and diversity. Shareholders increasingly view such stakeholder engagement not as corporate social responsibility theater, but as risk management tools that help companies identify potential problems before they become costly crises or regulatory interventions.[116]

Companies have also discovered that board-level oversight serves a dual function of ensuring management accountability while providing shareholders with confidence that social commitment implementation receives appropriate strategic attention. Effective boards regularly review executive decisions for consistency with stated commitments, hold management accountable for gaps between principles and practices, and ensure that social commitment implementation receives appropriate priority in strategic planning and resource allocation. This board involvement signals to shareholders that social commitments represent genuine strategic priorities rather than management pet projects or public relations initiatives that might divert resources from core business objectives.[117]

Finally, some companies have demonstrated their commitment to shareholders by linking executive compensation to successful implementation of social commitments through consistent decision-making. Such compensation linkages provide shareholders with assurance that management has personal financial incentives to follow through on stated commitments rather than abandoning them when implementation becomes costly or difficult. However, companies and their shareholders have learned that such linkages must be carefully designed to avoid creating perverse incentives that encourage form over substance, leading to increasingly sophisticated approaches that focus on meaningful outcomes rather than easily manipulated metrics.

3.3.3.4 The Ongoing Challenge of Authentic Implementation

The governance of executive decisions that implement corporate social commitments represents an evolving challenge that requires continuous adaptation and refinement. As stakeholder expectations continue to rise and scrutiny of corporate behavior intensifies, companies must develop increasingly sophisticated approaches to demonstrating authentic commitment through consistent decision-making. The companies that succeed will be those that embrace disclosure and accuracy not as compliance burdens but as opportunities to build lasting stakeholder trust through demonstrated integrity in translating principles into practice.[118]

The effectiveness of these governance mechanisms depends ultimately on corporate leadership's genuine commitment to the principles they have articulated. No governance system can substitute for authentic commitment, but this reality makes the governance challenge more urgent, not less important. In an era where virtually all major corporations have learned to reproduce the same compelling message, the critical question for shareholders and stakeholders has become how to distinguish between companies that genuinely embrace their stated principles and those that treat them primarily as strategic positioning tools.[119]

The answer lies precisely in examining the concrete implementation of executive decisions and the rigor of the processes that govern them. While companies can craft similar-sounding policy statements and rulemaking frameworks, their executive decisions reveal authentic priorities through resource allocation, trade-off management, and consistent implementation over time. Companies that have embedded social commitments into their actual decision-making processes demonstrate measurably different patterns of executive choice than those that treat such commitments as external constraints to be managed or marketing messages to be projected.[120]

Moreover, the decision-making processes themselves serve as predictive indicators of future performance. Companies that have developed systematic approaches to integrating social considerations into executive decisions, created robust accountability mechanisms, and established transparent measurement systems are more likely to maintain consistent implementation over time than those relying on ad hoc responses or management rhetoric. In an era of increasing stakeholder activism and public scrutiny, this distinction between authentic implementation and strategic positioning will likely determine not just corporate reputation but fundamental business sustainability and long-term financial performance.[121]

3.4 THE MONITORING FUNCTION IN CORPORATE GOVERNANCE

While corporate monitoring is traditionally associated with ensuring employee compliance with legal mandates, modern corporations have developed complex internal bureaucracies that serve a far broader set of principles. The focus is on tracking progress and alignment across a wide spectrum of commitments, from environmental goals to workplace equity, and from ethical sourcing to community impact. This expanded monitoring function represents the crucial final step in corporate governance: ensuring that principles articulated in corporate rulemaking frameworks actually translate into practice through executive decisions, and that these decisions are faithfully implemented throughout the organization.[122]

3.4.1 *The Expansive Reach of Modern Compliance*

What distinguishes contemporary corporate monitoring from its traditional counterpart is not merely its sophistication, but its remarkable scope. The modern compliance apparatus has evolved far beyond the conventional model of corporations as reluctant enforcers of externally imposed legal mandates. Today's monitoring systems encompass an extraordinary range of commitments that extend well into territories once considered purely strategic or aspirational. Companies now monitor adherence to self-imposed environmental targets, diversity and inclusion goals, supply chain ethical standards, data privacy commitments, community engagement promises, and broader stakeholder value propositions. Many of these goals do not result from direct legal mandates but emerge from business strategy, competitive positioning, investor expectations, or organizational values.[123]

This expansion reflects a fundamental shift in how corporations conceive of their monitoring obligations. Rather than simply transposing regulatory requirements into everyday corporate practice, companies now deploy sophisticated tracking mechanisms to oversee compliance with voluntary commitments that may be more stringent than legal minimums. A technology company might monitor not just its legal obligations under privacy law, but also its public commitments to data minimization that exceed regulatory requirements.[124] A manufacturing firm might track not only mandated emissions reporting but also progress toward self-imposed carbon neutrality goals.[125] A financial services company might monitor not just regulatory compliance with fair lending laws, but also voluntary commitments to community investment and financial inclusion.

This internal bureaucracy performs essential supervisory functions that extend well beyond conventional compliance, operating through an extraordinary level of managerial discretion exercised within sophisticated multilayered supervisory systems. At the operational level, companies deploy automated monitoring tools that track everything from employees' digital activities to factory emissions in real time. These systems feed into middle-tier review processes, where specialized compliance teams analyze patterns and flag potential issues. At the highest level, board committees and executive teams receive regular reports and metrics dashboards, creating a continuous flow of monitoring information up and down the corporate hierarchy.[126]

This tiered structure is further reinforced by an intricate web of internal and external oversight mechanisms. Internally, companies typically maintain multiple channels for monitoring and reporting: routine supervisory reviews, anonymous reporting hotlines, regular audits by internal teams, and specialized oversight committees. These internal systems are complemented by external verification through third-party auditors, certification bodies, and independent monitors. Many companies have also established sophisticated appeals processes that allow stakeholders to challenge decisions, often involving multiple levels of review and independent arbitrators.

3.4.2 *Managerial Discretion in Designing Comprehensive Monitoring*

Within this detailed framework, managers must make countless decisions about how to structure monitoring processes, what metrics to track, and how to respond to violations. They must determine how different monitoring systems interact, when to escalate issues between tiers, and how to balance the need for oversight with operational efficiency. These choices, which include everything from the frequency of audits to the composition of review panels, shape the effectiveness and impact of corporate commitments, both those mandated by law and those voluntarily undertaken.[127]

The scope of managerial discretion becomes apparent when examining specific monitoring challenges across key areas. In environmental monitoring, managers must decide how to account for carbon emissions: which calculation methodologies to use, what scope of emissions to include, and how to verify supplier data.

They face similar choices in water usage monitoring, particularly regarding supply chain impacts and regional variations in water stress.[128] In diversity initiatives, managers must determine how to measure progress across multiple dimensions: from basic metrics such as hiring and promotion rates to more nuanced measures of inclusion and intersectionality. Recent political developments, including executive actions and legal challenges, have further complicated these decisions by constraining the scope of permissible DEI programs in some jurisdictions. For ethical sourcing, they must choose how deep into the supply chain they should monitor, whether to rely on industry certifications or develop proprietary standards, and how to most effectively address violations. In privacy monitoring, they must balance thorough oversight of data handling with employee productivity and determine appropriate escalation protocols.[129]

These choices are rarely straightforward and often involve balancing competing priorities with practical constraints. Each decision shapes not only how monitoring is implemented but also what behaviors and outcomes the organization prioritizes. Perhaps most crucially, managers must design the processes for handling violations and appeals. They must decide who has the authority to investigate complaints, what evidence standards to apply, and how to protect both the accusers and the accused. They must determine appropriate sanctions for different types of violations and establish procedures for appeal and review. These decisions require careful consideration of fairness, effectiveness, and organizational culture.

3.4.3 *How Companies Adjust Monitoring without Changing Policy Goals: From #MeToo to ESG Backlash*

The examples later illuminate the distinction between corporate rulemaking and monitoring. While rulemaking establishes or changes a company's fundamental values and principles, monitoring purports to implement those values more rigorously, comprehensively, or from multiple perspectives without altering them. In the cases that follow, companies maintained their stated commitments to political neutrality, balanced discourse, workplace diversity, and other values while developing more sophisticated systems to track, measure, and demonstrate adherence to those principles. Yet the very significance of these monitoring changes, with their capacity to reshape corporate behavior, employee experiences, and stakeholder relationships, naturally raises questions about whether such adjustments truly leave underlying values unchanged. These doubts, however, rather than undermining the monitoring function, actually underscore its fundamental importance in corporate governance. The power of monitoring systems to influence organizational culture, decision-making processes, and practical outcomes reveals why the design and implementation of these systems represents such a critical exercise of managerial discretion, one that can determine whether corporate principles remain aspirational statements or become operational realities.

The transformation of corporate monitoring in response to the #MeToo movement exemplifies how the modern compliance apparatus expands beyond legal mandates to encompass broader organizational values and cultural commitments. Prohibitions against sexual harassment in the workplace had been in place since at least the 1970s, and the legal framework appeared well established before 2017. With no new legislation required, #MeToo prompted companies to voluntarily expand their monitoring apparatus in ways that carried out the law's mission more effectively. Some companies created new reporting channels, offering immediacy through hotlines and guaranteeing anonymity.[130] Others provided enhanced support mechanisms, establishing rehabilitation groups and offering access to outside assistance for victims. Many companies developed efforts to strengthen bonds and relationships among women in the workplace through mentorship programs, regular caucuses and town hall meetings, and diversity groups. Most publicly traded companies increased the number of female directors, often under significant pressure from investors, recognizing that diverse governance structures might enhance monitoring effectiveness.[131]

The #MeToo response also fundamentally altered the calculation for individual managers responsible for sanctioning violators. Before 2017, typical resolution of sexual harassment allegations against high-profile executives involved allowing them to leave the company while maintaining stock options and golden parachutes. After 2017, this exit option became much harder to sustain, as managers recognized that appearing to protect abusers would undermine both organizational culture and external legitimacy.[132]

These reforms illustrate the power and reach of voluntary compliance expansion. While entirely voluntary and arising from private initiative rather than legal mandate or fiduciary duty, these changes substantially strengthened enforcement frameworks and demonstrated the authority that corporations exercise in defining and implementing standards that exceed legal minimums. The cultural motivations driving #MeToo were channeled into institutional changes and individual choices that managers make, underscoring their role as key actors in expanding the scope and intensity of corporate monitoring beyond traditional legal compliance.[133]

The responsiveness of corporate monitoring systems to cultural and political pressures extends beyond progressive movements like #MeToo to encompass conservative values and priorities as well. Recent years have witnessed significant corporate adjustments in response to conservative criticism and organized pressure campaigns, demonstrating that the expansion and contraction of voluntary monitoring systems reflects broader stakeholder dynamics rather than a unidirectional progressive trend.[134]

The financial sector's response to "debanking" allegations illustrates how companies adjust their monitoring systems to better serve existing policy goals in response to conservative pressure. Following sustained criticism from Republican lawmakers and activists who alleged that banks were systematically discriminating against conservative customers and businesses, major financial institutions implemented enhanced monitoring procedures designed to ensure political neutrality in their business decisions.[135] Bank of America, JPMorgan Chase, and Wells Fargo all established new internal review mechanisms for account closures, creating multitiered oversight processes that require detailed documentation of business justifications for ending customer relationships. These banks developed specialized training programs for relationship managers and created escalation procedures that flag potential politically sensitive decisions for senior review. Some institutions established dedicated ombudsman offices specifically to handle complaints about alleged political bias in banking decisions, complete with independent review processes and appeals mechanisms. Crucially, these changes did not represent a shift in policy goals. Banks maintained their commitment to serving all qualified customers regardless of political affiliation, but implemented more robust monitoring systems to demonstrate and ensure adherence to that principle.

Technology companies have similarly adjusted their content moderation monitoring systems in response to conservative criticism about alleged anti-conservative bias, while maintaining their stated commitment to balanced discourse. Following congressional hearings and public pressure campaigns alleging systematic suppression of conservative viewpoints, platforms such as Facebook (Meta) and Twitter (before its acquisition) implemented enhanced review processes specifically designed to identify potential bias in content moderation decisions. These companies created specialized oversight teams tasked with monitoring the treatment of political content across the ideological spectrum, developed new appeal mechanisms for users who believe their content was wrongly removed, and established external advisory boards that include conservative voices. Some platforms implemented "red team" exercises where conservative employees or consultants specifically review content moderation decisions for potential bias. These monitoring enhancements aimed to better serve the same underlying goal of fair and balanced content policies rather than changing those policies themselves.[136]

Corporate hiring and workplace inclusion programs have also seen monitoring adjustments in response to conservative legal challenges, while maintaining commitments to diverse and inclusive workplaces. Following concerns about potential reverse discrimination and evolving legal interpretations of employment law, many companies have modified their diversity hiring monitoring systems to include enhanced documentation of candidate qualifications and selection criteria.[137] These companies developed new training programs for hiring managers that emphasize skills-based evaluation while maintaining diversity goals, created more detailed audit trails for hiring decisions, and established review mechanisms to ensure that diversity efforts do not inadvertently disadvantage any candidates based on protected characteristics.[138] Some organizations have expanded their diversity definitions to include veterans, first-generation college graduates, and employees from rural backgrounds, which may appeal more to conservative stakeholders while maintaining the fundamental commitment to workplace diversity.

3.4.4 *The Challenge of Performative Monitoring*

The expansion of corporate monitoring systems creates a fundamental tension between genuine oversight and performative compliance. Companies often respond to stakeholder pressure and regulatory expectations by layering on additional procedures, documentation requirements, and oversight roles without fundamentally altering decision-making processes or outcomes. This proliferation of monitoring apparatus can create an illusion of enhanced accountability while leaving underlying practices largely unchanged, a bureaucratic theater that generates extensive records but limited behavioral modification.

The distinction between effective and performative monitoring lies not in the formal structure of oversight systems, but in how companies design the practical mechanisms that translate monitoring into operational change. Organizations that successfully avoid performative compliance typically embed monitoring functions directly into business processes rather than treating them as parallel reporting exercises. They structure incentive systems that reward managers for substantive outcomes rather than procedural adherence, and they design escalation mechanisms that ensure identified problems trigger concrete remedial actions rather than additional documentation.[139]

Critically, the effectiveness of these systems rarely emerges from management intuition or ad hoc decision-making. Instead, companies develop systematic approaches to structuring monitoring relationships, defining escalation thresholds, allocating investigative resources, and measuring outcomes.[140] The substantial discretion that corporations exercise in designing these systems, from determining which issues warrant board-level attention to establishing protocols for employee reporting, shapes whether monitoring functions serve as genuine accountability mechanisms or elaborate performances.[141] The system Microsoft has put together to supervise responsible AI, described in Chapter 8, illustrates how to translate genuine commitments into oversight.

Corporate monitoring is thus an essential governance function, operating alongside rulemaking and executive action as distinct but interconnected mechanisms of organizational control. While rulemaking establishes the formal parameters of acceptable behavior and executive action drives day-to-day operations, monitoring provides the feedback mechanisms that determine whether stated policies translate into actual practice. Designed under management discretion, monitoring represents an area where companies make consequential choices about institutional structure with limited external guidance or standardization. Without analyzing how organizations construct their monitoring systems, observers cannot fully comprehend how corporate rulemaking and executive action function in practice, since monitoring provides the institutional architecture that connects formal commitments to operational reality.

3.5 BEYOND PURPOSE: CORPORATE GOVERNANCE AS INSTITUTIONAL ARCHITECTURE

The framework developed in this chapter, distinguishing corporate rulemaking, executive action, and monitoring functions, represents more than an analytical exercise. It fundamentally reframes how we understand corporate power, institutional design, and the relationship between business organizations and broader social ordering. The implications span multiple domains, from practical governance design to theoretical questions about the origins of legal authority itself.

3.5.1 *Revealing the True Scope of Corporate Institutional Work*

The tripartite analysis exposes a critical blind spot in contemporary corporate law scholarship, which has remained fixated on the binary question of whether corporations should pursue shareholder profits, stakeholder interests or broader social welfare. This debate, while generating substantial academic literature, obscures the far more complex reality of what corporations actually do. By applying the rulemaking-executive-monitoring framework, we see that corporate activity extends well beyond either profit maximization or stakeholder capitalism into the fundamental work of social ordering itself.

Corporations do not simply choose between shareholder primacy and stakeholder interests; they actively construct the institutional frameworks through which millions of people organize their daily lives. When Apple establishes App Store policies, Amazon designs fulfillment protocols, or Uber creates platform rules, these companies are not merely pursuing business strategies, but are building the infrastructure of modern economic and social relationships. The tripartite framework reveals this institution-building work as distinct from both traditional profit-seeking and conventional social responsibility, operating through mechanisms that function as de facto governance systems affecting billions of individual interactions.

This recognition fundamentally alters how we evaluate corporate performance and accountability. Rather than asking whether companies adequately balance competing interests, we must examine whether they have developed appropriate institutional capabilities for the governance functions they inevitably perform. The framework shifts analytical focus from outcomes to processes, from goals to institutional design, recognizing that the path from corporate intentions to social results travels through complex organizational machinery that requires sophisticated stewardship to function effectively.

The emphasis on institutional processes rather than declared purposes addresses a persistent weakness in corporate law scholarship, which tends to assume that properly aligned incentives will automatically produce desired outcomes. The tripartite analysis demonstrates that this assumption overlooks the critical role of institutional design in translating intentions into results. Even corporations with ideal incentive structures will fail to achieve their goals without governance systems appropriately calibrated to the distinct demands of rulemaking, executive action, and monitoring functions. The framework thus reveals corporate governance as fundamentally concerned with institutional architecture rather than simply incentive alignment.

3.5.2 *Practical Implications for Governance Design*

From a practical standpoint, the tripartite framework provides concrete guidance for designing more effective corporate governance systems. Current approaches to corporate oversight typically apply uniform mechanisms across fundamentally different types of corporate decisions, failing to recognize that rulemaking functions require different governance tools than executive actions, which in turn demand different approaches than monitoring activities.

The framework demonstrates why companies struggle when they apply identical governance approaches to fundamentally different corporate functions. Board committees designed for financial oversight may lack the stakeholder engagement capabilities necessary for effective rulemaking governance. Executive compensation systems optimized for strategic decision-making may poorly incentivize the independence and thoroughness required for effective monitoring. Disclosure requirements appropriate for routine business decisions may inadequately serve the transparency needs of executive actions implementing social commitments. The tripartite analysis provides a diagnostic tool for identifying these mismatches and developing more targeted governance solutions.

Legal practitioners and corporate advisors can use this framework to develop governance recommendations that match institutional tools to functional demands rather than relying on generic best practices. When companies face rulemaking decisions requiring broad stakeholder consultation, the framework suggests governance mechanisms focused on wide outreach and participatory processes. When they confront executive choices implementing stated commitments, it emphasizes disclosure and accuracy systems that build credibility through transparent communication. When they design monitoring systems for voluntary commitments, it highlights independence and investigative capacity as critical design elements.

The framework also helps explain why certain corporate governance reforms succeed while others fail. Reforms that align with functional requirements, such as stakeholder engagement processes for rulemaking decisions or independent oversight for monitoring functions, tend to enhance both corporate effectiveness and stakeholder satisfaction. On the other hand, reforms that ignore functional distinctions, such as applying uniform board oversight to all corporate decisions regardless of their different governance needs, often create compliance burdens without improving outcomes. Chapter 9 includes a broader discussion of governance implications for boards and managers, as well as suggestions for reforming our understanding of fiduciary duties.

3.5.3 *Reconceptualizing Corporate Legal Authority*

The tripartite framework has profound implications for understanding the relationship between corporate power and legal authority. Traditional accounts position corporations as subjects of law, created by state authority and constrained by regulatory frameworks. This subject-centered view treats corporate rule-creation as either contracted-for private ordering or problematic regulatory capture that undermines legitimate governmental authority.

The institutional perspective developed here suggests a more complex relationship in which corporations function as significant sources of legal ordering rather than merely subjects of it. When corporations establish frameworks of general and uniform applicability that govern millions of interactions, they are not simply exercising delegated authority or filling regulatory gaps. They are participating in the fundamental work of legal system construction. This participation operates through different mechanisms than state lawmaking, relying on economic leverage and contractual relationships rather than sovereign authority, but it produces similar outcomes in terms of behavioral coordination and social ordering.

This recognition has important implications for how we understand regulatory relationships. Rather than viewing regulation as the beginning of the legal process and corporations as passive recipients of externally imposed rules, the framework suggests that corporate ordering often precedes and shapes subsequent regulatory responses. Companies first develop internal governance systems for addressing social challenges, establish industry practices through their operational choices, and create de facto standards through their rulemaking activities. Regulatory intervention typically represents attempts to formalize, modify, or supplement these existing corporate governance systems rather than creating entirely new legal frameworks from scratch.

Understanding this sequence has practical implications for both corporate strategy and regulatory design. Companies that recognize their role as legal system builders can develop more sophisticated approaches to governance challenges, anticipating regulatory attention and designing internal systems that can serve as foundations for broader industry standards. Regulators who understand corporate governance as institutional construction can design interventions that build on existing corporate capabilities rather than attempting to impose external systems that ignore established organizational capacities.

3.5.4 *Advancing Corporate Law beyond Normative Stalemates*

Perhaps most importantly, the tripartite framework offers a path beyond the normative debates that have paralyzed corporate law scholarship for decades. Disputes about whether corporations should focus on shareholders or stakeholders, whether they should address social issues or stick to business fundamentals, and whether they represent solutions to governmental failures or threats to democratic authority echo through academic corridors without making much headway. These debates have prevented scholars from developing practical frameworks for evaluating and improving corporate governance where it actually operates.

The functional analysis developed here sidesteps these normative questions by focusing on institutional design rather than ultimate purposes. Rather than asking whether corporations should perform governance functions, it acknowledges that they inevitably do and examines how they can perform these functions more effectively. Rather than debating whether corporate social responsibility represents legitimate business activity, it analyzes what governance mechanisms best serve companies that have already decided to make social commitments. Rather than litigating whether corporate power threatens democratic values, it examines how corporate institutional design can better serve both business effectiveness and broader accountability.

This approach does not resolve normative questions about appropriate corporate purposes, but it makes progress on those questions by making them less necessary for developing better corporate governance. Companies with different values and priorities can benefit from the same institutional insights about matching governance mechanisms to functional demands. Progressive companies seeking to advance social justice goals and conservative companies focused on traditional business fundamentals both need effective governance systems for their rulemaking, executive, and monitoring functions, even though they may reach different conclusions about what those functions should accomplish.

The framework thus provides common ground for corporate governance improvement that transcends ideological divisions. By focusing on institutional effectiveness rather than ultimate goals, it offers practical guidance that can enhance corporate performance regardless of whether companies prioritize shareholder value, stakeholder interests, or other objectives. The tripartite framework reveals corporate governance as the fundamental institutional architecture that translates corporate intentions into social outcomes. This recognition opens new possibilities for corporate law scholarship and practice that move beyond tired debates about corporate purpose toward more sophisticated analysis of corporate capabilities and institutional design. In an era of increasing corporate influence and growing demands for corporate accountability, such analysis has never been more urgently needed.

4

Why Not Regulate?

Why not regulate? Regulation is the traditional approach our society would have followed to constrain or, sometimes, encourage private actions whose implications affect third parties.[1] We have built specialized agencies, some with increased safeguards of independence, in fields too technical for the median voter. We enable the institutions of representative democracy to channel the preferences of the populace, frame the mission for these agencies, and grant them powers accordingly. Agencies and legislatures aim to protect the public interest, while corporations, just like any other party, have strong incentives to put their own interests first. When private gains far outweigh public losses, our laws and regulations intervene to correct the mismatch through bans, fines, taxes, licensing restrictions, and other techniques. Corporate conduct is a prime target for regulatory restrictions. So, then, why not simply regulate?

The immediate answer to that question is straightforward: corporations are often the first ones with their hands on the issue, and their reaction – or lack thereof – constitutes a policy response. For example, corporations inevitably have transgender employees, and thus must set a policy for their bathrooms. Similarly, corporations set the pay for two employees hired to do the exact same job. If one employee is female and agrees to compensation lower than that of her male coworker, then the company might be seen as knowingly perpetuating a gender pay gap. The same is true outside human capital management issues. Climate change, to pick an obvious example, is progressing at a fast pace. Corporations know that understanding the extent to which their activities may be contributing to GHG emissions and the cost of transitioning to more sustainable production methods requires planning. Sometimes, corporate innovations themselves generate a need for regulatory intervention, as often happens with new technologies. Having won broad flexibility to make choices that drive our society's economic engine, corporations are expected to use it. The reality is that most corporate choices are recorded and will be assessed for their social implications. Stakeholders will judge them as conservative, progressive, woke, or however else their audience perceives them.[2] So, corporations are stuck making socially impactful choices, and so are we, at least until we mobilize to reverse them. To put it simply, we cannot regulate everything.

Rather than the end of the conversation, this realization is the launching point for this chapter. Chapter 1 has established an inescapable reality: corporations make choices with profound social consequences. They decide which communities to invest in, which environmental standards to meet, how to treat workers, and whether to amplify or moderate online speech. These decisions reshape our social landscape as surely as any legislative enactment. A corporation's choice to relocate a factory determines the economic fate of entire towns. Its decisions about data collection and algorithmic design structure how millions of people access information and form political opinions. Its employment practices set standards that ripple across industries and shape the distribution of economic opportunity. We cannot wish away this power, nor can we pretend that corporate choices are merely private matters without public consequence. The question is not whether corporations shape social policy, as they clearly do. The critical question that propels this chapter forward is different, and far more consequential: when should we trust corporations to make these socially significant choices themselves, and when should the state intervene to regulate them instead?

This is not an abstract theoretical problem. It goes to the heart of how we organize economic life in a democratic society. Every time a corporation announces a new sustainability initiative, a commitment to diversity and inclusion, or a policy governing speech on its platform, we face a choice. Do we allow the corporation to proceed with its self-regulatory effort, trusting that market pressures, reputational concerns, and internal governance will produce acceptable outcomes? Or do we conclude that corporate self-interest, even when enlightened, cannot substitute for democratic accountability, and that the state must step in to mandate specific conduct? The stakes are high on both sides. Premature or excessive government regulation can stifle innovation, impose uniform solutions on heterogeneous problems, and waste the valuable information that corporations possess about their own operations.[3] Yet deference to corporate self-regulation risks allowing powerful private actors to set social policy without democratic input, to pursue initiatives that serve their interests rather than the public good, and to abandon commitments the moment they become inconvenient or costly.[4]

The relationship between corporate self-regulation and government regulation is neither simple nor static. Corporate action might serve as a prelude to government regulation, with companies acting first and the state intervening later if corporate responses prove inadequate. The threat of government regulation might be the necessary catalyst that spurs corporate action in the first place. Alternatively, corporate self-regulation might function as a genuine substitute for government regulation, making state intervention unnecessary in certain domains. We must also consider corporate self-regulatory efforts that implement government directions or mandates, a form of public–private partnership where companies translate legislative intent into operational reality.[5] Or perhaps corporate action is simply a second-best solution, inferior to direct government regulation but pragmatically necessary given the state's limited resources and reach.

The tripartite distinction developed in Chapter 3 provides a framework for answering this dilemma by identifying the conditions under which corporate decision-making is likely to produce socially acceptable outcomes. Rather than assuming all corporate self-regulation is equally trustworthy or equally suspect, the framework focuses on the quality of corporate governance processes: the robustness of stakeholder engagement, the effectiveness of board oversight, and the depth of transparency mechanisms. These governance features determine whether corporate decision-makers have access to the information they need, face meaningful accountability for their choices, and operate under constraints that limit arbitrary action. When corporations exhibit strong governance along these dimensions, they are more likely to make decisions that serve broader social interests, even in the absence of government mandates. When governance is weak or merely symbolic, corporate self-regulation becomes unreliable, and state intervention becomes necessary. The framework thus transforms the abstract question of trust into a concrete inquiry about institutional design. It allows us to distinguish between corporations that have built genuine capacity for responsible self-regulation and those that have merely adopted the rhetoric without the substance. By examining governance quality, we can better assess which relationship between private corporate ordering and public regulation best serves the public interest in different contexts. In some instances, society might be better off if corporations act as pioneers testing new approaches. In other cases, corporations might serve public goals better as implementers of government performance standards, or subjects of prescriptive regulation that leaves them little discretion.

The first task for this chapter, then, is to situate corporations' self-regulatory efforts in our legal order and explore how they interact with other policymakers. To understand corporations' place in this regulatory ecosystem, we must first recognize that our legal order has always accommodated multiple sources of law and norm-setting beyond the state.[6] Corporations join a long tradition of private institutions, from medieval guilds to modern universities, that create binding norms for their constituents.[7] Competing regulators coexist in many fields, and a wide literature has explored their interaction, not just among states in corporate law, but also at a global scale.[8] Corporations, I argue, are just another player in this regulatory landscape, setting their preferred norms and initiatives to constrain their stakeholders' behavior. Stakeholders can try to defect if they object to corporate choices, while regulators and legislatures can intervene to reverse them.

The remainder of this chapter develops criteria for evaluating corporate self-regulation against efforts by other policymakers. First, I explore when corporate self-regulation can successfully substitute for government regulation, identifying two key factors: corporations' deep but narrow expertise in their operations, and the complementarity between their business goals and social concerns. When these align favorably, self-regulation can work; when they diverge, it fails. Second, I consider when voluntary corporate practices serve as templates that regulators ultimately adopt as mandatory policy, which depends on alignment with public interest and proximity to core business functions.

The analysis then turns to harder cases. When political gridlock or resource constraints mean corporate self-regulation is the only governance mechanism available, durability becomes critical. Corporations face a time inconsistency problem: the pressures that motivate adopting rules may not sustain enforcement over time. This requires institutional solutions – independent oversight mechanisms that persist even when issue salience fades. I also address the legitimacy concern that corporate self-regulation may simply reflect CEO personal agendas rather than genuine corporate interests, and examine how governance processes can distinguish between the two. Finally, I explore how corporations navigate increasingly divergent, and sometimes directly conflicting, requirements across jurisdictions, considering both the costs of fragmentation and corporations' role as unifying forces that may default to the strictest global standard.

4.1 CORPORATIONS IN OUR LEGAL ORDER: SELF-REGULATION BEYOND THE STATE

The formal architecture of lawmaking focuses on legislatures, regulatory agencies, and courts, thus providing only a partial account of how rules governing modern economic and social life actually come into being. Corporations occupy a powerful, if often overlooked, position in the creation of these rules. They do not simply follow the law; they shape it, respond to it, and at times effectively write the first draft of it.

This section examines the dynamic interplay between corporate self-regulation and formal government regulation. Rather than viewing corporations as passive subjects waiting to be regulated, or as external lobbyists merely seeking to influence lawmakers, this section explores how corporations function as active participants in an ongoing regulatory conversation. When new problems emerge, whether from technological innovation, evolving business models, or changing social expectations, corporations necessarily act first, developing their own frameworks and practices while formal lawmakers deliberate. These initial corporate choices establish precedents, define problems, and set baselines that shape all subsequent regulatory responses. Even after legislators intervene, corporations retain substantial discretion in translating vague mandates into concrete practices, determining how abstract legal requirements actually operate in the real world.

Understanding this interaction is essential because it reveals how the rules governing major societal issues actually come into being. The regulatory frameworks that structure financial markets, protect workers, safeguard consumer data, and address environmental challenges emerge not from legislative deliberation alone, but through an iterative process in which corporate governance choices play a constitutive role. Sometimes corporate self-regulation proves adequate and formal regulation never materializes. Other times, corporate frameworks fail dramatically, triggering governmental intervention. But even then, the resulting regulations bear the imprint of the corporate experimentation that preceded them.

The goal of this section is to map this interactive terrain: how corporations develop their own rules in the absence of regulation, how they implement or resist regulatory mandates once they arrive, and how governmental authorities respond to corporate successes and failures. Section 4.1.1 will turn to evaluation, examining when and under what conditions this interaction produces outcomes that serve broader societal needs, and when it falls short.

4.1.1 *Situating Corporate Ordering in the Constitutional Order*

Humans have long come together in institutions that create their own rules to better integrate, guide existing participants, and recruit new ones. Using a normative, rule-setting framework to organize individuals and resources into a single operation that serves a core mission is far from unique to states. Medieval merchants organized themselves into guilds to maintain quality standards, facilitate dispute resolution, and discourage outsiders.[9] Since the eighteenth century, stock exchanges have established rules for facilitating trades, building credibility among members, and assessing the quality of listing companies.[10] More recently, a variety of standard-setters, some national and some global, have developed frameworks and best practices that govern a wide range of issues, from human rights to accounting.[11]

Looking beyond the commercial sphere reveals even more extensive examples of private norm-creation. Universities have long established elaborate rules for assessing academic excellence, appointing and promoting personnel, regulating student conduct, and managing their resources.[12] The standards they create for tenure, academic integrity, and campus conduct operate with binding force within their communities, often with minimal state intervention. Even more conspicuously, the church has long exercised its own rule-setting function, translating religious guidance into rules of conduct and sometimes even supplanting state-created law in the process.[13] Canon law governed vast swaths of medieval life, from marriage to inheritance, operating as a complete legal system parallel to secular authorities. The literature on self-regulation explores these and many other examples of private institutions voluntarily undertaking the regulatory mantle, examining their motivations, conditions for success, and public reception of their frameworks.

As legal scholars understand well, constitutional orders establish a pyramid for the sources of law, but the reality is more complicated. Legislatures, regulators, courts, and enforcement agencies interact in ways that shape the content of the law they produce. Coexistence among different lawmakers and standard setters has both fascinated and perplexed legal scholars.

Federalism has described different states as laboratories of legal experimentation, where variation in political alliances promotes different solutions, allowing policymakers to learn from each other's successes and failures. In the corporate law context, state competition has been particularly influential. Carey[14] and Romano[15] have explored competition among U.S. states as the force shaping corporate law, while Roe contrasted Delaware's commitment to private ordering with Congress' more heavy-handed interventions after perceived failures due to Delaware's deferential stance.[16]

Yet the constitutional framework has never successfully contained all sources of binding norms within the formal pyramid of legislation, regulation, and judicial interpretation. Just like guilds, stock exchanges, universities, and religious institutions, corporations find themselves outside the constitutional sources of law, basing their influence instead on others' incentives to abide by it. Sometimes, third parties will adhere to the corporate regime because they are required to do so by contract, such as employees, suppliers, or collaborators. Other times, third parties will find themselves subjected to the implications of corporate choices even though they are not in privity of contract with the corporation, such as local communities, workers dependent on the continued success of the corporation, or large public goods like the environment.

4.1.2 *The Dynamic of Corporate Self-Regulation*

Like other private lawmakers, when corporations face a problem that has not been subject to formal regulation by legislators and government authorities, they will produce their own rules applicable to that problem. To do so, they must balance the interests of their various constituencies as best as they can understand them. Sometimes, each corporation will come up with its own institutional design. Other times, they will cooperate with each other to develop industry-wide best practices.

This initial corporate response is not made in a vacuum. Corporations operate within a competitive regulatory environment where their self-regulatory choices are constantly tested against three critical benchmarks: market acceptance, stakeholder satisfaction, and the threat of formal regulatory intervention. Their proposed solutions compete not only with the alternatives offered by other firms in their industry, but also with the latent regulatory frameworks that government authorities might impose if corporate efforts prove inadequate. This creates a dynamic where corporations are simultaneously experimenting with governance solutions and performing a high-stakes demonstration for potential regulators.

The temporal sequence here is crucial: corporations necessarily act first. When new problems emerge, there is an inherent regulatory lag before formal lawmakers can respond.[17] Legislators must identify the problem, understand its technical dimensions, navigate political obstacles, and draft appropriate rules. During this interval, which can last years or even decades, corporations are already operating, making choices, and establishing precedents. They are writing the first draft of the rules, even if the official legal system does not yet recognize it as a regulation. These initial corporate frameworks become the baseline against which all subsequent regulatory interventions take shape.[18]

If corporations manage to produce a set of rules that validates constituents' concerns, arrives at acceptable compromises, and puts in place a framework that allows the business to grow while addressing affected parties' needs, then formal lawmakers are unlikely to intervene. Successful corporate self-regulation may be imitated by competitors, diffuse throughout an industry, and crystallize into widely accepted best practices. In such cases, formal regulation may never materialize or may simply codify corporate practices that have already proven workable. The corporate solution, having survived market testing and stakeholder scrutiny, becomes the regulatory equilibrium. Conversely, other corporations facing similar problems may develop alternative approaches, creating a competitive marketplace of governance solutions. This competition generates information about what works, what does not, and what trade-offs different approaches require. This information may prove invaluable when formal regulators eventually consider intervention.

If, on the other hand, unsatisfied constituents manage to lobby other lawmakers successfully for a change, or a big crisis exposes fundamental problems in corporations' frameworks that harm aggregate social welfare, then other lawmakers will push forward their own preferred rules, overriding corporate choices. Yet even in these cases of regulatory override, the corporate first mover advantage often shapes the ultimate regulatory outcome.[19] Formal regulation emerges as a response to and reaction against the corporate framework that came before. Regulators identify gaps in corporate self-regulation, respond to its failures, and often build upon elements that worked while discarding those that did not. The architecture of formal regulation thus bears the imprint of the corporate experimentation that preceded it. Whether corporate self-regulation succeeds or fails, it defines the problem space, establishes the terms of debate, and influences the menu of solutions that regulators consider.

This dynamic suggests something fundamental about regulatory origins: regulation does not emerge ex nihilo from legislative deliberation but evolves through an iterative process in which corporate governance choices play a constitutive role. Corporations are not merely subjects of regulation; they are proto-regulators whose initial efforts at self-governance establish the factual and normative baseline from which formal regulation develops. Understanding regulation's origins thus requires understanding the corporate frameworks that preceded it, the problems those frameworks addressed or failed to address, and the constituencies whose satisfaction or dissatisfaction triggered regulatory intervention. The story of regulation is, in large part, the story of corporate self-regulation tested, refined, or rejected through market and political processes.

A recent example illustrates how this dynamic plays out in practice. The market for asset-backed securities was left largely to its own devices for decades until the 2007 financial crisis[20] revealed how corporate self-regulatory choices had compromised the stability of the financial system. Before 2007, corporations were able to set their own preferred contract terms, determine their own preferred due diligence levels, market the securities with little intervention by regulators, have them assessed for credit risk based on their own preferred standards, and utilize these ratings for capital adequacy purposes.[21] This corporate framework emerged incrementally over decades as financial institutions experimented with securitization techniques, developed market conventions, and established what they deemed to be adequate risk management practices. Crucial components of asset-backed transactions, like the derivative mechanisms, were based on industry-wide standardization through the International Swaps and Derivatives Association (ISDA). Other institutions observed what worked, imitated successful approaches, and adapted them to their own circumstances. The result was a largely self-regulated market that operated on corporate-designed rules.

After 2007, when it became catastrophically apparent that corporate self-regulation could not effectively police a burgeoning market, Congress and regulators intervened in many aspects of the asset-backed securities market.[22] Due diligence standards for the underlying assets became tighter and more closely enforced. Credit rating agencies became subject to tighter SEC supervision as their products were deemed systemically important.[23] Capital adequacy standards were significantly buttressed.[24]

Yet this regulatory response was fundamentally shaped by the corporate framework it displaced. Regulators identified specific failures in corporate due diligence, rating agency practices, and capital standards, and crafted rules designed to address those particular deficiencies. The postcrisis regulatory regime thus emerged as a direct response to the corporate self-regulatory system that had preceded it, bearing witness to how corporate first movers shape regulatory development even when their frameworks ultimately fail.

4.1.3 *Corporate Ordering When Implementing Legislative or Regulatory Mandates*

This dynamic of interaction between corporate self-regulation and formal lawmaking continues even after legislators intervene. Once Congress or other legislators enact laws that directly govern corporate conduct, another circle of interactions with corporations begins. Corporations are bound by these laws and cannot have policies in place that directly violate them. Nevertheless, implementation of these laws is far from a predetermined outcome.

Corporations still need to put in place the institutional framework that translates the legislative mandate into actual corporate practice. Often, legislative mandates are vague, leaving corporations with considerable discretion. Other times, legislators outlaw certain behavior but leave it up to the company to figure out a system that monitors whether this behavior occurs. Internal rulebooks and procedures, now ubiquitous in large U.S. corporations, are an example of corporate rulemaking, as they specify the precise actions and steps employees should take to ensure compliance. Through these rulebooks, corporations give specific meaning to legislative mandates. While they try to stick close to the intent of the legislators, they have also been criticized for failing to implement them.

4.1.3.1 The Choice between Design and Performance Standards

The degree of corporate discretion in implementing regulation depends significantly on the type of regulatory standard legislators choose. Regulators face a fundamental choice between two approaches: design standards and performance standards.[25] Design standards, also called specification standards or prescriptive standards, specify exactly how regulated entities must act to achieve desired outcomes. They prescribe particular technologies, methods, materials, or procedures that companies must follow. For instance, a prescriptive building code might specify exact construction materials and methods, or an environmental regulation might mandate installation of specific pollution control equipment.

Performance standards, by contrast, specify required outcomes or end-states but leave the means of achieving those outcomes to the regulated entity's discretion. An emissions performance standard, for example, might require that vehicles emit no more than a specified level of pollutants, but allow manufacturers to choose any technological approach to meet that limit, such as catalytic converters, engine redesign, or alternative fuels. The distinction is fundamental: design standards tell companies what to do, while performance standards tell them what to achieve.

Performance standards have gained widespread policy support, from U.S. presidential administrations to international organizations like the World Trade Organization and OECD, based on their theoretical advantages.[26] By giving firms discretion to choose compliance methods, performance standards allow companies to select approaches that fit their particular circumstances, whether they are large or small facilities, use old or new technology, or operate different production processes. This flexibility can yield substantial cost savings across regulated sectors and remove obstacles to innovation, as firms can adopt improved methods without requiring regulatory amendments.

However, this flexibility also means corporations retain significant initiative in determining how regulatory goals are actually implemented. When regulators set performance targets, companies must still design the specific systems, technologies, and practices that will achieve those targets. A firm facing air quality performance standards must decide which combination of technological controls, process modifications, or fuel switches to deploy. Different firms may make vastly different choices, creating diverse compliance landscapes even under uniform regulatory requirements. The corporate discretion inherent in performance standards thus represents another form of corporate lawmaking, as companies effectively write the operational rules that give concrete meaning to abstract regulatory goals.

Despite their theoretical appeal, performance standards face significant practical challenges that underscore their dependence on corporate cooperation. Most critically, performance standards require reliable measurement and monitoring of outcomes, which may be difficult or costly to establish. When outcomes cannot be verified continuously or accurately, companies may find ways to achieve technical compliance while undermining regulatory purposes, a phenomenon regulatory scholars call "teaching to the test."[27] The Volkswagen diesel emissions scandal[28] starkly illustrated this vulnerability: for seven years, vehicles passed regulatory performance tests while emitting up to forty times permissible levels during normal operation, because the company designed software that detected testing conditions and adjusted engine performance accordingly.

4.1.3.2 Culture over Compliance

Modern criminal law compliance emphasizes a company's culture rather than its adherence to a strict set of rules.[29] Strict adherence to compliance rulebooks can reduce a company's attention to a ticking-the-box mentality, making it too easy for underlying misconduct to evade detection. Critics have presented compliance as a superficial effort by corporations to fulfill their legal obligations on the surface while in fact permitting, if not surreptitiously encouraging, illegal conduct to continue unabated.[30] In criticizing corporate hypocrisy, these critics underline how central a role corporations play, since laws cannot really be enforced without their cooperation.

Instead, criminal enforcement authorities now require companies to enact a broader set of rules that direct supervisors to be mindful of irregularities, investigate red flags, and embrace and transmit the values underlying the law. Legislators and regulators cannot predict the pathways of misconduct, much less write laws, rules, and compliance handbooks that exhaustively track them. Rather, they recognize that this task must fall to the company and its management, which must embrace the law's mission, identify the critical junctures in its internal hierarchy, set up monitoring and internal reporting systems, and appropriately sanction violators. In practice, corporations must act as enforcement agencies themselves, in ways that authorities and courts would recognize as good faith efforts to implement broad legislative mandates.

What if corporate leaders disagree with the legislator's choice? In the case of the minimum wage, ascertaining compliance is easy since the law sets a clear numerical threshold. Violating it comes with severe sanctions a corporate leader cannot ignore without violating their fiduciary duties to the corporation and its shareholders. However, not all legal requirements are as straightforward. For example, after *Dobbs*[31], the Supreme Court ruling that reversed *Roe v. Wade*[32] and allowed states to make their own choices, many corporations have expressed their commitment to facilitating employees who wish to obtain an abortion, for example, by contributing to the cost of traveling across state borders to a provider operating legally.[33] Predictably, pro-life politicians are loathe to realize that their powers are more limited than previously thought and blame corporations for hampering their ability to impose their laws on persons that should have been subject to their jurisdiction.[34]

As emblematic of our era as *Dobbs* is, the corporate reaction to newly instituted abortion bans follows a familiar pattern. When lawmakers and regulators put forward initiatives that are not in line with corporate interests, companies comply to the extent required but also seek to undermine them. Without explicitly violating the law, companies utilize every shred of discretion left to them. Sometimes, companies will explore alternative corporate structures that steer clear of legal violations, often by offloading the potentially violative assets to a separate subsidiary or special purpose vehicle. Other times, companies will stick to the letter of the law, fully aware that these requirements will be proven to fall far short of lawmakers' intentions, as is often the case with anti-money laundering laws. Still other times, corporations may lobby lawmakers to change the regime, or undertake direct action to change it themselves were possible, as with Proposition 22 in California,[35] or with the implementation of Sarbanes-Oxley Section 404.[36] In all these options, corporate reaction undercut the effectiveness of a legal mandate or prohibition, particularly when compliance requires corporate cooperation.

4.1.4 *Corporate Ordering and Lobbying*

Any discussion of corporate self-regulation inevitably invites comparison to the long and controversial history of corporate lobbying. A vast literature has examined how firms seek to influence lawmakers and regulators, often framing lobbying as the principal mechanism of regulatory capture. Classic accounts, from Mancur Olson's analysis of concentrated interests[37] to Daniel Carpenter's work on bureaucratic reputation,[38] emphasize how corporations exploit informational advantages, deploy campaign contributions, and coordinate through trade associations to shape legal frameworks in their favor. Concerns about corporate influence intensified after *Citizens United v. FEC*,[39] which struck down restrictions on independent political spending and dramatically expanded opportunities for corporate political engagement. In the years since, political scientists, legal scholars, and the media have repeatedly highlighted how lobbying threatens democratic legitimacy by amplifying the voices of well-financed firms while muting the interests of diffuse publics.

This book does not seek to add to that literature. Its focus lies elsewhere: inward, on the internal governance practices through which corporations develop their own principles and frameworks of action. Whereas lobbying aims to persuade external lawmakers to adopt favorable rules, corporate self-regulation involves companies constructing rules for themselves, often with effects that reach employees, suppliers, customers, and communities at large. Lobbying aspires to shape official law; corporate self-regulation, by contrast, creates private frameworks that operate as de facto law within the corporate domain.

Yet lobbying and self-regulation, while distinct, are not disconnected. In lobbying, the fear is that corporate voices overwhelm democratic representation. Similarly, in self-regulation, the concern is that corporations impose unilateral rules on employees, suppliers, and customers with little opportunity for negotiation. In both settings, the familiar dynamics of capture and asymmetry resurface. Just as regulators get swayed by corporate resources, so too stakeholders inside and outside the firm find themselves subject to managerial framing of trade-offs without equal footing.

Moreover, the decision-making tools for which Chapter 3 advocates can help enhance the legitimacy concerns raised when companies lobby for them in the public sphere. Lobbying has traditionally relied on political contributions and closed-door access, modes that generate suspicion. Self-regulation increasingly depends on processes designed to demonstrate credibility: stakeholder consultation, disclosure of rationales, engagement with external experts, and independent monitoring.[40] These governance tools mirror the deliberative practices that independent policymakers themselves must follow, and when deployed effectively, they make corporate preferences more persuasive in subsequent regulatory debates. A corporation that can demonstrate how it has systematically gathered information, weighed competing claims, and transparently justified trade-offs is more likely to secure external acceptance of its proposed solutions, whether by investors, employees, or government officials. Properly designed, these tools not only protect shareholders and stakeholders from arbitrariness but also, as a by-product, strengthen the credibility of corporate advocacy in the public sphere.

4.1.5 *Corporate Self-Regulation and Law: Constant Interplay*

The constant interplay between corporations and government authorities is an indelible feature of our constitutional system, which delineates different spheres of power and autonomy for corporations, regulatory agencies, legislatures, states, and the executive. In a modern democracy, all these actors employ their distinct powers and capabilities in a constant fight to outsmart each other, assert their presence, and change the rules of interaction in society. But they also must abide by the limitations of their power, often in place to protect other actors' autonomy. As these actors clash with one another, the boundaries of their influence are constantly redrawn, but each actor's input contributes to the effectiveness of the outcome.

My contention is, then, that corporations' autonomy to create new rules, as well as to embrace or object to legislative or regulatory mandates, is valuable. Corporations are at once the central players in our economy and a key institutional link between the legislature and citizens. They have unique incentives in figuring out laws that maximize our society's production capacity, as well as direct insights on how laws affect citizens.[41] Asked to spearhead and monitor laws' implementation, they are the first to notice inconsistencies, gaps, misconceptions, and failures, as well as successes, complementarities, and moral affirmations. But corporations are also pioneers, veering into uncharted territories, noticing first the ethical and societal challenges awaiting the legislature as the economy moves at a fast pace toward tomorrow's world.

This interplay reveals corporations as autonomous self-regulatory actors. They are neither merely passive subjects of regulation nor simple extensions of state power, but independent participants in our polycentric lawmaking system. They compete and collaborate with legislatures, agencies, courts, and civil society organizations, each wielding distinct capabilities and constraints. Yet acknowledging corporations' valuable role in regulatory development does not mean embracing regulatory capture or abdicating public oversight. Corporations will not always get it right. Their profit motives may distort their judgment; their insularity may blind them to externalities; their power may enable them to entrench rules that serve private interests over public welfare.[42] The critical question, then, is not whether corporations should participate in lawmaking, because they unavoidably will. Rather, the challenge lies in clarifying under what conditions corporate self-regulation serves the public interest, and when it demands intervention by other institutional actors. The remainder of this chapter develops a framework for distinguishing productive corporate autonomy from problematic regulatory circumvention, identifying the structural features, competitive dynamics, and accountability mechanisms that determine whether corporate self-regulation enhances or undermines democratic governance.

To answer this question, I examine three distinct scenarios in which corporate self-regulation operates, each demanding different evaluative criteria. First, I explore instances where corporate self-regulation works so effectively that it substitutes for formal regulation. In these cases, regulatory authorities observe corporate initiatives and conclude that intervention is unnecessary because firms have adequately addressed the relevant concerns. Second, I consider situations where self-regulation serves as a prelude to regulation. Regulators identify best practices emerging from particular companies and mandate those solutions industry-wide, essentially codifying voluntary corporate innovation into binding legal requirements. Finally, I turn to the most complex scenario, which consists in evaluating self-regulation when government regulation is absent not by choice but by constraint. Here, political gridlock, resource limitations, jurisdictional ambiguities, or ideological disagreement prevent regulatory action, leaving corporate self-regulation as the only governance mechanism in play. Each scenario presents distinct advantages and risks, requiring us to assess corporate autonomy against different baselines and to consider what institutional safeguards might channel corporate rulemaking toward public-regarding outcomes.

4.2 WHEN CAN CORPORATE ORDERING ACT AS A SUCCESSFUL SUBSTITUTE FOR REGULATION?

The institutional features of corporate self-regulation raise a question that sits at the heart of regulatory theory and practice: is corporate self-regulation a substitute for regulation? This question has animated debates about the proper role of government oversight for decades, often framed as a choice between market-based solutions and command-and-control regulation.[43] Yet this framing suggests a false dichotomy. The question is not whether corporate self-regulation can or should entirely replace external government regulation, but rather under what conditions corporate efforts to self-regulate will be more successful, capturing rules that regulators and policymakers will accept and leave be, and under what conditions they are likely to fail, necessitating regulatory intervention.

The answer depends on understanding how corporations fare as self-regulating entities, comparing their distinctive strengths and limitations to other lawmakers. Two characteristics of corporations as rulemaking actors prove especially illuminating in predicting when self-regulation will succeed and when it will fall short: their deep and narrow focus, and the complementarity between their business goals and their regulatory responses. These conditions help explain the variable success of corporate self-regulation across different domains and over time, and they provide guidance for managers navigating their discretion.

4.2.1 *Deep and Narrow Focus*

Corporations are focused on a specific product or line of products and services, and aggregate expertise about all the necessary stages in developing that product. Compared to federal or state legislatures, or even to regulatory agencies, this represents a significantly narrower focus on certain elements of production. Moreover, the intensity of market competition often leads corporate managers to concentrate on key parameters of corporate production, which can help them reduce costs, offer improved products compared to industry averages, or target a niche corner of the market. Because of their product focus, companies' stakeholders are also a narrower subset of the electorate, or of society as a whole. Companies interact only with those workers who have chosen to work in their factories and offices, engage with citizens and authorities only in communities where they have established a presence, and communicate with regulators only in issue areas relevant to their own business. Even when launching initiatives in favor of universal goals, like reversing climate change or fighting systemic racism, they focus on how their specific operations relate to the goal in question. Managers must plan strategies, evaluate methods, and consider tradeoffs that might have differential impacts for their stakeholders and other groups.

This deep and narrow focus creates conditions favorable to successful self-regulation when the regulatory challenge falls squarely within the company's domain of expertise and stakeholder concerns.[44] By zeroing in on their companies' unique problems, managers develop superior understanding of operational idiosyncrasies and are better placed to respond to their challenges. Most other lawmakers are quite distanced from the issues or relationships they are trying to regulate and depend on others' input. In contrast, managers have direct oversight and are ideally situated to come up with practical, workable, and cost-effective solutions that are more easily integrated with the rest of the company. For example, managers know best where to turn to upgrade their packaging with biodegradable materials; what are the challenges to diversity in some of their departments; how best to organize transportation so as to minimize emissions per delivery. The pressure on managers to innovate in order to solve sustainability challenges is being regarded as a key driver for the success of sustainable business.[45] This expertise can lead managers to develop innovative solutions that less well-informed rulemakers, such as regulators or legislators, would not have otherwise conceived. Moreover, managers are more likely to capture accurately the costs and benefits of establishing a new rule or practice, thus striking a better balance when imposing constraints and obligations. In these circumstances, corporate self-regulation can genuinely substitute for external regulation, producing rules that align sufficiently with public interests that regulators find them acceptable or even preferable to legislated alternatives.

However, this same characteristic predicts failure when broader public interests diverge from the company's narrow stakeholder concerns.[46] The downside of managers' deep and narrow focus is, unsurprisingly, that their preferred solutions may not align with the interests or preferences of the electorate in general. Managers are tied to the interests of their own company's shareholders and stakeholders. Thus, solutions that work for one company may not necessarily be generalizable to other companies. In addition, a company's shareholders and stakeholders are only a subset of society, regardless of how broad a view one takes on stakeholderism. Thus, corporate rulemaking's claim to representation is a weak one, as important groups may be absent from the company's horizon or may not warrant as much weight as they would have gotten under a representative rulemaker. After all, what is good for the company may not necessarily be good for the nation.

This type of conflict signals that a company will have trouble addressing the issue on a voluntary basis without additional regulatory intervention, and that self-regulation is unlikely to succeed as a substitute for external rules. Content moderation in social media illustrates the difficulties associated with such a clash between corporate and public interests.[47] Admittedly, engagement with potentially offensive or otherwise violative posts helps the company gain traffic, and thus revenue. Moreover, it provides an outlet to certain users and to their followers. While it may enrage other users, or the public in general, it is hard for managers to assess how much weight they ought to put on negative reactions. Enraged users generally tend to continue engaging with the platform, even after temporary blockades. Free speech advocates provide a framework for justifying the company's position, also raising the stakes against removal choices. Without a massive exodus of users, or the threat of impending regulation or enforcement actions, the company's shareholders and stakeholders are unlikely to push management toward a solution that satisfies the broader public interest. In such cases, the narrow focus that gives corporations their expertise becomes precisely the limitation that prevents effective self-regulation.

4.2.2 *Complementarity*

Most other lawmakers do not have an independent activity directed at profit-making, which could present conflicts of interest for their lawmaking docket. Some may consider that rulemaking and profitmaking are incompatible, as entrusting rulemaking powers to a for-profit entity simply invites abuse.[48] Indeed, when some private rulemakers developed business-like activities or morphed into profit-making entities, legislators often forced them to forego some self-regulatory powers, introduce institutional separation, or submit to increased monitoring. Stock exchanges, for example, devolved their regulatory powers over their members once they demutualized, because they could be in competition with other financial intermediaries.[49] However, stock exchanges maintained power over listed companies, because ensuring high-quality listings was essential to the success of the market. As this example shows, rulemaking can often be complementary to the company's function, and this complementarity proves crucial in determining when self-regulation will succeed or fail.

For corporate managers, addressing ethical or societal dilemmas is complementary to their business goals rather than the primary focus of their actions. Thus, they are willing to confront such dilemmas to the extent that it helps promote their business or at least helps continue the smooth operation of the company without further disruption. Some clarification is due. Complementarity does not suggest that all management actions are constrained by a mandate to maximize profits. For example, managers may decide to sacrifice immediate profits and invest in costly but environmentally friendly production methods, believing that it is in the interest of shareholders to have the company be known as an early adopter. Or, they may decide that adopting a hard stance against sexual harassment is a necessary step for attracting female talent to the company, which may help the company overperform its peers. Although in both cases one can find a profit-making rationale, pinpointing specific benefits and profits is arguably elusive. Without a clear sense of how much profit is involved, profit maximization cannot be the motivation.[50]

When this complementarity is genuine and sustained, it creates favorable conditions for successful self-regulation. Complementarity between business and ethical or social issues helps managers grasp the consequences of their choices more fully. Issues that had not traditionally been the topic of board meetings but are proven central to the company's well-being, from parental leave benefits to supply chain human rights abuses, can come to the top of the agenda. This has been a key motivation behind the growth of the ESG movement, which underscored the social implications of many corporate choices.[51] Complementarity highlights that corporations are microcosms of our society, plagued by some of the same problems, biases, and unintended consequences. Ubiquitous as these problems are, they call for solutions in the specific institutional context in which they appear. Thus, complementarity's value is particularly evident in issues that find expression in the workplace, such as race and gender relations, which cannot be fully addressed without cooperation from the employers themselves and their managers.[52] Moreover, complementarity forces a rulemaker to think not only about the impact of a rule on the persons directly subject to it, but also about the broader company and its other stakeholders. In these situations, self-regulatory efforts are likely to be robust and sustained precisely because they serve the company's interests, making external regulation less necessary or even counterproductive.

But complementarity also illuminates when corporate self-regulation is likely to fail. To start, managers will focus only on social or ethical issues that help promote the company's business or substantially threaten to disrupt the company's performance. Not all social or ethical issues rise to that level, which suggests that stakeholders will need to mobilize in order to elevate the salience of an issue for managers. Arguably, issue salience is a challenge for all lawmakers, and potentially a costly one for stakeholders that must overcome collective action problems. It also suggests that shareholders or stakeholders who can grab managers' attention more readily are more likely to exercise pressure for issues important to them. It is no coincidence, for example, that Disney was particularly troubled by Florida's "Don't Say Gay" policy, as it had long cultivated an LGBT following for its resorts.[53] This dimension of complementarity may help explain why one might see trends in management attention. For example, when one company announces a social initiative that draws praise, other companies' managers may wish to imitate it. In contrast, when a company finds itself in trouble, other companies may take preventive measures to avoid similar fallout in their ranks.

More critically for the question of when self-regulation fails, management's attention will remain focused on an issue only to the extent that such an issue continues to benefit or challenge the company. Once its influence wanes, management is likely to direct its attention elsewhere, as new opportunities and concerns continue to arise. This presents a fundamental limitation on self-regulation as a substitute for external rules. To maintain the corporate machine's attention to that topic, stakeholders must ensure that it remains salient for management, or that the company puts in place important institutional reforms that ensure ongoing oversight. For example, a company may strive hard to obtain a green certification for its products or services but may decline to upgrade its operations once newer and better technology becomes available. Conversely, companies faced with a sexual harassment scandal may rush to take measures that help assuage employees' worries but fail to follow through with commitments once calmness returns to the workforce and headlines change. When complementarity is superficial or temporary, self-regulatory efforts are likely to atrophy without sustained external pressure, signaling to regulators that intervention remains necessary. The tight connection between business goals and self-regulatory responses makes corporate self-regulation powerful when interests align but also becomes the weakness that undermines it when that alignment dissolves.

4.3 WHEN CAN CORPORATE ACTION ACT AS PRELUDE TO REGULATION?

Understanding when corporate self-regulation succeeds or fails as a substitute for external regulation leads naturally to a related question: when can corporate action act as a prelude to regulation? That is, under what conditions are regulators likely to adopt corporate-made rules as mandatory public policy? This question examines a different dynamic than substitution.[54] Rather than asking whether self-regulation eliminates the need for government intervention, we are asking when private rule-making serves as a template or proving ground for public rulemaking, with regulators ultimately codifying voluntary corporate practices into binding law. Two conditions prove particularly important in determining this outcome: the alignment between corporate rules and public interest, and the proximity of those rules to the company's core business function.

4.3.1 *Alignment with Public Interest*

The most critical factor determining whether corporate rules become a prelude to regulation is the degree to which company goals overlap with the public interest, at least as understood by policymakers in power at the time. This alignment creates favorable conditions for regulators to look to corporate practices as models for mandatory policy. There are good reasons to expect such overlap, particularly when new areas of business activity emerge. Technological advances have fueled the rise of entirely new industries in recent years, whose success depends on customers' endorsement and continuous engagement. Companies are under pressure to deliver products, services, and environments that respect customers' expectations. The technical expertise for imagining how to incorporate justified rules and norms into their operation belongs, first and foremost, to the companies that designed them in the first place. When companies pioneer rules in these emerging domains, and those rules reflect genuine public interest concerns, regulators often find it efficient and effective to adopt these corporate innovations as the basis for mandatory requirements.

From a substantive perspective, it may be optimal to delegate initial rulemaking power to the corporate innovator precisely because the company's goals overlap with the public interest in these circumstances. Companies that have developed the technology or business model are best positioned to understand its operation, anticipate its challenges, and design workable solutions. When they voluntarily develop rules that balance innovation with customer protection or societal concerns, these rules demonstrate both technical feasibility and market acceptance. Regulators, observing this alignment, can build upon corporate practices that have already been tested and refined, rather than designing rules from scratch. In this way, corporate action genuinely serves as a prelude to regulation, with voluntary practices paving the way for mandatory standards that industry participants have already shown can work.

However, alignment with public interest cannot be assumed, and its absence creates conditions where corporate rules are unlikely to become the basis for regulation. The significant concerns associated with trusting corporate managers with broad rulemaking initiative become apparent when considering whether regulators should adopt their rules as public policy. Managers may have the technical expertise related to their product, and the vision about the company's future, but they are not necessarily well-placed to understand its ethical and social implications. Managers are chosen because of their business acumen and executive experience. These tasks do not necessarily nurture perceptive rulemakers, whose skills include sensitivity to differing perspectives and responsiveness to battling interest groups. Thus, managers are likely to miss or underestimate the public's reactions or the harm caused to specific stakeholders.

Moreover, managers' incentives may not be fully aligned with the public interest, which fundamentally undermines the potential for their rules to serve as templates for regulation. They may be inclined to avoid sound reform that could curtail their profit-making capacity, willing to bet that dissatisfied customers or unhappy stakeholders will be less detrimental to their bottom line in the end. Perhaps more simply, managers may be unwilling to engage with social or ethical issues, loathe about the additional corporate resources this requires. When regulators perceive that corporate rules are designed primarily to serve corporate interests or to forestall more stringent regulation, they are unlikely to adopt these rules as public policy. Instead, regulators may view voluntary corporate efforts with skepticism, seeing them as inadequate responses that justify more aggressive regulatory intervention rather than as models to be codified into law.

4.3.2 *Proximity to Core Business Function*

A second condition that determines whether corporate action serves as a prelude to regulation is the proximity of the rules to the company's core business function. This proximity affects both the legitimacy of managerial intervention and the credibility of corporate rules in the eyes of regulators. Since managers' rulemaking role, as well as expertise and background, are grounded in their business leadership, rules that are closely connected with the company's business operations are more likely to be viewed by regulators as legitimate and technically sound candidates for broader adoption.

When corporate rules address issues directly tied to the company's technical expertise and business operations, managers can explain and justify their intervention convincingly. These are areas where managers possess genuine knowledge advantages over legislators and regulators, and where their daily oversight gives them practical insights into what works and what does not. Regulators recognizing this expertise may look to these corporate practices as valuable sources of regulatory innovation. For instance, when companies develop internal protocols for data security, supply chain transparency, or workplace safety that directly relate to their production processes, these rules emerge from genuine operational knowledge. If these practices prove effective and gain industry-wide adoption, regulators may codify them into mandatory standards, confident that they represent feasible and well-tested approaches. The proximity to core business functions lends credibility to the rules and legitimacy to the managers who created them, making regulatory adoption more likely.

However, the farther the rule ventures into issues less directly connected with the company's business, the harder it will be for managers to explain or justify their intervention, and the less likely regulators will view these rules as appropriate models for public policy. Employees are a good example here. There are many aspects of employees' lives that managers may wish to support, prohibit, or control, arguing that they can affect productivity, ranging from family demands to religious beliefs and political involvement. Or, a company benefiting from a community resource, such as water, may find itself involved in many aspects of running that community that are not closely related to the company's business. In those instances, the broad discretion provided by corporate law may find the managers entering controversial territory where their expertise is questionable and their authority contested.

When corporate rules extend beyond core business functions into broader social or ethical domains, regulators face a different calculus in deciding whether to adopt them as public policy. The managerial claim to superior knowledge becomes weaker, and the concern that corporate rules serve private rather than public interests becomes stronger. Regulators may question whether managers have the appropriate perspective or incentives to craft rules in these areas, and may prefer to develop regulations through more representative processes that include diverse stakeholder input. In these circumstances, corporate action is unlikely to serve as a prelude to regulation. At best, corporate rules may demonstrate the existence of a problem that requires regulatory attention; at worst, they may be seen as corporate overreach that justifies limiting managerial discretion rather than codifying it into law.

4.4 CORPORATE ORDERING AS SECOND-BEST: WHEN DOES IT SUCCEED?

The analysis thus far has explored when corporate self-regulation can serve as a substitute for external regulation, and when corporate action can serve as a prelude to rules that regulators ultimately adopt as mandatory policy. Both questions assume, at least implicitly, that government regulation remains a realistic possibility. But we often find ourselves in a second-best world, where government regulation is absent either because policymakers lack the political motivation or resources to intervene, or due to political disagreements and gridlock.[55] Under these circumstances, corporate self-regulation is often the only option. The concerns expressed earlier regarding alignment with public interest and proximity to core business functions remain relevant. But an additional consideration becomes paramount: even when corporate self-regulation initially succeeds in addressing a problem, will it endure over time?

This question of durability distinguishes corporate self-regulation fundamentally from government regulation. Once enacted, government regulation persists regardless of the level of political attention or administrative enthusiasm at any given moment. Laws remain on the books, agencies continue to enforce them through bureaucratic routine, and compliance mechanisms become embedded in organizational practices across entire industries. Corporate self-regulation, by contrast, faces a powerful time inconsistency problem.[56] The conditions that motivate managers to establish rules may not be the same conditions that motivate them to enforce those rules rigorously over time. This temporal dynamic becomes especially critical when corporate self-regulation represents the only constraint on corporate conduct in a particular domain.

One might expect that corporations would be well primed to enforce rules that they themselves have set. However, compliance and enforcement are not necessarily as straightforward. The time inconsistency problem manifests in a predictable pattern. When faced with stakeholder demands, perhaps bolstered by a reputational crisis, managers may be willing to make promises or commit to standards that uphold outside expectations. The initial commitment phase can be quite robust, with managers devoting significant resources to designing comprehensive rules, establishing monitoring systems, and communicating new standards throughout the organization. Once the pressure abates, however, managers face different incentives. They will be loath to identify and publicize actions that prove or indicate moral misgivings or social blunders for their company. After working hard to build or restore a company's reputation, it might feel self-defeating to pinpoint their own failures. The very act of rigorous enforcement, which requires documenting violations, conducting investigations, and imposing sanctions, can generate precisely the kind of negative publicity that managers sought to avoid by adopting the rules in the first place.

This creates powerful incentives for managers to look for alternative ways to contain new failures without inciting further inquiry. For example, they may agree to voluntary retirement rather than public dismissal for executives violating codes of conduct, or they may withhold information about harmful repercussions of production techniques previously perceived as environmentally friendly. These responses allow managers to address specific problems quietly while maintaining the appearance of compliance with their publicly announced commitments. The time inconsistency problem may become more intense after management turnover, as new executives may feel less constrained by promises made under the previous team.[57] They inherit the costs of maintaining compliance systems without having personally experienced the reputational crisis or stakeholder pressure that motivated the original commitments.

The challenges of maintaining enforcement over time are compounded by the general difficulties of disciplining corporate conduct.[58] Enforcing laws against corporations suffers from well-known challenges derived from their collective character and the ensuing implications for manager liability. Disciplining an extensive workforce is not easy, and responsibility for different actions may be diffused among various workers with no single person subject to liability. Moreover, even if managers take notice of red flags, they may be better off suppressing them rather than addressing them to deflect liability for themselves. The corporate compliance literature has analyzed these challenges extensively, showing that enforcement authorities have played a critical role by establishing incentives for compliance and demanding institutional reforms that can better document violations. Building a compliance structure, however, comes at a significant cost, as it requires additional staffing, training, and commitment of effort and time by existing personnel that must adjust to new procedural safeguards. When external enforcement pressure is absent and corporate self-regulation truly represents the only rules in town, managers face these costs without the countervailing threat of regulatory sanctions for noncompliance.

Yet the time inconsistency problem is not insurmountable, and understanding when corporate self-regulation can endure provides insight into when it can genuinely serve as an effective substitute in the absence of government regulation. Overcoming the time inconsistency problem requires careful attention to conditions on the ground in combination with institutional reforms. Corporate rulemakers, particularly at the planning stage, benefit from their direct oversight of operations, which helps elucidate how problems arise. Thus, they are well-placed to design mechanisms that intervene early and appropriately, at once minimizing implementation costs and increasing effectiveness. The key is to build enforcement mechanisms that can operate independently of the fluctuating salience of the underlying issue and the changing composition of management teams.

Most scholars recognize that time inconsistency problems require institutional design solutions, typically through the creation of an independent oversight mechanism that is not subject to the same pressures that plague managers.[59] In the corporate context, independent board members can play this role, by overseeing internal control mechanisms designed to gather information, investigate, and enforce violations.[60] When companies establish compliance structures with genuine independence, perhaps through dedicated ethics officers reporting directly to independent board committees, or through third-party auditing arrangements that provide credible external verification, they create institutional constraints on their own future behavior. These structures make it more difficult for managers to quietly abandon enforcement when issue salience declines, because the compliance mechanism itself generates information and accountability that would be costly to suppress.

The effectiveness of such institutional solutions, however, depends critically on the initial design and ongoing commitment of resources. Independent oversight mechanisms require not only formal structural independence but also adequate funding, access to information, and organizational authority to conduct meaningful investigations and impose real consequences. When companies treat compliance infrastructure as mere window dressing, for example, by establishing ethics offices without adequate staff or authority, or creating board committees that meet infrequently and rely entirely on management for information, the time inconsistency problem resurfaces in full force. The institutional form exists, but the substance does not.

This analysis suggests that in a second-best world where corporate self-regulation represents the only constraint on corporate conduct, the durability of that self-regulation depends significantly on institutional design choices made at the outset. Companies that anticipate the time inconsistency problem and design robust, independent enforcement mechanisms are more likely to maintain meaningful self-regulation even as issue salience declines and management teams turn over. Companies that rely on managerial goodwill and stakeholder pressure alone are likely to see their self-regulatory commitments atrophy over time, as the immediate crisis that motivated reform fades from memory and new priorities claim management attention. Without the persistent, external pressure that government regulation provides, only those corporate self-regulatory efforts that institutionalize enforcement through independent structures are likely to endure.

4.5 CORPORATE ORDERING OR CEO POLICY AGENDA?

Recognizing corporations as autonomous self-regulatory actors raises a fundamental concern about legitimacy: when companies adopt rules or take positions on social issues, are these genuinely corporate decisions reflecting stakeholder interests and business needs, or are they simply the CEO's personal policy agenda dressed up as corporate action?[61] This concern becomes particularly acute because corporate leaders, unlike elected officials or appointed regulators, are not legitimized through official democratic channels. They are selected for business acumen and executive experience, not for their ability to represent diverse constituencies or navigate complex social and political issues. Yet once we acknowledge that managers make socially critical choices, we must confront the possibility that some corporate self-regulation may be less about the corporation's interests and more about individual executives wielding corporate resources to advance their personal views.

This concern is not merely theoretical. Whether corporate law comes to formally recognize managers' role in making socially critical choices or not, they are making them on the ground. Elon Musk's decision to have no restrictions on certain content on X (formerly Twitter),[62] or a CEO's decision to avoid the issue of transgender bathrooms, or a manager's decision to avoid measuring greenhouse gas emissions is, in fact, a socially critical choice, even if it is expressed as inaction. Once we recognize that companies can take meaningful action, then there is little denying that managers already possess that power. The question is not whether they should exercise it, but rather how they are exercising it, under what conditions, and with what goals. When a CEO uses the corporate platform to amplify personal political views, whether by restricting speech they personally find objectionable, by directing corporate donations to causes they support, or by taking public stands on contentious policy debates, the line between corporate self-regulation and individual agenda-setting becomes dangerously blurred.

The examples span the political spectrum, illustrating that this is not an issue confined to any particular ideological orientation. Hobby Lobby's leadership fought legal battles over contraception coverage based on the owners' religious convictions, ultimately winning the right to exempt their company from certain Affordable Care Act requirements.[63] Chick-fil-A faced boycotts and protests after its CEO made public statements opposing same-sex marriage,[64] raising questions about whether corporate charitable donations reflected genuine business strategy or personal religious beliefs. Goya Foods' CEO drew both praise and criticism after appearing at a Trump administration event and praising the former president, leading to both boycotts and "buycotts" from opposing political camps.[65] During the second Trump administration, several CEOs positioned their companies in relation to administration policies based on personal relationships or political alignments, sometimes breaking with industry consensus. MyPillow CEO Mike Lindell used his company's platform and resources to promote claims about election fraud, tying corporate brand identity directly to his personal political crusade.[66]

Progressive causes generate similar concerns. When Target's CEO decided first to display Pride Month merchandise prominently and then to remove it after backlash,[67] critics on both sides questioned whether these decisions reflected genuine corporate values or merely reactive capitulation to whichever group applied more pressure at the moment. Disney's extended battle with Florida Governor Ron DeSantis over the "Don't Say Gay" law raised questions about whether the company's opposition represented stakeholder interests or whether CEO Bob Chapek (and later Bob Iger) was advancing a particular cultural agenda.[68] When Sundar Pichai had to send multiple emails about Google's handling of sexual misconduct claims,[69] observers wondered whether the company's policies reflected a genuine commitment to addressing workplace harassment or whether they were hastily constructed responses to employee activism that caught leadership off guard.

By being oblivious about the real impact of managers' choices, corporate law misses the opportunity to submit them to meaningful restrictions. Any decision-maker brings to the table their own biases, predilections, motivations, and goals. Decisions may sound arbitrary, unjustified, or particularly harmful to certain groups. To go back to the X example, it falls upon Elon Musk to determine that the term "cisgender" is a slur and ban it, while permitting or even amplifying other controversial content. These choices reflect personal judgments about speech, civility, and social norms that have enormous practical impact given the platform's reach even though they emerge from one individual's worldview rather than any collective deliberation or established governance process. When managers make such choices in a vacuum, corporate self-regulation becomes indistinguishable from autocratic rule.

The legitimacy concern deepens when we consider that CEOs are neither trained nor selected on the basis of their social and political acumen. The number of CEO missteps over the years shows how easy it is to miscalculate. After employee protests over the favorable exit terms of a lead software engineer despite credible sexual misconduct claims, Sundar Pichai had to send a second email apologizing,[70] because the first one did not get the apology right. Netflix's CEO had to correct course after first seeming indifferent to accusations against comedian Dave Chappelle for transphobic jokes.[71] These are some of the instances where managers had to readjust their actions following controversies that reached the headlines. And then there are the huge controversies that led to fundamental changes in corporate governance and operations, like the Uber scandals of 2017.[72] These missteps reveal that managers often lack the expertise or perspective necessary to navigate complex social issues, yet corporate law grants them broad discretion to do so anyway. The possibility of a misfire is high, and when it occurs, the consequences extend beyond the CEO's personal reputation to affect employees, shareholders, customers, and communities.

However, recognizing the risk that corporate self-regulation might devolve into CEO policy agenda does not mean we should prohibit all corporate engagement with social issues. Rather, it suggests the need for governance processes that can distinguish between genuine corporate interests and individual executive preferences, and that can constrain arbitrary decision-making. In contrast to the vacuum in which many CEO decisions currently occur, corporate law can invite companies to build governance processes guiding managers through these questions. The governance process exposes them to views and considerations they might not have otherwise come across, information of which they were unaware, expert opinions reached after academic study or experience on the ground. Standardization can help consolidate these efforts into applicable rules, while transparency facilitates monitoring and accountability on an ongoing basis.

For these reasons, governance can lower concerns about arbitrary managerial decisions reflecting personal agendas rather than corporate interests. Managers are no longer making up their minds in a vacuum, deciding on the basis of personal principle, but are operating at the helm of an extensive effort to understand the social context around their choices. Rather than evoking broad rhetoric or personal mission statements to justify their choices, managers are now expected to point to specific inputs that have surfaced through the governance process. NGO recommendations, widely accepted standards, policy proposals by independent bodies or well-reputed international organizations can be used as sources supporting managers' decisions. Of course, managers are still free to steer the company toward their preferred direction. But, the hope is, this governance process can illuminate their choices and distinguish between decisions that emerge from genuine corporate deliberation and those that simply reflect executive fiat.

Many companies voluntarily engage in such governance processes precisely because they help navigate the legitimacy challenge. By convening expert groups when launching new and potentially controversial products, setting up new governance processes for reporting sexual misconduct independent of the company hierarchy, or following standards set by rigorous bodies, companies can get fresh ideas and hopefully avoid the worst. Following up on these ideas by adopting self-constraining devices such as public reporting or setting performance goals, companies limit their discretion even further. There is little doubt that by consulting experts, seeking feedback from stakeholders, and making public commitments, managers are limiting their discretion, since they create expectations about their ultimate choices. Yet, these moves make sense for managers because they provide positive signals to third parties, create accountability thresholds for insiders, and form a policy orientation that motivates other internal decisions.

From the manager's perspective, these moves help boost their leadership profile by introducing information they were previously lacking and helping them gain supporters among multiple stakeholder and shareholder groups. For managers, going through this governance process lowers the costs of decision-making, as it represents a built-in process for gathering intelligence and reaching conclusions. Moreover, managers are protecting themselves against potential criticisms, because they can show that they have studied the issue diligently and decided to weigh certain values over others. Essentially, managers are able to redirect any blame away from their personal performance and toward the governance process itself. Thus, for those managers who undertake restrictions voluntarily, these are welcome measures, because they help with decision-making and offer a defense against potential criticisms.

The governance solution is not perfect, of course. Well-designed processes can still be captured by determined executives who simply use them as window dressing for predetermined choices. And some social issues may be so divisive that no governance process can produce a resolution that satisfies all stakeholders or that clearly distinguishes corporate interest from executive preference. But allowing managers to make socially critical choices without any structured process, transparency, or accountability carries even greater risks. It invites exactly the concern this section addresses: that corporate self-regulation becomes merely a vehicle for CEO policy agendas, with the legitimacy and resources of the corporation deployed in service of individual beliefs rather than collective interests. By contrast, robust governance processes, even imperfect ones, help ensure that corporate self-regulation represents something more than executive autocracy dressed in corporate clothing.

4.6 CORPORATE ORDERING AT THE INTERSECTION OF CONFLICTING JURISDICTIONAL REQUIREMENTS

The tension between corporate preferences for uniform rules and the fragmented reality of multiple jurisdictions takes on new dimensions when different regulatory regimes do not merely differ but actively conflict with one another. This phenomenon has intensified following the 2024 U.S. presidential election, as policy shifts have placed American regulatory approaches in direct opposition to those of the European Union on issues ranging from data privacy and artificial intelligence governance[73] to environmental standards[74] and content moderation.[75] When jurisdictions impose diametrically opposing requirements, so that compliance with one jurisdiction's mandate necessarily entails violation of another's, corporations face a qualitatively different challenge than when they simply confront variations in regulatory stringency or approach.

These conflicts cannot be resolved purely through internal corporate mechanisms. Unlike situations where a company might voluntarily adopt uniform standards that exceed local requirements, active regulatory intervention by competing authorities constrains corporate autonomy. A company cannot simultaneously comply with an EU requirement to remove certain content and a U.S. prohibition on removing that same content; it cannot both disclose algorithmic decision-making processes as one jurisdiction demands and protect them as trade secrets as another requires. In such cases, the corporation's discretionary space, which forms the very foundation of its self-regulatory capacity, collapses.

In extreme circumstances, regulatory fragmentation may force structural solutions. Companies may find themselves fragmenting their own corporate hierarchies, establishing distinctly regulated subsidiaries with separate governance structures, personnel, and operations to ensure compliance with incompatible mandates.[76] This represents a profound shift from the integrated global enterprise that characterized peak globalization, and it carries significant costs: loss of economies of scale, duplication of administrative functions, barriers to internal knowledge transfer, and the weakening of unified corporate culture and values.

Yet even amid growing regulatory divergence, corporations retain their character as unifying forces in the global economy. At the height of globalization, multinational enterprises became powerful actors for diffusing common policies, practices, and norms across borders. This role has not disappeared; indeed, it may be more important than ever. Corporations often default to following the strictest rule among the jurisdictions in which they operate, not out of moral commitment alone but because uniformity and standardization tend to be more cost-efficient than maintaining parallel systems. The administrative burden of tailoring compliance programs, training materials, audit procedures, and technological systems to each jurisdiction's specific requirements generally exceeds the cost of elevating all operations to meet the highest standard.

This tendency toward regulatory homogenization at the top of the distribution has significant implications. When European data protection standards or environmental disclosure requirements become the de facto global standard because major corporations apply them worldwide, the EU effectively extends its regulatory reach beyond its formal jurisdiction.[77] This is not legal imperialism in the traditional sense; rather, it reflects corporate calculation that global uniformity is preferable to jurisdictional particularism. The result is a form of indirect regulatory export, where one jurisdiction's rules shape practices far beyond its borders through the intermediary of corporate self-regulation.

Corporations do not passively accept regulatory requirements, however, even when they ultimately comply. They actively engage with governments and regulators about their preferred positions, marshaling arguments about operational feasibility, economic impact, competitive effects, and alignment with stakeholder interests.[78] A company subject to conflicting requirements in different jurisdictions is well-positioned to highlight the costs and contradictions of regulatory fragmentation. Moreover, a corporation's cross-jurisdictional existence creates natural conditions for dialogue among policymakers who might otherwise operate in isolation. When a company explains to U.S. regulators that their proposed rule conflicts with an established EU requirement, or vice versa, it facilitates awareness of regulatory interaction effects that might otherwise escape notice. Corporations can serve as conduits for information about regulatory approaches in different jurisdictions, and their experiences implementing various regimes provide valuable data points for policymakers.

The effectiveness of this dialogue depends critically on governance. The better informed, more rigorously analyzed, and more carefully justified a company's position, the more likely it is to carry weight with policymakers. This requires corporations to invest in sophisticated regulatory affairs functions that understand not only the technical requirements of different jurisdictions but also the underlying policy objectives and political contexts. Companies must be able to explain not merely that a proposed rule conflicts with requirements elsewhere, but why that conflict matters, what alternatives might achieve regulatory objectives while reducing conflict, and what evidence supports their position. They must engage constructively rather than obstructively, offering solutions rather than mere resistance.

This governance capacity becomes a form of regulatory capital. Companies that develop reputations for good faith engagement, technical competence, and constructive problem-solving build relationships with regulators that can prove invaluable when conflicts arise.[79] Conversely, companies perceived as gaming the system, forum shopping, or making disingenuous arguments squander opportunities to shape regulatory outcomes. In an era of regulatory divergence, the quality of corporate governance – including how companies engage with multiple regulatory authorities and participate in policy development – may be as important to long-term success as the substantive choices companies make about their own internal rules and practices.

The interplay between corporate self-regulation and governmental regulation in a world of divergent jurisdictional requirements thus creates a complex dynamic. Corporations cannot escape governmental authority, and in cases of direct conflict they may face impossible choices or structural fragmentation. Yet their cross-jurisdictional presence, their tendency toward uniform standards, and their capacity for informed engagement also position them as important actors in the regulatory ecosystem – not merely subjects of regulation but participants in ongoing conversations about how regulatory divergence might be managed, reduced, or at least rendered more coherent. The outcome of these conversations will shape not only individual corporate compliance strategies but also the broader evolution of the global regulatory landscape.

4.7 CONCLUSION

This chapter has established corporations as autonomous self-regulatory actors whose rulemaking inevitably shapes social policy. Whether addressing new technologies, implementing vague legislative mandates, or confronting social issues where government regulation is absent, corporations make choices with profound public consequences. They write the first draft of rules in emerging domains, translate abstract legal requirements into concrete operational practices, and sometimes provide the only governance mechanism addressing pressing social concerns. This is not a normative claim about what corporations should do, but a descriptive reality about what they already do. The question is not whether to grant corporations this role but how to harness it in order to serve broader social interests.

The analysis reveals that corporate self-regulation succeeds under identifiable conditions. When corporations possess deep expertise in their domain and their business goals align with public interests, they can develop superior solutions that regulators might not conceive. When these conditions hold and corporations build robust enforcement mechanisms to overcome time inconsistency problems, self-regulation can genuinely substitute for government intervention. Conversely, when corporate incentives diverge from public welfare, when issues extend far beyond core business operations, or when initial commitments atrophy as stakeholder pressure wanes, self-regulation fails and regulatory intervention becomes necessary. Understanding these patterns allows us to distinguish productive corporate autonomy from problematic regulatory circumvention.

Yet recognizing corporations' contributions to our regulatory ecosystem does not mean endorsing all the rules they produce. This chapter identified genuine and consequential risks, such as regulatory capture, CEO personal agendas masquerading as corporate policy, time inconsistency problems, and the fundamental misalignment between profit motives and public welfare. Corporate self-regulation can serve private interests at public expense. Managers can exploit their discretion to advance personal beliefs rather than stakeholder interests. Companies can make bold commitments during crises only to quietly abandon them once attention shifts elsewhere. These are not hypothetical concerns but documented patterns that justify skepticism about corporate claims to serve the public good.

This is precisely why the governance machinery outlined in Chapter 3 proves essential. Stakeholder engagement, board oversight, and transparency mechanisms transform corporate self-regulation from arbitrary executive decision-making into a structured process that can be evaluated and lead to accountability. These governance tools serve dual purposes. For corporations themselves, they provide frameworks for gathering information, weighing competing interests, and justifying choices, thus making self-regulation more legitimate and effective. For regulators and policymakers, they provide observable signals about the quality of corporate decision-making, enabling more sophisticated assessments of when self-regulation can be trusted and when intervention is required.

The tripartite distinction developed in Chapter 3 thus becomes a diagnostic tool for navigating the relationship between corporate self-regulation and government regulation. Strong governance signals that a corporation has built genuine capacity for responsible self-regulation, while weak or merely symbolic governance suggests that state intervention may be necessary. This framework allows regulators to move beyond blanket assumptions that all corporate self-regulation is either inherently trustworthy or inherently suspect toward context-specific judgments based on observable institutional features. A corporation that has established robust stakeholder consultation processes, independent board oversight, and credible transparency mechanisms has demonstrated investment in responsible decision-making. One that adopts the rhetoric of self-regulation without the substance has not.

The governance approach advocated here also addresses the legitimacy concerns that corporate self-regulation inevitably raises in a democratic society. When corporations make socially significant choices through structured processes that gather information, consider diverse perspectives, and publicly justify trade-offs, they approximate the deliberative practices that legitimate official policymakers must follow. This does not make corporations equivalent to democratically elected legislators or accountable regulatory agencies. But it narrows the legitimacy gap by subjecting managerial discretion to procedural constraints and external scrutiny. Governance cannot eliminate the tension between corporate power and democratic accountability, but it can make that tension more manageable by ensuring corporate decision-making is neither arbitrary nor opaque.

Looking forward, the interplay between corporate self-regulation and government regulation will only intensify. Technological innovation, evolving business models, and shifting social expectations continue to outpace formal lawmaking, ensuring that corporations will remain first movers who establish precedents before regulators arrive. Regulatory divergence across jurisdictions creates spaces where corporate choices become the only source of global standards. Political gridlock increasingly means that corporate self-regulation operates as the sole governance mechanism in domains where public regulation has stalled. In this environment, the quality of corporate governance becomes not merely a matter of internal management but a question of public importance. The governance tools this book advocates are not corporate luxuries but essential infrastructure for a regulatory ecosystem in which corporations play an inescapable role. They enable both corporations and the public to navigate the uncomfortable reality that private actors wield public power, making that reality more legitimate, more accountable, and more aligned with democratic values.

5

Corporate Ordering

Past and Present

The corporate shaping of societal institutions through innovative business models may seem like a distinctly twenty-first-century phenomenon. Today's titans, whether it is Facebook algorithmically curating our social circles and defying our privacy,[1] or Amazon redefining consumer expectations,[2] or Monsanto introducing genetically modified crops onto our dinner table,[3] are landmark products of our era.[4] Without modern technological advances, Uber would not have been able to redesign urban transportation,[5] and Airbnb could not have altered tourism patterns and housing markets in cities globally.[6] In all these corporate efforts, previous chapters have argued, using law-like frameworks and processes has been key to success.[7] But while corporate influence might have reached breathtaking scope and velocity in recent years, this is not the first time in history in which private entities have claimed the mantel of social architects.[8]

This chapter draws connections between modern corporations' efforts to shape legal and societal norms and other instances of private initiative in law-making. Some of these examples are occurring as we speak. Industry efforts at self-regulation abound, from the financial industry[9] to the legal profession,[10] and from product safety specifications[11] to online advertising.[12] Sometimes, the role is outsourced to private certification providers, from b-certified companies to conflict diamond protocol certifiers.[13] Other times, international standard-setters take the lead in providing a regulatory regime that businesses can follow, either voluntarily or after being mandated to do so by national legislatures.[14] These different pathways have been a central focus of my earlier academic work, where I have analyzed their governance frameworks, rulemaking capabilities, and enforcement strategies.[15] As I noted, these bodies often employ governance structures reminiscent of those discussed in earlier chapters, designed to encourage feedback, foster transparency and accountability, develop a network of users that is the key to widespread market adoption.[16] Still, in all these private lawmaking initiatives, the entity creating the rules and those that must abide them are different. Typically, rule-creators strive hard to maintain the separation from rule-abiders, often through governance arrangements.

Yet, as this book notes, sometimes corporations abandon such separation and set the rules both for themselves and for a series of stakeholders. While this phenomenon has become widespread in recent years, there are examples throughout the history of corporate activity. This chapter discusses two striking instances where private corporations took the lead in designing regulatory regimes that subsequently became mandatory for all. The first example describes the very deliberate efforts to pave the road (pun intended) for the advent of motor vehicles, by reassigning the uses of streets and sidewalks, introducing streetlights and signage, and fashioning new norms of prohibited conduct such as jaywalking.[17] This massive transformation of city streets from public urban space to motorway occurred relatively quickly due to the coordinated efforts of private companies, which framed their products as addressing huge societal crises. As a growing city population utilized higher numbers of horses, tons of manure lined the streets, facilitating the spread of diseases and rodents.[18] Moreover, as carriages and cars sought to traverse the increasingly busy streets of new megacities, accidents had become commonplace, increasing the human toll. Responding to concerns by public health advocates, a coalition of car manufacturers seeking to sell more cars, insurance providers looking to cabin accident risks, and energy companies looking to create networks of gas stations joined forces and proposed the rules we now understand as vehicle and road codes.[19]

Contrary to the swift refashioning of road norms, it took many decades until the voluntary disclosures of public companies' financial and business conditions became mandatory. Pioneer companies started providing disclosures in the mid-nineteenth century, and while the information was primarily directed at investors, its importance for workers, competitors, local governments, and other stakeholders was quickly noted.[20] It took many successive iterations until the New York Stock Exchange (NYSE), then a membership organization, utilized its contracting power to adopt listing rules that greatly resembled private templates.[21] The exchange recognized the importance of disclosure for safeguarding the credibility of its marketplace, which would help attract more business. It was the 1929 collapse that precipitated the adoption of that template as the newly mandatory disclosure form S-1 in the 1933 Securities Act.[22]

Both road codes and mandatory disclosures were transformational not only for those directly affected but for society overall, yet they are controversial to this day. Many bemoan the takeover of city space by cars, the divide between city centers and suburbs, and the lack of investment in public transport.[23] Similarly, many see in the adoption of mandatory disclosure the influence of large corporations, which were better placed to implement these rules, against smaller upstarts, for whom the financial burden was prohibitive, thus shutting them off the public capital markets.[24] In both cases, critics point to shareholder gains from the spread of the model corporations supported.

The goal of this book is not to take a position in such debates, but to offer a new lens in evaluating some of these arguments. Examining the governance processes around the shaping and adoption of such rules can help establish the extent to which all stakeholders' concerns were considered, and the conditions under which policymakers chose to side with one set of arguments. For instance, while local communities were heavily involved in the early stages of considering driving code rules and enforcement, they were noticeably absent from the final push toward a single federal framework.[25] Without the opportunity to raise their concerns, their interests fell off policymakers' radar.[26]

The discussion of driving codes and mandatory disclosures brings to the forefront concerns about the lobbying power of corporations, or at least the very biggest of them, which seem to have pushed for the adoption of these reforms as law. Lobbying, and regulatory capture more generally, have been a central focus of social science research for decades.[27] Yet, they are distinct from the phenomenon discussed in this book. To start, lobbying involves the formal adoptions of laws or regulations by official authorities constitutionally authorized to enact them. This book, in contrast, tracks private companies' efforts to establish general frameworks that, though law-like in function, are based on these companies' individual autonomy. While some such efforts may end up inspiring formal laws, most of them will not reach that stage. Governments are not necessary actors in the phenomenon that this book is bringing to light. The governance efforts corporations undertake to bolster stakeholders' trust suggest that they seek to gain acceptance for their own decisions, rather than surreptitiously influence choices by official lawmakers.[28] Of course, there is a real risk that lobbyists will utilize corporate self-regulation efforts as an argument to placate lawmakers and stave off more stringent regulation. To distinguish between superficial corporate measures and deep commitments, examining the quality of governance efforts can offer a valuable guide.

This chapter proceeds in three parts. It first examines how automobile manufacturers helped develop modern traffic regulation, then turns to the emergence of corporate financial disclosure practices, and finally considers how these historical cases connect to contemporary debates around standard-setting and self-regulation.

5.1 CORPORATE ORDERING IN THE PAST: DRIVING CODES AND CORPORATE DISCLOSURES

The role that corporate practices play in shaping societal norms and legal frameworks is a recurring theme throughout modern history. This chapter examines two seminal cases that illuminate how private enterprises have shaped public policy and regulation: the development of driving codes in the early twentieth century and the emergence of corporate financial disclosure practices in the late nineteenth and early twentieth centuries. These examples, while distinct in their domains, share a common narrative of corporate-led innovation that ultimately crystallized into formal legal structures.

The driving code case study demonstrates the far-reaching impact of private industry in redesigning urban life. In the early twentieth century, rapid population growth presented American cities with unprecedented challenges of staggering proportions. Streets were inundated with tons of horse manure daily, breeding grounds for disease and vermin.[29] Traffic fatalities skyrocketed, with pedestrians, especially children, falling victim to chaotic and unregulated streets.[30] The scale of public health emergencies and traffic accidents demanded urgent action, as urban infrastructure designed for a slower pace of life buckled under the pressure of modernization. Initially, a diverse coalition of stakeholders came together to address these monumental issues. Local authorities, public health advocates, urban planners, citizen groups, and nascent automotive industries all contributed to the dialogue.[31] This phase was marked by a cacophony of voices and competing visions for urban reform.

However, as the process evolved, a more focused alliance emerged. Led by automotive interests, including car manufacturers, oil companies, and insurance providers, this coalition began to dominate the conversation. They skillfully presented a unified vision of urban transformation centered around the automobile, effectively sidelining alternative perspectives such as those favoring mass transit or traditional pedestrian rights.[32] The resulting framework, shaped primarily by this industry-led alliance, fundamentally altered the urban landscape. While it addressed immediate concerns of public health and traffic management, it also set in motion long-lasting changes to American culture and urban development. This transformation, though controversial, has endured for nearly a century, cementing the car's central role in American life while contributing to the urban-suburban divide and the decline of alternative transportation modes.[33] The close connections between Americans and their cars, which some praise as an emblem of personal liberty, and some decry for its environmental implications, date to that era.

The evolution of corporate financial disclosure practices presents a more nuanced and gradual narrative than the development of driving codes. Conventional accounts often highlight the pivotal role of the NYSE in shaping disclosure standards, which ultimately served as a foundation for the mandatory Form S-1 introduced by the Securities Act of 1933. However, the NYSE's influential standards were themselves inspired by the pioneering practices of individual companies that had already navigated a complex stakeholder landscape in developing their disclosure policies.[34] This chapter examines the multifaceted origins of corporate disclosure, revealing a landscape fraught with conflicting interests and competing motivations.[35]

Corporate managers were far from unified in their approach to disclosure.[36] Some viewed it as an opportunity to establish credibility and attract investment, while others resisted, seeing it as an unwelcome constraint on their autonomy. Similarly, shareholders were divided along lines of size and influence. Large shareholders often opposed expanded disclosure, fearing it would erode their informational advantages over smaller investors who lacked direct access to company information.[37] Beyond the corporate sphere, other stakeholders exerted significant influence on the evolution of disclosure practices. The emerging labor movement closely scrutinized corporate disclosures, using the information to inform their demands and negotiation strategies. Financial institutions pushed for greater transparency to facilitate share sales, while simultaneously trying to maintain relationships with influential large shareholders. Politicians viewed expanded disclosure as a means to democratize capitalism and broaden participation in financial markets, aligning with their vision of propelling the nation from its colonial past to global economic prominence.[38] By tracing the intricate interactions among these diverse stakeholders, the chapter illuminates how their competing interests and compromises shaped the development of disclosure practices. This evolutionary process ultimately produced the groundbreaking template that the NYSE would champion and that would later be codified into law by the Securities Act of 1933, fundamentally altering the landscape of corporate financial reporting and market regulation.

By reexamining these historical examples, this chapter aims to elucidate how a focus on governance can help us understand the processes by which corporate practices evolved into widely adopted norms and, ultimately, into codified law.[39] This analysis reveals why certain perspectives prevailed and how governance structures influenced the success of these corporate-led initiatives.[40] It is important to note that these cases are not presented as unequivocal successes or normative ideals. Indeed, both outcomes have faced significant criticism. Rather, they serve to illustrate how corporate governance efforts can establish precedents that shape stakeholder expectations and legal frameworks long before formal legislation is enacted.

This examination underscores the importance of studying the crucial phase of law development that precedes official codification.[41] By exploring interactions among the parties involved, we gain insight into both the efficacy of corporate strategies and the reasons why alternative stakeholder interests may have been marginalized.[42] Because the historical record from these earlier eras is not as comprehensive as contemporary digital documentation, the examples later trace and reconstruct parties' preferences and strategies from their public statements and the reactions they received from third parties. Private exchanges over letters or emails, minutes of meetings, or records of conversations similar to those found in Chapters 6–8 are harder to locate for the past. To the extent these were reported in the secondary sources that served as the base material for this chapter, they are included later.

5.2 THE INTRODUCTION OF THE AUTOMOBILE: INDUSTRY'S PIVOTAL ROLE

The automobile offers one of the earliest and clearest examples of corporate ordering in modern history. When cars first appeared in American cities, they entered streets that were chaotic, congested, and governed by fragmented local practices. There was no unified system of traffic regulation, no infrastructure built for speed, and little legal clarity about how cars should interact with existing street users.

For car manufacturers, this posed more than a public safety challenge. It was a barrier to market growth. If cars were to become desirable, they also had to become usable, and that meant rewriting the rules of the road. Manufacturers and their allies moved quickly to develop new traffic codes, propose design standards, and reshape public narratives around mobility and safety. They understood that the most effective way to clear the streets for cars was not through isolated fixes, but by constructing an entirely new framework for how roads were organized and used. That is the system they set out to build.

5.2.1 *Stakes: The Problem with Horses and Congestion*

In the late nineteenth and early twentieth centuries, American cities faced a growing crisis of urban transportation. Horse-drawn vehicles, the primary mode of transportation, was becoming increasingly problematic as cities expanded and populations grew. Horses produced enormous amounts of manure that piled up on city streets, creating unsanitary conditions and public health hazards. In New York City alone, horses deposited an estimated 2.5 million pounds of manure per day.[43] This waste attracted flies, spread disease, and created noxious odors that permeated urban areas.[44] Additionally, as traffic volumes increased, city streets became increasingly congested and dangerous. Horse-drawn vehicles moved slowly and unpredictably, leading to traffic jams and collisions. Pedestrian deaths from traffic accidents rose dramatically, with children being particularly vulnerable.[45] By the early 1900s, it was clear that horse-based transportation was inadequate for modern urban needs.

Amidst this crisis, a new invention was emerging that held the potential to revolutionize urban transportation: the automobile. These horseless carriages promised to be cleaner, faster, and more maneuverable than their equine predecessors. In theory, automobiles could reduce street congestion, improve sanitation, and enhance mobility for city dwellers.[46] However, as automobiles began to proliferate in the early twentieth century, they introduced a new set of challenges.[47] The number of cars on American roads grew rapidly, from roughly 8,000 in 1900 to over 8 million by 1920. This explosive growth led to a sharp rise in traffic fatalities. In the 1920s alone, over 200,000 Americans were killed in traffic accidents.[48]

The increasing presence of automobiles on city streets was exacerbated by a complete lack of traffic regulation infrastructure. Before 1903, no city had a comprehensive traffic code. There were virtually no traffic signs, stop signs, or other control devices to manage the flow of vehicles.[49] The first electric traffic signal was not installed until 1914 in Cleveland, Ohio.[50] Streets that had been designed for horses and pedestrians were now being shared with fast-moving machines, with no clear rules or systems in place to govern their interaction. Intersections became particularly dangerous, as there was no established right-of-way between vehicles or between vehicles and pedestrians.

This regulatory vacuum extended beyond just signage and traffic control devices. There were no standardized rules for which side of the road to drive on, how to signal turns, or how fast one could travel.[51] Speed limits, where they existed, varied widely and were often arbitrary. Enforcement was sporadic and inconsistent, as police forces were not equipped or trained to manage automobile traffic.[52] The lack of infrastructure was not limited to regulatory measures. Roads themselves were often inadequate for automobile traffic. Many were unpaved, becoming muddy quagmires in wet weather. Even paved roads were frequently too narrow or poorly maintained to safely accommodate both horse-drawn and motorized vehicles.[53]

In this context, the potential of the automobile to solve urban transportation problems remained largely theoretical. For cars to truly address issues of congestion and mobility, they would need to be integrated into a completely new system of traffic management and road infrastructure. This presented a significant challenge, requiring a reimagining of urban space and movement.

The situation created a complex set of stakes for various stakeholders. City officials faced pressure to reduce congestion and improve safety, but lacked the tools and frameworks to do so effectively.[54] The nascent auto industry saw tremendous opportunity, but needed a more hospitable urban environment for their products. The public was attracted to the convenience and status of automobiles, but also alarmed by their dangers. Addressing these intertwined challenges would require unprecedented cooperation between government, industry, and civil society. The stage was set for a dramatic transformation of American urban landscapes and transportation systems, with the automobile at the center of the storm.

5.2.2 *Heterogeneity of Preferences: Car Manufacturers versus Mass Transit*

The transition away from horse-based transportation revealed conflicting interests between various stakeholders. On one side were the emerging automobile manufacturers, who saw tremendous profit potential in personal vehicles becoming the dominant mode of urban transit. Companies such as Ford, General Motors, and others invested heavily in expanding production capacity and aggressively marketed cars as the future of transportation.

On the other side were proponents of mass transit systems, particularly electric streetcars and trolleys.[55] Many cities had extensive streetcar networks that efficiently moved large numbers of people.[56] Transit companies and urban reformers argued that expanding and improving mass transit was a better solution to urban congestion than private automobiles.[57]

A third crucial stakeholder group was local regulators and city officials, who found themselves overwhelmed by the rapid changes in urban transportation. These local authorities had to devote extraordinary resources to address the growing problems of congestion and traffic accidents. For example, the city of Grand Rapids, Michigan, found itself spending more than 36 percent of its police budget on traffic regulation at intersections alone.[58] This massive allocation of resources to traffic control came at the expense of other vital city services and strained municipal budgets. The burden extended beyond just policing. Local courts were inundated with traffic-related cases, creating significant backlogs and straining judicial resources. Judges often found themselves adjudicating complex disputes arising from accidents, with little precedent or standardized rules to guide their decisions. This not only taxed the court system but also led to inconsistent rulings, further complicating the regulatory landscape.[59]

Adding to the complexity was the fact that traffic norms and regulations varied widely between locations. Each city, and sometimes even individual neighborhoods within cities, had its own set of formal and informal rules governing road use. This lack of standardization was particularly problematic for drivers traveling between different areas, as they could find themselves unknowingly violating local customs or regulations. The resulting confusion and conflicts further taxed local law enforcement and judicial systems. City planners and engineers also found themselves grappling with the need to redesign urban infrastructure to accommodate automobiles while still serving other modes of transportation. This often involved costly and disruptive construction projects to widen streets, create parking areas, and install traffic control devices.

The heterogeneity of preferences among these powerful stakeholders shaped the trajectory of urban transportation development. Car manufacturers pushed for policies that would make cities more automobile-friendly, often at the expense of pedestrians and public transit. Transit companies lobbied to maintain their dominant position in urban transportation.[60] Meanwhile, local regulators struggled to balance these competing interests while also addressing immediate public safety concerns and budgetary constraints.

This clash of visions led to intense competition and maneuvering between auto interests, transit advocates, and city officials. The outcome of these conflicts would have profound implications for the future of American urban landscapes and transportation systems. As the situation grew increasingly complex and costly, it became clear that a more coordinated and standardized approach to urban transportation policy was needed. The challenge lay in finding a way to reconcile the divergent interests of these stakeholders while also addressing the pressing issues of congestion, safety, and urban mobility. This set the stage for new forms of cooperation between industry and government, as well as innovative approaches to traffic management and urban planning.[61]

5.2.3 *The Role of Private Individuals and Industry Cooperation*

Given the regulatory vacuum surrounding urban transportation in the early twentieth century, it largely fell to private parties to seek a pathway out of the chaos on the streets. While some individuals were motivated by idealistic visions of urban improvement, most were driven by practical concerns, such as the need to reduce costs associated with accidents and congestion and to create a more favorable environment for selling automobiles.

One key figure in this private-sector response was William Phelps Eno, a wealthy businessman who became fascinated with solving urban traffic problems. In 1903, Eno privately published the first comprehensive city traffic code for New York, introducing concepts like one-way streets, traffic circles, and pedestrian crosswalks.[62] He went on to design traffic plans for cities around the world, earning him the nickname "the father of traffic regulation."[63]

However, most efforts to address street chaos came from industry groups and local business interests. A pivotal development was the emergence of safety councils in cities across the United States. These were private organizations that brought together various stakeholders to address traffic safety issues. For example, the Chicago Association of Commerce formed a Street Traffic Committee in 1910, which worked to develop traffic regulations and promote safety education.[64] In St. Louis, the Automobile Club took the lead in organizing a vigilante effort to patrol city streets and report traffic violations. The membership of these safety councils often reflected a coalition of local business interests. In Cincinnati, the safety council included representatives from auto dealers, the chamber of commerce, and other civic organizations. These groups cooperated on initiatives like safety weeks, where they would distribute educational materials and conduct public awareness campaigns.

The automobile industry also recognized the need for better traffic management to ensure cars could operate efficiently in cities. In 1913, representatives from several auto companies formed the National Automobile Chamber of Commerce (NACC) to coordinate industry efforts on issues such as safety and urban planning. The NACC worked to shape traffic regulations, street design standards, and public perceptions of automobiles. Other industry groups like the American Automobile Association (AAA) emerged to advocate for drivers' interests. By the late 1920s, the AAA was supplying 50,000 teachers with monthly instructional materials on traffic safety, reaching an estimated 2 million school children.[65]

However, these industry-led efforts often conflicted with initiatives from citizens' groups supporting pedestrians' rights. In many cities, local residents resisted attempts to restrict pedestrian access to streets, viewing such measures as an infringement on traditional rights of way. For instance, in 1931, an Illinois judge struck down a city ordinance in Joliet that required pedestrians to cross streets only at right angles or on crosswalks, arguing that it unfairly restricted pedestrian movement. In some cases, these conflicting approaches led to heated public debates and legal battles.[66] In Cincinnati, a citizens' group gathered signatures for a ballot initiative to require speed governors on all cars, limiting their top speed to 25 mph. This was fiercely opposed by local auto dealers and other business interests, who mounted a successful campaign to defeat the measure.[67]

The result was a patchwork of local regulations and initiatives, often pulling in different directions. While industry groups generally pushed for measures that would facilitate automobile use, citizen groups frequently advocated for policies that would protect pedestrians and maintain traditional street uses. Other industry groups like the AAA emerged to advocate for drivers' interests. These organizations brought together car manufacturers, auto clubs, and other stakeholders to present a united front on transportation policy issues. This tension between different private interests highlighted the need for more coordinated approaches to traffic management.[68]

5.2.4 *Governance Measures: Industry-Government Conferences*

As the challenges of urban transportation grew more complex, and calls for regulation became more demanding, a more coordinated approach began to emerge from private industry. Automobile manufacturers and suppliers joined forces with the energy industry, transport and trucking, highway construction, and insurance industries, creating a coalition that came to be known as "Motordom."[69] The formation of Motordom was a response to the multiplicity of perspectives represented in local safety councils. While these councils had initially included diverse stakeholders, auto industry representatives began to see the need for a more unified voice to advance their interests. By the mid 1920s, auto clubs, dealers, and manufacturers had coalesced into a more cohesive social group, developing common strategies and rhetoric.

To boost its chances of success, Motordom further amplified the use of lawlike tools. A characteristic example can be seen in the drafting of a new traffic code for Los Angeles in 1925. The process was heavily influenced by Paul Hoffman, a prominent dealer for automobile manufacturer Studebaker. Hoffman saw the city's traffic problems as a threat to the auto industry's future and supported the work of Miller McClintock, an emerging traffic expert, to write the new code.[70] McClintock's approach favored the interests of motorists, arguing that "The old common law rule that every person, whether on foot or driving, has equal rights in all parts of the roadway must give way before the requirements of modern transportation."[71] This Los Angeles traffic code became influential nationwide, promoted by auto industry groups and incorporated into model ordinances. It represented a shift toward prioritizing automobile movement over traditional pedestrian rights, reflecting the growing power of Motordom in shaping urban transportation policy.

The culmination of these industry-led efforts was the series of National Conferences on Street and Highway Safety, organized by Commerce Secretary Herbert Hoover in the 1920s.[72] These conferences marked a turning point in the governance of urban transportation, bringing together diverse stakeholders under the auspices of the federal government.[73]

The first conference in 1924 attracted over 900 participants, including representatives from auto companies, safety organizations, engineering societies, insurance firms, and government agencies. Notably, the composition of these conferences reflected Hoover's belief that effective policymaking required input from all affected industries, rather than relying solely on ostensibly neutral experts. Hoover articulated this philosophy in his opening remarks, stating that the goal was "not representing any special group of interest" but rather opening the doors to "the representatives of all the industries that bear upon this problem." This approach marked a departure from previous attempts to address traffic issues through purely technical or bureaucratic means.[74]

Despite this inclusive approach, the influence of Motordom was evident in the conference proceedings. Auto industry representatives played key roles in crucial committees, often shaping the direction of policy recommendations. For example, the traffic control committee, described by one of Hoover's secretaries as "the heart of the whole business," was largely dominated by auto industry interests.[75] Interestingly, professional traffic engineers were notably underrepresented at these conferences. Out of 607 participants at the first conference, only about 7 percent were engineers, and many of these were affiliated with state highway commissions rather than urban traffic management.[76] This relative absence of technical experts further emphasized the conference's focus on industry perspectives.

The conferences produced influential model laws and policies that were widely adopted by state and local governments. For example, they developed a Uniform Vehicle Code that standardized traffic laws across jurisdictions. The conferences also established committees to continue work between meetings, creating an ongoing forum for public–private collaboration on transportation issues.[77]

This approach to governance, which prioritized stakeholder input over technical expertise, had far-reaching implications for urban transportation policy. It allowed private companies to play a central role in shaping the regulatory framework for automobiles, often in ways that prioritized the interests of drivers and car manufacturers over other street users. The national conferences thus represented both a solution to the fragmented approach of local safety councils and a consolidation of the auto industry's influence over transportation policy. They set the stage for a more uniform, car-centric approach to urban mobility that would dominate American cities for decades to come.

The outcome of these governance efforts was a highly determinative set of rules that not only regulated conduct on public streets by all users, but also established entirely new types of prohibited or allowed conduct. The term "jaywalking" exemplifies how these private efforts embraced legal techniques to affect norms and, ultimately, the law itself. In an effort to clear public streets from slow-moving pedestrians or children playing, jaywalking became a new offense with detailed legal contours, specific penalties, and enforcement measures.[78] Moreover, the campaign went beyond mere legal reform. Auto interests undertook extensive public relations efforts to convince people to conform their behavior to this new paradigm. This included educational campaigns in schools, public safety films, and even organized groups of children to shame adults who crossed streets mid-block. The term "jay," originally meaning a rural person unfamiliar with city ways, was weaponized to stigmatize those who didn't comply with the new rules.[79] This multipronged approach, which sought at once to define the offense, draft laws, suggest enforcement, and shape public opinion, demonstrates how jaywalking was established as both a social and a legal construct. The result was a radical reshaping of street use norms, criminalizing behavior that had been commonplace and accepted for centuries.[80]

The evolution of the term "parking" similarly reflects a coordinated effort to reshape public space for automotive use. Originally, "parking" referred to creating small areas of parkland or planting trees along streets. Municipal "parking" agencies were initially responsible for creating and maintaining green spaces. However, by the 1920s, these same agencies began "cutting down street trees and widening streets to accommodate the volume of cars, thereby replacing the original meaning of parking as a place for trees and greenery with parking as a place for automobiles to stop."[81] This linguistic shift accompanied and facilitated a massive reallocation of public space. Streets that had once been multipurpose public spaces, accommodating a variety of uses and users, were increasingly dedicated to the movement and storage of private vehicles. The repurposing of "parking" helped normalize this transformation, making it seem natural and inevitable that large portions of the public realm should be set aside for private car storage.[82]

5.2.5 *Clashes and Adoption by the Government*

A key outcome of these national conferences was the development of model laws intended to standardize traffic regulations across the country. One significant product was the proposed Uniform Vehicle Code, a model state code designed to replace the patchwork of existing state laws.[83] The drafting of this code was entrusted to a Committee on Uniformity of Laws and Regulations, chaired by a lawyer and assisted by a representative from the AAA. Notably, the actual writing of the proposed model state code was carried out by a staff lawyer from the Automobile Club of Southern California. This involvement of auto club representatives in drafting model legislation underscores the significant influence of motordom in shaping traffic laws. The Uniform Vehicle Code was presented to the second Hoover traffic conference in March 1926, after which local and state auto clubs organized efforts to push the code through their respective state legislatures.[84]

In addition to the state-level code, the conferences also produced a Model Municipal Traffic Ordinance.[85] This model ordinance was designed to provide a template for cities to adopt, further promoting uniformity in traffic regulation across the nation. The U.S. Department of Commerce issued the completed model ordinance in 1928, and it was widely circulated with the support of the NACC, which called the rules "a forward step in motor transportation."[86] The spread of this model ordinance was remarkably swift. By the end of 1928, over 100 cities had adopted it. By 1930, state legislatures in New Jersey and Wisconsin had adopted most of it for all their cities. In total, by 1930, twenty-three states had adopted all or part of the model ordinance.[87]

These model laws and ordinances represented a significant shift in how traffic regulations were developed and implemented. Rather than emerging organically from local conditions and preferences, traffic rules were now being shaped at a national level, with substantial input from auto industry interests. This approach facilitated greater uniformity in traffic laws across the country, which was beneficial for drivers traveling between jurisdictions. However, it also meant that local concerns and alternative perspectives on street use were often overridden in favor of a car-centric approach to urban mobility.

The rapid and widespread adoption of these model laws and ordinances demonstrates the effective collaboration between industry groups and government officials in reshaping the regulatory landscape for urban transportation. It also highlights the success of Motordom in advancing its vision for how city streets should be regulated and used. This standardization of traffic laws, driven largely by auto industry interests, played a crucial role in facilitating the dominance of automobiles in American cities. By creating a more uniform and predictable regulatory environment for driving, these model laws helped pave the way for the car-centric urban development that would characterize much of twentieth century America.

As the auto industry and its allies worked to reshape the regulatory landscape, they recognized the critical need to gain public support for their vision of urban mobility. This effort involved a multifaceted approach to shape public opinion and behavior, often using sophisticated marketing and public relations techniques. One key strategy was to frame automobile use in terms of personal freedom. The NACC began promoting the idea of "motor age freedom" in the mid 1920s.[88] This rhetoric positioned the automobile as a symbol of American individualism and liberty, contrasting it with the perceived constraints of public transit. By the 1930s, even traffic engineer Miller McClintock, once an advocate for strict regulation, was speaking against restrictions that would interfere with the "freedom … of automotive transportation."

Simultaneously, the industry worked to reshape public understanding of traffic safety issues. Rather than focusing on the inherent dangers of automobiles, they sought to frame accidents in terms of individual behavior, particularly "recklessness." This shift in emphasis allowed the industry to advocate for driver education and stricter enforcement against "bad" drivers, while deflecting attention from vehicle design or the overall increase in automobile traffic. The auto industry also made extensive use of press coverage to shape public perceptions. The NACC launched a central accident news service, supplying newspapers with standardized forms for reporting accidents.[89] This allowed the industry to control the narrative around traffic safety, often emphasizing pedestrian error over driver responsibility. Some local auto clubs went even further; for instance, the Chicago Motor Club began buying space in the Chicago Tribune for regular "Traffic Talks" that blamed "reckless pedestrians" for nearly 90 percent of collisions between cars and people.[90]

Public education campaigns formed another crucial element of this strategy. The AAA became a leading supplier of traffic safety education materials to schools across the country. By the 1928–29 school year, the AAA was providing monthly instructional materials to 50,000 teachers, reaching an estimated 2 million schoolchildren. These materials often emphasized pedestrian responsibility and proper street-crossing behavior, reinforcing the idea that streets were primarily for cars. The auto industry also supported the creation of school safety patrols, where older children helped younger ones cross streets safely. While ostensibly about protecting children, these programs also served to normalize the idea that pedestrians, even children, were responsible for avoiding cars rather than vice versa.

These efforts extended beyond schools. Auto clubs and manufacturers sponsored public safety campaigns, parades, and competitions to promote "proper" street behavior. They distributed millions of safety posters and pamphlets, all reinforcing the message that careful individual behavior, rather than restrictions on automobiles, was the key to traffic safety.

The industry's public relations efforts were remarkably successful in reshaping public attitudes and behaviors. Over time, the idea that streets were primarily for cars became widely accepted, and pedestrians increasingly internalized the responsibility to stay out of the way of automobiles. This shift in public perception was crucial in facilitating the broader regulatory changes that the auto industry sought. This approach not only helped to secure public support for pro-automobile policies but also laid the groundwork for the car-centric urban development that would dominate American cities for much of the twentieth century. The success of these public relations efforts demonstrates the power of coordinated messaging campaigns in shaping public opinion and behavior. It also highlights the critical role that public perception plays in facilitating regulatory change, especially in areas that affect everyday life as profoundly as urban transportation.

Overall, the introduction of the automobile and development of modern traffic systems was driven by a complex interplay between private industry, government, and civil society. While contentious at times, the frameworks for public–private cooperation established in this era laid the groundwork for the auto-centric transportation paradigm that would dominate twentieth century America. Understanding this history provides important context for current debates over the future of urban mobility and sustainability.

5.3 DEVELOPING CORPORATE DISCLOSURE

While the reshaping of urban transportation offers a vivid example of corporate ordering in the physical world, it is far from the only domain where private actors helped redefine the rules. If the automobile transformed how people moved through public space, the emergence of corporate financial disclosure reimagined how companies communicated with markets, regulators, and the wider public. Both stories show

how private enterprises, driven by strategic business goals, produced governance frameworks that prefigured formal law. But where the driving code was forged in response to urgent and visible crises, the evolution of financial reporting unfolded more slowly, shaped by decades of negotiation, experimentation, and the gradual convergence of stakeholder expectations.

This slower pace did not make the outcome less consequential. By the time the stock market crash of 1929 forced lawmakers to act, the basic template for corporate disclosure was already in place. Leading firms had been refining their practices, stock exchanges had begun imposing their own requirements, and investors had come to expect a certain level of transparency. What the crisis did was elevate and standardize what had already taken root in corporate ordering.

This next section traces the development of corporate disclosure practices, from their tentative beginnings to their widespread adoption. It examines the motivations that led companies to report more fully, the tensions between transparency and control, and the role of institutional actors in shaping norms that would later be codified into law. Like the reordering of the city street, this process reveals how corporate governance efforts can precede, and sometimes preempt, regulatory intervention.

5.3.1 *Stakes: The Costs of Attracting Investors*

The late nineteenth century marked a critical juncture in the evolution of corporate financial disclosure, with far-reaching implications for the United States' economic development and the health of its financial markets.[91] This era, characterized by rapid industrialization and the rise of large corporations, saw the emergence of new financial reporting practices that would prove instrumental in shaping the nation's economic trajectory.

At stake was nothing less than the country's ability to efficiently allocate capital and foster sustainable economic growth.[92] As the U.S. sought to establish itself as a global economic power, the development of robust and transparent financial markets became increasingly crucial. The quality and reliability of corporate financial disclosure played a pivotal role in this process, directly impacting the nation's capacity to fund large-scale industrial and infrastructure projects that were vital to its economic expansion. The health and integrity of the financial markets were fundamentally tied to the evolution of disclosure practices during this period. As the scale and complexity of business enterprises grew, particularly with the rise of railroads and other capital-intensive industries, the need for more sophisticated and standardized financial reporting became evident. The stakes were high: inadequate or misleading financial disclosure could lead to misallocation of resources, market instability, and a loss of investor confidence, potentially stifling economic growth and innovation.

The development of effective disclosure practices was also essential for democratizing access to investment opportunities.[93] As the U.S. economy matured, broadening participation in financial markets became increasingly important for both economic and social reasons. Improved financial disclosure had the potential to reduce information asymmetries, allowing a wider range of individuals and institutions to make informed investment decisions. The additional firepower that this previously untapped pool of funds brought to markets would be welcome in a period of rapid development and industrialization.

The expectations surrounding financial disclosure were evolving in tandem with the country's economic ambitions. There was a growing recognition that the development of sophisticated capital markets, capable of efficiently channeling savings into productive investments, required a foundation of reliable and comprehensive financial information. This created pressure for more extensive and standardized corporate reporting practices. At the same time, there were expectations that enhanced financial disclosure would contribute to the overall stability and resilience of the U.S. economy.[94] By providing investors and regulators with better tools to assess and monitor corporate performance and risk, improved disclosure practices had the potential to help prevent or mitigate financial crises, which could have devastating effects on national economic well-being.

5.3.2 *Heterogeneity of Preferences*

The late nineteenth century saw a complex interplay of expectations and desires among various stakeholders regarding corporate financial disclosure, often leading to clashes of interest and perspective. Companies and their managers generally sought to maintain flexibility and discretion in their reporting practices. Many viewed extensive disclosure as potentially harmful to their competitive position, fearing that too much transparency could reveal strategic information to rivals. Additionally, some companies were reluctant to fully disclose their financial position, particularly if it might reveal unfavorable information or volatility in earnings. Forward-thinking managers, like those at the Baltimore & Ohio Railroad (B&O), recognized that enhanced voluntary disclosure could attract investors and potentially lower their cost of capital.[95] However, the B&O case also shows some limits to transparency. The 1855 annual report included a detailed safety report with information on deaths and injuries, but this level of disclosure about accidents was not continued in subsequent years.

Managers were also concerned about the impact of financial disclosure on the worker movement.[96] At the time, labor relations were heated, as workers and their unions were seeking to negotiate higher wages and better conditions. If companies appeared financially profitable, the thinking went, workers would be emboldened to make even higher demands.

Investors, particularly individual shareholders, increasingly demanded more comprehensive and frequent financial information.[97] As investment opportunities expanded, they expected greater transparency to assess risks and potential returns. This group often found itself at odds with company management, pushing for more detailed disclosures and standardized reporting practices to facilitate comparisons between investment options. Large institutional investors and other shareholders with significant holdings often had different expectations than smaller, individual investors.[98] While they too desired accurate financial information, they sometimes had more direct access to management and might have been less insistent on public disclosures. In some cases, major shareholders might have aligned with management in resisting too much transparency, especially if it could negatively impact stock prices or reveal sensitive information.

Banks and financial intermediaries occupied a unique position.[99] On one hand, as lenders and underwriters, they benefited from having more detailed financial information about companies. On the other hand, many of these institutions also profited from information asymmetries in the market. Some banks, particularly those with close ties to specific companies, may have preferred to maintain their privileged access to information rather than support broader public disclosure.

These varying expectations and desires led to several areas of conflict. One significant clash was between the push for greater transparency from investors and the public versus the desire for discretion and limited disclosure from many companies and their managers. The practice of using retained earnings for reinvestment, noted in the B&O reports from 1849 onwards, illustrates a potential conflict between management's desire to grow the business and shareholders' expectations for dividends. This practice was reportedly criticized by some foreign investors, showing international differences in expectations.

Another area of tension existed between the needs of small, individual investors for standardized, easily understandable financial reports and the interests of more sophisticated investors or financial intermediaries who might have preferred, or been able to navigate, more complex disclosures. The National Association of Manufacturers' 1938 study reflects ongoing debates about disclosure.[100] It criticized many companies' reports as being full of "obscure accounting terms" not useful to ordinary people. This illustrates the clash between complex, technical disclosures preferred by some companies and the need for more accessible information for a broader investor base. Furthermore, there was an ongoing debate about the appropriate balance between voluntary disclosure and mandatory reporting requirements.[101] While some argued that market forces would naturally lead to optimal levels of disclosure, others pushed for more formalized and enforced standards.

5.3.3 *Corporate Ordering*

The evolution of corporate financial disclosure in the late nineteenth and early twentieth centuries was characterized by a gradual but significant shift in corporate reporting practices.[102] In a few decades, what began as basic balance sheet disclosures evolved into comprehensive annual reports that included detailed financial statements, operational statistics, market analyses, and forward-looking information.

This evolution laid the groundwork for the development of modern corporate reporting standards and practices in the twentieth century, shaping the landscape of financial disclosure we see today. The disclosures do not provide explicit details about interactions between the company, investors, government entities, and other stakeholders. However, the continuous expansion of the scope of disclosures, as well as the ongoing diffusion from few companies to the industry more generally, suggests that this expansion was positively received by investors and met with the public's demands. Moreover, the inclusion in the reports of information beyond what shareholders at the time could comprehend illustrates that companies reached out to a wider audience that included the railroad industry, the government, and local communities whose support was essential for the company.

The paragraphs below trace how investor pressures and managers' efforts to excel drove the evolution of disclosure norms in pioneering companies, exemplified by the reporting practices of three pioneers: the Quincy Mining Company (QMC), the B&O, and U.S. Steel.

5.3.3.1 Quincy Mining: Adoption and Retreat

If we applied today's parlance to the 1860s, the QMC would have been a unicorn. It was not yet profitable, but it operated big mines with a lot of potential. At first, its disclosures included only a balance sheet, an income statement, and a directors' report about the history of the company.[103] But as the company needed to shore up confidence and continue to attract investment, it expanded its disclosures. For example, in 1862, QMC expanded their Directors' Report to include data on copper and silver production volume, a brief on major undertakings, and an appraisal of its prospects for the following year. From 1863 to 1871, QMC introduced more detailed reporting on its mining cost and enhanced its productivity measurements, providing information on the cost of mining supply, the average monthly cost "per fathom stopped, per foot drifted and per foot sunk of shafts and winzes." This type of disclosure moves beyond financial information and presages the business section and forward-looking statements of modern disclosures. The goal was to portray a company that was well-managed, if not yet profitable. Moreover, it underlined the influence of professional managers, who had taken over control from major stakeholders.

Interestingly, in the 1880s, as QMC becomes more profitable, it changes ownership, starts providing higher dividends, and dramatically reduces the detail of financial disclosure it provides. As the company had become an attractive investment option, management no longer needed to persuade the market that it was efficiently run.

5.3.3.2 Baltimore and Ohio Railroad

The railroad industry, then at the height of its expansion, offers a good illustration of how pressures from investors, workers, governments, and other stakeholders shaped disclosure norms. Railroads require high upfront investment for expansion and maintenance, in exchange for the promise of profits once lines are established. Periodic reporting had grown common by the 1840s, including mostly financial statements very similar to a modern balance sheet and income statement. But by the 1860s, many companies' annual reports had expanded to over sixty pages, including information about engineering, operations, and legal matters alongside financial updates.

The rediscovery of annual reports from the (B&O), dating as early as 1827, as detailed by Previts and Samson (2000), allowed historians to study the evolution of reporting practices in this pioneering company.[104] B&O was a transportation technology innovator. It experimented with various sources of power, including wind and steam, with different configurations of wheels and tracks, and with different types of engines and cars. It also recognized early the importance of communications systems and used telegraphy as a tool, and engaged in extensive bridge and tunnel construction. To monitor this wide specter of activities, management set up a robust organizational structure with internal controls and built strong connections not only to the financial industry but also to political leaders. At the time, corporations chartered by state action were seen not simply as private profit-making entities, but also as custodians of communal assets. After all, many citizens of Baltimore owned shares, alongside local government entities. B&O's annual reports, which were hugely influential on other companies, as many historians have documented, had multiple audiences.

Initially, B&O strategically employed extensive disclosures primarily to attract investment capital and convince investors that the company was using its raised capital prudently. The company's first two presidents, Philip Thomas and Louis McLane, both had significant experience in banking and finance, which was crucial for this effort. Thomas, who was a banker and served as the president of the Mechanics Bank of Baltimore, initiated the publication of B&O's managerial reports in 1828. McLane, who had previously held the position of Secretary of the U.S. Treasury Department, further developed these reports by incorporating detailed discussions on operations, provided by the chief of transportation and the chief engineer. This practice not only became standard for B&O but also influenced other railroads, such as the Louisville & Nashville Railroad and the Illinois Central Railroad, to adopt similar practices.

But it quickly became clear that, if costs were the focus, the company had to provide information about the projects for which it was expending capital. As a result, reports quickly started developing sections that in modern times we would recognize as part of the business section, risk factors, or management's discussion and analysis. Construction projects were discussed, routes were mapped, passenger and freight data and projections were provided. Soon, specialized officers started being named, to shed light on the expertise and organizational efficiency of the company. The internal auditor, William Woodville, is named as early as 1830, and his work was credited as supervised by a committee of the board of directors. Similarly, the treasurer and the company secretary are also identified. In later years, the chief engineer provides data that allows comparisons between B&O and other U.S. railroads. Similarly, some years see the publication of special reports, including an engineering and routing report in 1828 and a two-page safety report in 1855.

Even at the time, it was widely acknowledged that the disclosures provided by B&O reached far beyond what shareholders would either need or even be able to understand and fully appreciate.[105] The detailed information about engineering, including the company's experimentations with different configurations, were informative for the wider industry and for the scientific community. The financing structures for B&O were soon imitated by other railroad companies. Similarly, other railroad companies also expanded their annual reports to include engineering and safety sections.

5.3.3.3 U.S. Steel

The formation of U.S. Steel in 1901 and its subsequent reporting practices represent a further iteration in this process, because they enhance the private governance structures associated with disclosure. Not only were U.S. Steel's early reports groundbreaking in their level of detail and transparency, as noted by Previts and Merino (1998), they also introduce the practice of third-party certification, thus strengthening private governance structures.[106]

The initial annual report of U.S. Steel in 1902 stands as a pioneering document in corporate financial disclosure, earning high praise from contemporaries for its comprehensive and detailed nature. As reported by Scientific American, this document was hailed as "the most complete and circumstantial report ever issued by any great American corporation" (p. 24).[107] It set a new standard for financial transparency by presenting the financial returns of a consolidated firm, a significant advancement at that time. A notable innovation introduced in this report was the inclusion of a certified audit report from Price Waterhouse & Co. (PWC). PWC's audit extended beyond the typical scope, as it also verified the "Properties Account," provisions for depreciation and bad debts, inventory valuation, and performed an in-depth analysis of cash accounts. The audit culminated in a certification of both the balance sheet and income statement, offering an unprecedented level of assurance for U.S. corporations.

The annual report was meticulously detailed, encompassing various elements such as a list of corporate directors and officers, a letter to shareholders discussing key financial aspects including income, retained earnings, quarterly profits, capital expenditures, and depreciation schedules, an audit certificate, comprehensive financial statements, and summaries of manufacturing plants, mines, and railroads, among others. From 1901 to 1926, U.S. Steel's annual reports were notably voluminous, with an average of fifty-two pages, dwarfing those of other leading companies.[108] For comparison, General Motors' reports ranged from 14 to 18 pages, DuPont's from 9 to 12 pages, and National Biscuit Company's typically less than ten pages.

This extensive disclosure practice by U.S. Steel garnered widespread acclaim, including from The Wall Street Journal, which praised the company for its leadership in providing timely and detailed financial information.[109] The Journal observed that the company had adopted the practice of giving monthly reports of profits and noted that if a corporation as large as U.S. Steel could produce such detailed financial statements promptly, it was unreasonable for smaller companies to claim that they could not do the same.

The ethos of full disclosure championed by U.S. Steel's President, Judge Elbert Gary, further underlined the company's commitment to transparency. Gary espoused the belief that corporations had a duty to be fully transparent with shareholders, driven by both ethical considerations and rising public concerns over antitrust issues. He famously stated that corporations could not operate behind "locked doors and shut lips," asserting that people had a right to know how businesses were being run and that greater transparency would ultimately benefit the business environment.[110] Gary's principles, later known as "The Gary Rules," emphasized honesty, fairness, and the importance of public opinion in business. He believed that success would ultimately come to those who adhered to these ethical standards.

But while the companies earlier were pioneers, there was significant variation among companies in their disclosure practices during the early twentieth century, as surveys of financial reporting of industrial firms in the 1920s demonstrate. Some companies voluntarily provided detailed financial statements, such as income statements and balance sheets, in response to investor demands for transparency and to attract capital.[111] However, other firms continued to disclose minimal information, influenced by factors like corporate governance structures and the economic environment. Investor dissatisfaction with these disclosures was evident, as reports from the period, such as those by Michael (1996) and Kohler (1926), highlighted concerns that less than 20 percent of balance sheets were useful for analysis, and incomplete income statements hindered financial analysis.[112] This dissatisfaction reflects the inconsistency in disclosure practices, where some companies responded to social pressures and investor demands, while others did not, leading to a fragmented and often inadequate supply of financial information. Generally, companies with a broader shareholder base that relied on professional managers provided more detailed disclosures, whereas companies whose officers controlled significant shareholding, were more circumspect in their disclosures.

5.3.4 *Industry Governance: The New York Stock Exchange*

While pioneering companies laid the foundation for modern disclosure practices, it was the institutions that connected these companies to investors, and particularly the NYSE, that began to formalize and standardize these efforts across the market. The NYSE, established in 1792, has long operated as a membership organization, providing access to its trading facilities only to brokers who were registered members of the exchange.[113] Initially focused on government securities, by the 1830s the stock exchange's trading had expanded to shares of banks, insurance companies, and later canal and railroad stocks. But inconsistencies in corporate disclosure practices posed a concern for members, as they represented a risk for members' own investments and could undermine investor confidence in the market as a whole. The lack of standardized reporting made it difficult for members to accurately assess the value and risks associated with various securities, potentially leading to mispricing and increased volatility. This growing awareness of the problems stemming from inadequate and inconsistent disclosure set the stage for the NYSE's gradual but significant push toward more comprehensive and uniform reporting standards. The NYSE quickly recognized that increased investor confidence could lead to higher trade volumes, directly impacting the exchange's revenue.[114] At the same time, the NYSE was also concerned about forgery, market manipulation, and other types of fraud.

In an effort to enhance its reputation and boost investor trust, the NYSE set out to use its strong bargaining position as a leading marketplace to extract promises of improved disclosure and governance reforms from corporations. Initially, these promises became the core of individualized listing agreements between each company and the exchange. Over time, the terms of these agreements became more uniform, and crystallized into listing requirements. The process of enhancing disclosure requirements was gradual, spanning several decades and encompassing various aspects of corporate reporting.

In the early years, listing requirements were minimal. In 1847, the Board merely resolved that stocks of regularly incorporated companies with transfer books in New York City could be listed at members' request. This laissez-faire approach, however, proved inadequate as the market grew and became more complex.[115] By 1856, more formal rules were established. Companies were required to apply directly to the Board, providing details on capital structure, number of shares, and resources. Additionally, companies had to maintain transfer books in New York City, a requirement that persists to this day. This marked the beginning of a trend toward greater transparency and standardization in listings.

A significant institutional development occurred in 1861 with the creation of the first standing Committee on Securities. This committee was tasked with handling listing applications and gathering information on listed securities, representing a more systematic approach to market oversight. But the Committee's efforts to collect more comprehensive financial information from listed companies were often met with resistance. A notable example is the 1866 correspondence between the Exchange and the Delaware, Lackawanna & Western Railroad Company, where the company flatly refused to provide any financial reports or statements.[116]

The turn of the century marked a new era in listing requirements, driven largely by the emergence of industrial companies seeking listings. These companies, eager for access to capital markets, were more willing to make extensive agreements regarding financial disclosures. The Glucose Sugar Refining Company's 1898 application, which included a promise to make public a detailed annual statement, was a harbinger of this trend. In 1900, the National Tube Company agreed to publish detailed annual statements of income, expenditures, and balance sheets.[117] However, it's worth noting that such agreements were not yet universal, particularly among railroads and utilities.

A significant shift occurred in 1910 when the NYSE abolished its Unlisted Department, where most industrial stocks were traded, and moved these issues to the main list. This change coincided with more comprehensive disclosure agreements. For instance, the Niagara Falls Power Company agreed to publish annual reports and quarterly income statements. Over the next few decades, a series of key agreements evolved, becoming increasingly standardized and comprehensive. Companies began agreeing to publish annual reports with detailed financial statements, including balance sheets and income statements. They committed to maintaining a transfer office in New York City, facilitating easier trading and shareholder recordkeeping. Firms agreed to notify the Exchange of significant corporate actions such as dividends, rights offerings, and changes in capital structure. An anti-speculation clause was introduced, with companies agreeing not to speculate in their own securities or those of subsidiaries, a measure aimed at preventing market manipulation.

The 1920s marked another period of progress in disclosure practices. By 1923, quarterly reporting agreements became increasingly common. Some companies, like the Metropolitan Edison Company in 1924, even agreed to publish monthly earnings statements. By 1928, the NYSE required annual financial statements to be audited by independent auditors, thus relying on third parties to enhance the reliability of their reporting. By the 1930s, disclosure agreements had become more standardized and comprehensive. The Continental Can Company's 1930 agreement, for example, required detailed financial reporting, including the publication of net profits after accounting for depreciation, depletion, income taxes, and interest. Firms also committed to notifying the Exchange of any changes in depreciation policies, recognizing the impact of such changes on financial statements. Additionally, companies agreed to report on any previously issued securities that had been reacquired, providing greater transparency on capital structure.

The disclosure practices introduced by the NYSE in the early twentieth century represent a formalization and broader application of the templates established by pioneering companies such as the QMC, B&O, and U.S. Steel. Rather than devising entirely new standards, the NYSE effectively developed and mandated practices that had already been proven successful by industry leaders. For instance, the comprehensive annual reports required by the NYSE mirrored the detailed disclosures voluntarily provided by B&O Railroad decades earlier. Similarly, the NYSE's push for quarterly reporting in the 1920s followed the example set by U.S. Steel's monthly profit reports.[118] The 1928 NYSE requirement for independent audits of annual financial statements essentially standardized the practice in the U.S. Steel had introduced it with its 1902 certified audit report from PWC. By 1933, approximately 80 percent of public companies were obtaining voluntary audits.[119] This pattern illustrates how the NYSE leveraged the successful reporting models developed by forward-thinking companies to create industry-wide standards, effectively turning voluntary best practices into formal requirements for listed companies.

However, because this was a system based on contractual arrangements negotiated separately between each company and the stock exchange, requirements were neither uniform nor universal. Many companies declined to provide even the most basic information, such as balance sheets and income statements. Moreover, it was left to the exchange to enforce noncompliance with the agreement, which would involve halting trading on the stocks and may have led to decreased trading volume and, consequently, lower commissions for members. Variability in disclosure standards further complicated enforcement, as investors were not always clear about what to expect from which company.

5.3.5 *Government Clashes*

After a financial crisis of tremendous proportions and the Great Depression, the New Deal era established a government-supervised mandatory disclosure system. The literature about the introduction of the 1933 and 1934 Acts is extensive, but the goal of the paragraphs below is to illustrate that the mandatory disclosure requirements did not emerge in a vacuum. The 1933 Securities Act largely codified, standardized, and expanded upon existing voluntary disclosure practices that had developed over the preceding decades, particularly those established by the NYSE.[120] In doing so, it compelled increased disclosure from more opaque firms, particularly smaller firms and those trading in less regulated markets. At the same time, the Act introduced important changes, most notably by making disclosure requirements universal and introducing robust enforcement through private class actions.

The similarities between the disclosure requirements of the Securities Act of 1933 and those previously established by the NYSE were substantial, reflecting the Act's roots in existing market practices. One of the most notable similarities was the requirement for companies to provide audited financial statements.[121] The NYSE had begun requiring annual audited financial statements for listed companies by 1928, recognizing the importance of independent verification in building investor confidence. The 1933 Act similarly mandated that registration statements include balance sheets and profit and loss statements certified by independent public accountants. Both the NYSE and the 1933 Act also emphasized the disclosure of a company's capital structure. The NYSE had long required companies to provide accurate information about their capitalization, including details on the number of shares, bonds, and other liabilities outstanding. The 1933 Act mirrored this focus, requiring comprehensive disclosure of a company's capital structure in the registration statement.

Another area of similarity was the emphasis on providing investors with a clear picture of a company's business operations.[122] The NYSE's listing requirements had evolved to include detailed information about a company's history, the nature of its business, and the location and extent of its properties. The 1933 Act echoed these requirements, mandating disclosure of the company's business model, competitive position, and material contracts.

The concept of ongoing disclosure was also present in both regimes.[123] While the NYSE had been pushing for quarterly reporting since the early 1920s, the 1933 Act, in conjunction with the Securities Exchange Act of 1934, established a system of regular, periodic reporting for public companies. This continuity reflects a shared understanding of the importance of keeping investors informed about a company's ongoing performance and material developments. Both systems also recognized the importance of disclosing management's interests and compensation. The NYSE had increasingly required disclosure of executive compensation and insider transactions, a practice that the 1933 Act formalized and expanded upon. The level of detail required in financial disclosures was another area of similarity. Both the NYSE and the 1933 Act pushed for greater granularity in financial reporting. For instance, by 1934, a significant portion of NYSE-listed companies were disclosing sales figures and cost of goods sold, practices that became mandatory under the new securities laws.[124] It's worth noting that the SEC's first disclosure forms, including the influential Form S-1, drew heavily from the NYSE's listing standards. This direct influence further illustrates the continuity between the voluntary disclosure regime developed by the NYSE and the mandatory system established by the 1933 Act. These similarities underscore that the 1933 Act, while revolutionary in its scope and legal enforceability, was evolutionary in its content. It built upon disclosure practices that had already been proven valuable in the marketplace. The Act's innovation lay not so much in inventing new disclosure requirements, but in extending these best practices to all public offerings and backing them with the force of law. This approach allowed the Act to leverage existing market wisdom while addressing the limitations of the voluntary system, particularly its lack of universality and enforcement mechanisms.

5.4 CORPORATE ORDERING AND OTHER COMPANY EFFORTS TO SHAPE REGULATION

The case studies of driving codes and corporate financial disclosures show that private actors have long sought to shape legal and regulatory environments to suit their goals. These early efforts relied on persuasion, alliance-building, and the strategic use of governance tools. Model laws, voluntary standards, and public messaging helped corporations build legitimacy for new norms that often preceded formal regulation.

In more recent decades, scholars have developed a rich literature on private standard-setting and transnational regulation. Beginning in the 1990s, this work highlighted how corporations played increasingly direct roles in creating frameworks that govern product safety, environmental conduct, financial markets, and labor practices. In many of these accounts, the emphasis shifted from informal influence to formal participation in rulemaking processes. Firms no longer merely shaped the margins of public law. They helped design the rules themselves through industry consortia, certification regimes, and multi-stakeholder bodies.

There are clear continuities between these more recent developments and the historical examples examined earlier. In both settings, private actors acted early and with intention, filling regulatory gaps before governments moved. They used legal techniques, coordination platforms, and claims to expertise to advance structures that reflected their interests. Yet important differences remain. Much of the later literature focuses on collective bodies with formal procedures for consultation and accountability. By contrast, the earlier cases involved more concentrated forms of corporate action, often without structured opportunities for stakeholder participation.

These differences help explain a recurring concern in both the historical and contemporary context. When private actors propose their own regulatory solutions, they often claim to be advancing efficiency, innovation, or public welfare. But they may also be seeking to forestall more stringent public regulation. The risk is that self-regulatory efforts, even when framed as governance, become tools of influence. They can offer a persuasive alternative to public oversight, especially when combined with lobbying or political contributions. In these cases, the line between responsible self-regulation and regulatory capture becomes difficult to draw.

The next section turns to collective industry bodies and international standard-setters. These organizations make more explicit use of governance procedures to build legitimacy and align with public expectations. Studying how they operate can offer a deeper understanding of the mechanisms through which private power continues to shape regulatory outcomes, and how these mechanisms can be distinguished from more familiar forms of political lobbying.

5.4.1 *Industry Bodies and Standard Setters*

The concept of market participants coalescing to establish self-regulatory regimes with quasi-legal features and procedures has antecedents dating to medieval guild structures.[125] In membership organizations, such as guilds, individuals or entities within a specific industry or profession form a voluntary association to pursue common interests, establish standards, and regulate their activities. This process of market creation and self-governance exhibits several common elements with the governance mechanisms elucidated in prior chapters, including enhancing credibility through transparency; mandating membership ratification for new regulations; implementing third-party accreditation and assurance processes; and enforcing standards via the threat of expulsion.[126] These governance tools serve to augment the reputation of the membership body vis-à-vis consumers and confer legitimacy upon its constituent members.

Contemporary exemplars of self-regulatory organizations (SROs) include professional associations such as the American Bar Association and industry bodies like the former National Association of Securities Dealers, which subsequently evolved into the Financial Industry Regulatory Authority.[127] In exchange for safeguarding public interests through stringent membership criteria and standards, these entities facilitate and protect the collective interests of their members within established trades. The motivations and operational dynamics of SROs diverge significantly from those of corporate entities primarily focused on launching innovative products in competitive markets. Scholars have long scrutinized the output of these self-regulatory bodies, with some lauding their practical, industry-specific expertise,[128] while others express reservations about potential conflicts of interest and inherent biases.[129]

Building upon the foundational concepts of self-regulation in financial markets, my earlier research has specifically focused on the governance processes implemented by stock exchanges in their capacity as market regulators. This work examines how exchanges have structured their self-regulatory powers to balance effective rulemaking and enforcement with the need to mitigate conflicts of interest inherent in their dual roles as market operators and overseers.[130]

A key finding of this research is the variation in governance structures adopted by different exchanges globally, as they were transitioning from membership organizations to private entities. For instance, some exchanges have established separate subsidiaries dedicated to regulatory functions, creating a degree of institutional separation between market operations and oversight activities. The New York Stock Exchange's NYSE Regulation, Inc. exemplifies this approach, operating as a not-for-profit subsidiary with an independent board of directors.[131] This structure aims to insulate regulatory decision-making from commercial pressures faced by the parent exchange.

Other exchanges have opted for internal governance mechanisms, such as creating dedicated regulatory committees within their board structures. These committees, often populated by independent directors, are tasked with overseeing the exchange's regulatory programs and ensuring compliance with statutory obligations.[132] The Australian Securities Exchange (ASX), for example, has implemented this model, with its regulatory oversight function embedded within its corporate governance framework.[133]

The goals served by these varied governance processes are multifaceted. Primarily, they seek to mitigate conflicts of interest by establishing structural or functional separations between regulatory and commercial activities. Additionally, these enhanced governance mechanisms aim to bolster the perceived integrity and effectiveness of the exchange's regulatory functions, both to market participants and external regulators.[134] Some governance structures are designed to facilitate more nimble regulatory responses to market developments, leveraging the exchange's proximity to market activities.[135] Furthermore, many governance processes incorporate reporting mechanisms to external regulators or public bodies, enhancing transparency and accountability in the self-regulatory process.[136] My research has also examined how these governance processes interact with broader regulatory frameworks, including the oversight role played by national securities regulators.[137] This interaction reveals a complex ecosystem of co-regulation, where self-regulatory activities of exchanges are subject to varying degrees of governmental supervision.[138]

Independent standard-setting bodies emerge as a potential remedy to the criticisms of industry bias and monopolization that frequently beset collective self-regulatory institutions. These entities, whether established through private initiatives or bolstered by governmental support, proffer cohesive regulatory frameworks that aim to safeguard specific public goods while providing structured clarity. Exemplars of such standard-setters include the Basel Committee, which establishes standards for banks' capital adequacy, and the International Organization for Standardization (ISO), which delineates technical specifications for products and processes across diverse industries.[139] These international standard-setters present an alternative paradigm to rules promulgated by individual national legislatures or regulatory bodies. Their efficacy lies in their capacity to transcend national boundaries and secure participation from a multitude of countries, thereby fostering more harmonized regulatory regimes on a global scale.[140]

In prior research, I have focused extensively on these bodies, particularly examining the diverse pathways through which standards become incorporated into national legal frameworks.[141] These pathways frequently involve governance approaches analogous to those discussed in Chapter 3 of the referenced work. Such approaches encompass comprehensive stakeholder consultation, robust notice and feedback mechanisms, initiatives to ensure inclusivity and establish representative assemblies, transparency measures, and accountability mechanisms. These governance approaches are designed to enhance the legitimacy and efficacy of the standards promulgated by these independent bodies. By employing these methodologies, standard-setters seek to mitigate the criticisms of industry capture and monopolization that often plague self-regulatory institutions, while simultaneously leveraging the expertise and engagement of relevant stakeholders.

The paragraphs earlier show that both self-regulatory industry bodies and international standard-setters rely extensively on governance arrangements that ensure broad consultation, provide transparency, and invite accountability and feedback.[142] It is not surprising to find these entities employing tools typically associated with legislatures, regulators, and other government lawmakers to gather information and build credibility.[143] Although neither SROs nor independent standard-setters are governmental in origin, they aim to emulate governments in their rule-making functions, partly by adopting similar methodologies.

This book, however, focuses specifically on private corporations and explores how they utilize similar approaches to gain acceptance for norms and practices inherent in their business models. While some specific instances of corporate legal innovation have been studied, such as Facebook's Oversight Board or responses to #MeToo investigations, there has been a lack of comprehensive analysis examining this as a broader trend among private companies.[144] The adoption of these governance methods by corporations for business purposes is a distinct phenomenon that has received little scholarly attention, particularly regarding its implications for corporate law. By investigating how private firms leverage these techniques to legitimize their operational norms, this book aims to fill a significant gap in our understanding of modern corporate governance and its wider societal impact.

5.4.2 *Governance or Lobbying?*

When considering corporate influence on lawmaking, legal scholars typically focus on lobbying. A substantial body of literature in law and political science examines how corporations expend resources to sway lawmakers, aiming to shape laws and regulations that favor their interests or minimize harm to them.[145] Some in the literature portray the interaction between corporations and governments as a regulatory "pendulum," a never-ending game of cat and mouse leading to a cyclical equilibrium that may even prove to be optimal.[146] But most scholars are far less optimistic.[147]

The landscape of corporate political contributions has garnered increased attention, especially following the Citizens United decision's impact on Political Action Committees (PACs).[148] Many worry that corporations' superior resources allow them to effectively appeal to lawmakers, persuade them of their positions, or offer financial support to political hopefuls, potentially tilting legislatures in their favor.[149] Recent reviews of empirical literature on lobbying emphasize that corporations typically target powerful legislators and worry that buying their votes is pervasive. Others point to the revolving door that allows retired CEOs to take over political positions.[150]

However, lobbying differs significantly from the corporate actions central to this book in terms of participants, methods, and outcomes. Lobbyists target public officials, particularly those constitutionally empowered to enact relevant laws or regulations. In contrast, the corporate initiatives discussed here require no specific constitutional authorization and fall within managers' discretion under general corporate law principles.[151] These actions do not represent an exercise of public authority but may take on a contractual form when necessary. They are directed at consumers, employees, supply chain subcontractors, and other corporate stakeholders. While lobbying often faces criticism for attempts to secure influence through campaign contributions, bribes, or lavish gifts, its goal is to shape formal laws or regulations. The corporate efforts examined in this book, however, aim to dictate behavior without necessarily involving formal lawmaking. Often, the purpose is to sidestep formal laws altogether, getting stakeholders to conform to corporations' desired model voluntarily.

That said, these corporate actions may occasionally lead to similar laws, either by emboldening policymakers to emulate them or by persuading them of their effectiveness through various means, including lobbying.[152] In the aftermath of a major crisis, for example, lawmakers are likely to be concerned with the social implications of corporate activity, and might look to companies that successfully weathered the storm as templates for mandatory laws.[153] Companies might also lobby to level the playing field with competitors.[154] Sometimes, the same social forces demanding corporate action – such as activists, consumer groups, and employees – may also pressure elected officials.[155] Sometimes, competitive pressures from other companies, or from abroad, might push lawmakers to align with corporate preferences to support the economy.[156]

The concern is that lobbyists will increasingly champion the virtues of corporate self-regulation as a strategic maneuver to avoid the imposition of more stringent external regulations. Instead of serving as a model for government regulation, corporate practices risk becoming a substitute, a lesser alternative, that sidesteps the need for robust oversight.[157] Corporate governance mechanisms, which are intended to shape responsible corporate behavior, may be co-opted by lobbyists as evidence of a company's commitment to the values in question.[158] This, in turn, strengthens their argument in favor of delaying or diluting more comprehensive regulatory frameworks. Tools like stakeholder outreach, feedback loops, transparency initiatives, and monitoring processes can be presented to lawmakers as comforting measures that supposedly ensure corporate accountability.[159] With these measures in mind, lawmakers might be more likely to consent to solutions that prioritize corporate interests above all else.

The risk of corporate hypocrisy is significant, and no single regulatory approach can entirely eliminate it.[160] However, during periods of heightened concern, it is important to recognize that governance measures are not simply a smokescreen to divert policymakers' attention from the underlying problem.[161] In contrast, these governance measures can offer policymakers a critical lens through which to differentiate between genuine mitigation efforts and superficial attempts to maintain the status quo. By scrutinizing corporate governance tools, policymakers can gain valuable insights into the diverse perspectives of various stakeholders and evaluate whether these voices were truly considered in the company's decision-making processes. Furthermore, these governance efforts can reveal the underlying motivations of corporate leadership, highlight the depth of their commitment to ethical practices, and contextualize the resources allocated to these efforts. Instruments such as comprehensive disclosures, alignment with recognized standards, independent third-party audits, and robust public consultations enable external observers to form a more nuanced understanding of a company's operations, especially before regulatory scrutiny intensifies.[162] While no single method is infallible, when combined, these approaches can collectively illuminate the reality of a company's practices and intentions.

5.5 CONCLUSION: THE HISTORICAL ROOTS OF CORPORATE ORDERING

Corporate ordering is not a recent invention. Long before today's platform companies and digital marketplaces, private enterprises were already experimenting with ways to shape the legal and institutional landscapes around them. This chapter examined two pivotal moments in that longer history. The first showed how car manufacturers and their allies helped define the rules of the modern street, reframing the public's relationship to urban space and traffic norms. The second traced how large corporations, stock exchanges, and financial stakeholders slowly built the practices that would eventually evolve into mandatory financial disclosure regimes. In both cases, private actors stepped into a regulatory vacuum, producing frameworks that began as voluntary or industry-led but eventually gained the force and legitimacy of law.

Still, the road to influence was far from smooth. In the past, corporate actors faced significant obstacles in coordinating across firms, reaching dispersed audiences, and responding to stakeholder expectations. Communication was slower. Visibility was limited. Even within firms, aligning interests and mobilizing support required time and effort. These early examples of corporate ordering were shaped by the constraints of their historical moment. They remind us that private rulemaking has always been possible, but that it once required sustained coordination and significant patience.

Today's environment is different. The challenges of the past have not disappeared entirely, but they have been dramatically reduced. Faster communication, broader reach, and more responsive feedback loops now make it easier for corporations to propose and promote new frameworks. The motivations remain familiar, but the tools have changed. What was once incremental can now spread quickly. As a result, corporate ordering is not only more visible in the modern era, but often more ambitious in scope.

The chapters that follow turn to this contemporary landscape. They examine how today's companies continue to construct rules, norms, and standards that shape society in ways that resemble those early efforts but also go beyond them. Understanding the governance structures behind these modern initiatives is key to recognizing both their power and their limits.

6

Safety in the Rideshare Industry

The emergence of ridesharing promised to transform urban transportation. Anyone could become a driver; anyone could summon a ride. The potential was revolutionary. But nothing about how this transformation would unfold was certain. Would these platforms develop governance capabilities adequate to the public challenges their business models created? Or would they simply "move fast and break things," as Silicon Valley's dominant ethos advised, leaving regulators to clean up the wreckage? The companies faced immense pressure, as venture capital demanded rapid growth, incumbents mobilized political opposition, and early regulatory encounters often proved hostile. Under these conditions, would management invest in the costly, time-consuming work of identifying governance problems, collecting operational data, engaging specialized expertise, building stakeholder coalitions, and developing comprehensive frameworks? The tripartite model of corporate governance outlined in Chapter 3 describes these deliberative processes as essential to successful corporate rulemaking. But pressure-tested startup companies racing toward scale might reasonably conclude that such investments were luxuries they could not afford.

The uncertainty extended beyond corporate strategy to regulatory substance. Ridesharing forced regulators to confront questions they had never systematically addressed: What insurance coverage should apply when personal vehicles transition between private and commercial use? How should platforms verify driver eligibility when traditional licensing regimes don't contemplate peer-to-peer transportation? What standards govern background checks when the entity conducting screening is neither an employer nor a government agency? These were not merely gaps in existing frameworks. They required genuine regulatory innovation across domains that had operated for decades under stable arrangements or had never been regulated at all.

Simultaneously, ridesharing collided with entrenched regulatory structures designed for entirely different transportation models. Taxi medallion systems, commercial licensing requirements, and municipal franchise agreements had evolved to govern professional drivers operating dedicated commercial vehicles. Ridesharing platforms coordinated casual drivers using personal cars, rendering existing categories conceptually inadequate. The result was immense conflict between platforms and regulators, between new entrants and incumbent industries, between competing visions of urban transportation's future.

This chapter examines two pivotal episodes where corporate policies ultimately shaped regulatory outcomes: insurance coverage frameworks and sexual harassment monitoring and reporting. In both instances, platform companies developed comprehensive solutions that regulators later embraced. These cases illuminate the interplay between corporate and regulatory governance more intimately than other studies in this book, revealing how companies and government agencies negotiate institutional boundaries in real time.

What emerges from these episodes is a distinctive pattern of corporate problem-solving. Companies do not begin with predetermined solutions. Instead, they identify governance challenges through operational experience, then actively collect information, engage specialized expertise, and solicit stakeholder feedback. Through this deliberative process, they arrive at frameworks that often differ substantially from initial assumptions. Lyft's insurance taxonomy began as a data organization exercise and evolved into the industry's definitional structure. The anti-harassment standards and practices that platforms championed emerged from sustained engagement with public safety advocates and technological constraints, not from Silicon Valley's initial regulatory skepticism.

These examples also demonstrate how corporate governance functions interweave in practice. The insurance case primarily involves rulemaking, creating standards of general applicability for thousands of drivers. The anti-harassment example combines rulemaking with executive functions, such as making case-by-case determinations about individual driver eligibility, as well as monitoring functions, such as conducting ongoing surveillance of driver behavior. Together, they reveal how companies exercise multiple governance functions simultaneously in addressing complex social challenges.

This chapter tells only a partial story. A comprehensive account of Uber and Lyft would require examining their labor practices, competitive dynamics, political strategies, and broader societal impacts. Such a complex undertaking is beyond this book's scope. What this focused analysis provides, however, is an illustration of the tripartite framework in operation. By observing how platforms navigate insurance gaps and screening requirements, we see rulemaking, executive, and monitoring functions not as abstract categories but as lived institutional practices, revealing both the possibilities and limitations of corporate governance in addressing public challenges.

6.1 STAKES: SCALING TRUST IN THE GIG ECONOMY

The emergence of ridesharing platforms represented a fundamental reimagining of both labor markets and urban transportation. Unlike the gradual evolution of most industries, the gig economy burst onto the scene with a disruptive business model that challenged decades of regulatory frameworks, labor classifications, and consumer expectations.[1] The stakes extended far beyond a single company's success or failure, as they encompassed the viability of an entirely new economic paradigm that would ultimately reshape how millions of people work and access services.

6.1.1 *The Platform Economy Challenge: Scale as Necessity*

The first fundamental challenge facing ridesharing companies was whether platform-based business models could maintain quality and safety standards across massive, fluid workforces. Traditional businesses build reliability through hierarchical management structures, standardized training protocols, and direct employment relationships. The gig economy inverted this model, creating networks of independent contractors whose numbers fluctuated daily and whose allegiance to any single platform remained tenuous at best.[2]

The scale imperative made this challenge particularly acute. Unlike traditional taxi companies that might employ dozens or hundreds of drivers in a given city, platforms such as Uber needed thousands of drivers to achieve the network effects that made their business model viable.[3] To have a ride available within minutes anywhere in the city required density that only massive scale could provide. Yet this very scale created unprecedented management challenges. How could a company ensure consistent service quality when drivers might work for multiple platforms simultaneously? How could safety standards be maintained when the workforce turned over constantly and driver onboarding needed to happen at breakneck speed?

These challenges were not unique to Uber. Across the emerging gig economy landscape, platforms grappled with similar tensions between scale and quality. Airbnb faced the challenge of ensuring property standards and guest safety across millions of unique listings, each with different hosts and varying levels of professionalism.[4] DoorDash and Instacart needed to guarantee food safety and accurate delivery when their workforces consisted of independent contractors with minimal oversight.[5] TaskRabbit had to maintain service quality across an impossibly diverse array of tasks, from furniture assembly to home repairs, performed by workers with varying skill levels and no traditional employment screening.[6]

The fundamental question underlying all these platforms was whether private companies could effectively manage these quality and safety concerns through technological solutions and reputation systems, or whether official regulatory processes and government oversight bodies would prove necessary. The gig economy model depended on answering this question in favor of private governance. If government regulators intervened, the cost structures and operational flexibility that made these platforms viable could collapse.

6.1.2 *The Trust Barrier: Convincing the World of a New Transportation Paradigm*

For Uber specifically, the challenge extended beyond general platform management to something more visceral and immediate: trust. The company was not simply asking people to try a new service, it was asking them to fundamentally reconsider their relationship with personal safety and urban mobility. The proposition required convincing millions of people to reject decades of safety conditioning and regulatory assurance in favor of a model that seemed, on its face, dangerously casual about risk.

The trust barrier operated on multiple levels. Most fundamentally, Uber asked riders to get into cars with complete strangers. These were not professional taxi drivers who had undergone background checks and licensing procedures mandated by official authorities, but ordinary individuals whose qualifications consisted of a personal vehicle, a smartphone, and whatever screening Uber itself chose to implement.[7] The psychological hurdle was substantial. Parents had spent generations warning children never to get into cars with strangers, but now a technology company was building a business model that required precisely this behavior.

The challenge worked in both directions. While riders needed to trust unknown drivers, those same drivers were being asked to operate in what traditional taxi regulation had always recognized as a vulnerable position. Drivers would invite strangers into their personal vehicles, often at night, sometimes in unfamiliar neighborhoods. They would have limited information about their passengers beyond a first name and a star rating. Their professional capacity, as not quite employees, not quite independent contractors, imbued additional ambiguity about what safety protocols and support systems they could rely upon.[8]

This trust challenge distinguished ridesharing from other gig economy platforms in crucial ways. When Airbnb asked people to stay in strangers' homes, at least the transaction happened in a fixed location with time for deliberation and investigation. When TaskRabbit connected people with service providers, the tasks typically occurred during daylight hours in public or semipublic contexts. But ridesharing required split-second decisions about personal safety in mobile, enclosed spaces. The vulnerability was immediate and intimate in ways that other platform transactions were not.

The magnitude of this trust barrier meant that safety failures would be catastrophic not just for individual users but for the entire business model. A single high-profile assault or serious safety incident could unravel consumer confidence and reinforce all the instinctive wariness that centuries of social conditioning had created around getting into vehicles with strangers. Uber's success depended not just on preventing safety incidents but on building and maintaining a public perception that its platform was as safe as, or even safer than, traditional alternatives.

6.1.3 *Regulatory Entrepreneurship: Changing the Law to Accommodate Innovation*

Beyond the challenges of scale and trust lay what legal scholars Elizabeth Pollman and Jordan Barry have termed "regulatory entrepreneurship," that is, the practice of building business models that explicitly depend on changing existing legal frameworks.[9] Unlike emerging technologies such as artificial intelligence or climate technology, which often develop in spaces where regulation has not yet been established, ridesharing entered markets where transportation services were already heavily regulated. In virtually every major jurisdiction, taxi services operated under comprehensive regulatory regimes mandating licensing procedures, insurance standards, fare structures, and accountability mechanisms designed to ensure driver competency, consumer protection, vehicle safety, and accessible transportation.[10]

Ridesharing platforms conflicted with these frameworks fundamentally. Their classification of drivers as independent contractors created ambiguity about responsibility for insurance and safety protocols.[11] Dynamic pricing clashed with regulated fare structures. Digital ratings replaced formal complaint mechanisms. The bypass of traditional licensing requirements appeared to regulators as either innovative efficiency or dangerous deregulation, depending on perspective.[12] This meant the rideshare business model required political as well as commercial success. Companies needed to demonstrate that their platforms could deliver the public goods that existing regulation aimed to protect at least as effectively as traditional taxi regulation.

The political dimension became particularly intense around worker classification.[13] In California and numerous other jurisdictions, fierce debates erupted over whether platform workers should be classified as employees or independent contractors.[14] These were not merely technical legal distinctions; they went to the heart of what the gig economy represented. Rideshare companies poured millions into ballot initiatives and lobbying campaigns, with stakes extending far beyond ridesharing itself.[15] Success would establish a template for how gig economy companies could operate across industries. Failure would collapse the entire business model, taking billions in investment and millions of gig economy jobs with it.

Critically, success in this regulatory entrepreneurship required public support. Rideshare companies needed consumers to actively prefer their services over traditional taxis on fundamental attributes such as safety and reliability, not just price or convenience. Without demonstrated public enthusiasm for the platform model, legislators and regulators would face little pressure to accommodate it. This meant that entering regulatory battles without first solving core safety issues could have been suicidal for the business model. Companies arguing that their platforms obviated the need for traditional safety regulation while simultaneously facing high-profile safety failures would find no sympathetic audience among policymakers or the public.

The combined challenge of platform scalability, trust in a new transportation paradigm, and regulatory transformation created an environment where safety was not simply a matter of ethical business practice or risk management. It became existential to the entire enterprise. Uber had to prove simultaneously that gig economy platforms could maintain quality at an unprecedented scale, that strangers could safely transport each other through cities, and that private governance mechanisms could serve public interests traditionally protected by government regulation. Failure on any of these fronts threatened not just one company's profitability but the viability of a new economic model that was rapidly expanding across industries and continents.

6.2 HETEROGENEITY OF PREFERENCES

The challenge of balancing rapid growth with responsible safety practices divided stakeholders not merely along predictable lines of workers versus management or consumers versus shareholders, but cut through the heart of Uber's own organizational culture and investor base.[16] The tension between "move fast and break things," the motto popularized by Mark Zuckerberg at Facebook that became emblematic of Silicon Valley startup culture, and "safety first" philosophies created deep organizational divides. Yet the preferences of different stakeholder groups reflected not merely a disagreement about the right path forward, but fundamentally different, albeit equally viable, business models. The tension was not between reckless immaturity and responsible stewardship, but between two coherent strategic approaches, each with its own logic, risks, and potential for success at any stage of company development. The crisis that engulfed Uber provides a rare opportunity to observe both paradigms operating within a single company at different moments, revealing the tradeoffs inherent in each approach.

6.2.1 *The Growth Imperative: The Kalanick Era and Venture Capital Logic*

The perspective favoring aggressive growth and rapid market penetration found its most forceful advocate in Travis Kalanick, Uber's cofounder and CEO through much of its explosive expansion phase.[17] Kalanick's leadership embodied a particular Silicon Valley philosophy that treated regulatory compliance, safety protocols, and deliberative decision-making as obstacles to be overcome rather than foundations to be carefully constructed.[18] Yet this approach represented a coherent business model with its own rationale rather than simply an immature phase that companies inevitably outgrow.

The logic underlying this approach was straightforward and, within the venture capital ecosystem, entirely defensible. Uber operated in a classic network effects business where value increased exponentially with scale.[19] A city with only a few dozen Uber drivers offered poor service due to long wait times, unreliable availability, or limited coverage area. But a city with thousands of drivers created a transformative experience where rides materialized within minutes anywhere in the urban core. This dynamic created a powerful first mover advantage: the first platform to achieve critical mass in a market would be extremely difficult to dislodge, as both drivers and riders would gravitate toward the platform with the most liquidity.

From this strategic perspective, quick growth was not merely desirable but potentially decisive for competitive positioning. Uber faced an established taxi industry with decades of regulated privileges, well-funded competitors such as Lyft in the United States, and even more aggressive rivals in international markets.[20] The company that established dominance first would likely maintain it indefinitely. Any delay from regulatory negotiations, safety protocol development, or careful deliberation about operational practices risked ceding markets to competitors who might prove either faster to scale or less concerned with such considerations.

The venture capital investors backing Uber strongly reinforced this perspective.[21] The VC model depends on a portfolio approach where a small number of massive successes compensate for numerous failures. Investors primarily seek exponential expansion that can turn millions in investment into billions in returns. This creates powerful incentives for aggressive risk-taking and rapid scaling. A company that grows cautiously might never achieve the transformative success that justifies venture investment, even if it avoids catastrophic failure.

From this perspective, corporate ordering, even if driven by the company itself, represented costly impediments. Developing comprehensive safety protocols required extensive deliberation, consultation with experts, testing and refinement, and careful tailoring of solutions to different contexts and jurisdictions.[22] All of this consumed time, attention, and resources that could otherwise be devoted to market expansion. The preferred strategy was clear: establish market dominance first, then use that position to address problems that emerged.

The Kalanick era exemplified this philosophy in practice. Uber's expansion was characterized by aggressive moves into new markets without seeking regulatory approval, confrontational relationships with local governments, and a corporate culture that celebrated rule-breaking and competitive ruthlessness. The company's internal culture, as later investigations would reveal, reflected these priorities in troubling ways, with reports of sexual harassment, discrimination, and a toxic work environment that showed little care for employee welfare and focused on growth metrics.

Importantly, this growth-first approach was not inevitable even for early stage rideshare companies. Lyft, operating in the same markets and facing similar competitive dynamics, made different strategic choices along the growth-safety spectrum. While also prioritizing expansion, Lyft cultivated a reputation for being more cooperative with regulators and more attentive to driver relations.[23] This suggests that the growth-first paradigm represented a strategic choice rather than a developmental necessity, one paradigm among viable alternatives, each with distinct tradeoffs.

6.2.2 *The Crisis: When Growth Collides with Reality*

The limitations of the growth-first approach became starkly apparent through a series of crises that revealed the costs inherent in prioritizing speed over systematic safeguards. The company became embroiled in controversy after controversy: allegations of sexual harassment within its corporate offices, reports of drivers assaulting passengers, accusations of aggressive surveillance of competitors, and revelations about a corporate culture that prioritized growth over virtually all other considerations.[24]

The safety crisis reached a critical inflection point when the scale of the problem became undeniable and quantifiable. In a terrifying leak to Buzzfeed, a screenshot suggested 5,000 messages concerning rape had reached Uber's customer support.[25] In India, a male Uber driver was arrested because of claims he had raped a female passenger.[26] These started looking less than isolated incidents and more like a pattern suggesting systematic failures in screening, monitoring, and responding to safety concerns. The sheer volume of incidents reflected a company that had scaled to millions of rides without developing proportionate safety infrastructure.

The paradox was that this crisis emerged precisely because of Uber's success in executing its chosen strategy. The company would not have accumulated hundreds of safety complaints if it had not become massively popular and conducted millions of rides. The problem was, in some sense, an outgrowth of the growth-at-all-costs strategy rather than a contradiction of it. Uber had achieved the scale and market dominance that its strategy sought; now it faced the consequences of having built that empire without adequate safeguards.

This moment of reckoning did not invalidate the growth-first model so much as quantify its costs in ways that changed the calculus for shareholders and stakeholders evaluating tradeoffs. What had been abstract concerns about potential safety issues became concrete data about actual harms. The crisis made it possible to weigh the benefits of rapid market capture against the demonstrable costs in safety incidents, legal liability, regulatory backlash, and reputational damage. For investors, executives, and employees who had supported aggressive growth, the question shifted from whether growth should be the priority to whether the achieved dominance justified the realized costs.[27]

Critically, this quantification of costs created conditions where a different strategic approach became viable, though not inevitable. The crisis opened space for transformation, but other rideshare companies navigated similar growth-safety tradeoffs without experiencing comparable public reckonings. Lyft and international competitors faced their own safety challenges but made different strategic choices about resource allocation and risk management at various points in their development.[28] Airbnb, operating in the broader gig economy space, implemented safety measures more proactively even as it pursued aggressive expansion.[29] These examples suggest that the crisis was not the only pathway to incorporating greater safety emphasis, but it was one particularly dramatic moment that made visible the tradeoffs that all platform companies confronted.

6.2.3 *The IPO Imperative: Shifting Incentives and Shareholder Composition*

The timing of Uber's strategic recalculation was not coincidental, though neither was it strictly determined by external forces. As the company moved toward its initial public offering, the composition and preferences of its shareholder base underwent fundamental transformation, creating new incentives that favored a different position on the growth-safety spectrum. The investors who had funded Uber through its growth phase, mostly venture capital firms comfortable with high risk and extended time horizons, wanted liquidity.[30] An IPO would allow them to realize returns on investments made years earlier. But going public meant opening ownership to a radically different type of investor.

Public market investors, on average, are considerably more risk-averse than venture capitalists.[31] They include pension funds, mutual funds, and individual investors seeking steady returns rather than moonshot bets.[32] These investors care deeply about reputation, regulatory risk, and potential liabilities.[33] A company mired in sexual assault scandals and regulatory battles presents the kind of risk profile that depresses valuations and drives investors away.

This shift in investor preferences created powerful incentives for Uber to adjust its position on the growth-safety tradeoff. The company needed to demonstrate that it had matured from a scrappy startup willing to operate in legal gray areas into a responsible corporate citizen capable of managing complex operations at a global scale. Safety problems that venture capital investors might have tolerated as growing pains became red flags that threatened to undermine the IPO.

Beyond investor composition, going public subjected Uber to enhanced scrutiny from securities regulators, media, and public interest groups. Private companies can maintain some opacity about their operations; public companies face continuous disclosure requirements and constant attention from analysts and journalists. Any safety incident at Uber would now be scrutinized not just as a customer service failure but as a potential securities issue affecting shareholder value. This dynamic revealed how market mechanisms and stakeholder preferences could drive corporate behavior even in the absence of direct government regulation. Uber did not improve its safety practices primarily because regulators forced its hand, but because the strategic calculus changed as the company's stakeholder base evolved. Different investors weighted growth and safety considerations differently, altering the balance of priorities within the organization.

The resolution of these competing preferences came not through deliberative consensus-building but through crisis and changing incentives prompting strategic recalibration. The departure of Kalanick and the arrival of new CEO Dara Khosrowshahi in 2017 marked a clear strategic pivot.[34] Khosrowshahi, previously the CEO of Expedia, brought a more measured, governance-focused approach that explicitly prioritized safety improvements and regulatory cooperation. The new leadership implemented sweeping changes: enhanced background check procedures, real time ID verification for drivers, continuous criminal monitoring, the creation of a dedicated safety team, partnerships with law enforcement, and eventually the publication of safety transparency reports.[35] These changes represented a significant shift in how the company positioned itself on the growth-safety spectrum, allocating substantially more resources to safeguards.

Critically, this transformation did not represent a wholesale rejection of the growth imperative so much as a recalibration of tradeoffs. The company continued to expand aggressively into new markets and invest heavily in technological development, but it simultaneously built more robust safety infrastructure.[36] The reformed Uber continued to pursue market dominance and achieved a successful IPO in 2019, demonstrating that these paradigms were not mutually exclusive absolutes but rather positions along a continuum.[37] The shift reflected a strategic choice to position the company differently, emphasizing safety more heavily while still prioritizing growth.

6.2.4 *How Unique Is the Uber Example? Heterogeneity of Preferences or Progression from Startup to Public Company?*

The dramatic arc of Uber's transformation, from aggressive growth under Kalanick through crisis and leadership upheaval to strategic recalibration under Khosrowshahi, might suggest that such changes require catastrophic failure and external pressure. The timing appears telling, as the shift came only after hundreds of safety complaints, a CEO's forced resignation, intense regulatory battles, and the looming demands of a public offering. This raises a crucial question: is Uber's story unique, or does it reveal something more general about how companies navigate growth-safety tradeoffs? Absent crisis and impending offerings, how likely are companies to install an internal safety-oriented governance system that embraces rulemaking, executive implementation, and monitoring?

A quick look at other gig economy companies suggests that growth-first and safety-conscious approaches represent genuine strategic alternatives available at any stage of company development, not a required sequence from one to the other. Consider Lyft, which cultivated a reputation for greater cooperation with regulators and more attention to driver relations from earlier in its lifecycle. As a smaller competitor facing the same network effects dynamics and venture capital pressures as Uber, Lyft theoretically had even stronger incentives to prioritize pure growth over all other considerations.[38] Yet the company made different strategic choices, positioning itself as the more responsible alternative to Uber.[39] This approach was viable even for a less dominant player, suggesting that emphasizing safety did not require market dominance or a crisis to justify it.

Airbnb's trajectory offers another instructive contrast. The company implemented systematic safety measures relatively proactively, including a 24/7 safety line, property verification systems, and host screening procedures, while still pursuing aggressive global expansion.[40] Though Airbnb faced its own safety incidents and cultural challenges, it did not experience a single catalyzing crisis comparable to Uber's 2017 reckoning.[41] Instead, it built its governance infrastructure incrementally alongside its growth, demonstrating that companies could allocate substantial resources to safeguards while maintaining expansion trajectories.

These examples reveal that multiple positions along the growth-safety spectrum can sustain viable businesses at various stages of development. Companies face similar tradeoffs but weight them differently based on leadership philosophy, stakeholder composition, competitive positioning, and strategic priorities. Some emphasize safety more heavily from the outset; others shift their emphasis after experiencing problems; still others maintain growth-focused approaches throughout. The variation suggests these are strategic choices rather than developmental inevitabilities.

This observation reframes the central regulatory question. Rather than asking "why not regulate" in the abstract, this book develops tools for assessing the quality of private governance efforts. The goal is not to prescribe where precisely the line between growth and safety should be drawn, as that will vary by context, technology, stage of development, and social values. Instead, the book explores whether and when private governance efforts should be recognized as genuine attempts to serve public interests.

When companies demonstrate substantive commitment to safety through transparent reporting, systematic improvements, responsive governance mechanisms, and meaningful accountability, regulatory frameworks might appropriately grant them greater flexibility in finding their own balance. Such recognition would reward companies that invest seriously in safety infrastructure while still pursuing growth, creating incentives for others to follow similar paths. The alternative, that is, rigid regulatory requirements that treat all companies as equally likely to prioritize growth over safety regardless of demonstrated commitment, may miss opportunities to reward and encourage genuine corporate stewardship while potentially stifling beneficial innovation.

6.3 UBER'S SAFETY REPORT: RULEMAKING, EXECUTIVE, AND MONITORING FUNCTIONS TESTED AGAINST REGULATORS

On December 5, 2019, Uber issued its first safety report, detailing sexual assault incidents, motor vehicle accidents, and fatalities related to Uber rides in the previous two years.[42] It was the first time any major technology company issued such a report, a particularly surprising move for a platform that relies on a plethora of gig workers operating largely without physical supervision while on rides. The report was, of course, a voluntary initiative, not required by any statute or rule in any of the jurisdictions that Uber spanned by 2018. Most companies would prefer to bury customers' negative experiences under a pile of positive reviews and exclamations of public satisfaction. But here was a company openly reporting data on some of the most painful experiences by its customers.

This section examines Uber's safety report as an example of the company's broader transformation precisely because it engages all three functions in the tripartite distinction of private governance: rulemaking, executive action, and monitoring. The safety report represents an executive decision, as it embodies the choice to publicly disclose safety data. But this disclosure could not occur in a vacuum. It required, as a precondition, the creation of substantive rules defining what counts as sexual misconduct, how to categorize incidents, and what procedures to follow when addressing reports. And critically, the entire edifice depends on monitoring and building the systems and processes necessary to ensure the accuracy and reliability of the information disclosed. The interplay among these three functions illuminates how private governance operates as an integrated system rather than as discrete, isolated acts.

But the incident is valuable for this book's argument because it also allows us to examine how regulatory agencies deal with a governance regime based on the tripartite distinction. When public regulators reviewed the report, they disapproved of the company's rulemaking and executive choices, especially the anonymity protections for incident reporting.[43] They would have preferred a different path, namely a fully eponymous referral to criminal authorities, and accused the company of harboring criminal action.[44] This objection threatened to undercut the entire effort, prompting the company to contest the regulators' stance in court.[45] The ensuing lawsuits and protracted legal battle necessitated a thorough investigation into the company's efforts and justifications, which led regulators to appreciate the company's rationale and change course.[46]

This episode reveals the example's dual value. First, it illuminates the comparative advantages and limitations of private versus public governance in addressing complex social problems, revealing both the potential of voluntary corporate action and the constraints that shape what companies will do absent regulatory mandates. Second, it demonstrates how a tripartite framework, grounded in thorough documentation, meaningful stakeholder engagement, and principled argumentation, can productively engage regulators who initially oppose a company's approach, potentially reshaping regulatory perspectives through the quality and comprehensiveness of the work itself.

6.3.1 *Motivation and Goals: The Executive Decision to Disclose*

Sexual assault concerns, either against riders or against drivers, were not new for Uber. After all, rideshare apps invite customers to enter a complete stranger's car, and controversies around sexual assault have continuously dogged the company. The decision to publicly disclose safety data represents a classic executive function, a strategic choice by company leadership about how to deploy organizational resources and shape public perception.

The path to this executive decision was paved with mounting pressure. In 2014, Uber introduced a "Safe Rider Fee" of about $1 to $2, claiming that proceeds would go toward background checks and other safety measures.[47] When this was revealed not to be the case, the company agreed to rename the fee, pay compensation to victims, and improve its background check process.[48] Uber's statement at the time may have retorted that "no form of transportation can ever be 100% safe," but many saw this behavior as betraying corporate cynicism.[49] Similarly, Uber settled a lawsuit by Los Angeles and San Francisco district attorneys, who claimed that Uber's vetting process for drivers was faulty, as it failed to uncover the criminal records for twenty-five drivers and did not use fingerprint-based background checks, considered the most comprehensive method.[50]

More worrisome was the pileup of individual lawsuits by victims, mostly women, who were assaulted by Uber drivers.[51] In most years, a number of riders would suffer headline-grabbing sexual violence crimes, such as rape, sexual assault, or kidnapping, and accuse the company of not doing enough to protect victims. Some claimed that Uber attempted to suppress information by forcing victims into arbitration.[52] In April 2018, CNN conducted a systematic analysis of police reports and court records, reporting that 103 Uber drivers and 18 Lyft drivers had been accused of sexually assaulting or abusing passengers over the previous four years.[53] The lawsuits mostly faulted the company's driver screening efforts and background checks, though they also demanded greater transparency about alleged sexual misconduct incidents involving drivers.

This mounting pressure created a critical juncture for Uber, and the stakes could not have been higher. The real threat was not simply legal liability or regulatory oversight, but the slow collapse of trust. If riders began to fear for their safety, if the brand became synonymous not with convenience but with risk, then no amount of venture capital or technological innovation could save the business model. Uber faced two starkly different paths forward. The first was to maintain the existing strategy and hope that the company could simply outrun the crisis and make it to the IPO before the next devastating story broke, before the public backlash reached critical mass.

The second option was to confront the problem head-on, to take control of the narrative before it consumed them entirely. Tony West, a former assistant attorney general in the Obama administration whom Dara Khosrowshahi had hired as general counsel, became the most forceful advocate for radical transparency.[54] He pushed for something unprecedented: the publication of a comprehensive safety report that would disclose all sexual assault and safety incidents in Uber rides to the extent they had been reported to the company.[55] The goal was not to spin or minimize, but to lay bare the reality of what was happening on the platform. Uber hoped, of course, that the data would reveal such incidents to be statistical rarities, thereby inspiring confidence rather than fear. But even if the numbers proved difficult or damaging, they would at minimum establish the true scope of the problem and transform speculation and anecdote into measurable reality.

Uber quickly realized that executing this disclosure would combine the exacting requirements of public company disclosures with the sensitivities around sexual harassment claims. Drafting public disclosures requires extensive due diligence, cross-checking sources of information, and debating language among professionals. It would be unlikely that statements in the safety report could be deemed material in a securities lawsuit, as the typical approach to materiality requires examining impact on annual turnover, which runs into billions of dollars. However, any misstatement or omission on such a sensitive issue would be hugely embarrassing for a company seeking to improve its reputation and would further boost concerns about overall safety.[56] Thus, the report would need to abide by the highest standards of accuracy, which meant that the executive decision to disclose necessitated robust rulemaking and monitoring infrastructure.

6.3.2 *Rulemaking as Precondition: Creating the Taxonomy of Sexual Violence*

The executive decision to issue a safety report could not be implemented without first establishing substantive rules. The company faced fundamental questions. What counts as sexual misconduct? How should incidents be categorized? What standards should govern data collection and classification? These are quintessential rulemaking challenges, because they demonstrate the need to create general, prospective standards that can be applied consistently across thousands of cases.

Going by conventional statutory definitions was challenging because they varied by jurisdiction, and no uniform standards had emerged in private industry either.[57] This variability highlighted a critical advantage of private governance: the ability to create tailored rules suited to a company's specific operational context.[58] Uber partnered with the National Sexual Violence Resource Center (NSVRC), a widely respected nonprofit, to create its own taxonomy of sexual violence.[59] Overall, Uber recruited help from over 200 gender-based experts, advocates, and NGOs such as the Rape, Abuse, & Incest National Network (RAINN), the National Alliance to End Sexual Violence, and the National Network to End Domestic Violence. The company relied on their guidance and opinion for many aspects of its reporting effort, as well as the handling of complaints internally.

In building their taxonomy, the company and its partners approached the issue in distinctly rule-like ways. The rulemaking process was bottom-up and iterative: reviewing customer reports, developing an initial categorization, and then implementing it in a pilot fashion across over 100,000 customer reports to make adjustments and modifications.[60] For example, they developed a detailed set of criteria for classifying attempts to touch nonsexual body parts, like a tap on the shoulder, which some people might not view as sexual while others might consider intrusive. They had to set scope boundaries for determining whether certain incidents were related to Uber, such as when they happened more than 48 hours after a trip had ended. These tasks represent an effort to provide a principled framework that can operate in a generalized and uniform manner across the board. The rules must be clear enough for drivers to understand, learn, and implement; for company monitors to utilize in internal reports; and for human resources staff to review and sanction violators.

This rulemaking function reveals both the flexibility and the limitations of private governance. Unlike legislative or administrative rulemaking, which must navigate public comment periods, political constraints, and procedural requirements, Uber could move quickly and adaptively. The pilot testing of the taxonomy on 100,000 reports allowed for rapid iteration, a responsiveness difficult to achieve in formal regulatory processes. The company could also draw on specialized expertise from advocacy organizations, incorporating their practical knowledge into rule design in ways that might be more cumbersome in a public regulatory context where formal advisory procedures and potential conflicts of interest might constrain such collaboration.

Seeking assistance from advocates that had spent their entire careers fighting corporations for failing to uproot sexual violence in the workplace was a move that could easily backfire. What if they provided recommendations that the company was unwilling to follow? The involvement of these organizations was itself a form of private governance innovation, as it enlisted civil society actors to provide legitimacy and expertise in lieu of government oversight. In the end, many of these organizations were happy to be named in the report and have their contributions described and recognized. NSVRC's CEO wrote a foreword, describing the report as "unprecedented."[61] Collaboration with these experts helped the company navigate a complicated set of concerns around victims, confidentiality, harm, and prevention. Moreover, the technocratic credentials of these experts added much-needed credibility to the report.

6.3.3 *Monitoring as Foundation: Ensuring Accuracy and Reliability*

The rulemaking function established what to count and how to categorize incidents, but the monitoring function determines whether the rules are actually applied correctly and whether the resulting data is trustworthy. Without robust monitoring, the executive decision to disclose would ring hollow, as the numbers would be meaningless if the underlying data collection and classification processes were unreliable.

The sheer magnitude of the company's business posed a unique challenge for data collection and screening. Nearly 4 million Uber trips happened every day in the US in 2018, amounting to more than 45 rides per second, according to the company.[62] The report describes at length the company's monitoring methodology, both for recording information from victims and for addressing the consequences of reported incidents. Sexual violence incidents are notoriously underreported, because victims may be reluctant to relive the experience of a traumatic event or may blame themselves in its aftermath.[63] If the company failed to appear credible to victims and convince them that reporting to Uber was a worthwhile exercise, the safety report would only be a pointless effort papering over an undetected problem.

To address this monitoring challenge, Uber created an Incident Response Team of about 300 professionals to address sexual violence reports.[64] This team performs a dual monitoring function: it both collects data about incidents and responds to them, creating a feedback loop between monitoring and executive action. The company also created a specialized audit team to review and categorize the data that went through hundreds of thousands of user reports (including non-safety ones). To ensure uniform application of the standards, the company created a curriculum and certification process for training its auditors and measures their classification accuracy. Moreover, the company established a process for resolving differences of opinion among auditors regarding classification.

This monitoring infrastructure illustrates how private governance must borrow legitimacy-enhancing techniques from legal and regulatory contexts. The methodology discussion in the report deploys concepts such as independent monitoring, reliance on outside auditors, confidentiality guarantees through anonymization, and other victim protection safeguards. It borrows concepts from compliance regimes, like the creation of hotlines, although not all actions covered constitute criminal violations. Monitoring mechanisms such as internal audit functions, quality control processes, documented procedures parallel what we might expect to find in a regulated industry. But here, they emerge voluntarily as part of the company's effort to make its disclosure credible.

The monitoring function also extends to enforcement against drivers who violate safety rules. Receiving a safety report against a driver triggers a review process within the company. The Incident Response Team must assess the severity of the report, investigate the circumstances of the incident, and determine an appropriate response. From Uber's perspective, deactivating a driver and banning their access to the platform is one of the most severe sanctions the company can impose. Functionally equivalent to getting fired, deactivation deprives drivers of opportunities that might be essential for earning their livelihood. In debates regarding drivers' status as employees or independent contractors, the company's power to deactivate their accounts for conduct violations was repeatedly mentioned as a factor illustrating drivers' dependence on the company.[65] For these reasons, the company put together a deactivation process that involves a high degree of formality and review to ensure that parties' interests are properly considered.

In cases where the safety shortfall is severe, or there is a pattern of risky conduct even if each single incident is not severe, the company can ban the driver from using the app to gain rides. With regard to sexual misconduct in particular, the company created teams of specialized agents who can better classify described actions, have access to information about the driver's history, and can explore whether continued infractions suggest further review and loss of access to the platform. According to the company, over 80,000 drivers have lost access to the platform due to its ongoing checks and safety deactivation process. Aware of the implications of this removal for many individuals, Uber has repeatedly stressed that no driver loses access without a human reviewing their file.[66]

This monitoring-enforcement nexus reveals a key distinction between private and public governance. In a regulatory regime, monitoring and enforcement are typically separated: agencies monitor compliance, and separate adjudicatory bodies impose sanctions. Uber, by contrast, integrates monitoring and enforcement within a single organizational structure. This integration can produce efficiency by leading to faster responses, better information flow, and more contextual judgment, but it also raises concerns about due process and accountability. Drivers facing deactivation have no independent tribunal to which they can appeal. The company is simultaneously investigator, prosecutor, and judge. While Uber has built procedural protections into its process (human review, specialized training, appeals mechanisms), these are self-imposed constraints that the company could, in theory, modify or discard.

6.3.4 *Reactions to Disclosure*

The key goal of any disclosure regime is to form the basis for an informed conversation around the issue in question by providing facts and analyzing trends and patterns that emerge as a result of management choices. Disclosure drafters, especially voluntary ones, have their own motivations in providing information. As discussed earlier, Uber's strategic objective was to dispel generalized concerns about safety while being open about weaknesses and committing to continuous improvement. But disclosure obtains its meaning because it reaches an audience that engages with its content, scrutinizes the information provided, and reacts to its content in ways that can influence the company's leadership. The power of disclosure lies in that it does not always elicit the response for which the company is hoping.

Uber's main argument, that safety incidents in its rides are extremely rare, is borne out by the data, as 99.9 percent of trips have no safety issues reported. For example, Uber reported 3,045 sexual violence incidents in 2018 out of over 1.3 billion trips in the US that year, corresponding to approximately one sexual violence incident in every 430,000 trips.[67] Uber admitted that this number was probably an underestimate, given that there are multiple barriers to reporting sexual violence incidents.[68] Still, this was an important baseline, particularly as Uber stated its intention to continue issuing the report biannually. Moreover, the report provided the company with the opportunity to highlight safety improvements it had made in the app, and others that it was in the process of making or considering.

But by choosing to issue the report, Uber also drew attention to the question of safety in rideshares, a high-stakes gamble that could easily backfire. The report required the company to essentially acknowledge that safety incidents, such as sexual assault, occur as a regular matter on its platform. The immediate reactions to the report were a double-edged sword.

The company received uniform praise for recognizing the centrality of safety in its services and for choosing to be transparent.[69] The company's willingness to issue the report and recognize that incidents do happen was seen as a departure from conventional corporate practices, which paper over complications and do not discuss problematic scenarios unless unavoidable. The fact that Uber's fatality rate was half the national average received significant recognition, with connections drawn to Uber's contribution to reducing the risks of drunk driving.[70] Widely acclaimed was Uber's partnership with advocacy experts whose credentials lent credibility to the report. Some press accounts saw the sexual violence taxonomy Uber created as a template for other companies faced with similar concerns.[71] In the long run, Uber's biggest competitor, Lyft, was pressured to follow its example, and thus the report evolved into an industry standard.[72] Moreover, Uber's open acknowledgement was seen as the first step toward generating accountability and taking actual steps to improve safety on rides.

But many saw the report as a somber reminder of how widespread sexual violence is in our culture, which brought up new criticisms and concerns. For some readers, the acknowledgment of the problems, and the complicated steps necessary to combat them, made the risks they face as they enter a stranger's car even more prevalent. The report also highlighted the so far unappreciated risk that drivers suffer, as 42 percent of reported safety incidents were submitted by drivers who were victims.[73] This raised questions about whether rideshare companies are doing everything they can to offer an equally safe workspace to everyone.

Some requested more information, for example, about safety incidents in other business lines like Uber Eats or other jurisdictions besides the US, the steps that Uber takes after receiving an incident report, or the most common reasons for suspension and deactivation from the platform.[74] Press coverage of the report also drew attention to lawsuits and other legal entanglements that often involve Uber, painting a different picture for the company. Uber is regularly named in sexual assault lawsuits and has continued to face criticisms about its driver authorization safeguards. In an infamous incident, it lost its license in London because it failed to detect 14,000 unauthorized drivers who had posed as authorized ones.[75]

The immediate sentiment in the market after the release of the report was negative. Telling the world that your company experienced 3,045 sexual assaults over the previous year sounded alarming, and the stock price dropped by nearly 3 percent, corresponding to an estimated loss of about $1.5 billion in capitalization.[76] Besides Lyft, other technology companies long criticized for secretive practices, such as Facebook, did not follow Uber's example in issuing a report.[77]

But Uber persevered. It issued a second report in 2022, covering 2019 and 2020, and a third one in 2024, covering 2021 and 2022.[78] The main takeaway remains that 99.9 percent of Uber trips occur with no safety incident. From the company's perspective, the commitment to provide ongoing information is testament to its ongoing efforts to improve its services but also raise awareness about these issues. The focus of the 2022 and 2024 reports is on execution and review rather than on rulemaking, since the company follows the taxonomy it had so heavily invested in creating for the purposes of its first report.

This shift from rulemaking to execution and monitoring illustrates the life cycle of corporate ordering initiatives. The initial report required intensive rulemaking to establish the taxonomy and monitoring infrastructure to collect reliable data. By the second report, those foundational elements were in place, and the emphasis shifted to demonstrating consistent application and continuous improvement. Uber mentions several improvements it made in terms of implementing its policies, such as creating emergency hotlines and providing easy access to 911. It also emphasizes an important review initiative, which consists of working together with Lyft and other platforms to share information about driver deactivation due to serious safety incidents.

This evolution toward industry collaboration represents a maturation of corporate ordering. What began as a unilateral disclosure by one company has evolved into a shared framework spanning multiple platforms. The information-sharing arrangement regarding deactivated drivers addresses a collective action problem: individual companies might hesitate to deactivate drivers who could simply move to competitors, undermining safety across the industry. By coordinating, platforms can make deactivation more effective while avoiding the competitive disadvantage of being the only company imposing strict standards. The persistence of the safety report suggests that, at least in this case, voluntary disclosure has achieved some durability.

6.4 UBER CLASHES WITH CPUC OVER ITS SAFETY REPORT

When companies undertake efforts to regulate their own conduct, concerns that their motivations might sabotage the desired outcome often end with a routine invocation: would government regulators have done a better job? In a clash between an all-knowing, public-spirited, well-resourced, and indefatigable regulator and a profit-maximizing, self-regarding, secretive, and lawyered-up corporation, our instincts are to side with the regulator. In practice, both regulators and companies rarely conform to these stereotypes, and the interactions between them are far more complex than this simple schematic allows.

Conventional wisdom suggests that when private self-regulatory efforts prove successful, regulators will respond in one of two ways: they will either stand back and allow the company's approach to continue voluntarily, or they will embrace the innovation and mandate it across the industry. But what happens when regulators fundamentally disagree with the company's self-regulatory choices? Such confrontations are rare, as company regulators typically prefer negotiation behind closed doors to public battles, making the clash between Uber and the California Public Utilities Commission all the more instructive.

This case demonstrates how the tripartite approach of principled rulemaking, rigorous implementation and disclosure, and enhanced monitoring, can yield dividends even in the most contentious circumstances. Uber's extensive rulemaking collaboration with victim advocacy groups like RAINN did not just help the company design better policies. It also equipped Uber to understand the complex policy tradeoffs at stake, to articulate them persuasively to skeptical regulators and judges, and ultimately to prevail through the strength of its reasoning rather than its lobbying power. Although regulators initially clashed with Uber over its refusal to disclose victim information, the company was eventually able to guide them away from their initial position precisely because of the alliances it had built with advocacy groups and the depth of expertise it had developed through meaningful collaboration. Watching this high-stakes regulatory confrontation play out in public filings and courtrooms, rather than in private negotiations, offers a rare privilege. We can observe the tripartite framework's persuasive power in action.

6.4.1 *The CPUC Early Demands*

The California Public Utilities Commission is an independent regulatory agency that oversees public utilities in the state of California. It is responsible for ensuring that customers receive safe, reliable, and affordable utility services, including electricity, natural gas, telecommunications, water, and transportation services.[79] Its independence is established on the principle that its commissioners, nominated by the Governor and confirmed by the state's Senate, can be removed only for cause.[80] It combines rulemaking authority, policy implementation powers, as well as an adjudicative function comprised of administrative law judges, who hear complaints by or against the CPUC. Since 2012, the CPUC has asserted its jurisdiction over rideshare companies, adopting regulations, investigating harassment claims and other complaints, and imposing certain reporting requirements.

The first publication of Uber's safety report alarmed the CPUC.[81] Here was a company that operated a key transportation service in California openly acknowledging a seemingly huge number of sexual violence incidents, as well as other safety incidents. Although the report did not specify how many incidents really concerned California riders and drivers, one could only assume, given California's size, that a significant proportion of them would have occurred within the CPUC's jurisdiction. Besides, Uber was headquartered in California.

On December 19, 2019, a mere fourteen days after the report's publication, a CPUC Administrative Law Judge issued an order demanding that Uber hand over to CPUC all records about the incidents that occurred in California in 2017, 2018, and 2019.[82] The CPUC demands covered the date, time, and place of each incident, a detailed description of the circumstances, each witness to each incident, and each person to whom this incident was reported. The CPUC also demanded information about the individuals who drafted the company's safety report, presumably because they had received complaints from victims but failed to refer them to the authorities. From CPUC's perspective, this was an essential step in investigating these incidents, identifying culprits, and imposing sanctions. Punishing perpetrators would be the most effective way of deterring these crimes in the future and protecting California riders.

6.4.2 *Uber's Response Highlights Differences between Corporate Ordering and Government Enforcement*

Stunned by finding itself at the target of another scandal involving sexual harassment, Uber management must have seen the move to issue the report as having massively backfired. Uber had issued the report to tell the world that it was safe and serious about fighting sexual harassment. Their stock price had tumbled at the news, unsure of what to make of all these disclosures when other companies simply said nothing. Uber faced a fundamental tension: it had voluntarily disclosed incident numbers to demonstrate transparency, yet now argued that further disclosure would harm victims. Critics might see this as having it both ways, taking credit for transparency while withholding the details that would enable accountability. And here was Uber's home state regulator appearing concerned about sexual harassment on the platform and accusing them of dealing with perpetrators secretly without releasing their names and allowing for retribution. This was quickly turning from a reputation-enhancing move into a liability.

Tony West, Uber's chief legal counsel, was convinced that handing over to the authorities whatever information the company possessed would nevertheless be the wrong move and would destroy the company's credibility in this area for good. Uber filed a motion for reconsideration before the entire commission, and an appeal against the ALJ's decision, requesting that the decision be reversed and explaining its logic.[83] The company organized its arguments around two main themes, which illuminate how company self-regulatory efforts can evolve in a different direction from regulation, both from a substantive perspective and from a procedural one.

Substantively, the company objected to disclosing victim information to the authorities because it believed it would be harmful for victims. Such disclosure, Uber explained, might further "violate people who have been already victimized … and risks re-traumatizing victims in various stages of healing." Moreover, the company was concerned that disclosure of personal information would put the victims in additional danger from their attackers. "One of the fundamental principles of managing sexual assault cases … is returning control and autonomy to victims." Uber had adopted an empathetic approach to report, of which anonymity was a keystone. Disclosing victims' information would force the company to betray its promise to them, destroy its credibility, and discourage future victims from turning to the company.

In defending the anonymity of these reports, Tony West was a convert himself. With his background as a prosecutor, he was initially in favor of the company collecting information about victims without any promise of confidentiality and disclosing that information if required.[84] But anonymized reporting was one of the key recommendations that emerged at the rulemaking process from the company's expert collaborators, the nonprofits, and advocacy groups that represented victims. In their view, anonymity would help victims overcome their resistance to revealing what had happened to them. Convinced by these arguments, forcefully made by many experts that had engaged with thousands of victims, Tony West ended up supporting the view that the reports should remain anonymous. He felt empowered to explain this rationale to the regulators too. His hope was that, once regulators were convinced that Uber was not withholding information maliciously, but rather acting to protect victims, they would see their interests as aligned with the company's and drop their demands.

The second theme in the company's response relates to the procedural safeguards Uber maintains in order to record sexual violence incidents and to initiate action against perpetrators. Uber stressed that, while it reaches out to all involved parties and witnesses, it does not seek to corroborate narrations or prove "beyond a reasonable doubt" that the victim suffered a sexual violence incident. If it demanded victim reports to meet that high standard, the company reasoned, it would often have to discard reports that, by virtue of the circumstances under which they happened, would fail. This would be ruinous, the company argued, as it would allow perpetrators to continue using the platform and commit further violations. Rather, in reporting these incidents, the company is largely relying on victims' version of the story. It gathers more information when it initiates a deactivation process, but it still does not aspire to reach the "beyond a reasonable doubt" standard. Based on the indications available, Uber's internal reviewers make an informed assessment of the risk the supposed perpetrator might represent for future rides.

The company's reasoning shows that, from its perspective, the motivation for enforcement is protecting its customers and its reputation, rather than exerting punishment for retribution or deterrence purposes. Since the sanctions a company can impose are not as burdensome as those imposed through our criminal or civil enforcement system, the process for doing so can also be more flexible. Corporate sanctions, like deactivation from Uber, do not purport to replace government penalties, but can be complementary to them or fulfill entirely different goals.

6.4.3 *Regulators Double Down with a $59 Million Fine and a Threat for Suspension*

Regulators remained unconvinced by Uber's arguments, seeing the company as simply unwilling to cooperate. On December 14, 2020, ALJ Mason imposed a $59 million fine on Uber, recommending that if it failed to provide the information within thirty days, it would have its operating license in California suspended.[85] Despite the fine, the ALJ did allow Uber to provide anonymized incident data as far as the victims are concerned, but not as regards the other requests by the CPUC. However, the ALJ described the company's efforts to avoid providing answers as "specious legal roadblocks" that seek to "frustrate the Commission's ability to gather information." News of the fine and the potential loss of Uber's license triggered another round of bad publicity for the company. The press saw it as "the latest development in Uber's long history of trouble with violence and assault between its drivers and passengers."[86] Another article mentioned that "Uber spent a year stonewalling state regulators' requests for additional information on sexual harassment or assault claims."[87]

6.4.4 *Uber Gets Support from Advocacy Groups, Regulators Reverse Course and Settle*

Uber immediately filed an appeal and entered into alternative dispute resolution.[88] The company seemed poised for compliance. The board was getting anxious, and the negative coverage was unrelenting. But Uber convinced RAINN, the advocacy group that was instrumental in setting the policies for the report, to file a Motion for Party Status with the CPUC, which the CPUC granted.[89] As one of the nation's largest anti-sexual violence organizations, RAINN's very open and public support for Uber's decision to not provide the data provided a heavyweight statement in favor of the company. RAINN reiterated that the decision to let the victims control the choice of when and to whom to talk about their experience was the correct policy call.[90] But it also criticized the decision to fine Uber, which essentially penalized the company for defending victims' rights against a CPUC order that seemed to disregard them. From RAINN's perspective, retraumatizing victims should be avoided at all costs. RAINN argued that the decision to impose a $59 million fine would deter other companies considering transparency efforts and urged CPUC to consult sexual violence prevention experts before shaping rules and policies on sexual assault.

Soon afterwards, CPUC settled the appeal in terms that grant Uber an unequivocal victory. The fine was reduced to a mere $150,000.[91] Uber agreed to pay an additional $9 million, of which $5 million went to the California Victim's Compensation Board to be used for victims of violence, and $4 million for efforts to address physical and sexual violence in the passenger carrier industry. Uber also agreed to provide CPUC sexual harassment and assault information in an anonymized fashion and to create an opt-in process for survivors to make more information available to CPUC.

6.4.5 *Lessons and Limitations*

This outcome seems a clear win not only for Uber, but also for the regulators and for all other parties involved. Uber managed to defend its reputation, make discernible progress toward addressing sexual violence in rides, and provide accurate information to consumers. It even managed to prevail in a high-stakes conflict with regulators, employing a rather optimistic strategy of striving to change regulators' mind. To do so, Uber had to convince regulators that its denial to comply with their requests was not mere posturing, as they believed when they decided to impose the fine. Rather, it was a principled decision based on its extensive research on sexual violence and the advice from experienced victim support organizations. Regulators, on the other hand, ended up with an improved understanding of the sensitivities around sexual violence reporting and prevention, which they had not appreciated in full. Once they recognized that anonymity was an essential condition for the success of the reporting effort, they entered negotiations with Uber only to find that the company was more cooperative than they had anticipated. The option to report to them directly through the app represents a facilitation they may not have conceived or sought to implement on their own. Striking the right balance on sexual violence prevention is, primarily, a win for victims and for our society overall, given the prevalence of these crimes around us.

How did Uber achieve this remarkable reversal? The answer lies in the groundwork it had laid through the tripartite process. By working closely with victim advocacy organizations from the outset, Uber accomplished two critical objectives. First, it developed policies that genuinely reflected best practices in the field, informed by organizations with decades of expertise and credibility. Second, it created allies who could vouch for the company's motivations and methods when regulators grew suspicious. These were independent bodies with established track records of mobilization against sexual violence, not corporate consultants or hired advocates. Their intervention helped Uber shed the presumption of self-regarding, profit-maximizing behavior that so often taints corporate self-regulatory efforts in the public domain.

The regulators, for their part, ended up with an improved understanding of the sensitivities around sexual violence reporting and prevention, including nuances they had not fully appreciated when they issued their initial demands. Once they recognized that anonymity was an essential condition for effective reporting, they entered negotiations only to find that Uber was more cooperative than they had anticipated. The company's willingness to share anonymized data and create an opt-in process represented a solution that balanced the regulator's need for oversight with victims' need for control.

The significance of this episode extends far beyond Uber's specific predicament, as it illustrates a crucial insight about effective corporate ordering. When companies engage meaningfully with expert stakeholders before regulators intervene, they develop better policies, as well as the credibility and expertise necessary to defend those policies against regulatory challenge. The tripartite approach transforms what might otherwise be dismissed as corporate foot-dragging into a principled defense of victim-centered policies, backed by the very organizations that regulators themselves should be consulting. In this case, the normally opaque world of regulatory negotiation played out in public filings, administrative proceedings, and court documents, offering a rare glimpse of how corporate ordering can equip companies to engage productively even with hostile regulators. Striking the right balance on sexual violence prevention is, ultimately, a win for victims and for society overall. But this case demonstrates that reaching that balance may require companies to stand firm against regulators' initial instincts, provided they have done the hard work beforehand.

The Uber-CPUC confrontation offers valuable lessons, yet its broader applicability deserves scrutiny. This case benefited from an unusually fortunate alignment: the victim advocacy organizations' recommendations, albeit counterintuitive at first, posed no fundamental conflict with Uber's business model. None of the expert-endorsed policies, such as anonymous reporting, victim autonomy, and deactivating users based on reasonable risk assessments, threatened Uber's core operations or profitability. Indeed, they arguably enhanced the company's commercial interests by encouraging reporting and bolstering its reputation.

To be sure, the tripartite framework is designed precisely to help companies explore potential alignments between business imperatives and stakeholder concerns, and to invent compromise solutions that might not be obvious at the outset. Through sustained dialogue with expert organizations and other stakeholders, companies can discover ways to reconcile seemingly competing demands or to restructure operations in ways that serve multiple goals. The framework's collaborative process creates space for creative problem-solving that neither companies nor advocates might achieve independently.

Yet profitability constraints ultimately impose limits on this exploration. When expert recommendations would require companies to sacrifice substantial revenues, abandon core features of their business model, or forgo significant competitive advantages, compromise solutions may not emerge, no matter how earnest the collaboration. Uber's success stemmed not only from its thorough rulemaking process, but also from the fortunate circumstance that following expert counsel exacted no significant business cost. In contexts where stakeholder interests and business profitability remain stubbornly at odds despite collaborative exploration, even the most carefully constructed tripartite process may reach an impasse.

6.5 HOW THREE POST-IT NOTES BECAME LAW: LYFT'S INSURANCE INNOVATION

In the early 2010s, the transportation revolution was still taking shape. Uber focused on connecting users with licensed black car services.[92] Lyft relied on voluntary donations rather than fares, positioning rides as friendly carpooling between community members. Neither company had yet settled on the business model that would transform urban mobility, but both recognized they were racing toward a fundamental restructuring of how people moved through cities.

Standing between these early experiments and that revolutionary potential was a seemingly mundane obstacle: insurance. Personal auto policies contained livery exclusions that denied coverage for commercial passenger transportation.[93] Rideshare drivers operated in regulatory gray zones, using personal vehicles for what would soon become obvious commercial purposes. Without a solution, the revolution would stall before it began. No drivers would accept uncompensated risk, no regulators would permit uninsured services, and no passengers would trust platforms that could not guarantee protection.

Resolving this insurance gap constituted a classic rulemaking problem in the taxonomy developed in Chapter 3. Any solution would need to establish standards of general and uniform applicability affecting thousands of drivers simultaneously, while navigating competing interests of platforms, drivers, passengers, insurers, and regulators. Yet Lyft and Uber, while facing similar market pressures, pursued markedly different paths, revealing how corporate rulemaking capabilities extend beyond mere incentive alignment. Lyft developed comprehensive solutions earlier by leveraging superior access to operational information and making systematic institutional investments in governance infrastructure. The company engaged specialized expertise, constructed novel analytical frameworks from granular operational data, and built stakeholder coalitions through deliberative processes that generated both technical solutions and political legitimacy. What began as three Post-It notes on an insurance broker's wall became the statutory framework adopted by jurisdictions nationwide, illustrating how organizational capabilities, leadership judgment, and institutional preparedness determine whether companies translate business challenges into effective governance solutions.

6.5.1 *Heterogeneous Preferences and the Insurance Challenge*

The emergence of ridesharing platforms in the early 2010s created a fundamental regulatory challenge: these services operated vehicles for commercial purposes under insurance arrangements designed exclusively for personal use.[94] Most personal insurance contracts contain a "livery exclusion" clause that denies coverage in those instances. This mismatch between business model and legal framework presented an existential threat to the industry's viability. Without adequate insurance coverage, platforms could neither attract drivers willing to assume uncompensated risk nor satisfy regulators concerned with public safety. Yet the industry's leading firms approached this challenge with characteristically different strategic orientations.

Lyft's leadership recognized that insurance would constitute the initial and most critical regulatory hurdle. The company's early operations relied on a donation-based model, which theoretically situated its activities within the scope of personal automobile insurance.[95] Drivers transported passengers but accepted only voluntary contributions, creating ambiguity about whether such arrangements constituted commercial activity subject to livery exclusions in personal insurance policies. While this gray area provided temporary operational flexibility, Lyft's executives understood that regulators and insurers would inevitably scrutinize this arrangement.

Uber, by contrast, faced no immediate insurance crisis during its initial phase of operations. The company exclusively contracted with licensed Transportation Charter-Party (TCP) carriers whose drivers maintained commercial insurance as a condition of their operating permits.[96] From Uber's institutional perspective, the insurance question appeared resolved within existing regulatory frameworks. This position aligned with the company's broader regulatory strategy, which advocated for maintaining traditional black car licensing requirements rather than creating new regulatory categories for peer-to-peer ridesharing.

These divergent approaches reflected deeper philosophical differences regarding regulatory engagement. Lyft's community-oriented brand identity necessitated proactive attention to safety and trust. Uber's disruptive innovation model prioritized rapid scaling and treated regulatory accommodation as secondary to market expansion. During early regulatory proceedings, Uber defended the black-car license as the only established option and urged the California Public Utilities Commission to regulate transportation network companies (TNCs) under existing frameworks rather than develop novel approaches. But when Lyft decided to operate rides driven by private individuals in their own cars for a fee, essentially replicating Uber's model at a lower price scale, Uber realized that it had to quickly follow suit.

The theoretical nature of the insurance debate ended abruptly on New Year's Eve 2013, when a collision in San Francisco transformed abstract policy concerns into tangible tragedy.[97] Sophia Liu, a six-year-old girl, was fatally struck while crossing an intersection with her mother and brother. The driver, Syed Muzaffar, was an Uber contractor who had logged into the platform's driver application but had not accepted a ride request at the time of the accident. Uber's initial response emphasized legal boundaries of corporate responsibility: "We can confirm that this tragedy did not involve a vehicle or provider doing a trip on the Uber system."[98] This statement made explicit what insurance experts had been warning, confirming a coverage gap during periods when drivers were available for rides but not actively transporting passengers. Neither personal insurance policies (which excluded commercial activity) nor platform-provided coverage (which applied only during active trips) addressed this intermediate state of partial engagement with platform operations.

The incident catalyzed regulatory attention and public scrutiny. What had been an abstract question of insurance policy design became an urgent matter of public safety. Both companies would be compelled to address the coverage gap, but Lyft had already begun developing systematic solutions months earlier.

6.5.2 *Corporate Rulemaking: Post-It Notes to Policy*

Prior to the Sophia Liu incident, Kristin Sverchek, Lyft's Chief Legal Officer, had adopted a strategy of regulatory anticipation rather than reactive compliance.[99] This approach centered on developing robust internal standards that could serve as templates for eventual regulatory requirements, while simultaneously building coalitions of stakeholders who would support these solutions in public proceedings. Implementing this strategy required specialized expertise that existed outside traditional insurance industry channels.

Lyft engaged Kate Sampson, an insurance broker who specialized in constructing coverage arrangements for unprecedented risk scenarios.[100] Sampson had recently designed the Airbnb Host Guarantee program, convincing insurers to provide coverage for a use case they had never contemplated, that is, homeowners temporarily converting residences into commercial lodging.[101] Her success in that context demonstrated capacity to bridge the gap between novel business models and conservative insurance underwriting practices. Lyft's challenge presented parallel difficulties: persuading insurers to cover personal vehicle owners who sporadically engaged in commercial passenger transportation.

Sampson approached the problem through systematic legal and actuarial analysis.[102] Her initial inquiry examined whether existing personal automobile insurance could provide any baseline coverage for rideshare activities. The critical question concerned livery exclusions, that is, provisions in personal policies that typically excluded coverage when vehicles were used for commercial passenger transportation. Sampson's analysis identified several potential ambiguities in how these exclusions might apply to ridesharing. First, personal insurance policies had not been drafted with ridesharing in mind, creating interpretive uncertainty about whether informal passenger transportation fell within the scope of traditional livery exclusions. Second, established principles of insurance law required that ambiguous policy language be construed in favor of the insured party. Third, many policies contained exceptions for expense-sharing arrangements, such as carpooling, which bore superficial similarity to donation-based ridesharing.

This analysis suggested that personal insurance might provide limited coverage during actual rides, at least until insurance companies modified their policy language to explicitly address ridesharing. However, this potential baseline coverage still left substantial gaps. Sampson identified two scenarios that fell entirely outside existing insurance frameworks. The first involved drivers who had accepted ride requests and were en route to passenger pickup locations. These drivers were clearly engaged in commercial activity but not yet transporting passengers. The second involved drivers who had merely activated the rideshare application and made themselves available for ride requests, a state of commercial readiness that had no precedent in insurance or transportation regulation. Traditional taxi drivers carried commercial insurance that provided continuous coverage during all periods of duty.[103] However, rideshare drivers used personal vehicles and worked intermittently, making traditional commercial insurance categories economically infeasible and conceptually inappropriate.

To address these unprecedented scenarios, Sampson developed a taxonomic framework that disaggregated rideshare operations into distinct temporal periods, each presenting different risk profiles and insurance needs. She designated these categories using three Post-It notes affixed to her office wall:

Period 1: Application activated, driver available for requests
Period 2: Request accepted, driver en route to passenger
Period 3: Passenger in vehicle

These categories served as organizational frameworks for comprehensive data collection. Each period required distinct actuarial analysis: typical duration, accident frequency, claim severity, and comparable risk data from existing transportation sectors. Sampson leveraged her extensive professional networks within the insurance industry, providing actuaries and underwriters with unprecedented access to Lyft's operational data. She supplemented platform-specific information with comparable data from commercial driving operations and traditional taxi services, enabling insurers to construct risk models for scenarios that had no direct historical precedents.

The resulting analysis demonstrated that Period 3, when passengers occupied vehicles, presented the most substantial exposure but also the most conventional insurance scenario. Period 2 involved clear commercial activity but relatively brief temporal exposure. Period 1 presented the most novel challenge, as drivers engaged in a form of work-readiness that generated some accident risk but did not involve actual transportation services.

Sampson secured insurance capacity through multiple channels. She negotiated with Marsh & McLennan, a global insurance brokerage and risk management firm.[104] Lyft announced coverage of $1 million in liability protection for Periods 2 and 3, a figure three times the minimum coverage required for traditional taxis.[105] This substantial coverage level served dual purposes: it provided robust protection for drivers and passengers while signaling to regulators and the public that rideshare companies would exceed rather than merely meet existing transportation safety standards. Subsequently, Lyft extended contingent coverage to Period 1, creating a comprehensive insurance framework spanning all operational states.[106]

Sampson's framework also addressed a technical problem in insurance coordination. When multiple policies potentially cover a single incident, insurance companies often dispute primary responsibility, creating extended claim resolution processes that burden injury victims while insurers engage in coordination-of-benefits litigation. By establishing clear primary coverage during Periods 2 and 3, Lyft eliminated this source of ambiguity, ensuring that both drivers and injured third parties would have clear recourse in accident scenarios.

6.5.3 *From Corporate Rulemaking to State Regulation*

The Sophia Liu incident placed Uber under intense public pressure to adopt comparable insurance protections. In early 2014, Uber implemented contingent coverage for Period 1, effectively adopting the three-period framework that Lyft had pioneered.[107] The company that had advocated for maintaining traditional regulatory categories now embraced the innovative framework it had previously resisted. This competitive dynamic created de facto industry standardization prior to formal regulatory intervention.

The California Department of Insurance convened a public hearing in March 2014 specifically addressing insurance coverage for TNCs.[108] This proceeding provided a formal venue for stakeholders to present evidence and proposals regarding appropriate insurance requirements. The hearing featured testimony from TNC representatives, insurance industry stakeholders, consumer advocates, and other interested parties. The central focus concerned the coverage gap during Period 1, when drivers had activated their applications but had not yet accepted ride requests.

At these proceedings, Lyft presented its comprehensive three-period framework as an operational solution that addressed regulatory concerns while maintaining economic viability. The company arrived at the hearing with a fully implemented system supported by actuarial data, claims experience, and demonstrated stakeholder acceptance. Uber, by contrast, had only recently extended its coverage in response to the Sophia Liu incident and attendant public criticism. The contrast between Lyft's proactive development of systematic solutions and Uber's reactive adjustments was evident to regulators and other participants. The hearings also revealed the role of stakeholder mobilization in regulatory proceedings. Lyft had cultivated relationships with driver and passenger communities, who provided testimony supporting the company's approach. This coalition-building strategy complemented Lyft's technical insurance solutions with political support that legitimized the company's regulatory proposals.

In September 2014, California enacted Assembly Bill 2293, which established mandatory insurance requirements for TNCs operating within the state.[109] The legislation explicitly adopted the three-period framework that had emerged from private sector innovation, mandating specific coverage levels for each operational phase, which became known as Period 1, 2, and 3. For Period 1, TNCs were required to provide contingent liability coverage of at least $50,000 per injury, $100,000 per incident, and $30,000 for property damage, with an additional $200,000 in excess liability coverage. For Periods 2 and 3, platforms were required to maintain $1 million in primary commercial liability coverage. The statute also required $1 million in uninsured/underinsured motorist coverage and established requirements for contingent collision and comprehensive coverage for drivers' vehicles.

Colorado enacted comparable legislation in June 2014, becoming the first state to codify comprehensive rideshare insurance requirements.[110] Within two years, dozens of jurisdictions adopted similar frameworks, all structured around the three-period taxonomy that Sampson had developed.[111] Traditional insurance companies began offering "rideshare endorsements" consisting of supplemental coverage options that personal policyholders could purchase to address gaps during rideshare activity.[112]

Sampson later observed that the three Post-It notes she had affixed to her wall in 2012 as organizational placeholders for data collection efforts regarding novel insurance challenges had become embedded in statutory law across multiple jurisdictions. What originated as a broker's analytical framework became the foundational architecture for an entire industry's regulatory structure.

6.5.4 *Implications: Corporate Rulemaking and Regulatory Development*

The rideshare insurance case exemplifies corporate rulemaking as defined in Chapter 3's tripartite framework. Lyft's three-period insurance taxonomy exhibited the defining characteristics of rulemaking functions: it created standards of general and uniform applicability affecting thousands of drivers simultaneously, navigated heterogeneous stakeholder preferences across diverse constituencies, and established frameworks that ultimately shaped regulatory responses. The framework's visibility and aggregated impact made corporate choices focal points for stakeholder attention, positioning them as statements about industry values and predictions of regulatory direction. This case thus illustrates how corporations engage in institutional construction that functions as de facto social policy, precisely the phenomenon Chapter 3 identifies as central to understanding modern corporate influence.

The case illuminates a critical advantage corporations possess in rulemaking functions: superior access to operational information that reveals governance challenges before they become apparent to external observers. Lyft understood that insurance would be the central consideration for the public and regulators through direct experience with driver concerns and regulatory inquiries, not abstract analysis. Kate Sampson's identification of three distinct temporal periods emerged from detailed understanding of how drivers actually used the platform, what risks materialized during different operational phases, and how existing insurance categories failed to map onto rideshare reality. This granular operational knowledge enabled precise problem decomposition that would have been difficult for external regulators operating at greater distance from daily business realities.

Moreover, Sampson provided insurers with platform-specific data about driver behavior patterns, accident frequencies, and claim characteristics that simply did not exist in any external database. This data generation capacity allowed Lyft to move beyond speculation toward actuarially grounded solutions, demonstrating how corporate information systems can serve public functions by illuminating previously opaque operational domains. The case thus challenges simplistic accounts positioning corporations merely as self-interested advocates, revealing instead that companies can perform essential epistemic work by identifying governance gaps, analyzing their operational dimensions, and developing information infrastructure necessary for evidence-based solutions.

Equally significant was the framework's success in building public trust through deliberative processes incorporating stakeholder input without sacrificing managerial authority. Sampson's extensive consultation with insurance professionals, provision of data access, and willingness to engage comparative information demonstrated how corporate rulemaking can achieve procedural legitimacy. The company's mobilization of drivers and passengers to support its framework at regulatory hearings illustrated how stakeholder engagement generates political support facilitating regulatory acceptance.

6.5.5 *Beyond Incentives: The Insufficiency of Structural Alignment*

Perhaps most critically, the case demonstrates that properly aligned incentives are a necessary but insufficient condition for effective corporate governance of social challenges. Both Lyft and Uber faced identical market pressures regarding insurance, since both needed to attract drivers, satisfy passengers, address regulatory concerns, and manage liability exposure. Both possessed strong incentives to develop workable solutions. Yet the companies followed markedly different paths and timelines in addressing the insurance challenge, with Lyft developing a comprehensive framework earlier in its operational trajectory while Uber's systematic engagement came later, accelerating significantly after the Sophia Liu tragedy brought heightened public and regulatory attention.

This divergence cannot be explained through incentive analysis alone. The standard economic account of corporate behavior predicts that firms facing similar market conditions and possessing comparable information should converge on similar solutions. The rideshare insurance case reveals instead that organizational capabilities, leadership judgment, and deliberative processes mediate between incentives and outcomes in ways that fundamentally shape both the timing and character of corporate responses to governance challenges.

Lyft's earlier development of comprehensive insurance solutions stemmed from systematic institutional investments that extended beyond immediate market pressures. The company's engagement of Kate Sampson represented a deliberate commitment to specialized expertise. Sampson's opted for a methodical approach through identifying distinct operational periods, gathering comprehensive data, consulting industry experts, and providing transparent information to stakeholders. This approach reflected organizational choices about governance processes that required dedicated resources and sustained attention. The company's partnerships with global brokers demonstrated long-term institutional thinking and willingness to invest in governance infrastructure. Lyft's proactive framework development reflected not superior incentives but rather prior investments in institutional architecture capable of translating business challenges into systematic governance solutions.

The case thus reveals a fundamental insight about corporate governance that extends beyond the rideshare context: while properly structured incentives may be necessary for effective corporate behavior, they are insufficient without corresponding institutional capabilities. Companies require not just motivation to address social challenges, but also organizational structures, deliberative processes, expertise networks, and leadership judgment capable of recognizing problems early, developing comprehensive solutions, and implementing frameworks effectively. The presence of strong incentives does not automatically generate these capabilities, which must instead be deliberately constructed through sustained institutional investment.

This distinction between incentive alignment and institutional capacity has important implications for corporate governance theory and practice. It suggests that improving corporate responses to social challenges requires attention not merely to structuring appropriate incentives through regulation, shareholder pressure, or market competition, but also to developing organizational capabilities that allow companies to translate those incentives into effective action. The rideshare insurance case supports Chapter 3's emphasis on institutional architecture rather than incentive alignment as the central challenge of corporate governance, demonstrating how companies with similar motivations can achieve markedly different outcomes based on their institutional preparedness and governance capabilities.

7

A Corporate Framework for Sustainability

For more than three decades, climate change has divided the corporate world along lines that cannot be reduced to simple economic self-interest. Some companies have broken ranks with industry peers to develop measurement frameworks and commit to emissions reductions. Others have doubled down on fossil fuel expansion despite shareholder pressure and regulatory threats. Political support for climate action has waxed and waned. Recent years have brought regulatory retrenchment, with the Trump administration dismissing climate change as a priority[1] and the EU scaling back sustainability reporting requirements.[2] Yet despite this sustained contestation, a governance regime has taken hold. Standardized frameworks for measuring and disclosing corporate emissions now structure investment decisions, regulatory mandates, and corporate strategy across global markets.

Corporate sustainability became entangled with ESG politics and culture war battles,[3] but it represents something more fundamental and enduring than these recent controversies suggest. Corporate attention to climate began in the late 1980s, decades before ESG emerged as a political flashpoint. The recent backlash reflects political cycles and tactical overreach rather than resolution of the underlying challenge. If climate scientists are right about the physical risks and their business implications, climate governance will remain a corporate concern long after current debates over ESG investing have faded.[4] The measurement and disclosure frameworks examined in this chapter emerged from sustained engagement with climate as a distinct problem requiring specialized technical solutions.

The regime's persistence through political opposition reveals something important about how corporate ordering operates under contested conditions. Governance frameworks have gained authority not by eliminating disagreement but by surviving it through adaptation and coalition-building. When companies began defecting from organized climate denial in the late 1990s, they did not act alone. British Petroleum (BP) partnered with the World Resources Institute, an environmental nonprofit, to develop what would become the Greenhouse Gas Protocol.[5] This unlikely collaboration established a model of multi-stakeholder engagement that proved essential to the regime's development. The framework's creators deliberately structured the process to be open, transparent, and inclusive, inviting participation from corporations, environmental organizations, industry associations, and government agencies.[6] Corporate technical expertise combined with environmental credibility to produce standards that could claim both scientific rigor and practical applicability.

Private initiatives like the Carbon Disclosure Project transformed these voluntary efforts into market infrastructure by mobilizing institutional investors who demanded standardized emissions data from portfolio companies.[7] Different stakeholders brought different motivations to this coalition. Some companies saw competitive advantage in emerging clean technology markets. Others faced pressure from consumers and regulators in jurisdictions with stronger environmental expectations. Employees in talent-competitive industries demanded that their employers pursue purposeful work on climate. These diverse motivations created a coalition held together not by shared values but by overlapping interests in standardized measurement and disclosure. This stakeholder model gave the frameworks legitimacy that helped them survive subsequent political backlash. When regulatory mandates were scaled back, the underlying measurement infrastructure persisted because it served multiple constituencies with competing priorities.

The climate challenge presents a paradigmatic application for corporate ordering because it demands innovation across all three functions examined in Chapter 3. Companies must develop rulemaking frameworks for climate accountability, establishing scientifically sound definitions, protocols, and methodologies for emissions tracking. These choices about what constitutes an emission, which categories to track, and how to calculate carbon equivalencies directly affect reported outcomes and comparability across firms. Executive action transforms these frameworks into operational reality through consequential resource allocation decisions about which technologies to deploy, how many specialists to hire, and how to prioritize competing sustainability initiatives. Without sufficient investment in personnel, systems, and training, even the most rigorous frameworks remain theoretical. Monitoring mechanisms like public disclosure create the feedback loops necessary for accountability, enabling both internal tracking and external scrutiny from investors who increasingly evaluate companies based on climate performance.

Given the long tradition of environmental regulation, one might expect government bodies to take the lead in setting rules for corporate climate action. Yet at the industry-wide level, it was private companies that took the initiative in exploring what a response to deteriorating climate conditions would look like.[8] Translating abstract climate goals into concrete company-level action required new frameworks that governments alone were hardly equipped to create. Moving from national emissions targets to specific corporate inventories demanded technical expertise, industry knowledge, and practical testing that only companies themselves could provide. The chapter outlines how private companies worked with nonprofit partners to develop the first comprehensive standards for measuring and recording greenhouse gas emissions, the key driver for global warming and climate change. This extensive rulemaking effort culminated in the Greenhouse Gas Protocol, which has become the world's most widely adopted framework for corporate emissions measurement and reporting.[9] Nine out of ten Fortune 500 companies now utilize it in their disclosures. Regulators around the world, including the European Union and California, have endorsed it as the key classification system for emissions reporting.

This chapter examines corporate ordering across all three functions in the context of contested climate governance. It first documents the heterogeneity of corporate preferences that created both fierce opposition and strategic defection, enabling unlikely coalitions between companies and environmental organizations. The chapter then traces how these coalitions spearheaded industry-wide development of the GHG Protocol and examines its remarkable spread across national boundaries and corporate cultures despite sustained political resistance. Special attention falls on the Scope 3 Standard's evolution from voluntary exploratory tool to mandatory regulatory infrastructure and its current redesign under political pressure.[10] This trajectory illustrates how corporate ordering advances not by eliminating contestation but by developing mechanisms that accommodate ongoing disagreement about scope, responsibility, and ambition. The chapter concludes with a granular examination of how Salesforce translated broad international frameworks into operational reality, developing sophisticated internal mechanisms for measurement, supplier engagement, and public disclosure that extended its governance reach throughout its global value chain.[11]

Understanding these developments requires grasping how businesses navigate climate transition through governance approaches that span rulemaking, implementation and monitoring. More fundamentally, it requires recognizing that private initiative has shaped the evolving landscape of corporate climate action with implications extending far beyond individual companies to influence global standards, regulatory frameworks, and investment practices. This influence operates through coalition-building and stakeholder engagement as much as through corporate self-interest, creating governance mechanisms that survive political backlash by proving their value to multiple constituencies even as those constituencies continue fighting over the proper scope and ambition of climate action.

7.1 HETEROGENEITY OF PREFERENCES

Conventional wisdom holds that corporations are keen to oppose environmental regulations that threaten to increase operational costs and reduce profit margins. This economic logic appeared to explain corporate resistance to climate action in the late twentieth century, as mounting evidence of global warming prompted calls for emissions reductions that would fundamentally challenge existing business models. Yet this simple economic calculus fails to capture the complex dynamics that emerged as scientific consensus around climate change strengthened. Instead of the united front that this explanation predicts, managers and shareholders developed vastly different preferences toward climate change.

7.1.1 *Companies Break Rank: Private Push for Sustainability*

The establishment of the Intergovernmental Panel on Climate Change (IPCC) in 1988,[12] coupled with NASA climatologist James Hansen's watershed Congressional testimony confirming the reality of global warming,[13] created unprecedented pressure on the corporate world to respond. The business community's initial reaction was to organize resistance through the Global Climate Coalition (GCC), formed in 1989. This powerful lobbying group, representing approximately forty companies and industry associations, exemplified how corporations sought to protect their economic interests through coordinated opposition to climate science and policy. The coalition employed a sophisticated strategy of scientific skepticism, effectively transforming the scientific principle of uncertainty into a tool for policy paralysis. It challenged anthropogenic climate change, amplified minor uncertainties in climate models into supposed major doubts, and advocated for endless research as a substitute for immediate action. One of GCC's greater successes was blocking the Clinton administration from ratifying the 1997 Kyoto Protocol, describing it as a "terrible deal" for America.[14]

Yet within this seemingly unified corporate opposition, fissures had begun to appear by the mid 1990s. The most dramatic and consequential break from industrial solidarity came from BP, whose transformation would reshape the landscape of corporate climate politics.[15] BP's evolution from climate skeptic to environmental advocate represents a watershed moment in corporate environmental history, not only for its defection from the established orthodoxy of denial, but more importantly for taking the first steps toward a rigorous, quantitative framework for corporate climate action. By developing the first comprehensive system for measuring and managing corporate emissions, BP created a template that would transform how businesses approach climate change, moving them from rhetorical opposition to data-driven accountability. This methodological innovation provided a disciplined path forward, replacing vague promises with scientific targets and systematic measurement. Thus, it became the foundation for the modern system of emissions disclosure.[16]

BP's transformation was remarkable both in its scope and execution. Under the leadership of CEO John Browne, the company undertook a series of initiatives that would fundamentally alter its relationship with climate science and environmental policy. The catalyst for this transformation came in the mid 1990s, when BP developed an ambitious internal emissions trading system with the goal of reducing its emissions by 10 percent from 1990 levels by 2010. This initiative required the company to venture into uncharted territory and create a comprehensive system for measuring and reporting corporate emissions.[17] Within months of announcing the initiative, BP had developed a groundbreaking CO_2 reporting protocol and completed a thorough inventory of its greenhouse gas emissions for multiple benchmark years (1990, 1994, 1995, and 1996).[18] This pioneering effort to account for corporate-level carbon emissions would have a lasting impact on business practices and environmental discourse. Indeed, while the term "ecological footprint" had been coined by ecologist William Rees in the early 1990s,[19] it was BP that introduced and popularized the now-ubiquitous concept of the "carbon footprint."[20]

This technical innovation was accompanied by bold political moves, such as BP's resignation from the GCC in 1997 and Browne's landmark Stanford speech acknowledging the reality of climate change. In his speech, Browne skillfully reframed the climate debate away from the binary choice between business-as-usual and draconian regulation. Instead, he positioned BP as a pragmatic innovator, arguing that climate action need not require the economic disruption of an outright fossil fuel ban. By advocating for a collaborative approach between industry, government, and other stakeholders, Browne positioned BP to influence the emerging climate regime rather than resist it. This strategy was designed to appeal to business interests. By emphasizing the compatibility of climate action with profitability, and calling for collective action rather than unilateral sacrifice, Browne offered other corporations a viable alternative to the Global Climate Coalition's increasingly untenable position of denial. Through this careful positioning, BP managed to present itself as both environmentally responsible and commercially pragmatic, effectively pioneering a new model of corporate environmentalism that promised to preserve profitability while adapting to climate constraints.[21]

BP's strategic transformation provides a compelling framework for understanding the varied responses of other major corporations to climate change. General Motors, despite having conducted early climate research through its own laboratories in the late 1960s, followed a more tortuous path toward environmental responsibility. Unlike BP's decisive break with climate skepticism, GM maintained an ambivalent stance well into the late 1990s.[22] GM's eventual departure from the GCC in 2000 reflected not just this new reliance on environmental expertise, but also the realities of operating in a global marketplace.[23] With operations spanning fifty-three countries, GM faced pressure from consumers and regulators in Europe and Asia, where environmental concerns carried far greater weight than in the United States.[24] This global exposure pushed GM, like other multinational brands, to adapt to the highest common denominator of environmental standards rather than maintain the American industry's traditional resistance to climate action.

Monsanto's experience illustrates a different dimension of corporate environmental strategy. Under CEO Robert Shapiro's leadership, Monsanto approached sustainability not merely as an environmental challenge, but as an opportunity for technological innovation that became entangled with broader societal concerns.[25] While the company initially focused on the scientific merits of its sustainability initiatives, particularly in biotechnology, it soon encountered resistance that transcended purely environmental considerations. As Shapiro later acknowledged, the company had failed to appreciate that environmental sustainability could not be divorced from ethical, religious, cultural, and social concerns.[26] This hard-learned lesson about the interplay between environmental and societal responsibility came when Monsanto's genetically modified crops, despite their potential environmental benefits, sparked intense ethical and cultural debates. Shapiro's admission that "there is often a very fine line between scientific confidence on the one hand and corporate arrogance on the other" reveals how environmental initiatives must navigate a complex terrain where scientific solutions intersect with deeply held societal values.[27]

BP's strategic reinvention, GM's globally driven evolution and embrace of external expertise, and Monsanto's complex navigation of scientific and societal concerns illustrate the multifaceted challenges corporations face in addressing environmental issues. BP's success lay not merely in being first to break ranks with climate skeptics, but in seeking to create a practical framework for corporate climate action that other companies could emulate. By developing rigorous emissions measurement protocols and linking environmental responsibility to business opportunity, BP pioneered a template that helped transform corporate climate action from an adversarial stance to a management challenge. This legacy continues to influence how companies approach environmental challenges, suggesting that meaningful corporate responses to climate change require not just acknowledgment of the problem, but the development of systematic, measurable approaches to addressing it – all while remaining attuned to the complex interplay of global market pressures and societal expectations.

7.1.2 *American Oil Giants: Resisting Change Despite Investor Pressure*

In the global oil industry, the strategies adopted by major companies in response to climate change have diverged significantly since the 1990s, shaping their distinct trajectories to this day. While European energy giants initially embraced renewable transitions,[28] American counterparts like ExxonMobil have largely doubled down on their traditional focus on oil and natural gas, making only modest investments in innovative climate-oriented technologies.[29] This strategic divergence reveals a fundamental difference in how these companies envision their roles in a carbon-constrained future.

ExxonMobil, in particular, has maintained an unwavering commitment to fossil fuels despite mounting pressure from various stakeholders.[30] In 2021, the company faced a watershed moment when activist investor Engine No. 1, despite holding only a 0.02 percent stake, successfully waged a proxy battle to install three directors on ExxonMobil's board to push the energy giant to reduce its carbon footprint. This remarkable victory would not have been possible without the unprecedented support of some of Exxon's biggest institutional investors, including BlackRock,

Vanguard, and State Street, who voted against Exxon's leadership. The boardroom coup appeared to represent a turning point in how American oil companies would respond to climate concerns.

In response to this shareholder rebellion, ExxonMobil announced plans to enhance its focus on reducing greenhouse gas emissions and exploring low-carbon technologies.[31] However, the company's subsequent actions reveal a dramatically different trajectory that reaffirms its fundamental commitment to fossil fuel expansion. In October 2023, Exxon agreed to acquire West Texas fracking giant Pioneer Natural Resources for approximately $64.5 billion in stock, in one of the largest oil and gas acquisitions in recent years.[32] This mammoth deal would combine Pioneer's 856,000 acres in the Midland Basin with ExxonMobil's 570,000 net acres in the adjacent Delaware and Midland Basins, resulting in an estimated 16 billion barrels of oil equivalent resources in the Permian Basin. ExxonMobil's stated rationale emphasized transforming its upstream portfolio and creating "an industry-leading, high-quality, high-return undeveloped U.S. unconventional inventory position," clearly cementing its long-term commitment to fossil fuel extraction rather than transitioning toward renewable alternatives.

The ExxonMobil-Pioneer acquisition was merely the opening salvo in what would become a sweeping consolidation wave across the American oil sector, with each transaction further demonstrating these companies' determination to expand fossil fuel production. Just one week after ExxonMobil's announcement, Chevron revealed its own major acquisition, wagering about $53 billion in stock for Hess, which has a stake in a large Exxon-led oil project off the coast of Guyana.[33] This was followed by Occidental's acquisition of CrownRock[34] and a merger between Chesapeake Energy and Southwestern Energy.[35] Collectively, these transactions represent a massive recommitment to fossil fuel assets at precisely the moment when global climate imperatives suggest these companies should be diversifying away from carbon-intensive operations. The timing and magnitude of this merger wave serve as compelling evidence that American oil giants view their future prosperity as inextricably linked to expanded fossil fuel production, regardless of climate considerations or the energy transition occurring elsewhere in the global market.

Other forms of investor activism have similarly failed to substantially shift the American oil giants' trajectory. In August 2020, Storebrand Asset Management, Norway's largest private money manager, divested from ExxonMobil and Chevron under its new climate change policy, citing concerns with lobbying, coal, and oil sands.[36] Despite these growing pressures from major financial institutions, the American oil majors remain firmly committed to their traditional business models in stark contrast to their European counterparts. This persistent strategic divergence underscores the American oil industry's continued resistance to fundamentally reimagining its core business despite mounting environmental concerns, regulatory pressures, and shareholder activism. While paying lip service to climate initiatives, their capital allocation decisions tell the true story of companies betting their futures on the continued dominance of fossil fuels rather than leading the transition to a low-carbon economy.

7.1.3 *The Ebb and Flow of Company Strategies in a Volatile Energy Landscape*

The contrasting strategies of oil companies continue to play out in a dynamic market environment where fortunes rise and fall with geopolitical events, market disruptions, and shifting investor priorities. This constant ebb and flow reveals that neither approach has proven definitively superior, as companies on both sides of the strategic divide experience periods of triumph and difficulty.

The Russia-Ukraine war vividly illustrated this volatility, dramatically reshaping the energy landscape and delivering a windfall to American oil companies focused on fossil fuels. ExxonMobil and Chevron capitalized on surging oil prices, achieving record-breaking profits and returning more than $155 billion to shareholders through dividends and share repurchases since early 2022.[37] "In 2023, we returned more cash to shareholders and produced more oil and natural gas than any year in the company's history," Chevron Chief Executive Mike Wirth proudly declared.

Meanwhile, European companies that had previously led renewable energy transitions found their strategies less financially rewarding in the short term. BP's market valuation stands at less than half that of its American counterparts, creating intense pressure from shareholders dissatisfied with the company's renewable energy focus.[38] This pressure ultimately led to a dramatic strategic reversal, with BP CEO Murray Auchincloss announcing a hiring freeze and pause in new wind energy investments in mid 2024.[39] BP is now preparing to abandon its ambitious target to cut oil and gas production by 40 percent by 2030, a cornerstone of its climate strategy announced in 2020. Shell has similarly retreated from its renewable energy commitments, abandoning a key climate target for 2035 and weakening another goal for 2030.[40] Both companies are redirecting capital toward their core oil and gas business units, seemingly vindicating the more conservative approach maintained by American companies.

Yet this apparent American victory may prove temporary. The ExxonMobil-Pioneer deal has sparked significant debate about its implications for climate change and the energy transition.[41] Proponents argue that industry consolidation creates efficiency, with short-cycle shale investments offering flexibility to respond to demand changes. Critics counter that these massive investments in fossil fuel assets further complicate any potential pivot to low-carbon alternatives as the energy transition accelerates.

As the global energy landscape continues to evolve, competing business strategies will generate demand for adjustments at unprecedented scales. Companies pursuing fossil fuel optimization and those embracing renewable transformation will both face massive capital reallocation challenges. Regardless of strategic direction, energy firms must develop sophisticated institutional structures to effectively communicate with shareholders and stakeholders about their transition approaches. This requires robust frameworks for articulating strategic motivations, methodological choices, financial implications, resource allocation plans, and long-term impact assessments.

The energy transition will unfold unevenly, with market disruptions alternately favoring traditional and emerging energy models. Rather than a single "correct" path, success will likely come to organizations that build internal capabilities for strategic agility and transparent stakeholder engagement. More than any specific energy portfolio, these institutional competencies may ultimately determine which companies thrive through decades of volatile transformation ahead.

The sections below illustrate how energy companies have created robust institutional frameworks specifically designed to address climate challenges. By establishing sophisticated mechanisms for setting and tracking emissions metrics, as well as communicating progress transparently, these organizations have fundamentally reshaped the regulatory landscape. What began as internal corporate governance innovations has evolved into the foundation for industry-wide disclosure frameworks, standardizing how companies report their climate impacts and transition strategies. This institutional infrastructure serves as both an internal governance effort and a roadmap for regulatory innovation, as jurisdictions around the world are introducing mandatory requirements that embrace the private initiatives spearheaded by these companies.

7.2 FROM HETEROGENEOUS PREFERENCES TO PRIVATE GOVERNANCE: THE GHG PROTOCOL

Despite repeated calls to action by international organizations and world leaders, fighting climate change remained an abstract and somewhat chimeric objective until corporations got involved. While the 1990s saw major international agreements like the Kyoto Protocol establish emissions targets for developed nations, when it came to translating these high-level goals into specific regulatory targets, governments were at a loss. To make any progress, it would be necessary to move from abstract national targets to concrete company-level inventories of greenhouse gas emissions. With their emissions tracked and measured, companies would be able to understand their specific risks in a carbon-constrained economy while identifying opportunities for innovation and efficiency. However, this crucial step required new frameworks that governments alone were hardly equipped to create.

Corporations that sought to establish their climate change credentials have pioneered a strategy that uses disclosure as a tool for self-commitment, demonstrating year-over-year emissions reductions to stakeholders. However, this approach requires sophisticated governance across all three key functions. First, corporate rulemaking is essential to establish scientifically sound definitions, protocols, and methodologies for emissions tracking. Companies must develop consistent frameworks that determine what constitutes an emission, which categories to track, and how to calculate carbon equivalencies. These choices directly affect reported outcomes and comparability across firms. Second, executive action transforms these frameworks into operational reality through critical resource allocation decisions. Leaders must determine which technologies to deploy, how many specialists to hire, and how to prioritize competing sustainability initiatives. Without sufficient investment in personnel, systems, and training, even the most rigorous frameworks remain theoretical. Finally, monitoring mechanisms like public disclosure create the feedback loops necessary for accountability. By regularly publishing emissions data according to standardized protocols, companies enable both internal tracking and external scrutiny from investors, who increasingly demand climate performance improvements. This comprehensive approach to corporate ordering represents a significant institutional innovation, yet remains challenging due to the world's still-evolving carbon accounting systems and the inherent complexity of emissions measurement across global operations and supply chains.

It was in response to this critical need that BP, along with other companies, joined forces with the World Resources Institute (WRI), a nonprofit organization with no formal governmental authority.[42] Their collaboration would lead to the creation of the Greenhouse Gas Protocol (GHG Protocol), which has become the world's most widely adopted framework for measuring and reporting corporate emissions.[43] The Protocol has become widely recognized as the "gold standard" for corporate carbon reporting, with 9 out of 10 Fortune 500 companies utilizing in their disclosures. In addition, the Protocol has gained such widespread acceptance that regulators around the world, including the European Union and the state of California, as well as standard-setters like the ISSB, have endorsed it as the key classification system for emissions reporting.[44]

The paragraphs later discuss the GHG Protocol as an exemplary case of corporate governance that integrates all three critical functions. As a rulemaking initiative, the Protocol established scientifically rigorous frameworks for measuring carbon impacts, creating standardized definitions and methodologies that provided consistency across industries and regions.[45] Unlike frameworks developed by individual corporations, the GHG Protocol emerged from a collaborative process where companies such as BP, GM, and Monsanto partnered with the World Resources Institute to signal their shift from climate denial toward data-driven sustainability.[46] The rulemaking phase represented recognition that meaningful climate action required establishing measurement standards accepted by both scientific and business communities, creating a common language for evaluating environmental performance.

Executive action proved equally essential to the Protocol's development, as participating companies committed substantial resources toward implementation, making strategic decisions about testing methodologies, providing technical expertise, and adapting the framework to their operations. These companies deployed executives and technical specialists to "road-test" the emerging standards, contributed detailed feedback through formal review processes, and allocated capital toward developing sector-specific adaptations.[47] This phase transformed abstract principles into operational tools that businesses could feasibly implement, addressing practical challenges from data collection to verification methodologies. Without this executive commitment, the Protocol would have remained a theoretical construct rather than a functional system for carbon accounting.

The monitoring function completed this governance framework through standardized disclosure mechanisms that enabled both internal progress tracking and external accountability. By establishing clear reporting expectations and verification processes, the Protocol created the infrastructure for stakeholder oversight while giving companies tools to monitor their own performance. Though still evolving when pioneer corporations first joined the initiative, the Protocol's transparent, participatory development process allowed companies to actively shape the standards while simultaneously committing themselves to follow them. This integration of rulemaking, executive action, and monitoring created a governance structure that has fundamentally transformed how corporations approach climate change, moving from political opposition to systematic engagement with emissions management across global operations.

7.2.1 *Corporate Rulemaking: A New Measuring System for Emissions*

The GHG Protocol's origins demonstrate how private corporations drove rulemaking innovation in climate accounting. The breakthrough came from BP's pioneering initiative in the mid 1990s, when the company took the unprecedented step of developing its own internal emissions measurement system to support an innovative corporate emissions trading program. However, BP recognized that a single company's measurement system would have limited impact in addressing the broader climate challenge. They needed a partner with environmental expertise and credibility to help develop standards that could be widely adopted. This led them to the World Resources Institute (WRI), a nonprofit organization dedicated to environmental research and policy analysis, which was already establishing itself as a leader in environmental reporting through its work on the Global Reporting Initiative (GRI).[48] The partnership made strategic sense – BP brought practical business experience in emissions measurement, while WRI contributed its technical expertise in environmental standards and its reputation as a respected research organization. This collaboration between a major oil company and a leading environmental NGO marked a significant shift in how climate solutions could be developed, demonstrating that corporate and environmental interests could align to create practical tools for climate action.

The momentum grew as other major corporations recognized both the risks and opportunities in climate action. General Motors and Monsanto joined BP and WRI in a landmark initiative that would lay the foundation for the GHG Protocol. In October 1998, these organizations launched the "Safe Climate, Sound Business: An Action Agenda," which explicitly positioned business as a positive force in climate protection through policy development, technological innovation, and emissions reduction.[49] The agenda's first priority was telling. These corporate leaders committed to developing a joint protocol for measuring and reporting greenhouse gas emissions, marking the first formal step toward the GHG Protocol.

This was not merely a public relations exercise. As Steven W. Percy, chairman and CEO of BP America, emphasized, it was fundamentally about business competitiveness: "By acknowledging climate change and changing our business as usual approach, we are aiming to keep at bay not controversy, but competition. This is about being competitive in long-term markets – renewables, solar, fuel cells and natural gas."[50]

The initiative gained further momentum when WRI partnered with the World Business Council for Sustainable Development (WBCSD), a Geneva-based coalition of over 200 international companies. While WRI provided technical expertise, WBCSD's extensive corporate network helped secure vital private sector support and participation. Major corporations not only funded the initiative but also contributed their practical expertise and resources. But the private sector's involvement went far beyond mere financial support, embracing a deeply collaborative approach that WRI's Vice-President Janet Ranganathan would later identify as key to the Protocol's success.[51] The development process was deliberately structured to be "open, transparent, and inclusive," welcoming participation from all interested parties.[52] While this included NGOs, environmental groups (such as WWF and Pew Center on Global Climate Change), academia, and some government authorities like the EPA, corporations were central participants throughout the drafting process.

Companies contributed in multiple crucial ways. First, 23 corporations agreed to "road-test" the initial standards, providing vital feedback to ensure real-world applicability.[53] This practical testing phase was crucial. As Pankaj Bhatia, WRI's Greenhouse Gas Protocol Director, noted, "I am both surprised and inspired to see how much businesses are committed to the GHG Protocol and what a difference it makes when they are involved in finding solutions. Our partnership with WBCSD brings access to the world's leading companies, many of whom contribute to, road test, and use the standards."[54] Beyond testing, companies participated through a formal "Structured Feedback" process, providing systematic evaluations of the standards. Professional services firms, particularly accounting companies such as KPMG, conducted peer reviews to ensure consistency and replicability of the standards.

Perhaps most significantly, corporations played a crucial role in adapting the Protocol to specific industry needs. WRI and WBCSD collaborated extensively with industry associations to develop sector-specific tools and guidelines. This resulted in the creation of a dozen specialized tools for industries including aluminum, cement, and wood products, many of which became standard for their respective sectors. Throughout this process, participants contributed as technical experts rather than merely representing their organizational interests, ensuring the final standards were both rigorous and practical. As one analysis noted, "This is not to say that the discussions were not without contention, but that they were governed by good-faith negotiation to create a rigorous methodology rather than one that would favor certain groups."[55]

This corporate engagement has not diminished over time. Today, major technology companies, including Microsoft, Meta, Google, Amazon, and Salesforce are key supporters, demonstrating the Protocol's ongoing relevance in the modern economy.[56] Their involvement continues to shape new developments, such as the Land Sector and Removals Standard and Guidance, set for release by the end of 2025, which will guide companies in accounting for emissions from land management, biogenic products, and carbon dioxide removal technologies.[57] This sustained corporate involvement ensures the Protocol remains both practical and forward-looking, adapting to new challenges and opportunities in corporate climate action.

7.2.2 *An Illustration: The Corporate Value Chain (Scope 3) Standard*

The evolution of the Corporate Value Chain or Scope 3 Standard provides a concrete illustration of the collaborative process that characterizes the GHG Protocol. Developed through private initiative and sustained by multi stakeholder participation, Scope 3 demonstrates how corporate practices can shape regulatory agendas while also revealing the pressures that arise once those practices attract legal and political reliance.

7.2.2.1 Goals, Design Philosophy, and Early Success

The Corporate Value Chain (Scope 3) Standard marked a decisive shift in the architecture of corporate climate governance. Unlike earlier accounting frameworks, which focused narrowly on emissions generated by a firm's own operations or purchased energy, Scope 3 expanded the analytical frame to encompass the entire value chain.[58] Emissions were no longer treated as the by-product of discrete corporate activities, but as the cumulative effect of participation in a global network of suppliers, logistics providers, consumers, and financiers.

The appeal of Scope 3 lay precisely in this ambition. It provided companies, investors, and regulators with a common language to discuss supply chain decarbonization, product design, procurement strategy, and portfolio alignment. For many firms, Scope 3 accounting was the first tool that made visible the climate implications of outsourcing, global sourcing, and downstream product use.[59] While these tools had long been central to corporate strategy, their impact in environmental reporting had been largely overlooked.

The early success of Scope 3 was inseparable from its origins as a voluntary, coproduced standard, developed through a collaborative process. Over sixty global companies participated in its creation, contributing valuable insights into the practical challenges and requirements of measuring value chain emissions.[60] These companies, including Walmart, Unilever, and Shell, provided technical expertise and real-world perspectives that shaped the standard's guidelines.[61] Pilot testing with organizations such as PepsiCo and BASF allowed for refinement of the methodologies, ensuring they were both scientifically rigorous and operationally feasible.[62] After several rounds of public consultation, the final standard was released in 2011, accompanied by detailed guidance to support its implementation.[63]

During this initial phase, Scope 3 functioned primarily as an indicative tool. It was designed to support learning, experimentation, and internal awareness rather than precision or enforcement. Estimation was not a defect but a feature. Spend-based averages, proxies, and high-level assumptions were accepted as reasonable starting points in a domain where perfect data was neither available nor expected. This voluntary context mattered. Early adopters were typically large, sophisticated firms with internal sustainability teams and an interest in signaling climate leadership. For them, Scope 3 accounting was less about compliance than about orientation: mapping emissions hotspots, engaging suppliers, and identifying strategic levers for long-term decarbonization. Comparability across firms was secondary to momentum.

That design choice proved powerful, as Scope 3 diffused rapidly through corporate practice.[64] Walmart, for example, has used the standard to guide its Project Gigaton initiative, which aims to reduce one gigaton of emissions from its supply chain by 2030.[65] Similarly, Microsoft has integrated Scope 3 accounting into its sustainability strategy, targeting emissions from product use and end-of-life treatment as part of its broader carbon neutrality goals.[66] Unilever has committed to achieving net-zero emissions across its value chain by 2039, a target informed by the methodologies provided by the Scope 3 Standard.[67] Adoption of the standard has also been facilitated by initiatives such as the Science Based Targets Initiative (SBTi), which aligns corporate emissions reduction goals with the global climate objectives of the Paris Agreement.[68]

7.2.2.2 From Indicative Framework to Enforceable Standard

The rapid adoption of Scope 3 across corporate sustainability practices quickly reshaped expectations around its use. As Scope 3 disclosures proliferated, financial institutions and large asset managers began to rely on them to assess climate risk, evaluate transition strategies, and inform portfolio alignment decisions. What had initially functioned as a voluntary and exploratory accounting exercise increasingly became a tool used to support investment judgment and risk management.

Policymakers followed this shift. In the European Union, Scope 3 disclosures were incorporated into the Corporate Sustainability Reporting Directive (CSRD),[69] embedding value chain emissions within mandatory corporate reporting. Under the Biden administration, the SEC proposed including Scope 3 as part of mandatory climate reporting proposal. At the state level, California has similarly embraced mandatory Scope 3 reporting through SB 253, affecting over 5,300 companies doing business in the state.[70] Together, these developments signaled that Scope 3 information was no longer merely aspirational but increasingly central to market considerations and regulatory oversight.

As reliance on Scope 3 disclosures expanded, expectations changed. Estimates that had been acceptable when Scope 3 served an indicative function became problematic once disclosures were expected to be accurate, comparable, auditable, and enforceable. The framework's original tolerance for approximation now sat uneasily with the demands of regulatory scrutiny and legal accountability. What had been designed to guide learning and engagement was increasingly treated as decision-grade infrastructure, exposing the tension between Scope 3's conceptual ambition and its operational readiness.

Once Scope 3 was treated as mandatory infrastructure rather than voluntary guidance, its limitations became difficult to ignore. The complex task of measuring emissions across sprawling global value chains presents a fundamental challenge, with organizations frequently encountering data gaps that necessitate estimation.[71] As a result, companies relied heavily on averages and generic emission factors, producing results that were difficult to verify and compare. Critics raised concerns about the enormous costs of compliance, arguing that the requirements would disproportionately burden small and medium-sized businesses and would potentially force larger companies to cease doing business with smaller suppliers unable to meet reporting demands. The financial industry was particularly vocal, highlighting the challenges of double-counting emissions and the lack of standardized methodologies for measuring financed emissions.

Governance concerns followed. Firms were expected to discipline global supply chains, extract data from smaller partners, and influence emissions over which they lacked direct control. This effectively positioned companies as regulators without clear authority, guidance, or safe harbors. Legal exposure amplified resistance. As Scope 3 disclosures entered securities filings and public statements, firms faced liability risk for estimates derived from incomplete information.

7.2.2.3 Legislative Retrenchment and Global Divergence

Since 2023, the regulatory trajectory of Scope 3 has been marked by fragmentation and retrenchment rather than convergence. While the framework has not been abandoned outright, its incorporation into binding law has been repeatedly narrowed, delayed, and recalibrated as political and operational concerns intensified.

In the United States, Scope 3 disclosure was explicitly abandoned at the federal level when the Securities and Exchange Commission removed it from its final climate disclosure rule.[72] Ultimately, the Trump administration discarded the entire mandatory climate disclosure rule.[73] At the state level, the California regime is forging ahead with implementation but has faced a litigation challenge by the U.S.

Chamber of Commerce, asserting that the laws violate the U.S. constitution on various grounds, including claims that they compel speech contrary to the First Amendment.[74] So far, courts have not agreed to stay implementation of SB 253, but the lawsuit is still pending.[75]

Beginning in 2024, the E.U. has undertaken a sweeping reconsideration of the scope and intensity of climate reporting obligations under the CSRD through a series of simplification initiatives commonly referred to as the Omnibus packages. These efforts culminated in a provisional agreement between the European Parliament and the Council in December 2025.[76] Under the agreement, the CSRD now applies only to companies with more than 1,000 employees and more than 450 million euros in net turnover. As a result, more than 80 percent of companies previously expected to report under the CSRD are excluded from mandatory sustainability reporting. In several member states, estimates suggest that fewer than forty companies remain within scope. Crucially for Scope 3 governance, the Omnibus agreement sharply restricted the information that companies may request from business partners in their value chains to data contained in the voluntary sustainability reporting standard for small and medium sized enterprises.[77]

7.2.2.4 GHG Protocol Overhauls Scope 3

As the political backlash brought to light the structural mismatch between the original design of Scope 3 and the roles it was increasingly expected to perform, the GHG Protocol initiated a strategic overhaul of the standard through a multi-year process.[78] A defining feature of the overhaul is a shift in emphasis from outcomes to processes. Under the original framework, credibility was associated with the breadth of emissions coverage and the completeness of inventories. Under the revised approach, credibility increasingly turns on how companies identify material categories, document assumptions, explain exclusions, and demonstrate consistent decision-making over time. Rather than treating uncertainty as a failure, the revised framework seeks to discipline how uncertainty is managed.

Materiality or significance thresholds are central to this effort. The new thresholds allow companies to exclude categories that contribute only marginally to total emissions, provided those exclusions are explained and documented.[79] This responds directly to corporate concerns about disproportionate reporting burdens. It also reflects regulatory logic. Once Scope 3 disclosures carry legal consequences, it becomes necessary to define what counts as significant. The overhaul also places greater emphasis on documentation, data quality, and boundary clarity. Companies are expected to disclose data sources, estimation methods, assumptions, and limitations with greater specificity. The focus shifts from headline numbers to the integrity of the underlying process. Boundary clarification serves a similar purpose. By refining category definitions and allocation rules, the revised framework aims to reduce double counting and inconsistent treatment of the same emissions across firms.

The process of revision is itself revealing. The overhaul is being conducted through multi stakeholder technical working groups, public consultations, and staged releases.[80] Corporations, auditors, regulators, and civil society organizations all participate. The Protocol is effectively mediating between competing demands for ambition, feasibility, legal defensibility, and comparability. In this sense, the revision process functions as a site of institutional negotiation over how responsibility for value chain emissions should be allocated and governed.

7.2.2.5 Corporate Ordering through Contestation

At first glance, the trajectory of the Scope 3 Standard looks like retrenchment. What began as a bold expansion of corporate climate accountability encountered sustained political resistance, prompting legislators to narrow obligations, regulators to step back from enforcement, and companies to recalibrate public commitments. On this reading, Scope 3 appears to confirm a familiar critique of corporate ordering. Private governance, the argument goes, survives only so long as political actors tolerate it. Once corporate practices generate real costs or threaten powerful interests, political opposition prevails and ordering collapses.

This interpretation captures part of what occurred, but it fails to take note of the current state of emissions reporting. Scope 3 did not disappear. Its most expansive legal manifestations were narrowed, but the underlying concept of value chain emissions endured across markets, private standards, and regulatory discourse.[81] Resistance emerged at a specific point, not against the idea that value chain emissions matter, but against the expectation that an exploratory and flexible framework could suddenly function as binding regulatory infrastructure. The framework was asked to support enforcement and liability before its operational architecture had matured. Ambiguity around boundaries, methodologies, and responsibility created exposure.[82] Firms were expected to disclose emissions they could not reliably measure, discipline supply chains they did not control, and assume legal risk for estimates derived from incomplete information.[83] Political opposition succeeded because these conditions made Scope 3 vulnerable.

The response to that opposition reveals something important about corporate ordering. The overhaul of the Scope 3 Standard by the GHG Protocol does not represent abandonment. It represents adaptation. Rather than retreating from value chain accountability, the redesign seeks to make it governable under conditions of contestation. The shift from comprehensive coverage to materiality, from headline numbers to documentation, and from uniform expectations to sector differentiation reflects a deeper logic. Corporate ordering becomes durable not by insulating itself from politics, but by developing procedures, thresholds, and justificatory practices that allow governance to persist amid disagreement.

This dynamic also reflects a broader feature of corporate ordering emphasized earlier in the book. Corporate ordering does not operate in a legal vacuum. It develops in constant interaction with legislatures, regulators, courts, and electoral politics, each of which asserts competing claims to authority. As Chapter 4 explains, corporate ordering often advances alongside public law, sometimes filling gaps, sometimes supplying templates, and sometimes provoking resistance that reshapes its trajectory. Scope 3 illustrates this competitive coexistence. As private standards, investor expectations, and internal corporate practices expanded, public authorities selectively incorporated those tools, recalibrated them, or pushed back against them. The resulting governance landscape is not hierarchical but plural, shaped by overlapping and sometimes conflicting sources of norm creation.

Importantly, this account does not treat corporate ordering as a straight line or as a process insulated from contestation. Resistance, critique, and adjustment are not signs of failure but integral features of how corporate ordering evolves. Ambitious practices generate pressure, pressure triggers scrutiny, and scrutiny forces refinement. The history of Scope 3 shows that corporate ordering advances through iteration rather than accumulation, with moments of expansion followed by correction and redesign.[84] What matters for the theory is not the absence of opposition, but whether ordering survives opposition by reorganizing itself in ways that continue to structure behavior and decision-making over time.

7.2.3 *Implementation and Monitoring: Widespread Adoption Spurs Internal Governance Transformation*

The widespread adoption of the GHG Protocol triggered an equally widespread effort inside firms to translate voluntary climate standards into operational practice. What had initially functioned as an exploratory exercise in measurement and orientation increasingly came to be treated as decision-grade infrastructure. As investor reliance grew and regulatory mandates loomed, companies faced mounting pressure to produce emissions data that was not merely indicative, but accurate, comparable, and auditable. It was at this point that the full architecture of corporate ordering came into view. The ambition of corporate rulemaking could not be sustained by standards alone. Implementation and monitoring exposed the scale of organizational labor, coordination, and risk required to make those rules operational. This shift fundamentally altered the calculation about the internal organization of corporate climate governance and contributed to the backlash discussed in Section 7.2.2.3.

7.2.3.1 The Build Up: Scaling Measurement and Sustainability Teams as Disclosure Engines

What began as a voluntary initiative embraced by a small cohort of environmentally progressive firms has evolved into a mainstream business practice through strategic multi-stakeholder engagement. The WRI and WBCSD worked diligently to expand adoption through multi-stakeholder dialogues, training courses, and international events, while organizations like the Pew Center on Global Climate Change promoted the compatibility of environmental stewardship with business success.[85] The Carbon Disclosure Project's emergence in 2002 fundamentally altered the landscape, as this consortium of over 300 institutional investors with $41 trillion in assets began systematically requesting emissions disclosures from the world's largest firms according to the GHG Protocol.[86] Their influence proved immediately substantial, as 71 percent of FT Global 500 firms participated in the first CDP cycle, with 45 percent providing full responses.[87] By the fourth cycle, participation had surged to 91 percent, with 72 percent offering complete responses. In the U.S., 56 percent of companies disclosing climate information to CDP reported Scope 3 emissions, a reporting rate lower than that of other regions, like Europe.[88]

The escalation of disclosure expectations catalyzed a rapid expansion of internal sustainability teams. What had once been small units focused on environmental compliance or corporate responsibility reporting evolved into cross-functional operations involving sustainability specialists, finance teams, legal counsel, risk managers, and operational staff.[89] These teams were tasked with gathering emissions data across business units and value chains, coordinating responses to multiple disclosure frameworks, and preparing reports that would increasingly be scrutinized by investors, auditors, and regulators.[90]

The scale of this collective effort was substantial. In 1997, two-thirds of large businesses produced no sustainability report whatsoever.[91] By 2022, according to the Global Reporting Initiative, this practice had become nearly universal among large multinational companies. The Governance & Accountability Institute's analysis reveals this transformation clearly: in 2011, just 20 percent of S&P 500 companies published sustainability reports.[92] By 2023, 9 out of 10 Russell 1,000 companies were publishing increasingly substantial sustainability reports.[93] These reports have grown significantly in both length and detail, as the average U.S. sustainability report increased from seventy pages in 2021 to eighty-three pages in 2024, according to research from Teneo.[94] Academic research examining over 210,000 annual reports from 24,271 public firms across thirty international countries found that environmental and social disclosures have expanded more than sixfold since 2001.[95]

This expansion reflected not a settled regulatory design, but collective mobilization under uncertainty. Prompted by the ESG wave, sustainability teams were building reporting systems while standards, methodologies, and regulatory expectations remained in flux. By 2022, over 18,700 companies submitted climate disclosures through CDP, amounting to a 42 percent increase from 2021 and more than triple the number when the Paris Agreement was signed in 2015.[96] Sustainability teams became disclosure machines, striving to meet escalating demands for precision while still figuring out how emissions could be measured reliably across complex global operations.

7.2.3.2 The Push toward Decision-Grade Governance and Organizational Overextension

As sustainability reporting migrated from voluntary reports into regulated filings and assurance processes, expectations hardened. Disclosure was no longer primarily about learning or signaling. It was increasingly treated as decision-grade infrastructure supporting investment judgment, risk management, and regulatory oversight. This shift imposed new burdens on internal teams. Firms were expected to deliver emissions data that was consistent across years, comparable across firms, and defensible under audit, even when underlying data remained incomplete or highly estimated.

The elevation of sustainability to executive leadership reflected an effort to meet these demands. The role of Chief Sustainability Officer became increasingly prominent in top management, marking a significant shift in how companies approach environmental governance. According to a 2023 report by Spencer Stuart, nearly 50 percent of Fortune 500 companies created a senior-level sustainability executive like a CSO.[97] By 2021, more than 30 percent of firms in the ISS Executive Compensation Analytics database had incorporated ESG metrics into executive pay, up from just 3 percent in 2010.[98] These moves signaled that climate governance had become a core managerial concern rather than a peripheral corporate responsibility issue.

Yet this institutional elevation also exposed sustainability teams to heightened scrutiny and risk. As emissions disclosures entered securities filings and were subjected to external assurance, sustainability functions increasingly bore responsibility for managing legal exposure and reputational risk. Assurance markets expanded rapidly. By 2022, more than half of large companies globally subjected at least some of their environmental disclosures to external audit, and 70 percent of S&P 500 companies that reported ESG information obtained third-party assurance.[99] Greenhouse gas emissions were by far the most commonly assured metric, often including Scope 3 categories.

Market evaluation systems emerged as the final component in the Protocol-driven institutional ecosystem, creating external pressures that reinforce internal governance changes. Major players such as Bloomberg ESG Data Services, Sustainalytics, Thomson Reuters, and RepRisk use sophisticated methodologies, including artificial intelligence and machine learning, to evaluate thousands of companies globally.[100]

This period of rapid expansion, fueled by the ESG wave of the early 2020s, also produced predictable excesses. As climate disclosure and investor attention intensified, many companies moved quickly to adopt ambitious net-zero commitments before developing credible strategies for achieving them.[101] Long-dated targets proliferated despite widespread criticism about their feasibility, internal coordination requirements, and reliance on uncertain technological pathways.[102] In many cases, commitments outpaced implementation capacity. Firms announced goals covering entire value chains without clear plans for supplier engagement, capital allocation, or governance oversight.[103] Branding and rhetoric assumed an outsized role, as sustainability reports and public commitments became tools for signaling alignment rather than vehicles for disciplined planning. Disclosure volume often substituted for strategic clarity, and comparability masked significant variation in underlying assumptions and methodologies.

These objections did not reflect bad faith so much as the absence of a settled governance model. In an environment where expectations were rising faster than operational guidance, companies relied on aspirational commitments and expansive narratives as placeholders while implementation frameworks were still taking shape. The result was a period in which ambition was visible and costly, but execution remained provisional. What appeared as momentum often concealed unresolved questions about responsibility, sequencing, and control. Precisely because rulemaking raced ahead, the importance of implementation and monitoring came sharply into focus. At the same time, the gap between aspiration and operational readiness opened the door to criticism and backlash.

7.2.3.3 Retrenchment and Redesign

The pressure to make climate governance decision-grade eventually exposed the limits of the expansive organizational structures built during the disclosure acceleration phase. As emissions reporting migrated into regulated filings, assurance regimes, and politically salient debates, sustainability teams increasingly bore responsibility for managing legal exposure, compliance costs, and reputational risk under conditions of methodological uncertainty. What had begun as a collective effort to scale measurement capacity gradually became a source of organizational strain. By 2024, as policymakers started retreating from mandatory disclosure requirements amidst ongoing complaints, many firms began reassessing the scale, authority, and visibility of their sustainability functions. This reassessment coincided with rising costs of disclosure and assurance, heightened litigation risk, and an increasingly polarized political environment. Particularly in the United States, President Trump's election signaled a shift in priorities.

Organizational retrenchment took multiple forms. Companies reduced the size of sustainability teams as part of broader cost-containment efforts, with notable layoffs at firms such as Nike,[104] Amazon,[105] Zendesk,[106] S&P Global, and Southwest Airlines.[107] Industry surveys suggest that these reductions were not isolated. According to a recent briefing by Leafr, two-thirds of companies now operate with sustainability teams of three or fewer employees, often reporting that remaining staff are pushed beyond their technical expertise as disclosure and monitoring demands continue to rise.[108] These contractions followed a period of rapid expansion in which sustainability teams had been scaled quickly to meet escalating expectations, often without settled methodologies or stable regulatory endpoints.

Changes at the leadership level reflect the same recalibration. Senior sustainability roles have not disappeared, but they have become more fluid and constrained.

Several large financial institutions downgraded or narrowed top sustainability positions, removed them from executive committees, or chose not to replace departing leaders.[109] At the same time, new appointments continue, particularly in sectors facing intensive disclosure and regulatory pressure. In the first half of 2025, more than forty companies appointed senior sustainability executives, even as turnover increased and mandates narrowed.[110] Survey evidence captures this ambivalence. Most large firms continue to maintain senior sustainability leadership and report growing executive engagement, yet fewer executives report having built a robust internal business case for sustainability initiatives, and confidence in measuring return on investment has declined sharply.[111] The result is not abandonment, but tighter coupling between sustainability roles and core reporting, risk, and compliance functions.

Taken together, these developments point to recalibration rather than retreat. Efforts aimed at comprehensive and uniform disclosure across all firms and value-chain relationships are being scaled back, but this narrowing has not erased the core achievements of the past decade. A large share of companies continue to report emissions and comply with disclosure expectations, and the firms with the greatest climate impact remain subject to the most demanding obligations.[112] For these companies, climate governance has not receded. It has become more structured, more scrutinized, and more tightly integrated into financial, legal, and risk management systems. Retrenchment has reduced breadth, but it has also clarified priorities.

What is emerging is a more focused phase of corporate ordering. Metrics are being refined and recalibrated rather than discarded, with increasing attention to materiality, boundary definition, and methodological transparency. The shared language of sustainability continues to develop, shaping how firms explain emissions, risks, and transition strategies to investors, regulators, and the public. At the same time, implementation and monitoring have underscored the importance of justification. Companies are now expected not merely to disclose numbers, but to explain how those numbers are produced, what they capture, and where their limits lie. The demand for data has not diminished; it has become more exacting. Corporate ordering is now headed away from expansive but fragile claims of completeness, and toward governance practices that prioritize understanding, defensibility, and durability under sustained political and regulatory scrutiny.

7.3 RULEMAKING, IMPLEMENTATION AND MONITORING AT THE INDIVIDUAL COMPANY LEVEL: SALESFORCE

International cooperation among companies, nonprofits, and standard-setters has provided voluntary frameworks that set broad directions for sustainability reporting and action. Initiatives like the Greenhouse Gas Protocol offer important guidance for organizations seeking to measure and disclose their environmental impact. However, translating these international frameworks into operational reality presents an enormous challenge that requires companies to develop sophisticated internal governance mechanisms.

The case study that follows examines how corporations must deploy three distinct but interconnected functions to implement effective sustainability reporting: rulemaking (establishing consistent methodologies and standards), executive action (making strategic decisions about implementation and resource allocation), and monitoring (ensuring accurate tracking and verification). Using Salesforce as a focal example, this study reveals how a leading technology company confronted the complexities of carbon accounting by developing internal protocols, making critical implementation decisions, and building robust monitoring systems. When all three functions operate in concert, they give rise to an important pole in the company's organizational chart that affects choices throughout the hierarchy, transforming sustainability from an abstract commitment into a tangible operational reality that shapes decision-making across the enterprise.

7.3.1 *Sustainability as a Business Advantage for Salesforce*

Salesforce, a global leader in customer relationship management (CRM) software commanding 21.7 percent of the worldwide market, has established itself as both a technological innovator and a corporate climate leader.[113] Founded in 1999 by Marc Benioff and his partners,[114] the company revolutionized the tech industry with its software-as-a-service (SaaS) model and has grown to report revenues of $34.86 billion in fiscal year 2024,[115] ranking 133rd on the Fortune 500 list.[116]

Salesforce's environmental strategy reflects a fundamental business philosophy articulated by CEO Marc Benioff: "The great miscalculation of the age is the idea that businesses have to make a choice; to become profitable, or to become platforms for change. This is not the case."[117] This principle has guided the company's approach to climate action since fiscal year 2012, when Salesforce became an early pioneer in the tech industry by voluntarily disclosing emissions across all scopes (1, 2, and 3) and responding to the Carbon Disclosure Project's Investor Information request.[118] Starting at a time when few companies were addressing their carbon footprint with such transparency, Salesforce's initial disclosure efforts have since matured into a sophisticated and comprehensive monitoring strategy with audited metrics tracking a wide range of environmental impacts. This early commitment to measurement and accountability laid the groundwork for the company's increasingly ambitious climate initiatives in the years that followed.

The company's climate initiatives are grounded in a clear-eyed assessment of business risks, as Benioff explains: "More than half of global GDP is exposed to risk from the nature loss effects of climate change. And it will only get worse unless we collectively take bold steps now to limit global warming. We need to apply every strategy possible to protect and preserve our planet."[119] This understanding has driven Salesforce to develop ambitious climate targets, including achieving net-zero emissions and transitioning to 100 percent renewable energy for global operations.[120]

Salesforce's environmental leadership serves as a competitive advantage in the talent-driven tech industry. As Benioff notes, "In a competitive business such as tech, where luring top talent can be the difference between profit and loss, it's often something intangible – like a diverse, inclusive, values-driven culture – that determines where the best and brightest decide to work."[121] The company's climate commitments have become an integral part of its corporate identity, helping to attract and retain employees who seek purposeful work.

Beyond talent acquisition, Salesforce views sustainability as a catalyst for innovation and future growth opportunities. "We're on the threshold of one of the greatest moments of innovation in the world – it's going to be in the area of the environment," Benioff states, highlighting the company's forward-thinking approach.[122] What began as emissions reporting has evolved into a comprehensive Climate Action Plan with audited metrics, positioning Salesforce at the forefront of corporate environmental leadership while enhancing its brand reputation and market position.

7.3.2 *Salesforce's Governance Initiatives for Environmental Reporting*

When Salesforce began measuring and reporting its carbon emissions, the company faced significant challenges due to the complexity of its global operations. With more than 100 offices spanning the Americas, Europe, Asia, Africa, and Australia and serving more than 150,000 companies worldwide in 2024, Salesforce encountered substantial difficulty in accurately calculating emissions across its vast network.[123] The diversity of its customer base, ranging from small businesses to multinational corporations across financial services, healthcare, retail, manufacturing, and technology sectors, further complicated efforts to assess value chain contributions, even when using industry benchmarks as guidelines.[124]

This complexity was compounded by the inherent limitations of the Greenhouse Gas (GHG) Protocol itself. While widely accepted as a framework for carbon accounting and reporting, the GHG Protocol grants companies considerable flexibility in implementation, creating challenges for consistency and comparability. The Protocol allows organizations to selectively adopt components that align with their objectives rather than requiring comprehensive implementation. Companies must navigate numerous technical decisions, including how to define organizational boundaries, whether based on equity share or control (financial or operational) in a given operation.[125] They must also determine how to categorize and calculate various types of emissions, from direct emissions to indirect emissions from purchased electricity, as well as emissions generated throughout their value chain.

Particularly challenging is the management of Scope 3 emissions, which are notoriously difficult to measure accurately. These emissions, occurring in a company's value chain but outside its direct control, require organizations to develop methods for gathering data from distant facilities and suppliers, and to determine how to integrate this information with industry estimates. This process demands significant discretion and operationalization by the company, as the GHG Protocol provides guidance but leaves the specific implementation methods to individual organizations.

To address these challenges and enhance data accuracy for supporting its environmental claims and targets, Salesforce implemented two major initiatives that transformed its governance structures and impacted nearly the entire organization. First, the company developed sophisticated automated carbon accounting tools to replace outdated, spreadsheet-based methods previously used for emissions tracking.[126] Second, Salesforce created a Sustainability Exhibit, a contractual framework that embeds specific, binding climate obligations into supplier agreements.

These initiatives were designed to overcome the limitations in the GHG Protocol's flexible approach. By establishing more standardized methodologies for emissions management, Salesforce sought to improve the accuracy and reliability of its environmental reporting while addressing the discretionary aspects of carbon accounting that often lead to inconsistencies across organizations.

Precise carbon accounting and reporting are crucial for several reasons. Inaccurate reporting exposes companies to multiple vulnerabilities, including litigation risks as climate-related lawsuits have risen significantly in recent years.[127] As demonstrated by Salesforce's inclusion of climate-related disclosures in its 2020 10-K filing, companies face increased regulatory scrutiny when reporting emissions data.[128] Accurate information prevents misleading shareholders and stakeholders, which could otherwise lead to securities fraud claims and reputational damage. Furthermore, proper accounting enables companies to effectively contribute to combating global warming and addressing systemic business threats.

Joe Allanson, former executive vice president of finance ESG at Salesforce, emphasized the importance of standardized reporting when supporting the SEC climate disclosure proposal in 2022: "I vividly recall the internal deliberations five years ago about how much we should report on climate in our SEC financial filings, what to say about our risks, and what legal exposure we might take on by doing so voluntarily. It was personal to me as one of the co-signers on Form 10-K."[129] At the time of these deliberations, Salesforce faced a significant asymmetric risk: the company could potentially be sued for information it voluntarily disclosed, but faced no legal repercussions for omitting information since there was no regulatory obligation to report. This created a challenging risk calculus where greater transparency paradoxically meant consciously expanding litigation exposure. While truthful disclosures would theoretically minimize the risk of paying damages, this was largely an untested legal proposition at the time, placing companies like Salesforce in uncharted territory when deciding to voluntarily include climate-related information in their financial filings.

7.3.3 *Automating Carbon Accounting Tools: The Rulemaking Challenge*

Salesforce's journey toward effective carbon accounting began with confronting a fundamental challenge: highly fragmented emissions-related data. As a large enterprise, the company needed to collect information from diverse sources, such as office buildings, data centers, and cloud service providers, which were delivering data in incompatible formats, at irregular intervals, and with varying levels of detail.[130] Patrick Flynn aptly described this fragmentation: "We were mining the data from the data centers, from the network, from the utility, from the structured contract data, customer feedback – all trying to improve the quality of our services and the environmental impact of our services."[131]

The company faced a critical decision point: how to design a system that could effectively aggregate and verify this disparate information. This required fundamentally a rulemaking exercise, where Salesforce executives needed to establish internal protocols that would govern how data was collected and processed across departments, jurisdictions, and reporting periods. Without such a system, emissions tracking remained labor-intensive and error-prone, with Salesforce leadership having significant discretion over which data sources to prioritize and how to resolve inconsistencies.

Even after collecting the raw data, Salesforce encountered another significant obstacle: inconsistent measurement standards across business units. The company discovered wide variation in how different locations and vendors reported energy consumption, as some used kilowatt-hours (kWh), others megawatt-hours (MWh), and still others British Thermal Units (BTUs). These inconsistencies extended to reporting timelines, with data available monthly, quarterly, or annually, depending on the source. As Scher noted, "There was no single source of truth or guiding set of calculations that everyone was following."[132] This lack of standardization meant that Salesforce executives needed to create a company-wide rulebook for emissions accounting. Effectively, this set of standards would function such as internal regulations, determining how various business units would measure and report their environmental impact. These decisions about which metrics to prioritize and how to reconcile discrepancies would directly impact the reliability, efficiency, and comparability of reported emissions.

A third major challenge involved determining consistent calculation methodologies. While the GHG Protocol offered a general framework, it provided guidance rather than prescriptive rules, leaving Salesforce with substantial discretion in selecting which emissions factors to apply for different activities.[133] For example, calculating carbon dioxide equivalent (CO_2e) emissions from natural gas heating systems required choosing specific emissions factors to convert fuel consumption into CO_2e values.[134] Multiple authoritative sources offered slightly different emissions factors, including the U.S. Environmental Protection Agency (EPA), the IPCC, and various regional regulatory bodies.[135] Similarly, for electricity consumption, Salesforce had to decide between location-based emissions factors (reflecting regional energy grid mixes) or market-based factors (accounting for purchased renewable energy).[136] These seemingly technical choices carried significant implications for the company's reported carbon footprint. Different methodological decisions could yield substantially different emissions totals, highlighting how the design of the accounting system itself shaped environmental reporting outcomes.

7.3.4 *The Skills Gap: Executive Decisions for Implementation*

Compounding the challenges described earlier was a significant skills gap that required executive intervention at two distinct levels. The challenges outlined earlier were fundamentally of a rulemaking nature, as Salesforce needed to establish consistent protocols for data collection, measurement, and calculation. However, crafting this governance framework was only the first step. Once rules were established, significant implementation challenges lay ahead, requiring different sets of specialized capabilities to transform theoretical frameworks into functioning systems. Yet Salesforce discovered that many personnel tasked with carbon accounting responsibilities lacked the specialized knowledge in environmental science, data analytics, and regulatory compliance needed to design these rules effectively.

Even more critically, once rules were established, implementing them through robust systems required technical capabilities that were scarce within the organization. As Scher observed, the process was "very dependent on numerous third parties, data getting handed off from here to there, black boxes, and multiple spreadsheets woven together."[137] This implementation challenge meant that executive decisions about technical infrastructure were as important as decisions about the accounting rules themselves.

Salesforce's leadership faced a multifaceted resource allocation challenge. First, they needed to decide how to acquire the expertise necessary to design appropriate carbon accounting rules. This challenge required environmental science knowledge, regulatory expertise, and familiarity with emerging industry standards. Second, they needed to determine how to build the technical capabilities required to implement these rules consistently across the organization. In turn, this challenge demanded data engineering skills, software development expertise, and systems integration capabilities.

This technical capacity shortage meant that Salesforce's executive leadership faced a critical resource allocation decision. They could choose to invest in training existing staff, hire specialized talent, or outsource the work to external consultants. This was not merely a tactical choice but a strategic executive decision about where to direct company resources and how to build institutional capabilities. Each approach would significantly influence not only how thoroughly emissions were tracked and reported but also how the company's internal carbon governance would evolve over time.

7.3.5 *Solutions: Executive Investment in Team-Building and System Design*

Recognizing these challenges, Salesforce's leadership made a series of characteristic executive decisions that reflected their priorities and would shape the company's approach to environmental governance. In 2015, the company made a significant resource commitment by hiring Patrick Flynn as Vice President of Sustainability to lead its carbon accounting efforts, thus establishing a dedicated leadership position that signaled the importance of this work.[138] By 2017, with executive backing, Flynn had expanded the team to include Shengyuan Su, an analyst with specialized expertise in environmental accounting and software development.

Facing an impending deadline for incorporating climate metrics into the company's 10-K financial disclosure, Salesforce's leadership took a decisive path. Rather than adopting third-party software, the company would invest in leveraging its own technology platform to create a customized solution. This choice reflected a classic "build versus buy" executive decision and gave Salesforce maximum control over the design and implementation of its carbon accounting system. Essentially, the company would write its own rulebook for environmental reporting while aligning the solution with their existing technology ecosystem.

With executive backing and resources secured, the team embarked on building a comprehensive environmental governance infrastructure. At the heart of their solution was a centralized sustainability app that functioned as the company's system of record, standardizing how emissions data was stored and managed across all business units. This central repository established uniform reporting rules that every department would follow, eliminating the fragmentation that had previously plagued their efforts. Complementing this foundation, the team developed an automated carbon conversion tool that brought mathematical consistency to the process, translating diverse energy data from various sources into standardized carbon equivalents. This tool embodied the uniform calculation methodologies that would now apply across the entire organization, replacing the inconsistent approaches of the past. To complete the system, they created a real time emissions tracking dashboard that made the company's carbon footprint visible and understandable, categorized by scope and accessible to decision-makers. This dashboard served as a common reference point for environmental performance, standardizing how success would be measured and creating accountability across the organization.

These interconnected technical components, backed by significant investment of company resources, dramatically transformed Salesforce's carbon accounting process. What had once taken six months to compile could now be completed in just six weeks, an efficiency gain that represented a direct return on the executive decision to allocate talent and capital to the problem.[139] The system's modular architecture proved particularly valuable, as it was designed with expandability in mind from the outset. Initially, the team strategically focused on direct emissions (Scope 1) and selected indirect emissions (Scope 2) to demonstrate quick wins and establish credibility. However, the flexible framework they had constructed allowed for seamless incorporation of additional data sources and calculation methodologies over time. This built-in scalability meant that when Salesforce later needed to address the more complex and data-intensive Scope 3 emissions categories, which involve the entire value chain, they could extend rather than replace their existing system. This phased, expandable implementation approach reflected not only strategic prioritization of immediate resources but also foresight in creating a foundation that could evolve alongside increasingly demanding environmental reporting requirements.

7.3.6 *Executive Decision to Commercialize the Solution*

Recognizing the broader potential of its carbon accounting tools, Salesforce's leadership made another characteristic executive decision in 2020. The company would transform what began as an internal compliance solution into a revenue-generating commercial offering called Salesforce Sustainability Cloud (later rebranded as Net Zero Cloud).[140] This represented a strategic pivot that leveraged the company's investment in internal rulemaking to create a product that would effectively export Salesforce's environmental governance model to other organizations. This subscription-based product enabled other businesses and governments to adopt Salesforce's approach to tracking, analyzing, and reporting environmental data.

The company's statement that "We believe that our technology can play an important role in helping to drive climate action to accelerate the world's efforts towards carbon neutrality" reflected not just an environmental aspiration but a strategic business decision to position Salesforce as a rule-maker and standard-setter in the emerging field of corporate environmental governance.[141]

Throughout this journey, Salesforce exercised considerable discretion in determining how to structure its carbon accounting systems and how to allocate corporate resources. Each executive decision, from which data sources to prioritize, to which calculation methodologies to employ, to how to present the resulting information, to how many specialists to hire, shaped not only the efficiency of the process but also the reliability and comparability of the outcomes across departments, jurisdictions, and time periods. The company's experience illustrates how executive choices about resource allocation and internal rulemaking can profoundly influence environmental reporting and ultimately transform internal compliance challenges into strategic business opportunities.

7.3.7 *Sustainability Exhibit: The Supply Chain Challenge*

In April 2021, Salesforce unveiled a strategy to address its Scope 3 emissions by introducing the "Sustainability Exhibit," a contractual addition mandating climate obligations for all its suppliers.[142] This initiative represents a remarkable example of corporate rulemaking at scale, where a single company's policies function similarly to governmental regulations, cascading throughout an extensive supply chain and affecting numerous businesses. With Scope 3 emissions constituting 80 percent of Salesforce's total carbon footprint, and suppliers accounting for 74 percent of that impact, the company effectively created a regulatory framework extending far beyond its corporate boundaries.[143]

The development and implementation of the Sustainability Exhibit closely mirrors how governmental regulatory bodies craft and enforce rules. The process began through specific contract negotiations in 2020, where, according to VP of Sustainability Patrick Flynn, Salesforce was "motivated to try to get those suppliers accelerated on their climate action journey."[144] This initial concept evolved into a formal three-page contractual document establishing specific requirements: suppliers must publicly disclose Scopes 1, 2, and 3 emissions within one year, set science-based emissions reduction targets, deliver carbon-neutral products and services, and share third-party sustainability scorecards annually.

Before widespread implementation, Salesforce engaged in practices reminiscent of regulatory field testing and stakeholder consultation. Major suppliers participated in trials of the agreement, providing feedback that shaped the final version. Herman Miller, an office furniture company with its own supply chain sustainability experience dating back to 2013, was among those that field-tested the Exhibit. Other companies such as Atlassian had been engaging with Salesforce on climate initiatives prior to the Exhibit's release, while Marriott International had been reporting sustainability data to Salesforce for years, creating a foundation for the new requirements.[145] This consultative approach parallels how regulators often seek input from affected parties before finalizing new rules.

Salesforce further embraced evidence-based rulemaking by conducting a formal survey among priority suppliers in late 2020.[146] This research assessed their familiarity with science-based targets (SBTs) and identified potential implementation barriers. The survey revealed that while over 90 percent of suppliers were familiar with SBTs, only 37 percent reported actively exploring them. Among those not yet exploring SBTs, only 15 percent had taken the fundamental step of measuring their emissions. Suppliers cited lack of internal resources (41 percent), inadequate data management tools (30 percent), and limited control over their own supply chains as primary challenges.

Like sophisticated regulatory regimes, Salesforce used this evidence to modify its requirements and develop differentiated approaches based on supplier capabilities. Recognizing the resource constraints identified in the survey, Salesforce created alternatives to strict compliance.[147] While encouraging the SBTs initiative (SBTi) validation, they developed an alternative attestation form for suppliers unable to secure formal validation but willing to align with SBTi criteria. For small and medium enterprises with more limited resources, Salesforce created a dedicated six-month Sustainability Accelerator program in 2022, including subsidized greenhouse gas inventory development. Additionally, they published guidance documents through their online learning platform, enabling potential suppliers to understand compliance requirements, similar to regulatory implementation guides issued by regulators.[148]

The implementation phase further demonstrates structures reminiscent of formal regulatory systems. Salesforce established a dedicated supplier sustainability leadership position within procurement, effectively creating an internal "regulatory body" to oversee compliance.[149] This leader coordinates across procurement, sourcing, legal, and sustainability teams to ensure aligned execution. When the Exhibit became a standard contract component, the legal team conducted training sessions and developed a detailed reference playbook to help procurement teams understand, communicate, and negotiate the new requirements.

To ensure organizational commitment to enforcement, Salesforce tied executive variable compensation to ESG metrics, including increased spend with suppliers incorporating climate commitments through the Sustainability Exhibit.[150] This created internal accountability for rule enforcement, similar to how regulatory agencies establish performance metrics for their enforcement divisions.

The Exhibit's enforcement provisions mirror regulatory compliance mechanisms. Noncompliance triggers a "Climate Breach" designation, resulting in "Climate Remediation Fees" calculated at either the cost of carbon offsets or 0.5 percent of annual contract value. In severe cases, Salesforce reserves the right to terminate contracts, particularly when a supplier's practices "pose a material risk" to the company's reputation or conflict with its sustainability commitments.[151]

Despite this sophisticated regulatory-like framework, Salesforce faces implementation challenges similar to governmental bodies. While targeting suppliers representing 60 percent of applicable Scope 3 emissions to establish SBTs by FY25, as of FY24, only 25 percent of these emissions were from suppliers with validated SBTs, with an additional 14 percent from suppliers committed to setting such targets, totaling 39 percent progress toward the goal.[152]

The Sustainability Exhibit has also driven methodological innovation in carbon accounting. Salesforce has transitioned from relying solely on industry estimates (Environmentally Extended Input-Output methodology) to a hybrid approach incorporating supplier-specific data.[153] This methodological shift enables more accurate emissions accounting and reveals targeted decarbonization opportunities that would remain hidden under generic industry-based calculations.

The Salesforce case illustrates how corporate rulemaking, when implemented at sufficient scale, necessarily adopts the sophisticated characteristics of public regulatory systems, such as consultation, evidence gathering, compliance flexibility, enforcement mechanisms, and continuous improvement based on implementation feedback. As large corporations increasingly influence global supply chains through such sustainability requirements, understanding these processes as de facto regulatory regimes becomes essential for comprehending modern environmental governance.

7.4 CONCLUSION

The climate change case study presented in this chapter offers a comprehensive illustration of the book's central thesis. Sophisticated corporate governance requires the integration of rulemaking, executive action, and monitoring functions to address complex social challenges. Climate action represents perhaps the most vivid example of this framework's necessity and potential.

The development of the Greenhouse Gas Protocol demonstrates how rulemaking transforms seemingly intractable challenges into actionable frameworks. Without the pioneering efforts of companies such as BP, GM, and Monsanto working alongside nonprofit organizations, we would lack the standardized carbon accounting methods that now form the foundation of climate governance worldwide. This rulemaking function created a common language for measuring environmental impact, establishing not just terminology and categories, but also methodological approaches that balance scientific rigor with practical applicability.

Implementation reveals equally significant challenges, demanding substantial resource commitments that only executive action can authorize. Salesforce's journey illustrates how companies must make strategic decisions about technological investments, personnel allocation, and organizational priorities to operationalize environmental frameworks. These are not merely technical choices but fundamental business decisions that reshape corporate capabilities and competitive positioning. The significant disparities between American and European oil companies further highlight how executive preferences about resource allocation lead to dramatically different environmental trajectories.

The monitoring function, while perhaps less visible, proves equally essential. Without standardized disclosure protocols and verification systems, climate governance would lack accountability. The Carbon Disclosure Project's transformation of voluntary initiatives into market expectations demonstrates how external monitoring mechanisms drive internal company behavior. As investors have increasingly embraced climate metrics in their evaluation of corporate performance, monitoring has expanded from a passive reporting function to an active governance mechanism.

Climate governance also illuminates the heterogeneity of preferences among shareholders, a complexity that will likely intensify as climate impacts become more apparent. Engine No. 1's campaign against ExxonMobil, contrasted with the retreat of European oil giants from their renewable commitments, reveals profound disagreements about the proper corporate response to climate challenges. These tensions are further complicated by political headwinds, competitive pressures, and geopolitical considerations that create a constantly shifting landscape for corporate climate action.

What becomes clear through this analysis is that without significant corporate endorsement from the outset, climate governance would have remained stalled in abstract political debates rather than evolving into operational frameworks. Within just two decades, this corporate-led initiative has fundamentally transformed how shareholders, asset managers, regulators, and market professionals approach environmental responsibility. The sophistication of climate governance continues to advance across all three functions, with rules becoming more precise, implementation becoming more efficient, and monitoring becoming more rigorous.

Looking forward, continued progress will require further innovation across all three governance domains. Rulemaking must evolve to address emerging challenges like carbon removal accounting and transition planning. Executive action must navigate increasingly complex trade-offs between short-term profitability and long-term resilience. Monitoring systems must balance standardization with flexibility as climate science and policy continue to develop. Despite these challenges, the climate governance case reveals how corporate leadership, when exercised through sophisticated institutional frameworks, can drive systematic progress on even the most complex social challenges.

8

How to Govern AI?

The general counsel of a major AI company got the telephone call that all in-house lawyers fret.[1] The U.S. Department of Defense wanted to invite the company to a meeting, in D.C., to talk about the implications of artificial intelligence for national security. It was a few months after OpenAI had released ChatGPT for free, taking the world by storm.[2] Suddenly, everyone had been left amazed by how articulate and knowledgeable it seemed. There was a lot of excitement about potential applications, from providing content and education to facilitating menial support tasks.[3] There were also concerns about misinformation, ethics, and the reinforcing of harmful stereotypes, the revolutionization of industries, and the replacement of humans by machines.[4] But national security was an issue with an entirely different set of considerations, because it affected the integrity of the country itself.[5]

It was also an issue about which any AI company would have thought only in passing at the time. Yet, management felt that they had to go to D.C. and answer the military's questions. To take the extraordinary step of inviting them, they must have done something to enter their radar.[6] But what could that possibly be? They were determined to be prepared. When national security considerations enter the scene, the government has a lot of extraordinary, far-reaching powers that they could use against the company. They needed to be ready to put down as many fires as possible. So, the general counsel worked hard to be briefed about various aspects of the company's operations, the people who accessed its platform, and the sources of information it utilized. They traveled to D.C. and entered the meeting ready to defend the company and determined to be truthful. After the initial introductions and pleasantries, the senior military officers went to the heart of the topic. They had seen AI grab the world's attention and they were worried about the future. So, they thought, they should be proactive and ask AI companies: in their view, how could AI impact national security?[7] Management immediately realized that they knew a lot more about the topic than the military officers across the table. They went on to have a very engaging meeting.

It sounds almost like a truism that government often finds itself one step behind the industry.[8] Particularly in areas such as technology or finance, which bring together some of the best minds in the world with capital exploring investment opportunities, regulators often find themselves struggling to follow developments.[9] Still, the incident above is extraordinary because it shows not only how far behind governments can fall, but also how much they must rely on private companies to find their way. The U.S. military is, one would hope, far more sophisticated and well-resourced than the average regulatory agency.[10] Still, when developments occur at breakneck speeds, governments have little option apart from turning to companies for information, analysis, and guidance.

This chapter explores two different pathways for governing AI. In the conventional regulatory model, AI companies become regulated entities subject to compliance and disclosure obligations and, possibly, licensing requirements.[11] Federal agencies supervise various AI products and aspects of the firm's operations, governance, and board personnel. In the corporate ordering model, AI companies establish their own internal governance regimes, disclosing their contours and inviting accountability and engagement. They may also come together, possibly in an industry-funded regulatory body, to set standards about their products and services.[12] Groups of experts in different fields collaborate to propose standards in their respective areas. The standard-setting process is transparent with input from governments, citizens' groups, NGOs, and other interested parties, informing the public about developments.

When faced with two different regulatory models, conventional legal analysis would contrast them by highlighting their strengths and weaknesses. My goal in this chapter is to argue that viewing this as a dilemma is misconstrued. Not only can the two models coexist, but in fact, the corporate ordering effort is a necessary precondition for any official regulatory regime. Corporations must do the legwork of preparing for regulation, for the simple reason that they understand better than anyone how their activity may impact other groups. This is particularly true in areas where technological developments disrupt existing industry structures at a very quick pace, like in AI. Moreover, corporations will also be required to implement any solutions to social concerns, so their input in designing them is crucial.

One might worry that, if the substantive core of a regulatory obligation originates from the regulated entity, that is, the company, then the likelihood of capture is extremely high. This concern is central to any self-regulatory effort. Addressing it requires corporations to implement measures that enhance their credibility, help them take into account other parties' views, and increase their legitimacy. The chapter offers some examples of how governance can help in this direction. But it also highlights that, if corporate ordering fails, then governments might remain in the dark and stakeholders may continue to suffer harm.

8.1 STAKES: INNOVATION AT FULL SPEED, SAFETY AND STEWARDSHIP

Few technological developments have elicited language as apocalyptic as artificial intelligence. The stakes could not have been higher, as AI is on track to revolutionize the economy and throw the workforce into chaos. From a political economy perspective, lawmakers and tech moguls, progressives and conservatives, elite thinkers, and working class advocates are united in the belief that the risks posed by AI are too severe to be left unchecked.[13] As governments worldwide race to establish regulatory frameworks, a fundamental tension lies at the heart of AI development: the conflict between rapid innovation and responsible stewardship. This tension crystallizes the competing imperatives of accelerated technological advancement and careful safety considerations in an era of unprecedented change. It also illustrates why AI is a hard case for the argument this book is advancing. Given the magnitude of the challenges, one would not expect private companies to be the ones taking the lead in setting up appropriate frameworks.

8.1.1 *The Stewardship Imperative: Safeguarding the Future*

The case for careful stewardship of AI development rests on an intricate web of concerns, ranging from existential threats to immediate societal risks. At the most fundamental level, stewardship advocates worry about AI systems that could become uncontrollable and act against human interests.[14] There is a real possibility that highly developed systems may actively resist human oversight and pursue goals that conflict with human values. The challenge of ensuring these systems remain subordinate to human control becomes exponentially more complex as their capabilities increase.[15] Industry leaders such as Bill Gates and Elon Musk have raised alarm about these existential threats, arguing that even though catastrophic scenarios might be decades away, the groundwork for prevention must be laid now.[16] Their concern stems from a crucial insight: once superintelligent AI systems exist, implementing controls might be impossible.[17] This creates an asymmetric risk scenario where the cost of moving too quickly far outweighs the benefits of rapid development.

The stewardship perspective gains additional urgency from more immediate threats. AI systems already demonstrate alarming capabilities for malicious deployment. Advanced AI can automate the discovery of software vulnerabilities, potentially compromising critical systems faster than human defenders can respond.[18] The threat extends beyond traditional cybersecurity, as AI-powered systems could orchestrate sophisticated disinformation campaigns, manipulating public discourse and undermining democratic institutions at unprecedented scales.[19]

Critical infrastructure faces particular risks. AI-powered cyber intrusions could simultaneously target multiple systems, creating cascading failures across interconnected networks.[20] A coordinated attack could disable financial systems, disrupt energy grids, and paralyze transportation networks, causing widespread societal disruption. The automation and scale possible with AI attacks make traditional security measures increasingly inadequate.

Perhaps most insidiously, AI enables unprecedented surveillance capabilities. By aggregating data across multiple domains, including social media, financial transactions, location data, and communication metadata, AI systems can create detailed profiles of individuals and groups.[21] This mass surveillance capability threatens not just privacy but fundamental human liberties, potentially enabling social control mechanisms that would be impossible without AI.[22] The combination of bulk data access and sophisticated analysis tools creates surveillance possibilities that even George Orwell could not have imagined.

8.1.2 *The Speed Imperative: Innovation as Economic and Strategic Necessity*

The argument for rapid AI development presents its own compelling logic, grounded in economic necessity and geopolitical reality. AI is not just another technological advance, but rather represents a fundamental transformation of human productive capabilities. The technology is already revolutionizing the workforce in ways that previous automation waves never approached.[23] Unlike earlier technological shifts that primarily affected routine manual labor, AI is disrupting professions that were thought to require uniquely human capabilities.[24]

The scope of this disruption is staggering. Legal analysis, medical diagnosis, creative writing, and artistic production, all domains previously considered safe from automation, are being transformed by AI capabilities.[25] The recent Hollywood writers' strike highlights how AI is reshaping even creative industries.[26] With one in five U.S. workers facing potential job displacement or transformation, the economic imperative for rapid development becomes clear: those who fail to adapt quickly risk being left behind.[27]

This transformation extends beyond domestic economic concerns into the realm of global power dynamics. Nations and organizations that successfully deploy AI gain unprecedented advantages in productivity and capability.[28] In critical sectors such as defense, transportation, and healthcare, AI advantages could become decisive. Military applications, from autonomous weapons to strategic planning systems, could shift the balance of global power.[29] Healthcare breakthroughs enabled by AI could provide dramatic advantages in life expectancy and quality of life.[30]

The global race for AI supremacy creates a prisoner's dilemma in international relations. While all nations might benefit from careful, coordinated AI development, the potential advantages of pulling ahead create strong incentives for rapid deployment.[31] The U.S. restriction on exporting advanced AI chips to China[32] exemplifies this dynamic. While motivated by security concerns, U.S. policies also reflect the recognition that AI capabilities have become central to national power.

This tension between speed and stewardship reflects a singular challenge in human technological development. The same capabilities that promise extraordinary benefits also create equally novel risks. As public anxiety about AI grows, with Americans expressing more concern than excitement, rising from 37 percent in 2021 to 52 percent in 2023,[33] the challenge of balancing innovation and safety becomes increasingly urgent. Yet, governments are in a significant disadvantage in grasping the full range of concerns AI rises, as well as coming up with rules that would address very different needs. Thus, it falls on companies at the forefront of AI development to determine how to best address these challenges. The following section explores how this abstract debate manifests in concrete organizational decisions, with different shareholders and stakeholders holding varying views.

8.2 HETEROGENEITY OF PREFERENCES

The differing perspectives on how to address AI concerns divide not only public opinion, but also some of the key actors spearheading the AI revolution. Throughout the business world, managers, investors, financiers, and employees take different positions regarding the necessity of stewardship and the urgency of adjusting to new realities. The November 2023 leadership crisis at OpenAI, one of the pioneers in LLMs, serves as a compelling illustration of how heterogeneous preferences among stakeholders can create significant organizational tensions in artificial intelligence development.[34] This section analyzes how divergent stakeholder priorities regarding AI safety, commercial development, and governance led to one of the most dramatic corporate conflicts in recent technology history.

The crisis began on November 17, 2023, when OpenAI's board abruptly fired CEO Sam Altman, citing concerns about his candor in communications.[35] This decision triggered a cascade of events that exposed deep-seated tensions between different stakeholder groups. The board's initial statement claimed that Altman "was not consistently candid in his communications with the board, hindering its ability to exercise its responsibilities."[36] However, this dramatic action revealed fundamental disagreements about OpenAI's direction and governance that had been brewing beneath the surface.[37]

The immediate aftermath demonstrated the complex web of shareholder and stakeholder interests, with each group bringing distinct preferences and priorities to the forefront. The board, led by independent directors, emphasized their unique governance mandate, noting that unlike traditional companies, they weren't tasked with maximizing shareholder value. Instead, their stated mission focused on ensuring the creation of "broadly beneficial" artificial general intelligence.[38] But faced with opposition from key funders, who were ready to redirect their resources elsewhere, and the threat of an en masse resignation by the company's employees, the board had little option but to retreat.[39] With Altman reinstated, board members resigned and paved the way for a leadership reshuffle and direction realignment.[40]

8.2.1 *Stewardship Advocates*

The perspective of stewardship advocates represents a fundamental commitment to ensuring artificial intelligence development serves humanity's long-term interests.

This stakeholder group, including Helen Toner, Ilya Sutskever, and Elon Musk, prioritizes the careful governance and responsible development of AI over commercial or technological imperatives.[41]

Helen Toner's position, as articulated through her academic work and board actions, emphasized the paramount importance of responsible AI development.[42] Her paper "Decoding Intentions: AI and Costly Signals" had criticized OpenAI's rapid deployment of technologies like GPT-4, arguing that commercial pressures were compromising essential safety protocols.[43] The tension between Toner and Altman reached a critical point when Altman attempted to remove her from the board due to her paper's criticisms of OpenAI's approach.[44] Toner's later statement that "*even OpenAI's potential self-destruction might align with the mission*" of ensuring AGI benefits humanity demonstrates the depth of the safety-first perspective.[45] This view was so fundamental that when an OpenAI lawyer suggested the board's decision might lead to the company's downfall, Toner maintained her position, arguing that such an outcome could still serve the broader mission of ensuring beneficial AGI development.

Elon Musk, an original cofounder of OpenAI, represents perhaps the most forceful articulation of the stewardship position. His 2024 lawsuit against OpenAI alleged that the organization had "*strayed from its original mission of developing AGI for the benefit of humanity*."[46] Musk's legal action argued that the shift to a for-profit model fundamentally compromised OpenAI's founding principles. His consistent warnings about AI's existential risks and his criticism that OpenAI's current focus on commercialization only exacerbates these dangers align closely with Toner's concerns about prioritizing market success over responsible development.[47]

Ilya Sutskever's role in the crisis particularly illuminates the complexity of the stewardship position. As OpenAI's chief scientist, Sutskever initially supported Altman's removal, arguing during a company all-hands meeting that the action was "necessary" to protect OpenAI's mission of "making AI beneficial to humanity."[48] However, his subsequent reversal and public regret over participating in Altman's removal highlight the challenging balance between technological progress and responsible oversight.[49]

8.2.2 *Commercialization and Speed Supporters*

The perspective favoring rapid development and market release of AI technologies represents a distinct philosophy about how AI development should proceed, most prominently championed by Sam Altman and strongly supported by OpenAI's technical workforce. This viewpoint emphasizes the importance of practical deployment and swift iteration while attempting to maintain alignment with the broader mission of beneficial AI development.[50]

Sam Altman's leadership at OpenAI embodied a complex vision that sought to bridge rapid technological advancement with responsible development.[51]

His approach centered on the belief that practical deployment was essential for understanding and improving AI systems.[52] When addressing OpenAI's mission, Altman consistently framed it in terms of both technological progress and societal benefit, stating that ensuring artificial general intelligence benefits all of humanity was not just a corporate objective but a moral imperative. In 2019, Altman defended the shift of OpenAI from a nonprofit to a capped-profit model.[53] He stated that OpenAI would need to "invest billions of dollars in upcoming years into large-scale cloud compute, attracting and retaining talented people, and building AI supercomputers," making commercialization necessary to support this massive scale.

The perspective of senior technical leaders further reinforced this position. The resignation of key figures like research director Jakub Pachocki and head of preparedness Aleksander Madry suggested that those closest to the technical work saw Altman's leadership style as crucial for meaningful progress.[54] Research scientist Andrej Karpathy's public statement that "The board had a chance to explain their drastic actions and they did not take it" reflected the technical community's skepticism of the board's more cautious approach.[55]

Microsoft's substantial investment in OpenAI aligned closely with this rapid deployment perspective. Their $10 billion investment, structured significantly around cloud computing resources, demonstrated a belief in the importance of scaling AI development and deployment.[56] Satya Nadella's vision for the partnership emphasized both technological advancement and practical application, seeing rapid deployment as crucial for progress. His statement that "Microsoft's partnership with OpenAI is built on a foundation of ethical AI development" while simultaneously pushing for accelerated development and integration of OpenAI's technologies into Microsoft's products reveals the attempt to balance speed with responsibility.[57]

This perspective gains particular support from market-oriented stakeholders, including venture capital firms such as Khosla Ventures. Vinod Khosla's description of Altman as a "once in a generation CEO" whose "positive mark on the world will be indelible" reflects the belief that rapid, market-oriented development under visionary leadership is crucial for realizing AI's potential benefits.[58]

8.2.3 *Crisis and Overhaul*

The tension between rapid deployment and careful oversight came to a head during the leadership crisis in November 2023. The board's initial decision to remove Altman, citing concerns about his candor in communications, reflected deep-seated anxieties about the pace and direction of development. However, the swift and nearly universal backlash from employees, investors, and industry partners suggested strong support for the rapid development approach.

The employee response to Altman's removal provided crucial validation of his approach to AI development. The near-unanimous workforce reaction, with over 650 of approximately 770 employees threatening to resign, demonstrated remarkable alignment with Altman's vision.[59] The employee letter to the board offered a detailed defense of this perspective on AI development: "OpenAI is the world's leading AI company. We, the employees of OpenAI, have developed the best models and pushed the field to new frontiers. Our work on AI safety and governance shapes global norms. The products we built are used by millions of people around the world. Until now, the company we work for and cherish has never been in a stronger position."[60] This statement reveals how the technical workforce viewed rapid development and deployment as complementary to, rather than in conflict with, responsible AI development. Their assertion that the board's actions had "jeopardized all of this work and undermined our mission and company" suggests they saw no contradiction between swift progress and ethical considerations.

The depth of employee commitment to this vision became particularly clear in their ultimatum to the board: "We are unable to work for or with people that lack competence, judgment and care for our mission and employees." The fact that Microsoft extended job offers to all OpenAI employees, and that many were prepared to follow Altman to a new venture, demonstrated how deeply the technical workforce aligned with his approach to AI development.[61]

The crisis resolution, including Altman's reinstatement and the reorganization of the board, represented an attempt to find a sustainable balance between speed and oversight. Microsoft's gaining of a nonvoting board observer position through Dee Templeton highlighted the formal recognition of the importance of maintaining development momentum while establishing new governance guardrails.[62]

This speed and market release perspective fundamentally differs from both the stewardship view and pure commercial interests. It represents a belief that rapid development and deployment of AI technologies, when properly managed, serve both the advancement of the technology and the broader mission of ensuring AI benefits humanity. The perspective acknowledges risks but argues that these are best understood and mitigated through practical experience and iterative improvement rather than primarily through theoretical consideration and cautious deployment.

8.3 PRIVATE GOVERNANCE IN SPECIALIZED AI: ALPHAFOLD

AlphaFold is an artificial intelligence program developed by DeepMind, a subsidiary of Alphabet Inc. (Google's parent company).[63] It represents a significant advancement in the field of structural biology. AlphaFold's primary function is to predict the three-dimensional structures of proteins based on their amino acid sequences. This capability is a major breakthrough because understanding a protein's structure is crucial for comprehending its function and subsequently utilizing it in applications like drug discovery and vaccine development.

Before AlphaFold, determining protein structures was a time-consuming and complex process, often requiring years of experimental work.[64] AlphaFold, however, can predict structures with a level of accuracy comparable to laboratory methods, and it does so in a matter of days or even hours. This efficiency opens up new possibilities for scientific research, particularly in understanding biological processes and developing new treatments for diseases. AlphaFold's success is largely due to its advanced machine learning algorithms, which were trained on a vast dataset of known protein structures. In 2020, AlphaFold demonstrated its capabilities by achieving remarkable success in the Critical Assessment of Structure Prediction (CASP), a biennial competition in protein structure prediction.[65] The program's predictions were so accurate that they were described as a solution to a fifty-year-old grand challenge in biology.[66] Matthew Higgins, a biochemistry professor at Oxford University, stated to the Financial Times: "The use of AlphaFold was really transformational, giving us a sharp view of [a] malaria surface protein."[67]

8.3.1 *Risks Associated with the Development of AlphaFold*

Like any advanced technological tool, the development of AlphaFold brings with it several potential risks, emanating both from the successful application of its findings as well as from the limitations or potential misuse of this technology.[68] A key concern is that the quality and validity of AlphaFold's protein structure predictions have not been fully established.[69] While the structures look promising, critics argue they may produce false leads that delay research progress. Experts warn researchers not to assume these structures are completely accurate without rigorous experimental validation.[70] Experimental methods validate and enrich our understanding of protein structures, and overreliance on computational methods could undermine these traditional approaches. Overreliance on computational models without sufficient experimental checks could lead to the propagation of inaccuracies or oversights in scientific research.

There is also a risk that the promises and hype surrounding AlphaFold may be exaggerated. While the system represents an impressive technical feat, some experts caution that translating these molecular structures into clinically useful insights or treatments could still be far off.[71] Overstating AlphaFold's readiness for guiding medical therapies risks premature application.[72] Similarly, AlphaFold's success with certain types of proteins might inadvertently bias research toward those proteins that are more amenable to prediction by the tool, potentially neglecting important proteins that are less predictable but equally significant.[73]

More broadly, deploying AI technologies such as AlphaFold within complex domains like drug discovery and genomics research raises ethical questions. AlphaFold's training and operation require large datasets, some of which may contain sensitive information.[74] Ensuring the privacy and security of this data is essential to prevent misuse or unauthorized access. As datasets grow in size and scope, issues around informed consent, responsible data sharing, privacy protection, and fair access become more pressing. Ownership, control, and patenting of information derived from human genomic databases are fraught with controversy and still being actively debated. The ability to predict protein structures accurately could accelerate research in genetic engineering and synthetic biology. This raises ethical questions about the limits of modifying biological systems, potential environmental impacts, and unintended consequences.

The risks from potential misuse of AlphaFold are even more acute. For example, understanding protein structures could help create more effective toxins or bioweapons.[75] AlphaFold can provide detailed insights into the structures and functions of proteins, including those that might be critical to the pathogenicity or virulence of harmful microorganisms.[76] This knowledge could, in theory, be used to modify existing pathogens or create new ones. By understanding how specific proteins interact with human biology, it could become possible to design biological agents that are more selective, potent, or resistant to existing medical treatments. This prospect becomes even more threatening given the speed and efficiency of AI-driven tools. The rapid and automated nature of AI-driven predictions could potentially bypass some of the traditional checkpoints and balances in scientific research, which might normally help to identify and mitigate potentially harmful research products.

8.3.2 *DeepMind's Governance Approach to Mitigate Concerns*

The benefits and the risks of developing AlphaFold were painfully apparent to DeepMind from the beginning of this project. In 2020, DeepMind was preparing for a prediction test, widely known in the fields of bioinformatics and structural biology as CASP. In CASP, participating teams use computational methods to predict the three-dimensional structure of proteins from their amino acid sequence.[77] These predictions are then compared to experimental results, which are kept secret until after the predictions are submitted. This comparison helps in assessing the accuracy and effectiveness of the prediction methods. The insights gained from these competitions often lead to improved methods for predicting protein structures, which is crucial for understanding biological processes and developing new pharmaceuticals. The team believed that AlphaFold would take the scientific community by storm, because of its higher-than-anticipated accuracy. But they were far less clear about the moral and social implications of their product.

For years, DeepMind had developed AlphaFold while trying to align with the operating principles established by their parent, Alphabet.[78] Google's AI Community Standards require avoiding technologies that cause harm, facilitate injury to people, enable surveillance violating norms, or contravene human rights principles. They also focus on equity and inclusiveness in AI and call for designing systems carefully to avoid amplifying human biases. But moving from general principles to specific applications is always challenging, particularly when the same products could be at once hugely beneficial and broadly harmful. The team recognized the immense potential of its AlphaFold system to solve this longstanding scientific problem. However, they also grappled with analyzing the wider implications of releasing such a capable technology openly. They also realized that releasing AlphaFold could present risks across areas where DeepMind lacked expertise.

To gain a broader perspective, DeepMind consulted over thirty external leaders spanning biology, biosecurity, bioethics, human rights, and related domains, thus making a concerted effort to incorporate diverse voices. Several consistent themes surfaced through these expansive discussions. On the concern of potential harm, experts largely argued AlphaFold itself did not fundamentally lower practical barriers to misuse. With thoughtful safeguards in place, experts contended, open information access would catalyze scientific progress. Biologists also stressed the importance of DeepMind providing clear confidence metrics to guide responsible application of AlphaFold's predictions. Additionally, experts strongly advised DeepMind to consider partnerships and hands-on support for researchers tackling historically underfunded challenges such as neglected diseases in order to equitably share benefits.

By proactively consulting a spectrum of disciplines on AlphaFold's release, DeepMind looked beyond technical considerations to broader societal implications, so as to maximize upside opportunities while conscientiously assessing risks. This guided an approach focused on transparency, equity, and enabling broad access to create a widespread public good. To reassure the scientific community about AlphaFold's accuracy, DeepMind secured peer-reviewed publications, including two in Nature, that applied the typical rigorous standards in the field. Through the peer-review process, DeepMind provided to researchers clear confidence measures about AlphaFold's predictions, which highlighted both its strengths and its limitations, and open source code, which allows researchers to incorporate it into their tools more readily.[79] In addition, they partnered with the European Molecular Biology Laboratory – European Bioinformatics Institute (EMBL-EBI), part of an intergovernmental research organization funded by over twenty states and widely considered the industry leader in big data biological research.[80] Together, they released predicted shapes for every protein in the human body, later expanded to nearly all cataloged proteins known to science.[81] This information is available for free, accompanied by support resources. To further focus on equity concerns, they continue to partner with other nonprofit organizations supporting research on marginalized issues, such as the Drugs for Neglected Disease Initiative.

AlphaFold's release was not without its criticisms. While AlphaFold has been successful in predicting protein structures, its ability to aid in drug discovery is not fully realized. A study from MIT highlighted that AlphaFold is useful in structure prediction but lacks capabilities in other stages of drug discovery, such as modeling how drugs and proteins interact physically.[82] Derek Lowe, a drug discovery chemist, emphasized that knowing protein structures does not significantly aid in drug discovery, as the major challenges lie in choosing the right targets and early warnings about toxicity.[83] Others point to a general misunderstanding of what has been accomplished by AlphaFold and claim that the algorithm struggles with disordered protein regions, which are beyond its computational technique.[84]

These and other criticisms, however, revolve around AlphaFold's limitations as a research tool, an important conversation in any such release. The ethical and social considerations associated with its release have not surfaced with any rigor either in conversations in the scientific community or in the public press. This suggests that, at least at first glance, DeepMind's efforts have succeeded in reassuring concerned parties that it intends to uphold principles of transparency and equity.

8.4 HYBRID CORPORATE FORMS AS A SOLUTION TO GOVERNING LLMS

The development of large language models (LLMs) presents governance challenges that traditional corporate structures struggle to address effectively. These increasingly powerful systems offer revolutionary benefits in knowledge access, creative assistance, and information processing,[85] but also carry unique and potentially catastrophic risks.[86] LLMs can generate convincing misinformation at unprecedented scale, facilitate sophisticated cyberattacks, amplify harmful social biases and, as they grow more capable, potentially develop emergent behaviors that their creators neither intended nor fully understand. Unlike traditional software products, these models can be deployed globally in minutes, can influence billions of users simultaneously, and operate as increasingly autonomous reasoning systems rather than simple tools. The stakes involved in LLM development are significantly greater than in conventional industries, creating intense pressure on companies developing these systems to demonstrate credible commitment to responsible innovation.[87]

Against this backdrop, hybrid governance structures have emerged as a promising solution. Hybrid forms constitute a fundamental departure from conventional corporations operating under shareholder primacy doctrine, where managers are legally obligated to prioritize profit maximization and shareholder returns above all else.[88] While traditional corporations must justify every decision through the lens of financial benefit to shareholders, hybrid structures intentionally realign incentives between managers and shareholders, creating protected space for executives to pursue missions that extend beyond the bottom line. Hybrid structures purport to free management from the relentless pressure of quarterly earnings and short-term stock performance, enabling them to make decisions that prioritize broader societal values such as safety, quality, ethics, and long-term sustainability.

The appeal of hybrid governance is rooted in its simplicity. These structures focus their innovation almost exclusively at the top, intervening at the level of management incentives and board composition, in the hopes that managers will then transform company operations in their image. Where the process outlined in this book calls for internal norm-creation, detailed procedural safeguards, extensive documentation requirements, and complex monitoring mechanisms that permeate throughout the organization, hybrid structures offer a refreshingly minimalist alternative. They promise to solve the governance challenge[89] through a single, elegant intervention at the incentive level. Rather than building intricate institutional architectures to constrain executive behavior within a fundamentally profit-driven structure, hybrid organizations simply rewrite the foundational contract. By adopting charter provisions that explicitly prioritize public-oriented missions and installing leadership philosophically committed to those principles, they aim to align manager incentives directly with broader societal benefit. The simplicity is undeniably seductive: correct the incentives at the source, select virtuous leadership, and trust their largely unconstrained discretion to advance the mission.

Leading AI innovators have adopted these hybrid structures as commitment devices regarding their values and priorities. While government regulation is the traditional alternative to self-regulation in most industries, hybrid structures have emerged as a third path, particularly popular among AI developers. By signaling ethical boundaries and commitment to safety, these structures attempt to convince skeptics while still accessing the capital markets and talent pools necessary for cutting-edge research and development.

The paragraphs later describe the experiences of OpenAI and Anthropic, two leading LLM developers that have adopted distinct hybrid governance models, to reveal the limitations of this simplified approach. Modifying foundational documents and restructuring boards does not substitute for the challenging work of translating abstract values and principles into operational reality. These cases demonstrate that even when managers are freed from pure profit-maximization imperatives, they still require robust processes to surface emerging ethical issues, incorporate diverse perspectives, make principled tradeoffs, and implement consistent safeguards throughout the organization. The governance mechanisms described in earlier chapters prove even more necessary, not less, in these mission-driven organizations. Far from being rendered obsolete by innovative corporate structures, these operational governance practices provide an essential roadmap for well-intentioned managers struggling to navigate the complex ethical terrain of advanced AI development.

8.4.1 *OpenAI's Capped-Profit Model*

OpenAI was founded in December 2015 as a nonprofit organization with the explicit mission to ensure that artificial general intelligence benefits all of humanity. In 2019, the organization transitioned to a capped-profit model by establishing OpenAI LP, a for-profit subsidiary governed by the nonprofit parent, OpenAI Inc.[90] This structural transformation was essential for the company's growth strategy, enabling OpenAI to attract and retain top talent by offering employees equity-like compensation through stock options, a necessity in the competitive AI talent market. The restructuring also proved critical in securing massive investment from Microsoft, who committed billions to the company while formally accepting the limitations on their potential returns.[91]

This capped-profit structure allows investors to earn returns up to 100 times their investment, which Sam Altman defended as modest given the "incomprehensibly enormous" potential impact of AGI.[92] As Altman explained: "We've made a soft promise to investors that, 'Once we build a generally intelligent system, that basically we will ask it to figure out a way to make an investment return for you.'" The nonprofit board maintains control over OpenAI LP, theoretically ensuring that the mission remains central to operations. This arrangement attempts to thread a delicate needle, accessing the capital and talent advantages of for-profit entities while maintaining the mission-oriented governance of a nonprofit.

However, OpenAI's governance model has faced significant challenges that highlight the fundamental limitations of structural solutions. Far from resolving the heterogeneity of preferences among stakeholders, the hybrid structure may have actually intensified conflicts by creating parallel power centers with competing visions for the company's direction.[93] The November 2023 leadership crisis dramatically illustrated how these deep divisions between safety advocates and deployment enthusiasts remained unresolved under the hybrid governance model.

Despite the theoretical checks provided by the nonprofit board, Altman maintained extraordinary discretion over critical strategic and operational decisions.[94] He managed the OpenAI Startup Fund personally, raising serious conflict of interest concerns.[95] The board discovered this arrangement only after hearing complaints that profits weren't flowing to OpenAI investors. When questioned, "OpenAI executives first said it had been for tax reasons, then eventually explained Altman had set up the fund because it was faster and only a 'temporary' arrangement."[96] This episode revealed how easily the hybrid structure's intended guardrails could be circumvented through peripheral management decisions that gradually sidelined the nonprofit's oversight role.

Even more concerning was Altman's ability to bypass established safety protocols at will. He claimed to have secured approval from the Microsoft-OpenAI joint safety board for controversial GPT-4 features, when in fact "only one had actually been approved." This misrepresentation demonstrates how the hybrid structure failed to create meaningful constraints on executive decision-making when it came to the core tension between rapid deployment and careful safety considerations.

The internal dynamics with key executives further exposed the governance model's inadequacy. Mira Murati, OpenAI's CTO, found herself unable to effectively perform her role due to what she described as "the dynamic between Altman and Brockman – who reported to her but would go to Altman anytime she tried to rein him in – made it almost impossible for her to do her job."[97] This organizational dysfunction reveals how the mission was not consistently articulated and implemented throughout different levels of the company, with parallel power structures undermining formal reporting relationships.

When the board finally attempted to exercise its authority by removing Altman, citing concerns about his candor in communications, the limitations of the hybrid structure became starkly apparent. Over 700 employees signed a letter demanding Altman's return and declared publicly that "OpenAI is nothing without its people."[98] Microsoft, as the primary investor, reportedly threatened to hire all departing employees unless Altman was reinstated.[99] These actions effectively nullified the board's formal authority, demonstrating how the alignment between the CEO, major investors, and employees could override the governance mechanisms established in the hybrid structure. The crisis resolution, which achieved Altman's reinstatement and a board restructuring, represents not the triumph of the hybrid model but its fundamental recalibration toward more conventional corporate governance.

8.4.2 *Anthropic's Public Benefit Corporation and Long-Term Benefit Trust*

Anthropic, founded in 2021 by former OpenAI researchers including Dario Amodei, took a different approach to hybrid governance.[100] Structured as a Public Benefit Corporation (PBC), Anthropic integrated its ethical mission directly into its legal charter, which explicitly states that the company's purpose is "the responsible development and maintenance of advanced AI for the long-term benefit of humanity."[101] This PBC status creates a legal foundation for considering impacts beyond shareholder value, but Anthropic recognized that this alone would be insufficient to ensure ethical decision-making as the company scaled. As they stated, while the PBC released managers and directors from the constraints of profit maximization, it did not necessarily render them "directly accountable to other stakeholders or align their incentives with the interests of the general public."

To strengthen its governance model, Anthropic established the Long-Term Benefit Trust (LTBT), a novel structure designed to provide additional safeguards for its mission. The LTBT consists of five independent, financially disinterested trustees selected from backgrounds in public health, AI alignment, national security, and policy. These trustees hold specialized Class T stock that grants them formal board control, with increasing authority over time. While the LTBT could not remove the CEO or president, it initially elects a subset of the board and will eventually elect a majority of Anthropic's board within four years.[102]

Anthropic's approach deliberately attempts to create a more robust check against mission drift than OpenAI's model, emphasizing the role of independent, disinterested parties in governance.[103] By placing future board control in the hands of trustees who have no financial stake in the company's success, Anthropic aimed to avoid the conflicts that might arise when board members must balance their fiduciary duty to shareholders with broader ethical considerations. This model represents a promising evolution in hybrid governance structures, but as we will see, even this more sophisticated approach leaves critical questions about operational governance unresolved.

8.4.3 *Why Hybrid Structures Are Not Sufficient*

Hybrid governance structures represent an important innovation in corporate design, but they substitute the declaration of values for their implementation. Enshrining principles such as safety, responsibility, and human benefit in founding documents is a necessary first step, but it hardly guarantees that these values will shape the organization's actual behavior. The real work of responsible AI governance happens not in crafting mission statements or designing board structures, but in the countless day-to-day decisions that translate abstract principles into concrete actions. This translation process is where hybrid structures alone prove ultimately insufficient.

The gap between declared values and organizational practice emerges from a fundamental reality: values do not implement themselves. A charter provision stating that AI should benefit humanity provides no operational guidance on what capabilities to prioritize, what safeguards to implement, what deployment timelines are appropriate, or how to resolve conflicts between competing goods.[104] These crucial decisions depend on how managers exercise their discretion in interpreting and applying the organization's stated mission. At OpenAI, we saw this discretion manifest in Altman's management of the startup fund and his representation of safety approvals.[105] Despite the nonprofit board's theoretical oversight, his personal interpretation of how best to achieve the mission shaped the organization's trajectory far more than its formal governance structure.

The discretion afforded to managers in hybrid structures is both their greatest strength and most significant vulnerability. All leading AI companies, including Google DeepMind, Microsoft, OpenAI, and Anthropic, ostensibly pursue similar missions of beneficial AI development, yet their practical approaches differ dramatically.[106] These differences stem not from their experimentations with hybrid governance, but from how their leadership teams translate abstract values into strategic and operational decisions.[107] Managers determine which research directions to fund, which safety concerns to prioritize, which stakeholder voices merit attention, and how to balance speed with caution. Hybrid structures provide no inherent mechanism for guiding or constraining this expansive discretion beyond the blunt instrument of board oversight, which proved to be easily circumvented or neutralized when tested in the OpenAI crisis.

As organizations scale, the challenge of maintaining alignment with stated values intensifies exponentially. A single visionary leader or small leadership team cannot personally oversee the translation of principles into practice across hundreds or thousands of employees working on increasingly complex systems. This reality necessitates sophisticated governance infrastructure, such as structured processes for surfacing ethical concerns, clear guidelines for resolving conflicts between values, robust monitoring systems to detect misalignment, and meaningful escalation paths when lower-level resolution proves impossible. The dysfunctional dynamic between OpenAI's executives illustrates what happens when informal power relationships undermine formal reporting structures, creating organizational confusion about how to implement the mission consistently.

Perhaps the most problematic assumption underlying hybrid governance models is that the right manager with the right incentives will automatically establish appropriate implementation structures.[108] This assumption fundamentally misunderstands the complexity of operationalizing abstract values in rapidly evolving technological environments. Even the most ethically minded leaders may lack the expertise, perspective, or institutional capacity to design comprehensive governance systems that effectively translate values into practice across diverse contexts. The complexity of AI governance demands specialized knowledge from multiple disciplines, from ethics and law to computer science, sociology, and psychology, that no single leader or leadership team can fully possess.

Moreover, the very process of designing effective governance systems requires precisely the practices that the system itself should foster: consultation with diverse stakeholders, deliberation about competing values, negotiation between different perspectives, and transparent communication about tradeoffs and limitations.[109] Managers operating within hybrid structures may sincerely believe they have sufficient insight to design these systems unilaterally, but this confidence often proves unwarranted. The cognitive limitations, institutional blindspots, and personal biases that governance systems aim to counterbalance affect the designers themselves. This recursive challenge cannot be resolved through structural innovation alone.

Rather than assuming well-intentioned managers will spontaneously create appropriate governance structures, organizations need systems that verify managers have engaged in the necessary consultation, deliberation, and communication with all relevant stakeholders. Independent board oversight, external advisory councils, formal stakeholder engagement processes, regular governance reviews, and other mechanisms serve not just as constraints on managerial overreach but as essential resources for developing more effective governance. These mechanisms complement hybrid structures rather than competing with them, providing the accountability and perspective necessary to translate abstract values into consistent practice.

OpenAI's board discovered too late that its formal authority offered little protection against the aligned interests of the CEO, major investors, and employees.[110] The hybrid structure that was meant to preserve mission integrity ultimately proved inadequate in the face of commercial pressures and executive influence. This outcome does not invalidate the importance of mission-driven governance structures, but it does highlight their limitations when not accompanied by robust operational governance mechanisms throughout the organization.[111] The lesson is clear: hybrid structures may create protected space for ethical decision-making, but they do not inherently fill that space with the governance processes necessary for translating values into practice.

8.4.4 *Corporate Ordering Solutions*

If hybrid structures alone cannot ensure responsible AI development, what can? The answer lies in the daily decisions and operational practices that translate abstract values into tangible governance. AI companies themselves have pioneered a remarkable array of governance innovations to address the ethical complexity their technologies present. Long before regulators were around to mandate them, these practices emerged through private sector experimentation as companies sought to build trust, mitigate risks, and demonstrate responsible stewardship. Many of these methods represent applications of fundamental corporate governance tools discussed in earlier chapters. For example, red teaming embodies the principle of external validation, system cards implement disclosure and accountability, while constitutional AI represents an ambitious exercise in corporate rulemaking. These private governance innovations are now informing the regulatory landscape. As lawmakers around the world develop AI legislation, they are essentially codifying best practices first developed within companies themselves.[112] Through this iterative process, private governance becomes the foundation for law. The goal of this chapter is not to evaluate how effectively individual companies implement these tools, but rather to understand how a collective effort to develop governance mechanisms is establishing industry standards that both complement hybrid structures and provide a blueprint for effective regulation.

8.4.4.1 Red Teaming Relies on External Validation

Red teaming has emerged as a critical governance practice that deliberately introduces external accountability into AI development processes. Unlike internal testing, red teaming deliberately invites adversarial perspectives from outside experts tasked with breaking, manipulating, or otherwise exposing vulnerabilities in AI systems before they reach the public.[113] OpenAI's approach to red teaming GPT-4 exemplifies this practice, with the company engaging over 100 independent experts across twenty-nine countries to stress-test the model through simulated adversarial attacks, jailbreaking attempts, and probes for harmful outputs.[114] These external experts include ethicists, safety researchers, and specialists in domains like cybersecurity and disinformation. Because they are not regular employees, they operate without the institutional biases that might blind internal testers to certain risks.

The findings from these red team exercises directly inform crucial decisions about model capabilities, limitations, and deployment timelines. Anthropic has further formalized this approach through its Responsible Scaling Policy, which establishes graduated AI Safety Levels (ASLs) that determine the intensity and scope of required red teaming before models can be deployed at increasing scales.[115] This represents a significant evolution from traditional quality assurance toward a more adversarial security mindset that recognizes the inherent limitations of self-assessment. By institutionalizing external criticism, red teaming creates a crucial counterbalance to the natural optimism and enthusiasm of AI developers.

8.4.4.2 System Cards Promote Disclosure and Accountability

System cards represent another essential governance mechanism, embedding transparency and public accountability into AI development processes. These detailed technical documents serve as the equivalent of nutritional labels or pharmaceutical package inserts for AI systems, documenting known limitations, biases, performance boundaries, and potential risks associated with each model.[116] Unlike marketing materials designed to highlight strengths, system cards deliberately focus on weaknesses, risks, and boundaries of appropriate use.

OpenAI, Anthropic, and Meta have all adopted system cards as standard practice for major model releases, creating a consistent framework for communicating critical information to users, researchers, and the public.[117] These documents typically include quantitative evaluations across multiple dimensions: performance degradation across demographic groups, sensitivity to adversarial inputs, tendency toward hallucination in specific domains, and susceptibility to prompt manipulation. System cards provide information for diverse external stakeholders, from researchers to enterprise customers to civil society organizations. With this information, they can make informed decisions about model adoption and implement appropriate safeguards in downstream applications.

Anthropic's approach to system cards exemplifies their governance value, as the company intentionally delayed Claude's market release to complete thorough documentation of its capabilities and limitations. This deliberate restraint was praised as "a costly signal" demonstrating genuine commitment to safety over market advantage. By establishing system cards as a prerequisite for release rather than a retrospective documentation exercise, Anthropic embedded accountability directly into its product development cycle.

8.4.4.3 Constitutional AI and Value Alignment

Constitutional AI represents a groundbreaking approach to embedding ethical principles directly into model development rather than merely imposing restrictions after training. At its core, constitutional AI attempts to solve the fundamental value alignment problem: how to ensure that increasingly powerful AI systems optimize for human values rather than pursuing goals that might technically satisfy their programming but violate deeper ethical principles.

The approach, pioneered by Anthropic, involves developing a set of fundamental principles, termed a "constitution," that guides the model's behavior throughout training and operation.[118] Rather than relying solely on post-training filters or safeguards, constitutional AI integrates these principles into the foundation of how models learn. Anthropic's Claude was trained using a constitution developed in collaboration with the Collective Intelligence Project, deliberately incorporating diverse perspectives through public input processes to ensure the embedded values reflect democratic principles rather than merely the preferences of Anthropic's engineers.

This constitutional framework functions as a form of self-supervision during training, where the model learns to critique its own outputs according to the established principles. When generating responses, the AI system first produces a draft, then evaluates that draft against constitutional principles, identifies potential violations, and refines its output accordingly.[119] This recursive self-improvement process creates an internal deliberative mechanism analogous to human ethical reasoning.

What makes constitutional AI particularly significant from a governance perspective is its transparency and modifiability. Unlike black box safety mechanisms, the constitutional principles can be publicly documented, debated, and revised based on stakeholder input and emerging ethical consensus. This approach received substantial praise for its emphasis on principled restraint rather than rushing to market, with observers such as Open AI's Helen Toner noting that Anthropic's decision to keep their product off the market was a costly signal of restraint, enhancing the credibility of its commitments to AI safety. By building ethical reasoning into the core of model development rather than treating it as an external constraint, constitutional AI represents a paradigm shift in how AI systems can be aligned with human values.

8.4.4.4 The Need for Governance Tools in Hybrid Corporate Structures

Hybrid governance structures like those pioneered by OpenAI and Anthropic represent meaningful attempts to address the unique challenges posed by advanced AI development. By creating formal mechanisms that prioritize broader societal benefit alongside commercial considerations, these structures establish an important foundation for responsible innovation. They signal to stakeholders, employees, and the public a serious commitment to developing AI that serves humanity's interests rather than merely maximizing shareholder returns.

Yet as the analysis earlier demonstrates, these structural innovations function best when complemented by robust operational governance practices. The translation of abstract principles into consistent organizational behavior requires more than well-crafted mission statements or innovative board compositions. It demands the patient, deliberate development of governance mechanisms that guide daily decision-making at all levels of the organization. Red teaming introduces essential external perspectives that counter institutional blindspots, system cards create transparency and accountability around model capabilities and limitations, and approaches like constitutional AI embed ethical reasoning into the technical development process itself.

8.5 CORPORATE ORDERING IN A LARGE CORPORATION: MICROSOFT

For a large corporation like Microsoft, implementing responsible AI governance presents distinct organizational challenges. AI technologies inevitably appear across multiple products and software applications with widely varying commercial uses and contexts. Maintaining a consistent ethical approach across this diverse portfolio is a significant challenge in itself. Moreover, certain strategic decisions about acceptable uses and technological boundaries must be made centrally, while ensuring alignment among employees with vastly different skillsets and priorities, from engineers focused on innovation to legal teams concerned with compliance and risk.[120] As CEO Satya Nadella stated, "we learned that we needed to create a governance model that was inclusive and encouraged engineers, researchers, and policy practitioners to work shoulder to shoulder to uphold our AI principles. A single team or a single discipline tasked with responsible or ethical AI was not going to meet our objectives."[121] This insight drove the development of a comprehensive governance structure at Microsoft that integrates three essential functions: corporate rulemaking, executive decision-making, and continuous monitoring.

The success of Microsoft's approach stems from its ability to combine a principles-based framework with operational reach across the organization. By establishing clear ethical guidelines through its Responsible AI Standard, Microsoft created a common language for evaluating AI systems while extending implementation through a hub-and-spoke model of AI champions embedded across engineering teams. This structure ensures consistent application of principles while maintaining flexibility for diverse technical contexts. When difficult tradeoffs arise, Microsoft's Sensitive Uses review process functions as a quasi-judicial system, creating precedents that guide future development with clear escalation paths to the highest levels of the organization.[122]

The paragraphs below discuss three core components of Microsoft's governance structure. First, the corporate rulemaking efforts that establish standards, including the development of the Responsible AI Principles and Standard through the Aether Committee. Second, the executive decision-making functions that operationalize these principles through the Office of Responsible AI and its hub-and-spoke network of champions. Finally, the monitoring process is embodied by the Sensitive Uses review, which subjects potentially problematic AI applications to rigorous scrutiny and makes principled choices about tradeoffs between innovation and responsibility.

8.5.1 *Microsoft's AI Strategy: Values as Business Imperatives*

In 2016, Microsoft CEO Satya Nadella published a pioneering article in Slate titled "The Partnership of the Future," establishing the company's early commitment to artificial intelligence development.[123] This piece reveals how, years before the current AI boom, Microsoft was already formulating a strategic approach to AI that placed values at its core. Nadella's vision transcended the simplistic narrative of computers versus humans, instead proposing a future where "human and machine work together to solve society's greatest challenges such as beating disease, ignorance, and poverty."

What distinguishes Nadella's approach is his recognition that values are not peripheral considerations but fundamental to AI's business viability. He powerfully cites John Markoff's observation that "The best way to answer the hard questions about control in a world full of smart machines is by understanding the values of those who are actually building these systems." This insight forms the cornerstone of Microsoft's AI philosophy, which posits that technological development and values-based considerations are inseparable, with the latter directly determining market success. Without appropriate value systems guiding development, Nadella implicitly acknowledges that society might reject AI technologies, impose restrictive regulations, or ban applications altogether, effectively limiting AI's commercial potential.

Nadella frames this values-first approach through several interconnected principles: AI must augment rather than replace human capabilities; systems must be transparent and understandable; privacy and security protections must be built-in; and technology must preserve human dignity while maximizing efficiency.[124] These are not presented merely as ethical ideals but as practical business requirements that will determine whether AI technologies gain widespread acceptance. By emphasizing that AI must be designed with "algorithmic accountability" and against bias, Nadella positions responsible AI as a market imperative rather than a regulatory burden.

The business tradeoffs in AI development are addressed with similar nuance. Nadella acknowledges the tension between automation that displaces workers and technology that enhances human capabilities, suggesting that business leaders must "replace our labor-saving and automation mindset with a maker-and-creation mindset."[125] This reflects his understanding that AI's commercial potential depends on societal acceptance, which requires addressing legitimate economic concerns. For Nadella, establishing an "ethical and empathic framework" for AI design is not just morally appropriate, but it is first and foremost the essential foundation for realizing AI's business potential and securing Microsoft's position in this emerging market. His approach demonstrates remarkable foresight in recognizing that embedded values would become central to AI's commercial viability, a perspective that has only gained relevance in today's rapidly evolving AI landscape.

8.5.2 *Corporate Rulemaking: Responsible AI Principles and Standard*

Microsoft understood that to translate ethical aspirations into responsible practice, they first needed to identify key principles, and then develop these principles into actionable items. This corporate rulemaking effort began with defining core principles, which then evolved into the Responsible AI Standard, initially introduced in 2018 and later revised in 2022.[126]

Microsoft recognized early that waiting for regulatory guidance was not an option. They needed to take the initiative themselves, not only because regulatory timelines would be impractically slow for their development cycles, but because they needed to independently determine what the critical ethical issues were in the first place.[127] This proactive approach led them to establish a deliberate process of soliciting input from external stakeholders.[128] They actively consulted scholars, researchers, and academics to inform their emerging ethical framework.[129] They strategically expanded their knowledge base by drawing insights from adjacent communities focused on human rights, privacy, and related fields.

This external consultation phase was crucial in helping Microsoft develop standards that would be both robust and practical, and thus widely accepted and adopted. By channeling this diverse external input into their internal processes, they were able to create guidelines that had legitimacy both within and outside the company. Engineering teams, arguably the most influential group at Microsoft due to their product development capabilities, needed to be convinced of the framework's value and practicality.

As regulators eventually began showing interest in AI governance, Microsoft's approach evolved further. Their early investment in ethical frameworks positioned them to not only anticipate regulatory requirements but also to participate meaningfully in shaping the regulatory process itself.[130] While legal requirements would only establish a minimum threshold, Microsoft's proactive stance meant they were already operating beyond that floor. This forward-looking perspective has proven valuable, as the threat of regulation has served as a helpful motivator for organizational alignment around responsible AI practices. This methodical progression from conceptual frameworks to operational guidelines represents Microsoft's systematic approach to ensuring their AI technologies align with human values and societal needs.

8.5.2.1 The Microsoft Responsible AI Standard

The foundational premise of Microsoft's strategy was that AI technologies would gain market acceptance if they addressed user concerns and societal implications.[131] Thus, the goal of the rulemaking framework would be to identify and categorize these concerns, so that they form a cohesive set of guidelines for the company's software engineers. The Microsoft Responsible AI Standard operationalizes six core AI principles: accountability, transparency, fairness, reliability and safety, privacy and security, and inclusiveness.[132] Each principle, as the paragraphs later discuss, seeks to broaden the commercial appeal of the company's products by ensuring they address the concerns that might otherwise limit market acceptance and adoption.

At its heart, the standard recognizes that accountable AI systems require rigorous assessment of potential impacts on different populations.[133] Microsoft implements this through structured Impact Assessments during early development, helping teams identify and address potential negative effects before they manifest. This approach reduces legal and reputational risks while positioning Microsoft's products favorably for earning consumer confidence and navigating potential regulatory concerns.

Hand in hand with accountability comes transparency, which allows end users to understand what information forms the basis for their interactions with AI systems. Through Transparency Notes, users gain insight into an AI system's capabilities, limitations, and appropriate uses.[134] This principle reduces uncertainty about AI operations and enables informed decisions. Commercially, transparent AI systems address concerns about "black box" decision-making, potentially increasing adoption rates.[135] Businesses are more likely to invest in AI solutions when they understand how these tools make decisions that affect their operations.

The standard places equal emphasis on fairness, which ensures AI systems provide a consistent quality of service across different demographic groups, including marginalized communities. This principle enhances commercial value by expanding the market reach of AI products. Fair systems work effectively for diverse user bases, opening additional market segments.[136] Moreover, companies with demonstrably fair AI systems are better positioned to win contracts that require equitable treatment of all users, particularly in sectors such as finance, healthcare, and government services.

Reliability and safety form another cornerstone of the framework, focusing on predictable performance even under varied conditions. Microsoft understood that AI systems that fail unexpectedly or operate inconsistently quickly lose market share regardless of their technical sophistication. By emphasizing these qualities, Microsoft positions its AI offerings as dependable business tools rather than experimental technologies, allowing them to command premium pricing in mission-critical applications where reliability justifies higher investment.

Privacy and security concerns have emerged as significant barriers to AI adoption, which Microsoft addresses through strict data governance and management practices.[137] The standard mandates comprehensive protocols for data collection, processing, and storage that protect user information from misuse.[138] Beyond addressing user concerns, these practices ensure compliance with global regulations such as GDPR and CCPA, expanding Microsoft's market reach while avoiding costly penalties.[139]

Rounding out the framework, Microsoft emphasizes inclusiveness by actively collaborating with diverse communities throughout the development process.[140] This approach ensures AI systems work effectively across global markets and varied user groups, opening new opportunities and use cases that might otherwise remain unexplored. Products designed with inclusivity from the ground up naturally align with the values of socially conscious consumers and investors, creating additional market advantages.[141]

The release of Microsoft's Responsible AI Standard in 2022 has garnered significant attention within the industry and press.[142] Commentators have widely recognized it as a leading example of translating high-level ethical principles into enforceable, operational requirements.[143] The Standard has drawn particular praise for its depth, specificity, and rigorous oversight mechanisms, with many highlighting its emphasis on continuous evaluation, human oversight, and transparency as setting a benchmark for the industry.[144] Microsoft's approach to fairness, especially in essential domains such as healthcare, finance, and employment, has been noted as a meaningful step toward mitigating algorithmic bias. However, critics have pointed to challenges in implementation, with some industry observers expressing concern about the complexity and resource demands of such a thorough standard, particularly for smaller organizations with limited resources.[145] There is also ongoing debate about enforcement mechanisms, with questions raised about whether external audits or regulatory oversight might ultimately be necessary to ensure compliance industry-wide.[146]

8.5.2.2 The Aether Committee as Corporate Rulemaker: A Pioneering Multidisciplinary Brain Trust

Behind Microsoft's development of these AI principles and standards is the Aether Committee, a pioneering body essentially functioning as an internal think tank and policymaker.[147] AETHER stands for AI, Ethics, and Effects in Engineering and Research. This internal advisory body is dedicated to guiding the ethical development and deployment of artificial intelligence technologies.

The Committee consists of approximately forty top executives drawn from research, policy, and engineering teams, creating a multidisciplinary brain trust that combines technical knowledge with policy and ethical expertise. Co-led by Brad Smith, Microsoft's Board Chairman and former chief legal officer, and Kevin Scott, the company's Chief Technology Officer, the Committee meets monthly to submit to ORA progress and coordinate AI initiatives.[148] Their discussions range from evaluating specific high-risk applications to debating broader ethical frameworks, with division leaders sharing implementation updates while subject matter experts in fields ranging from machine learning to human rights law provide guidance. The Committee's influence was evident from its earliest days. It formulated Microsoft's first AI principles, which the company formally adopted in 2018, establishing the foundation for all subsequent governance efforts. The principles represented a quintessential example of corporate rulemaking, establishing uniform, generally applicable standards that would govern all of Microsoft's AI development.

The effort to combine multiple disciplines reflects the understanding that input from all perspectives is necessary for responsible AI development. Aether serves as a cross-disciplinary forum, bringing together experts from technology, ethics, law, and policy to evaluate the societal implications of AI technologies. The committee provides recommendations on policies, processes, and best practices to ensure that AI systems are developed and deployed responsibly.[149] It functions in an advisory capacity to Microsoft's senior leadership and the Office of Responsible AI, influencing decisions on AI-related initiatives and customer engagements.

To address the multifaceted challenges of AI ethics, Aether comprises several specialized working groups, each focusing on specific areas such as fairness and inclusiveness, reliability and safety, privacy and security, transparency, and accountability.[150] These working groups develop tools, best practices, and implementation guidance to operationalize responsible AI across Microsoft's products and services.

But the institutional experimentation does not stop there. Once the company established executive teams dedicated to implementing the standard, it also designed channels for providing feedback from these teams into the corporate rulemaking effort. The Aether Committee participates in the Responsible AI Council, which convenes representatives from research, policy, engineering, and business. These forums are described as both "challenging and refreshing," fostering collective wisdom and generating new ideas through the combination of diverse viewpoints.[151] The committee's processes are iterative, with ongoing dialogue and feedback loops, allowing for the identification of blind spots, the surfacing of new risks, and the adaptation of policies as technology and societal expectations evolve.

8.5.3 *Executive Decision-Making: The Office of Responsible AI*

With a set of AI principles established by 2019, Microsoft was ready to take the next step in responsible AI governance by creating a dedicated team designed to bring these principles into practice. This team took shape as the Office of Responsible AI (ORA), established in 2019 as the heart of Microsoft's governance structure for responsible AI.[152] The ORA is structured under Corporate External Legal Affairs (CELA), though not all members are practicing lawyers. It has evolved into a hybrid organization combining legal expertise, technical knowledge, and policy experience.[153] Its staff includes lawyers and compliance professionals alongside engineers, ethicists, and policy experts who can engage meaningfully with development teams on technical questions while maintaining focus on ethical and societal impacts. As of early 2025, Microsoft has invested significantly in this area, with over 400 employees working on responsible AI initiatives, of which approximately half are dedicated full-time to ORA, and the other half dispersed around the company on various teams working on AI.[154]

While this might sound like a traditional compliance department, the ORA represents a significant departure in both structure and function. Unlike conventional legal or compliance teams that typically react to problems after they arise, the ORA works proactively with engineering teams during the development process. This required a fundamental shift in how oversight functions operate within the company. A crucial part of the ORA's operation is its daily engagement with engineers to build a compliance platform for all teams to submit their AI uses, partially automating the oversight process. Through this hybrid structure, the ORA effectively combines executive decision-making functions with continuous monitoring to ensure those decisions align with Microsoft's ethical principles and standards.

This institutional hybrid was Microsoft's answer to a key challenge: how to gain buy-in from the company's famed engineering teams, which wield exceptional influence due to their central role in product development. In a company that prizes innovation above all, presenting a set of principles that not only appears consistent but also evolves alongside products without stifling future developments was crucial. This approach was essential to establishing legitimacy and building the close collaboration necessary to ensure that ethical standards became embedded in technical processes rather than remaining abstract principles.

8.5.3.1 Hub and Spoke: Embedding Responsibility throughout the Company

Microsoft employs a "hub-and-spoke" governance model for responsible AI that seeks to integrate privacy, security, and accessibility into Microsoft's products and services. This model allows Microsoft to centralize key governance functions while distributing implementation responsibilities throughout the organization.

At the center of this model, the Office of Responsible AI serves as the primary hub, connecting to two other essential components: the Aether Committee, which leverages top scientific and engineering talent for subject-matter expertise, and the Responsible AI Strategy in Engineering (RAISE) group, which enables engineering groups to implement responsible AI processes through systems and tools.[155] This interconnected hub ensures that issues identified by the ORA provide direct input to the company's policymaking efforts, creating a continuous feedback loop between practical implementation challenges and policy development. Together, these three groups set a consistent bar for responsible AI across the company.

From this central hub, the "spokes" extend outward through a network of "Responsible AI Champions," that is, senior employees embedded across different engineering and sales teams. These Champions, appointed by company leadership, serve as the eyes and ears of the responsible AI program on the ground. They actively raise awareness about Microsoft's approach to responsible AI, help teams assess ethical and societal considerations in their specific contexts, and cultivate a culture of responsible innovation within their units.

When engineering teams encounter potential ethical challenges or need to evaluate the implications of new AI applications, Champions serve as their first point of contact, helping to navigate the company's responsible AI requirements and connecting them with appropriate resources from the ORA. This structure reflects Microsoft's recognition that effective AI governance requires both centralized expertise and distributed implementation capabilities.

8.5.3.2 Operationalizing "Fit for Purpose" through the Champion Network

The "Fit for Purpose" standard serves as the key mechanism through which engineers interact with the Office of Responsible AI, ensuring their AI systems remain responsible throughout development and deployment.[156] Microsoft defines this standard as the requirement that AI systems must provide valid solutions to the problems they are designed to solve. This means each system should effectively address its intended use cases, with evidence supporting that it is an appropriate and effective solution for those specific problems.

Microsoft operationalizes "Fit for Purpose" through its Responsible AI Standard and associated Impact Assessment process.[157] Engineering teams must engage with the ORA through this process, explicitly assessing and documenting how their AI systems will solve the problems posed by their intended uses. The documentation process becomes the primary interface between technical teams and the governance structure, creating accountability at every stage of development.

The documentation process flows through a comprehensive and structured Impact Assessment for each AI system. Teams must articulate a clear definition of the problem being solved for each intended use, provide detailed documentation of the model's inputs and how well they represent the intended concepts and limitations, and document the model's outputs and their validity in representing the target phenomena. They must also assess the model's generalizability based on its training and testing data, define performance metrics and thresholds for responsible release, and identify error types and acceptable error rates.

Evidence requirements create another layer of interaction between engineers and the governance framework. Teams engage with multiple stakeholders and research methodologies to gather support for their system's fitness.[158] This may involve soliciting input from domain experts, gathering results from user studies, focus groups, or surveys, and conducting experiments or systematic research showing the system's effectiveness compared to alternatives.

To illustrate how this works in practice, consider an AI system designed to allocate hospital beds. The engineering team would work with the ORA through the Champions network to document how the system's predictions help solve the bed allocation problem. They would gather evidence through pilot studies or expert feedback demonstrating that the system improves efficiency compared to existing methods. Throughout this process, they would acknowledge any limitations in the model's predictions or generalizability, creating a transparent record of the system's capabilities and constraints.

This ongoing dialogue between engineers and the ORA is facilitated by the Champions, who guide teams through probing questions that encourage critical thinking about AI systems. Questions like "What is the problem to be solved for this intended use?" and "What evidence will establish that the system is fit for this intended use?" prompt engineers to consider the ethical and practical implications of their work. The Champions ensure that teams justify their design decisions with evidence and stakeholder input, legitimizing AI development through a rigorous review process that the ORA ultimately approves. This continuous interaction between technical development and ethical oversight is what distinguishes Microsoft's approach to responsible AI governance.

8.5.3.3 From Ground-Level Implementation to Board Oversight

Microsoft's responsible AI governance structure creates a clear line of accountability from day-to-day engineering decisions all the way to board-level oversight. The ORA has a governance and enablement team that connects to the board through two key leaders who embody the cross-disciplinary approach necessary for effective AI governance. Brad Smith, the board chairman and former chief legal officer, represents the legal and strategy perspective, while the Chief Technology Officer, Kevin Scott, represents the engineering perspective. These two executives serve as the primary conduit to the board, ensuring that both ethical and technical considerations inform the highest level of decision-making. Importantly, the Environmental, Social, and Public Policy Committee of the Microsoft Board provides oversight of the responsible AI program, establishing a direct line to board-level governance.[159]

Below these executives sits the Responsible AI Council, consisting of approximately forty corporate vice presidents who meet monthly to set the agenda, coordinate efforts, share progress, and serve as division leads. They function as the ORA's eyes and ears on the ground, helping to adopt policies in practice and providing feedback. They also connect with internal audit and other oversight functions to ensure comprehensive coverage of AI governance issues. The Aether Committee also participates in the Responsible AI Council. This governance structure has evolved organically over time in response to the growing importance of AI in Microsoft's business. Each addition to the governance framework has built upon earlier structures, creating a progressively more robust system for ensuring responsible AI development. The Responsible AI Council now serves as a forum for leadership alignment and accountability in implementing Microsoft's responsible AI program across the entire organization.[160]

This multilayered approach creates a governance structure that balances centralized expertise with distributed implementation, connecting board-level oversight to day-to-day engineering decisions through multiple layers of engagement. By taking feedback from governments, public policy teams, civil society, and international stakeholders, Microsoft's responsible AI governance demonstrates how corporate oversight can be both internally effective and externally responsive. The result is a sophisticated response to the unique challenges of overseeing AI development and deployment, a governance structure that can adapt to the evolving landscape of AI technology while maintaining a focus on responsible innovation.

8.5.4 *Monitoring and Review: Sensitive Uses*

Microsoft's governance structure faces its true test in handling sensitive use cases, where competing priorities and complex tradeoffs demand careful navigation.[161] The sensitive uses process exemplifies how Microsoft's three governance functions work together in practice: rulemaking through the standards that define sensitive uses, executive decision-making in determinations about whether to launch specific products, and monitoring through the multilayered review and appeal process for sensitive uses. In 2019, Microsoft founded the program to subject its most sensitive and novel AI use cases to rigorous, specialized review that results in tailored guidance. Since its establishment, the Sensitive Uses team has processed over 900 submissions, with the pace accelerating dramatically to 300 cases in 2023 alone, nearly 70 percent of them related to generative AI. This surge reflects both the rapid advancement of AI technology and Microsoft's expanding efforts to scrutinize its applications.

The paragraphs below describe the review process for identifying and assessing sensitive uses, highlighting that the effort for careful calibration of diverse considerations and thorough documentation lend it a quasi-judicial character. Some landmark examples of that review process in practice illustrate how this process serves the company's business strategy.

8.5.4.1 The Sensitive Uses Review Process: A Quasi-Judicial Approach

The review process itself operates like a sophisticated filtering system, with multiple levels of scrutiny that reach all the way to the top of the organization. It begins when an employee flags a potential sensitive use through a central submission tool. The system captures cases involving AI applications that could deny individuals access to consequential services such as healthcare or financial support, create risks of physical or psychological harm (particularly for vulnerable populations), or infringe on fundamental human rights such as freedom of expression or privacy. This scope, aligned with Microsoft's Responsible AI Standard, ensures that Microsoft identifies not just obvious risks but also subtle ways AI might impact human welfare.

Once submitted, the case is first routed to a local Responsible AI Champion, who serves as an initial assessor. The Champion, working closely with the Office of Responsible AI and the project team, investigates the case details and checks whether similar scenarios have previously been addressed. For familiar situations with established precedent, they can apply existing guidance. But when they encounter novel challenges, as often happens with rapidly evolving technologies such as generative AI, the case moves to the Sensitive Uses Working Group for deeper evaluation.[162]

This working group represents Microsoft's brain trust for ethical AI development, bringing together diverse experts to deliberate on complex cases. Besides technical feasibility, they consider broader societal implications and potential unintended consequences. For particularly thorny issues, or issues where there are disagreements between the engineers and the Office of Responsible AI, cases can be escalated all the way to the Aether Committee itself, ensuring the company's most senior leaders weigh in on precedent-setting decisions. If disagreements persist, the case will go to the CEO, in a clear indication of just how seriously Microsoft takes these issues and how the very top of the organization is involved in responsible AI governance.[163] This escalation path from a local champion to working groups to committees and ultimately to the CEO demonstrates Microsoft's commitment to ethical AI at every level of the organization.

The outcome is not simply a yes or no verdict. The Sensitive Uses team provides detailed, practical guidance tailored to each project's specific challenges. These recommendations might include technical safeguards, additional employee training, or modifications to the project's scope. Sometimes, when the risks appear unmanageable, teams are directed to abandon projects entirely. This is a clear indication that Microsoft's commitment to responsible AI development can trump commercial opportunities.

Microsoft's Sensitive Uses Review Program bears a striking resemblance to formal legal proceedings in both structure and function. Like a judicial system, it applies broad principles such as privacy, safety, or human rights to specific technological applications, creating a body of precedent that guides future decisions. The program's multilayered review process mimics the hierarchical structure of courts, with initial assessments by Responsible AI Champions serving as a "first instance" review, the Sensitive Uses Working Group functioning as an appellate body, and the Aether Committee representing a supreme court of sorts, with the CEO as the final authority. This structure ensures a degree of independence from the engineering teams developing the products, similar to how judicial independence separates legal judgment from the interested parties in a case. The rigorous documentation requirements parallel legal briefs and opinions, forcing teams to articulate their reasoning and consider counterarguments. Like court proceedings, the process allows all stakeholders to present their perspectives and concerns, with dissenting voices having a path to escalate their objections. Even the outcome, which consists in detailed guidance with specific requirements rather than simple approval or rejection, resembles judicial remedies that often include specific conditions and limitations. This quasi-judicial approach lends legitimacy to Microsoft's decisions, establishing a governance system that, while internal to the company, mimics the procedural fairness we typically associate with formal legal institutions.

8.5.4.2 Example: Facial Recognition in Law Enforcement

A landmark example of the Sensitive Uses review process in action emerged through Microsoft's handling of facial recognition technology in law enforcement. When faced with requests to deploy real time facial recognition on police body cameras, the case went through this review process and ultimately reached the highest levels of consideration.[164]

The outcome might have seemed unthinkable in an earlier era of tech development: Microsoft said no. The company knew this decision would spark intense controversy. While facial recognition technology promised to enhance public safety and aid law enforcement, it also raised serious ethical concerns.[165] The technology had shown significant accuracy problems, with particularly high misidentification rates for women, young people, and people of color, potentially subjecting these groups to unwarranted police scrutiny. Beyond accuracy issues, the technology's deployment would enable unprecedented levels of public surveillance, allowing for pervasive monitoring of citizens without their consent. There were also valid concerns about potential abuse, as the technology could be used for discriminatory targeting or unauthorized tracking of individuals' movements and activities.

Microsoft determined such applications were premature given both technical limitations and societal implications. The decision extended beyond considerations of technical readiness, reflecting Microsoft's recognition that the deployment of facial recognition technology in law enforcement applications necessitated comprehensive societal dialogue and robust regulatory frameworks.

In the wake of Microsoft's decision, other companies moved to fill the market gap. Most notably, Axon, which had evolved from its origins as a taser manufacturer into a comprehensive law enforcement technology provider, expanded aggressively into the police technology space. By 2024, Axon had further extended its reach by incorporating advanced AI capabilities into its body camera systems, including automated audio summarization powered by LLMs. The contrast between Microsoft's cautious approach and Axon's expansion illustrates how the Sensitive Uses process helps Microsoft navigate complex tradeoffs between commercial opportunities and potential societal harm, even when competitors choose different paths.

Microsoft's stance on facial recognition technology has continued to evolve. As recently as May 2024, the company expanded its prohibition to include "any real-time facial recognition on mobile cameras used by any law enforcement globally," strengthening its previous restrictions.[166] This policy adjustment came shortly after Axon announced a new AI technology utilizing OpenAI's GPT-4 to translate audio captured by body cameras into police reports, demonstrating Microsoft's ongoing vigilance regarding how its AI technologies might be deployed.[167]

Microsoft's decision to decline the opportunity to provide facial recognition technology for police body cameras represented a calculated strategic choice. While the company recognized the significant revenue potential in equipping police forces with this technology, Microsoft's leadership made a deliberate assessment that the reputational risks outweighed the short-term financial gains. By saying no to what could have been a lucrative market, Microsoft prioritized its long-term brand positioning as a leader in responsible AI, a differentiator they viewed as increasingly valuable in a competitive tech landscape. This difficult decision reflected Microsoft's understanding that maintaining trust with consumers, enterprise clients, and regulators would ultimately yield greater returns than pursuing every possible AI application regardless of societal impact. Rather than seeing responsible AI governance as merely a compliance function, Microsoft positioned ethical considerations as a core competitive advantage, betting that their restraint would enhance their credibility when offering AI solutions in more sensitive sectors such as healthcare, finance, and government services where trust is paramount. The decision demonstrated how responsible AI practices had become integrated not just into Microsoft's ethical framework, but into its fundamental business strategy.

8.5.4.3 Azure Custom Neural Voice: Balancing Innovation and Safeguards

Azure AI's Custom Neural Voice represents another important case where Microsoft's Sensitive Uses review process demonstrated its value.[168] This innovative speech technology enables the creation of synthetic voices that sound nearly identical to the original source. This technology is already used by enterprise customers like AT&T and Progressive, with promising applications in education, accessibility, and entertainment. However, the potential for abuse through inappropriate impersonation and listener deception required careful consideration.

Consistent with Microsoft's measured approach for higher-risk AI systems, Custom Neural Voice underwent several Sensitive Uses reviews as it evolved toward broader availability. These reviews led to the adoption of a layered control framework for Custom Neural Voice. Microsoft limited customer access to the service, ensured acceptable use cases were defined and communicated through an application form, implemented speaker consent mechanisms, created specific terms of use, published transparency documentation detailing risks and limitations, and established technical guardrails to help ensure the speaker's active participation when creating a synthetic voice.[169] Through these and other controls, Microsoft is helping protect against misuse while maintaining beneficial uses of the technology. One such beneficial use includes what is known as voice banking, allowing people who are at risk of losing their voice to "bank" their voice for later use by training a synthetic voice model through Custom Neural Voice.[170]

8.5.4.4 Fairness in Speech-to-Text Technology

Microsoft's Responsible AI Standard has also been instrumental in addressing fairness issues in speech-to-text technology. This technology can improve individuals' lives, from sending hands-free texts to helping people with hearing loss communicate. Yet an academic study revealed that this technology produced nearly double the error rates for members of some Black and African American communities than for white users.[171]

These results spurred Microsoft to take a closer look at the AI systems that power its speech-to-text technologies, to ensure they had been sufficiently trained on the rich diversity of speech patterns.[172] The company turned to an expert sociolinguist and expanded its data collection efforts to narrow the performance gap in its solutions. During the process, Microsoft involved stakeholders from outside the company, such as experts and people from diverse communities. These lessons were invaluable, and have since been incorporated into the Responsible AI Standard to further articulate specific steps teams must take to ensure Microsoft AI systems are designed to provide a similar quality of service for identified demographic groups, including marginalized groups, to help the company and other organizations harness the benefits of these technologies and avoid potential harms in the future.

8.6 SPEED AND STEWARDSHIP: WHAT CAN REGULATION CONTRIBUTE?

The tension between speed and stewardship that defines corporate governance in AI also shapes governmental approaches. States, like corporations, face the same foundational dilemma: whether to privilege innovation and competitiveness or to institutionalize deliberation and restraint. The underlying logic is not uniquely public, as it originates within corporate environments that first grapple with the challenges of deploying high-risk technologies. Governments enter later, adopting the conceptual vocabulary and operational routines already developed by companies to manage AI risk. What distinguishes the public sphere is not its orientation but its instrument. States possess superior tools for coordination, enforcement, and subsidization that enable them to amplify or contain private action.

This section traces how different governmental entities have responded to the dilemma. It begins with the Trump Administration, whose approach to AI regulation exemplifies the speed imperative in its most explicit form. The federal government there uses its distinctive tools to support rapid technological development through deregulation and subsidization, constructing what might be called a state-managed accelerationism. It then turns to California, where lawmakers have built a countermodel organized around transparency, auditing, and public reporting, a model that converges in design and ambition with the European Union's Artificial Intelligence Act (AIA). The juxtaposition highlights how both state and supranational institutions extend, rather than replace, corporate practices of governance: whether accelerating or deliberating, they institutionalize frameworks that first emerged within private enterprise.

8.6.1 *Tools for Boosting Speed: The Trump Administration's Approach*

The Trump Administration exemplifies a government that governs artificial intelligence through the speed imperative: the conviction that technological leadership depends on accelerating development faster than any rival can respond.[173] In this view, AI policy becomes a competitive instrument of national power rather than a site of public deliberation. The administration operationalizes this imperative through two tools: deregulation and subsidization. The first removes procedural friction, while the second channels public resources toward private acceleration.

Together, they define a model of the government as financier and deregulatory catalyst of technological expansion.

8.6.1.1 Deregulation: Removing Friction

Federal AI policy has evolved rapidly across administrations, reflecting different judgments about how government should relate to technological development. During the Biden Administration, the prevailing emphasis was on stewardship: ensuring that innovation unfolded alongside ethical, labor, and environmental considerations. Executive actions and agency initiatives, particularly from the Office of Science and Technology Policy (OSTP) and the National Institute of Standards and Technology (NIST), sought to create a coordinated framework for responsible AI, centered on transparency, accountability, and risk management.[174] These measures aimed to guide rather than constrain private innovation, using standards and interagency coordination to shape early norms in an emerging field even in the absence of legislation.

The Trump Administration redirected this approach. Through a series of executive orders, it shifted the language of AI policy from stewardship to speed. The most emblematic, Removing Barriers to American Leadership in Artificial Intelligence, rescinded many of the prior executive measures and instructed agencies to identify and remove regulatory obstacles to deployment. OSTP and NIST were encouraged to promote adoption and competitiveness. In effect, the Administration redefined the federal role: from framing rules for responsible innovation to advancing the speed of technological progress.

The deregulatory pivot also introduced a cultural dimension. Some executive orders discouraged or eliminated references to diversity, equity, inclusion, and climate change in federal funding and procurement programs. For supporters, this signaled a commitment to ideological neutrality and market focus; for critics, it blurred the boundary between administrative simplification and cultural intervention. What remained consistent across both administrations was the assumption that government could shape AI development indirectly, either by coordinating standards or by accelerating implementation, but not by building an elaborate regulatory apparatus through legislative intervention.[175]

8.6.1.2 Subsidization: Financing Speed

While deregulation reduced procedural friction, subsidization sought to build the underlying momentum. The Trump Administration's emphasis on speed did not simply involve removing constraints, but it also reoriented the use of federal resources toward expansion. The idea was that state investment could amplify innovation where private markets alone might move too slowly, using fiscal capacity as a competitive instrument.

This orientation took its most explicit form in *Winning the Race*, a policy document that recast AI strategy as an investment agenda rather than a regulatory framework.[176] Drafted under the supervision of Michael Kratsios and David Sacks, the report proposed that the United States secure technological leadership not primarily by tightening oversight, but by scaling infrastructure and funding. It called for increased federal grants, public–private partnerships, and procurement programs to accelerate AI adoption across industry, defense, and research. Agencies were encouraged to prioritize projects consistent with national competitiveness goals, and to avoid duplicative or "burdensome" oversight efforts. In this way, fiscal coordination replaced administrative regulation as the government's preferred mode of influence.

The report also framed AI as a domain of strategic competition. It argued that the United States could not lead in the global race without a robust domestic foundation in computing power, semiconductor production, and data infrastructure. Public funding, therefore, was not merely economic support but a tool of industrial resilience and geopolitical positioning. Yet this approach also introduced a degree of centralization. While the document promoted deregulation, it simultaneously concentrated discretion within the Executive Office to decide where and how federal resources should be allocated. The result was a hybrid model, market-driven in rhetoric, state-directed in practice.

Elements of this strategy were codified in the *Big Beautiful Bill*.[177] Although Congress removed its most ambitious deregulatory proposal, a decade-long moratorium on state AI regulation, the final statute institutionalized large-scale federal investment in AI infrastructure. It provided funding for domestic data centers, semiconductor manufacturing, and supply chain expansion, and included restrictions on participation by foreign entities.[178] These provisions linked acceleration to industrial policy, embedding speed within a framework of economic nationalism. By tying eligibility for subsidies to compliance with sourcing and governance requirements, the Big Beautiful Bill blurred the boundary between market autonomy and state direction. Public funds were deployed not to constrain or command but to incentivize. The government selected which sectors and partnerships would advance most rapidly, using capital allocation as its organizing mechanism.

Subsidization also carried a cultural dimension. In documents such as *Winning the Race*, funding was linked not only to technical capacity but also to a broader notion of "ideological neutrality."[179] Federal support was conditioned on projects and jurisdictions perceived as free from what the administration described as politicized or value-laden approaches to technology, such as references to diversity, equity, or environmental impact. This framing reflected an effort to align technological development with a particular vision of neutrality: innovation unencumbered by social programming. While its practical implications were uneven, the linkage illustrates how fiscal instruments can be used not only to accelerate production but also to signal the cultural and political orientation that public investment is meant to promote.

Subsidization also carried a cultural dimension. In documents such as Winning the Race, funding was linked not only to technical capacity but also to a broader notion of "ideological neutrality." Federal support was conditioned on projects and jurisdictions perceived as free from what the administration described as politicized or value-laden approaches to technology, such as references to diversity, equity, or environmental impact. This framing reflected an effort to align technological development with a particular vision of neutrality: innovation unencumbered by social programming. While its practical implications were uneven, the linkage illustrates how fiscal instruments can be used not only to accelerate production but also to signal the cultural and political orientation that public investment is meant to promote.

8.6.2 *California's Countermodel and the European Parallel*

California has taken the opposite approach, constructing a deliberative model of AI governance that parallels the European Union's AIA, as discussed later. The state's legislative initiatives, most notably SB 53, the Transparency in Frontier AI Act, and the Privacy Protection AI package, reflect an effort to define processes and responsibilities rather than prescribe outcomes. SB 53 requires developers of frontier or foundation models to prepare and publicly disclose safety and security protocols, conduct catastrophic-risk assessments, and report serious incidents to state authorities. It also calls for independent audits and annual updates to risk-management frameworks beginning later in the decade. The accompanying Privacy Protection AI regulations extend this procedural logic to automated decision-making systems, introducing risk assessments, opt-out rights, and audit requirements for significant uses of AI in employment, finance, housing, and healthcare.[180]

California's framework treats review and documentation as the infrastructure of trust. Where the federal model defines efficiency as the removal of delay, California defines safety as the product of testing and revision. Its architecture parallels the EU's administrative approach to AI governance: both institutionalize foresight through risk assessment, conformity testing, and documentation. The result is an emerging transatlantic convergence around procedural regulation, in contrast to the federal accelerationism that prioritizes immediate deployment. California's deliberative model thus acts as the domestic counterpart to the EU's rule-based system: each constructs legitimacy through procedure rather than velocity.

8.6.3 *The EU's Effort to Regulate AI: Institutionalizing Best Practices*

For many in the EU, a mandatory regulatory regime for AI is a no brainer. According to Dragoş Tudorache, the co-leading negotiator for the European parliament, AI "is a pioneering technology and we need to harness it, which means putting rules in place. Self-due diligence by companies is not enough."[181] First proposed by the

European Commission in April 2021, the AIA introduced a graded system of oversight, classifying AI systems according to the level of risk they pose, from minimal to prohibited. Policymakers initially conceived of it as a form of consumer-safety regulation, requiring developers to test and certify the quality of the data their systems use, and to inform users about the nature and limits of the technology.[182] But this early approach, which resembled product safety law, was quickly overtaken by the pace of innovation. The unveiling of ChatGPT and similar systems in late 2022 transformed the debate, revealing the broad reach of foundation models capable of generating complex text, code, and imagery from vast and largely unfiltered datasets. Concerns that such systems could be used to manipulate human behavior, evade cybersecurity controls, or even design biological weapons led the European Parliament to expand the scope of the Act substantially. Following two years of negotiation, it was approved in late 2023, ushering in the EU's first comprehensive framework for regulating artificial intelligence.

A key feature of the AIA is its explicit prohibition of certain AI practices, alongside its careful distinction between high-risk and lower-risk applications. The prohibited category reflects issues of fundamental rights and human dignity, encompassing activities such as social scoring that could determine access to services, emotion recognition in workplaces or schools, and remote biometric identification in public spaces, except under narrow law-enforcement exceptions. These prohibitions signal a broader European concern that algorithmic systems, when deployed without constraint, can intrude upon privacy, amplify discrimination, or erode individual autonomy.[183]

Lower-risk systems, by contrast, are primarily subject to transparency obligations. Consumers must be able to tell when they are interacting with a machine, when images or voices are synthetically generated, or when outputs draw upon copyrighted materials. The Act's provisions on transparency extend to the developers of foundation models themselves, who must provide summaries of the data used in training and disclose whether it includes protected content. Regulators are expected to develop further guidance for such systems, encouraging companies to adopt voluntary codes of conduct covering human oversight, data accuracy, and fairness in algorithmic design. In this sense, the AIA not only prescribes mandatory standards but also invites a broader process of self-governance aligned with its objectives.[184]

The central thrust of the regulatory regime for high-risk systems, however, goes beyond disclosure. It establishes an extensive compliance architecture that binds companies to conduct a detailed assessment of the risks their systems pose, evaluate their likelihood and severity, and adopt proportionate mitigation measures. These requirements operate alongside preexisting legal duties in areas such as data protection, consumer protection, and nondiscrimination, but they add new dimensions that are specifically attuned to the epistemic and moral risks of machine learning.[185] Providers must document every stage of this process, maintain traceability logs, and continuously monitor and update their systems once they are deployed. For larger organizations, compliance will require building internal audit and ethics functions, designating personnel responsible for AI safety, and sometimes undergoing external conformity assessments administered by independent bodies accredited by national regulators.[186] In cases involving critical uses of biometric or safety-related data, external certification will be mandatory. The European Commission retains the power to update these conformity mechanisms through delegated legislation, ensuring that regulatory standards evolve in parallel with technological capabilities.[187]

Enforcement will follow the typical EU model, relying on national supervisory authorities to implement and monitor compliance while coordination and standard-setting occur at the European level. A newly created European Artificial Intelligence Office, supported by a board of representatives from member states and an expert panel, will guide implementation, issue interpretive guidance, and facilitate uniform application across the Union. The office will also oversee the development of shared practices for high-risk and foundation models, balancing enforcement with capacity-building and cooperation among regulators.[188]

Criticism of the AIA has focused largely on its costs and on the potential chilling effect on innovation. Some estimates, such as those from the Center for Data Innovation, have placed the cost of compliance for the European economy in the tens of billions, though the European Commission itself expects the burden to be considerably lower. The concern remains, however, that the effort to document, justify, and monitor AI systems could exhaust the limited resources of smaller firms or startups.[189] OpenAI's early statements that the obligations might make it impossible to operate in Europe, captured a broader anxiety among technology entrepreneurs, especially in Germany and France, where fledgling AI sectors face steep competition from American platforms.[190] Yet the Act's supporters argue that such fears overlook the long-term benefits of predictability, safety, and public trust. By imposing clear boundaries on what is acceptable, and by formalizing the obligations of those who design and deploy high-impact systems, the AIA seeks not to suppress innovation but to stabilize it within a framework of accountability.

8.6.4 *From Corporate Ordering to Public Law: Corporate Templates and the EU AIA Act*

The AIA Act's risk-based structure, described earlier, reflects a broader EU aspiration to make technological progress compatible with fundamental rights, as Anu Bradford has argued.[191] Yet the Act's method for achieving this balance, through procedures of consultation, documentation, and review, did not emerge in a vacuum. It evolved in dialogue with the practices of leading firms that had already begun to develop internal governance mechanisms for artificial intelligence. The Act can thus be read not only as a legislative innovation but also as an act of institutional borrowing. It translates corporate self-regulation into a coordinated public framework, retaining many of its underlying features while adding enforcement and coherence across jurisdictions.

The governance architectures at Microsoft and DeepMind exemplify this convergence. Both companies had begun to construct procedural systems that mirrored public administrative functions. DeepMind's work on AlphaFold relied on engagement with domain experts, publication of confidence metrics, and staged data release. These steps, while voluntary, resembled the stages of public rulemaking: consultation with stakeholders, deliberation over risks, and publication of clear parameters for responsible use.[192] Microsoft's internal system, anchored in the Office of Responsible AI, the Aether Committee, and a network of responsible AI "champions," performed a similar role on the decision-making and oversight side.[193] It established structured review, escalation protocols, and documentation duties, producing a framework that internalized many of the features of regulatory administration.

The AIA Act reproduces this tripartite structure – rulemaking, executive decision-making, and oversight – almost intact. Its risk management provisions require consultation with relevant expertise and documentation of design choices; its conformity assessment mechanisms parallel corporate escalation pathways; and its emphasis on independent review finds a counterpart in the requirement for external certification of certain high-risk systems. The procedural grammar is remarkably similar. What changes is the locus of authority. The Act takes the internal governance practices of a few pioneering companies and turns them into a shared baseline for all market participants.

This alignment does not mean the Act lacks significance. By embedding these practices in law, it replaces discretion with obligation and ensures a level of coordination that private governance could not readily achieve on its own. The European AI Office and national supervisory authorities mirror the internal committees and oversight boards of large firms, but they also link them across organizational boundaries, allowing for exchange of information, consistent interpretation, and collective learning. The Act thereby turns an individualized model of responsibility into a public system of mutual accountability.

Still, the continuity between private and public governance is striking. The AIA Act does not create a new model so much as it stabilizes one that already existed in the private sphere. Its contribution lies in extending these practices to firms that might not have adopted them voluntarily and in formalizing coordination among those that have. The distance between self-regulation and state regulation is, in this respect, smaller than often assumed, less a gap than a gradient. Both rely on similar mechanisms of consultation, documentation, and oversight; both seek legitimacy through transparency and reason-giving. The Act's primary intervention is to ensure that what was once a matter of corporate commitment becomes an expectation of all.

In this sense, the AIA Act represents a process of translation rather than rupture. It takes the procedural norms that firms such as Microsoft and DeepMind had already internalized and embeds them in a framework of public enforcement and institutional coordination. The result is a system that preserves the logic of private governance while distributing it more widely and binding it to collective authority.

The line between corporate self-regulation and public regulation, though formally present, becomes thin enough that in practice it often appears continuous.

This alignment does not mean the Act lacks significance. By embedding these practices in law, it replaces discretion with obligation and ensures a level of coordination that private governance could not readily achieve on its own. The European AI Office and national supervisory authorities mirror the internal committees and oversight boards of large firms, but they also link them across organizational boundaries, allowing for exchange of information, consistent interpretation, and collective learning. The Act thereby turns an individualized model of responsibility into a public system of mutual accountability.

Still, the continuity between private and public governance is striking. The AIA Act does not create a new model so much as it stabilizes one that already existed in the private sphere. Its contribution lies in extending these practices to firms that might not have adopted them voluntarily and in formalizing coordination among those that have. The distance between self-regulation and state regulation is, in this respect, smaller than often assumed, less a gap than a gradient. Both rely on similar mechanisms of consultation, documentation, and oversight; both seek legitimacy through transparency and reason-giving. The Act's primary intervention is to ensure that what was once a matter of corporate commitment becomes an expectation of all.

In this sense, the AIA Act represents a process of translation rather than rupture. It takes the procedural norms that firms such as Microsoft and DeepMind had already internalized and embeds them in a framework of public enforcement and institutional coordination. The result is a system that preserves the logic of private governance while distributing it more widely and binding it to collective authority. The line between corporate self-regulation and public regulation, though formally present, becomes thin enough that in practice it often appears continuous.

8.7 CONCLUSION: BUILDING AI GOVERNANCE FROM WITHIN

The story of AI governance to date is not one of regulatory foresight but of private initiative, compelled less by idealism than by necessity. It was the magnitude of what AI might become, its potential to transform industries, reshape societies, and pose existential risks, that pushed private firms to act. What began as a pragmatic response to technological power is evolving into something far more ambitious: an attempt to build governance from the inside out. These companies came to understand that building trustworthy AI required building the procedural and institutional infrastructure to oversee it, treating governance not as a compliance task but as a core function. They recognized that without internal rulemaking, formalized decision rights, and transparent mechanisms for dissent and review, their principled aspirations would remain rhetorical, valuable, but ultimately unenforceable.

These efforts emerged in response to real tensions within organizations, especially the growing divergence of views among investors, boards, and technical leaders.

The push to move quickly and secure strategic advantage has often collided with concerns about safety, long-term impact, and reputational risk. In this context, governance has become the channel through which firms negotiate and recalibrate between stewardship and speed, innovation and risk, profit and protection. Through governance, companies make decisions that are specific, calibrated, and grounded in the realities of each product and use case, rather than abstract pronouncements crafted for political stages. Governance, in this view, is not a matter of public signaling but of internal alignment, an ongoing process of choosing, adapting, and adjusting as the technology evolves.

This emerging architecture is still evolving. It is uneven, sometimes improvised, and far from complete. But it represents a serious attempt to reconcile the demands of speed with the responsibilities of stewardship. As governments move to develop formal regulation, they are finding that many of the tools already exist, built not in the halls of policymaking but in product meetings, engineering reviews, and internal deliberations. These are not a substitute for public oversight, but they may well shape its direction. In the case of AI, governance has not followed from regulation. It has followed from the challenges that arise when innovative companies face conflicting priorities, and from the recognition that without structure, neither speed nor safety can be sustained.

9

A New Fiduciary Standard

Corporations today make decisions that shape how millions of people work, communicate, and move through the world. They set standards for online speech, design algorithms that determine who gets hired, and establish frameworks that govern climate accountability across global supply chains. These decisions carry profound social consequences, yet corporate law offers directors remarkably little guidance about how to make them. Courts reviewing such choices have historically confined themselves to assessing whether directors acted in good faith and on an informed basis, leaving the substance of that inquiry undefined.[1] The result is a governance paradox. Boards exercise vast discretion over socially consequential decisions through processes that corporate law has never specified or scrutinized.

The absence of legal standards has not meant an absence of governance. The preceding case studies revealed that when confronted with profound social uncertainty, leading corporations have built procedural frameworks to organize their discretion. Consider the three trajectories explored in Chapters 6, 7, and 8.

When Uber and Lyft confronted questions about passenger safety and sexual assault reporting, they faced a predicament that traditional transportation law had not anticipated. Their business model strained the categories of employment, transportation, and insurance that had long organized urban mobility. Rather than wait for regulators to prescribe solutions, these companies built governance tools to bridge innovation and consumer protection. They partnered with criminologists and safety experts to design ride-audit protocols and data systems for documentation and reporting.[2] They created new insurance products that redefined coverage between personal and commercial use.[3] In effect, they built the evidentiary basis for regulatory frameworks that were still emerging, turning operational risk into a campaign to demonstrate responsible governance.

Climate emissions presented a different challenge. Confronted with a paradigmatically intractable problem, BP and General Motors worked with environmental scientists and policy experts to design the Greenhouse Gas Protocol, converting atmospheric chemistry into accounting categories.[4] This corporate rulemaking established how climate commitments should be measured and what evidence would make claims credible. Companies then built managerial systems that translated those rules into daily practice through carbon accounting and supplier-contract clauses, creating feedback loops that joined data accuracy with executive accountability.

Artificial-intelligence governance pushes this trajectory further and faster than any other field. AI has become the operating system of modern decision-making, a technology that shapes how information is created, interpreted, and exchanged across every sector. It is at once existential and pedantic: questions of bias, transparency, and control coexist with the minutiae of data labeling and model documentation.[5] Faced with this paradox, companies such as Microsoft have built internal regimes that combine rulemaking, implementation, and oversight within a single institutional framework.[6] Principles like fairness and accountability function not as aspirational slogans but as procedural triggers: each invokes a review, an impact assessment, or an audit before a system can be deployed. Specialized committees examine use cases; monitoring teams collect post-deployment evidence; the findings cycle back into revised guidance.

These examples reveal a consistent pattern. When confronted with social uncertainty, corporations built procedural frameworks to organize their discretion. They created consultation mechanisms to gather expertise, verification systems to test claims, monitoring infrastructure to track implementation, and documentation practices to create accountability. These are operational necessities, ways to make contested decisions intelligible and defensible when neither markets nor law provides clear guidance. Yet corporate law has never analyzed these practices or specified what constitutes adequate deliberation over social conflict. The vast discretion that boards exercise in these domains has remained invisible to legal doctrine, neither defined nor evaluated.

This chapter makes that discretion visible. It distills the practices observed in the case studies into an analytical framework, translating institutional logic into a procedural grammar that can guide corporate deliberation across contexts. It specifies what sophisticated social deliberation requires in each of the three functional domains of rulemaking, executive action, and oversight, identifying the core procedural elements that distinguish genuine engagement from systematic failure. This analytical work represents a methodological contribution. Corporate law scholarship has debated whether corporations should address social conflicts but has not examined how boards actually exercise discretion when they do. This chapter provides that analysis.

Yet presenting best practices raises a deeper question. If sophisticated firms already adopt deliberative procedures when facing significant social conflicts, why should corporate law mandate what voluntary practice has achieved? The answer connects directly to the problem of unexamined discretion. Without formalization, deliberative excellence remains optional, creating competitive pressures that reward governance shortcuts. Firms that invest in robust social deliberation face disadvantages against competitors who avoid such costs. More troubling still, the absence of legal analysis means that boards have no baseline for what adequate deliberation requires. Some firms develop sophisticated procedures while others operate through intuition or avoidance, yet corporate law treats both approaches identically because it has never specified how this form of discretion should be exercised.

This chapter closes that gap. It argues that the deliberative practices documented in the case studies should become mandatory fiduciary obligations, integrated into the duty of care that corporate law already imposes. This is not a radical departure but a natural evolution. Courts have repeatedly absorbed new procedural technologies when decision-making contexts demanded them. They incorporated fairness opinions into merger review, independent committees into conflict transactions, and monitoring systems into compliance oversight. Each time, corporate law moved from treating certain forms of discretion as unexamined black boxes to specifying how that discretion should be exercised. Social conflicts now warrant the same recognition.

The chapter proceeds in three parts. The first distills from the examples and theoretical framework a procedural grammar for social deliberation, specifying what sophisticated deliberation looks like across rulemaking, executive action, and oversight functions. The second makes the normative case for formalizing these practices as fiduciary obligations, addressing agency problems, risk identification failures, coordination problems, legitimacy concerns, and doctrinal coherence. The third addresses implementation, asking when the duty to deliberate applies, what constitutes breach, how courts should review deliberative adequacy, and what remedies are appropriate when procedures prove deficient.

9.1 FROM DISCRETION TO DELIBERATION: BEST PRACTICES

Modern corporate governance grants directors and officers vast discretion over how their firms navigate social controversy. Courts reviewing such choices have historically confined themselves to assessing whether directors acted in good faith and on an informed basis, leaving the content of that information undefined. As a result, when boards deliberate over social conflict, whether to adopt an environmental pledge, take a position on legislation, or respond to public pressure, they operate within a zone of near-complete doctrinal silence.[7] This state of affairs resembles fiduciary law before the corporate governance reforms of the late 1980s and 1990s: the duty of care existed in name and spirit but lacked procedural structure.[8]

This chapter's first task is to distill from the examples and theory that preceded a procedural grammar for social deliberation, one that translates principles into actionable guidance for corporate directors and officers. Chapters 3, 6, 7, 8 developed a theoretical framework for understanding corporate deliberation and documented how companies navigate social conflict. This section synthesizes these insights into best practices: specifying what sophisticated social deliberation looks like when corporations take social governance seriously and identifying the procedural elements that distinguish good faith efforts from systematic failure. A core methodological contribution of this book lies in making this move from analysis to practical guidance, articulating a toolset that can guide boards in exercising their discretion over how they navigate social controversy.

This section proposes such a toolset by identifying the core procedural elements required across the tripartite framework introduced in Chapter 3: the distinct deliberative infrastructures for rulemaking, executive action, and oversight. Each function addresses different social governance contexts and therefore calls for different procedural configurations. Rulemaking contexts demand broad consultation because such rules affect diverse constituencies with competing interests. Executive decisions require informed, high-quality decision-making that demonstrates engagement with material social dimensions and the values at stake. Oversight functions demand institutional independence and continuous investigation to ensure implementation and identify systematic problems before they escalate.

9.1.1 *Rulemaking Functions: Outreach, Consultation, and the Feedback Loop*

Rulemaking describes those moments when corporations articulate norms of general and uniform applicability, such as codes of conduct, sustainability commitments, supplier standards, or content-moderation principles. These decisions resemble legislative acts. They define rules by which internal and external stakeholders will interact with the firm, and they project the company's social stance to a wide public. Because the consequences of such rules are diffuse and often unpredictable, the central procedural risk is insularity: a narrow informational base incapable of capturing the heterogeneity of affected interests.

An adequate process of rulemaking thus begins with wide outreach to both experts and stakeholders. Directors should ensure that draft frameworks are informed by relevant technical, scientific, and legal expertise, while also exposing those frameworks to the lived experiences of those they will govern. External advisors can assess feasibility, regulatory alignment, and risk. Stakeholder consultations reveal distributional and reputational implications invisible from within the firm. This dual outreach is not a concession to managerial limitations but a manifestation of fiduciary diligence: recognizing that no board can be expert in all things, it institutionalizes the means by which informational asymmetries, whether technical or social, are responsibly overcome.

To institutionalize this outreach, corporations should adopt procedures analogous to notice-and-comment in administrative law.[9] Proposed standards could be circulated internally and externally for comment, accompanied by a defined period during which interested parties may submit observations. The object is not to democratize decision-making but to discipline it: a structured invitation for input compels directors to anticipate objections and refine reasoning.[10] The process should culminate in a feedback loop, whereby the board or responsible committee summarizes the comments received, indicates how they were addressed, and explains the rationale for the final policy. Publication of this summary, whether in corporate-governance reports or sustainability disclosures, demonstrates responsiveness and provides an evidentiary record of informed deliberation.[11]

Consider the example of a pharmaceutical company that faces a recurring question about how it should respond to requests for access from populations that cannot afford market prices. Rather than deciding ad hoc for each drug, the board establishes an Access Framework, a set of principles and procedures governing such decisions. Adequate rulemaking would involve extensive outreach, consultations, and forums through a special committee that consults global health experts, intellectual property considerations, and relevant pharmaceutical organizations to understand contemporary best industry practices.

The committee drafts a framework proposing tiered pricing based on country income levels, expedited applications for humanitarian emergencies, voluntary licensing in generic markets for specified markets, and income-based patient assistance. This draft is circulated for comment to relevant departments and external stakeholders. Feedback reveals complications, as pharmaceutical manufacturers fail to capture within-country inequality, and definitions of country income-based patient assistance terms need clearer boundaries. The committee documents these responses, revises the framework, and explains changes in a published summary. The final policy is adopted with a commitment to review implementation after two years.

This constitutes deliberative rulemaking through structured consultation that brings multiple types of expertise and stakeholder perspectives into conversation, a reasoned response to feedback, and written documentation for learning through periodic review. Contrast this with an inadequate process where management drafts an access policy focused primarily on tax benefits and public relations value, and a board committee approves it without expert input or stakeholder consultation. No feedback mechanism is provided, and the policy is largely unused because operational departments lack guidance on how to apply it.

9.1.2 *Executive Functions: Accuracy and Disclosure*

Executive decisions differ from rulemaking in tempo and texture. They involve the implementation of policy, the management of crises, and the calibration of corporate action in real time. Examples include withdrawing from a controversial jurisdiction, making a political contribution, launching a sensitive product, or responding to allegations of discrimination. In these contexts, deliberation is often constrained by urgency, and the principal risk is hypocrisy: that executive actions will contradict commitments made during rulemaking, or that corporate rhetoric will outpace actual deliberation.[12] Companies may announce principles without creating processes to implement them, or make public claims that lack grounding in verified analysis. This produces the phenomenon critics call corporate washing, describing sustainability commitments without operational change, diversity pledges without hiring reforms, ethical principles without enforcement mechanisms.[13]

The procedural safeguard here lies in two complementary requirements: disclosure, which creates accountability through public commitment, and accuracy, which fulfills that commitment through verified information. Disclosure creates expectations that subsequent performance must meet. This public commitment generates internal pressure for verification: once a claim is made externally, the corporation must ensure it can substantiate that claim with evidence. Disclosure thus functions as the impetus for internal reform, transforming aspirational statements into operational demands.

Accuracy fulfills the commitment that disclosure creates. It requires corporations to establish internal teams and mechanisms that collect and verify information systematically.[14] When management proposes executive action with evident social stakes, the board's role is to ensure that systems exist that not only implement substantive commitments but also generate reliable data evidencing the implementation. This may involve creating cross-functional working groups that coordinate between legal, operations, and public affairs departments; establishing data collection protocols that track implementation metrics; or designating specific officers responsible for verification.

Return to the pharmaceutical company that has established its Access Framework. The Indian government approaches the company seeking a voluntary license that would allow local generic manufacturers to produce a breakthrough treatment at significantly lower cost for the Indian market. This decision carries substantial social dimensions, as thousands of Indian patients could gain access, and the decision sets precedent for future middle-income country requests. Yet risks abound. Licensed generics might leak into wealthy markets. Quality control failures could damage reputation. Granting this license may generate pressure for similar arrangements elsewhere. Corporate washing risks are acute.[15]

If the company discloses this decision publicly, committing to expand patient access and reporting on implementation progress, that disclosure creates pressure for accuracy. The company must establish internal mechanisms to substantiate its claims. This might require creating a cross-functional task force that evaluates potential licensees, designs quality monitoring protocols, establishes anti-diversion controls, and creates patient access tracking systems. The board receives documentation of this verification infrastructure before approving disclosure. Only after establishing these accuracy mechanisms does the company make its public commitment. The disclosure and accuracy work together: the announcement creates accountability, while the internal systems provide capacity to fulfill it.

Contrast this with inadequate process. The company issues a press release announcing a voluntary license "consistent with our Access Framework principles" without establishing verification mechanisms. No task force evaluated implementation feasibility. The board approved the announcement based on public relations value rather than operational assessment. Months later, the license remains largely symbolic: no licensed generics have reached patients, yet the company continues citing the announcement as evidence of its access commitment. The gap between disclosed rhetoric and operational reality demonstrates that accuracy mechanisms are essential infrastructure, not optional features. Without them, executive deliberation fails its fundamental obligation: ensuring that corporate action aligns with corporate speech.

9.1.3 *Review and Oversight Functions: Independence and Investigation*

The third domain of deliberation concerns ongoing oversight of how corporate rules and executive decisions are implemented and whether the systems that support them continue to function as intended. Oversight is not confined to moments of crisis or misconduct. It is a continuous process through which boards ensure that adopted corporate rules are implemented faithfully and that the information on which future decisions depend remains accurate.[16] This function closes the deliberative loop by translating rules into practice, testing implementation against policy, and generating data that feed back into revised rulemaking. Without such supervision, even carefully designed deliberative processes risk becoming aspirational rather than operational.

To perform this function credibly, oversight must be institutionally separate from management. The corporation should establish a distinct organizational unit whose exclusive mandate is supervision, such as monitoring the application of rules, evaluating the performance of internal systems, and ensuring the reliability of data that inform executive action. This separation ensures that those responsible for implementation are not the same as those responsible for verification. The model parallels the creation of audit and compliance divisions after Sarbanes-Oxley reforms: internal yet autonomous bodies empowered to observe, assess, and report.[17] By design, their authority derives from the board rather than from management hierarchy, and their accountability runs to independent directors or board committees charged with governance and risk oversight.

For investigation to serve this purpose, it must rest on specialized competence and procedural rigor.[18] The supervisory department should employ professionals with expertise required to assess implementation in their respective domains, such as compliance officers, auditors, data scientists, or human rights analysts, supported by clear methodologies for sampling, testing, and documentation. Their findings should be systematically recorded and presented to the board, accompanied by management responses and follow up actions. Where confidentiality allows, corporations should disclose summaries of these reviews to external audiences, thereby demonstrating that supervision is ongoing and structurally credible.

Imagine that the pharmaceutical company's Access Framework is now operational, but oversight determines whether it achieves its intended purposes. The board establishes an Access Monitoring Unit, independent from the marketing and pricing teams, to track implementation. The Unit collects data on access requests received, approval rates, processing times, and whether approved programs reach intended beneficiaries. It audits voluntary licenses to ensure quality standards are maintained and investigates whether patient assistance programs function as designed.

Six months into implementation, the Unit reports to the board's governance committee. Humanitarian requests are processed efficiently. The voluntary license to India is functioning, though quality audits revealed one subcontractor using substandard ingredients, prompting corrective action. This oversight enables learning. The board directs management to add enhanced quality-monitoring provisions to future voluntary licensing agreements. The Framework itself is revised based on implementation experience.

Contrast this with inadequate oversight. The company announces its Access Framework and India program but establishes no monitoring mechanisms. The board receives annual reports from marketing stating that "access programs are operational" without verification. When media investigations later reveal that the India program relies on faulty ingredients, the board has no documentary record of having monitored implementation, no data on program performance, and no institutional capacity to have identified problems before external pressure forced a response.

9.1.4 *Why Deliberation Works*

What unites these three functions is a commitment to making corporate reasoning visible and testable. When corporations establish rules through structured consultation, they create expectations that constrain future action. When they make executive decisions based on verified information, they generate records that can be evaluated for coherence and honesty. When they monitor implementation through independent oversight, they demonstrate that commitments are operational rather than symbolic. Together, these practices constitute a system of corporate accountability that operates through deliberation rather than through substantive mandates. The law does not dictate what corporations must decide about access to medicines, climate strategy, or algorithmic fairness. It requires that such decisions emerge from processes designed to inform judgment, test assumptions, and enable learning. This is the essence of governance: not the elimination of discretion, but its disciplined exercise through procedures that make power answerable to reason.

This raises the central question that motivates the remainder of this chapter. The deliberative practices outlined earlier remain aspirational tools that firms may adopt at their discretion rather than mandatory fiduciary obligations. Whether and how to address social conflicts is a decision that lies firmly within business judgment. The issue is whether, when boards do confront such conflicts, corporate law should specify how they exercise that judgment. Put differently, the vast discretion that boards possess over socially consequential decisions currently operates as an unexamined black box. The remainder of this chapter argues that fiduciary duty should absorb the procedural logic that the case studies have revealed, translating best practices into legal obligations.

9.2 THE CASE FOR EXTENDING A FIDUCIARY DUTY OBLIGATION

Corporate law evaluates managerial discretion through decision-making quality. Its premise holds that directors must decide well, not necessarily right; their judgments must arise from processes designed to inform, test, and justify choice.[19] This procedural conception of care has allowed fiduciary doctrine to adapt repeatedly as the informational environment of business has changed. The present moment, defined by the drive for efficiency at scale, constant scrutiny in the digital age, and heterogeneous preferences among shareholders, requires a further turn in that evolution.

The adaptability of fiduciary duty is not a concession to external pressures but an intrinsic feature of corporate doctrine. At critical inflection points in corporate history, courts have incorporated new tools of reasoning into the definition of due care. When *Smith v. Van Gorkom* castigated the superficiality of uninformed judgments, directors responded by institutionalizing expert evaluation.[20] The fairness opinion became a technology of care, an external validation that directors had tested the economic logic of their decisions. Subsequent Delaware cases refined that expectation, clarifying that expertise must be both independent and interrogated.[21] Boards were to obtain advice from qualified sources but also to challenge it, document their engagement, and ensure that competing valuations had been considered. The duty of care thus evolved from a standard of intuition to a discipline of method.

A parallel transformation occurred in the domain of loyalty. In *Kahn v. M&F* Worldwide, the Delaware Supreme Court held that conflicted transactions could receive business-judgment deference if boards employed specific procedural protections: an independent committee; informed negotiation; and majority-of-the-minority shareholder approval.[22] MFW did not change the substance of fiduciary law but clarified what diligence and independence look like when tested by conflict. The court effectively rewarded good process with deference, turning procedural integrity into a safe harbor for managerial discretion. This logic treats independence and expertise as twin pillars of credible judgment, insulating decisions not because they are substantively correct but because they emerged from structures designed to discipline self-interest.

The duty to monitor followed a similar trajectory. Caremark established that directors must ensure the existence of information systems adequate for monitoring corporate legal compliance.[23] *Stone v. Ritter* clarified that liability attaches when boards either fail to implement any reporting system or consciously disregard red flags. The duty does not require perfect oversight or guarantee that violations will never occur. It demands that boards establish reasonable procedures for information flow and respond to warning signs. *Marchand* extended this logic to encompass broader risk management, requiring that the board establish governance structures that systematically gather information about critical operational, reputational, and strategic threats.[24]

These evolutions share a common structure. Courts confronted business environments where traditional expectations of director attention proved insufficient. Hostile takeovers and financial engineering created valuation disputes that boards could not resolve through general business acumen alone. Conflicted transactions between controlling shareholders and public companies demanded safeguards beyond ordinary deliberation. Complex regulatory regimes and operational scale meant boards could no longer monitor compliance through casual inquiry. Courts did not second-guess substantive choices or impose outcome-based liability. They updated procedural expectations, requiring boards to deploy new institutional tools. Once these tools became available and their reliability demonstrated, courts incorporated them into the evidentiary standard of care.

This pattern reveals a jurisprudence that does not invent new duties but continually refines what fiduciary competence requires. The underlying principle remains constant, declaring that directors exercise informed judgment when they create or oversee processes capable of gathering relevant information, testing assumptions, and documenting reasoning. What changes is the content of those processes, which must evolve to match the character of risks that corporations confront. Fiduciary law adapts not by expanding liability but by recognizing that new decision-making contexts demand new deliberative technologies.

That same logic now applies to social deliberation. The challenges that dominate board agendas today differ in subject matter but not in structure from those that prompted earlier evolutions. Issues such as climate strategy, artificial intelligence deployment, data ethics, and workplace culture are high-stakes, uncertain, and often irreducible to financial metrics. What fiduciary law once demanded for valuation and agency conflict, it must now demand for social complexity, by ensuring that boards create, or at least oversee, processes capable of integrating specialized knowledge, considering diverse perspectives, and enabling ongoing review. The standard remains procedural. The content of procedures evolves to match contemporary risk.

This evolution would not politicize fiduciary duty but modernize it. Courts need not judge whether a company's climate targets are ambitious enough or whether its artificial intelligence policies are ethically optimal. They should ask instead whether directors established systems to gather relevant information, consulted necessary expertise, and deliberated before acting. The doctrinal machinery is already in place. The object of its inquiry has broadened. Seen in this light, the governance mechanisms documented in the case studies are not departures from fiduciary tradition but its continuation.

Fiduciary law evolves through recognition. Once courts acknowledge that a decision-making technology reliably improves the informational basis of judgment, that technology becomes part of the evidentiary canon of care. The transition from intuitive assessment to expert validation in merger contexts, from informal negotiation to structured independence in conflict transactions, and from episodic oversight to systematic monitoring in compliance all followed this pattern. Social deliberation represents the next iteration. The tools exist, their value is demonstrable, and the risks they address have become central to corporate performance. What remains is for legal doctrine to absorb these practices into its definition of informed judgment, completing the evolution that earlier courts began.

9.2.1 *Why Fiduciary Duty Should Require Social Deliberation*

As Chapter 1 showed, many corporations already engage in social deliberation voluntarily, adopting governance tools to help with decision-making. One might conclude that legal intervention is unwarranted if firms find deliberation valuable. This chapter argues otherwise. It proposes that corporate law incorporate social deliberation into the duty of care, transforming what are now optional best practices into mandatory fiduciary obligations. Before examining when this duty applies, we must establish the foundations for mandatory deliberation. The case rests on institutional design rather than moral commitment or corporate purpose.

9.2.1.1 Agency Costs and Managerial Discretion

When corporations confront social conflicts on which shareholders, stakeholders, and society hold heterogeneous views, managers exercise a distinctive form of discretion. Unlike ordinary business decisions, where market feedback and financial performance provide discipline, social decisions often lack clear evaluative metrics. A manager's choice to take a public stance on legislation, adopt a controversial supplier standard, or respond to activist pressure may reflect genuine business judgment. It may also reflect personal ideology, short-term reputational concerns, or conflict avoidance. Without structured processes, no reliable mechanism exists to distinguish motivated reasoning from informed judgment.

Procedural obligations reduce this agency problem by requiring that decisions pass through filters designed to surface information and test assumptions.[25] When boards must consult experts, document alternatives, and explain reasoning, choices based on hidden preferences or untested intuitions become more difficult to sustain. The process preserves managerial discretion entirely. Boards retain full authority to weigh competing considerations and reach conclusions reflecting their strategic priorities. Yet that discretion becomes more transparent and accountable. This function has always characterized fiduciary duties in financial contexts. The obligation to obtain fairness opinions in conflict transactions does not dictate deal terms. It ensures that valuation claims face testing against independent expertise. Social deliberation serves the same disciplining function in domains where conflicts concern not self-dealing but the interpretation of ambiguous and contested risks.

9.2.1.2 Risk Identification and Harm Prevention

Beyond the agency problem lies a related concern about institutional capacity. Companies lacking deliberative structures may fail to recognize the harms they cause or may respond in ways that prove counterproductive. Consider the reputational crises that have engulfed major corporations in recent decades. When Uber's workplace culture became the subject of widespread criticism, the absence of structures for hearing employee concerns meant the company lacked information about patterns of misconduct until external pressure forced investigation.[26] When Facebook confronted the Cambridge Analytica scandal, the company had not developed processes for systematically evaluating how third-party data access might be exploited in ways the company had not anticipated.[27]

These examples share a common pattern. They involved not malicious intent but failures of deliberation. Without structured inquiry, companies could not identify the harms their operations created, could not distinguish between serious risks and manageable frictions, and could not develop responses calibrated to actual problems rather than perceived public relations challenges. The Uber safety case documented in Chapter 6 illustrates this dynamic particularly well. The chief legal officer's initial instinct was to cooperate fully with law enforcement in sexual assault cases, treating transparency and legal compliance as paramount. Only through systematic consultation with victim advocates and criminologists did the company discover that this approach was counterintuitive and harmful. Victims would likely refuse to report incidents if doing so meant automatic police involvement, fearing retaliation or immigration consequences.[28] The correct response of maintaining confidentiality even from authorities while creating alternative accountability mechanisms emerged only through deliberative processes that incorporated expertise the companies did not initially possess.

Mandatory standards address this feedback gap by ensuring that companies build the capacity to identify harms, understand their sources, and develop responses informed by those most affected. The concern extends beyond financial consequences from mismanagement. Without deliberation, firms will continue causing social harm precisely because they lack the institutional structures to recognize it or to discover solutions that may run counter to managerial intuition.

9.2.1.3 Coordination Problems and Competitive Dynamics

The case for formalization extends to collective action problems that voluntary adoption cannot resolve.[29] When some firms invest in sophisticated governance structures while others decline to do so, markets may penalize the former for incurring costs without immediate financial returns. This dynamic is familiar from the history of financial disclosure and internal controls. Before legal mandates, firms that voluntarily adopted rigorous practices faced competitive disadvantages relative to those that minimized such investments. Mandatory standards prevent this race to the bottom. They ensure that all firms internalize the costs of credible governance and that competition occurs on the basis of operational performance rather than willingness to take governance shortcuts. Over time, universal expectations raise baseline deliberation quality across markets, generating positive spillovers as firms learn from one another and convergence around effective structures occurs.

9.2.1.4 Corporate Legitimacy and Regulatory Pressure

The argument also encompasses legitimacy concerns essential to sustaining corporate autonomy.[30] As corporations exercise increasing influence over domains of intense social impact, setting standards for online speech, shaping labor markets, and influencing environmental outcomes, their business model depends on social acceptance. That acceptance requires perceiving corporate leadership as operating responsibly and accountably. Procedural obligations provide visible accountability mechanisms, signaling to regulators, investors, and the public that corporate decisions rest on structured reasoning rather than arbitrary choice. This is not cosmetic. It constitutes the foundation of continued corporate discretion. When firms demonstrate that they govern their social impacts deliberately, the case for prescriptive regulation weakens. Conversely, when governance appears ad hoc or purely reactive, political pressure for detailed mandates intensifies. Fiduciary formalization thus operates as institutional self-preservation, maintaining discretion by making its exercise legible and defensible.

9.2.1.5 Doctrinal Coherence

Finally, internal consistency within corporate law requires this extension. Corporate law already mandates deliberation in domains characterized by high stakes, uncertainty, and complexity. Financial transactions, conflict-of-interest situations, and compliance monitoring all trigger heightened procedural expectations. Social conflicts now routinely meet identical criteria. They affect substantial value, involve contested evidence, and require specialized knowledge. Current doctrine creates an arbitrary gap. It demands that directors inform themselves about market conditions and competitive threats while permitting them to remain uninformed about reputational, regulatory, and operational risks arising from social conflict. This gap reflects not principle but doctrinal lag. Extending the procedural logic of care and oversight to social deliberation completes rather than expands fiduciary duty, ensuring that all issues with significant social dimensions receive commensurate attention.

These justifications converge on a common insight. Formalizing deliberation as a fiduciary expectation provides the legal architecture necessary for corporations to reason publicly about their decisions. It aligns corporate governance with the demands of an environment in which business and society intertwine inextricably. The proposal recognizes that power operating through structured reasoning maintains legitimacy, while power exercised through unconstrained discretion invites constraint.

9.2.2 *The Threshold Question: When Does Deliberation Become Obligatory?*

Any procedural standard must identify the conditions under which it applies. The social-deliberation standard imposes an obligation when credible evidence suggests that a matter carries significant social dimensions that may bear on corporate operations, reputation, or long-term value. The duty at this threshold is not to conclude that the matter carries social weight; it is to deliberate about whether it does. This distinction preserves managerial discretion while ensuring that decisions rest on inquiry rather than assumption. A board exercises informed judgment when it investigates whether an issue warrants structured attention, consults relevant sources of knowledge, considers its firm's specific circumstances, and reaches a reasoned conclusion about the issue's social consequences. A board that dismisses the same question without investigation, asserting that social matters lie outside its concern, substitutes assumption for deliberation. The former approach receives judicial deference. The latter does not.

A critic might argue that this formulation collapses into circularity. If boards must deliberate when deliberation reveals they should deliberate, the threshold for triggering the duty depends on exercising the very judgment the duty is meant to structure. However, legal standards routinely require contextual judgment without becoming circular. Negligence and materiality both depend on reasonableness determinations yet function effectively because they possess practical traction, as they can distinguish clear cases of diligence from neglect, even when borderline cases require discretion.[31]

The social deliberation standard operates within this same tradition. The obligation to deliberate arises not from esoteric determinations of true social significance but from observable signals that reasonable directors, attentive to fiduciary obligations, would recognize as warranting structured attention. These signals are familiar to corporate practice. Sustained shareholder engagement through proposals, investor letters, or voting patterns indicates that significant capital providers consider the matter important. Emerging regulatory activity suggests that voluntary practices may harden into legal requirements. Peer company actions reveal industry-wide recognition of an issue's social weight. Reputational incidents involving the firm or close competitors demonstrate tangible business consequences. Persistent stakeholder concerns affect operations, recruitment, or market position.

When such signals converge, the board faces an obligation to inquire. Consider a technology company confronting concerns about algorithmic bias in its hiring platform. Civil rights organizations raise concerns, academic studies document disparate impacts in similar systems, and peer companies adopt fairness audits. These constitute credible signals. The board need not immediately conclude that bias exists or that the platform requires redesign. Yet it cannot responsibly ignore the matter. At minimum, directors must ensure that management has investigated the concern, consulted technical experts on detection methods, and evaluated whether current systems adequately address potential risks. If, following such inquiry, the board concludes that existing practices suffice, that judgment receives deference. A board that never inquires because it views bias as political rather than operational would not receive such deference.

One might observe that this framework grants boards significant discretion in determining what requires deliberation and that directors with different perspectives will reach different threshold judgments. This observation is correct but not problematic. Fiduciary law has always entrusted boards with discretion precisely because judgment remains necessary. What prevents discretion from becoming arbitrary is not the elimination of judgment but its proceduralization.[32] Boards must explain, with reference to observable facts, why they concluded that deliberation was or was not warranted. This constitutes accountability through reasoning, the core discipline of fiduciary obligation. When that reasoning is absent, when boards dismiss issues without inquiry or avoid them through silence, the threshold for judicial scrutiny is crossed.

Establishing that deliberation should be mandatory leaves critical implementation questions. The duty must specify when it applies, what conduct constitutes breach, and how courts should review deliberative adequacy without becoming entangled in the merits of contested social issues. These implementation questions require translating the analytical framework and normative justifications into a workable standard of review, one that preserves business judgment deference while ensuring that boards exercise judgment rather than avoid it. Section 9.2.3 turns to that task.

9.2.3 *The Standard of Review*

The proposed standard does not require comprehensive stakeholder consultation for every decision with social dimensions, nor mandate that every corporate commitment be verified through elaborate accuracy mechanisms, nor require that every policy be monitored through independent oversight units. What it requires is evidence that the board took the matter seriously, that it made a good-faith effort to understand the issue and its implications, and that it reached its decision through a process designed to inform judgment rather than ratify predetermined conclusions. The standard is reasonableness and good faith, not perfection or exhaustive procedure.

9.2.3.1 What Would Constitute a Breach

The proposed standard recognizes two circumstances in which boards fail to satisfy their deliberative obligations. The first involves systematic inattention, which arises when boards create no institutional capacity whatsoever to consider social risks relevant to their operations. The second involves process so cursory that it cannot be characterized as deliberation at all. These breach conditions are intentionally narrow. The goal is not to second-guess reasonable judgments or penalize boards for choosing one deliberative approach over another. It is to identify the outer boundaries of acceptable governance, the point at which inaction or superficiality crosses into fiduciary neglect.

9.2.3.2 Failure to Establish Any Structure for Considering Social Risks

Boards breach their duty when they have no structure whatsoever for considering social issues relevant to their operations, such that material concerns are systematically overlooked. This is a minimal obligation to ensure that social conflicts plausibly connected to corporate operations do not fall into a governance void where they receive no consideration at all. The standard here is structural capacity, not substantive outcome. A board does not breach this duty by concluding, after deliberation, that a particular issue does not warrant policy changes. It breaches the duty by creating no mechanism through which the issue could reach the board's attention in the first place.

Consider several examples. A corporation deploying facial recognition technology across multiple jurisdictions that has never established any mechanism, formal or informal, for considering bias, privacy, or civil liberties concerns demonstrates systematic failure.[33] The technology's social implications are obvious and well-documented; the absence of any governance structure suggests conscious avoidance rather than reasoned judgment. Similarly, a company with extensive overseas supply chains that has no means of learning about labor conditions in its manufacturing facilities – no audits, no hotlines, no stakeholder engagement – fails to meet even minimal expectations. The risks of labor exploitation in global supply chains are widely known; systematic ignorance is not defensible as business judgment.[34]

Importantly, the breach lies not in failing to detect every problem or establish elaborate monitoring systems, but in creating no capacity whatsoever to think systematically about a category of risk clearly relevant to the business. Boards need not create dedicated committees or hire specialized staff for every domain of potential social conflict. They must ensure that, for issues obviously connected to their industry and operations, someone within the governance structure has responsibility for awareness, and the board receives at least periodic information. This might involve charging an existing committee with oversight, requiring management to include social risk in enterprise risk management frameworks, or establishing routine reporting on stakeholder concerns. The form matters less than the existence of some institutional means by which relevant issues reach the board's attention rather than being systematically ignored.

What would not constitute a breach under this standard? A board that considers algorithmic bias concerns, consults with technical experts, reviews the company's detection protocols, and concludes that existing systems adequately address the risks has not breached its duty, even if subsequent events prove that judgment wrong. The standard is procedural, not substantive. Similarly, a board that establishes a committee to monitor supply chain labor practices, receives quarterly reports, and adjusts policies based on findings has satisfied its obligation, even if individual violations occur. The duty is to create deliberative capacity, not to guarantee perfect outcomes.

9.2.3.3 Processes So Deficient They Amount to No Process

Liability attaches when the board's decision-making is so cursory, so lacking in substance, that it cannot be characterized as informed deliberation at all. The standard here resembles *Van Gorkom*: just as a board cannot satisfy the duty of care by approving a merger after a two-hour meeting with no valuation analysis, a board cannot satisfy its deliberative obligation by rubber-stamping a controversial social commitment without meaningful inquiry. The question is whether the process was genuine or pretextual.

Examples of inadequate process include a board that adopts a public commitment on a controversial social issue after minimal discussion, without consulting anyone with relevant expertise, without documenting any reasoning, and without establishing implementation mechanisms. Or a board that responds to credible signals of significant social risk, such as shareholder proposals backed by major investors, regulatory investigations, or peer company actions, by dismissing the matter in a cursory five-minute discussion as "not our concern" or "political rather than business-related." These scenarios suggest that the board did not deliberate, it simply ratified management's preferred course or avoided engagement entirely.

Crucially, this standard distinguishes between inadequate process and substantive disagreement. Boards and courts may reasonably disagree about the significance of particular social issues. Some directors may view climate risk as paramount, while others prioritize other concerns. The deliberation standard does not require boards to reach particular conclusions or adopt particular policies. It requires that they engage meaningfully with issues that credible evidence suggests carry material social dimensions. A board that deliberates seriously and concludes that a given social issue does not warrant policy changes has exercised business judgment. A board that never deliberates has not.

9.2.4 *Remedies*

The purpose of process-based review is not to penalize error but to ensure that corporate judgment is exercised under conditions conducive to reasoned decision-making. When courts assess fiduciary adequacy in the social domain, the appropriate remedy for a deficient process is not necessarily liability but recalibration. Thus, a judicial order might direct the board to complete or strengthen the deliberative procedures that were lacking. In this sense, enforcement is remedial rather than punitive, restorative rather than substitutive. The court's task is to restore the procedural balance that fiduciary law presupposes, by making a decision on the basis of adequate information, expertise, and reflection.

This remedial approach follows established patterns in corporate law. When Delaware courts find that boards failed to satisfy procedural requirements in merger contexts, they rarely invalidate transactions outright.[35] Instead, they may order additional disclosure to shareholders, require boards to obtain supplemental expert opinions, or mandate extended negotiation periods.[36] The remedy addresses the process deficiency directly. It first cures the informational gap, and then allows the board to decide. Social deliberation cases would follow this model. Courts might direct the board to obtain additional expert analysis,[37] consult affected stakeholders,[38] disclose relevant uncertainties, or conduct independent verification of key data.[39] These measures do not dictate outcomes, but enhance the conditions under which directors make them.

A remedial order might take several forms, depending on the nature of the deficiency. If a board adopted a controversial policy without adequate consultation, the court might require the board to engage specified experts or stakeholder groups, document their input, and reconsider the policy in light of that information. If a board made public commitments without establishing verification mechanisms, the court might order the creation of specific monitoring systems and require periodic reporting to an independent committee. If a board systematically ignored an issue despite credible signals of its significance, the court might mandate that the matter be placed on the board's agenda, that management prepare a briefing addressing specified questions, and that the board document its deliberation and reasoning.

These orders would typically require a renewed board vote following the augmented process, accompanied by documentation demonstrating that the new deliberation addressed prior deficiencies. The court does not dictate what the board must decide, but it ensures that the decision emerges from adequate process. If, after completing the required deliberation, the board reaches the same conclusion as before, that judgment would receive deference. The remedy compels the missing element of fiduciary care, that is, the inquiry or consultation that should have occurred initially, rather than a particular substantive outcome.

This form of iterative review aligns judicial authority with the informational logic of fiduciary duty. Rather than positioning the court as an arbiter of corporate morality or social policy, it treats the judiciary as a guarantor of deliberative completeness. The underlying assumption is that better processes, not judicially imposed solutions, are the most legitimate path toward sound corporate decisions. This assumption reflects both epistemic humility, as courts lack the expertise to resolve complex social conflicts, and institutional respect for the business judgment rule. Courts should not substitute their judgment for that of boards. They should ensure that boards exercise judgment rather than avoiding it.

Such orders resemble the equitable remedies familiar from the transactional context. Just as courts mandate process corrections in conflict-of-interest transactions without displacing management's discretion to decide on deal terms,[40] they can mandate deliberative corrections in social governance without dictating social policy. The court thereby preserves the integrity of business judgment while ensuring that the conditions of that judgment meet fiduciary expectations. This approach also addresses a common objection to heightened procedural standards: that they will increase litigation and judicial interference in business decisions. By focusing remedies on process correction rather than damages or injunctive relief prohibiting particular actions, courts can enforce deliberative standards without becoming enmeshed in the merits of social controversies.

Recalibration also creates incentives for internal reform. Boards aware that inadequate procedures may prompt a judicial directive to revisit decisions have reason to establish robust deliberative systems preemptively. The prospect of redeliberating under judicial supervision provides stronger incentive for thorough initial deliberation than the threat of damages, which liability insurance often covers. Over time, this remedial framework should reduce rather than increase litigation, as boards adopt procedures that immunize their decisions from challenge. The goal is not to proliferate lawsuits but to institutionalize deliberation, rendering judicial intervention unnecessary except in cases of genuine failure.

9.3 PROCESS WITHOUT PREDETERMINED OUTCOMES

This chapter completes the analytical project that animates this book. Corporate law has long recognized that boards exercise vast discretion, yet it has never examined how that discretion operates when corporations confront social conflict. The case studies in Chapters 6, 7, and 8 made that discretion visible, documenting the procedural frameworks through which sophisticated firms organize their judgment over socially consequential decisions. This chapter has translated those observations into legal architecture. It distilled best practices into a procedural grammar spanning rulemaking, executive action, and oversight functions. It established why these practices should become mandatory fiduciary obligations rather than remain voluntary. And it specified how courts can enforce deliberative standards without displacing business judgment or entangling themselves in substantive social controversies. Together, these elements provide what corporate law has lacked in this domain: a way to hold boards accountable for how they exercise discretion without dictating what they decide.

The proposal's goal is to resolve the governance paradox identified at the outset. Boards make decisions with significant social consequences, yet the processes through which they make such decisions have remained invisible to legal scrutiny. By incorporating the procedural logic revealed in the case studies into fiduciary duty, corporate law can treat social deliberation as it has treated other forms of high-stakes decision-making. It can articulate what constitutes adequate process, distinguish between genuine engagement and systematic failure, and create incentives for boards to deliberate seriously rather than avoid difficult questions. This represents evolution rather than revolution, adapting existing fiduciary principles to ensure that the discretion boards exercise over their most consequential decisions operates through the same deliberative discipline that corporate law has always demanded.

The proposal does not seek to weigh the scales one way or another, and it will disappoint those looking for specific outcomes, progressives and conservatives alike. It does not resolve normative debates about corporate purpose[41] or determine which social issues corporations should prioritize. It does not guarantee that corporations will adopt progressive policies on climate change, algorithmic fairness, or labor practices. Those remain questions of business judgment. Yet this is not what corporate governance does. Corporate law has avoided dictating substantive outcomes in domains of managerial discretion. Instead, it has specified the processes through which discretion must be exercised, ensuring that decisions emerge from informed deliberation rather than arbitrary choice, systematic avoidance, or untested assumption. The social deliberation standard follows this tradition precisely. It preserves full managerial autonomy over what to decide while ensuring that boards actually deliberate before deciding.

Formalization marks only the beginning of doctrinal development. Courts will need to refine these standards through cases, determining how deliberative adequacy applies across industries and contexts. Yet this evolutionary process is itself characteristic of corporate law, which develops through incremental specifications of what responsible discretion requires. This chapter identifies the next iteration in that evolution, one that recognizes social conflicts as decision-making contexts demanding the same procedural discipline that corporate law applies to financial transactions, agency conflicts, and compliance monitoring. The result is a fiduciary standard adapted to contemporary governance challenges, one that preserves managerial autonomy while ensuring that autonomy operates through an accountable process.

Conclusion

Reason and Authority

Corporate governance is no longer merely a system of managerial control or financial oversight. It has become a form of public reasoning. Corporations today adjudicate questions once reserved for democratic institutions, including about climate, labor, technology, equity, and the common good. Their decisions are not just economically consequential, they are also morally, socially, and politically charged. As society's expectations grow more complex,[1] corporate influence increasingly depends not on who decides, but on how decisions are made. This book began with a simple but pressing question: how can corporations make business choices when their decisions shape public life? What has emerged is not a call for consensus, but a framework grounded in deliberation as the institutional discipline of gathering knowledge, confronting conflict, and explaining choices in ways that others can understand.

Chapter 1 introduced this predicament as the unavoidable condition of modern corporate life. It observed that governance, once thought simply the ordinary business of running a corporation, has become inseparable from social conflict. Subsequent chapters traced how law and practice have struggled to adjust. Chapter 2 showed that our traditional fiduciary vocabulary, born in an era of homogeneity, falters in a world of competing values. Our established corporate governance tools presuppose alignment on what is valuable[2] but offer little guidance when directors must choose between conflicting moral claims or incommensurable metrics of success.

To fill that gap, Chapter 3 articulated a new model of governance built around three functions: rulemaking, execution, and monitoring. Together, these three functions constitute deliberation as a unifying discipline. Deliberation here means not a meeting or ritual, but a structure of reasoning, an institutional commitment to gather knowledge widely, question assumptions, and justify decisions transparently. These processes do not dictate outcomes, but they make good judgment possible. Chapter 4 examined the complementary role of law and government. It recognized that while regulation remains essential, corporations act first, as they encounter emerging conflicts before legislatures can define them. Corporate responses form the raw material of future legal regimes.

The book's case studies illuminate this deliberative dynamic across contemporary and historical contexts. Chapter 6 examines how Uber and Lyft confronted regulatory gaps in rideshare safety and insurance, developing hybrid coverage frameworks and misconduct-reporting protocols that regulators later codified as they sought to legitimate their novel business models.[3] Chapter 7 traces corporate leadership in climate governance, showing how BP and General Motors collaborated with environmental scientists to create the Greenhouse Gas Protocol, the world's dominant emissions measurement framework,[4] and how individual firms such as Salesforce translated these standards into automated carbon accounting systems and supplier contract clauses that cascaded climate obligations throughout supply chains.[5] Chapter 8 explores AI governance at the technological frontier, where companies such as Microsoft built internal regimes combining rulemaking, implementation, and oversight into continuous deliberative loops, deploying fairness principles not as aspirational slogans but as procedural triggers that mandate impact assessments before system deployment.[6]

Yet this pattern is not new. Chapter 5 reveals how early twentieth-century corporations designed the road codes, traffic rules, and financial disclosure templates that governments subsequently formalized into law, demonstrating that private norm-creation has long preceded public codification, though never at today's velocity or scale. Finally, Chapter 9 translates these empirical findings into doctrinal reform, proposing a social-deliberation standard that would embed these deliberative practices within fiduciary law itself, making deliberative quality, rather than substantive outcomes, the measure of directorial care when corporations navigate social conflict.

C.1 WHY HETEROGENEITY OF PREFERENCES DEMANDS A PRACTICE OF REASONING

At the heart of this transformation lies heterogeneity of preferences among shareholders, the defining challenge of the modern corporate enterprise.[7] Corporations now bring together people and institutions with profoundly different goals, beliefs, and constraints. Shareholders disagree about time horizons and risk. Employees differ in their values and ambitions. Customers and communities press moral claims that often resist quantification. These differences are not marginal, but rather inherent in the manner in which modern corporations operate.

The modern corporation inherits a structure built for homogeneity. Hierarchy presupposes that those at the top can discern a single "corporate interest" and that those below, recognizing the legitimacy of command, will align their efforts accordingly. This assumption worked tolerably well in an era when investors shared relatively uniform expectations about returns, employees expected security and advancement, and social consensus shielded business from political contestation. It falters in a world where the corporation has become a meeting ground for radically different value systems between generations, geographies, and worldviews.

Heterogeneity of preferences disrupts hierarchy in two distinct ways. First, it erodes epistemic authority: the idea that management knows best. When shareholders, workers, and consumers possess their own information, networks, and normative commitments, managerial expertise loses its monopoly on defining what counts as rational or desirable. Second, it erodes moral authority: the willingness of subordinates to obey even when they disagree. Individuals who see corporate decisions as conflicting with their ethical or civic identities experience obedience as complicity. What once appeared as organizational discipline now feels like moral submission.

The result is not open revolt but quiet corrosion. Employees comply selectively, customers mobilize through social media, and investors use disclosure demands to reopen questions that management thought settled. Hierarchical control becomes less a chain of command and more a negotiation conducted in real time across porous boundaries. Authority persists, but it must now be continually justified. Legitimacy becomes procedural rather than positional.

Classical corporate theory treats such pluralism as noise to be suppressed. The task of governance is to unify purpose and align incentives, that is, to translate many preferences into one objective function. That project worked so long as disagreement could be reduced to economic terms. Today, the conflicts that unsettle corporations may present as different business models but often betray deeper clashes on worldviews. They cannot be resolved by incentives alone because they concern the meaning of the enterprise itself, diverging on questions like what the firm should produce, whom it should serve, what risks it may impose on others. Under such conditions, hierarchy without deliberation breeds distrust. It invites the perception that managerial authority masks private interest, ideology, or inertia.

Deliberation, by contrast, provides a language through which heterogeneity can be acknowledged without paralysis. It turns difference into data, dissent into feedback. When managers open their reasoning to scrutiny, they do not dissolve hierarchy but recalibrate it. Authority becomes conditional on justification. The board's role shifts from command to orchestration, from issuing directives to organizing the processes that make decisions intelligible and defensible. The legitimacy of the hierarchy is thus reconstituted through reason-giving, not through ownership or control.

Seen this way, the modern corporation faces the same legitimacy challenge as democratic government, namely to transform disparate perspectives into decisions without erasing the plurality that gives those decisions meaning. Hierarchy remains indispensable for coordination, but only deliberation can sustain its acceptance. The two together form the new architecture of governance, in which authority is anchored in reason.

The case studies in this book demonstrate that reasoning, when institutionalized, restores coherence without demanding consensus. In the rideshare industry, companies learned that legitimacy could not be purchased through compliance alone, but had to be earned through systematic consultation with safety experts, insurers, and advocacy groups. In climate governance, firms discovered that scenario analysis and disclosure were not bureaucratic exercises but disciplines for thinking, methods for reconciling ambition with evidence. In AI, firms realized that a revolutionary technology called for a radical rethinking of substantive values and an extensive architecture of monitoring implementation and refining standards. Across these settings, deliberation provided the structure through which heterogeneity could become productive rather than paralyzing.

C.2 CORPORATIONS AS DELIBERATIVE INSTITUTIONS: A BLINDSPOT BETWEEN PUBLIC AND PRIVATE LAW

Corporations today occupy a position unlike any other institution in modern life. They stand at the center of our most consequential choices, such as how to respond to climate change, how to structure work and compensation, how to govern artificial intelligence, how to balance privacy with innovation, how to design systems of communication that shape public discourse itself.[8] These questions define the boundaries of our collective future. The reason corporations draw such intense scrutiny, and often such sharp criticism, is precisely that they have become the sites where these conflicts are confronted first.

It is easy to view this prominence as overreach, where private entities are assuming powers once reserved for legislatures and governments. Critics see hubris, opportunism, and self-interest, and those tendencies are indeed real. But to stop there is to miss a deeper reality. Corporations are not simply occupying these spaces. They are filling the regulatory void because no other institution currently possesses the knowledge, scale, or immediacy to do so.[9] Corporations are designing the frameworks by which entire domains of human activity become intelligible. The challenge, and the achievement, lie in how they have built mechanisms to reason through these problems under extraordinary uncertainty.

The argument of this book is that modern corporations have evolved into deliberative institutions, systems organized not only for production and profit but also for reasoning at scale. Their structures of governance include conventional tools such as boards, committees, and disclosure regimes, but also voluntary reporting frameworks, audit trails, and stakeholder consultations. Together, they form an architecture of collective thought. Within these structures, corporations continuously identify problems, gather expertise, weigh competing claims, and justify their actions to multiple audiences. They are, in effect, the largest deliberative systems humanity has ever created.

This transformation is often invisible because it does not fit the romantic image of deliberation as open debate or civic dialogue. Corporate reasoning takes place through spreadsheets, risk matrices, board presentations, sustainability disclosures, and crisis-response protocols. Yet these technical forms are where some of the most sophisticated moral and epistemic judgments of our time are made. When a company models the cost of decarbonization across its global operations, when it evaluates human rights risk in supply chains, or when it sets parameters for algorithmic fairness, it is engaging in structured deliberation, translating moral uncertainty into institutional procedure. These exercises are imperfect, but they represent a remarkable organizational achievement: the institutionalization of reflection itself.

To acknowledge this achievement does not mean ignoring the shortcomings. Many corporate deliberations are narrow, self-protective, or cosmetic. But even these failures confirm the fact that stakeholders demand deliberation, transparent processes, and responsiveness precisely because society now expects corporations to reason publicly about their choices. Managers are judged not only for what they decide but also for how they decide. That expectation, and the systems that have arisen to meet it, are new. They mark a turning point in the history of governance.

Across the book's chapters, we have seen this deliberative capacity develop. In present and past, companies in early capital markets created disclosure practices that prefigured modern securities law, demonstrating how private frameworks could become the language of public trust. In the Rideshare Case Study, firms built safety and insurance standards that regulators later adopted, showing how corporate reasoning can generate new categories of law. In the Climate Case Study, the slow convergence around emissions measurement and scenario analysis illustrated how iterative corporate deliberation can anchor global norms even before they become legally mandatory. Each of these examples reflects not unaccountable power, but a form of organized reasoning through which corporations have contributed to social order.

Yet these contributions often go unacknowledged because they do not fit the binary categories through which law and politics traditionally evaluate power. We are used to seeing corporations as either subjects of regulation or objects of critique. We lack an analytical category for understanding them as institutions that, however imperfectly, generate the frameworks that govern our shared problems. This book's purpose has been to make that analytical step possible, to reveal the corporation not as an intruder in the realm of social governance, but as one of its most capable practitioners.

Recognizing corporations as deliberative institutions changes what we ask of them. It does not mean absolving them of accountability, but assessing them by a different standard, which focuses on the quality of their reasoning rather than the purity of their motives. Do they seek out knowledge widely? Do they confront evidence honestly? Do they explain their decisions in ways that make sense to those affected by them? These are the questions by which corporate leadership should now be judged.

Corporate law, too, must evolve to support this reality. Its role is not to dictate outcomes, but to nurture the conditions under which deliberation can thrive, to ensure that corporate reasoning remains informed, transparent, and contestable. Fiduciary duties, disclosure requirements, and board procedures should be understood as tools for cultivating institutional intelligence. Law cannot produce wisdom directly, but it can make wisdom possible.

Seen in this light, the corporation's dual identity as both private enterprise and deliberative institution becomes a defining feature of twenty-first-century governance. It explains both the intensity of public scrutiny and the persistence of corporate influence. The very reason corporations are criticized so much is that they now sit at the heart of society's most difficult questions. But that centrality also means they are uniquely positioned to contribute to their resolution. Their deliberative achievements, however imperfect or incremental, deserve to be studied, strengthened, and extended.

To understand corporations in this way is to take them seriously as institutions of reasoning, not merely of power. They are the world's largest laboratories of decision-making, constantly translating uncertainty into action. Their mistakes have global reach, but so do their successes. Recognizing both is essential if we are to improve the systems on which modern life depends.

C.3 BEYOND GOVERNANCE: IMPLICATIONS

This book has been about governance. It explores how managers, directors, and other practitioners can better navigate the social conflicts that now define corporate life. Its ambition has been to show how decision-makers can confront moral and political complexity without losing clarity, and how organizations can build processes that turn disagreement into insight rather than paralysis. Throughout, the book has treated governance not as a system of command, but as a discipline of reasoning and a way to structure judgment when facts are uncertain, values are contested, and outcomes are fraught with consequence.

But the journey of developing this framework has also carried the argument far beyond the mechanics of boardrooms and management committees. The cases and examples explored here, whether dealing with environmental controversies, labor practices, or the dilemmas of technology governance, touch on questions that reach the core of modern public life. As the analysis unfolded, it became evident that understanding how corporations deliberate is inseparable from understanding how societies govern themselves. The challenges that directors face in balancing competing claims are, in miniature, the challenges that democracies face in sustaining legitimacy under pluralism.[10]

This final section turns to those broader questions. It does not seek to resolve them, nor could it. Some threads will need to be followed in future work. Yet the theory and examples developed here inevitably point toward wider implications. They suggest new ways to think about the relationship between corporations and democracy, about the changing role of corporations in society, and about the origins of law itself. The reflections that follow sketch how a project conceived to help practitioners reason better within their institutions also sheds light on how authority, legitimacy, and law are evolving in the twenty-first century.

C.3.1 *Implications for Corporations and Democracy: Can Process Substitute Representation?*

Recasting fiduciary law as a discipline of deliberation carries implications far beyond doctrinal reform. It offers a new foundation for corporate legitimacy in a fractured public sphere.[11] The growing expectation that corporations will engage with climate change, diversity, labor rights, and the ethics of technology reflects not only demands for substantive outcomes but also demands for voice and reason. Citizens and investors alike seek reassurance that corporate decisions are not arbitrary, partisan, or opaque. The deliberative model responds to this need by shifting the source of legitimacy away from alignment with any particular constituency and toward the quality of the reasoning process itself. When corporations can demonstrate that they have sought knowledge widely, listened seriously, and explained transparently, they command respect even amid disagreement.

This conception reframes the relationship between corporations and democracy. Corporations are not substitutes for public institutions, but they can complement them by embodying democratic virtues such as reason-giving, participation, and accountability within their own domain.[12] As public law's procedural ideals migrate into the corporate sphere, the corporation becomes an arena in which plural interests are mediated through deliberation rather than force or fiat. The social-deliberation standard proposed here provides an analog to democratic decision-making because it makes deliberation, rather than profit or philanthropy, the measure of responsible corporate citizenship. When fiduciary duty is interpreted as an obligation to deliberate conscientiously under conditions of heterogeneity, corporate law assumes a quasi-constitutional role, ensuring that discretion, wherever it is exercised, remains accountable to reason.

Yet this analogy also exposes what may be called the democratic deficit of corporate law.[13] Once we recognize corporations as rulemakers that aggregate and impose preferences on others, the absence of democratic authorization becomes central. Managerial discretion today shapes citizens' environments of work, nutrition, communication, and even belief. It reaches deeply into the domains that democratic politics once claimed as its own. Because these decisions occur largely within the penumbra of private ordering, critics question both their majoritarian legitimacy, that is, whether corporate elites represent the will of the people, and their countermajoritarian role, that is, whether they protect values that majorities might threaten. The corporation thus stands at a constitutional frontier, since it forms an undoubtedly powerful law-making actor, but also one lacking the democratic pedigree of the institutions it increasingly resembles.

Skeptics might readily discard the procedural steps this book embraces as inadequate to cure this democratic deficit.[14] For them, no amount of procedural refinement can substitute for unelected power. Deliberation may change how corporations justify their decisions, but it does not change who holds the power to decide. True legitimacy requires not better processes but different actors, such as elected representatives, worker councils, or democratically accountable boards. Until corporations derive authority from stakeholder representation, their internal reasoning remains nothing more than a sophisticated form of public relations, legitimation theater designed to make private power palatable. From this perspective, deliberative procedures not only fail, but may actively obscure the problem by making arbitrary authority seem rational, consultative, and therefore, acceptable.

The critique identifies a genuine limit. Deliberative procedures cannot transform corporate influence into democratically legitimate authority. A corporation with perfect deliberative practices remains an institution making consequential decisions without electoral mandate. But this critique misunderstands the challenge through which corporations gain their influence. Governments have no choice but to act after corporations have already entered and shaped a domain. Corporations are the institutions imagining new economic activities, be it the gig economy, social media platforms, algorithmic management, or synthetic biology. Democratic institutions follow behind, attempting to govern arrangements already operating at scale.[15] By the time legislatures understand what platform work entails, millions of workers have been reclassified. By the time regulators comprehend what algorithmic feeds do to political discourse, entire publics have been restructured. This priority reflects how market institutions generate novelty faster than political institutions can deliberate about it. The question, then, is not whether corporate influence can be made democratically legitimate, but what safeguards can help guide it.

This is where deliberative governance matters. What it establishes are defensive mechanisms that make corporate experimentation governable rather than opaque. It creates accountability touchpoints where decisions must be articulated and justified, generating records that can later be scrutinized. It fights arbitrary decision-making by requiring managers to articulate reasons and consider conflicts. It makes trade-offs visible, turning private choices into public facts that stakeholders and regulators can identify and contest. Most critically, it generates the evidence base for intervention by documenting harms, mapping affected parties, revealing patterns that regulators would have trouble unveiling by themselves. These are not solutions to the legitimacy problem but practical necessities for governing corporate influence that needs to move faster than law.

C.3.2 *Implications for the Role of Corporations in Society: Can Process Counteract Incentives?*

This book casts corporate governance not as a system of control but as a system of collective reasoning. Managers and directors are not merely agents of shareholders or stewards of capital, they are also custodians of institutions whose decisions shape the social and moral environment. Corporate ordering frames how this custodial role takes form. Rulemaking gives deliberation a forward-looking dimension by requiring institutions to anticipate social consequences and incorporate diverse expertise before commitments harden into practice. Execution brings deliberation into motion by testing rules against real-world complexity and forcing adjustments through implementation. Monitoring completes the cycle by converting experience into reflection, thus transforming information about errors and impacts into institutional memory. Together, these functions make deliberation continuous rather than episodic. They turn corporate governance from a sequence of decisions into a living system of reasoning.

This procedural turn is both modest and ambitious. It is modest in refusing to dictate outcomes, but ambitious in redefining what it means to govern well. It asks corporations to earn their autonomy through reasoned transparency and to view legitimacy as an ongoing conversation between expertise and society. This evolution reflects a deeper truth. Managerial discretion, long justified by ownership and later by agency, now requires justification through reason.

Under this model, the corporation's role in society changes fundamentally. It becomes not merely an engine of economic production but an institution of social interpretation, translating plural values into operational choices. The board's purpose is no longer to impose unity upon diversity but to navigate among competing claims in a manner that is intelligible and defensible. In doing so, corporate governance internalizes the very processes by which democratic societies maintain legitimacy amid disagreement.

Still, one might worry that deliberation must contend with the realities of the market. Corporations operate within incentive systems that reward decisiveness and short-term performance, not patience or reflection.[16] However sophisticated their reasoning processes, managers remain accountable to investors whose primary metric of success is profit maximization.[17] In such conditions, deliberation risks becoming either too costly or practically impossible. When competitive pressure mounts or crisis erupts, there may be no room for maneuver, no time for consultation, no budget for analysis, no patience for uncertainty. The pursuit of profit might leave no room for flexibility.

This objection has force, and any defense of deliberation must answer it directly. One response points to changing market dynamics, as corporate legitimacy itself is increasingly priced as an asset. Reputational damage, regulatory exposure, and stakeholder backlash translate into costs of capital and constraints on autonomy[18]. Disclosure regimes for climate transition, human rights, and AI governance now require corporations to expose their reasoning and explain how they weigh evidence, consider alternatives, and justify trade-offs. Under these conditions, deliberation acquires economic form, a signal of institutional competence that markets can reward.

But this response, while true, is incomplete. It remains trapped within the instrumentalist frame of the objection itself, suggesting deliberation is merely a technique for managing reputational risk or satisfying disclosure requirements. The deeper answer is that deliberation changes what decision-makers know and believe. Structured reasoning pushes directors and managers to surface assumptions, test evidence, consult expertise, and explore alternatives. They may discover options they had not considered, recognize risks they had overlooked, and revise their judgments about what serves the enterprise. The information revealed through the deliberative process cannot be known in advance. Incentives set the boundaries of decision-making, but deliberation reveals how to navigate within them and sometimes exposes how those boundaries themselves might be redrawn.

This tension is structural, not moral. Markets prize clarity and speed, while deliberation requires ambiguity and time. Yet it is precisely this friction that reimagines deliberation not as a constraint on efficiency, but as the mechanism through which firms discover what efficiency actually demands under conditions of complexity and uncertainty. The challenge ahead is to align legal architecture with this reality, to make deliberative quality not merely defensible under fiduciary law, but structurally necessary for credible judgment. Law cannot dictate outcomes, but it can ensure that reasoning processes are robust enough to generate the knowledge that outcomes require.

C.3.3 *Implications for the Origins of Law*

Although this project is not about the origins of law in a general sense, its analysis reveals something striking about how law now comes into being. Modern legislators are seldom the architects of new regimes. Rather, they inherit systems already built within corporate hierarchies and professional networks. When governments regulate emerging domains, from artificial intelligence to sustainability, they often adopt templates first designed by firms. Corporate leaders, consultants, and industry groups draft codes of conduct, reporting frameworks, and verification procedures that public authorities later formalize. In this way, corporate governance functions as an incubator of legality. It generates the norms, structures, and vocabularies that law subsequently ratifies.

This insight challenges a central premise of legal scholarship, that the state is the primary unit of legal creation. By the time regulators intervene, the basic architecture of compliance, metrics, and accountability often exists in private form. Legal scholars who study regulation after it reaches the statute book may therefore be analyzing only the codification of norms whose formative moment occurred elsewhere. Corporate governance, with its reliance on deliberation, internal rulemaking, and moral reasoning, is one of those formative sites.

Recognizing this dynamic aligns corporate law with other fields that have traced the migration of normative power from public to private hands. Sarah Light's work on "corporate environmental law" shows how firms develop internal systems that parallel environmental regulation.[19] Josh Macey's and Aneil Kovvali's analyses of energy and financial governance similarly depict private actors constructing regulatory frameworks before the state.[20] The theory advanced here unifies these strands. It understands corporate law not merely as a mechanism for managing internal conflicts but as a framework through which those conflicts radiate outward, shaping the normative environment in which both business and government operate.

The implications for legal theory are substantial. To grasp law's contemporary origins, scholars must look not only to legislatures and courts but also to corporate deliberation itself. The procedures that firms design to navigate pluralism, from risk management systems to AI ethics committees, are not merely compliance tools, but sources of law in embryonic form. They embody the same logic that fiduciary deliberation aims to formalize, ensuring that legitimacy flows from reasoned process, even in the absence of state coercion.

In this sense, the corporation becomes both subject and author of law. It governs not only itself but, indirectly, the social and economic systems upon which modern life depends. Appreciating this dual role allows us to see corporate law as the connective tissue between private governance and public order. In this domain, the boundaries between managers and governments, or morality and legality, are constantly redrawn.

C.4 CONCLUSION: WHAT WE KNOW, WHAT WE OWE, WHERE WE LOOK

This book has operated on three levels, each with distinct implications for how we understand corporate governance in the twenty-first century.

C.4.1 *The Contemporary Account of Corporate Ordering*

As a descriptive matter, the book documents how corporate ordering has become a formative site of legal creation. The basic architecture of compliance systems, reporting frameworks, and verification procedures increasingly originates in corporate hierarchies before governments formalize them into law. This is neither regulatory capture nor privatization. Rather, corporations function as laboratories where the norms, metrics, and vocabularies of future regulation take shape. By the time legislators intervene, they often inherit templates already operating at scale. Understanding this dynamic requires scholars to look beyond statutes and court decisions to the boardrooms, compliance departments, and stakeholder consultations where regulatory frameworks first emerge. The descriptive claim thus redirects attention from law's moment of codification to its sites of formation.

C.4.2 *The Normative Argument about Corporate Ordering*

Normatively, the book argues that legitimacy in corporate decision-making flows from deliberative quality rather than ownership or democratic authorization. When corporations exercise authority over matters of genuine social consequence, such as sustainability, AI, or labor standards, they cannot claim legitimacy through shareholder primacy or market efficiency alone. Instead, legitimacy depends on the rigor of reasoning, asking whether managers and directors seek knowledge widely, engage competing claims seriously, and justify their choices transparently. This standard does not eliminate the democratic deficit inherent in corporate power, but it establishes what corporations owe in exchange for their autonomy. Fiduciary deliberation becomes the mechanism through which unelected authority can be made accountable to reason, even when it cannot be made accountable to voters. The normative claim thus reimagines corporate governance as a discipline of justification, not merely a system of control.

C.4.3 *The Methodological Intervention*

Methodologically, the book calls for legal scholarship that treats corporate governance not as a peripheral subject but as central to understanding how contemporary societies actually govern themselves. If the formative work of regulation increasingly occurs in private deliberation, then understanding law requires understanding those deliberative processes. This demands institutional eclecticism. We should look beyond formal legal institutions to the networks, professional communities, and epistemic authorities that shape corporate practice. We should pay attention to process over outcomes, developing tools to evaluate whether stakeholder consultation is genuine, whether board deliberation reflects careful value-balancing, and which institutional structures support rigorous reasoning. The methodological proposal thus argues for scholarship that is more empirical about how norms emerge, more attentive to the sociology of norm production, and more willing to treat corporations as sites of legal creation rather than merely legal subjects.

These three dimensions converge on a single insight. We are entering a new era in corporate governance, one that elevates decision-making quality from aspiration to necessity. From owner-management to professional management, from managerial authority to shareholder accountability, from shareholder primacy to social conflict management, each transition reflected changed conditions and redistributed authority differently. The current evolution marks another fundamental reordering, from governance by consent or ownership to governance by reason. What distinguishes this era is that deliberative rigor has become the criterion of legitimacy itself. Corporations earn their autonomy not through ownership rights or contractual efficiency but through demonstrating that their processes are robust enough to navigate moral and epistemic complexity.

This is not idealism but recognition of structural necessity. In a world where corporate decisions shape public outcomes, and where those decisions cannot be democratically authorized, deliberative quality becomes the mechanism through which authority is justified. The work ahead is to institutionalize these practices, making them standard rather than exceptional, embedding them in legal architecture, and holding corporations accountable not only for what they decide but also for how they decide. This book has sought to show why that work matters and what shape it might take.

Notes

INTRODUCTION

1. Meta, "Meta's efforts regarding the Israel–Hamas war," October 18, 2023, https://about.fb.com/news/2023/10/metas-efforts-regarding-israel-hamas-war/ (last accessed November 15, 2025).
2. Oversight Board, "Content moderation in a new era for AI and automation," September 2024, www.oversightboard.com/wp-content/uploads/2024/09/Oversight-Board-Content-Moderation-in-a-New-Era-for-AI-and-Automation-September-2024.pdf (last accessed November 15, 2025).
3. Evelyn Douek, "Content moderation as systems thinking," in press, *Harvard Law Review* 136, https://ssrn.com/abstract=4005326 (last accessed November 23, 2025); Kate Klonick, "The new governors" (2018) 131 *Harvard Law Review* 1598–670.
4. Mike Isaac, "Social media users accuse Facebook and Instagram of suppressing pro-Palestinian posts," The New York Times, October 16, 2023, www.nytimes.com/2023/10/16/world/middleeast/israel-hamas-war-social-media.html (last accessed November 23, 2025).
5. Elle Caruso Fitzgerald, "JLens' Meta shareholder proposal garners support from nearly half of independent investors," ETF Trends, July 3, 2025, www.etftrends.com/faith-based-investing-content-hub/jlens-meta-shareholder-proposal-garners-support-half-independent-investors/ (last accessed November 24, 2025); Leslie P. Norton, "Why Meta's new content moderation policy could pose risks to its stock," Morningstar, March 18, 2025, https://global.morningstar.com/en-gb/sustainable-investing/why-metas-new-content-moderation-policy-could-pose-risks-its-stock (last accessed November 24, 2025).
6. Kari Paul, "Rights groups urge Meta shareholders to end pro-Palestinian content 'censorship'," The Guardian, May 29, 2024, www.theguardian.com/technology/article/2024/may/29/meta-censorship-palestine (last accessed November 23, 2025).
7. Will Duffield, "A libertarian vision for digital expression," Libertarianism.org, March 31, 2020, www.libertarianism.org/essays/libertarian-vision-for-digital-expression (last accessed November 23, 2025).
8. Annie Correal, "Eyes, not tech, led police to suspect in C.E.O. killing," The New York Times, December 11, 2024, www.nytimes.com/2024/12/09/nyregion/uhc-ceo-suspect-photos-facial-recognition.html (last accessed November 23, 2025).
9. Jessica Glenza, "Brian Thompson's killing sparks outrage over state of US health-care," The Guardian, December 5, 2024, www.theguardian.com/us-news/2024/dec/05/unitedhealthcare-brian-thompson-killing-online-reaction (last accessed November 23, 2025).

10. Chen Li et al., "Delay, deny, and defend: Public outrage at health insurance companies and stock market debacle," 20 PLoS One e0334399, 2025, https://doi.org/10.1371/journal.pone.0334399 (last accessed November 23, 2025).
11. Milton Friedman, "The social responsibility of business is to increase its profits," The New York Times Magazine, September 13, 1970, 32–33.
12. Lucian A. Bebchuk and Roberto Tallarita, "The illusory promise of stakeholder governance" (2020) 106 *Cornell Law Review* 91–178.
13. Elizabeth Pollman, "Corporate social responsibility, ESG, and compliance," in Benjamin van Rooij and D. Daniel Sokol (eds.), *The Cambridge Handbook of Compliance* (Cambridge: Cambridge University Press, 2021).
14. Gwladys Fouche, "Norway pauses wealth fund's ethical divestments," Reuters, November 4, 2025, www.reuters.com/business/finance/norway-poised-pause-wealth-funds-ethical-divestments-2025-11-04/ (last accessed November 23, 2025).
15. Bloomberg, "Global ESG assets predicted to hit $40 trillion by 2030, despite challenging environment, forecasts Bloomberg Intelligence," February 8, 2024, www.bloomberg.com/company/press/global-esg-assets-predicted-to-hit-40-trillion-by-2030-despite-challenging-environment-forecasts-bloomberg-intelligence/ (last accessed November 23, 2025).
16. Andrew Edgecliffe-Johnson, "The war on 'woke capitalism'," Financial Times, May 27, 2022, www.ft.com/content/e4a818e5-4039-46d9-abe0-b703f33d0f9b (last accessed November 23, 2025); Jennifer S. Fan, "Woke capital: The role of corporations in social movements" (2019) 9 *Harvard Business Law Review* 441–504.
17. Karin Rives, "Dozens of new state anti-ESG bills introduced; federal legislation expected," S&P Global, January 31, 2025, www.spglobal.com/market-intelligence/en/news-insights/articles/2025/1/dozens-of-new-state-antiesg-bills-introduced-federal-legislation-expected-87342102 (last accessed November 23, 2025).
18. Lamar Johnson, "State AGs threaten financial institutions over ESG, DEI policies," ESG Dive, January 27, 2025, www.esgdive.com/news/state-ags-threaten-financial-institutions-over-esg-dei-policies/738385/ (last accessed November 23, 2025).
19. Silla Brush, Saijel Kishan, and Alastair Marsh, "BlackRock exits major climate group amid Wall Street exodus," Bloomberg Law, January 10, 2025, https://news.bloomberglaw.com/ip-law/blackrock-exits-major-climate-group-amid-wall-street-exodus (last accessed November 23, 2025).
20. William T. McEnroe, Amanda B. Robinson, and Rachel Mann, "Antitrust scrutiny of ESG initiatives by state attorneys general heats up," Morgan Lewis, August 5, 2025, www.morganlewis.com/pubs/2025/08/antitrust-scrutiny-of-esg-initiatives-by-state-attorneys-general-heats-up (last accessed November 23, 2025).
21. Austyn Gaffney, "Supreme Court rejects an effort to block states from suing oil giants," The New York Times, March 10, 2025, www.nytimes.com/2025/03/10/climate/supreme-court-climate-lawsuits-states.html (last accessed November 23, 2025).
22. Kirk McDaniel, "Tensions over climate change, activist investors spark controversy at Exxon shareholder meeting," Courthouse News Service, May 29, 2024, www.courthousenews.com/tensions-over-climate-change-activist-investors-spark-controversy-at-exxon-shareholder-meeting/ (last accessed November 23, 2025).
23. Beth Sasfai, Michael Mencher, and Emma Bichet, "EU adopts long-awaited mandatory ESG reporting standards," Harvard Law School Forum on Corporate Governance, August 23, 2023, https://corpgov.law.harvard.edu/2023/08/23/eu-adopts-long-awaited-mandatory-esg-reporting-standards/ (last accessed November 23, 2025).
24. US Securities and Exchange Commission, "SEC votes to end defense of climate disclosure rules," March 27, 2025, www.sec.gov/newsroom/press-releases/2025-58 (last accessed November 23, 2025).

25. Alma Petras and Charles Wehland, "Both convergence and divergence seen in emerging state climate disclosure bills," JD Supra, September 4, 2025, www.jdsupra.com/legalnews/both-convergence-and-divergence-seen-in-6953438/ (last accessed November 23, 2025); Sophie Austin, "Appeals court pauses California law requiring companies to report climate-related financial risk," Associated Press, November 18, 2025, https://apnews.com/article/california-climate-disclosure-law-paused-court-appeal-42708d5fc7ed15001f4ac5a870eb105d (last accessed November 23, 2025).
26. William W. Bratton and Michael L. Wachter, "Shareholder primacy's corporatist origins: Adolf Berle and *The Modern Corporation*" (2008) 34 *Journal of Corporation Law* 99–152; Henry Hansmann and Reinier Kraakman, "The end of history for corporate law" (2001) 89 *Georgetown Law Journal* 439–68.
27. Friedman, "The social responsibility of business."
28. Margaret M. Blair and Lynn A. Stout, "A team production theory of corporate law" (1999) 85 *Virginia Law Review* 247–328.
29. Business Roundtable, "Business Roundtable redefines the purpose of a corporation to promote 'an economy that serves all Americans,'" August 19, 2019, www.businessroundtable.org/business-roundtable-redefines-the-purpose-of-a-corporation-to-promote-an-economy-that-serves-all-americans (last accessed November 23, 2025).
30. Elizabeth Pollman, "The making and meaning of ESG" (2024) 14 *Harvard Business Law Review* 403–53 (giving an overview of the rise of the ESG movement and the strategic goals behind it).
31. David A. Cifrino, "The politicization of ESG investing," Harvard ALI Social Impact Review, January 24, 2024, www.sir.advancedleadership.harvard.edu/articles/politicization-of-esg-investing (last accessed November 23, 2025).
32. Kenneth W. Abbott and Duncan Snidal, "International regulation without international government: Improving IO performance through orchestration" (2010) 5 *Review of International Organizations* 315–44; Michael P. Vandenbergh, "Private environmental governance" (2013) 99 *Cornell Law Review* 129–99; and Michael P. Vandenbergh and Jonathan M. Gilligan, *Beyond Politics: The Private Governance Response to Climate Change* (Cambridge: Cambridge University Press, 2017) (all analyzing the conditions under which companies function as de facto regulators).
33. Patrick Bolton and Marcin T. Kacperczyk, "Do investors care about carbon risk?" (2021) 142 *Journal of Financial Economics* 517–49.
34. James Brusseau, "Acceleration AI ethics, the debate between innovation and safety, and stability AI's diffusion versus OpenAI's DALL-E," AI Ethics Working Paper, 2022, https://philarchive.org/archive/BRUAAE (last accessed November 23, 2025).
35. Dorothy S. Lund, "Toward a dynamic view of corporate purpose" (2025) 109 *Minnesota Law Review* 2088–161.
36. Jeffrey N. Gordon, "The rise of independent directors in the United States, 1950–2005: Of shareholder value and stock market prices" (2007) 59 *Stanford Law Review* 1465–568.
37. George J. Benston and Alicia L. Hartgraves, "Enron: What happened and what we can learn from it" (2002) 21 *Journal of Accounting and Public Policy* 105–27.
38. Gil Sadka, "The economic consequences of accounting fraud in product markets: Theory and a case from the U.S. telecommunication industry (WorldCom)" (2006) 8 *American Law and Economics Review* 439–75.
39. Roberta Romano, "The Sarbanes-Oxley Act and the making of quack corporate governance" (2005) 114 *Yale Law Journal* 1521–611.
40. Lyman Johnson, "The modest business judgment rule" (2000) 55 *Business Lawyer* 625–52.

41. Stavros Gadinis and Chris Havasy, "The quest for legitimacy: A public law blueprint for corporate governance" (2024) 57 *UC Davis Law Review* 1581–655.
42. Stavros Gadinis and Amelia Miazad, "Corporate law and social risk" (2020) 73 *Vanderbilt Law Review* 1401–39 (discussing the epistemic benefits from managerial engagement with stakeholders).
43. Colin Mayer, "Shareholderism versus stakeholderism – A misconceived contradiction: A comment on 'The illusory promise of stakeholder governance' by Lucian Bebchuk and Roberto Tallarita," European Corporate Governance Institute Law Working Paper No. 522/2020, 2020, https://ssrn.com/abstract=3617847 (last accessed November 23, 2025) (arguing that daily managerial choices operationalize corporate values and inherently require balancing among stakeholder interests).
44. Andrew F. Tuch, "Multiple gatekeepers" (2010) 96 *Virginia Law Review* 1583–648 at 1592–97 (discussing the role of external gatekeepers, including auditors and outside experts, to provide trustworthy verification on companies' information).
45. The business judgment rule protects managers from liability for decisions made for "any rational business purpose." *Unocal Corp. v. Mesa Petroleum Co.*, 493 A2d 946 at 954 (Del. 1985) (quoting *Sinclair Oil Corp. v. Levien*, 280 A2d 717 at 720 (Del. 1971)); *Gagliardi v. TriFoods International, Inc.*, 683 A2d 1049 at 1051 (Del. Ch. 1996) (stating that, absent "self-dealing or improper motive, a corporate officer or director is not legally responsible to the corporation for losses that may be suffered as a result of a decision that an officer made or that directors authorized in good faith").
46. Nicolas Schmid et al., "Governing complex societal problems: The impact of private on public regulation through technological change" (2020) 15 *Regulation & Governance* 840–55 (documenting how private regulatory schemes pioneer technological and procedural templates that public regulators later adopt and formalize).
47. Securities Act of 1933, Pub. L. No. 73–22, 48 Stat. 74 (1933), codified at 15 USC §§ 77a–77aa.
48. Ryan Lawler, "On-demand ridesharing startup Lyft adds insurance between rides," TechCrunch, March 13, 2014, https://techcrunch.com/2014/03/13/lyft-insurance-between-rides/ (last accessed November 15, 2025).
49. Janine M. Zweig and Emily Tiry, "Three lessons businesses can learn from Uber's collecting and reporting sexual assault data," Urban Wire, December 6, 2019, www.urban.org/urban-wire/three-lessons-businesses-can-learn-ubers-collecting-and-reporting-sexual-assault-data (last accessed November 13, 2025).
50. Tony West, "Delivering on our safety commitments," Uber, December 4, 2020, www.uber.com/newsroom/delivering-on-safety-commitments/ (last accessed November 24, 2025) (explaining Uber's engagement with many stakeholders, including RAINN, the advocacy group that was instrumental in setting the policies for its safety reports).
51. David G. Victor and Joshua C. House, "BP's emissions trading system" (2006) 34 *Energy Policy* 2100–12.
52. Salesforce, "What is a sustainable supply chain?" www.salesforce.com/net-zero/cloud/what-is-sustainable-supply-chain/ (last accessed October 19, 2025).
53. Dean Carignan, "Lessons from Microsoft's responsible AI journey," Emerj, February 15, 2023, https://emerj.com/lessons-from-microsofts-responsible-ai-journey-dean-carignan-microsoft/ (last accessed October 6, 2025).
54. Evelyn Douek, "The Meta oversight board and the empty promise of legitimacy" (2024) 37(2) *Harvard Journal of Law & Technology* 374–445.
55. Michael C. Jensen and William H. Meckling, "Theory of the firm: Managerial behavior, agency costs and ownership structure" (1976) 3 *Journal of Financial Economics* 305–60.

56. Steven Bernstein and Benjamin Cashore, "Can non-state global governance be legitimate?" (2007) 1 *Regulation & Governance* 347–71.
57. David Vogel, "The private regulation of global corporate conduct" (2010) 49 *Business & Society* 68–87.
58. Tim Büthe and Walter Mattli, *The New Global Rulers: The Privatization of Regulation in the World Economy* (Princeton: Princeton University Press, 2011).
59. Andreas Georg Scherer, Dorothée Baumann-Pauly, and Anselm Schneider, "Democratizing corporate governance: Compensating for the democratic deficit of corporate political activity and corporate citizenship" (2013) 52 *Business & Society* 473–514; Guido Palazzo and Andreas G. Scherer, "Corporate social responsibility, democracy, and the politicization of the corporation" (2008) 33 *Academy of Management Review* 773–75 (arguing that corporations increasingly exercise public power, creating democratic legitimacy deficits that governance structures – not substantive priorities – must address).

1 THE SOCIAL IMPACT CHALLENGE

1. Melissa Repko, "Target rolls back DEI initiatives, the latest big company to retreat," CNBC, January 1, 2025, www.cnbc.com/2025/01/24/target-rolls-back-major-dei-initiatives.html (last accessed September 29, 2025).
2. BBC, "Bud Light boycott over trans influencer Dylan Mulvaney hits beer giant's sales," August 3, 2023, www.bbc.com/news/business-66398296 (last accessed September 29, 2025).
3. Scott Shane and Daisuke Wakabayashi, "'The business of war': Google employees protest work for the Pentagon," The New York Times, April 4, 2018, www.nytimes.com/2018/04/04/technology/google-letter-ceo-pentagon-project.html (last accessed September 29, 2025).
4. Jensen and Meckling, "Theory of the firm."
5. Bebchuk and Tallarita, "The illusory promise of stakeholder governance."
6. Elizabeth Napolitano, "UnitedHealth uses faulty AI to deny elderly patients medically necessary coverage, lawsuit claims," CBS News, November 20, 2023. www.cbsnews.com/news/unitedhealth-lawsuit-ai-deny-claims-medicare-advantage-health-insurance-denials/ (last accessed September 29, 2025).
7. Jonathan Stray, "What Meta's new studies do – and don't – reveal about social media and polarization," Wired, August 3, 2023, www.wired.com/story/meta-social-media-polarization/ (last accessed September 29, 2025).
8. Bernard J. White and B. Ruth Montgomery, "Corporate codes of conduct" (1980) 23 *California Management Review* 80–87.
9. Adnan V. Ertemel, "Consumer insight as competitive advantage using big data and analytics" (2015) 1 *International Journal of Commerce and Finance* 45–51.
10. David Shepardson and Makini Brice, "Tech CEOs told 'you have blood on your hands' at US Senate child safety hearing," Reuters, January 31, 2024, www.reuters.com/technology/meta-tiktok-x-ceos-face-tough-questions-child-safety-us-senate-hearing-2024-01-31/ (last accessed February 10, 2025).
11. Annie Palmer, "Amazon warehouse workers suffer serious injuries at twice the rate of rivals, study finds," CNBC, April 12, 2022, www.cnbc.com/2022/04/12/study-amazon-workers-suffer-serious-injuries-at-twice-rate-of-rivals.html (last accessed September 29, 2025).
12. Associated Press, "Exxon Mobil accurately predicted warming since 1970s, study finds," January 12, 2023, www.nbcnews.com/science/environment/exxon-mobil-accurately-predicted-warming-1970s-study-finds-rcna65583 (last accessed September 29, 2029).

13. Aimee Picchi, "Cracker Barrel loses almost $100 million in value as stock plunges after new logo release," CBS News, August 25, 2025, www.cbsnews.com/news/cracker-barrel-cbrl-stock-down-200-million-loss-new-logo-change/ (last accessed September 29, 2029).
14. Peter Beaumont, "'I feel utter anger': From Canada to Europe, a movement to boycott US goods is spreading," The Guardian, March 12, 2025, www.theguardian.com/us-news/2025/mar/12/i-feel-utter-anger-from-canada-to-europe-a-movement-to-boycott-us-goods-is-spreading?utm_source=chatgpt.com (last accessed September 29, 2025).
15. Skadden, "Activist investing in Europe," 2025, www.skadden.com/-/media/files/publications/2025/01/activist_investing_in_europe_2025.pdf (last accessed September 29, 2025).
16. Cache McClay, "Goya Foods: Hispanic brand faces boycott for praising Trump," BBC, July 10, 2020, www.bbc.com/news/world-us-canada-53371392 (last accessed September 29, 2025).
17. Shane and Wakabayashi, "'The business of war'."
18. Mike Isaac, "Dissent erupts at Facebook over hands-off stance on political ads," The New York Times, October 28, 2019, www.nytimes.com/2019/10/28/technology/facebook-mark-zuckerberg-political-ads.html (last accessed September 29, 2025).
19. Jonathan Watts, "Just 57 companies linked to 80% of greenhouse gas emissions since 2016," The Guardian, April 3, 2024, www.theguardian.com/environment/2024/apr/04/just-57-companies-linked-to-80-of-greenhouse-gas-emissions-since-2016 (last accessed September 29, 2025).
20. Eric Sylvers, "Airbnb is conquering Italy. One city is fighting back," *The Wall Street Journal*, November 30, 2023, www.wsj.com/business/hospitality/airbnb-is-conquering-italy-one-city-is-fighting-back-eea8fee5 (last accessed January 9, 2025).
21. Laura Hall, "What does a world without Airbnb look like?" BBC, July 2, 2024, www.bbc.com/travel/article/20240701-what-does-a-world-without-airbnb-look-like (last accessed September 29, 2025).
22. Mihir Zaveri, "New York City's Crackdown on Airbnb Is Starting. Here's What to Expect," The New York Times, September 5, 2023, www.nytimes.com/2023/09/05/nyregion/airbnb-regulations-nyc-housing.html (last accessed September 29, 2025).
23. Stray, "What Meta's new studies do – and don't – reveal about social media and polarization."
24. Udit Madan, "Amazon investing $4B in rural America to expand our delivery network, offer even faster delivery, and create more than 100,000 new jobs," Amazon, April 30, 2025, www.aboutamazon.com/news/transportation/amazon-investment-delivery-network-small-town-rural-us (last accessed September 29, 2029).
25. Sarbanes–Oxley Act of 2002, Pub. L. No. 107-204, 116 Stat. 745 (2002), codified at 15 USC §§ 7201–7266.
26. Dodd–Frank Wall Street Reform and Consumer Protection Act, Pub. L. No. 111-203, 124 Stat. 1376 (2010), codified at 12 USC § 5301 et seq.
27. Sopen Shah et al., "California Supreme Court upholds proposition 22," Perkins Coie LLP, August 21, 2024, https://perkinscoie.com/insights/update/california-supreme-court-upholds-proposition-22?utm (last accessed September 29, 2025).
28. Apple, "App review guidelines," June 9, 2025, https://developer.apple.com/app-store/review/guidelines/ (last accessed September 29, 2025).
29. Brian Fung, "Twitter bans President Trump permanently," CNN Business, January 9, 2021, www.cnn.com/2021/01/08/tech/trump-twitter-ban (last accessed September 29, 2025).
30. Ertemel, "Consumer insight as competitive advantage using big data and analytics."

31. Fred Lambert, "Tesla finally released Autopilot safety data after more than a year," Electrek, May 22, 2024, https://electrek.co/2024/05/22/tesla-finally-releases-autopilot-safety-data-after-more-than-a-year/ (last accessed September 29, 2025).
32. Elham F. Mohamed and Gamal Awad, "Development of nano-sensor and biosensor as an air pollution detection technique for the foreseeable future" (2022) 99 *Comprehensive Analytical Chemistry* 163–88 at 165.
33. Jensen and Meckling, "Theory of the firm."
34. Georgette Green, "Ford implements the moving assembly line," Library of Congress, September 16, 2024, https://guides.loc.gov/this-month-in-business-history/October/Ford (last accessed September 29, 2025).
35. Ronald H. Coase, "The nature of the firm" (1937) 4 *Economica* 386–405 (introducing the concept that firms arise to reduce transaction costs associated with market exchanges, leading to hierarchical organizational structures).
36. White and Montgomery, "Corporate codes of conduct."
37. Coase, "The nature of the firm."
38. Apple, "App review guidelines."
39. Kif Leswing, "Here's what Apple had to change as a result of the Epic Games legal battle," CNBC, January 16, 2024, www.cnbc.com/2024/01/16/what-apple-had-to-change-as-a-result-of-the-epic-games-legal-battle.html (last accessed September 29, 2025).
40. Meta, "Community standards," https://transparency.meta.com/policies/community-standards/ (last accessed September 29, 2025).
41. Casey Newton, "The deep inequalities of Facebook's secretive cross-check moderation program," The Verge, December 7, 2022, www.theverge.com/2022/12/7/23498030/facebook-moderation-scandal-xcheck-cross-check (last accessed September 29, 2025).
42. Federica Liberini et al., "Politics in the Facebook Era. Evidence from the 2016 US presidential elections" (2025) 87 *European Journal of Political Economy* 102641.
43. Natalie-Anne Hall, "Understanding Brexit on Facebook: Developing close-up, qualitative methodologies for social media research" (2021) 27 *British Sociological Association* 707–23.
44. Oguchi O. Ajaegbu and Chigozirim Ajaegbu, "The new democratisation: Social media impact on the political process in Sub-Saharan Africa" (2024) 9 *Frontiers in Communication* 1–6; Global Witness, "Facebook fails to tackle election disinformation ads ahead of tense Brazilian election," August 15, 2022. www.globalwitness.org/en/campaigns/digital-threats/facebook-fails-tackle-election-disinformation-ads-ahead-tense-brazilian-election/ (last accessed October 9, 2025).
45. Fergus Ryan, "TikTok algorithm: Why it isn't really a social media app," Vision of Humanity, March 17, 2021, www.visionofhumanity.org/why-tiktok-isnt-really-a-social-media-app/?utm (last accessed September 29, 2025).
46. World Population Review, "TikTok users by country 2025," 2025, https://worldpopulationreview.com/country-rankings/tiktok-users-by-country (last accessed September 29, 2025) (showing that TikTok has a large volume of TikTok users in both India and the Middle East).
47. Meaghan Tobin, "TikTok is facing legal backlash around the world," The New York Times, January 10, 2025, www.nytimes.com/2025/01/09/technology/tiktok-ban-global-legal-battles.html (last accessed September 29, 2025).
48. Manish Singh, "India bands TikTok, dozens of other Chinese apps," TechCrunch, June 29, 2020, https://techcrunch.com/2020/06/29/india-bans-tiktok-dozens-of-other-chinese-apps/?utm (last accessed September 29, 2025).
49. Reuters, "U.S. ready to ban TikTok if deal on divestiture cannot be reached," September 15, 2025, www.reuters.com/world/china/us-ready-ban-tiktok-if-deal-divestiture-cannot-be-reached-2025-09-15/?utm (last accessed September 29, 2025).

50. Dan Milmo, "EU opens investigation into TikTok over online content and child safeguarding," The Guardian, February 19, 2024, www.theguardian.com/technology/2024/feb/19/eu-investigation-tiktok-online-content-child-safeguarding?utm (last accessed September 29, 2025).
51. Alex Rosenblat, "The truth about how Uber's app manages drivers," Harvard Business Review, April 6, 2016, https://hbr.org/2016/04/the-truth-about-how-ubers-app-manages-drivers?utm (last accessed September 29, 2025).
52. Dina Klimkina and Bobby Silverstein, "California Proposition 22 overturns employee classification for rideshare and delivery 'gig workers'," The Council of State Governments, December 2, 2020, https://seed.csg.org/california-proposition-22-overturns-employee-classification-for-rideshare-and-delivery-gig-workers/ (last accessed September 29, 2025).
53. Levi Sumagaysay, "Uber, Lyft, DoorDash workers remain contractors due to California Supreme Court ruling," CalMatters, July 25, 2024, www.marketplace.org/2024/07/25/uber-lyft-doordash-workers-remain-contractors-california-supreme-court-ruling/ (last accessed November 26, 2025).
54. Amazon Science, "The evolution of Amazon's inventory planning system," October 1, 2021, www.amazon.science/latest-news/the-evolution-of-amazons-inventory-planning-system?utm (last accessed September 29, 2025).
55. Palmer, "Amazon warehouse workers suffer serious injuries at twice the rate of rivals, study finds."
56. Jeremy Asuncion et al., "Benefits and effects of Tesla's direct-to-customer sales model" (2023) *Proceedings of 6th European Conference on Industrial Engineering and Operations Management Lisbon, Portugal* 1710–17.
57. Tesla, "Supercharger," www.tesla.com/supercharger?utm (last accessed October 4, 2025).
58. Apple, "United Nations Guiding Principles on Business and Human Rights – 2024 mapping of the Apple supply chain," 2024, https://s203.q4cdn.com/367071867/files/doc_downloads/2024/04/Apple-UNGP-Mapping.pdf?utm at 25 (last accessed October 4, 2025) (confirming that people's rights are respected "throughout the entirety of their employment journey, regardless of their job, their location, or how they were hired").
59. Apple, "Apple supplier code of conduct," 2022, www.apple.com/hk/supplier-responsibility/pdf/Apple-Supplier-Code-of-Conduct-and-Supplier-Responsibility-Standards.pdf?utm (last accessed October 4, 2025).
60. Reed Albergotti, "Apple accused of worker violations in Chinese factories," The Washington Post, September 9, 2019, www.washingtonpost.com/technology/2019/09/09/apple-accused-worker-violations-chinese-factories-by-labor-rights-group/?utm (last accessed October 4, 2025).
61. Walmart, "Supplier requirements," https://corporate.walmart.com/suppliers/requirements?utm (last accessed October 4, 2025).
62. J. Dara Bloom, "Standards for development: Food safety and sustainability in Wal-Mart's Honduran produce supply chains" (2015) 80 *Rural Sociology* 198–227.
63. Benjamin A. Evans, "Accord on fire and building safety in Bangladesh: An international response to Bangladesh labor conditions" (2015) 40 *North Carolina Journal of International Law* 597–627 at 606.
64. Darian McBain, "Tracing traceability," Thai Union, www.thaiunion.com/en/blog/sustainability/546/tracing-traceability?utm (last accessed October 4, 2025).
65. Nestle, "Responsible sourcing of seafood at Nestle," 2020, www.nestle.com/sites/default/files/2021-03/nestle-responsible-sourcing-seafood-progress-report-2020.pdf?utm (last accessed October 4, 2025).

66. International Maritime Organization, "Global limit on sulphur in ships, fuel reduced from January 1, 2020," December 20, 2019, www.imo.org/en/mediacentre/pressbriefings/pages/34-imo-2020-sulphur-limit-.aspx (last accessed October 4, 2025).
67. International Maritime Organization, "IMO 2020 – cutting sulphur oxide emissions," www.imo.org/en/mediacentre/hottopics/pages/sulphur-2020.aspx (last accessed October 10, 2025).
68. Jamie Friedman, "Cement and concrete companies leading the net-zero transition," Center for American Progress, July 11, 2024, www.americanprogress.org/article/cement-and-concrete-companies-leading-the-net-zero-transition/?utm (last accessed October 4, 2025).
69. ArcelorMittal, "Climate change," https://corporate.arcelormittal.com/sustainability/approach/climate-change?utm (last accessed October 4, 2025).
70. Changing Markets Foundation, "Faster fashion: Growing use of polluting textiles revealed," September 17, 2025, https://changingmarkets.org/press-releases/faster-fashion-growing-use-of-polluting-textiles-revealed-2/?utm (last accessed October 4, 2025).
71. UN Environment Programme, "UN Report: Time to seize opportunity, tackle challenge of e-waste," January 24, 2019, www.unep.org/news-and-stories/press-release/un-report-time-seize-opportunity-tackle-challenge-e-waste?utm (last accessed October 4, 2025).
72. Teo Lombardo, "Aviation," International Energy Agency, January 16, 2025, www.iea.org/energy-system/transport/aviation (last accessed October 4, 2025).
73. Christopher Mims, "The way Amazon uses tech to squeeze performance out of workers deserves its own name: Bezosism," *The Wall Street Journal*, September 11, 2021, www.wsj.com/articles/the-way-amazon-uses-tech-to-squeeze-performance-out-of-workers-deserves-its-own-name-bezosism-11631332821 (last accessed October 4, 2025).
74. Walmart, "Food traceability requirements," https://public.walmart.com/content/food-safety/en_us/food-safety-requirements/food-traceability.html (last accessed October 4, 2025).
75. Natalie Taylor, "Walmart sets new traceability requirement for leafy green suppliers," Supermarket News, September 24, 2018, www.supermarketnews.com/independents-regional-grocers/walmart-sets-new-traceability-requirement-for-leafy-green-suppliers (last accessed October 4, 2025).
76. JP Morgan, "Silent night: Behind the scenes of peak payments season," July 28, 2025, www.jpmorgan.com/payments/newsroom/behind-the-scenes-peak-payments-season (last accessed October 4, 2025).
77. Julia C. Wong, "Uber CEO Travis Kalanick caught on video arguing with driver about fares," The Guardian, March 1, 2017, www.theguardian.com/technology/2017/feb/28/uber-ceo-travis-kalanick-driver-argument-video-fare-prices (last accessed October 4, 2025).
78. Bloomberg, "#MeToo movement has singled out more than 400 high-profile people," Los Angeles Times, June 25, 2018, www.latimes.com/business/la-fi-metoo-executives-20180625-story.html?utm (last accessed October 4, 2025).
79. Amelia Miazad, "Sex, power, and corporate governance" (2021) 54 *University of California, Davis Law Review* 1913–98.
80. Albert Hirschman, *Exit, Voice, and Loyalty* (Cambridge, MA: Harvard University Press, 1972).
81. Girish Dhamane, "Did you know … Google processes 8.5 billion searches daily? Here's what people search most," Medium, August 4, 2025, https://medium.com/bloody-sweet-writers/did-you-know-google-processes-8-5-billion-searches-daily-heres-what-people-search-most-a4ee9ee472e7 (last accessed October 4, 2025).
82. StatCounter, "Mobile operating system market share worldwide," 2025, https://gs.statcounter.com/os-market-share/mobile/worldwide (last accessed October 4, 2025).

83. Kerry Flynn, "#DeleteUber campaign inspired 500,000 to delete accounts in one week: NYTimes," Mashable, March 22, 2017, https://mashable.com/article/uber-delete-account-500000 (last accessed October 4, 2025).
84. Uber Technologies, "Uber announces results for fourth quarter and full year 2022," February 8, 2023, https://investor.uber.com/news-events/news/press-release-details/2023/Uber-Announces-Results-for-Fourth-Quarter-and-Full-Year-2022/default.aspx (last accessed October 9, 2025).
85. CBS News, "#DeleteFacebook trends amid Cambridge Analytica scandal," March 21, 2018, www.cbsnews.com/news/deletefacebook-trends-amid-cambridge-analytica-scandal/ (last accessed October 4, 2025).
86. Consumer Reports, "Cost of organic food," March 19, 2015, www.consumerreports.org/cro/news/2015/03/cost-of-organic-food/index.htm (last accessed October 10, 2025); Megan F. Lee et al., "How much more to pay? A study of retail prices of organic versus conventional vegetarian foods in an Australian regional area" (2021) 52 *Journal of Food Distribution Research* 46–62.
87. Thibault Spirlet et al., "Amazon CEO Andy Jassy just got brutally honest about AI – and other bosses may follow his lead," Yahoo News, June 18, 2025, www.yahoo.com/news/amazon-ceo-andy-jassy-just-223950540.html?utm (last accessed October 10, 2025).
88. Joseph Parilla, "U.S. cities compete for Amazon: Will tax incentives deliver HQ2?" Brookings, December 1, 2017, www.brookings.edu/articles/u-s-cities-compete-for-amazon-will-tax-incentives-deliver-hq2/?utm (last accessed October 10, 2025).
89. Riley Edwards, "Breaking down the Amazon HQ2 deal," Citizens Budget Commission (CBC), November 21, 2018, https://cbcny.org/research/breaking-down-amazon-hq2-deal?utm (last accessed October 10, 2025).
90. Tommy Andres and Tracey Samuelson, "How the closings of two auto plants changed the Hamtramck and Detroit's Poletown," Marketplace, August 14, 2019, www.marketplace.org/story/2019/08/14/how-the-closings-of-two-auto-plants-changed-hamtramck-and-detroits-poletown (last accessed October 10, 2025).
91. UN Principles for Responsible Investment, "Climate Action 100+," www.unpri.org/collaborative-engagements/climate-action-100/6285.article (last accessed October 10, 2025).
92. Matt Phillips, "Exxon's board defeat signals the rise of social-good activists," The New York Times, June 9, 2021, www.nytimes.com/2021/06/09/business/exxon-mobil-engine-no1-activist.html (last accessed October 10, 2025).
93. Matteo Tonello, "The evolving landscape of DEI shareholder proposals," Harvard Law School Forum on Corporate Governance, April 25, 2025, https://corpgov.law.harvard.edu/2025/04/25/the-evolving-landscape-of-dei-shareholder-proposals/?utm (last accessed October 10, 2025).
94. Arjun Panchadar and Paresh Dave, "Google hears protesters, changes sexual harassment policies," Reuters, November 8, 2018, www.reuters.com/article/technology/google-hears-protesters-changes-sexual-harassment-policies-idUSKCN1ND2ZL/ (last accessed October 11, 2025).
95. Johana Bhuiyan, "The Google walkout: What protestors demanded and what they got," Los Angeles Times, November 6, 2019, www.latimes.com/business/technology/story/2019-11-06/google-walkout-demands (last accessed October 10, 2025).
96. Kate Conger and Daisuke Wakabayashi, "Google employees protest secret work on censored search engine for China," The New York Times, August 16, 2018, www.nytimes.com/2018/08/16/technology/google-employees-protest-search-censored-china.html (last accessed October 10, 2025).

97. Zoe C. Jones, "Netflix employees stage walkout over Dave Chappelle special," CBS News, October 25, 2021, www.cbsnews.com/news/dave-chappelle-netflix-employees-walkout/ (last accessed October 10, 2025).
98. Alina Selyukh, "Amazon warehouse workers in Alabama might get a third try at unionizing," NPR, April 25, 2024, www.npr.org/2024/04/25/1246423390/amazon warehouse-alabama-union-vote (last accessed October 10, 2025).
99. Daniel Victor and Matt Stevens, "United Airlines passenger is dragged from an overbooked flight," The New York Times, www.nytimes.com/2017/04/10/business/united-flight-passenger-dragged.html (last accessed October 15, 2025).
100. Wong, "Uber CEO Travis Kalanick caught on video arguing with driver about fares."
101. Klimkina and Silverstein, "California Proposition 22 overturns employee classification for rideshare and delivery 'gig workers'."
102. Jesus Jiménez and Brooks Barnes, "What we know about the DeSantis-Disney dispute," The New York Times, May 19, 2023, www.nytimes.com/article/disney-florida-desantis.html (last accessed October 20, 2025).
103. Shane and Wakabayashi, "'The business of war'."
104. Petere Hoskins, "Ben & Jerry's co-founder quits over social activism row," BBC, September 17, 2025, www.bbc.com/news/articles/c4g58xx1eero (last accessed October 15, 2025).
105. Ertemel, "Consumer insight as competitive advantage using big data and analytics."
106. Shepardson and Brice, "Tech CEOs told 'you have blood on your hands'."
107. Emilee Coblentz, "'It killed him': Families of victims of big tech, present at Senate hearing, share their stories," USA Today, February 8, 2024, www.usatoday.com/story/tech/2024/01/31/big-tech-hearing-victims/72429122007/ (last accessed October 20, 2025).
108. Kari Paul et al., "Meta sued by 33 states over claims youth mental health endangered by Instagram," The Guardian, October 24, 2023, www.theguardian.com/technology/2023/oct/24/instagram-lawsuit-meta-sued-teen-mental-health-us?utm (last accessed October 20, 2025).
109. Brian Fung, "Mark Zuckerberg personally rejected Meta's proposals to improve teen mental health, court documents allege," CNN Business, November 10, 2023, www.cnn.com/2023/11/08/tech/meta-facebook-instagram-teen-safety/index.html (last accessed October 20, 2025).
110. Nicholas Confessore, "Cambridge Analytica and Facebook: The scandal and the fallout so far," The New York Times, April 4, 2018, www.nytimes.com/2018/04/04/us/politics/cambridge-analytica-scandal-fallout.html (last accessed October 20, 2025).
111. Dan Milmo, "TikTok's ties to China: why concerns over your data are here to stay," The Guardian, November 8, 2022, www.theguardian.com/technology/2022/nov/07/tiktoks-china-bytedance-data-concerns (last accessed October 12, 2025).
112. Kashmir Hill, "How Target figured out a teen girl was pregnant before her father did," Forbes, February 16, 2012, www.forbes.com/sites/kashmirhill/2012/02/16/how-target-figured-out-a-teen-girl-was-pregnant-before-her-father-did/ (last accessed October 20, 2025).
113. Federal Trade Commission, "Developer of popular women's fertility-tracking app settles FTC allegations that it misled consumers about the disclosure of their health data," January 13, 2021, www.ftc.gov/news-events/news/press-releases/2021/01/developer-popular-womens-fertility-tracking-app-settles-ftc-allegations-it-misled-consumers-about (last accessed October 20, 2025).
114. Lily Hay Newman, "23andMe user data stolen in targeted attack on Ashkenazi Jews," Wired, October 6, 2023, www.wired.com/story/23andme-credential-stuffing-data-stolen/ (last accessed October 20, 2025).

115. Sam Gruet, "Amazon fined for" "excessive" "surveillance of workers," BBC, January 23, 2024, www.bbc.com/news/business-68067022 (last accessed October 20, 2025).
116. Lucy McNulty and Trista Kelly, "PwC under fire for tech that tracks traders' loo breaks," Financial News, June 15, 2020, www.fnlondon.com/articles/pwc-under-fire-for-tech-that-tracks-traders-loo-breaks-20200615 (last accessed October 25, 2025).
117. Laurel Wamsley, "Uber ends its controversial post-ride tracking of users' "location," NPR, August 29, 2017, www.npr.org/sections/thetwo-way/2017/08/29/547113818/uber-ends-its-controversial-post-ride-tracking-of-users-location (last accessed October 25, 2025).
118. Lambert, "Tesla finally released Autopilot safety data after more than a year."
119. Mohamed and Awad, "Development of nano-sensor and biosensor."
120. Geoffrey Supran, Stefan Rahmstorf, and Naomi Oreskes, "Assessing ExxonMobil's global warming projections" (2023) 379 *Science* eabk0063, www.science.org/doi/epdf/10.1126/science.abk0063 (last accessed November 10, 2025).
121. Abrahm Lustgarten and Ryan Knutson, "Years of internal BP probes warned that neglect could lead to accidents," ProPublica, June 7, 2010, www.propublica.org/article/years-of-internal-bp-probes-warned-that-neglect-could-lead-to-accidents?utm (last accessed October 20, 2025).
122. Chevron Corporation, "Evidence summary: Documents relevant to the case of the Lago Agrio plaintiffs," January 2012, https://chevroninecuador.org/assets/docs/2012-01-evidence-summary.pdf (last accessed October 10, 2025).
123. Amy D. Sorkin, "United's unfriendly skies," The New Yorker, April 11, 2017, www.newyorker.com/news/amy-davidson/uniteds-unfriendly-skies?utm (last accessed October 25, 2025).
124. Sorkin, "United's unfriendly skies."
125. CBS News, "United Airlines faces backlash after dragging man from plane," April 11, 2017, www.cbsnews.com/news/united-airlines-faces-backlash-after-dragging-man-from-plane/ (last accessed October 25, 2025).
126. PR Week, "Communicator of the year 2017," March 17, 2017, www.prweek.com/article/1427604/communicator-year-2017 (last accessed October 10, 2025).
127. Pete Vernon, "Q&A: Former LA Times reporter on story that led to $185 million Wells Fargo fine," *Columbia Journalism Review*, September 12, 2016, www.cjr.org/q_and_a/wells_fargo_la_times_accounts.php?utm (last accessed October 20, 2025).
128. Anna Wiener, "A perfect storm at Uber," The New Yorker, February 28, 2017, www.newyorker.com/business/currency/a-perfect-storm-at-uber (last accessed October 20, 2025).
129. Dave Lee, "Uber fires 20 staff after harassment investigation," BBC, June 6, 2017, www.bbc.com/news/business-40179472 (last accessed October 20, 2025).
130. Mike Isaac, "Uber founder Travis Kalanick resigns as C.E.O.," The New York Times, June 21, 2017, www.nytimes.com/2017/06/21/technology/uber-ceo-travis-kalanick.html (last accessed October 25, 2025).
131. BBC, "Bud Light boycott over trans influencer Dylan Mulvaney hits beer giant's sales."
132. Amanda Holpuch, "Behind the backlash against Bud Light," The New York Times, November 21, 2023, www.nytimes.com/article/bud-light-boycott.html (last accessed October 25, 2025).
133. Steve Rose, "How Disney found its pride – and riled the American right," The Guardian, May 7, 2022, www.theguardian.com/film/2022/may/07/disney-lgbtq-community-gay-days-american-conservatives (last accessed October 20, 2025).
134. Alex Hern, "Third of advertisers may boycott Facebook in hate speech revolt," The Guardian, June 30, 2020, www.theguardian.com/technology/2020/jun/30/third-of-advertisers-may-boycott-facebook-in-hate-speech-revolt (last accessed October 20, 2025).

135. Al Jazeera, "Global fashion brands exploiting Bangladesh workers: Study," January 11, 2023, www.aljazeera.com/news/2023/1/11/fashion-brands-paid-less-than-production-cost-to-bangladesh-firms (last accessed October 20, 2025).
136. Dana Farrington, "Petition calls for boycott of Target's 'inclusive' bathroom policy," NPR, April 25, 2016, www.npr.org/sections/thetwo-way/2016/04/25/475624646/petition-calls-for-boycott-of-targets-inclusive-bathroom-policy (last accessed October 20, 2025).
137. Li Zhou, "Conservatives think Chick-fil-A is woke now?" Vox, May 31, 2023, www.vox.com/politics/2023/5/31/23742373/chick-fil-a-boycott-controversy-conservative-backlash (last accessed October 20, 2025).
138. U.S. Securities Exchange Commission, "Information about submitting a whistleblower tip," September 30, 2025, www.sec.gov/enforcement-litigation/whistleblower-program/information-about-submitting-whistleblower-tip (last accessed October 25, 2025).
139. Chapman, "SEC's new climate disclosure rules face legal challenges," March 19, 2024, www.chapman.com/publication-secs-new-climate-disclosure-rules-face-legal-challenges (last accessed October 25, 2025).
140. FINRA, "Institutional investors and 'smart money,'" October 15, 2024, www.finra.org/investors/insights/institutional-investors-and-smart-money?utm (last accessed October 20, 2025).
141. Jeffrey N. Gordon, "Systematic stewardship" (2022) 47 *Journal of Corporation Law* 627–73.
142. Dorothy S. Lund, "Asset managers as regulators" (2023) 171 *University of Pennsylvania Law Review* 77–146 at 143.
143. Amelia Miazad, "Investor climate alliances" (2025) 102 *Washington University Law Review* 797–857.
144. Brigette Lumpkins, "The evolution of impact investing: Aligning financial returns with positive change," Chartered Alternative Investment Analyst Association (CAIA), May 19, 2025, https://caia.org/blog/2025/05/19/evolution-impact-investing-aligning-financial-returns-positive-change (last accessed October 20, 2025).
145. Lumpkins, "The evolution of impact investing."
146. Abby Schultz, "Impact investors hold US$228 billion in assets," Barron's, June 6, 2018, www.barrons.com/articles/impact-investors-hold-us-228-billion-in-assets-1528294454 (last accessed October 20, 2025).
147. Dean Hand et al., "Sizing the impact investing market 2024," Global Impact Investing Network, October 2024, https://s3.amazonaws.com/giin-web-assets/giin/assets/publication/giin-sizingtheimpactinvestingmarket-2024.pdf (last accessed October 20, 2025).
148. KBV Research, "The impact investing market is predicted to reach USD 2.34 trillion by 2032, at a CAGR of 7.5%," July 21, 2025, www.kbvresearch.com/press-release/impact-investing-market/ (last accessed November 12, 2025).
149. Zach Church, "For Bloomberg's new ESG scores, ideas from across industries," MIT Sloan School of Management, December 7, 2020, https://mitsloan.mit.edu/ideas-made-to-matter/bloombergs-new-esg-scores-ideas-across-industries?utm (last accessed October 20, 2025).
150. Henri Torbey and Ju-Hon Kwek, "Asset management 2025: The great convergence," McKinsey & Company, September 18, 2025, www.mckinsey.com/industries/financial-services/our-insights/asset-management-2025-the-great-convergence (last accessed October 20, 2025).
151. Jeffrey Petit, "Millennials and their spending power," Brkthru, July 17, 2023, https://brkthru.com/millennials-and-their-spending-power/ (last accessed October 20, 2025).

152. Geraldine Ang, “The trillion dollar question,” Chartered Banker Institute, September 12, 2019, www.charteredbanker.com/resource_listing/news/the-trillion-dollar-question.html (last accessed October 25, 2025); Nick Lichtenberg, “The $124 trillion great wealth transfer is bigger than ever – and millennials will get the biggest cut,” Fortune, July 23, 2025, https://fortune.com/2025/07/23/great-wealth-transfer-124-trillion-bigger-than-ever-millennials-gen-x/ (last accessed October 20, 2025).
153. Phenix Capital, “2022 impact fund universe report,” January 2022, www.financialinvestigator.nl/l/en/library/download/urn:uuid:4f4c3f59-54b2-4a9c-90b9-ef3b849f3b07/phenix+capital+-+2022+impact+fund+universe+report.pdf (last accessed October 25, 2025).
154. SEC, “SEC votes to end defense of climate disclosure rules.”
155. Darcy Song, “US Department of Labor slams OECD on ‘Marxist’ ESG policies,” Top1000Funds.com, September 11, 2025, www.top1000funds.com/2025/09/us-department-of-labor-slams-oecd-on-marxist-esg-policies/ (last accessed October 20, 2025).
156. Executive Order 14151, “Ending radical and wasteful government DEI programs and preferencing,” 90 FR 8339 (2025).
157. Noah Yim and Matthew Cranston, “Firms abandon ‘woke’ signaling in annual reports,” The Australian, September 8, 2025, www.senatorpaterson.com.au/news/firms-abandon-woke-signalling-in-annual-reports (last accessed October 25, 2025); Eva Xiao, Taylor Nicole, Rogers and Clara Murray, “US companies drop DEI from annual reports as Trump targets corporate values,” Financial Times, March 15, 2025, www.ft.com/content/c2320415-dcf6-4b69-acd4-3187507d762c (last accessed November 25, 2025).
158. Hortense Bioy, “Investors turn away from ESG funds in record numbers in Q1 2025,” Morningstar, May 6, 2025, https://global.morningstar.com/en-gb/sustainable-investing/investors-turn-away-esg-funds-record-numbers-q1-2025 (last accessed October 20, 2025).
159. Kalyeena Makortoff, “Support for ESG proposals at record low driven by US investors, report shows,” The Guardian, February 17, 2025, www.theguardian.com/business/2025/feb/18/support-for-esg-proposals-at-record-low-driven-by-us-investors-report-shows?utm (last accessed October 20, 2025).
160. Lydia Moynihan, “New fund rejects ‘woke’ investing as it touts ‘EIG’ economy,” New York Post, June 8, 2023, https://nypost.com/2023/06/08/new-fund-rejects-woke-investing-as-it-touts-eig-economy/ (last accessed October 25, 2025).
161. Phillips, “Exxon’s board defeat signals the rise of social-good activists.”
162. Robert G. Eccles, “Unilever’s purpose and sustainability test of its shareholders,” Forbes, February 10, 2022, www.forbes.com/sites/bobeccles/2022/02/10/unilevers-purpose-and-sustainability-test-of-its-shareholders/ (last accessed October 20, 2025).

2 GOVERNANCE GAP

1. Mark Zuckerberg, “It’s time to get back to our roots around free expression,” Facebook, September 15, 2025, www.facebook.com/zuck/videos/its-time-to-get-back-to-our-roots-around-free-expression-were-replacing-fact-che/1525382954801931 (last accessed September 16, 2025).
2. Joel Kaplan, “More speech and fewer mistakes,” Meta, January 7, 2025, https://about.fb.com/news/2025/01/meta-more-speech-fewer-mistakes (last accessed September 16, 2025).
3. Claire Duffy, “Meta is getting rid of fact checkers: Zuckerberg acknowledged more harmful content will appear on the platforms now,” CNN Business, January 7, 2025, www.cnn.com/2025/01/07/tech/meta-censorship-moderation (last accessed September 16, 2025).

4. Ryne Weiss, "Meta's content moderation changes closely align with FIRE recommendations," The Fire, January 9, 2025, www.thefire.org/news/metas-content-moderation-changes-closely-align-fire-recommendations (last accessed September 16, 2025).
5. Jillian C. York, Paige Collings, and David Greene, "Meta's new content policy will harm vulnerable users. If it really valued free speech, it would make these changes," Electronic Frontier Foundation, January 9, 2025, www.eff.org/deeplinks/2025/01/metas-new-content-policy-will-harm-vulnerable-users-if-it-really-valued-free (last accessed September 16, 2025).
6. David A. Cifrino, "The future of corporate sustainability and climate action in the anti-'woke' era," Harvard A.L.I. Social Impact Review, February 2018, www.sir.advancedleadership.harvard.edu/articles/future-corporate-sustainability-climate-action-in-anti-woke-era (last accessed September 16, 2025).
7. Greenpeace, "Unilever's 'greenwashing' and vulnerability to brand damage: Briefing for investors," www.greenpeace.org.uk/resources/unilever-greenwash-investor-briefing (last accessed September 16, 2025); Rob Davies, "Unilever to scale back environmental and social pledges," The Guardian, April 19, 2024, www.theguardian.com/business/2024/apr/19/unilever-to-scale-back-environmental-and-social-pledges (last accessed September 16, 2025).
8. Ben Maiden, "The week in GRC: Unilever CEO says corporate purpose can be 'unwelcome distraction' and group appeals decision upholding Nasdaq's board diversity rule," Governance Intelligence, October 27, 2023, www.governance-intelligence.com/regulatory-compliance/week-grc-unilever-ceo-says-corporate-purpose-can-be-unwelcome-distraction-and (last accessed September 16, 2025).
9. Dasha Afanasieva, "Nestle's scaled back goals highlight world's plastic pollution problem," Bloomberg, July 10, 2024, www.bloomberg.com/news/features/2024-07-11/nestle-s-scaled-back-recycling-goals-highlight-world-s-plastic-pollution-problem (last accessed September 16, 2025).
10. Isabel O"Brien, "Data center emissions probably 662% higher than big tech claims. Can it keep up the ruse?" The Guardian, September 15, 2024, www.theguardian.com/technology/2024/sep/15/data-center-gas-emissions-tech (last accessed September 16, 2025).
11. Thomas Le Goff, "Not greenwashing, but still … a closer look at big tech's 2025 sustainability reports," Internet Policy Review, August 7, 2025, https://policyreview.info/articles/news/big-techs-2025-sustainability-reports/2027 (last accessed September 16, 2025).
12. Carlo Di Mao et al., "An examination of net-zero commitments by the world's largest banks," European Central Bank, Occasional Paper Series No. 334, 2023, www.ecb.europa.eu/pub/pdf/scpops/ecb.op334~4ddaea487d.en.pdf (last accessed September 16, 2025).
13. L. Michael Buchsbaum, "Shell games: Dodging lawsuits and greenwashing charges on both sides of the Atlantic," Energy Transition, November 9, 2023, https://energytransition.org/2023/11/shell-games-dodging-lawsuits-and-greenwashing-charges-on-both-sides-of-the-atlantic/ (last accessed September 16, 2025).
14. Blair and Stout, "A team production theory of corporate law."
15. Stephen M. Bainbridge, "The business judgment rule as abstention doctrine" (2004) 57 *Vanderbilt Law Review* 83–130.
16. Daniel R. Fischel, "The business judgment rule and the Trans Union case" (1985) 40 *Business Lawyer* 1437–55.
17. Friedman, "The social responsibility of business," p. 32.
18. Dorothy S. Lund and Elizabeth Pollman, "The corporate governance machine" (2021) 121 *Columbia Law Review* 2563–650.
19. Delaware General Corporation Law, 8 Del. C. § 141.

20. Carter McNamara, "Overview of roles and responsibilities of corporate board of directors," Free Management Library, www.sig.org/srcdocuments/overview-roles-and-responsibilities-corporate-board-directors (last accessed September 16, 2025).
21. Jay W. Lorsch and Elizabeth MacIver, *Pawns or Potentates: The Reality of America's Corporate Boards* (Boston: Harvard Business School Press, 1989).
22. 8 Del. C. §§ 141(a), 141(c) and 251.
23. Stephen M. Bainbridge, "Director primacy: The means and ends of corporate governance" (2003) 97 *Northwestern University Law Review* 547–606.
24. Business Roundtable, "Principles of corporate governance," Harvard Law School Forum on Corporate Governance, September 8, 2016, https://corpgov.law.harvard.edu/2016/09/08/principles-of-corporate-governance (last accessed September 16, 2025).
25. Adolf A. Berle and Gardiner C. Means, *The Modern Corporation and Private Property* (New York: Macmillan, 1932).
26. Jensen and Meckling, "Theory of the firm."
27. Stephen M. Bainbridge, "The case for limited shareholder voting rights" (2006) 53 *UCLA Law Review* 601–36.
28. Bainbridge, "Business judgment rule as abstention doctrine," 603.
29. Jonathan R. Macey, "Corporate law as myth" (2020) 93 *Southern California Law Review* 923–62 at 926.
30. *Smith v. Van Gorkom*, 488 A.2d 858 (Del. 1985).
31. Kelly Huang, Meng Li, and Stanimir Markov, "What do employees know? Evidence from a social media platform" (2020) 95 *Accounting Review* 199–226.
32. Melvin A. Eisenberg, "The divergence of standards of conduct and standards of review in corporate law" (1993) 62 *Fordham Law Review* 437–72.
33. Lyman Johnson, "The modest business judgment rule" (2000) 55 *Business Lawyer* 625–60.
34. *Kamin v. American Express Co.*, 83 N.Y.S.2d 807 (N.Y. Sup. Ct. 1976).
35. *Shlensky v. Wrigley*, 237 N.E.2d 776 (Ill. App. Ct. 1968).
36. Einer Elhauge, "Sacrificing corporate profits in the public interest" (2005) 80 *New York University Law Review* 733–869.
37. Leo E. Strine Jr., "Making it easier for directors to 'do the right thing'" (2015) 4 *Harvard Business Law Review* 235–53.
38. Lynn A. Stout, "Why we should stop teaching Dodge v. Ford" (2008) 3 *Virginia Law & Business Review* 163–94.
39. *eBay Domestic Holdings, Inc. v. Newmark*, 16 A.3d 1 at 33 (Del. Ch. 2010).
40. *Simeone v. Walt Disney Co.*, 302 A.3d 956 (Del. Ch. 2023).
41. *Citizens United v. Federal Election Commission*, 558 US 310 (2010).
42. *Burwell v. Hobby Lobby Stores, Inc.*, 573 US 682 (2014).
43. Adam B. Badawi, "The business judgment rule," in Gerrit De Geest (ed.), *Encyclopedia of Law and Economics*, 2nd ed. (Cheltenham: Edward Elgar, 2023).
44. *Simeone v. The Walt Disney Co.*, C.A. No. 2022-1120-LWW, 2023 WL 4197374 at *2 (Del. Ch. June 27, 2023), https://courts.delaware.gov/Opinions/Download.aspx?id=349140 (last accessed September 16, 2025).
45. Ronald P. O'Hanley, "Long-term value begins at the board," Harvard Law School Forum on Corporate Governance, March 20, 2017, https://corpgov.law.harvard.edu/2017/03/20/long-term-value-begins-at-the-board (last accessed September 16, 2025).
46. Bebchuk and Tallarita, "The illusory promise of stakeholder governance."
47. Steven M. Davidoff, "Fairness Opinions" (2006) 55 *American University Law Review* 1557–625 at 1569.

48. Dalia T. Mitchell, "Proceduralism: Delaware's legacy" (2023) 2(2) *University of Chicago Business Law Review* 333–90.
49. Mitchell, "Proceduralism," 341.
50. *Van Gorkom* at 872.
51. *Aronson v. Lewis*, 473 A.2d 805 at 812 (Del. 1984).
52. *Brehm v. Eisner*, 746 A.2d 244 at 264 (Del. 2000).
53. *Van Gorkom* at 876–77, 880–81.
54. 8 Del. C. § 102(b)(7).
55. Ethan Klingsberg and Oliver Board, "DGCL amendment merits amending charters and engagement with institutional shareholders," Harvard Law School Forum on Corporate Governance, September 4, 2022, https://corpgov.law.harvard.edu/2022/09/04/dgcl-amendment-merits-amending-charters-and-engagement-with-institutional-shareholders (last accessed September 16, 2025).
56. Bernard S. Black and Reinier Kraakman, "A self-enforcing model of corporate law" (1996) 109 *Harvard Law Review* 1911–82.
57. Gordon, "The rise of independent directors in the United States, 1950–2005."
58. Donald C. Langevoort, "The human nature of corporate boards: Law, norms, and the unintended consequences of independence and accountability" (2001) 89 *Georgetown Law Journal* 797–832; American Law Institute, *Principles of Corporate Governance: Analysis and Recommendations* (St. Paul: American Law Institute, 1994), § 3A.01.
59. NYSE Listed Company Manual § 303A.07(b); NASDAQ Listing Rules r. 5605(c).
60. Sherron Watkins and Cynthia Cooper, "We exposed fraud at Enron and WorldCom. Don't let history repeat itself.," The New York Times, May 27, 2025, www.nytimes.com/2025/05/27/opinion/enron-worldcom-fraud-pcaob.html (last accessed September 16, 2025).
61. Sarbanes–Oxley Act, § 301.
62. Sarbanes–Oxley Act, § 101.
63. Sarbanes–Oxley Act, § 301.
64. Sarbanes–Oxley Act, § 302.
65. *Weinberger v. UOP, Inc.*, 457 A.2d 701 (Del. 1983).
66. *Weinberger* at 709–10; *Kahn v. Lynch Communication Systems, Inc.*, 638 A.2d 1110 (Del. 1994); *Emerald Partners v. Berlin*, 726 A.2d 1215 (Del. 1999); *In re Southern Peru Copper Corp. Shareholder Derivative Litigation*, 52 A.3d 761 (Del. Ch. 2011).
67. *Kahn v. M&F Worldwide Corp.*, 88 A.3d 635 (Del. 2014).
68. *Corwin v. KKR Financial Holdings LLC*, 125 A.3d 304 (Del. 2015).
69. Alex J. Pollock, "Addressing the unintended burdens of the Sarbanes-Oxley Act," American Enterprise Institute, April 5, 2006, www.aei.org/research-products/testimony/addressing-the-unintended-burdens-of-the-sarbanes-oxley-act (last accessed September 16, 2025); Soyoung Ho, "House panel revisits Sarbanes-Oxley as smaller companies cite rising burdens," Thomson Reuters, July 2, 2025, https://tax.thomsonreuters.com/news/house-panel-revisits-sarbanes-oxley-as-smaller-companies-cite-rising-burdens (last accessed September 16, 2025).
70. Delaware Senate Bill 21, 152nd Gen. Assemb. (2023), https://legis.delaware.gov/json/BillDetail/GenerateHtmlDocument?legislationId=140262&legislationTypeId=1&docTypeId=2 (last accessed September 16, 2025).
71. John C. Coffee, *Gatekeepers: The Professions and Corporate Governance* (Oxford: Oxford University Press, 2006); Michael W. Peregrine & Charles W. Elson, "The important legacy of the Sarbanes-Oxley Act," Harvard Law School Forum on Corporate Governance, August 30, 2022, https://corpgov.law.harvard.edu/2022/08/30/the-important-legacy-of-the-sarbanes-oxley-act (last accessed September 16, 2025).

72. Keri Calagna, Kristen Sullivan, and Asma Qureshi, "Integrated ERM and the audit committee: Questions to consider," *The Wall Street Journal*, November 7, 2022, https://deloitte.wsj.com/riskandcompliance/integrated-erm-and-the-audit-committee-questions-to-consider-01667511321 (last accessed September 16, 2025); The Center for Audit Quality, "Audit committees prioritize cybersecurity, enterprise risk management in new survey," March 12, 2024, www.thecaq.org/acpr24 (last accessed September 16, 2025).
73. *Simeone* at 2.
74. Florida House Bill 1577, Midway Fire District, Santa Rosa County, 2024 Reg. Sess., www.flsenate.gov/Session/Bill/2024/1577 (last accessed September 16, 2025).
75. Dawn Chmielewski, "Disney CEO, responding to LGBTQ employees, says company's stories promote inclusion," Reuters, March 7, 2022, www.reuters.com/business/media-telecom/disney-ceo-responding-lgbtq-employees-says-companys-stories-promote-inclusion-2022-03-07 (last accessed September 16, 2025); Selome Hailu, "Disney employees slam Bob Chapek's memo on 'Don't Say Gay' bill: 'Silence Is Unacceptable'," Variety, March 7, 2022, https://variety.com/2022/film/news/disney-dont-say-gay-bill-bob-chapek-reactions-1235198226 (last accessed September 16, 2025).
76. Cydney S. Posner, "Disney: Speaking out on issues of social significance within board's business judgment," Harvard Law School Forum on Corporate Governance, July 18, 2023, https://corpgov.law.harvard.edu/2023/07/18/disney-speaking-out-on-issues-of-social-significance-within-boards-business-judgment (last accessed September 16, 2025).
77. Brooks Barnes, "Disney CEO says company is 'opposed' to Florida's 'Don't Say Gay' bill," The New York Times, March 9, 2022, www.nytimes.com/2022/03/09/business/disney-ceo-florida-lgbtq-bill.html (last accessed September 16, 2025).
78. Eugene Volokh, "Court rejects Disney shareholder's demand for corporate documents related to controversy over Florida law," Reason, June 29, 2023, https://reason.com/volokh/2023/06/29/court-rejects-disney-shareholders-demand-for-corporate-documents-related-to-controversy-over-florida-law (last accessed September 16, 2025).
79. Ulrike Malmendier, Vincenzo Pezone, and Hui Zheng, "Managerial duties and managerial biases" (2023) 69 *Management Science* 3157–79.
80. Jim DeLoach, "Blind spots in the C-suite and boardroom," Corporate Compliance Insights, August 27, 2024, www.corporatecomplianceinsights.com/blind-spots-c-suite-boardroom (last accessed September 16, 2025).
81. Lenore Palladino and Kristina Karlsson, "Towards accountable capitalism: Remaking corporate law through stakeholder governance," Harvard Law School Forum on Corporate Governance, February 11, 2019, https://corpgov.law.harvard.edu/2019/02/11/towards-accountable-capitalism-remaking-corporate-law-through-stakeholder-governance (last accessed September 16, 2025).
82. Lucian A. Bebchuk, Kobi Kastiel, and Roberto Tallarita, "For whom corporate leaders bargain" (2021) 94 *Southern California Law Review* 1467–560.
83. Lund and Pollman, "The corporate governance machine."
84. Pollman, "Corporate social responsibility, ESG, and compliance," 668.
85. *In re Caremark International Inc. Derivative Litigation*, 698 A.2d 959 at 961 (Del. Ch. 1996).
86. *Stone v. Ritter*, 2006 WL 302558 at *1 (Del. Ch. January 26, 2006).
87. *In re Citigroup Inc. Shareholder Derivative Litigation*, 964 A.2d 106 (Del. 2009).
88. *Marchand v. Barnhill*, 212 A.3d 805 (Del. 2019).
89. Roy Shapira, "A new Caremark era: Causes and consequences" (2021) 98 *Washington University Law Review* 1857–96.

90. Kilian Moote and Kiran Vasantham, "Global institutional investor survey 2024 report," Harvard Law School Forum on Corporate Governance, March 17, 2025, https://corpgov.law.harvard.edu/2025/03/17/global-institutional-investor-survey-2024-report (last accessed September 16, 2025).
91. CalPERS, "Addressing climate change risk, CalPERS" first response to Senate Bill 964," December 2019, www.calpers.ca.gov/documents/addressing-climate-change-risk/download (last accessed September 16, 2025).
92. Ross Kerber and Jessica DiNapoli, "BlackRock adds diversity target for U.S. boardrooms," Reuters, December 18, 2021, www.reuters.com/markets/us/blackrock-adds-diversity-target-us-boardrooms-2021-12-14 (last accessed September 16, 2025).
93. Niklas Kreander and Ken McPhail, "State investments and human rights? The case of the Norwegian Government Pension Fund Global" (2019) 32(6) *Accounting, Auditing & Accountability Journal* 1742–70; Business and Human Rights Clinic, "Pension funds and human rights: A study of human rights considerations of pension funds," 2018, www.humanrightscolumbia.org/sites/default/files/bhr_pension_funds_2018.pdf (last accessed September 16, 2025).
94. *Wenske v. Blue Bell Creameries, Inc.*, 2018 WL 3337531 (Del. Ch. July 6, 2018).
95. *In re Clovis Oncology, Inc. Derivative Litigation*, 2019 WL 4850188 at *1 (Del. Ch. October 1, 2019).
96. *In re Boeing Co. Derivative Litigation*, 2021 WL 4059934 at *1 (Del. Ch. September 7, 2021).
97. Shapira, "A new Caremark era," pp. 1865–66.
98. Food Safety Modernization Act, Pub. L. No. 111–353, 124 Stat. 3885 (2011).
99. Virginia Furness and Marc Jones, "Basel Committee makes climate risk disclosure for bank regulators voluntary," Reuters, June 13, 2025, www.reuters.com/sustainability/cop/basel-committee-makes-climate-risk-disclosure-bank-regulators-voluntary-2025-06-13 (last accessed September 16, 2025).
100. *Caremark* at 971; *Stone* at 370; *Marchand* at 809–10.
101. Elizabeth Pollman, "Corporate oversight and disobedience" (2019) 72 *Vanderbilt Law Review* 2013–46 (noting that Caremark liability is limited to failures of legal compliance, and that Delaware courts avoid second-guessing board judgments in areas lacking clear legal standards).
102. H. Justin Pace and Lawrence J. Trautman, "Mission critical: Caremark, Blue Bell, and director responsibility for cybersecurity governance" (2022) *Wisconsin Law Review* 887–952.
103. Subodh Mishra, "U.S. shareholder proposals: A decade in motion," Harvard Law School Forum on Corporate Governance, November 18, 2024, https://corpgov.law.harvard.edu/2024/11/18/u-s-shareholder-proposals-a-decade-in-motion (last accessed August 22, 2025).
104. Lindsey Stewart and River Meng, "Investor views on AI oversight: What do proxy votes tell us," Harvard Law School Forum on Corporate Governance, May 30, 2025, https://corpgov.law.harvard.edu/2025/05/30/investor-views-on-ai-oversight-what-do-proxy-votes-tell-us (last accessed September 16, 2025).
105. Bram van der Kroft et al., "Timing sustainable shareholder proposals in real asset investments," MIT Center for Real Estate, Research Paper No. 24/09 (2025), https://ssrn.com/abstract=4883596 (last accessed September 16, 2025).
106. 8 Del. C. § 141(a).
107. 8 Del. C. §§ 211(b) and 251(c).
108. Rule 14a-8, 17 C.F.R. § 240.14a-8.

109. Rule 14a-8(i)(7); *Trinity Wall Street v. Wal-Mart Stores, Inc.*, 792 F.3d 323 at 344 (3d Cir. 2015); *Business Roundtable v. SEC*, 905 F.2d 406 at 408 (D.C. Cir. 1990).
110. Rule 14a-8(d).
111. Mishra, "U.S. shareholder proposals: A decade in motion."
112. George Serafeim, "Social-impact efforts that create real value," Harvard Business Review, September 2020, https://hbr.org/2020/09/social-impact-efforts-that-create-real-value (last accessed August 25, 2025).
113. The Conference Board, "Environmental shareholder proposals increasingly focus on climate," October 22, 2021, www.conference-board.org/research/environmental-social-governance-briefs/environmental-shareholder-proposals-focus-on-climate (last accessed September 16, 2025).
114. Richard Fields and Cal Smith, "Human capital management during and after the COVID era," BoardMember, 2021, https://boardmember.com/human-capital-management-during-and-after-the-covid-era (last accessed September 16, 2025); Ben Maiden, "COVID-19 puts spotlight on human capital," Governance Intelligence, August 3, 2020, www.governance-intelligence.com/esg/covid-19-puts-spotlight-human-capital (last accessed September 16, 2025).
115. U.S. Securities and Exchange Commission, "Staff Legal Bulletin No. 14L," 2021, www.sec.gov/rules-regulations/staff-guidance/staff-legal-bulletins/shareholder-proposals-staff-legal-bulletin-no-14l-cf (last accessed August 25, 2025).
116. U.S. Securities and Exchange Commission, "Staff Legal Bulletin No. 14M" (2025), www.sec.gov/about/shareholder-proposals-staff-legal-bulletin-no-14m-cf (last accessed August 25, 2025).
117. Jamie Smith, "2025 proxy season review: Four key takeaways," Harvard Law School Forum on Corporate Governance, August 6, 2025, https://corpgov.law.harvard.edu/2025/08/06/2025-proxy-season-review-four-key-takeaways/ (last accessed August 25, 2025).
118. Matteo Tonello, "The evolving landscape of DEI shareholder proposals," Harvard Law School Forum on Corporate Governance, April 25, 2025, https://corpgov.law.harvard.edu/2025/04/25/the-evolving-landscape-of-dei-shareholder-proposals/ (last accessed August 25, 2025).
119. Paul Washington and Merel Spierings, "2023 proxy season: More proposals, lower support," Harvard Law School Forum on Corporate Governance, June 1, 2023, https://corpgov.law.harvard.edu/2023/06/01/2023-proxy-season-more-proposals-lower-support/ (last accessed September 16, 2025).
120. Subodh Mishra, "Climate shareholder proposals: A more sophisticated discourse," Harvard Law School Forum on Corporate Governance, October 10, 2024, https://corpgov.law.harvard.edu/2024/10/10/climate-shareholder-proposals-a-more-sophisticated-discourse (last accessed September 16, 2025).
121. Kilian Moote and Kiran Vasantham, "Global institutional investor survey 2024 report," Harvard Law School Forum on Corporate Governance, March 17, 2025, https://corpgov.law.harvard.edu/2025/03/17/global-institutional-investor-survey-2024-report (last accessed September 16, 2025) (reporting that institutional investors' top priorities for 2025 include executive pay, shareholder rights, climate transition, and human capital management, reflecting a focus on issues with clear business relevance).
122. Jeremy Ho, "Anti-ESG proposals have increased in volume, but fare poorly," Harvard Law School Forum on Corporate Governance, February 6, 2025, https://corpgov.law.harvard.edu/2025/02/06/anti-esg-proposals-have-increased-in-volume-but-fare-poorly (last accessed September 16, 2025).

123. Mishra, "U.S. shareholder proposals: A decade in motion."
124. Sanford Lewis, "Analysis and recommendations on shareholder proposal decision making under the SEC no-action process," Harvard Law School Forum on Corporate Governance, July 26, 2018, https://corpgov.law.harvard.edu/2018/07/26/analysis-and-recommendations-on-shareholder-proposal-decision-making-under-the-sec-no-action process (last accessed August 25, 2025).
125. Jill E. Fisch, "Making sustainability disclosure sustainable" (2019) 107 *Georgetown Law Journal* 923–66 (noting that shareholder proposals and voluntary disclosure tend to prioritize visible ESG issues while neglecting systemic risks such as biodiversity, water, and broader human capital impacts).
126. Subodh Mishra, "AI in focus in 2025: Boards and shareholders set their sights on AI," Harvard Law School Forum on Corporate Governance, April 2, 2025, https://corpgov.law.harvard.edu/2025/04/02/ai-in-focus-in-2025-boards-and-shareholders-set-their-sights-on-ai (last accessed September 16, 2025).
127. Neil P. Stronski and Richard J. Grossman, "Lessons from the first few contests under the universal proxy rules, and the outlook for 2023," Skadden, January 4, 2023, www.skadden.com/insights/publications/2023/01/lessons-from-the-first-few-contests-under-the-universal-proxy-rules (last accessed September 16, 2025).
128. U.S. Securities and Exchange Commission, "Fact sheet: Universal proxy rules for director elections," www.sec.gov/files/34-93596-fact-sheet.pdf (last accessed September 16, 2025).
129. Matt Phillips, "Exxon's board defeat signals the rise of social-good activists," The New York Times, June 9, 2021, www.nytimes.com/2021/06/09/business/exxon-mobil-engine-no1-activist.html (last accessed January 14, 2025).
130. Collin Eaton and Benoît Morenne, "Exxon to buy pioneer in $60 billion deal to create shale giant," *The Wall Street Journal*, October 11, 2023, www.wsj.com/business/energy-oil/exxon-pioneer-deal-60-billion-60b-2023-10-11 (last accessed September 16, 2025).
131. Bernard S. Sharfman, "The illusion of success: A critique of Engine No. 1's proxy fight at ExxonMobil" (2021) 12 *Harvard Business Law Review*, Online art 3, https://journals.law.harvard.edu/hblr/hblr-online-volume-12/ (last accessed September 16, 2025).
132. ECGI, "ESG evolution & backlash timeline," www.ecgi.global/projects/responsible-capitalism/esg-evolution-backlash-timeline (last accessed September 16, 2025).
133. Isla Binnie, "BlackRock's Fink says he's stopped using 'weaponised' term ESG," Reuters, June 26, 2023, www.reuters.com/business/finance/blackrocks-fink-says-hes-stopped-using-weaponised-term-esg-2023-06-26 (last accessed September 16, 2025).
134. Lisa M. Fairfax, "ESG's death-defying future: Predicting the future of ESG through the lens of current ESG disclosure" (2024) 26 *University of Pennsylvania Journal of Business Law* 1019–57.
135. Philipp Krueger, Zacharias Sautner, and Laura T. Starks, "The importance of climate risks for institutional investors" (2020) 33 *Review of Financial Studies* 1067–111.
136. BlackRock Investment Stewardship, "Climate-related risks and the low-carbon transition," January 2025, www.blackrock.com/corporate/literature/publication/blk-commentary-climate-risk-and-energy-transition.pdf (last accessed September 16, 2025).
137. Mishra, "AI in Focus in 2025."
138. Steven Hyland, "Labor rights: Engagement trends and shareholder proposals," Glass Lewis, November 21, 2024, www.glasslewis.com/article/labor-rights-engagement-trends-and-shareholder-proposals (last accessed September 16, 2025); ISS-Corporate, "Shareholder proposals on nature: Resurgence and new frameworks," November 5, 2024, https://insights.issgovernance.com/posts/shareholder-proposals-on-nature-resurgence-and-new-frameworks (last accessed September 16, 2025) (describing the rise of biodiversity

and nature-related proposals reframed through TNFD and ESRS standards to emphasize financial and operational risks).

139. T. Rowe Price, "For or against? The year in shareholder resolutions – 2023," Harvard Law School Forum on Corporate Governance, April 29, 2024, https://corpgov.law.harvard.edu/2024/04/29/for-or-against-the-year-in-shareholder-resolutions-2023 (last accessed September 16, 2025).
140. Yazhou Ellen He, Bige Kahraman, and Michelle Lowry, "ES risks and shareholder voice," European Corporate Governance Institute (ECGI) Finance Working Paper No. 786/2021, 2023, www.ecgi.global/sites/default/files/working_papers/documents/esrisksandshareholdervoice.pdf (last accessed September 16, 2025) (finding that higher support for failed E&S proposals predicts subsequent ESG risk incidents and negative abnormal returns, showing investors focus on business risk rather than ideology).
141. Jill E. Fisch and Adriana Robertson, "Shareholder proposals and the debate over sustainability disclosure," in *Board–Shareholder Dialogue: Policy Debate, Legal Constraints and Best Practices* (Cambridge: Cambridge University Press, 2024), pp. 475–501 (finding that proposals framed in terms of materiality and disclosure gain more traction than purely advocacy-oriented proposals).
142. Benjamin E. Hermalin, "Transparency and corporate governance," in Zenichi Shishido (ed.), *Enterprise Law* (Cheltenham: Edward Elgar, 2014), pp. 342–48 (arguing that greater transparency reduces information asymmetry between managers and outsiders, improves valuation, and strengthens governance oversight).
143. Christopher S. Armstrong, Wayne R. Guay, and Joseph P. Weber, "The role of information and financial reporting in corporate governance and debt contracting" (2010) 50(2–3) *Journal of Accounting and Economics* 179–234.
144. Alexander Platt, "Beyond 'market transparency': Investor disclosure and corporate governance" (2022) 74 *Stanford Law Review* 1393–477.
145. Georgios Karamatzanis, Anna Tilba, and Konstantinos Nikolopoulos, "Corporate governance reporting, disclosures, monitoring, and decision-making: The role of big data analytics and technological tools" (2025) *Corporate Governance: An International Review* 1–16.
146. Securities Act of 1933; Securities Exchange Act of 1934, Pub L No. 73–291, 48 Stat 881 (1934), codified at 15 USC §§ 78a–78qq.
147. *TSC Industries, Inc. v. Northway, Inc.*, 426 US 438 (1976).
148. Joan MacLeod Heminway, "The materiality of ESG information: Why it may matter" (2024) 84 *Louisiana Law Review* 1363–403 (arguing that existing U.S. materiality doctrine can encompass ESG and social issues when viewed holistically in context).
149. Leah Feor, Amelia Clarke, and Ilona Dougherty, "Social impact measurement: A systematic literature review and future research directions" (2023) 4 *World* 816–37.
150. Mohini Singh and Sandra Peters, "The case for quarterly and environmental, social, and governance reporting," CFA Institute, 2019, https://corpgov.law.harvard.edu/wp-content/uploads/2019/08/financial-reporting-quarterly-and-esg-2019.pdf (last accessed September 22, 2025) (arguing that quarterly reporting cycles constrain meaningful disclosure of ESG and social performance metrics, which often cannot be updated or assessed on the same cadence as financial data).
151. Bing Zhou, "ESG in the headlines: Media-driven reputational risk and stock performance" (2025) 82 *Journal of Corporate Finance* 102558 (finding that ESG controversies revealed through media coverage significantly affect firm valuations, demonstrating that social impacts often become visible only after public exposure).

152. Jens K. Roehrich, Johanne Grosvold, and Stefan U. Hoejmose, "Reputational risks and sustainable supply chain management: Decision making under bounded rationality" (2014) 34(5) *International Journal of Operations & Production Management* 695–718 (showing that reputational risks often become evident only later, once stakeholders or the public uncover labor or environmental issues in supply chains).
153. Manuel C. Kathan et al., "What you see is not what you get: ESG scores and greenwashing risk" (2025) 74 *Finance Research Letters* 106710 (documenting that companies with high ESG scores often use vague or overly generalized disclosures that mask gaps between apparent and actual performance, protecting against legal challenge).
154. David Hackett et al., "Growing ESG risks: The rise of litigation" (2020) 50 *Environmental Law Reporter* 10849 (observing that many early ESG disclosures were vague, limiting liability, while legal risk increases when companies provide specific, verifiable claims that may later be challenged).
155. Barbara Ballan and Jason J. Czarnezki, "Disclosure, greenwashing and the future of ESG litigation" (2024) 81(2) *Washington and Lee Law Review* 411–74 (arguing that companies often choose broad, voluntary ESG disclosures to demonstrate responsiveness while avoiding the legal exposure created by specific, measurable claims).
156. RepRisk, "On the rise: Navigating the wave of greenwashing and social washing," October 23, 2023, www.reprisk.com/research-insights/reports/on-the-rise-navigating-the-wave-of-greenwashing-and-social-washing (last accessed January 20, 2025).
157. Directive 2014/95/EU of the European Parliament and of the Council of October 22, 2014, amending Directive 2013/34/EU as regards disclosure of non-financial and diversity information by certain large undertakings and groups, OJ 2014 No. L330/1.
158. European Parliament, "Non-financial reporting directive: Overview and state of play," January 2021, www.europarl.europa.eu/RegData/etudes/BRIE/2021/654213/EPRS_BRI(2021)654213_EN.pdf (last accessed September 16, 2025).
159. Directive (EU) 2022/2464 of the European Parliament and of the Council of December 14, 2022 amending Regulation (EU) No. 537/2014, Directive 2004/109/EC, Directive 2006/43/EC and Directive 2013/34/EU as regards corporate sustainability reporting, OJ 2022 No. L322/15.
160. Jill E. Fisch, Keith L. Johnson, and Cynthia A. Williams, "Why corporate sustainability disclosure has become a mainstream demand," University of Pennsylvania Institute for Law & Economics Research Paper No. 19–13, 2019, www.law.nyu.edu/sites/default/files/Corporate%20Sustainability%20Disclosure%20by%20Fisch%20Johnson%20Williams%209.18.pdf (last accessed September 16, 2025) (arguing that voluntary sustainability disclosure has become widespread but remains inconsistent).
161. Task Force on Climate-related Financial Disclosures (TCFD), "Recommendations of the task force on climate-related financial disclosures," Financial Stability Board, June 2017, https://assets.bbhub.io/company/sites/60/2021/10/FINAL-2017-TCFD-Report.pdf (last accessed September 16, 2025).
162. World Resources Institute (WRI) and World Business Council for Sustainable Development (WBCSD), "The greenhouse gas protocol: A corporate accounting and reporting standard," 2004, https://ghgprotocol.org/corporate-standard (last accessed September 16, 2025).
163. Jill E. Fisch and Steven Davidoff Solomon, "Should corporations have a purpose?" (2021) 99(5) *Texas Law Review* 1309–46.
164. William W. Bratton and Michael L. Wachter, "Shareholder primacy's corporatist origins: Adolf Berle and The Modern Corporation" (2008) 34(1) *Journal of Corporation Law* 99–152 (arguing that shareholder primacy was shaped by corporatist debates surrounding

Berle and Means); Henry Hansmann and Reinier Kraakman, "The end of history for corporate law" (2001) 89(2) *Georgetown Law Journal* 439–68 (asserting that shareholder primacy had become the dominant and "end of history" model for corporate law).

165. Blair and Stout, "A team production theory of corporate law" (presenting the stakeholderist "team production" theory of the firm as an alternative to shareholder primacy).
166. Business Roundtable, "Business Roundtable redefines the purpose of a corporation."
167. Larry Fink, "A sense of purpose," BlackRock, 2018, www.blackrock.com/corporate/investor-relations/2018-larry-fink-ceo-letter (last accessed September 16, 2025).
168. Larry Fink, "A fundamental reshaping of finance," BlackRock, 2020, www.blackrock.com/corporate/investor-relations/2020-larry-fink-ceo-letter (last accessed September 16, 2025).
169. Global Sustainable Investment Alliance (GSIA), "Global sustainable investment review 2020," July 2021, www.gsi-alliance.org/wp-content/uploads/2021/08/GSIR-20201.pdf (last accessed September 16, 2025).
170. Center for Audit Quality, "S&P 500 sustainability reporting and assurance analysis," June 2025, www.thecaq.org/sp-500-and-esg-reporting (last accessed September 16, 2025) (finding that 99% of S&P 500 companies disclosed sustainability-related information in 2023).
171. Ross Douthat, "The rise of woke capital," The New York Times, February 28, 2018, www.nytimes.com/2018/02/28/opinion/corporate-america-activism.html (last accessed September 16, 2025).
172. Carl Rhodes, *Woke Capitalism: How Corporate Morality Is Sabotaging Democracy* (Bristol: Bristol University Press, 2021).
173. Morrison & Foerster, "Anti-ESG legislation," www.mofo.com/esg-resources/anti-esg-legislation (last accessed February 10, 2025).
174. Florida, CS/CS/HB 3 (2023), Laws of Florida ch. 28 (prohibiting consideration of ESG or other non-pecuniary factors in state and local investment decisions and requiring exclusive reliance on pecuniary factors); Texas, SB 13 (2021) (requiring the state comptroller to identify financial firms that "boycott" fossil fuel companies and prohibiting state investment in, or contracting with, such firms).
175. Lawrence A. Cunningham, "What the volume and diversity of comment letters to the SEC say about its climate proposal," Harvard Law School Forum on Corporate Governance, July 3, 2022, https://corpgov.law.harvard.edu/2022/07/03/what-the-volume-and-diversity-of-comment-letters-to-the-sec-say-about-its-climate-proposal/ (last accessed February 6, 2025).
176. Jacob H. Hupart, "SEC expected to drop Scope 3 GHG emissions disclosure requirements from final climate rule," *National Law Review*, February 26, 2024, https://natlawreview.com/article/sec-expected-drop-scope-3-ghg-emissions-disclosure-requirements-final-climate-rule (last accessed February 6, 2025).
177. Evan Williams, "The chamber fights back against counterproductive corporate disclosure requirements," U.S. Chamber of Commerce, January 30, 2024, www.uschamber.com/finance/corporate-governance/effective-material-corporate-disclosure-is-the-cornerstone-of-u-s-capital-markets (last accessed February 6, 2025); National Association of Manufacturers, "Comment letter on SEC proposed rule: The enhancement and standardization of climate-related disclosures for investors," June 6, 2022, https://documents.nam.org/tax/nam_comments_sec_climate_rule.pdf (last accessed February 6, 2025).
178. Shannon Goff Kukulka, "Fiduciary update: DOL reverses course on ESG and cryptocurrency investment policies," Holland & Knight, July 2, 2025, www.hklaw.com/en/insights/publications/2025/07/fiduciary-update-dol-reverses-course-on-esg-and-cryptocurrency (last accessed September 16, 2025).

179. Morgan Stanley, "Sustainable fund returns lag peers' in second half of 2024," March 4, 2025, www.morganstanley.com/insights/articles/sustainable-funds-performance-second-half-2024 (last accessed September 16, 2025).
180. Silla Brush, Saijel Kishan, and Alastair Marsh, "BlackRock exits major climate group amid Wall Street exodus," Bloomberg Law, January 10, 2025, https://news.bloomberglaw.com/ip-law/blackrock-exits-major-climate-group-amid-wall-street-exodus (last accessed February 6, 2025).
181. Nathaniel Meyersohn, "Walmart rolls back DEI programs after right-wing backlash," CNN, November 26, 2024, www.cnn.com/2024/11/26/business/walmart-diversity-dei-programs-backlash (last accessed September 16, 2025).
182. Pamela N. Danziger, "Disney shifts away from DEI to return to its entertainment business mission," Forbes, February 13, 2025, www.forbes.com/sites/pamdanziger/2025/02/13/disney-shifts-away-from-dei-to-return-to-its-primary-business-mission/ (last accessed September 16, 2025).
183. Colin Hilson, "Climate change and the politicization of ESG in the US" (2024) 6 *Frontiers in Political Science* 1332399.
184. Virginia E. Harper Ho, "Corporate climate governance," European Corporate Governance Institute Law Working Paper No. 804/2024, 2024, https://ssrn.com/abstract=4934244 (last accessed September 16, 2025) (emphasizing governance structures and risk management as pragmatic approaches to climate issues).
185. Bainbridge, "Business judgment rule as abstention doctrine."
186. *Simeone* at 980.
187. Zohar Goshen and Richard Squire, "Principal costs: A new theory for corporate law and governance" (2017) 117 *Columbia Law Review* 767–829 (arguing that shareholder heterogeneity produces divergent preferences, meaning that empowering shareholders directly may increase governance costs); Edward B. Rock, "The logic and (uncertain) significance of institutional shareholder activism" (1991) 79 *Georgetown Law Journal* 445–506 (arguing that institutional investors differ from retail shareholders in their time horizons and policy goals, complicating assumptions of unified shareholder preferences).
188. *Van Gorkom* at 872–73 (holding that directors breach their duty of care if they approve a merger without adequate information or deliberation).
189. Bebchuk, Kastiel, and Tallarita, "For whom corporate leaders bargain" (showing that corporate leaders primarily prioritize shareholder and managerial interests in dealmaking, while stakeholder perspectives are often excluded from the decision-making process).
190. *Caremark* at 971.
191. Frank H. Easterbrook and Daniel R. Fischel, *The Economic Structure of Corporate Law* (Cambridge, MA: Harvard University Press, 1991) (presenting corporate law as a set of standardized frameworks that enhance efficiency and adapt flexibly across organizational contexts); Reinier Kraakman et al., *The Anatomy of Corporate Law: A Comparative and Functional Approach*, 3rd ed. (Oxford: Oxford University Press, 2017).

3 CORPORATE ORDERING FOR SOCIAL CONFLICTS

1. *Aronson v. Lewis*, 473 A.2d 805 at 812 (Del. 1984).
2. Bainbridge, "Business judgment rule as abstention doctrine," 90.
3. Bainbridge, "Director primacy," 555.
4. Bainbridge, "Director primacy," 556.
5. *Van Gorkom* at 872, 874–75.

6. Stephen Grace Jr., Lawrence Prendergast, and Susan Koski-Grafer, "Corporate governance and information gaps: Importance of internal reporting for board oversight," Business Law Today, January 15, 2018, https://businesslawtoday.org/2018/01/corporate-governance-and-information-gaps-importance-of-internal-reporting-for-board-oversight/ (last accessed November 26, 2025).
7. Stephen M. Bainbridge and M. Todd Henderson, "Boards-R-Us: Reconceptualizing corporate boards" (2014) 66(5) *Stanford Law Review* 1051–119 at 1092.
8. Marco Da Rin, Thomas Hellmann, and Manju Puri, "A survey of venture capital research," NBER Working Paper No. 17523, 2011, www.nber.org/papers/w17523 (last accessed November 26, 2025).
9. Joshua D. Krebs, "The rating agencies: Where we have been and where do we go from here?" (2009) 3 *Journal of Business, Entrepreneurship & Law* 134–63 at 134.
10. Thomas A. Uebler, "Reinterpreting section 141(e) of Delaware's General Corporation Law: Why interested directors should be 'fully protected' in relying on expert advice" (2020) 65 *The Business Lawyer* 1023–54.
11. Thomas W. France, "Complying with oversight fiduciary duty obligations in Delaware," Venable Insights, June 4, 2020, www.venable.com/insights/publications/2020/06/complying-with-oversight-fiduciary-duty-obligat (last accessed November 15, 2025).
12. Matteo Gatti, "Corporate governing: Promises and risks of corporations as socio-economic reformers," ECGI Law Working Paper No. 730/2023, 2023, www.ecgi.global/sites/default/files/working_papers/documents/corporategoverning_0.pdf (last accessed November 21, 2025).
13. Heiko Spitzeck and Erik G. Hansen, "Stakeholder governance: How stakeholders influence corporate decision making" (2010) 10(4) *Corporate Governance* 378–91.
14. Business Roundtable, "Principles of corporate governance."
15. Michael Mangum, "The power of corporate governance (part 1 of 2)," FMI Insights, September 2019, https://fmicorp.com/insights/thought-leadership/the-power-of-corporate-governance-part-1-of-2/ (last accessed October 22, 2025).
16. Iain Stewart, "Aristotle, Montesquieu and Dicey on 'Separation of Powers'" (2004) 4 *Macquarie Law Journal* 187–223 at 192.
17. Alex Zhang, "Separation of structures" (2024) 10 *Virginia Law Review* 599–689 at 630.
18. Rutger Claassen, "Political theories of the business corporation" (2023) 18 *Philosophy & Social Criticism* 1–13 at 2.
19. Bryan D. Jones, "Bounded rationality and public policy: Herbert A. Simon and the decisional foundation of collective choice" (2002) 35 *Policy Sciences* 269–84 at 275–76.
20. Bas Hillebrand, Paul H. Driessen, and Oliver Koll, "Stakeholder marketing: Theoretical foundations and required capabilities" (2015) 43 *Journal of the Academy of Marketing Science* 411–28 at 414.
21. Spitzeck and Hansen, "Stakeholder governance," 380–81.
22. Charl de Villiers and Ruth Dimes, "Determinants, mechanisms and consequences of corporate governance reporting: A research framework" (2020) 25 *Journal of Management and Governance* 7–26 at 13–14.
23. Stephen M. Bainbridge, "Why a board? Group decision-making in corporate governance" (2002) 55 *Vanderbilt Law Review* 1–34 at 7.
24. Marie-Estelle Rey, "The role of board-level committees in corporate governance," OECD Corporate Governance Working Papers No. 24, 2022, www.oecd.org/content/dam/oecd/en/publications/reports/2022/09/the-role-of-board-level-committees-in-corporate-governance_907d0a67/8a97a3f6-en.pdf at 6 (last accessed October 22, 2025).

25. Dinara Davlembayeva and Savvas Papagiannidis, "Platform-provider relationship dynamics in the sharing economy: Challenges and implications" (2023) 111 *Industrial Marketing Management* 242–56 at 252–54.
26. Harsh V. Singh and Olivia Zeydler, "Why the net-zero transition needs a transparency boost," World Economic Forum, November 10, 2022, www.weforum.org/stories/2022/11/net-zero-transition-transparency-cop27-climate-change (last accessed October 25, 2025).
27. George S. Georgiev, "Disclosure as a corporate governance tool: Channels and challenges," in Jeffrey N. Gordon and Wolf-Georg Ringe (eds.), *The Oxford Handbook of Corporate Law and Governance* (Oxford: Oxford University Press, 2025), pp. 2–39.
28. John M. Holcomb, "Ethics and compliance committees of corporate boards: An exploratory study" (2017) 14 *Corporate Ownership & Control* 114–21 at 115.
29. Tom Moore, "The corporate power reset that makes *Citizens United* irrelevant," Center for American Progress, September 15, 2025, www.americanprogress.org/article/the-corporate-power-reset-that-makes-citizens-united-irrelevant/ (last accessed October 24, 2025).
30. Brian Libgober, "Meetings, comments, and the distributive politics of rulemaking" (2020) 15 *Quarterly Journal of Political Science* 449–81 at 451.
31. Lee Drutman, "How corporate lobbyists conquered American democracy," The Atlantic, April 20, 2015, www.theatlantic.com/business/archive/2015/04/how-corporate-lobbyists-conquered-american-democracy/390822/ (last accessed October 24, 2025).
32. Eliska Drapalova and Kai Wegrich, "Platforms' regulatory disruptiveness and local regulatory outcomes in Europe" (2024) 13 *Internet Policy Review* 2–28 at 11.
33. Alex Hern, "Facebook releases content moderation guidelines – rules for posts made by billions of users," The Guardian, April 24, 2018, www.theguardian.com/technology/2018/apr/24/facebook-releases-content-moderation-guidelines-secret-rules (last accessed October 22, 2025); Derek Khanna, "Tesla and the car dealers' lobby," Cato Institute Regulation, Summer 2014, www.cato.org/regulation/summer-2014/tesla-car-dealers-lobby (last accessed October 24, 2025).
34. Alexander Benlian et al., "Algorithmic management" (2022) 64 *Business & Information Systems Engineering* 825–39 at 834.
35. Drapalova and Wegrich, "Platforms' regulatory disruptiveness."
36. Michael Klausner, "The contractarian theory of corporate law: A generation later" (2006) 31 *Journal of Corporation Law* 779–900 at 782.
37. Finn Janning, Wafa Khlif, and Coral Ingley, "Transparency is (full) disclosure in corporate governance," in Finn Janning, Wafa Khlif, and Coral Ingley (eds.), *The Illusion of Transparency in Corporate Governance: Does Transparency Help or Hinder True Ethical Conduct?* (London: Palgrave Macmillan, 2020), pp. 57–82.
38. John G. Ruggie, "Multinationals, corporate social responsibility and public regulation: A perspective on corporate self-regulation in the global economy" (2017) 12 *Regulation & Governance* 317–33 at 320.
39. Brett H. McDonnell, "Stakeholder engagement" (2022) 51 *Florida State University Law Review* 305–72 at 316–8.
40. Economic Policy Institute, "Unequal power: How the assumption of equal bargaining power in the workplace undermines freedom, fairness, and democracy," www.epi.org/unequalpower/home/ (last accessed October 26, 2025).
41. McDonnell, "Stakeholder engagement," 318.
42. Coase, "The nature of the firm."
43. Coline Serres, Marek Hudon, and François Maon, "Social corporations under the spotlight: A governance perspective" (2022) 37 *Journal of Business Venturing* 106192 at 2–3.

44. David Cray, "Control and coordination in multinational corporations" (1984) 15 *Journal of International Business Studies* 85–97 at 86.
45. Raphael Amit and Christoph Zott, "Value creation in e-business" (2001) 22 *Strategic Management Journal* 493–520 at 498.
46. Christian Homburg, Danijel Jozić, and Christina Kuehnl, "Customer experience management: Toward implementing an evolving marketing concept" (2017) 45 *Journal of the Academy of Marketing Science* 377–401 at 379.
47. Michel Wedel and P.K. Kannan, "Marketing analytics for data-rich environments" (2016) 80 *Journal of Marketing* 97–121 at 99–100.
48. Lina M. Khan, "The separation of platforms and commerce" (2019) 119 *Columbia Law Review* 973–1098 at 1004.
49. Julie E. Cohen, "Turning privacy inside out" (2019) 20 *Theoretical Inquiries in Law* 1–37 at 26.
50. Michele Micheletti and Dietlind Stolle, "Mobilizing consumers to take responsibility for global social justice" (2007) 6 *Annals of the American Academy of Political and Social Science* 157–75 at 169.
51. Amitai Etzioni, "The limits of transparency," in Emmanuel Alloa & Dieter Thomä (eds.), *Transparency, Society and Subjectivity: Critical Perspectives* (London: Palgrave Macmillan, 2018), pp. 176–201.
52. Pauline T. Kim, "Beyond principal–agent theories: Law and the judicial regulation of workers" (1997) 1997 *Law and Contemporary Problems* 535–75 at 544.
53. Robert Klonoski, "Defining employee benefits: A managerial perspective" (2016) 6 *International Journal of Human Resource Studies* 52–72 at 59.
54. Roger Friedland and Robert R. Alford, "Bringing society back in: Symbols, practices, and institutional contradictions," in W. W. Powell and P. J. DiMaggio (eds.), *The New Institutionalism in Organizational Analysis* (Chicago: University of Chicago Press, 1991), pp. 232–67.
55. Panikos Georgallis, "The link between social movements and corporate social initiatives: Toward a multi-level theory" (2017) 142 *Journal of Business Ethics* 735–51 at 736.
56. Todd Corley, Vontrese (Voni) Pamphile, and Katina Sawyer, "What has (and hasn't) changed about being a chief diversity officer," Harvard Business Review, September 23, 2022, https://hbr.org/2022/09/what-has-and-hasnt-changed-about-being-a-chief-diversity-officer (last accessed October 24, 2025).
57. Umesh Chandra Tiwari, "DEI metrics in executive compensation," Harvard Law School Forum on Corporate Governance, June 26, 2024, https://corpgov.law.harvard.edu/2024/06/26/dei-metrics-in-executive-compensation/ (last accessed October 24, 2025).
58. Eric Lau and Taylor Telford, "'DEI' vanishing from corporate filings, mirroring business world's retreat," The Washington Post, April 30, 2025, www.washingtonpost.com/business/interactive/2025/dei-companies-sec-filings/ (last accessed October 24, 2025).
59. Lara A. Flath, David E. Schwartz, and Amy Van Gelder, "Corporate DEI policies face scrutiny following SCOTUS affirmative action decision," Skadden Insights, September 2023, www.skadden.com/insights/publications/2023/09/quarterly-insights/corporate-dei-polices-face-scrutiny (last accessed October 24, 2025); Michael Hatcher et al., "Ten state attorneys general launch inquiry into major financial institutions" DEI/ESG programs', Jackson Lewis P. C., January 29, 2025, www.jacksonlewis.com/insights/ten-state-attorneys-general-launch-inquiry-major-financial-institutions-dei-esg-programs (last accessed November 21, 2025); Taylor Telford, "The growing battle over corporate diversity practices, explained," The Washington Post, October 2, 2023, www.washingtonpost.com/business/2023/10/02/corporate-diversity-inclusion-affirmative-action-ruling/ (last accessed October 24, 2025).

60. Geri Stengel, "Black Lives Matter protests move corporate D&I initiatives into the spotlight," Forbes, June 17, 2020, www.forbes.com/sites/geristengel/2020/06/17/black-lives-matter-protests-moves-corporate-di-initiatives-into-the-spotlight/ (last accessed October 24, 2025).
61. Maria Aspan, "Corporate America's retreat from DEI has eliminated thousands of jobs," NPR, May 27, 2025, www.npr.org/2025/05/27/nx-s1-5307319/dei-jobs-trump (last accessed October 24, 2025).
62. Anurada Jain, "The gig economy: Disruption, innovation, and economic evolution" (2024) 30 *Educational Administration Theory and Practice Journal* 5133–40 at 5135.
63. Airbnb, "Official codification of party ban," June 28, 2022, https://news.airbnb.com/official-codification-of-party-ban/ (last accessed October 31, 2025); Airbnb.org, "Airbnb.org expands temporary housing support for refugees," June 20, 2024, https://news.airbnb.com/airbnb-org-expands-temporary-housing-support-for-refugees/ (last accessed October 31, 2025).
64. Audrea Chen, "Employee or independent contractor? A legal analysis of Uber's worker misclassification," Columbia Law Review Online, September 5, 2024, www.culawreview.org/current-events-2/employee-or-independent-contractor-a-legal-analysis-of-ubers-worker-misclassification (last accessed October 31, 2025).
65. Faiza Patel and Laura Hecht-Felella, "Facebook's content moderation rules are a mess," Brennan Center for Justice, February 22, 2021, www.brennancenter.org/our-work/analysis-opinion/facebooks-content-moderation-rules-are-mess (last accessed October 31, 2025).
66. Jeroen K. G. Hopster and Matthijs M. Maas, "The technology triad: Disruptive AI, regulatory gaps and value change" (2024) 4 *AI and Ethics* 1051–65 at 1064.
67. Abdullah Alsaleh, "The impact of technological advancement on culture and society" (2024) 14 *Scientific Reports* 32140 at 4.
68. Kezia Farnham, "Corporate governance rules: What they are & why they matter," Diligent Corporation, May 21, 2024, www.diligent.com/resources/blog/corporate-governance-rules (last accessed November 1, 2025).
69. Eduardo Schiehll, Henrique Castro Martins, and Krista B. Lewellyn, "Symbolic or substantive? How shareholder heterogeneity shapes the purpose of the corporation" (2025) 58 *Long Range Planning* 102582 at 19–20.
70. Robert P. Bartlett and Ryan Bubb, "Corporate social responsibility through shareholder governance," ECGI Working Paper Series in Law No. 677, 2023, www.ecgi.global/sites/default/files/working_papers/documents/corporatesocialresponsibilitythroughshareholdergovernance_0.pdf (last accessed November 21, 2025).
71. Marisa McVey, "Untangling the authority of external experts in the corporate implementation of the UN Guiding Principles on Business and Human Rights" (2022) 21 *Journal of Human Rights* 620–38 at 627.
72. McVey, "Untangling the authority of external experts," 627.
73. Spitzeck and Hansen, "Stakeholder governance," 378.
74. Starbucks, "C.A.F.E. Practices: Starbucks' approach to ethically sourcing coffee," February 28, 2024, https://stories.starbucks.com/stories/2024/cafe-practices-starbucks-approach-to-ethically-sourcing-coffee (last accessed November 1, 2025).
75. Starbucks, "Sustainability at the heart of Starbucks coffee sourcing," https://athome.starbucks.com/story/sustainability-heart-starbucks-coffee-sourcing/ (last accessed November 1, 2025).
76. Paul Wiegmann et al., "Competing standard-setting organizations: A choice architecture for innovators?" (2022) 51 *Research Policy* 1–15 at 11–12.
77. World Resources Institute and World Business Council for Sustainable Development, "About GHG Protocol," https://ghgprotocol.org/about-us (last accessed November 1, 2025).

78. Olivier Serrat, "A primer on corporate values," in *Knowledge Solutions: Tools, Methods, and Approaches to Drive Organizational Performance* (Singapore: Springer 2017), pp. 701–09.
79. Giorgia Profumo, Lara Penco, and Ilaria Tutore, "Mission statements and the sustainability communication" (2019) 2 *Symphonya: Emerging Issues in Management* 95–108 at 97–100.
80. Alperen Afşin Gözlügöl, "Blinded by 'fairness': Why we need (strong) procedural safeguards in screening self-dealing and obtaining a fair price is not the answer" (2022) *European Business Organisation Law Review* 23(4) 634–67 at 634.
81. Ratna Sari and Muslim Muslim, "Corporate transparency and environmental reporting: Trends and benefits" (2024) 4 *Amkop Management Accounting Review* 1–18 at 14.
82. Ingo Pies et al., "Trade-offs in stakeholder theory: An ordonomic perspective" (2024) 20 *Society and Business Review* 975–95 at 976.
83. Simone de Colle, "A stakeholder management model for ethical decision making" (2005) 6 *International Journal of Management and Decision Making* 299–314 at 312–13.
84. Marwan Mansour et al., "The relationship between corporate governance quality and firm performance" (2022) 14 *Sustainability* 1–25 at 4.
85. Renata Wandroski Peris et al., "Does better corporate governance increase operational performance?" (2017) 17 *Corporate Governance: The International Journal of Business in Society* 524–37.
86. Timothy J. McClimon, "Bluewashing joins greenwashing as the new corporate whitewashing," Forbes, October 3, 2022, www.forbes.com/sites/timothyjmcclimon/2022/10/03/bluewashing-joins-greenwashing-as-the-new-corporate-whitewashing/ (last accessed November 1, 2025).
87. Aaron K. Chatterji and Michael W. Toffel, "The new CEO activists," Harvard Business Review, March–April 2018, https://hbr.org/2018/01/the-new-ceo-activists (last accessed November 1, 2025).
88. Lisa M. Fairfax, "Stakeholderism, corporate purpose, and credible commitment" (2022) 108 *Virginia Law Review* 1163–247 at 1166.
89. Bloomberg, "Corporate America promised to hire more people of color – it did," September 27, 2023, www.bloomberg.com/graphics/2023-black-lives-matter-equal-opportunity-corporate-diversity/ (last accessed November 3, 2025).
90. Ioannis Ioannou, "What the ESG backlash reveals – and what comes next" (2025), Forbes, March 25, 2025, www.forbes.com/sites/lbsbusinessstrategyreview/2025/03/25/what-the-esg-backlash-reveals-and-what-comes-next/ (last accessed November 3, 2025).
91. David A. Cifrino, "The future of corporate sustainability and climate action in the anti-'woke' era," *Harvard Advanced Leadership Initiative Social Impact Review*, February 8, 2025, www.sir.advancedleadership.harvard.edu/articles/future-corporate-sustainability-climate-action-in-anti-woke-era/ (last accessed November 4, 2025).
92. Yale Chief Executive Leadership Institute, "Over 1,000 companies have curtailed operations in Russia – but some remain," January 28, 2024 (updated regularly since 2022), https://som.yale.edu/story/2022/over-1000-companies-have-curtailed-operations-russia-some-remain (last accessed November 4, 2025).
93. Michael A. Witt, "Corporate responses to the war in Ukraine: Moral principles, strategic rationales, and stakeholder pressures" (2022) 48 *Financial Research Letters* 1–4.
94. Cifrino, "The future of corporate sustainability and climate action."
95. Kathleen Rehbein et al., "Corporate social responsibility and the issue environment: A longitudinal analysis" (2006) 111 *Business & Society Review* 175–91 at 182–85.
96. Ronald Mitchell et al., "Toward a theory of stakeholder identification and salience: Defining the principle of who and what really counts" (1997) 22 *Academy of Management Review* 853–86 at 869.

97. Organisation for Economic Co-operation and Development, "G20/OECD Principles of Corporate Governance," 2023, www.oecd.org/content/dam/oecd/en/publications/reports/2023/09/g20-oecd-principles-of-corporate-governance-2023_60836fcb/ed750b30-en.pdf (last accessed November 15, 2025).
98. R. Edward Freeman, *Strategic Management: A Stakeholder Approach* (Cambridge: Cambridge University Press, 2015), pp. 25–26.
99. Fairfax, "Stakeholderism, corporate purpose, and credible commitment," p. 1166.
100. McClimon, "Bluewashing joins greenwashing."
101. OECD, "G20/OECD Principles of Corporate Governance," p. 23.
102. Nicole Dando and Tracey Swift, "Transparency and assurance: Minding the credibility gap" (2003) 44 *Journal of Business Ethics* 195–200 at 196.
103. McVey, "Untangling the authority of external experts," p. 627.
104. Thi Hong Van Hoang et al., "Environmental transparency and performance: Does the quality of ESG disclosure matter?" (2021) 10 *Corporate Governance: The International Journal of Business in Society* 1–11 at 6.
105. Alex Edmans, *Grow the Pie: How Great Companies Deliver Both Purpose and Profit* (Cambridge: Cambridge University Press, 2020).
106. Russ Banham, "Shareholders: The new rules of engagement,' Corporate BoardMember, https://boardmember.com/shareholders-the-new-rules-of-engagement/ (last accessed 7 November 2025).
107. Zhiyang Liu et al., "Stakeholders and ESG disclosure strategies adoption: The roles of firm and stakeholder characteristics" (2022) 10 *Elementa: Science of the Anthropocene* 1–12 at 3–4.
108. Joanna Krasodomska et al., "The impact of companies' trust-building efforts on sustainability reporting and assurance quality: Insights from Europe" (2024) 33 *Meditari Accountancy Research* 246–79 at 249.
109. Bentleys, "ESG reporting: Key insights for accurate and effective disclosure," April 1, 2025, www.bentleys.com.au/resources/esg-reporting-key-insights-for-accurate-and-effective-disclosure/ (last accessed November 4, 2025).
110. Deloitte, "Using the COSO framework to establish internal controls over sustainability reporting (ICSR)" April 21, 2023, https://dart.deloitte.com/USDART/home/publications/deloitte/heads-up/2023/coso-framework-for-internal-controls-over-sustainability (last accessed November 4, 2025).
111. Reiner Quick et al., "Assurance on CSR reports impact on credibility perceptions of non-financial information by bank directors" 28 *Meditari Accountancy Research* 833–62 at 833.
112. Marta Isabel Garcia-Rivas et al., "Corporate social responsibility reports: A review of the evolution, approaches and prospects" (2023) 9 *Heliyon* 1–18 at 13–14.
113. Merle Ojasoo, "CSR reporting, stakeholder engagement and preventing hypocrisy in corporations" (2016) 6 *Journal of Global Entrepreneurship Research* 1–14 at 3–7.
114. Simone Altoe, Carmen Simion, and Martin Wennerström, "ESG-linked compensation: Driving action on sustainability," Sustainalytics, April 3, 2024, www.sustainalytics.com/esg-research/resource/investors-esg-blog/incentivizing-change--how-esg-linked-compensation-can-advance-sustainability-initiatives (last accessed November 4, 2025).
115. Sarah Marschlich et al., "The effect of third-party certifications on corporate social responsibility communication authenticity and credibility" (2025) 9 *Corporate Communications: An International Journal* 1–20 at 5.
116. Ayes Saka-Helmhout et al., "Stakeholder engagement strategies for impactful corporate social innovation initiatives by multinational enterprises" (2024) 30 *Journal of International Management* 1–20 at 9–11.

117. OECD, "G20/OECD Principles of Corporate Governance," p. 47.
118. Faiza Siddiqui et al., "The role of corporate governance and reputation in the disclosure of corporate social responsibility and firm performance" (2023) 9 *Heliyon* 1–14 at 4–5.
119. Erica Steckler et al., "Authenticity and corporate governance" 114 *Journal of Business Ethics* 951–63 at 955–6.
120. Tamanna Fatima and Said Elbanna, "Corporate social responsibility (CSR) implementation: A systematic review of 122 empirical studies" (2022) 31 *Business Ethics: A European Review* 678–95.
121. Fatima and Elbanna, "Corporate social responsibility (CSR) implementation," p. 682.
122. Alan S. Gutterman, "CSR governance and organizational culture," ResearchGate, June 14, 2023, www.researchgate.net/publication/371680183_CSR_Governance_and_Organizational_Culture (last accessed November 5, 2025).
123. Fatima and Elbanna, "Corporate social responsibility (CSR) implementation," p. 679.
124. Associated Press, "Microsoft lets cloud users keep personal data within Europe to ease privacy fears," January 11, 2024, https://apnews.com/article/70e50c9051b57794f6074f1562 4a000f (last accessed November 8, 2025).
125. Simon Jessop, "Companies setting climate transition plans up 44% in 2023, research shows," Reuters, June 18, 2024, www.reuters.com/sustainability/climate-energy/companies-setting-climate-transition-plans-up-44-2023-research-shows-2024-06-18/ (last accessed November 8, 2025).
126. Oliver G. Kayas, "Workplace surveillance: A systematic review, integrative framework, and research agenda" (2023) 168 *Journal of Business Research* 1–16 at 6.
127. Bernd Manz, "Corporate governance reporting, disclosures, monitoring and analytics" (2025) 33(2) *Corporate Governance: An International Review* 145–62 at 150.
128. Kristin Burnham, "Scope 3 emissions top supply chain sustainability challenges," MIT Sloan Ideas Made to Matter, December 18, 2024, https://mitsloan.mit.edu/ideas-made-to-matter/scope-3-emissions-top-supply-chain-sustainability-challenges (last accessed 14 November 2025).
129. Adwoa Bagalini, "5 ways intersectionality affects diversity and inclusion at work," World Economic Forum, July 22, 2020, www.weforum.org/stories/2020/07/diversity-inclusion-equality-intersectionality/ (last accessed November 8, 2025).
130. Lauren Weber and Emily Glazer, "Sex scandals. Accounting fraud. It's all showing up on the corporate hotline," *The Wall Street Journal*, September 12, 2025, www.wsj .com/business/nestle-employee-complaint-hotline-74ac4fde (last accessed November 8, 2025).
131. Patrick Temple-West, "More women make it on to US company boards but fewer reach the C-suite," Financial Times, May 20, 2024, www.ft.com/content/a586a0d6-d299-463c-a531-22539446ff87 (last accessed 14 November 2025).
132. Rachel Arnow-Richman, James Hicks, and Steven Davidoff Solomon, "Do social movements spur corporate change? The rise of 'MeToo termination rights' in CEO contracts" (2022) 98 *Indiana Law Journal* 125–74 at 151.
133. Weber and Glazer, "Sex scandals."
134. Patrick Temple-West, "Companies drop DEI targets from bonus plans on pressure from conservatives," Financial Times, July 21, 2024, www.ft.com/content/63ac21a5-9929-4bc3-9089-03299f023bcd (last accessed November 10, 2025).
135. Ross Kerber, "Just 35 complaints of debanking cite political bias despite Trump order," Reuters, August 19, 2025, www.reuters.com/legal/transactional/just-35-complaints-debanking-cite-political-bias-despite-trump-order-2025-08-19/ (last accessed November 10, 2025).

136. Jay Peters, "Zuckerberg says he's moving Meta moderators to Texas because California seems too 'biased'," The Verge, January 7, 2025, www.theverge.com/2025/1/7/24338305/meta-mark-zuckerberg-moving-meta-moderators-texas-california-bias (last accessed November 14, 2025); Lauren Goode, "Twitter's former head of trust and safety finally breaks her silence," Wired, November 21, 2023, www.wired.com/story/del-harvey-twitter-trust-and-safety-breaks-her-silence/ (last accessed November 14, 2025).
137. Ariel Zients, "Companies expand DEI programs to include first-generation professionals," Bloomberg Law, April 5, 2024, https://news.bloomberglaw.com/esg/companies-expand-dei-programs-to-include-first-generation-professionals (last accessed November 14, 2025).
138. Society for Human Resource Management, "Regularly monitoring, using DE&I data is key to closing organizational gaps," September 11, 2021, www.shrm.org/topics-tools/news/inclusion-diversity/regularly-monitoring-using-dei-data-key-to-closing-organizational-gaps (last accessed November 14, 2025).
139. Miriam H. Baer, "Governing corporate compliance" (2009) 50 *Boston College Law Review* 949–1019 at 1001.
140. Jean-Michel Ferat and Shelly Mady, "The significance of audit and monitoring in a compliance programme," Global Investigations Review, August 7, 2024, https://globalinvestigationsreview.com/guide/the-guide-compliance-archived/third-edition/article/the-significance-of-audit-and-monitoring-in-compliance-programme (last accessed November 14, 2025).
141. Francesco Prencipe, "Accountability between compliance and legitimacy: A structured conceptual review of sustainability governance" (2025) 17 *Sustainability* 9305–24 at 9310.

4 WHY NOT REGULATE?

1. John C. Coffee, "'No soul to damn, no body to kick': An unscandalized inquiry into the problem of corporate punishment" (1981) 79 *Michigan Law Review* 386–459; Cary Coglianese and David Lazer, "Management-based regulation: Prescribing private management to achieve public goals" (2003) 37 *Law & Society Review* 691–730 (together explaining that regulation has long been the primary tool for addressing divergences between private incentives and public welfare, particularly when corporate behavior imposes externalities).
2. Jill E. Fisch and Jeff Schwartz, "How did corporations get stuck in politics and can they escape?" (2024) 3 *University of Chicago Business Law Review* 325–60.
3. Jonathan B. Wiener, "The regulation of technology, and the technology of regulation" (2004) 26 *Technology in Society* 483–500; Coglianese and Lazer, "Management-based regulation," 700.
4. Ian Ayres and John Braithwaite, *Responsive Regulation: Transcending the Deregulation Debate* (Oxford: Oxford University Press, 1992), pp. 7–10.
5. John Braithwaite, "Enforced self-regulation: A new strategy for corporate crime control" (1982) 80 *Michigan Law Review* 1466–507.
6. Gunther Teubner, "Global Bukowina: Legal pluralism in the world-society," in Gunther Teubner (ed.), *Global Law without a State* (Aldershot: Dartmouth, 1996), pp. 3–28; Brian Tamanaha, "A non-essentialist version of legal pluralism" (2000) 27 *Journal of Law and Society* 296–321.

7. Robert C. Ellickson, *Order without Law: How Neighbors Settle Disputes* (Cambridge, MA: Harvard University Press, 1991) (showing how communities generate and enforce their own normative orders, an analogy frequently invoked to illustrate how corporate and institutional actors produce internal rule systems); Marion Fourcade and Kieran Healy, "Seeing like a market" (2017) 15 *Socio-Economic Review* 9–29 (analyzing how modern private institutions, including universities, rating agencies, and corporations, construct normative classifications and metrics that operate as de facto governance systems).
8. Roberta Romano, "Law as product: Some pieces of the incorporation puzzle" (1985) 1 *Journal of Law, Economics, & Organization* 225–83 (discussing regulatory competition within U.S. corporate law, particularly the dynamics between Delaware and other states); Anne-Marie Slaughter, *A New World Order* (Princeton, NJ: Princeton University Press, 2004) (analyzing how transgovernmental regulatory networks cooperate and compete across borders in a multi-level global governance system).
9. Gary Richardson, "Guilds, laws, and markets for manufactured merchandise in late-medieval England" (2001) 56 *Explorations in Economic History* 1–25.
10. Jonathan R. Macey and Maureen O'Hara, "Regulating exchanges and alternative trading systems: A law and economics perspective" (1999) 28 *Journal of Legal Studies* 17–54; Joel Seligman, *The Transformation of Wall Street* (3rd ed., New York: Aspen Publishers, 2003) (providing a historical account of stock exchanges as self-regulating institutions prior to federal securities law).
11. John Braithwaite and Peter Drahos, *Global Business Regulation* (Cambridge: Cambridge University Press, 2000); Kenneth W. Abbott and Duncan Snidal, "The governance triangle: Regulatory standards institutions and the shadow of the state," in Walter Mattli and Ngaire Woods (eds.), *The Politics of Global Regulation* (Princeton: Princeton University Press, 2009), pp. 44–88.
12. Sheila Slaughter and Larry L. Leslie, *Academic Capitalism: Politics, Policies, and the Entrepreneurial University* (Baltimore: Johns Hopkins University Press, 1997).
13. Harold J. Berman, *Law and Revolution: The Formation of the Western Legal Tradition* (Cambridge, MA: Harvard University Press, 1983).
14. William L. Cary, "Federalism and corporate law: Reflections upon Delaware" (1974) 83 *Yale Law Journal* 663–705.
15. Roberta Romano, "The state competition debate in corporate law" (1987) 8 *Cardozo Law Review* 709–57.
16. Mark J. Roe, "Delaware's competition" (2003) 117 *Harvard Law Review* 588–646.
17. Bloomberg Law, "Regulation and legislation lag behind constantly evolving technology," September 27, 2019, https://pro.bloomberglaw.com/insights/technology/regulation-and-legislation-lag-behind-technology/ (last accessed November 20, 2025).
18. Tim Büthe, "Private regulation in the global economy: A (p)review" (2010) 12 *Business and Politics* 1–38.
19. Guillaume Beaumier, "Novelty and the demand for private regulation: Evidence from data privacy governance" (2023) 25 *Business and Politics* 371–92 (arguing that American companies seek a first-mover advantage or reputational benefit when they use private regulation to set themselves apart and shape the rules of the game).
20. Brian Duignan, "Financial crisis of 2007–08," Britannica Money, July 2, 2025, www.britannica.com/money/financial-crisis-of-2007-2008 (last accessed 20 November 2025).
21. Anne K. Barnett-Hart, "The story of the CDO market meltdown: An empirical analysis," M-RCBG Associate Working Paper Series No. 4, 2009, www.hks.harvard.edu/sites/default/files/centers/mrcbg/files/Barnett-Hart_2009.pdf (last accessed November 22, 2025).

22. Noah Berman, "What is the Dodd-Frank Act?" Council on Foreign Relations, May 8, 2023, www.cfr.org/backgrounder/what-dodd-frank-act (last accessed November 20, 2025).
23. US Securities and Exchange Commission, "SEC adopts credit rating agency reform rules," August 27, 2014, www.sec.gov/news/press-release/2014-178 (last accessed November 30, 2025) (implementing the Dodd–Frank Act's post-crisis mandate to strengthen internal-control, transparency, and disclosure obligations for NRSROs).
24. Jan-Peter Siedlarek, "The evolution of US bank capital around the implementation of Basel III," Federal Reserve Bank of Cleveland, March 26, 2024, www.clevelandfed.org/publications/economic-commentary/2024/ec-202407 (last accessed November 30, 2025).
25. Cary Coglianese, Jennifer Nash, and Todd Olmstead, "Performance-based regulation: Prospects and limitations in health, safety, and environmental regulation" (2003) 55 *Administrative Law Review* 705–29.
26. World Trade Organization, "Agreement on Technical Barriers to Trade, Annex 3," 1995, www.wto.org/english/docs_e/legal_e/17-tbt_e.htm (last accessed November 30, 2025); Organisation for Economic Co-operation and Development, "Regulatory policies in OECD countries," 2002, www.oecd.org/gov/regulatory-policy/Regulatory-Policies-in-OECD-Countries.pdf (last accessed November 30, 2025).
27. Donald Moynihan, *The Dynamics of Performance Management: Constructing Information and Reform* (Washington, DC: Georgetown University Press, 2008).
28. Russell Hotten, "Volkswagen: The scandal explained," BBC, December 10, 2015, www.bbc.com/news/business-34324772 (last accessed November 20, 2025).
29. Mihailis Diamantis, "Corporate criminal minds" (2019) 91 *University of Colorado Law Review* 635–707.
30. Samuel W. Buell, *Capital Offenses: Business Crime and Punishment in America's Corporate Age* (New York: W.W. Norton, 2016).
31. *Dobbs v. Jackson Women's Health Organization*, 597 US 215 (2022).
32. *Roe v. Wade*, 410 US 113 (1973).
33. Emma Goldberg, "These companies will cover travel expenses for employee abortions," The New York Times, June 27, 2022, www.nytimes.com/2022/06/27/business/abortion-travel-expenses-companies.html (last accessed November 30, 2025).
34. Stephanie Kirchgaessner and Lauren Aratani, "These companies claim to support abortion rights. They are backing anti-abortion Republicans," The Guardian, November 6, 2022, www.theguardian.com/world/2022/nov/06/us-companies-abortion-rights-donation-anti-abortion-republicans (last accessed November 30, 2025).
35. Levi Sumagaysay, "Uber, Lyft, DoorDash workers remain contractors due to California Supreme Court ruling," CalMatters, July 25, 2024, https://calmatters.org/economy/2024/07/prop-22-california-gig-work-law-upheld/ (last accessed November 13, 2025).
36. Sarbanes–Oxley Act.
37. Mancur Olson, *The Logic of Collective Action: Public Goods and the Theory of Groups* (Cambridge, MA: Harvard University Press, 1965).
38. Daniel Carpenter, *The Forging of Bureaucratic Autonomy: Reputations, Networks, and Policy Innovation in Executive Agencies* (Princeton: Princeton University Press, 2001), pp. 1862–928.
39. *Citizens United v. Federal Election Commission*, 558 US 310 (2010).
40. Abbott and Snidal, "The governance triangle."
41. Neil Gunningham, Peter Grabosky, and Darren Sinclair, *Smart Regulation: Designing Environmental Policy* (Oxford: Oxford University Press, 1998) (arguing that corporations are core actors in regulatory systems, with unique incentives and specialized knowledge that governments lack).

42. Donald C. Langevoort, "Behavioral ethics, behavioral compliance," in Jennifer Arlen (ed.), *Research Handbook on Corporate Crime and Financial Misdealing* (Cheltenham: Edward Elgar, 2018).
43. Stephen Breyer, *Regulation and Its Reform* (Cambridge, MA: Harvard University Press, 1982).
44. Michael C. Dorf and Charles F. Sabel, "A constitution of democratic experimentalism" (1998) 98 *Columbia Law Review* 267–473.
45. Ram Nidumolu, C. K. Prahalad, and Manjula R. Rangaswami, "Why sustainability is now the key driver of innovation," Harvard Business Review, September 2009, https://hbr.org/2009/09/why-sustainability-is-now-the-key-driver-of-innovation (last accessed November 22, 2025); Michael E. Porter and Claas van der Linde, "Green and competitive: Ending the stalemate," Harvard Business Review, September–October 1995, https://hbr.org/1995/09/green-and-competitive-ending-the-stalemate (last accessed November 22, 2025).
46. Robert Baldwin, Martin Cave, and Martin Lodge, *Understanding Regulation: Theory, Strategy, and Practice* (Oxford: Oxford University Press, 2012).
47. Kate Klonick, "The new governors: The people, rules, and processes governing online speech" (2018) 131 *Harvard Law Review* 1598–670.
48. Roberta Romano, "The need for competition in international securities regulation" (2001) 2 *Theoretical Inquiries in Law* 387–562.
49. Jonathan R. Macey and Maureen O'Hara, "The economics of stock exchange governance" (2005) 21 *Journal of Financial Intermediation* 297–319.
50. Michael C. Jensen, "Value maximization, stakeholder theory, and the corporate objective function" (2002) 12 *Business Ethics Quarterly* 235–56.
51. Pollman, "The making and meaning of ESG," 414 (describing the formulation of the business rationale for ESG).
52. Frank Dobbin and Alexandra Kalev, "Why diversity programs fail," Harvard Business Review, July–August 2016, https://hbr.org/2016/07/why-diversity-programs-fail (last accessed November 22, 2025) (showing that workplace reforms around gender and race succeed only when they complement organizational incentives and internal managerial interests).
53. Elizabeth Blair, "After protests, Disney CEO speaks out against Florida's 'Don't Say Gay' bill," NPR, March 10, 2022, www.npr.org/2022/03/08/1085130633/disney-response-florida-bill-dont-say-gay (last accessed November 14, 2025).
54. David Vogel, "The private regulation of global corporate conduct" (2010) 49 *Business & Society* 68–87 (analyzing when private regulatory schemes substitute for, and when they are incorporated into, public regulation).
55. Tim Bartley, "Institutional emergence in an era of globalization: The rise of transnational private regulation of labor and environmental conditions" (2007) 113 *American Journal of Sociology* 297–351 (arguing that private regulatory schemes arise in political contexts where governments lack the will or capacity to regulate).
56. Christine Parker, *The Open Corporation: Effective Self-Regulation and Democracy* (Cambridge: Cambridge University Press, 2002) (discussing the tendency of voluntary corporate commitments to deteriorate once public scrutiny or regulatory pressure wanes).
57. Brett W. Lewis, Judith L. Walls, and Glen W. Dowell, "Difference in degrees: CEO characteristics and firm environmental disclosure" (2014) 35 *Strategic Management Journal* 712–22 (finding that changes in leadership alter the firm's environmental commitments and disclosure practices).
58. Coffee, "No soul to damn, no body to kick"; Buell, Capital Offenses (together explaining the difficulty of disciplining corporations due to their collective structure and the challenge of attributing fault to specific managers).

59. Reinier R. Kraakman et al., *The Anatomy of Corporate Law: A Comparative and Functional Approach* (3rd ed., Oxford: Oxford University Press, 2017) (explaining that independent directors and supervisory bodies function as institutional responses to managerial conflicts of interest and weak internal enforcement).
60. Stephen M. Bainbridge, *Corporate Governance after the Financial Crisis* (Oxford: Oxford University Press, 2012) (explaining that independent directors serve as an institutional response to managerial agency problems by providing oversight of compliance, internal controls, and enforcement).
61. Gadinis and Havasy, "The quest for legitimacy."
62. Marianna Spring, "Elon Musk's 'social experiment on humanity': How X evolved in 2024," BBC, December 26, 2024, www.bbc.com/news/articles/c1elddq34p70 (last accessed 18 November 2025).
63. Leah Rutman, "The Hobby Lobby decision: Imposing religious beliefs on employees," ACLU Washington, August 11, 2014, www.aclu-wa.org/news/hobby-lobby-decision-imposing-religious-beliefs-employees/ (last accessed November 19, 2025).
64. Sarah Aarthun, "Chick-fil-A wades into a fast-food fight over same-sex marriage rights," CNN, July 28, 2012, www.cnn.com/2012/07/27/us/chick-fil-a-controversy (last accessed November 15, 2025).
65. Cache McClay, "Goya foods: Hispanic brand faces boycott for praising Trump," BBC, July 10, 2020, www.bbc.com/news/world-us-canada-53371392 (last accessed September 29, 2025).
66. Associated Press, "MyPillow founder Mike Lindell is ordered to pay $5M in election fraud challenge," NPR, April 21, 2023, www.npr.org/2023/04/21/1171193932/mypillow-founder-mike-lindell-is-ordered-to-pay-5m-in-election-fraud-challenge (last accessed November 19, 2025).
67. Jordan Valinsky, "Target is dialing back on pride merchandise after right-wing backlash," CNN, May 10, 2024, www.cnn.com/2024/05/10/business/target-pride-merchandise-june-2024 (last accessed November 19, 2025).
68. Jesus Jiménez and Brooks Barnes, "What we know about the Desantis-Disney dispute," The New York Times, May 19, 2023, www.nytimes.com/article/disney-florida-desantis.html (last accessed October 20, 2025).
69. Valeri Bolden-Barrett, "After #googlewalkout, Google CEO rolls out new sexual harassment policies," HR Dive, November 9, 2019, www.hrdive.com/news/after-googlewalkout-google-ceo-rolls-out-new-sexual-harassment-policies/541833/ (last accessed November 18, 2025).
70. Aimee Picchi, "Google CEO: Apology for harassment 'wasn't enough'," CBS News, October 13, 2018, www.cbsnews.com/news/google-ceo-sundar-pichai-apology-for-harassment-wasnt-enough/ (last accessed November 19, 2025).
71. Hannah J. Davies, "Netflix CEO says he 'screwed up' over Dave Chappelle memos," The Guardian, October 20, 2021, www.theguardian.com/tv-and-radio/2021/oct/20/ted-sarandos-netflix-dave-chappelle (last accessed November 22, 2025).
72. Julia Carrie Wong and Sam Morris, "Collision course: Uber's terrible 2017," The Guardian, December 27, 2017, www.theguardian.com/technology/ng-interactive/2017/dec/27/uber-2017-scandals-investigation (last accessed November 23, 2025).
73. Bejamin C. Larsen and Sabrina Küspert, "Regulating general-purpose AI: Areas of convergence and divergence across the EU and the US," Brookings, May 21, 2024, www.brookings.edu/articles/regulating-general-purpose-ai-areas-of-convergence-and-divergence-across-the-eu-and-the-us/?utm%27 (last accessed November 20, 2025).
74. Stavros Gadinis and Silvia Fregoni, "Beyond the Brussels effect: The surprising rise of the International Sustainability Standards Board," in press, *Journal of International Economic Law*, European Corporate Governance Institute – Law Working Paper No. 886/2025, 2025, https://ssrn.com/abstract=5777602 (last accessed November 30, 2025).

75. Richard Wennberg, "Does the EU's Digital Services Act violate freedom of speech?" Center for Strategic & International Studies, September 22, 2025, www.csis.org/blogs/europe-corner/does-eus-digital-services-act-violate-freedom-speech (last accessed November 30, 2025).
76. Julie Brill and Erin Chapple, "Microsoft announces the phased rollout of the EU Data Boundary for the Microsoft Cloud begins January 1, 2023," Microsoft EU Policy Blog, December 15, 2022, https://blogs.microsoft.com/eupolicy/2022/12/15/eu-data-boundary-cloud-rollout/ (last accessed November 30, 2025) (describing the creation of a separately governed EU cloud environment to comply with European data-sovereignty rules).
77. Anu Bradford, *The Brussels Effect: How the European Union Rules the World* (Oxford: Oxford University Press, 2020).
78. Deloitte, "Executive summary of the SEC's landmark climate disclosure rule," April 8, 2024, https://dart.deloitte.com/USDART/home/publications/deloitte/heads-up/2024/sec-climate-disclosure-requirements-ghg-emissions-executive-summary (last accessed November 30, 2025) (showing that the SEC received record levels of feedback on the proposed rule with registrants raising significant concerns).
79. Abbott and Snidal, "The governance triangle"; Vogel, "The private regulation of global corporate conduct" (together explaining how firms build reputational and governance capacities that enhance their credibility with regulators and strengthen their influence over regulatory outcomes).

5 CORPORATE ORDERING: PAST AND PRESENT

1. Zeynep Tufekci, "Algorithmic harms beyond Facebook and Google: Emergent challenges of computational agency" (2015) 13 *Colorado Technology Law Journal* 203–18.
2. Agostino Vollero, Domenico Sardanelli, and Alfonso Siano, "Exploring the role of the Amazon effect on customer expectations: An analysis of user-generated content in consumer electronics retailing" (2021) 22 *Journal of Consumer Behaviour* 1062–73.
3. Wyatte Grantham-Philips, "Georgia jury orders Monsanto parent to pay nearly $2.1 billion in Roundup weed-killer lawsuit," AP News, March 24, 2025, https://apnews.com/article/7f903acb350dd6f6ce09b102914eabc1 (last accessed October 26, 2025).
4. Shoshana Zuboff, *The Age of Surveillance Capitalism: The Fight for a Human Future at the New Frontier of Power* (New York: PublicAffairs, 2019).
5. Jonathan Hall, Craig Palsson, and Joseph Price, "Is Uber a substitute or complement for public transit?" (2018) 66 *Transport Policy* 45–56.
6. Gary Barker, "The Airbnb effect on housing and rent," Forbes, February 21, 2020, www.forbes.com/sites/garybarker/2020/02/21/the-airbnb-effect-on-housing-and-rent (last accessed October 26, 2025).
7. Julia Black, "Constitutionalising self-regulation" (1996) 59 *Modern Law Review* 24–55.
8. David L. Engel, "An approach to corporate social responsibility" (1979) 32 *Stanford Law Review* 1–98.
9. Rajeev R. Bhattacharyay and Mahendra R. Gupta, "Impact of self-regulation on financial markets," December 4, 2025, https://ssrn.com/abstract=4490828 (last accessed November 30, 2025).
10. John Macey, "Occupation Code 541110: Lawyers, self-regulation, and the idea of a profession" (2005) 69 *Fordham Law Review* 969–1018.
11. Mohan Reddy, "Product self-regulation: A paradox of technology policy" (1990) 38 *Technological Forecasting and Social Change* 49–63.

12. Ron F. Jabal, "Keeping it clean: Self-regulation in the advertising industry," BusinessWorld Online, September 6, 2024, www.bworldonline.com/opinion/2024/09/06/618927/keeping-it-clean-self-regulation-in-the-advertising-industry/ (last accessed October 26, 2025).
13. Virginia Haufler, "The Kimberley Process Certification Scheme: An innovation in global governance and conflict prevention" (2010) 89 *Journal of Business Ethics* 403–17.
14. Büthe and Mattli, The New Global Rulers.
15. Stavros Gadinis, "Three pathways to global standards: Private, regulator, and ministry networks" (2015) 109 *American Journal of International Law* 1–57; Stavros Gadinis, "The Financial Stability Board: The new politics of international financial regulation" (2012) 48 *Texas International Law Journal* 157–218.
16. Gadinis, "Three pathways to global standards."
17. Peter D. Norton, *Fighting Traffic: The Dawn of the Motor Age in the American City* (Cambridge, MA: MIT Press, 2008).
18. Clay McShane and Joel A. Tarr, *The Horse in the City: Living Machines in the Nineteenth Century* (Baltimore: Johns Hopkins University Press, 2007).
19. U.S. Department of Commerce, *Report of the National Conference on Street and Highway Safety* (Washington, DC: Government Printing Office, 1924).
20. Rodney R. Michael, "Voluntary disclosure in a nineteenth-century American corporation: The demise of managerial information as a significant element of financial reporting" (1996) 23 *Accounting Historians Journal* 1–33.
21. Stavros Gadinis and Howell E. Jackson, "Markets as regulators: A survey" (2007) 80 *Southern California Law Review* 1239–300 at 1251–3.
22. Seligman, The Transformation of Wall Street; Roberta S. Karmel, *Regulation by Prosecution: The Securities and Exchange Commission vs. Corporate America* (New York: Simon & Schuster, 1982), pp. 19–25.
23. Susan Handy, "Smart growth and the transportation-land use connection: What does the research tell us?" (2005) 25 *International Regional Science Review* 3–22.
24. Paul G. Mahoney, "The political economy of the Securities Act of 1933" (2001) 30 *Journal of Legal Studies* 1–31.
25. Norton, Fighting Traffic, pp. 110–35.
26. Clay McShane, *Down the Asphalt Path: The Automobile and the American City* (New York: Columbia University Press, 1994).
27. Daniel Carpenter and David A. Moss (eds.), *Preventing Regulatory Capture: Special Interest Influence and How to Limit It* (Cambridge: Cambridge University Press, 2014); Frank R. Baumgartner and Beth L. Leech, *Basic Interests: The Importance of Groups in Politics and in Political Science* (Princeton, NJ: Princeton University Press, 1998).
28. Colin Mayer, *Prosperity: Better Business Makes the Greater Good* (Oxford: Oxford University Press, 2018) (arguing that corporations can self-govern through internal norms and accountability mechanisms that perform law-like functions independent of the state).
29. McShane and Tarr, The Horse in the City.
30. Norton, Fighting Traffic.
31. Paul Barrett, *The Automobile and Urban Transit: The Formation of Public Policy in Chicago, 1900–1930* (Philadelphia: Temple University Press, 1983), pp. 45–67.
32. Kenneth T. Jackson, *Crabgrass Frontier: The Suburbanization of the United States* (New York: Oxford University Press, 1985).
33. Sarah A. Seo, *Policing the Open Road: How Cars Transformed American Freedom* (Cambridge, MA: Harvard University Press, 2019).
34. John C. Coffee, "Market failure and the economic case for a mandatory disclosure system" (1984) 70 *Virginia Law Review* 717–53 at 735–42.

35. Roberta Romano, *The Genius of American Corporate Law* (Washington, DC: American Enterprise Institute, 1993), pp. 45–9.
36. George J. Benston, "Required disclosure and the stock market: An evaluation of the Securities Exchange Act of 1934" (1973) 63 *American Economic Review* 132–55 at 138–45.
37. Frank H. Easterbrook and Daniel R. Fischel, "Mandatory disclosure and the protection of investors" (1984) 70 *Virginia Law Review* 669–715 at 685–90.
38. William G. Roy, *Socializing Capital: The Rise of the Large Industrial Corporation in America* (Princeton, NJ: Princeton University Press, 1997), pp. 178–203; Thomas K. McCraw, *Prophets of Regulation: Charles Francis Adams, Louis D. Brandeis, James M. Landis, Alfred E. Kahn* (Cambridge, MA: Harvard University Press, 1984), pp. 153–78.
39. Curtis J. Milhaupt and Katharina Pistor, *Law and Capitalism: What Corporate Crises Reveal about Legal Systems and Economic Development around the World* (Chicago: University of Chicago Press, 2008) (arguing that corporate practice and crisis responses often evolve into formal legal norms).
40. Mark J. Roe, *Strong Managers, Weak Owners: The Political Roots of American Corporate Finance* (Princeton, NJ: Princeton University Press, 1994), pp. 45–67 (showing how political and institutional governance arrangements shaped the trajectory of U.S. corporate law).
41. Marc Bloch, *The Historian's Craft* (Manchester: Manchester University Press, 1954) (highlighting the analytical value of examining the evolution of practices and ideas prior to their formal codification).
42. Roy, Socializing Capital (tracing how early industrial firms influenced the institutionalization of corporate law).
43. McShane and Tarr, The Horse in the City, pp. 152–60 (illustrating how technological innovation shaped urban governance before regulatory codification).
44. Martin V. Melosi, *The Sanitary City: Environmental Services in Urban America from Colonial Times to the Present* (Pittsburgh, PA: University of Pittsburgh Press, 2000).
45. Seo, Policing the Open Road, pp. 17–33 (situating early traffic dangers within the emergence of policing and regulatory control).
46. James J. Flink, *The Automobile Age* (Cambridge, MA: MIT Press, 1988).
47. Ruth Schwartz Cowan, *More Work for Mother: The Ironies of Household Technology from the Open Hearth to the Microwave* (New York: Basic Books, 1983).
48. U.S. Census Bureau, *Statistical Abstract of the United States: 1921* (Washington, DC: Government Printing Office, 1922), p. 432.
49. Seo, Policing the Open Road, pp. 60–66.
50. William Phelps Eno, *The Story of Highway Traffic Control, 1899–1939* (Westport, CT: Eno Foundation, 1939).
51. McShane, Down the Asphalt Path, pp. 157–73.
52. Seo, Policing the Open Road.
53. Bruce E. Seely, *Building the American Highway System: Engineers as Policy Makers* (Philadelphia: Temple University Press, 1987).
54. Paul Barrett, *The Automobile and Urban Transit: The Formation of Public Policy in Chicago, 1900–1930* (Philadelphia: Temple University Press, 1983).
55. Colin Divall and Winstan Bond, *Suburbanizing the Masses: Public Transport and Urban Expansion in the United States* (New York: Routledge, 2004).
56. George W. Hilton and John F. Due, *The Electric Interurban Railways in America* (Stanford, CA: Stanford University Press, 1960).
57. Barrett, Automobile and Urban Transit.
58. National Transportation Library, *Proceedings of the First National Conference on Street and Highway Safety* (Washington, DC: Government Printing Office, 1924).

59. Lawrence M. Friedman, *A History of American Law* (3rd ed., New York: Simon & Schuster, 2005).
60. Scott L. Bottles, *Los Angeles and the Automobile: The Making of the Modern City* (Berkeley: University of California Press, 1987).
61. Seely, Building the American Highway System.
62. Eno, Story of Highway Traffic Control.
63. Ann Henebery, "The rules of the road: Then versus now," Eno Center for Transportation, October 6, 2015, www.enotrans.org/article/the-rules-of-the-road-then-versus-now/ (last accessed October 30, 2025) (noting that William P. Eno was internationally recognized as a pioneer of traffic regulation and safety and referred to as the "Father of Traffic Safety").
64. McShane, Down the Asphalt Path, pp. 149–50.
65. AAA Foundation for Traffic Safety, "Our History," https://aaafoundation.org/about/our-history/ (last accessed August 13, 2025).
66. McShane, Down the Asphalt Path.
67. Norton, Fighting Traffic.
68. Seo, Policing the Open Road.
69. Norton, Fighting Traffic.
70. Miller McClintock, *Street Traffic Control* (New York: McGraw-Hill, 1925), p. 34.
71. Norton, Fighting Traffic, p. 205.
72. Herbert Hoover, "Address to the first national conference on street and highway safety."
73. McShane, Down the Asphalt Path.
74. Hoover, "Address to the first national conference on street and highway safety."
75. Norton, Fighting Traffic.
76. Seely, Building the American Highway System.
77. National Conference on Street and Highway Safety, *Uniform Vehicle Code* (Washington, DC 1926).
78. Seo, Policing the Open Road, pp. 102–06.
79. Norton, Fighting Traffic.
80. Miller McClintock, *Report and Recommendations of the Metropolitan Street Traffic Survey* (Chicago: Chicago Association of Commerce, 1926), p. 133.
81. Kirk Savage, *Monument Wars: Washington, D.C., the National Mall, and the Transformation of the Memorial Landscape* (Berkeley: University of California Press, 2009).
82. David W. Jones, *Mass Motorization and Mass Transit: An American History and Policy Analysis* (Bloomington: Indiana University Press, 2008).
83. National Committee on Uniform Traffic Laws and Ordinances, *Uniform Vehicle Code* (1969 ed., Washington, DC, 1969).
84. Federal Highway Administration, "Chapter 3: Traffic Laws and Regulations," FHWA Operations, https://ops.fhwa.dot.gov/publications/fhwahop20013/ch3.htm (last accessed October 30, 2025).
85. National Conference on Street and Highway Safety, *Model Municipal Traffic Ordinance* (Washington, DC: U.S. Department of Commerce, 1928).
86. "Model Traffic Code Indorsed," Los Angeles Times, October 7, 1928.
87. Norton, Fighting Traffic, p. 193.
88. Peter D. Norton, "Fighting traffic: The dawn of the motor age in the American city," PhD thesis, University of Virginia (2002), p. 242.
89. Peter D. Norton, "Street rivals: Jaywalking and the invention of the motor age street" (2007) 48 *Technology and Culture* 331–59 at 356.
90. Michael Lewyn, "The criminalization of walking" (2017) 2017(3) *Illinois Law Review* 1167–94 at 1170–71.

91. Michael, "Voluntary disclosure in a nineteenth-century American corporation," 74.
92. Albert Fishlow, "Capital markets during the nineteenth century and the interwar period" (1985) 39 *Explorations in Economic History* 227–53.
93. Alejandro Komai and Gary Richardson, "A brief history of regulations regarding financial markets in the United States: 1789 to 2009," NBER Working Paper No. 17443, 2011, www.nber.org/system/files/working_papers/w17443/w17443.pdf (last accessed November 13, 2025).
94. Joel Seligman, The Transformation of Wall Street.
95. Gary John Previts and William D. Samson, "Reporting for success: The Baltimore and Ohio railroad" (1999) 28 *Business History* 235–54.
96. Alfred D. Chandler Jr., *The Visible Hand: The Managerial Revolution in American Business* (Cambridge, MA: Harvard University Press, 1977), pp. 291–6, 319–22.
97. Richard Sylla and Robert E. Wright, "Corporate governance and stockholder democracy: The role of financial disclosure, 1790–1930," in Richard Sylla, Robert E. Wright, and David Cowen (eds.), *The Origins, History, and Future of the Federal Reserve: A Return to Jekyll Island* (Cambridge: Cambridge University Press, 2010), pp. 85–88.
98. Mark J. Roe, Strong Managers, Weak Owners.
99. Naomi R. Lamoreaux, *Insider Lending: Banks, Personal Connections, and Economic Development in Industrial New England* (Cambridge: Cambridge University Press, 1994).
100. National Association of Manufacturers, *Financial Statements: Their Use and Abuse* (New York 1938), p. 4.
101. Coffee, "Market failure," 719–22.
102. Mary O'Sullivan, *Dividends of Development: Securities Markets in the History of U.S. Capitalism, 1866–1922* (Oxford: Oxford University Press, 2016), pp. 118–22.
103. Gary John Previts and Barbara D. Merino, A *History of Accountancy in the United States: The Cultural Significance of Accounting* (Athens, OH: Ohio University Press, 1998), pp. 73–76.
104. Gary John Previts and William D. Samson, "Exploring the contents of the Baltimore and Ohio railroad annual reports: 1827–1856" (2000) 27 *Accounting Historians Journal* 1–42.
105. Paul J. Miranti Jr., "Corporate financial disclosure in the United States: 1850–1930" (1989) 13 *Accounting Historians Journal* 1–37 at 8–10.
106. Previts and Merino, A History of Accountancy in the United States.
107. "The United States Steel Corporation's annual report," *Scientific American*, 1902, p. 24.
108. Previts and Merino, A History of Accountancy in the United States, pp. 192–93.
109. "Prompt corporate accounting," *The Wall Street Journal*, May 23, 1902, p. 1.
110. "Judge Gary pleads for open business," The New York Times, November 13, 1910, p. 1.
111. Michael, "Voluntary disclosure in a nineteenth-century American corporation."
112. Jeffrey J. Archambault and Marie E. Archambault, "Financial reporting in 1920: The case of industrial companies" (2010) 37 *Accounting Historians Journal* 53–80.
113. New York Stock Exchange, "History of the NYSE," www.nyse.com/history-of-nyse (last accessed November 11, 2025).
114. Paul G. Mahoney, "The exchange as regulator" (1997) 83 *Virginia Law Review* 1453–500.
115. Robert Sobel, *N.Y.S.E.: A History of the New York Stock Exchange, 1935–1975* (New York: Weybright and Talley, 1975), pp. 17–18.
116. New York Stock Exchange, "Minutes of the governing committee," Entry for February 27, 1866 (New York Stock Exchange Archives, New York).
117. Birl E. Shultz, *Stock Exchange Procedure* (New York: New York Stock Exchange Institute, 1936).

118. Marty Butler, Arthur Kraft, and Ira S. Weiss, "The effect of reporting frequency on the timeliness of earnings: The cases of voluntary and mandatory interim reports" (2007) 43 *Journal of Accounting and Economics* 181–217.
119. Stephen A. Zeff, "Truth in accounting: The ordeal of Kenneth MacNeal" (1982) 57 *The Accounting Review* 528–53.
120. Thomas Bourveau et al., "Public company auditing around the Securities Exchange Act: Historical lessons for ESG assurance," Columbia Business School Research Paper No. 2021-04, 2025, https://business.columbia.edu/sites/default/files-efs/pubfiles/28461/BBKS_WP_2021.pdf (last accessed November 13, 2025).
121. Robert J. Daines and Charles M. Jones, "Truth or consequences: Mandatory disclosure and the impact of the 1934 act," Stanford Law and Finance Working Paper, 2012, https://law.stanford.edu/publications/truth-or-consequences-mandatory-disclosure-and-the-impact-of-the-1934-act/ at 14 (last accessed November 13, 2025).
122. Paul G. Mahoney and Jianping Mei, "Mandatory vs. contractual disclosure in securities markets: Evidence from the 1930s," University of Virginia Law School John M. Olin Program in Law and Economics Working Paper No. 25, 2006, https://law.bepress.com/cgi/viewcontent.cgi?article=1069&context=uvalwps (last accessed November 13, 2025).
123. Benston, "Required disclosure and the stock market."
124. Oliver Binz and John Graham, "The information content of corporate earnings: Evidence from the Securities Exchange Act of 1934," NBER Working Paper No. 29747, 2022, www.nber.org/papers/w29747 (last accessed November 13, 2025).
125. Paul Milgrom, Douglass North, and Barry Weingast, "The role of institutions in the revival of trade: The law merchant, private judges, and the champagne fairs" (1990) 2 *Economics & Politics* 1–23.
126. Stephen J. Choi and Andrew T. Guzman, "Portable reciprocity: Rethinking the international reach of private regulation" (1998) 71 *Southern California Law Review* 903–72.
127. Chris Brummer, *Soft Law and the Global Financial System: Rule Making in the 21st Century* (Cambridge: Cambridge University Press, 2012); Howell E. Jackson, "Regulation in a multisectored financial services industry: An exploratory essay" (1999) 77 *Washington University Law Quarterly* 319–97.
128. Reinier Kraakman, "Corporate liability strategies and the costs of legal controls" (1984) 93 *Yale Law Journal* 857–98; Eilís Ferran, *Building an EU Securities Market* (Cambridge: Cambridge University Press, 2004).
129. Jonathan R. Macey and Caroline Novogrod, "Enforcing self-regulatory organization's penalties and the nature of self-regulation" (1999) 40 *Hofstra Law Review* 963–1002; Roberta S. Karmel, "Should securities industry self-regulatory organizations be considered government agencies?" (2008) 14 *Stanford Journal of Law, Business & Finance* 151–200.
130. Gadinis and Jackson, "Markets as regulators," 1251–56; Gadinis, "The financial stability board," 162–68.
131. New York Stock Exchange, "Regulation," www.nyse.com/regulation (last accessed October 26, 2025).
132. 17 CFR § 240.19d-1 (2023) (providing the statutory framework requiring securities exchanges to maintain disciplinary and compliance mechanisms).
133. Jennifer G. Hill, "Regulatory responses to global corporate scandals" (2005) 23 *Wisconsin International Law Journal* 367–406 at 392–98.
134. Karmel, "Should securities industry self-regulatory organizations be considered government agencies?"; Saule T. Omarova, "Rethinking the future of self-regulation in the financial industry" (2010) 35 *Brooklyn Journal of International Law* 665–747.

135. Howell E. Jackson, "Centralization, competition, and privatization in financial regulation" (2001) 2 *Theoretical Inquiries in Law* 649–87.
136. 17 CFR § 240.19d-1 (2023).
137. Gadinis, "The financial stability board," 157–215.
138. Eilís Ferran, Elizabeth Howell, and Felix Steffek, *Principles of Corporate Finance Law* (3rd ed., Oxford: Oxford University Press, 2023), pp. 240–45.
139. Charles Goodhart, *The Basel Committee on Banking Supervision: A History of the Early Years 1974–1997* (Cambridge: Cambridge University Press, 2011); Büthe and Mattli, The New Global Rulers.
140. Walter Mattli and Tim Büthe, "Setting international standards: Technological rationality or primacy of power?" (2003) 56 *World Politics* 1–42.
141. Gadinis, "Three pathways to global standards."
142. Abbott and Snidal, "The governance triangle."
143. Black, "Constitutionalising self-regulation," 35–38.
144. Evelyn Goh and Lucille Chia, "Facebook's oversight board: Move fast with stable infrastructure and humility" (2021) 9 *Stanford Technology Law Review* 1–45.
145. Carpenter and Moss (eds.), *Preventing Regulatory Capture*.
146. Edward J. Kane, *The Regulatory Dialectic: Theory and Evidence in the Evolution of Financial Regulation* (San Francisco: Federal Reserve Bank of San Francisco, 1981); Coffee, Gatekeepers, pp. 215–22.
147. Marver H. Bernstein, *Regulating Business by Independent Commission* (Princeton, NJ: Princeton University Press, 1955); Steven Croley, *Regulation and Public Interests: The Possibility of Good Regulatory Government* (Princeton, NJ: Princeton University Press, 2008).
148. Richard L. Hasen, *Plutocrats United: Campaign Money, the Supreme Court, and the Distortion of American Elections* (New Haven, CT: Yale University Press, 2016), pp. 85–92.
149. Lee Drutman, *The Business of America Is Lobbying: How Corporations became Politicized and Politics became More Corporate* (Oxford: Oxford University Press, 2015).
150. Revolving Door Working Group, *A Matter of Trust: How the Revolving Door Undermines Public Confidence in Government – and What to Do about It* (Washington, DC: Government Accountability Project, 2005).
151. Elhauge, "Sacrificing corporate profits in the public interest," 745–50.
152. Kenneth W. Abbott et al. (eds), *International Organizations as Orchestrators* (Cambridge: Cambridge University Press, 2015).
153. Hill, "Regulatory responses to global corporate scandals," 392–98.
154. David P. Baron, *Business and Its Environment* (7th ed., Upper Saddle River, NJ: Pearson, 2013).
155. Neil Gunningham, Robert A. Kagan, and Dorothy Thornton, *Shades of Green: Business, Regulation, and Environment* (Stanford, CA: Stanford University Press, 2003).
156. David Vogel, *The Politics of Precaution: Regulating Health, Safety, and Environmental Risks in Europe and the United States* (Princeton, NJ: Princeton University Press, 2012).
157. David Vogel, *The Market for Virtue: The Potential and Limits of Corporate Social Responsibility* (Washington, DC: Brookings Institution Press, 2005), pp. 102–07 (explaining how CSR initiatives may substitute for more stringent legal regulation).
158. Cynthia A. Williams, "The Securities and Exchange Commission and corporate social transparency" (1999) 112 *Harvard Law Review* 1197–311 at 1220–35.
159. Bebchuk and Tallarita, "The illusory promise of stakeholder governance" (arguing that stakeholder-oriented governance rhetoric allows managers to avoid genuine accountability while appealing to policymakers).

160. Guido Berens, Cees B.M. van Riel, and Marius M. van Riel, "Corporate hypocrisy: When do consumers perceive a difference between corporate social responsibility and corporate social performance?" (2007) 44 *Journal of Business Ethics* 1–13.
161. Merritt B. Fox, "Required disclosure and corporate governance" (1999) 62(3) *Law & Contemporary Problems* 113–50.
162. Gunningham, Kagan, and Thornton, "Shades of green," pp. 215–18.

6 SAFETY IN THE RIDESHARE INDUSTRY

1. Jacques Bughin and Jan Mischke, "Exploding myths about the gig economy," McKinsey Global Institute, November 28, 2016, www.mckinsey.com/mgi/media-center/exploding-myths-about-the-gig-economy (last accessed October 27, 2025).
2. Ian Hathaway and Mark Muro, "Tracking the gig economy: New numbers," Brookings Institute, October 13, 2016, www.brookings.edu/articles/tracking-the-gig-economy-new-numbers (last accessed October 27, 2025).
3. Neil Irwin, "Can Uber live up to its $40 billion valuation?" The New York Times, June 13, 2014, www.nytimes.com/2014/06/14/upshot/ubers-real-challenge-leveraging-the-network-effect.html (last accessed October 27, 2025).
4. Dorine von Briel and Sara Dolnicar, "The evolution of Airbnb regulations," in Sara Dolnicar (ed.), *Airbnb Before, During and After COVID-19* (Brisbane: University of Queensland Press, 2021).
5. "United States Food and Drug Administration: New era of smarter food safety summit on e-commerce: Ensuring the safety of foods ordered online and delivered directly to consumers," October 19, 2021, www.fda.gov/media/154859/download (last accessed October 27, 2025).
6. Matt Beier, "Home improvements 101: Meet the taskers," TaskRabbit, April 8, 2020, www.taskrabbit.ca/blog/home-improvements-101-meet-the-taskers (last accessed October 27, 2025).
7. Moira McGregor et al., "On-demand taxi driving: Labour conditions, surveillance, and exclusion," Oxford Internet Institute, September 2015, https://blogs.oii.ox.ac.uk/ipp-conference/sites/ipp/files/documents/McGregor_Uber%2520paper%2520Sept%25201%2520PDF.pdf (last accessed October 27, 2025).
8. "Driving Danger: How Uber and Lyft create a safety crisis for their drivers," Strategic Organizing Center, April 2023, https://thesoc.org/wp-content/uploads/sites/342/SOC_RideshareDrivers_rpt-042023.pdf (last accessed October 27, 2025).
9. Elizabeth Pollman and Jordan M. Barry, "Regulatory entrepreneurship" (2017) 90 *Southern California Law Review* 383–448.
10. Michael D. Farren, Christopher Koopman, and Matthew D. Mitchell, "Rethinking taxi regulations: The case for fundamental reform," Mercatus Center, July 19, 2016, www.mercatus.org/research/research-papers/rethinking-taxi-regulations-case-fundamental-reform (last accessed October 28, 2025).
11. Lloyd's, "US: The emerging regulation of transportation network companies," April 24, 2015, www.lloyds.com/market-resources/regulatory-communications/news-articles/the-emerging-regulation-of-transportation-network-companies (last accessed October 28, 2025).
12. Rex Deighton-Smith, "Case 4. Ridesourcing services: regulatory challenges and regulatory approaches," in OECD/KDI, *Case Studies on the Regulatory Challenges Raised by Innovation and the Regulatory Responses* (Paris: OECD Publishing, 2021), pp. 77–95.

13. Jack Karsten and Darrell M. West, "Who protects workers in the on-demand economy?" Brookings Institute, August 27, 2015, www.brookings.edu/articles/who-protects-workers-in-the-on-demand-economy/ (last accessed October 28, 2025).
14. Rachel Zheliabovskii, "Gig work in California: Fueling the classification debate," Society for Human Resource Management, April 15, 2025, www.shrm.org/topics-tools/employment-law-compliance/gig-work-california-fueling-classification-debate (last accessed October 28, 2025).
15. Christopher Cadelago, "Uber to counter California's labor muscle with $30M political spend," Politico, January 24, 2024, www.politico.com/news/2024/01/24/uber-counter-california-labor-muscle-00137562 (last accessed October 28, 2025); Suhauna Hussain, Johana Bhuiyan, and Ryan Menezes, "How Uber and Lyft persuaded California to vote their way," Los Angeles Times, November 13, 2020, www.latimes.com/business/technology/story/2020-11-13/how-uber-lyft-doordash-won-proposition-22 (last accessed October 28, 2025).
16. David F. Larcker and Brian Tayan, "Governance gone wild: Epic misbehavior at Uber Technologies," in Rock Center for Corporate Governance at Stanford University (ed.), *Stanford Closer Look Series: Topics, Issues and Controversies in Corporate Governance* (Stanford, CA 2017), pp. 1–15.
17. Forbes, "Travis Kalanick," www.forbes.com/profile/travis-kalanick/ (last accessed October 28, 2025).
18. Ingrid Lunden, "Uber's Travis Kalanick on regulators: You have to grit your teeth, be a warrior, or do something less disruptive," TechCrunch, September 12, 2012, https://techcrunch.com/2012/09/12/ubers-travis-kalanick-on-regulators-you-have-to-grit-your-teeth-be-a-warrior-or-do-something-less-disruptive/ (last accessed October 28, 2025).
19. Peter Fisk, "Metcalfe's Law explains how the value of networks grows exponentially … exploring the 'network effects' of businesses such as Apple, Facebook, Trulia and Uber," February 17, 2020, www.peterfisk.com/2020/02/metcalfes-law-explains-how-the-value-of-networks-grow-exponentially-there-are-5-types-of-network-effects/ (last accessed October 29, 2025).
20. Eric Newcomer, "Lyft gaining on Uber as it spends big on growth," SFGate, April 15, 2016, www.sfgate.com/business/article/Lyft-gaining-on-Uber-as-it-spends-big-on-growth-7251625.php (last accessed October 29, 2025); Sydney P. Freedberg et al., "How Uber won access to world leaders, deceived investigators and exploited violence against its drivers in battle for global dominance," *International Consortium of Investigative Journalists*, July 10, 2022, www.icij.org/investigations/uber-files/uber-global-rise-lobbying-violence-technology/ (last accessed October 29, 2025).
21. Conor Sen, "Growing at the speed of Uber always comes at a cost," Bloomberg, July 10, 2017, www.bloomberg.com/opinion/articles/2017-07-10/growing-at-the-speed-of-uber-always-comes-at-a-cost (last accessed October 29, 2025).
22. Toby Graham, "A step-by-step guide to transforming your company's safety culture," KPA, August 6, 2025, https://kpa.io/blog/a-step-by-step-guide-to-transforming-your-companys-safety-culture/ (last accessed October 29, 2025).
23. Joy Borkholder et al., "Uber state interference: How transportation network companies buy, bully, and bamboozle their way to deregulation," National Employment Law Project, January 2018, www.nelp.org/app/uploads/2018/01/Uber-State-Interference-How-Transportation-Network-Companies-Buy-Bully-Bamboozle-Their-Way-to-Deregulation.pdf (last accessed October 29, 2025); Aarti Shahani, "In the battle between Lyft and Uber, the focus is on drivers," KQED, July 15, 2024, www.kqed.org/news/10837826/in-the-battle-between-lyft-and-uber-the-focus-is-on-drivers (last accessed October 29, 2025).

24. Susan Fowler, "Reflecting on one very, very strange year at Uber," February 19, 2017, www.susanjfowler.com/blog/2017/2/19/reflecting-on-one-very-strange-year-at-uber (last accessed October 29, 2025); Emily Steel, "Uber's festering sexual assault problem," The New York Times, August 6, 2025, www.nytimes.com/2025/08/06/business/uber-sexual-assault.html (last accessed October 29, 2025); Kate Conger, "Uber survived the spying scandal. Some careers didn't," The New York Times, November 28, 2021, www.nytimes.com/2021/12/06/technology/uber-spying-allegations.html (last accessed October 29, 2025).
25. BBC, "Uber discloses rape data after leak," March 7, 2016, www.bbc.com/news/technology-35746405 (last accessed December 8, 2025).
26. ABC News, "Uber driver accused of rape to India's shame," December 8, 2014, https://abcnews.go.com/International/uber-driver-accused-rape-indias-shame/story?id=27450040 (last accessed December 8, 2025).
27. Hubert Horan, "The Uber bubble: Why is a company that lost $20 billion claimed to be successful?" ProMarket, November 20, 2019, www.promarket.org/2019/11/20/the-uber-bubble-why-is-a-company-that-lost-20-billion-claimed-to-be-successful/ (last accessed October 30, 2025).
28. Lyft, "2020–2022 safety transparency report," 2024, https://assets.ctfassets.net/vz6nkkbc6q75/3yrOoaP4mPfTTvyaUZHJfJ/f77d145864edc540aa9f7fe530c6bcec/Safety_Transparency_Report_2020-2022.pdf (last accessed October 29, 2025).
29. Lauren Feiner, "Airbnb pushes new safety measures days after deadly party-house shooting," CNBC, November 6, 2019, www.cnbc.com/2019/11/06/airbnb-is-pushing-major-safety-changes.html (last accessed October 30, 2025).
30. Diana Milanesi, "The rise of the secondary trading of private company shares in the United States, Europe, and the United Kingdom: New opportunities and unique challenges," Stanford–Vienna TTLF Working Paper No. 46, 2019, https://law.stanford.edu/wp-content/uploads/2019/11/milanesi_wp46_.pdf (last accessed October 30, 2025).
31. Claire Brunel, "Comparing the investment behavior of public and private firms," *National Bureau of Economic Research*, January 1, 2012, www.nber.org/digest/jan12/comparing-investment-behavior-public-and-private-firms (last accessed October 30, 2025).
32. Manuel Calvente Orden, "What types of investors are there in financial markets?" BBVA, September 3, 2021, www.bbva.com/en/financial-health/what-types-of-investors-are-there-in-financial-markets/ (last accessed October 30, 2025).
33. Gordon L. Clark, "Risk management and institutional investors," in Gordon L. Clark et al. (eds.), *Managing Financial Risks: From Global to Local* (Oxford: Oxford University Press, 2009).
34. Saheli Roy Choudhury, "Uber officially announces Dara Khosrowshahi will be its new CEO," CNBC, August 29, 2017, www.cnbc.com/2017/08/29/uber-new-ceo-dara-khosrowshahi-officially-announced-as-new-chief.html (last accessed November 5, 2025).
35. Dara Khosrowshahi, "Getting serious about safety," Uber, April 12, 2018, www.uber.com/newsroom/getting-serious-safety/ (last accessed November 5, 2025).
36. Nat Levy, "Uber releases IPO documents, reports $11.3B in 2018 revenue, up 42% from 2017," GeekWire, April 11, 2019, www.geekwire.com/2019/uber-releases-ipo-documents-reports-11-3b-revenue-42-2017/ (last accessed November 5, 2025).
37. Michael J. de la Merced and Kate Conger, "Uber I.P.O. values ride-hailing giant at $82.4 billion," The New York Times, May 9, 2019, www.nytimes.com/2019/05/09/technology/uber-ipo-stock-price.html (last accessed November 5, 2025).
38. Alison Griswold, "How Lyft stacks up against Uber," Quartz, July 20, 2022, https://qz.com/1563536/how-lyft-stacks-up-against-uber (last accessed November 5, 2025).

39. Simon Mainwaring, “How Lyft drives growth through purpose,” Sustainable Brands, November 16, 2018, https://sustainablebrands.com/read/how-lyft-drives-growth-through-purpose (last accessed November 5, 2025).
40. “Host and guest safety,” Airbnb, www.airbnb.com/help/article/3063 (last accessed November 5, 2025); Joel Dreyfuss, “The Airbnb effect: Fueling start-up ecosystems around the world,” CNBC, May 22, 2018, www.cnbc.com/2018/05/22/the-airbnb-effect-fueling-start-up-ecosystems-around-the-world.html (last accessed November 5, 2025).
41. Laura Begley Bloom, “Is Airbnb safe? New report exposes scams, bug infestations, discrimination,” Forbes, October 11, 2021, www.forbes.com/sites/laurabegleybloom/2021/10/11/is-airbnb-safe-new-report-exposes-scams-bug-infestations-and-more/ (last accessed November 5, 2025).
42. Uber, “2017–2018 US safety report,” 2019, https://tb-static.uber.com/prod/udam-assets/drclg/UberUSSafetyReport_201718_FullReport.pdf (last accessed November 5, 2025).
43. Seth Rosenfeld, “CPUC proposes repealing secrecy of Uber, Lyft accident data,” San Francisco Public Press, February 11, 2020, www.sfpublicpress.org/cpuc-proposes-repealing-secrecy-of-uber-lyft-accident-data/ (last accessed November 5, 2025).
44. Greg Bensinger, “Sen. Blumenthal assails how Uber and Lyft deal with driver misconduct following Washington Post report,” The Washington Post, September 25, 2019, www.washingtonpost.com/technology/2019/09/25/sen-blumenthal-assails-how-uber-lyft-deal-with-driver-misconduct-following-washington-post-report/ (last accessed November 5, 2025).
45. Brittany Anthony, “Uber appeals California Public Utilities Commission ruling to protect privacy of sexual assault survivors,” Uber, January 14, 2021, www.uber.com/newsroom/protecting-survivor-privacy/ (last accessed November 5, 2025).
46. California Public Utilities Commission, “CPUC approves $9 million settlement with Uber,” December 2, 2021, www.cpuc.ca.gov/news-and-updates/all-news/cpuc-approves-9-million-settlement-with-uber (last accessed November 5, 2025).
47. Graham Rapier, “Uber made nearly $500 million from a ‘safe rides fee’ – and that money went straight to the company’s pockets,” Business Insider, August 27, 2019, www.businessinsider.com/uber-safe-rides-fee-500-million-profit-super-pumped-book-2019-8 (last accessed November 5, 2025).
48. Ellen Huet and Joel Rosenblatt, “Uber settles claims its ‘safe rides fee’ misled passengers,” Bloomberg, February 11, 2016, www.bloomberg.com/news/articles/2016-02-11/uber-settles-claims-its-safe-rides-fee-misled-passengers (last accessed November 5, 2025).
49. Tony West, “Uber delivers U.S. safety report,” Uber, December 6, 2019, www.uber.com/en-IL/newsroom/2019-us-safety-report/ (last accessed November 5, 2025).
50. Bryan Goebel, “Uber settles lawsuit with S.F. and L.A. District Attorneys,” KQED, April 7, 2016, www.kqed.org/news/10923008/uber-settles-lawsuit-with-s-f-and-l-a-district-attorneys (last accessed November 12, 2025).
51. Rebecca Bellan, “Uber facing lawsuit from dozens of women over sexual assaults by drivers,” TechCrunch, July 13, 2022, https://techcrunch.com/2022/07/13/uber-sued-by-550-women-and-counting-over-sexual-assaults-by-drivers (last accessed November 12, 2025).
52. Natasha Lomas, “Uber ends policy of forced arbitration for individual sexual assault claims,” TechCrunch, May 15, 2018, https://techcrunch.com/2018/05/15/uber-ends-policy-of-forced-arbitration-for-individual-sexual-assault-clams (last accessed November 12, 2025).
53. Sara Ashley O’Brien et al., “CNN investigation: 103 Uber drivers accused of sexual assault or abuse,” CNN Business, April 30, 2018, www.cnn.com/2018/09/28/tech/uber-driver-sexual-assault (last accessed November 12, 2025).

54. Mark Matousek, "Uber's top lawyer rejected the company's attempts to recruit him twice. Here's how CEO Dara Khosrowshahi finally won him over," Business Insider, April 22, 2021, www.businessinsider.com/tony-west-uber-dara-khosrowshahi-pepsi-2021-4 (last accessed November 12, 2025).
55. Andrew Cohen, "Uber Chief Legal Officer Tony West shares insights and lessons with Berkeley Law students," UC Berkeley Law, October 7, 2022, www.law.berkeley.edu/article/uber-chief-legal-officer-tony-west-shares-insights-and-lessons-with-berkeley-law-students/ (last accessed November 12, 2025).
56. Noam Noked, "Materiality and the fraud-on-the-market presumption," Harvard Law School Forum on Corporate Governance, October 16, 2012, https://corpgov.law.harvard.edu/2012/10/16/materiality-and-the-fraud-on-the-market-presumption (last accessed November 12, 2025).
57. Reinsurance Association of America, "Sexual misconduct," www.reinsurance.org/RAA/RAA/Legal-Tools/Insurance-Risks-Database/Active/Sexual%20Misconduct.aspx (last accessed November 12, 2025).
58. Jill E. Fisch, "Stealth governance: Shareholder agreements and private ordering" (2021) 99 *Washington University Law Review* 913–60.
59. Chad Sniffen, Julia Durnan, and Janine Zweig, "Helping industries to classify reports of sexual harassment, sexual misconduct, and sexual assault," National Sexual Violence Resource Center, November 12, 2018, www.raliance.org/wp-content/uploads/2018/11/helping-industries.pdf (last accessed November 12, 2025).
60. Uber, "2017–2018 US safety report," 41.
61. Uber, "2017–2018 US safety report," 6.
62. Uber, "2017–2018 US safety report," 10.
63. Cameron Kimble and Inimai M. Chettiar, "Sexual assault remains dramatically underreported," Brennan Center for Justice, October 4, 2018, www.brennancenter.org/our-work/analysis-opinion/sexual-assault-remains-dramatically-underreported (last accessed November 12, 2025).
64. Uber, "2017–2018 US safety report," 25.
65. Tad Devlin and Stacey Chiu, "Is your Uber driver or Lyfter an employee or independent contractor and why does it matter?" Thomson Reuters, June 2017, www.kaufmandolowich.com/wp-content/uploads/2017/07/Westlaw-Shared-Economy-Is-Uber-Driver-an-Employee-or-Independent-Devlin-June-2017.pdf (last accessed November 12, 2025).
66. Uber, "2019–2020 US safety report," 2022, https://drive.google.com/file/d/1r2gUgnux2MzM4YMi6D3nwHJb2UaZ5Yjv/view (last accessed November 12, 2025).
67. Bani Sapra, "Uber safety report reveals over 3,000 sexual assaults in US rides in 2018," Business Insider, December 5, 2019, www.businessinsider.com/uber-said-3000-sexual-assaults-reported-in-us-last-year-2019-12 (last accessed November 13, 2025).
68. Faiz Siddiqui, "Uber discloses 3,000 reports of sexual assault on U.S. rides last year in its long-awaited safety study," The Washington Post, December 5, 2019, www.washingtonpost.com/technology/2019/12/05/uber-disclosed-sexual-assaults-us-rides-last-year-its-long-awaited-safety-report/ (last accessed November 13, 2025).
69. Aarian Marshall, "A criminologist says Uber's crime report is 'highly alarming'," Wired, December 6, 2019, www.wired.com/story/criminologist-uber-crime-report-highly-alarming/ (last accessed November 13, 2025) (stating that "[a]ssault survivor advocacy groups praised Uber's release of the safety report, hailing the company' efforts as a high-water mark in transparency").
70. Matthew Feeney, "Study: Uber reduces drunk driving, increases vehicle theft," Cato Institute, June 2, 2016, www.cato.org/blog/study-uber-reduces-drunk-driving-increases-vehicle-theft (last accessed November 13, 2025).

71. Janine M. Zweig and Emily Tiry, "Three lessons businesses can learn from Uber's collecting and reporting sexual assault data," Urban Wire, December 6, 2019, www.urban.org/urban-wire/three-lessons-businesses-can-learn-ubers-collecting-and-reporting-sexual-assault-data (last accessed November 13, 2025).
72. Lyft, "Community safety report," October 20, 2021, www.lyft.com/blog/posts/lyfts-community-safety-report (last accessed November 13, 2025).
73. Uber, "2017–2018 US safety report," 61.
74. Spandana Singh, "Breaking down Uber's first safety transparency report," New America, December 6, 2019, www.newamerica.org/oti/blog/breaking-down-ubers-first-safety-transparency-report/ (last accessed November 13, 2025).
75. Bill Chappell, "London won't renew Uber's license, saying unauthorized drivers took 14,000 trips," NPR, November 25, 2019, www.npr.org/2019/11/25/782559740/london-wont-renew-uber-s-license-saying-unauthorized-drivers-took-14-000-trips (last accessed November 13, 2025).
76. Jason Wingard, "Uber's transparency gamble: How troubling safety disclosures are actually helping the company," Forbes, December 13, 2019, www.forbes.com/sites/jasonwingard/2019/12/13/ubers-transparency-gamble-how-troubling-safety-disclosures-are-actually-helping-the-company/ (last accessed November 13, 2025).
77. Jaclyn Diaz, "Facebook's new whistleblower is renewing scrutiny of the social media giant," NPR, October 4, 2021, www.npr.org/2021/10/04/1042921981/facebook-whistleblower-renewing-scrutiny-of-social-media-giant (last accessed November 13, 2025).
78. Uber, "2021–2022 US safety report," 2023, https://uber.app.box.com/s/lea3xzb70bp2wxe3k3dgk2ghcyr687x3 (last accessed November 13, 2025).
79. California Public Utilities Commission, "About the California Public Utilities Commission (CPUC)," www.cpuc.ca.gov/about-cpuc/cpuc-overview/about-us (last accessed November 13, 2025).
80. Ballotpedia, "California Public Utilities Commission," https://ballotpedia.org/California_Public_Utilities_Commission (last accessed November 13, 2025).
81. California Public Utilities Commission, "Presiding officer's decision imposing penalties against Uber Technologies, Inc. for violating the assigned administrative law judge's December 19, 2019 and January 27, 2020 rulings requiring information regarding sexual assault and sexual harassment claims," December 14, 2020, https://docs.cpuc.ca.gov/PublishedDocs/Efile/G000/M354/K636/354636771.PDF (last accessed November 13, 2025).
82. California Public Utilities Commission, "Administrative law judge's ruling ordering Uber Technologies, Inc. to file and serve its US safety report for 2017–2018 and to answer questions regarding alleged sexual assault and sexual misconduct incidents," December 19, 2019, https://docs.cpuc.ca.gov/PublishedDocs/Efile/G000/M322/K122/322122212.PDF (last accessed November 13, 2025).
83. California Public Utilities Commission, "Response of Uber Technologies, Inc. to the December 19, 2020 ALJ ruling ordering Uber Technologies, Inc. to file and serve its US safety report," December 20, 2021, https://docs.cpuc.ca.gov/PublishedDocs/Efile/G000/M326/K933/326933699.PDF (last accessed November 13, 2025).
84. Interview with the author, November 2, 2023, notes on file with the author.
85. California Public Utilities Commission, "Presiding officer's decision imposing penalties against Uber Technologies, Inc.," 2, 69.
86. Sean O'Kane, "Uber fined $59 million for dodging questions about sexual assaults," The Verge, December 14, 2020, www.theverge.cwwom/2020/12/14/22174943/uber-sexual-assault-fine-california-public-utility-commission-report-59-million (last accessed November 13, 2025).

87. Suhauna Hussain, "Judge fines Uber $59 million, threatens license in California over assault data," Los Angeles Times, December 15, 2020, www.latimes.com/business/technology/story/2020-12-15/california-fines-uber-59-million-threatens-license-over-refusal-to-disclose-sexual-assault-data (last accessed November 13, 2025).
88. California Public Utilities Commission, "Uber Technologies, Inc. appeal of presiding officer's decision imposing penalties against Uber Technologies, Inc.," December 20, 2012, https://docs.cpuc.ca.gov/PublishedDocs/Efile/G000/M359/K864/359864659.PDF (last accessed November 13, 2025).
89. California Public Utilities Commission, "E-mail ruling granting Rape, Abuse & Incest National Network motion for party status," August 28, 2020, https://docs.cpuc.ca.gov/PublishedDocs/Efile/G000/M345/K925/345925956.PDF (last accessed November 13, 2025).
90. Rape, Abuse & Incest National Network (RAINN), "RAINN's appeal of presiding officer's decision imposing penalties against Uber Technologies, Inc. for violating the assigned administrative law judge's 19 December 2019 and 27 January 2020 rulings requiring information regarding sexual assault and sexual harassment claims," January 11, 2021, https://perma.cc/MU8E-8B47 (last accessed November 13, 2025).
91. California Public Utilities Commission, "Decision adopting the settlement agreement between the Consumer Protection and Enforcement Division, Uber Technologies, Inc., and the Rape, Abuse & Incest National Network, Inc.," October 29, 2021, https://docs.cpuc.ca.gov/PublishedDocs/Published/G000/M427/K636/427636880.PDF (last accessed November 13, 2025).
92. Lisa Rayle and Onesimo Flores, "The 3 factors behind Uber and Lyft's regulatory win in California," TechCrunch, April 17, 2016, https://techcrunch.com/2016/04/17/the-3-factors-behind-uber-and-lyfts-regulatory-win-in-california/ (last accessed November 14, 2025).
93. National Association of Insurance Commissioners, "Commercial ride-sharing: Background," October 23, 2024, https://content.naic.org/insurance-topics/commercial-ride-sharing (last accessed November 14, 2025).
94. Insurance Information Institute, "Ride-sharing and insurance: Q&A," www.iii.org/article/ride-sharing-and-insurance-qa (last accessed November 14, 2025).
95. Annie Lowrey, "Can Lyft pull an Avis?" New York Magazine, June 30, 2015, https://nymag.com/intelligencer/2015/06/can-lyft-pull-an-avis.html (last accessed November 15, 2025).
96. California Public Utilities Commission, "Comments of Uber Technologies, Inc. on order instituting rulemaking," January 28, 2013, www.taxi-library.org/cpuc-2013/uber.pdf (last accessed November 15, 2025).
97. Kale Williams and Kurtis Alexander, "Uber sued over girl's death in S.F.," SFGate, January 28, 2014, www.sfgate.com/bayarea/article/uber-sued-over-girl-s-death-in-s-f-5178921.php (last accessed November 15, 2025).
98. Josh Constine, "Uber's denial of liability in girl's death raises accident accountability questions," TechCrunch, January 2, 2014, https://techcrunch.com/2014/01/02/should-car-services-provide-insurance-whenever-their-driver-app-is-open/ (last accessed November 15, 2025).
99. Yoonji Han, "How Lyft's lead lawyer built up an 'in-house law firm' to navigate the ridesharing company through tricky legal and regulatory pressures," Business Insider, September 2, 2020, www.businessinsider.com/lyft-general-counsel-svercheck-background-ridesharing-company-2020-8 (last accessed November 15, 2025).
100. Andrew G. Simpson, "If they try it, they'll like it: How ridesharing, autonomous cars will win over the public," *Insurance Journal*, January 23, 2018, www.insurancejournal.com/news/national/2018/01/23/478073.htm (last accessed November 15, 2025).

101. Anthony R. O'Donnell, "Kate Sampson joins REIN's advisory board," Insurance Innovation Reporter, October 16, 2019, https://iireporter.com/kate-sampson-joins-reins-advisory-board/ (accessed November 19, 2025).
102. Interview with author, October 23, 2025.
103. New York City Taxi and Limousine Commission, "Notice of promulgation," January 29, 2025, www.nyc.gov/assets/tlc/downloads/pdf/insurance_rule.pdf (last accessed November 15, 2025).
104. Marsh McLennan, "Marsh McLennan is the world's leading professional services firm in risk, strategy and people," www.marshmclennan.com/ (last accessed November 15, 2025).
105. Lyft, "All things insurance, all in one place," www.lyft.com/driver/insurance (last accessed November 15, 2025); State of California Department of Motor Vehicles, "Insurance requirements," www.dmv.ca.gov/portal/vehicle-registration/insurance-requirements/ (last accessed November 15, 2025).
106. Ryan Lawler, "On-demand ridesharing startup Lyft adds insurance between rides," TechCrunch, March 13, 2014, https://techcrunch.com/2014/03/13/lyft-insurance-between-rides/ (last accessed November 15, 2025).
107. Ingrid Lunden, "Following Lyft, Uber offers coverage to its U.S. drivers to close the 'insurance gap'," TechCrunch, March 14, 2014, https://techcrunch.com/2014/03/14/following-lyft-uber-offers-insurance-gap-coverage/ (last accessed November 15, 2025).
108. California Department of Insurance, "Insurance and Transportation Network Companies: Solving the insurance challenges so passengers, drivers, pedestrians and property owners are adequately protected," March 21, 2014, www.insurance.ca.gov/01-consumers/105-type/82-TNC-Ridesharing/upload/TNCBackground.pdf (last accessed November 15, 2025).
109. Senate Insurance Committee, "Bill analysis," www.leginfo.ca.gov/pub/13-14/bill/asm/ab_2251-2300/ab_2293_cfa_20140623_201427_sen_comm.html (last accessed November 15, 2025).
110. Colorado Public Radio, "Uber, Lyft become regulated in Colorado," June 6, 2014, www.cpr.org/2014/06/06/uber-lyft-become-regulated-in-colorado/ (last accessed November 15, 2025).
111. Uber, "Unfair rideshare insurance requirements raise costs for riders and affect drivers' ability to earn," www.uber.com/us/en/u/fair-insurance/ (last accessed November 15, 2025).
112. Allstate, "Occasional rideshare driving? Here's what to know about insurance," August 2025, www.allstate.com/resources/car-insurance/part-time-rideshare-insurance#:~:text=What%20is%20a%20rideshare%20endorsement,policy%20(which%20is%20more%20expensive) (last accessed November 15, 2025).

7 A CORPORATE FRAMEWORK FOR SUSTAINABILITY

1. Nate Perez and Rachel Waldholz, "Trump is withdrawing from Paris Agreement (again), reversing US climate policy," NPR, January 21, 2025, www.npr.org/2025/01/21/nx-s1-5266207/trump-paris-agreement-biden-climate-change (last accessed November 6, 2025).
2. European Commission, "Commission proposes to cut red tape and simplify business environment," February 26, 2025, https://commission.europa.eu/news/commission-proposes-cut-red-tape-and-simplify-business-environment-2025-02-26_en (last accessed November 6, 2025).

3. David A. Cifrino, "The politicization of ESG investing," Harvard ALI Social Impact Review, January 24, 2024, www.sir.advancedleadership.harvard.edu/articles/politicization-of-esg-investing (last accessed November 6, 2025).
4. Fairfax, "ESG's death defying future."
5. Greenhouse Gas Protocol, "Standards & guidance," https://ghgprotocol.org/standards-guidance (last accessed September 29, 2025).
6. Jessica F. Green, "Private standards in the climate regime: The Greenhouse Gas Protocol" (2010) 12 *Business & Politics* 1–37.
7. Su-Yol Lee, Yun-Seon Park, and Robert D. Klassen, "Market responses to firms' voluntary climate change information disclosure and carbon communication" (2015) 22 *Corporate Social Responsibility & Environmental Management* 1–12 at 2.
8. Daniel A. Farber, "Going private: Climate action by businesses and individuals" (2018) 71 *Vanderbilt Law Review En Banc* 197–218 at 203.
9. Pankaj Bhatia and Janet Ranganathan, "GHG Protocol: The gold standard for accounting for greenhouse gas emissions," Greenhouse Gas Protocol, October 4, 2011, https://ghgprotocol.org/blog/ghg-protocol-gold-standard-accounting-greenhouse-gas-emissions.
10. Carbon Trust, "What are Scope 3 emissions and why do they matter?" www.carbontrust.com/our-work-and-impact/guides-reports-and-tools/what-are-scope-3-emissions-and-why-do-they-matter (last accessed November 6, 2025).
11. Salesforce, "Accelerating value chain decarbonization by integrating supplier carbon data," www.salesforce.com/en-us/wp-content/uploads/sites/4/documents/white-papers/integrating-supplier-carbon-data-whitepaper.pdf (last accessed November 18, 2025).
12. Intergovernmental Panel on Climate Change, "About the IPCC," www.ipcc.ch/about/ (last accessed September 29, 2025).
13. Philip Shabecoff, "Global warming has begun, expert tells senate," The New York Times, June 24, 1988, www.nytimes.com/1988/06/24/us/global-warming-has-begun-expert-tells-senate.html (last accessed November 18, 2025).
14. Robert J. Brulle, "Advocating inaction: A historical analysis of the global climate coalition" (2023) 32 *Environmental Politics* 185–206.
15. John Browne, "Climate change – A new responsibility," Speech at Stanford University, May 19, 1997, bp-john-browne-stanford-1997-climate-change-speech-1.pdf (last accessed March 10, 2025).
16. David G. Victor and Joshua C. House, "BP's emissions trading system" (2006) 34 *Energy Policy* 2100–12.
17. John Browne, "Leading a global company: The case of BP," Speech, Yale School of Management (September 18, 1998).
18. Victor and House, "BP's emissions trading system," 2102.
19. Post Carbon Institute, "William Rees," www.postcarbon.org/our-people/william-rees/ (last accessed September 29, 2025).
20. Pam Reynolds, "The truth about carbon footprints," Conservation Law Foundation, May 5, 2025, www.clf.org/blog/the-truth-about-carbon-footprints/ (last accessed November 18, 2025).
21. Browne, "Climate change – a new responsibility."
22. Maxine Joselow, "Exclusive: GM, Ford knew about climate change 50 years ago," E&E News, October 26, 2020, www.eenews.net/articles/exclusive-gm-ford-knew-about-climate-change-50-years-ago/ (last accessed November 18, 2025).
23. Joselow, "GM, Ford knew about climate change 50 years ago."
24. Meredith Wadman, "Car maker joins exodus from anti-Kyoto coalition" (2000) 404 *Nature* 322.

25. Joan Magretta, "Growth through global sustainability: An interview with Monsanto's CEO, Robert B. Shapiro," Harvard Business Review, January–February 1997, https://hbr.org/1997/01/growth-through-global-sustainability-an-interview-with-monsantos-ceo-robert-b-shapiro (last accessed November 18, 2025).
26. Robert Shapiro, "The welcome tension of technology: The need for dialogue about agricultural biotechnology," in *Business Leaders: Thought and Action CEO Series*, Issue 37 (St. Louis: Center for the Study of American Business, Washington University, 2000), as cited in Jeremy Hall, Stelvia Matos, and Cooper H. Langford, "Social exclusion and transgenic technology: The case of Brazilian agriculture" (2008) 77 *Journal of Business Ethics* 45–63 at 49.
27. Kurt Eichenwald, "Redesigning nature: Hard lessons learned; Biotechnology food: From the lab to a debacle," The New York Times, January 25, 2001, www.nytimes.com/2001/01/25/business/redesigning-nature-hard-lessons-learned-biotechnology-food-lab-debacle.html (last accessed November 18, 2025).
28. European Commission, "2050 long-term strategy," https://climate.ec.europa.eu/eu-action/climate-strategies-targets/2050-long-term-strategy_en (last accessed October 2, 2025).
29. Reclaim Finance, "Assessment of ExxonMobil's climate strategy," May 2024. https://reclaimfinance.org/site/wp-content/uploads/2024/05/202405_Assessment-of-ExxonMobils-climate-strategy.pdf (last accessed October 2, 2025).
30. Matt Phillips, "Exxon's board defeat signals the rise of social-good activists," The New York Times, June 9, 2021, www.nytimes.com/2021/06/09/business/exxon-mobil-engine-no1-activist.html (last accessed November 18, 2025).
31. ExxonMobil, "Growing low carbon solutions," April 30, 2025, https://corporate.exxonmobil.com/sustainability-and-reports/advancing-climate-solutions/growing-low-carbon-solutions (last accessed September 30, 2025).
32. ExxonMobil, "ExxonMobil announces merger with Pioneer Natural Resources in an all-stock transaction," October 11, 2023, https://corporate.exxonmobil.com/news/news-releases/2023/1011_exxonmobil-announces-merger-with-pioneer-natural-resources-in-an-all-stock-transaction (last accessed September 30, 2025).
33. Chevron, "Chevron announces agreement to acquire Hess," October 23, 2023, www.chevron.com/newsroom/2023/q4/chevron-announces-agreement-to-acquire-hess (last accessed October 2, 2025).
34. Occidental, "Occidental to acquire CrownRock, strengthening its U.S. onshore portfolio with premier Permian Basin assets," December 11, 2023, www.oxy.com/news/news-releases/occidental-to-acquire-crownrock-strengthening-its-u.s.-onshore-portfolio-with-premier-permian-basin-assets (last accessed October 2, 2025).
35. Expand Energy, "Chesapeake Energy Corporation and Southwestern Energy to combine to accelerate America's energy reach," January 11, 2024, https://investors.expandenergy.com/news-releases/news-release-details/chesapeake-energy-corporation-and-southwestern-energy-combine (last accessed October 2, 2025).
36. Dieter Holger, "Norway's biggest private money manager exits from Exxon, Chevron over climate change," *The Wall Street Journal*, August 24, 2020, www.wsj.com/articles/norways-biggest-private-money-manager-exits-from-exxon-chevron-over-climate-change-11598294780 (last accessed November 18, 2025).
37. Stanley Reed, "Oil giants pump their way to bumper profits," The New York Times, February 2, 2024, www.nytimes.com/2024/02/02/business/oil-gas-companies-profits.html (last accessed November 18, 2025).
38. Gaurav Sharma, "A shareholders' revolt and 30% stock slump: Where next for BP?" Forbes, April 20, 2025, www.forbes.com/sites/gauravsharma/2025/04/20/a-shareholders-revolt-and-30-stock-slump-where-next-for-bp/ (last accessed November 18, 2025).

39. Ron Bousso, "BP halts hiring, slows renewables roll-out to win over investors," Reuters, June 27, 2024, www.reuters.com/business/energy/bp-halts-hiring-slows-renewables-roll-out-win-over-investors-2024-06-27/ (last accessed November 18, 2025).
40. Ron Bousso, "Shell weakens 2030 carbon emissions reduction target," Reuters, March 14, 2024, www.reuters.com/sustainability/climate-energy/shell-loosens-2030-carbon-emissions-target-2024-03-14/ (last accessed November 18, 2025).
41. Robert G. Eccles, "Is ExxonMobil's acquisition of Pioneer good news or bad news for climate change?" Forbes, January 20, 2024, www.forbes.com/sites/bobeccles/2024/01/20/is-exxonmobils-acquisition-of-pioneer-good-news-or-bad-news-for-climate-change/ (last accessed November 18, 2025).
42. World Resources Institute, "About us," www.wri.org/about (last accessed October 2, 2025).
43. Greenhouse Gas Protocol, "Standards & guidance," https://ghgprotocol.org/standards-guidance (last accessed October 2, 2025).
44. Hannah Momblanco, Kyla Aiuto, and Sarah Huckins, "Overview of GHG Protocol integration in regulatory climate disclosure rules," Greenhouse Gas Protocol, March 2024, https://ghgprotocol.org/sites/default/files/2024-03/GHG-Protocol-Integration.pdf (last accessed November 18, 2025).
45. Greenhouse Gas Protocol, "About us," https://ghgprotocol.org/about-us (last accessed October 4, 2025).
46. Green, "Private standards in the climate regime," 8.
47. Thomas Hickmann, "Voluntary global business initiatives and the international climate negotiations: A case study of the Greenhouse Gas Protocol" (2017) 169 *Journal of Cleaner Production* 94–104 at 97.
48. Bhatia and Ranganathan, "GHG Protocol: The gold standard."
49. World Resources Institute, "Safe climate, sound business: An action agenda," October 1, 1998, www.wri.org/research/safe-climate-sound-business (last accessed November 27, 2025)
50. Knight, "Greenhouse gangsters vs. climate justice."
51. Bhatia and Ranganathan, "GHG Protocol: The gold standard."
52. Florence Daviet and Margaret B. Yamashita (eds.), *The Greenhouse Gas Protocol: Designing a Customized Greenhouse Gas Calculation Tool* (Washington, DC: World Resources Institute, 2006), p. 4.
53. Hickmann, "Voluntary global business initiatives and the international climate negotiations," 97.
54. Bhatia and Ranganathan, "GHG Protocol: The gold standard."
55. Green, "Private standards in the climate regime," 10.
56. Greenhouse Gas Protocol, "Funders," https://ghgprotocol.org/funders (last accessed October 6, 2025).
57. Greenhouse Gas Protocol, "Land sector and removals guidance," https://ghgprotocol.org/land-sector-and-removals-guidance (last accessed October 6, 2025).
58. Greenhouse Gas Protocol, "Technical guidance for calculating scope 3 emissions," 2013, https://ghgprotocol.org/sites/default/files/standards/Scope3_Calculation_Guidance_0.pdf (last accessed October 7, 2025).
59. Madison Condon, "What's Scope 3 good for?" (2023) 56 *UC Davis Law Review* 1921–61.
60. Greenhouse Gas Protocol, "Companies complete road testing of new global greenhouse gas accounting standards," March 24, 2017, https://ghgprotocol.org/blog/companies-complete-road-testing-new-global-greenhouse-gas-accounting-standards (last accessed October 7, 2025).
61. Greenhouse Gas Protocol, "Product and scope 3 accounting and reporting standards," https://ghgprotocol.org/partners (last accessed October 7, 2025).

62. Greenhouse Gas Protocol, "List of final Scope 3 standard and product standard road testers," February 2010, https://ghgprotocol.org/sites/default/files/ghgp/list-of-roadtesters.pdf (last accessed October 7, 2025).
63. Greenhouse Gas Protocol, "History of the Corporate Value Chain Standard Development Process," https://ghgprotocol.org/history-corporate-value-chain-standard-development-process (last accessed October 7, 2025).
64. Greenhouse Gas Protocol, "Scope 3 standard (corporate value chain accounting and reporting standard), second edition," December 20, 2024, https://ghgprotocol.org/sites/default/files/2025-01/S3-SDP-20241220.pdf (last accessed October 7, 2025).
65. Kathleen McLaughlin, "Walmart suppliers lead the charge, help deliver Project Gigaton goal more than six years early," Walmart, February 21, 2024, https://corporate.walmart.com/news/2024/02/21/walmart-suppliers-lead-the-charge-help-deliver-project-gigaton-goal-more-than-six-years-early (last accessed November 18, 2025).
66. Microsoft, "Scope 3 emissions," December 11, 2024, https://learn.microsoft.com/en-us/industry/sustainability/calculate-scope3 (last accessed October 8, 2025).
67. Unilever, "Our climate transition action plan," 2024, www.unilever.com/sustainability/climate/our-climate-transition-action-plan/ (last accessed October 8, 2025).
68. Science Based Targets Initiative, "How to set science-based targets," https://sciencebasedtargets.org/how-to-set-science-based-targets (last accessed October 8, 2025).
69. Directive (EU) 2022/2464 of the European Parliament and of the Council of December 14, 2022 amending Regulation (EU) No 537/2014, Directive 2004/109/EC, Directive 2006/43/EC and Directive 2013/34/EU as regards corporate sustainability reporting (Corporate Sustainability Reporting Directive), OJ 2022 L 322, December 16, 2022, 15–80.
70. California Senate Bill 253, Climate Corporate Data Accountability Act (2023).
71. Josué C. Velázquez Martinez and Victoria Arnold (eds), *State of Supply Chain Sustainability 2024* (Cambridge, Mass. and Lombard, Ill.: MIT Center for Transportation & Logistics and Council of Supply Chain Management Professionals, 2024).
72. Hiroko Tabuchi, Ephrat Livni, and David Gelles, "S.E.C. approves new climate rules far weaker than originally proposed," The New York Times, March 6, 2024, www.nytimes.com/2024/03/06/climate/sec-climate-disclosure-regulations.html (last accessed May 15, 2025).
73. Yusuf Khan, "SEC votes to end defense of climate disclosure rules," *The Wall Street Journal*, March 28, 2025, www.wsj.com/articles/sec-votes-to-end-defense-of-climate-disclosure-rules-fc9091ba (last accessed November 6, 2025).
74. *Chamber of Commerce of the United States of America v. Randolph*, No. 2:24-cv-00801-ODW-PVC (CD Cal. 2024).
75. Andrew Ramonas, "California climate reporting law passed by Ninth Circuit," Bloomberg Law, November 18, 2025, https://news.bloomberglaw.com/esg/california-climate-disclosure-law-paused-by-ninth-circuit (last accessed December 15, 2025).
76. Council of the European Union, "Council and Parliament strike a deal to simplify sustainability reporting and due diligence requirements and boost EU competitiveness," December 9, 2025, www.consilium.europa.eu/en/press/press-releases/2025/12/09/council-and-parliament-strike-a-deal-to-simplify-sustainability-reporting-and-due-diligence-requirements-and-boost-eu-competitiveness/ (last accessed December 9, 2025).
77. Mark Segal, "EU lawmakers strike deal to cut sustainability reporting, due diligence laws," ESG Today, December 9, 2025, www.esgtoday.com/eu-lawmakers-strike-deal-to-cut-sustainability-reporting-due-diligence-laws/ (last accessed December 15, 2025).
78. Greenhouse Gas Protocol, "Corporate suite of standards and guidance update process," https://ghgprotocol.org/ghg-protocol-corporate-suite-standards-and-guidance-update-process (last accessed December 15, 2025).

79. Greenhouse Gas Protocol, "Scope 3 standard."
80. Greenhouse Gas Protocol, "GHG Protocol announces inaugural steering committee and independent standards board members," September 19, 2024, https://ghgprotocol.org/blog/release-ghg-protocol-announces-inaugural-steering-committee-and-independent-standards-board (last accessed December 15, 2025).
81. Hannah Momblanco, Kyla Aiuto, and Sarah Huckins, "Overview of GHG Protocol integration in regulatory climate disclosure rules," Greenhouse Gas Protocol, March 2024, https://ghgprotocol.org/sites/default/files/2024-03/GHG-Protocol-Integration.pdf (last accessed February 6, 2025).
82. National Association of Manufacturers, "Comment letter on SEC proposed rule" (warning that uncertainty and data limitations surrounding Scope 3 emissions would expose companies to heightened liability risk); Business Roundtable, "Comment letter on SEC proposed rule: The enhancement and standardization of climate-related disclosures for investors," June 17, 2022, https://s3.amazonaws.com/brt.org/2022.06.17-BRT.Countryman.TheEnhancementandStandardizationofClimate-RelatedDisclosuresforInvestors3.pdf (last accessed February 6, 2025) (contending that the SEC's Scope 3 disclosure requirement would be unduly burdensome, unlikely to yield consistent or decision-useful information for investors, and would heighten firms' legal and compliance exposure).
83. Tobias Busch, Matthew Johnson, and Timo Pioch, "Corporate carbon performance data: Quo vadis?" (2022) 26 *Journal of Industrial Ecology* 350–63 (noting that data stemming directly from reporting companies are significantly more reliable than secondary data from survey data, third-party estimation methods, or global average emission factors).
84. Terence C. Halliday and Gregory Shaffer, *Transnational Legal Orders* (Cambridge: Cambridge University Press, 2015) (explaining that transnational norms develop through recursive cycles of adoption, contestation, and revision rather than through linear accumulation).
85. Global System for Sustainable Development, "Pew Center on global climate change," https://gssd.mit.edu/search-gssd/site/pew-center-global-climate-change-53111-mon-07-23-2012-0903 (last accessed October 9, 2025).
86. Lee, Park, and Klassen, "Market responses to firms' voluntary climate change information," 1–2.
87. Eun-Hee Kim and Thomas Lyon, "When does institutional investor activism increase shareholder value? The Carbon Disclosure Project" (2011) 11 *The B.E. Journal of Economic Analysis & Policy* 1–29 at 3.
88. Maida Hadziosmanovic, Kian Rahimi, and Pankaj Bhatia, "Trends show companies are ready for Scope 3 reporting with US climate disclosure rule," World Resources Institute, June 24, 2022, www.wri.org/update/trends-show-companies-are-ready-scope-3-reporting-us-climate-disclosure-rule (last accessed October 9, 2025).
89. Robert G. Eccles and Alison Taylor, "The evolving role of chief sustainability officers," Harvard Business Review, July–August 2023, https://hbr.org/2023/07/the-evolving-role-of-chief-sustainability-officers (last accessed November 18, 2025).
90. Chitra Singla, "Key departments in an ESG team: Building a comprehensive strategy for sustainability," OneStop ESG, May 31, 2025, https://onestopesg.com/esg-news/key-departments-in-an-esg-team-building-a-comprehensive-strategy-for-sustainability-1748711729074 (last accessed October 19, 2025).
91. Global Reporting Initiative, "25 years of empowering sustainable decisions," September 15, 2022, www.globalreporting.org/news/news-center/25-years-of-empowering-sustainable-decisions/ (last accessed October 20, 2025).

92. Governance & Accountability Institute, "2020 S&P 500 flash report," July 16, 2020, www.ga-institute.com/research/research/sustainability-reporting-trends/2020-sp-500-flash-report/ (last accessed October 25, 2025).
93. Governance & Accountability Institute, "Sustainability reporting in focus," 2025, www.ga-institute.com/research/research/sustainability-reporting-trends/2025-sustainability-reporting-in-focus/ (last accessed December 12, 2025).
94. Teneo, "Stand by ESG? Our annual state of U.S. sustainability reports," September 2024, www.teneo.com/app/uploads/2024/09/Stand-by-ESG-Our-Annual-State-of-US-Sustainability-Reports.pdf (last accessed October 9, 2025).
95. Yan Lin et al., "Global evolution of environmental and social disclosure in annual reports" (2024) 62(5) *Journal of Accounting Research* 1941–88.
96. Kyla Aiuto, Sarah Huckins, and Hannah Momblanco, "What are greenhouse gas accounting and corporate climate disclosures? 6 questions, answered," World Resources Institute, March 7, 2024, www.wri.org/insights/ghg-accounting-corporate-climate-disclosures-explained (last accessed October 9, 2025).
97. Spencer Stuart, "Fortune 500 C-suite snapshot: Profiles in functional leadership," December 2023, file:///mnt/data/df0e1867-155b-4cba-8265-1a26ac424a13.pdf (last accessed October 9, 2025).
98. Adam B. Badawi and Robert Bartlett, "ESG overperformance? Assessing the use of ESG targets in executive compensation plans," Stanford Law and Economics Olin Working Paper No. 592, August 2024, file:///mnt/data/df0e1867-155b-4cba-8265-1a26ac424a13.pdf at 9 (last accessed October 9, 2025).
99. Center for Audit Quality, "S&P 500 and ESG reporting," June 2024, www.thecaq.org/sp-500-and-esg-reporting (last accessed October 19, 2025).
100. Brian Tayan, "ESG ratings: A compass without direction," Harvard Law School Forum on Corporate Governance, August 24, 2022, https://corpgov.law.harvard.edu/2022/08/24/esg-ratings-a-compass-without-direction/ (last accessed March 3, 2025); Florian Berg, Julian F. Koelbel, and Roberto Rigobon, "Aggregate confusion: The divergence of ESG ratings" (2022) 26 *Review of Finance* 1315–44.
101. Investor Group on Climate Change, "Companies' climate ambition contrasted by lack of detailed action plans," October 18, 2023, https://igcc.org.au/climate-action-100-assessments-of-global-companies-2023/ (last accessed December 15, 2025).
102. Albert C. Lin, "Making net zero matter" (2022) 79 *Washington and Lee Law Review* 679–767.
103. Desmond Butler and Steven Mufson, "Can the market save the planet? FedEx is the latest brand-name firm to say it's trying," The Washington Post, March 5, 2021, www.washingtonpost.com/climate-environment/2021/03/05/more-than-50-companies-have-vowed-be-carbon-neutral-by-2040/ (last accessed December 15, 2025) (quoting UC San Diego professor David Victor: "Net zero does not mean efficiency; it means complete transformation, and that's the challenge").
104. Institute of Sustainability Studies, "Nike CEO steps down following major cuts to sustainability team," October 30, 2024, https://instituteofsustainabilitystudies.com/insights/news-analysis/nike-ceo-steps-down-following-major-cuts-to-sustainability-team/ (last accessed December 15, 2025).
105. Annie Palmer, "Amazon lays off 'small number' of employees in communications and sustainability units," CNBC, January 29, 2025, www.cnbc.com/2025/01/29/amazon-cuts-some-jobs-in-its-communications-sustainability-units.html (last accessed December 15, 2025).
106. Heather Clancy, "Zendesk layoffs include director of sustainability," Trellis, March 3, 2025, https://trellis.net/article/zendesk-layoffs-include-director-of-sustainability/ (last accessed December 15, 2025).

107. Heather Clancy, "Sustainability pros join jobless ranks as ESG priorities shift," Trellis, March 6, 2025, https://trellis.net/article/sustainability-pros-join-historic-jobless-ranks/ (last accessed December 15, 2025).
108. Leafr, "The true state of sustainability," 2025, www.leafr.com/the-true-state-of-sustainability-2025-read-report (last accessed December 15, 2025).
109. Kenza Bryan, "Banks downgrade top sustainability roles," Financial Times, February 23, 2025, www.ft.com/content/f70876d6-b8f9-49b4-a6c3-206dfac9a210 (last accessed December 15, 2025).
110. Melodie Michel, "Is there really a recession in sustainability recruitment?" CSO Futures, October 1, 2025, www.csofutures.com/news/is-there-really-a-recession-in-sustainability-recruitment/ (last accessed December 15, 2025).
111. Kara Stiles, "New survey: Sustainability stays central to C-suite's vision amid global unrest, but leaders struggle to prove its ROI," Forbes, April 14, 2025, www.forbes.com/sites/forbes-research/2025/04/14/new-survey-sustainability-stays-central-to-c-suites-vision-amid-global-unrest-but-leaders-struggle-to-prove-its-roi/ (last accessed December 15, 2025).
112. Center for Corporate Environmental Performance, "The state of corporate sustainability disclosure 2025," 2025, www.ioes.ucla.edu/project/the-state-of-corporate-sustainability-disclosure-2025/ (last accessed December 15, 2025) (documenting increased uptake of climate-related disclosure among S&P 500 companies, with 69.5% now reporting Scope 3 emissions).
113. Salesforce, "Salesforce ranked #1 CRM provider for 11th consecutive year," May 1, 2024, www.salesforce.com/news/stories/idc-crm-market-share-ranking-2024/ (last accessed October 19, 2025).
114. Salesforce, "The history of Salesforce," www.salesforce.com/news/stories/the-history-of-salesforce/ (last accessed October 19, 2025).
115. Salesforce, "Salesforce announces strong fourth quarter fiscal 2024 results," February 28, 2024, www.salesforce.com/news/press-releases/2024/02/28/fy24-q4-earnings/ (last accessed October 19, 2025).
116. Fortune, "Fortune 500 full list (2024)," 2024, www.50pros.com/fortune500 (last accessed December 9, 2024).
117. Marc Benioff, *Trailblazer: The Power of Business as the Greatest Platform for Change* (New York: Crown Currency, 2019).
118. Salesforce, "Sustainability report FY2012," www.responsibilityreports.com/HostedData/ResponsibilityReportArchive/s/NYSE_CRM_2012.pdf (last accessed October 19, 2025).
119. Salesforce, "Marc and Lynne Benioff, Salesforce announce $300 million in investments to accelerate ecosystem restoration and climate justice," October 28, 2021, www.salesforce.com/news/press-releases/2021/10/28/marc-and-lynne-benioff-and-salesforce-announce-investment-to-accelerate-ecosystem-restoration-and-climate-justice/ (last accessed October 19, 2025).
120. Salesforce, "Salesforce achieves net zero residual emissions across its value chain and 100% renewable energy," September 21, 2021, www.salesforce.com/news/press-releases/2021/09/21/salesforce-achieves-net-zero-across-its-full-value-chain/ (last accessed October 19, 2025).
121. Benioff, Trailblazer.
122. Salesforce, "Marc Benioff speaks on planet's 'Climate Action, Silicon Valley, and the Road to COP26' panel," July 13, 2021, www.salesforce.com/news/stories/marc-benioff-speaks-on-planets-climate-action-silicon-valley-and-the-road-to-cop26-panel/ (last accessed October 19, 2025).

123. Salesforce, "12 Salesforce facts and figures you might not know," April 2025, www.salesforce.com/news/stories/salesforce-company-facts/ (last accessed October 19, 2025); Salesforce, "Our story," www.salesforce.com/company/our-story/ (last accessed October 19, 2025).
124. Salesforce, "Customer Stories," www.salesforce.com/customer-stories/ (last accessed October 19, 2025).
125. Green, "Private standards in the climate regime," 4.
126. Mick Brady, "Case study: Retooling carbon accounting – better business, healthier planet," *ISACA Journal*, vol 4 (2021), June 30, 2021, www.isaca.org/-/media/files/isacadp/project/isaca/articles/journal/2021/volume-4/retooling-carbon-accounting_joa_eng_0721.pdf (last accessed November 15, 2025).
127. Lyle Moran, "Climate lawsuits against largest fossil fuel producers have almost tripled," ESG Dive, September 25, 2024, www.esgdive.com/news/climate-lawsuits-against-largest-fossil-fuel-producers-have-almost-tripled/728069/ (last accessed November 18, 2025).
128. U.S. Securities and Exchange Commission, "Salesforce.com, Inc., Form 10-K for the Fiscal Year Ended January 31, 2020," www.sec.gov/ix?doc=/Archives/edgar/data/1108524/000110852420000014/crm-20200131.htm (last accessed October 19, 2025).
129. Joe Allanson, "Why Salesforce is urging corporations to support the SEC's climate disclosure rule," Salesforce, June 15, 2022, www.salesforce.com/news/stories/why-salesforce-is-urging-corporations-to-support-the-secs-climate-disclosure-rule/ (last accessed October 19, 2025).
130. Salesforce, "The mission to track emissions: Why we created Salesforce Sustainability Cloud," September 18, 2019, www.salesforce.com/news/stories/the-mission-to-track-emissions-why-we-created-salesforce-net-zero-cloud/ (last accessed October 19, 2025).
131. Brady, "Retooling carbon accounting," 36.
132. Salesforce, "The mission to track emissions."
133. Greenhouse Gas Protocol, "The Greenhouse Gas Protocol for the U.S. public sector," October 2010, https://ghgprotocol.org/sites/default/files/2022-12/us-public-sector-protocol_final_oct13.pdf (last accessed October 19, 2025).
134. Brady, "Retooling carbon accounting," 38.
135. U.S. Environmental Protection Agency, "GHG emission factors hub," January 16, 2025, www.epa.gov/climateleadership/ghg-emission-factors-hub (last accessed October 19, 2025); Intergovernmental Panel on Climate Change, "Fifth assessment report," www.ipcc.ch/assessment-report/ar5/ (last accessed October 19, 2025).
136. Brady, "Retooling carbon accounting," 38.
137. Salesforce, "The mission to track emissions."
138. Salesforce, "The mission to track emissions."
139. Brady, "Retooling carbon accounting," 41.
140. Salesforce, "Net Zero Cloud," www.salesforce.com/net-zero/cloud/ (last accessed March 3, 2025).
141. Salesforce, "Notice of the 2022 annual meeting and 2022 proxy statement," April 28, 2022, https://s205.q4cdn.com/626266368/files/doc_financials/2022/ar/Salesforce-2022-Proxy-Statement-1.pdf (last accessed October 19, 2025).
142. Salesforce, "Sustainability Exhibit," April 2022, www.salesforce.com/en-us/wp-content/uploads/sites/4/documents/legal/no-index/sustainability-exhibit.pdf (last accessed October 9, 2025).
143. Salesforce, "What is a sustainable supply chain?" www.salesforce.com/net-zero/cloud/what-is-sustainable-supply-chain/ (last accessed October 19, 2025).
144. Joel Makower, "Inside Salesforce's bold play for supply-chain leadership," Trellis, May 3, 2021. https://trellis.net/article/inside-salesforces-bold-play-supply-chain-leadership/ (last accessed October 19, 2025).

145. Tovin Lapan, "How Salesforce wants to make its supply chain more sustainable," Fortune, June 22, 2021, https://fortune.com/2021/06/22/salesforce-supply-chain-sustainability/ (last accessed October 9, 2025).
146. Salesforce, "Reducing value chain emissions by enabling supplier action," 2021, https://relayto.com/explore/reducing-value-chain-emissions-by-enabling-supplier-action-vquyorv5nx334/qwf7urGh1 (last accessed October 21, 2025).
147. Science Based Targets initiative, "Supplier engagement case study – Salesforce," https://sciencebasedtargets.org/companies-taking-action/case-studies/supplier-engagement-case-study-salesforce (last accessed January 8, 2025).
148. Salesforce, "Supplier sustainability," www.salesforce.com/company/supplier-sustainability/ (last accessed October 21, 2025).
149. Salesforce, "Reducing value chain emissions by enabling supplier action," 2021, www.salesforce.com/content/dam/web/en_us/www/documents/white-papers/salesforce-emissions-supplier-enablement.pdf (last accessed October 9, 2025).
150. Salesforce, "FY24 stakeholder impact report," 2024, www.salesforce.com/en-us/wp-content/uploads/sites/4/documents/white-papers/salesforce-fy24-stakeholder-impact-report.pdf (last accessed October 21, 2025).
151. Salesforce, "Sustainability Exhibit," 4.
152. Salesforce, "FY24 stakeholder impact report," 12.
153. Salesforce, "Schedules of selected environmental and social metrics," 2024, www.salesforce.com/en-us/wp-content/uploads/sites/4/documents/white-papers/salesforce-fy24-stakeholder-impact-report.pdf (last accessed October 21, 2025).

8 HOW TO GOVERN AI?

1. Interview with the author, October 10, 2023, notes on file with the author.
2. Bernard Marr, "A short history of ChatGPT: How we got to where we are today," Forbes, 19 May 2023, www.forbes.com/sites/bernardmarr/2023/05/19/a-short-history-of-chatgpt-how-we-got-to-where-we-are-today/ (last accessed September 22, 2025).
3. Sarah Kessler and Ephrat Livni, "The optimist's guide to artificial intelligence and work," The New York Times, May 20, 2023, www.nytimes.com/2023/05/20/business/dealbook/the-optimists-guide-to-artificial-intelligence-and-work.html (last accessed September 22, 2025).
4. Cade Metz, "What exactly are the dangers posed by A.I.?" The New York Times, May 1, 2023, www.nytimes.com/2023/05/01/technology/ai-problems-danger-chatgpt.html (last accessed September 22, 2025).
5. Emmet Lyons, "DeepSeek AI raises national security concerns, U.S. officials say," CBS News, January 29, 2025, www.cbsnews.com/news/deepseek-ai-raises-national-security-concerns-trump/ (last accessed September 22, 2025).
6. Interview with the author.
7. Interview with the author.
8. Jonathan B. Wiener, "The regulation of technology, and the technology of regulation" (2004) 26 *Technology in Society* 483–500.
9. Kevin Wei et al., "How do AI companies 'fine-tune' policy? Examining regulatory capture in AI governance" (2024) *Proceedings of the AAAI/ACM Conference on AI, Ethics, and Society* 1539–55 (observing that in rapidly evolving fields like AI, regulators struggle to keep pace and often rely on industry input, heightening risks of regulatory capture).

10. US Department of Defense, "Department of Defense releases the President's Fiscal Year 2025 defense budget," March 11, 2024, www.defense.gov/News/Releases/Release/Article/3703410/department-of-defense-releases-the-presidents-fiscal-year-2025-defense-budget/ (last accessed September 22, 2025).
11. Claudio Novelli et al., "A robust governance for the AI Act: AI Office, AI Board, Scientific Panel, and national authorities" (2025) 16 *European Journal of Risk Regulation* 566–90 (reporting an example of the conventional regulatory model, establishing compliance obligations, disclosure duties, and supervisory bodies for regulated AI systems).
12. Daniel E. Walters and Hannah J. Wiseman, "Self-regulation in emerging and innovative industries" (2025) 62 *Houston Law Review* 543–610 (documenting an example of the self-regulatory model, showing how companies can form industry-funded bodies to set standards and incorporate expert input).
13. Dario Amodei, "Anthropic CEO: Don't let AI companies off the hook," The New York Times, June 5, 2025, www.nytimes.com/2025/06/05/opinion/anthropic-ceo-regulate-transparency.html (last accessed September 22, 2025).
14. Judd Rosenblatt, "AI is learning to escape human control," *The Wall Street Journal*, June 1, 2025, www.wsj.com/opinion/ai-is-learning-to-escape-human-control-technology-model-code-programming-066b3ec5 (last accessed September 22, 2025).
15. Stuart Russell, "Provably beneficial artificial intelligence," in *The Next Step: Exponential Life* (Madrid: BBVA OpenMind, 2017), pp. 1–15.
16. Bill Gates, "The risks of AI are real but manageable," Gates Notes, July 11, 2023, www.gatesnotes.com/meet-bill/tech-thinking/reader/the-risks-of-ai-are-real-but-manageable (last accessed September 29, 2025); Marco Quiroz-Gutierrez, "Elon Musk says there's a 10%–20% chance AI 'goes bad'," Fortune, October 30, 2024, https://fortune.com/2024/10/30/elon-musk-ai-could-go-bad-existential-threat-xai-fundraising/ (last accessed September 29, 2025).
17. Damita Menezes, "AI will be smarter than humans in 20 years, 'godfather of AI' warns," NewsNation, August 4, 2025, www.newsnationnow.com/cuomo-show/ai-humans-20-years-godfather-of-ai-warns/ (last accessed September 29, 2025).
18. Maanak Gupta et al., "From ChatGPT to ThreatGPT: Impact of generative AI in cybersecurity and privacy" (2023) 11 *IEEE Access* 80218–45.
19. Daniel Thilo Schroeder et al., "How malicious AI swarms can threaten democracy," OSF Preprints, 2025, https://doi.org/10.31219/osf.io/qm9yk_v2 (last accessed October 10, 2025) (arguing that coordinated AI systems can fabricate messages, infiltrate communities, and manipulate public discourse at scale, posing systemic risks to democracy).
20. U.S. Department of Homeland Security, "DHS publishes guidelines and report to secure critical infrastructure and weapons of mass destruction from AI-related threats," April 29, 2024, www.dhs.gov/news/2024/04/29/dhs-publishes-guidelines-and-report-secure-critical-infrastructure-and-weapons-mass (last accessed September 29, 2025).
21. Darrell M. West, "How AI can enable public surveillance," Brookings, April 15, 2025, www.brookings.edu/articles/how-ai-can-enable-public-surveillance/ (last accessed September 30, 2025).
22. Charlie Savage, "Spy agency memo sets rules for artificial intelligence and Americans' private data," The New York Times, November 14, 2024, www.nytimes.com/2024/11/14/us/ai-privacy-guidelines-intelligence.html (last accessed September 30, 2025).
23. Jordyn Holman and Jeanna Smialek, "Will A.I. boost productivity? Companies sure hope so," The New York Times, April 1, 2024, www.nytimes.com/2024/04/01/business/economy/artificial-intelligence-productivity.html (last accessed September 30, 2025).
24. Noam Scheiber, "Which workers will A.I. hurt most: The young or the experienced?" The New York Times, July 7, 2025, www.nytimes.com/2025/07/07/business/ai-job-cuts.html (last accessed September 30, 2025).

25. Alexa Mikhail, "Microsoft claims its AI tool can diagnose complex medical cases four times more accurately than doctors," Fortune, July 3, 2025, https://fortune.com/2025/07/03/microsoft-ai-diagnostic-orchestrator-diagnosing-complex-cases-medical-doctors/ (last accessed September 30, 2025); Noam Scheiber, "Will A.I. upend white-collar work? Consider the Hollywood editor," The New York Times, July 30, 2024, www.nytimes.com/2024/07/30/business/economy/artificial-intelligence-hollywood-unions.html (last accessed September 30, 2025).
26. Jake Coyle, "In Hollywood writers' battle against AI, humans win (for now)," Associated Press, September 27, 2023, https://apnews.com/article/hollywood-ai-strike-wga-artificial-intelligence-39ab72582c3a15f77510c9c30a45ffc8 (last accessed September 30, 2025).
27. Molly Kinder et al., "Generative AI, the American worker, and the future of work," Brookings, October 10, 2024, www.brookings.edu/articles/generative-ai-the-american-worker-and-the-future-of-work/ (last accessed September 30, 2025).
28. Adam Satariano and Paul Mozur, "The global A.I. divide," The New York Times, June 21, 2025, www.nytimes.com/interactive/2025/06/23/technology/ai-computing-global-divide.html (last accessed September 30, 2025).
29. Sheera Frenkel, "The militarization of Silicon Valley," The New York Times, August 4, 2025, www.nytimes.com/2025/08/04/technology/google-meta-openai-military-war.html (last accessed September 30, 2025).
30. Lisa D. Ellis, "The benefits of the latest AI technologies for patients and clinicians," Harvard Medical School, August 30, 2024, https://learn.hms.harvard.edu/insights/all-insights/benefits-latest-ai-technologies-patients-and-clinicians (last accessed September 30, 2025).
31. Kevin Lynch, "The race for AI supremacy: A new frontier of international competition," Forbes, July 28, 2025, www.forbes.com/councils/forbestechcouncil/2025/07/28/the-race-for-ai-supremacy-a-new-frontier-of-international-competition/ (last accessed September 30, 2025).
32. Tripp Mickle, "Nvidia says U.S. will restrict sales of more of its A.I. chips to China," The New York Times, April 15, 2025, www.nytimes.com/2025/04/15/technology/nvidia-h20-chip-china-restrictions.html (last accessed September 30, 2025).
33. Alec Tyson and Emma Kikuchi, "Growing public concern about the role of artificial intelligence in daily life," Pew Research Center, August 28, 2023, www.pewresearch.org/short-reads/2023/08/28/growing-public-concern-about-the-role-of-artificial-intelligence-in-daily-life/ (last accessed September 30, 2025).
34. David Goldman, "How OpenAI so royally screwed up the Sam Altman firing," CNN, November 20, 2023, www.cnn.com/2023/11/19/tech/sam-altman-open-ai-firing-board (last accessed September 30, 2025).
35. Matt O'Brien, "ChatGPT-maker OpenAI fires CEO Sam Altman, the face of the AI boom, for lack of candor with company," Associated Press, November 18, 2023, https://apnews.com/article/altman-ai-chatgpt-murati-893e4a460c10eb3a8f1afefa6156eca3 (last accessed September 30, 2025).
36. OpenAI, "OpenAI announces leadership transition," November 17, 2023, https://openai.com/index/openai-announces-leadership-transition/ (last accessed September 30, 2025).
37. Matt O'Brien and Haleluya Hadero, "OpenAI brings back Sam Altman as CEO just days after his firing unleashed chaos," Associated Press, November 22, 2023, https://apnews.com/article/altman-openai-chatgpt-31187f7f6eca8ff9d0eef7585aac6ace (last accessed September 30, 2025).
38. OpenAI, "Our structure," 2023, https://openai.com/our-structure (last accessed September 30, 2025); OpenAI, "Introducing OpenAI," December 11, 2015, https://openai.com/index/introducing-openai/ (last accessed September 30, 2025).

39. Ty Roush, "More than 700 OpenAI employees threaten to quit – and join Microsoft – unless board resigns," Forbes, November 20, 2023, www.forbes.com/sites/tylerroush/2023/11/20/more-than-500-openai-employees-threaten-to-quit-over-sam-altmans-removal/ (last accessed September 30, 2025).
40. Deepa Seetharaman and Tom Dotan, "Sam Altman rejoins OpenAI board along with three new directors," *The Wall Street Journal*, March 8, 2024, www.wsj.com/tech/ai/openai-board-brings-sam-altman-back-adds-three-new-members-bbdb4807 (last accessed September 30, 2025).
41. Medium, "OpenAI in the context of steward-ownership – blog post 1 on the 'OpenAI saga'," December 20, 2023, https://medium.com/@purpose_network/openai-in-the-context-of-steward-ownership-blog-post-1-on-the-openai-saga-dd07fea9eecd (last accessed September 30, 2025).
42. OpenAI, "Helen Toner joins OpenAI's board of directors," September 8, 2021, https://openai.com/index/helen-toner-joins/ (last accessed September 30, 2025).
43. Andrew Imbrie, Owen J. Daniels, and Helen Toner, "Decoding intentions: artificial intelligence and costly signals," Center for Security and Emerging Technology, 2023, https://cset.georgetown.edu/wp-content/uploads/CSET-Decoding-Intentions.pdf at 27 (last accessed September 30, 2025).
44. Cade Metz, Tripp Mickle, and Mike Isaac, "Before Altman's ouster, OpenAI's board was divided and feuding," The New York Times, November 21, 2023, www.nytimes.com/2023/11/21/technology/openai-altman-board-fight.html (last accessed September 30, 2025).
45. Meghan Bobrowsky and Deepa Seetharaman, "The OpenAI board member who clashed with Sam Altman shares her side," *The Wall Street Journal*, December 7, 2023, www.wsj.com/tech/ai/helen-toner-openai-board-2e4031ef (last accessed September 30, 2025).
46. Jemma Green, "Elon Musk's lawsuit against OpenAI sparks debate over AI transparency," Forbes, March 7, 2024, www.forbes.com/sites/jemmagreen/2024/03/07/elon-musks-lawsuit-against-openai-sparks-debate-over-ai-transparency/ (last accessed September 30, 2025).
47. Adi Robertson, "Elon Musk sues OpenAI for abandoning its mission to benefit humanity," The Verge, March 1, 2024, www.theverge.com/2024/3/1/24087473/elon-musk-openai-lawsuit-nonprofit-mission (last accessed September 30, 2025); Elon Musk v. OpenAI et al., *Complaint* (Superior Court of California, County of San Francisco, February 29, 2024), www.courthousenews.com/wp-content/uploads/2024/02/musk-v-altman-openai-complaint-sf.pdf (last accessed September 30, 2025).
48. Kyle Wiggers, "Most of OpenAI's employees threaten to quit if Sam Altman isn't reappointed CEO," TechCrunch, November 20, 2023, https://techcrunch.com/2023/11/20/most-of-openais-employees-threaten-to-quit-if-sam-altman-isnt-reappointed-ceo/ (last accessed September 30, 2025).
49. Cade Metz, "OpenAI's chief scientist and co-founder is leaving the company," The New York Times, May 14, 2024, www.nytimes.com/2024/05/14/technology/ilya-sutskever-leaving-openai.html (last accessed September 30, 2025).
50. Gerrit De Vynck and Nitasha Tiku, "AI execs used to beg for regulation. Not anymore," The Washington Post, May 8, 2025, www.washingtonpost.com/technology/2025/05/08/altman-congress-openai-regulation/ (last accessed September 30, 2025).
51. Sam Altman, "Sam Altman on the future of AI and humanity," TED, January 7, 2025, www.ted.com/pages/sam-altman-on-the-future-of-ai-and-humanity-transcript (last accessed September 30, 2025).
52. Sam Altman, "The intelligence age," September 23, 2024, https://ia.samaltman.com/ (last accessed September 30, 2025).

53. OpenAI, "OpenAI LP," March 11, 2019, https://openai.com/index/openai-lp/ (last accessed September 30, 2025).
54. Livemint, "Three senior OpenAI researchers resign after CEO Sam Altman ousted," November 18, 2023, www.livemint.com/ai/artificial-intelligence/sam-altman-ousted-tthree-senior-openai-researchers-resign-11700299676106.html (last accessed September 30, 2025).
55. Andrej Karpathy, X, November 19, 2023, https://x.com/karpathy/status/1726289070345855126 (last accessed September 30, 2025).
56. Cade Metz and Karen Weise, "Microsoft to invest $10 billion in OpenAI, the creator of ChatGPT," The New York Times, January 23, 2023, www.nytimes.com/2023/01/23/business/microsoft-chatgpt-artificial-intelligence.html (last accessed September 30, 2025).
57. Microsoft, "OpenAI forms exclusive computing partnership with Microsoft to build new Azure AI supercomputing technologies," July 22, 2019, https://news.microsoft.com/source/2019/07/22/openai-forms-exclusive-computing-partnership-with-microsoft-to-build-new-azure-ai-supercomputing-technologies/ (last accessed September 30, 2025).
58. Shanthi Rexaline, "Microsoft, investors stand solidly behind 'once in a generation' CEO Sam Altman, putting OpenAI board under pressure," Benzinga, November 19, 2023, www.benzinga.com/analyst-ratings/analyst-color/23/11/35865361/microsoft-investors-stand-solidly-behind-once-in-a-generation-ceo-sam-altman-puttin (last accessed September 30, 2025).
59. Jacob Kastrenakes and Tom Warren, "Hundreds of OpenAI employees threaten to resign and join Microsoft," The Verge, November 20, 2023, www.theverge.com/2023/11/20/23968988/openai-employees-resignation-letter-microsoft-sam-altman (last accessed September 30, 2025).
60. OpenAI Employees, "Letter to the OpenAI board," DocumentCloud, November 20, 2023, www.documentcloud.org/documents/24172377-letter-to-the-openai-board (last accessed September 30, 2025).
61. Tom Gerken, "Microsoft offers to match pay of all OpenAI staff," BBC, November 21, 2023, www.bbc.com/news/technology-67484455 (last accessed September 30, 2025).
62. Dina Bass and Rachel Metz, "Microsoft picks Dee Templeton as OpenAI board observer," Bloomberg Law, January 5, 2024, https://news.bloomberglaw.com/artificial-intelligence/microsoft-picks-dee-templeton-as-openai-board-observer (last accessed September 30, 2025).
63. Jeremy Khan, "DeepMind spins out new Alphabet company focused on drug discovery," Fortune, November 4, 2021, https://fortune.com/2021/11/04/deepmind-spins-out-alphabet-company-isomorphic-drug-discovery-company/ (last accessed September 30, 2025).
64. John Jumper et al., "Highly accurate protein structure prediction with AlphaFold" (2021) 596 *Nature* 583–89.
65. Protein Structure Prediction Center, "CASP14 press release," December 1, 2020, https://predictioncenter.org/casp14/doc/CASP14_press_release.html (last accessed September 30, 2025).
66. DeepMind, "AlphaFold: A solution to a 50-year-old grand challenge in biology," Google DeepMind Blog, November 30, 2020, https://deepmind.google/discover/blog/alphafold-a-solution-to-a-50-year-old-grand-challenge-in-biology/ (last accessed September 30, 2025).
67. Madhumita Murgia, "DeepMind research cracks structure of almost every known protein," Financial Times, July 28, 2022, www.ft.com/content/6a088953-66d7-48db-b61c-79005a0a351a (last accessed September 30, 2025).
68. Anastassis Perrakis and Titia K. Sixma, "AI revolutions in biology: The joys and perils of AlphaFold" (2021) 28 *Nature Structural & Molecular Biology* 649–50.

69. Thomas C. Terwilliger et al., "AlphaFold predictions are valuable hypotheses and accelerate but do not replace experimental structure determination" (2024) 21 *Nature Methods* 13–24.
70. Priscila S. F. C. Gomes, Diego E. B. Gomes, and Rafael C. Bernardi, "Protein structure prediction in the era of AI: Challenges and limitations when applying to *in silico* force spectroscopy" (2022) 2 *Frontiers in Bioinformatics* 983306.
71. Derek Lowe, "AlphaFold's place in the world," *Science*, December 11, 2023, www.science.org/content/blog-post/alphafold-s-place-world (last accessed September 30, 2025).
72. Oleg Kovalevskiy, Juan Mateos-Garcia, and Kathryn Tunyasuvunakool, "AlphaFold two years on: Validation and impact" (2024) 121 *Proceedings of the National Academy of Sciences* e2315002121.
73. Pankaj Malik et al., "Utilizing AlphaFold predictions to understand protein function and dynamics," ResearchGate, January 2024, www.researchgate.net/publication/377895875_utilizing_alphafold_predictions_to_understand_protein_function_and_dynamics (last accessed September 30, 2025).
74. Ali Burak Ünal, Nico Pfeifer, and Mete Akgün, "A privacy-preserving approach for cloud-based protein fold recognition" (2024) 5 *Patterns* 101023.
75. Ewen Callaway, "Could AI-designed proteins be weaponized? Scientists lay out safety guidelines," *Nature*, March 8, 2024, www.nature.com/articles/d41586-024-00699-0 (last accessed September 30, 2025).
76. Brendan Bordelon, "The fight over AI biosecurity risk takes a twist," *Politico*, February 6, 2024, www.politico.com/newsletters/digital-future-daily/2024/02/06/the-fight-over-ai-biosecurity-risk-takes-a-twist-00139945 (last accessed September 30, 2025).
77. Andriy Kryshtafovych et al., "Critical Assessment of Methods of Protein Structure Prediction (CASP) – round XIII" (2019) 27 *Proteins: Structure, Function, and Bioinformatics* 323–38.
78. Koray Kavukcuoglu et al., "How our principles helped define AlphaFold's release," Google DeepMind Blog, September 14, 2022, https://deepmind.google/discover/blog/how-our-principles-helped-define-alphafolds-release/ (last accessed September 30, 2025).
79. Andrew W. Senior et al., "Improved protein structure prediction using potentials from deep learning" (2020) 577 *Nature* 706–10.
80. EMBL-EBI, "About us," www.ebi.ac.uk/about/ (last accessed September 30, 2025).
81. Mihaly Varadi et al., "AlphaFold protein structure database: massively expanding the structural coverage of protein-sequence space with high-accuracy models" (2022) 50 *Nucleic Acids Research* D439–44.
82. Anne Trafton, "Analyzing the potential of AlphaFold in drug discovery," MIT News, September 6, 2022, https://news.mit.edu/2022/alphafold-potential-protein-drug-0906 (last accessed September 30, 2025).
83. Derek Lowe, "Why AlphaFold won't revolutionize drug discovery," *Chemistry World*, August 5, 2022, www.chemistryworld.com/opinion/why-alphafold-wont-revolutionise-drug-discovery/4016051.article (last accessed September 30, 2025).
84. Perrakis and Sixma, "AI revolutions in biology."
85. Olivia Shone, "5 key features and benefits of large language models," Microsoft Blog, October 9, 2024, www.microsoft.com/en-us/microsoft-cloud/blog/2024/10/09/5-key-features-and-benefits-of-large-language-models/ (last accessed September 30, 2025).
86. Cade Metz and Karen Weise, "A.I. is getting more powerful, but its hallucinations are getting worse," The New York Times, May 5, 2025, www.nytimes.com/2025/05/05/technology/ai-hallucinations-chatgpt-google.html (last accessed September 30, 2025).

87. Muhammad Muzammil Rawjan, "The ethical AI imperative: How OpenAI is leading the way in responsible development," RT Insights, February 21, 2024, www.rtinsights.com/the-ethical-ai-imperative-how-openai-is-leading-the-way-in-responsible-development/ (last accessed September 30, 2025).
88. "Amoral drift in AI corporate governance" (2025) 138 *Harvard Law Review* 1633–56 at 1634.
89. Natalia Garrido-Skurkowicz, Rafael Wittek, and Chaïm la Roi, "Performance of hybrid organizations: Challenges and opportunities for social and commercial enterprises" (2022) 15 *Journal of Social Entrepreneurship* 1058–87 (drawing on empirical evidence to examine the governance challenges and tensions hybrid organizations face in balancing social and commercial logics).
90. Devin Coldewey, "OpenAI shifts from nonprofit to 'capped-profit' to attract capital," TechCrunch, March 11, 2019, https://techcrunch.com/2019/03/11/openai-shifts-from-nonprofit-to-capped-profit-to-attract-capital/ (last accessed September 30, 2025).
91. Microsoft, "Microsoft and OpenAI extend partnership," January 23, 2023, https://blogs.microsoft.com/blog/2023/01/23/microsoftandopenaiextendpartnership/ (last accessed September 30, 2025).
92. Connie Loizos, "Sam Altman's leap of faith," TechCrunch, May 18, 2019, https://techcrunch.com/2019/05/18/sam-altmans-leap-of-faith/ (last accessed September 30, 2025).
93. Sigal Samuel, "OpenAI as we knew it is dead," Vox, September 26, 2024, www.vox.com/future-perfect/374275/openai-just-sold-you-out (last accessed September 30, 2025).
94. Gary Marcus, "OpenAI's Sam Altman is becoming one of the most powerful people on earth. We should be very afraid," The Guardian, August 3, 2024, www.theguardian.com/technology/article/2024/aug/03/open-ai-sam-altman-chatgpt-gary-marcus-taming-silicon-valley (last accessed September 30, 2025).
95. Robert Hart, "Sam Altman cut from OpenAI's startup fund – here's what the ChatGPT maker invests in," Forbes, April 2, 2024, www.forbes.com/sites/roberthart/2024/04/02/sam-altman-cut-from-openais-startup-fund-heres-what-the-chatgpt-maker-invests-in/ (last accessed September 30, 2025).
96. Keach Hagey, "The secrets and misdirection behind Sam Altman's firing from OpenAI," *The Wall Street Journal*, March 28, 2025, www.wsj.com/tech/ai/the-real-story-behind-sam-altman-firing-from-openai-efd51a5d (last accessed September 30, 2025).
97. Hagey, "The secrets and misdirection behind Sam Altman's firing from OpenAI."
98. Wired, "More than 730 OpenAI staff threaten to quit after Sam Altman ouster," November 20, 2023, www.wired.com/story/openai-staff-walk-protest-sam-altman (last accessed September 30, 2025).
99. Max Zahn, "Sam Altman hired by Microsoft, 600 OpenAI employees threaten to quit in protest of his ouster," ABC News, November 20, 2023, https://abcnews.go.com/Business/sam-altman-hired-microsoft-600-openai-employees-threaten/story?id=104942311 (last accessed September 30, 2025).
100. Ellen Glover, "Anthropic: What we know about the company behind Claude AI," Built In, November 12, 2025, https://builtin.com/artificial-intelligence/anthropic-ai (last accessed November 15, 2025).
101. Anthropic, "The long-term benefit trust," May 29, 2023, www.anthropic.com/news/the-long-term-benefit-trust (last accessed September 30, 2025).
102. Billy Perrigo, "How Anthropic designed itself to avoid OpenAI's mistakes," Time, May 30, 2024, https://time.com/6983420/anthropic-structure-openai-incentives (last accessed September 30, 2025).

103. Alex Kantrowitz, "After OpenAI's chaos, Anthropic has an opportunity (and its own untraditional board)," Big Technology, December 1, 2023, www.bigtechnology.com/p/after-openais-chaos-anthropic-has (last accessed September 30, 2025).
104. Bebchuk and Tallarita, "The illusory promise of stakeholder governance," 100–05 (arguing that broad stakeholder commitments lack operational content and fail to provide managers with concrete guidance for resolving trade-offs).
105. Krystal Hu, "OpenAI removes Sam Altman's ownership of its startup fund," Reuters, April 1, 2024, www.reuters.com/technology/openai-removes-sam-altmans-ownership-its-startup-fund-2024-04-01 (last accessed October 1, 2025).
106. Anca Dragan et al., "Taking a responsible path to AGI," DeepMind Blog, April 2, 2025, https://deepmind.google/blog/taking-a-responsible-path-to-agi/ (last accessed September 30, 2025).
107. Jonas Schuett et al., "Towards best practices in AGI safety and governance: A survey of expert opinion," arXiv, May 11, 2023, https://doi.org/10.48550/arXiv.2305.07153 (last accessed September 30, 2025).
108. Anne-Claire Pache, Julie Battilana, and Channing Spencer, "An integrative model of hybrid governance: The role of boards in helping sustain organizational hybridity" (2024) 67(2) *Academy of Management Journal* 437–67 (arguing that sustaining hybrid organizations requires governance mechanisms beyond managerial discretion, as boards must actively manage trade-offs between competing logics).
109. Fernando Delgado et al., "Stakeholder participation in AI: Beyond 'add diverse stakeholders and stir'," arXiv, November 1, 2021, https://arxiv.org/abs/2111.01122 (last accessed September 30, 2025) (arguing that effective governance requires not just including diverse stakeholders but also structuring deliberation, negotiation, and communication about trade-offs).
110. Reuters, "OpenAI responds to warnings of self-governance by former board members, the Economist Reports," May 30, 2024, www.reuters.com/technology/openai-responds-warnings-self-governance-by-former-board-members-economist-2024-05-30 (last accessed October 1, 2025).
111. Anup Banerjee, Martin Carlsson-Wall, and Mattias Nordqvist, "Hybrid board governance: Exploring the challenges in implementing social impact measurements" (2024) 56(5) *The British Accounting Review* 101359 (arguing that hybrid governance structures can provide space for social mission but struggle with implementation, measurement, and accountability); Liliana Ávila and Marlene Amorim, "Operational challenges in hybrid organizations: Insights for future research," in João Reis, Marlene Amorim, Nuno Melão, and Paulo Matos (eds.), *Operations and Service Management* (Hershey, PA: IGI Global, 2017) 955–73 (discussing how hybrid organizations face inherent tensions in aligning social and commercial goals, creating complexity in translating missions into practice).
112. Qinghua Lu et al., "Responsible AI pattern catalogue: A collection of best practices for AI governance and engineering" (2024) 56(7) *ACM Computing Surveys* Art 173, 1–35.
113. Jacob Metcalf and Ranjit Singh, "Scaling up mischief: Red-teaming AI and distributing governance" (2024) 6(2) *Harvard Data Science Review* 1–7.
114. OpenAI, "GPT-4o system card," August 8, 2024, https://openai.com/index/gpt-4o-system-card (last accessed October 1, 2025).
115. Anthropic, "Anthropic's Responsible Scaling Policy," September 19, 2023, www.anthropic.com/news/anthropics-responsible-scaling-policy (last accessed October 1, 2025).
116. Margaret Mitchell et al., "Model cards for model reporting" (2019) *Proceedings of the Conference on Fairness, Accountability, and Transparency (FAT*)* 220–29.

117. OpenAI, "GPT-4 system card," 2023, https://cdn.openai.com/papers/gpt-4-system-card .pdf (last accessed October 1, 2025); Anthropic, "System card: Claude Opus 4 & Claude Sonnet 4," https://anthropic.com/model-card (last accessed October 1, 2025); Meta, "System cards: A new resource for understanding how AI systems work," November 16, 2022, https://ai.meta.com/blog/system-cards-a-new-resource-for-understanding-how-ai-systems-work (last accessed October 1, 2025).
118. Yuntao Bai et al., "Constitutional AI: Harmlessness from AI feedback," arXiv, 2022, https://arxiv.org/abs/2212.08073 (last accessed September 30, 2025).
119. Anthropic, "Collective constitutional AI: Aligning a language model with public input," October 17, 2023, www.anthropic.com/research/collective-constitutional-ai-aligning-a-language-model-with-public-input (last accessed October 1, 2025).
120. Ian W. Eisenberg, Lucía Gamboa, and Eli Sherman, "The unified control framework: Establishing a common foundation for enterprise AI governance, risk management and regulatory compliance," arXiv, 2025, https://arxiv.org/abs/2503.05937 (last accessed September 30, 2025).
121. Natasha Crampton, "Reflecting on our responsible AI program: Three critical elements for progress," Microsoft, May 1, 2023, https://blogs.microsoft.com/on-the-issues/2023/05/01/responsible-ai-standards-principles-governance-progress (last accessed October 1, 2025).
122. Natasha Crampton, "Microsoft's framework for building AI systems responsibly," Microsoft, June 21, 2022, https://blogs.microsoft.com/on-the-issues/2022/06/21/microsofts-framework-for-building-ai-systems-responsibly (last accessed October 1, 2025).
123. Satya Nadella, "The partnership of the future," Slate, June 18, 2016, https://slate.com/technology/2016/06/microsoft-ceo-satya-nadella-humans-and-a-i-can-work-together-to-solve-societys-challenges.html (last accessed October 1, 2025).
124. Mike Murphy, "Microsoft CEO Satya Nadella has 10 commandments for how AI and humans should act," Quartz, July 20, 2022, https://qz.com/microsoft-ceo-satya-nadella-has-10-commandments-for-how-ai-and-humans-should-act-1849195111 (last accessed October 1, 2025).
125. Nadella, "The partnership of the future."
126. Microsoft, "Responsible AI Standard: Reference guide, version 2," June 2022, https://it1.com/wp-content/uploads/2024/03/Microsoft-Responsible-AI-Standard-Reference-Guide.pdf (last accessed October 1, 2025).
127. Brad Smith, "Meeting the AI moment: Advancing the future through responsible AI," Microsoft, February 2, 2023, https://blogs.microsoft.com/on-the-issues/2023/02/02/responsible-ai-chatgpt-artificial-intelligence (last accessed October 1, 2025).
128. Microsoft, "Responsible AI transparency report 2025," 2025, https://cdn-dynmedia-1 .microsoft.com/is/content/microsoftcorp/microsoft/msc/documents/presentations/CSR/Responsible-AI-Transparency-Report-2025-vertical.pdf#page=31 at 31 (last accessed October 1, 2025).
129. Natasha Crampton, "Advancing AI responsibly," Microsoft, 2023, https://unlocked .microsoft.com/responsible-ai (last accessed October 1, 2025).
130. Teresa Hudson and Natasha Crampton, "Our 2025 responsible AI transparency report: How we build, support our customers, and grow," Microsoft, June 20, 2025, https://blogs .microsoft.com/on-the-issues/2025/06/20/our-2025-responsible-ai-transparency-report (last accessed October 1, 2025).
131. Microsoft Research Asia, "Societal AI: Research challenges and opportunities," March 2025, www.microsoft.com/en-us/research/wp-content/uploads/2025/03/Societal-AI-Research-Challenges-and-Opportunities.pdf at 12 (last accessed October 1, 2025).

132. Microsoft, "AI principles and approach," www.microsoft.com/en-us/ai/principles-and-approach (last accessed August 12, 2025).
133. Microsoft, "Responsible AI standard v2 – general requirements," June 2022, https://msblogs.thesourcemediaassets.com/sites/5/2022/06/Microsoft-Responsible-AI-Standard-v2-General-Requirements-3.pdf at 4 (last accessed October 1, 2025).
134. Microsoft, "Transparency note for Microsoft 365 Copilot," August 6, 2025, https://learn.microsoft.com/en-us/copilot/microsoft-365/microsoft-365-copilot-transparency-note (last accessed October 1, 2025).
135. Carlo Giovine et al., "Building AI trust: The key role of explainability," QuantumBlack, November 26, 2024, www.mckinsey.com/capabilities/quantumblack/our-insights/building-ai-trust-the-key-role-of-explainability (last accessed October 1, 2025).
136. Greg Satell and Yassmin Abdel-Magied, "AI fairness isn't just an ethical issue," Harvard Business Review, October 20, 2020, https://hbr.org/2020/10/ai-fairness-isnt-just-an-ethical-issue (last accessed October 6, 2025).
137. Daria Korobenko, Anastasija Nikiforova, and Rajesh Sharma, "Towards a privacy and security-aware framework for ethical AI: Guiding the development and assessment of AI systems," *Proceedings of the 25th Annual International Conference on Digital Government Research* (ACM 2024).
138. Microsoft Azure, "Chapter 1: Understanding security and responsible AI," Security and Responsible AI Guide, 2025, https://azure.github.io/Security-and-Responsible-AI-Guide/chapters/chapter_01_understanding_security_and_responsible_ai (last accessed October 6, 2025).
139. Alex Fleck, "Responsible AI: Why it matters and how we're infusing it into our internal AI projects at Microsoft," Microsoft Blog, June 5, 2025, www.microsoft.com/insidetrack/blog/responsible-ai-why-it-matters-and-how-were-infusing-it-into-our-internal-ai-projects-at-microsoft/ (last accessed October 6, 2025).
140. Joyce Chou, Roger Ibars, and Oscar Murillo, "In pursuit of inclusive AI," Microsoft Inclusive Design, 2023, https://inclusive.microsoft.design/tools-and-activities/InPursuitofInclusiveAI.pdf (last accessed October 6, 2025).
141. Lama Lteif et al., "A conceptual framework for marketplace inclusion" (2025) 44(2) *Journal of Public Policy & Marketing* 214–31 (arguing that inclusive design and marketing practices expand participation by addressing exclusionary barriers and creating access for diverse consumer groups).
142. Dean Carignan, "Lessons from Microsoft's responsible AI journey," Emerj, February 15, 2023, https://emerj.com/lessons-from-microsofts-responsible-ai-journey-dean-carignan-microsoft/ (last accessed October 6, 2025).
143. James Darley, "Inside Microsoft's 2025 responsible AI transparency report," AImagazine, June 24, 2025, https://aimagazine.com/articles/inside-microsofts-2025-responsible-ai-transparency-report (last accessed October 6, 2025) (highlighting Microsoft's steps toward openness and accountability as regulators and customers scrutinize AI governance more intensely).
144. Casey Ross and Brittany Trang, "Microsoft is selling AI in health care, and helping to set its standards: is that a problem?" STAT+, April 18, 2024, www.statnews.com/2024/04/18/microsoft-health-care-artificial-intelligence-regulatory-capture/ (last accessed October 6, 2025).
145. Malak Sadek et al., "Challenges of responsible AI in practice: scoping review and recommended actions" (2025) 40 *AI & Society* 199–215.
146. Edwin A. Farley and Christian R. Lansang, "AI auditing: First steps towards the effective regulation of artificial intelligence systems" (2025) 38 *Harvard Journal of Law & Technology Digest* (Spring) 1–41 at 38 (proposing government-mandated AI auditing as a

necessary foundation for enforceable regulatory oversight); Brian Judge, Mark Nitzberg, and Stuart Russell, "When code isn't law: Rethinking regulation for artificial intelligence" (2025) 44 *Policy & Society* 85–97 (arguing that AI's scale and opacity demand direct governmental regulation and oversight rather than reliance on voluntary or industry-led self-regulation).

147. Eric Horvitz, "The Aether Committee at Microsoft," erichorvitz.com, 2019, https://erichorvitz.com/Aether_Committee_Microsoft.htm (last accessed October 6, 2025).
148. Crampton, "Reflecting on our responsible AI program."
149. Todd Bishop, "Microsoft is turning down some sales over AI ethics, top researcher Eric Horvitz says," GeekWire, October 30, 2018, www.geekwire.com/2018/microsoft-cutting-off-sales-ai-ethics-top-researcher-eric-horvitz-says/ (last accessed October 6, 2025).
150. Natasha Crampton, "The building blocks of Microsoft's responsible AI program," Microsoft, January 19, 2021, https://blogs.microsoft.com/on-the-issues/2021/01/19/microsoft-responsible-ai-program/ (last accessed December 17, 2025).
151. Crampton, "Reflecting on our responsible AI program."
152. Ernie Fernandez, "7 top questions government leaders are asking about AI," Microsoft, 2023, https://wwps.microsoft.com/blog/top-questions-ai (last accessed October 6, 2025).
153. Microsoft, "Artificial intelligence overview," 2025, https://learn.microsoft.com/en-us/compliance/assurance/assurance-artificial-intelligence (last accessed October 6, 2025).
154. Microsoft, "Responsible AI transparency report 2024," May 2024, https://cdn-dynmedia-1.microsoft.com/is/content/microsoftcorp/microsoft/msc/documents/presentations/CSR/Responsible-AI-Transparency-Report-2024.pdf (last accessed November 18, 2025).
155. Microsoft, "AI RMF RFI comments," 2022, www.nist.gov/document/ai-rmf-rfi-comments-microsoft (last accessed October 6, 2025).
156. Microsoft, "Responsible AI standard v2 – general requirements," 6.
157. Microsoft, "Microsoft responsible AI impact assessment template," 2022, https://msblogs.thesourcemediaassets.com/sites/5/2022/06/Microsoft-RAI-Impact-Assessment-Template.pdf (last accessed October 6, 2025).
158. Microsoft, "Responsible AI standard v2 – general requirements," A1.1.
159. Microsoft, "Artificial intelligence overview."
160. Microsoft, "Reflecting on our responsible AI program."
161. Microsoft, "Responsible AI transparency report 2025."
162. Microsoft, "Governing AI: A blueprint for the future," May 25, 2023, https://cdn-dynmedia-1.microsoft.com/is/content/microsoftcorp/microsoft/msc/documents/presentations/CSR/Governing-AI-A-Blueprint-for-the-Future.pdf at 10 (last accessed October 6, 2025).
163. Microsoft, "Putting principles into practice: How we approach responsible AI at Microsoft," 2020, www.microsoft.com/cms/api/am/binary/RE4pKH5 at 12 (last accessed October 6, 2025).
164. Microsoft, "Governing AI: A blueprint for the future," 34.
165. Michael Smith and Seumas Miller, "The ethical application of biometric facial recognition technology" (2022) 37 *AI & Society* 167–75; Robin A. Waelen, "The struggle for recognition in the age of facial recognition technology" (2023) 3 *AI and Ethics* 215–22.
166. Microsoft, "Code of conduct for Microsoft AI services," 2025, https://learn.microsoft.com/en-us/legal/ai-code-of-conduct at § 19 (last accessed October 13, 2025); Masha Borak, "Microsoft further limits law enforcement use of its facial recognition," Biometric Update, May 3, 2024, www.biometricupdate.com/202405/microsoft-further-limits-law-enforcement-use-of-its-facial-recognition (last accessed October 13, 2025).
167. Axon, "How Axon is using AI responsibly," 2024, www.axon.com/resources/how-axon-is-using-ai-responsibly (last accessed October 13, 2025); Axon, "A closer look at Draft One," 2024, www.axon.com/resources/closer-look-draft-one (last accessed October 13, 2025).

168. Leah Culler, "Are you talking to me? Azure AI brings iconic characters to life with custom neural voice," Microsoft, February 3, 2021, https://news.microsoft.com/source/features/ai/custom-neural-voice-ga/ (last accessed October 7, 2025).
169. Eric Hal Schwartz, "Microsoft restricts custom voice and facial recognition AI access," Voicebot.ai (Synthedia), June 21, 2022, https://voicebot.ai/2022/06/21/microsoft-restricts-custom-voice-and-facial-recognition-ai-access/ (last accessed October 13, 2025).
170. Betsy Weber, "Tech for food: Giving a voice to the voiceless," Microsoft Tech Community, August 20, 2024, https://techcommunity.microsoft.com/blog/mvpawardprogramblog/tech-for-good-giving-a-voice-to-the-voiceless/4217303 (last accessed October 7, 2025).
171. Allison Koenecke et al., "Racial disparities in automated speech recognition" (2020) 117 *Proceedings of the National Academy of Sciences* 7684–89.
172. Shaun Sutner, "Microsoft reins in AI facial and voice recognition tech," TechTarget, June 23, 2022, www.techtarget.com/searchenterpriseai/news/252521952/Microsoft-reins-in-AI-facial-and-voice-recognition-tech (last accessed October 13, 2025).
173. The White House, "Winning the race: America's AI action plan," July 2025, www.whitehouse.gov/wp-content/uploads/2025/07/Americas-AI-Action-Plan.pdf (last accessed November 23, 2025).
174. United States, Preparing Americans for high-paying skilled-trade jobs of the future, 90 Fed. Reg. 26148 (28 April 2025); The White House, "Removing barriers to American leadership in artificial intelligence," January 23, 2025, www.whitehouse.gov/presidential-actions/2025/01/removing-barriers-to-american-leadership-in-artificial-intelligence/ (last accessed November 23, 2025).
175. Bobby Allyn, "Trump's new AI policies keep culture war focus on tech companies," NPR, 23 July 2025, www.npr.org/2025/07/23/nx-s1-5476771/trump-artificial-intelligence-woke-eo (last accessed November 23, 2025).
176. The White House, "Winning the race: America's AI action plan."
177. One Big Beautiful Bill Act, Pub. L. No. 119–21, 139 Stat. 72 (2025).
178. Will Oremus, "In dramatic reversal, Senate votes to kill AI-law moratorium," The Washington Post, July 1, 2025 www.washingtonpost.com/politics/2025/07/01/ai-moratorium-big-beautiful-bill/ (last accessed November 23, 2025); Regina Sam Penti and Ama A. Adams, "AI and tech under the One Big Beautiful Bill Act: Key restrictions, risks and opportunities," *Ropes & Gray*, July 14, 2025, www.ropesgray.com/en/insights/alerts/2025/07/ai-and-tech-under-the-one-big-beautiful-bill-act-key-restrictions-risks-and-opportunities (last accessed November 25, 2025).
179. The White House, "Winning the race: America's AI action plan," 2.
180. Office of the Governor of California, "Governor Newsom signs SB 53, advancing California's world-leading artificial intelligence industry," September 29, 2025, www.gov.ca.gov/2025/09/29/governor-newsom-signs-sb-53-advancing-californias-world-leading-artificial-intelligence-industry/ (last accessed November 25, 2025); Erin M. Bosman et al., "At the frontier – California enacts AI safety and transparency regulation TFAIA (SB 53)," Morrison & Foerster, October 1, 2025, www.mofo.com/resources/insights/251001-california-enacts-ai-safety-transparency-regulation-tfaia-sb-53 (last accessed November 22, 2025).
181. Javier Espinoza, "EU agrees landmark rules on artificial intelligence," Financial Times, December 9, 2023, www.ft.com/content/cc8a1b0d-e676-44b2-a4ab-69a8b28232a5 (last accessed November 25, 2025).
182. European Commission, "Regulatory framework proposal on artificial intelligence: Questions & answers," April 21, 2021, https://ec.europa.eu/commission/presscorner/detail/en/qanda_21_1683 (last accessed November 22, 2025).

183. European Union, "Article 5: Prohibited AI practices," AI Act Service Desk, https://ai-act-service-desk.ec.europa.eu/en/ai-act/article-5 (last accessed November 23, 2025); European Parliament, "Texts adopted – Artificial Intelligence Act," June 14, 2023, www.europarl.europa.eu/docco/document/TA-9-2023-0236_EN.html (last accessed November 25, 2025).
184. Regulation (EU) 2024/1689 of the European Parliament and of the Council of June 13, 2024 laying down harmonised rules on artificial intelligence (Artificial Intelligence Act), OJ L, July 12, 2024.
185. AIA, Arts 9 and 17.
186. AIA, Art 12.
187. AIA, Arts 19–21.
188. European Union, "The AI Office: What is it, and how does it work?" March 21, 2024, https://artificialintelligenceact.eu/the-ai-office-summary/ (last accessed November 25, 2025).
189. Benjamin Mueller, "How much will the (EU) AI Act cost?" Center for Data Innovation, July 2021, www2.datainnovation.org/2021-aia-costs.pdf (last accessed November 25, 2025).
190. Pascale Davies, "Why OpenAI's voice mode, Meta's Llama and Apple's AI won't be coming to Europe yet," Euronews, October 8, 2024, www.euronews.com/next/2024/10/08/why-openais-voice-mode-metas-llama-and-apples-ai-wont-be-coming-to-europe-yet (last accessed November 25, 2025).
191. Anu Bradford, *Digital Empires: The Global Battle to Regulate Technology* (Oxford: Oxford University Press, 2023).
192. DeepMind, "How our principles helped define AlphaFold's release," September 14, 2022, https://deepmind.google/en/blog/how-our-principles-helped-define-alphafolds-release/ (last accessed November 25 2025).
193. Microsoft, "Our approach to responsible AI," 2023, www.microsoft.com/en-us/ai/responsible-ai (last accessed November 25 2025).

9 A NEW FIDUCIARY STANDARD

1. Melvin A. Eisenberg, "The divergence of standards of conduct and standards of review in corporate law" (1993) 62 *Fordham Law Review* 437–503.
2. Tony West, "Uber delivers U.S. Safety Report," Uber, December 6, 2019, www.uber.com/en-IL/newsroom/2019-us-safety-report/ (last accessed November 5, 2025).
3. Ryan Lawler, "On-demand ridesharing startup Lyft adds insurance between rides," TechCrunch, March 13, 2014, https://techcrunch.com/2014/03/13/lyft-insurance-between-rides/ (last accessed November 15, 2025).
4. World Resources Institute, "Safe climate, sound business" (describing a collaborative effort by GM, BP, the World Resources Institute, and Monsanto that initiated the partnerships later leading to the Greenhouse Gas Protocol).
5. Esmat Zaidan and Imad Antoine Ibrahim, "AI governance in a complex and rapidly changing regulatory landscape: A global perspective" (2024) 11 *Humanities and Social Sciences Communications* 1–18.
6. Crampton, "Microsoft's framework for building AI systems responsibly."
7. Elhauge, "Sacrificing corporate profits in the public interest."
8. Charles Hansen, "The duty of care, the business judgment rule, and the American Law Institute corporate governance project" (1993) 48 *The Business Lawyer* 1355–76; Bernard Black, Brian Cheffins, and Michael Klausner, "Outside director liability" (2006) 58 *Stanford Law Review* 1055–160.

9. Jacob E. Gersen, "Legislative rules revisited" (2007) 74 *University of Chicago Law Review* 1705–22 at 1720 (discussing the goal of notice-and-comment as ensuring that agencies face public input before producing important policies).
10. Ethan R. Burris, James R. Detert, and Alexander C. Romney, "Speaking up vs being heard: The disagreement around and outcomes of employee voice" (2013) 24 *Organizational Science* 22–38; James R. Detert et al., "Voice flows to and around leaders: understanding when units are helped or hurt by employee voice" (2013) 58 *Administrative Science Quarterly* 624–68; and Chak Fu Lam and David M. Mayer, "When do employees speak up for their customers? A model of voice in a customer service context" (2014) 67 *Personnel Psychology* 637–66.
11. Williams, "The Securities and Exchange Commission and corporate social transparency" (noting that transparency has long been foundational in securities regulation and has increasingly shaped sustainability disclosure practices).
12. Nils Brunsson, *The Organization of Hypocrisy: Talk, Decisions and Actions in Organizations* (Chichester: John Wiley & Sons, 1989).
13. Aneesh Raghunandan and Shivaram Rajgopal, "Do socially responsible firms walk the talk?" (2024) 67 *Journal of Law and Economics* 731–986.
14. George S. Georgiev, "Too big to disclose: Firm size and materiality blindspots in securities regulation" (2017) 64 *UCLA Law Review* 602–48 at 646–8 (explaining how securities disclosure obligations strengthen internal governance by requiring firms to build systems for collecting and validating information).
15. Konstantina Ragazou et al., *Transparency and Corporate Washing in the Age of Sustainability: An Operational Research Agenda to Evaluate Corporate Sustainability Disclosure* (Cham: Springer Nature, 2025) (discussing how sustainability rhetoric often exceeds underlying implementation capacity, producing various forms of corporate washing).
16. Claire A. Hill and Brett H. McDonnell, "Stone v Ritter and the expanding duty of oversight" (2007) 62 *Minnesota Law Review* 1769–96 (arguing that the Caremark duty of oversight requires ongoing monitoring of corporate information and compliance systems to ensure that policies are implemented in practice rather than remaining merely aspirational).
17. Robert A. Prentice, "Sarbanes-Oxley: The evidence regarding the impact of SOX 404" (2007) 29 *Cardozo Law Review* 703–63.
18. Sean J. Griffith, "Corporate governance in an era of compliance" (2016) 57 *William & Mary Law Review* 2075–140 (emphasizing that credible internal investigations require specialized expertise, systematic methodologies, and rigorous documentation presented to independent directors).
19. Bainbridge, "Business judgment rule as abstention doctrine" (conceptualizing fiduciary review as a procedural inquiry).
20. Stephen J. Lubben and Alana J. Darnell, "Delaware's duty of care" (2006) 31 *Delaware Journal of Corporate Law* 589–630.
21. Alexandros N. Rokas, "Reliance on experts from a corporate law perspective" (2013) 2 *American University Business Law Review* 323–51.
22. Zohar Goshen, Assaf Hamdani, and Dorothy S. Lund, "Fixing MFW: Fairness and vision in controller self-dealing" (2025) 15 *Harvard Business Law Review* 577–633.
23. Stephen M. Bainbridge, "Caremark and enterprise risk management" (2009) 34 *Journal of Corporation Law* 967–90.
24. Katherine M. King, "Marchand v. Barnhill's impact on the duty of oversight: New factors to assess directors' liability for breaching the duty of oversight" (2021) 62 *Boston College Law Review* 1925–68.

25. Eugene F. Fama, "Agency problems and the theory of the firm" (1980) 88 *Journal of Political Economy* 288–307 at 290.
26. David F. Larcker and Brian Tayan, "Governance gone wild: Epic misbehavior at Uber Technologies," Rock Center for Corporate Governance at Stanford University Closer Look Series, No. CGRP-70, 2017, https://ssrn.com/abstract=3087371 (last accessed November 29, 2025).
27. Christophe Olivier Schneble, Bernice Simone Elger, and David Shaw, "The Cambridge Analytica affair and Internet-mediated research" (2018) 19 *EMBO Reports* e46579.
28. Anthony, "Uber appeals California Public Utilities Commission ruling to protect privacy of sexual assault survivors."
29. Coffee, "Market failure" (explaining that voluntary disclosure creates collective action problems and that mandatory standards prevent competitive disadvantages for early adopters).
30. Gadinis and Havasy, "The quest for legitimacy in corporate governance."
31. Benjamin C. Zipursky, "Reasonableness in and out of negligence law" (2015) 163 *University of Pennsylvania Law Review* 2131–70; Tom C. W. Lin, "Reasonable investor(s)" (2015) 95 *Boston University Law Review* 461–518.
32. Lynn A. Stout, "In praise of procedure: An economic and behavioral defense of Smith v. Van Gorkom and the business judgment rule" (2002) 96 *Northwestern University Law Review* 675–94.
33. Lilian Edwards and Michael Veale, "Slave to the algorithm? Why a right to an explanation is probably not the remedy you are looking for" (2017) 16 *Duke Law & Technology Review* 18–84 (discussing the well-documented risks that emerging algorithmic technologies pose to privacy, fairness, and other rights).
34. Patricia Feeney, "Business and human rights: The struggle for accountability in the UN and the future direction of the advocacy agenda" (2009) 6 *Sur International Journal of Human Rights* 161–89 (explaining that labor abuses in global supply chains are well documented and that companies have a basic responsibility to implement monitoring systems to learn about conditions in overseas facilities).
35. Charles Korsmo, "Delaware's retreat from judicial scrutiny of mergers" (2019) 10 *UC Irvine Law Review* 55–106.
36. *Eisenberg v. Chicago Milwaukee Corp*, 537 A.2d 1051 (Del. Ch. 1987) (ordering corrective disclosure rather than invalidating the transaction); *In re Netsmart Technologies, Inc. Shareholders Litigation*, 924 A.2d 171 (Del. Ch. 2007) (issuing a tailored injunction requiring supplemental disclosures and a delayed vote – rather than blocking the deal – to cure informational and procedural deficiencies).
37. *Dell, Inc. v. Magnetar Global Event Driven Master Fund Ltd.*, 177 A.3d 1 (Del. 2017) (emphasizing that boards must rely on independent financial advisers capable of producing credible valuation analyses – such as discounted cash flow, comparable company, and precedent-transaction methodologies – when assessing the financial fairness of a transaction); *In re Nine Systems Corp. Shareholders Litigation*, 2014 WL 4383127 (Del. Ch. 2014) (criticizing directors for failing to obtain independent valuation expertise, making clear that this omission alone could undermine the fairness of a transaction); *In re PLX Technology Inc. Stockholders Litigation*, 2018 WL 5018535 (Del. Ch. 2018) (underscoring that boards must not only engage qualified financial advisers but also use that expertise to evaluate alternative strategic options that might provide greater value).
38. *Paramount Communications Inc. v. Time Inc.*, 571 A.2d 1140 (Del. 1989) (recognizing that it may be appropriate for directors to consider the interests and perspectives of affected constituencies when evaluating major corporate decisions, so long as this judgment is connected to long-term shareholder welfare).

39. *In re Dole Food Co., Inc. Stockholder Litigation*, 2015 WL 5052214 (Del. Ch. 2015) (underscoring the need for independent verification of critical data and finding that misleading information undermines the integrity of the process).
40. *Kahn v. Lynch Communication Systems, Inc.*, 638 A.2d 1110 (Del. 1994) (requiring a controlling-shareholder transaction to be reviewed under entire fairness unless an independent committee with real bargaining power is used, thereby employing process safeguards without dictating substantive deal terms); *Weinberger v. UOP, Inc.*, 457 A.2d 701 (Del. 1983) (emphasizing the need for robust procedural protections in a controlling-shareholder merger, including independent valuation and fairness opinions, while articulating the modern entire-fairness framework without prohibiting freeze-out transactions).
41. Fisch and Solomon, "Should corporations have a purpose?"; Edward B. Rock, "For whom is the corporation managed in 2020? The debate over corporate purpose" (2021) 76 *Business Lawyer* 363–406.

CONCLUSION: REASON AND AUTHORITY

1. Edelman, "2025 Edelman Trust Barometer special report: Brand trust – from we to me," 2025, www.edelman.com/trust/2025/trust-barometer/special-report-brands (last accessed November 24, 2025).
2. Henry Hansmann, *The Ownership of Enterprise* (Cambridge, MA: Harvard University Press, 1996) (discussing the costs of implementing corporate governance mechanisms to broaden corporate constituencies).
3. Lunden, "Following Lyft, Uber offers coverage to its U.S. drivers to close the 'insurance gap'."
4. Greenhouse Gas Protocol, "Standards & guidance."
5. Brady, "Retooling carbon accounting."
6. Microsoft, "Governing AI: a blueprint for the future."
7. Michal Barzuza, Quinn Curtis, and David H. Webber, "Shareholder value(s): Index fund ESG activism and the new millennial corporate governance" (2020) 93 *Southern California Law Review* 1243–321 (discussing the investing preferences of millennials and how their investing preferences diverge from previous generations).
8. Shoshana Zuboff, *The Age of Surveillance Capitalism* (New York: PublicAffairs, 2019).
9. Vandenbergh, "Private environmental governance."
10. Joshua Cohen, "Moral pluralism and political consensus," in *Philosophy, Politics, and Democracy* (Cambridge, MA: Harvard University Press, 2009), p. 38; Will Kymlicka, *Multicultural Citizenship: A Liberal Theory of Minority Rights* (Oxford: Oxford University Press, 1995); and Jeremy Waldron, *Law and Disagreement* (Oxford: Oxford University Press, 1999) (all discussing the problem of moral pluralism in the modern democratic state).
11. Cass R. Sunstein, *#Republic: Divided Democracy in the Age of Social Media* (Princeton: Princeton University Press, 2017); Jürgen Habermas, *The Structural Transformation of the Public Sphere* (Cambridge, MA: MIT Press, 1989).
12. James O. Freedman, *Crisis and Legitimacy: The Administrative Process and American Government* (Cambridge, MA: Cambridge University Press, 1978); James M. Landis, *The Administrative Process* (New Haven: Yale University Press, 1938); and Daniel E. Walters, "The administrative agon: A democratic theory for a conflictual regulatory state" (2022) 132 *Yale Law Journal* 1–88 (all analyzing the foundations and limits of public institutional legitimacy, and explaining why democratic authorization cannot be replicated by private entities).

13. Jeffrey Moriarty and Waheed Hussain, "Corporations, the democratic deficit, and voting" (2014) 12 *Georgetown Journal of Law & Public Policy* 429–50; Allan C. Hutchinson, "Hurly-Berle – corporate governance, commercial profits, and democratic deficits" (2011) 34 *Seattle University Law Review* 1219–58.
14. Elizabeth Anderson, *Private Government: How Employers Rule Our Lives and Why We Don"t Talk About It* (Princeton: Princeton University Press, 2017) (arguing that corporations exercise arbitrary, undemocratic authority that procedural reforms cannot cure).
15. Matteo Gatti, "Corporate governing: Understanding corporations as agents of socioeconomic change" (2024) 50 *Journal of Corporation Law* 1–58.
16. Mark J. Roe, "Corporate short-termism – in the boardroom and in the courtroom" (2013) 68 *Business Lawyer* 977–1006; Bengt Holmström, "Agency costs and innovation" (1989) 3 *Journal of Economic Behavior & Organization* 305–27; Alfie Kohn, "Why incentive plans cannot work," Harvard Business Review, September–October 1993, https://hbr.org/1993/09/why-incentive-plans-cannot-work (last accessed December 17, 2025) (together explaining that incentive plans push managers toward short-term, easily quantifiable achievements rather than thoughtful, reflective decision-making).
17. Lund and Pollman, "The corporate governance machine" (arguing that corporate governance structures channel managerial accountability primarily to investors and reinforce profit-centered performance metrics).
18. John Armour, Colin Mayer, and Andrea Polo, "Regulatory sanctions and reputational damage in financial markets" (2017) 52 *Journal of Financial and Quantitative Analysis* 1429–58.
19. Sarah E. Light, "The law of the corporation as environmental law" (2019) 71 *Stanford Law Review* 137–213.
20. Aneil Kovvali and Josh C. Macey, "Private profits and public business" (2025) 103 *Texas Law Review* 711–83.

Index

AAA. *See* American Automobile Association (AAA)
abstention, from social considerations, 22–24
  business strategies as factor in, 23
  core business models as factor for, 23
  profit maximization as factor in, 25
accountability mechanisms
  Corporate Accountability International, 39
  materiality doctrine and, 81
  at Microsoft, 280
  at Open AI, 275
  at OpenAI, 275
  Salesforce Accountability Cloud, 252
Aether Committee, 277, 281–82, 285, 286–87
agriculture industries, standardization of, 30
AI. *See* artificial intelligence (AI), governance of
AIA. *See* Artificial Intelligence Act (AIA), in EU (2021)
Airbnb, 23
  corporate ordering and, 160
  safety frameworks for, 198–99, 201
algorithms
  content moderation, 2–3
  for Meta
    engagement optimization, 3
    social impacts of, 20
  for UnitedHealthcare, 2
    healthcare access determinations, 3
    social impacts of, 20
Allanson, Joe, 248
AlphaFold, 264–68
  CASP competition, 265, 266
  DeepMind and, 264, 266–68
  developmental risks with, 265–66
  limitations of, 267–68
  mitigation approaches within, 266–68
  transparency principles, 267–68
alternative assets, in social impact investing, 50
Altman, Sam, 261, 262–64, 270. *See also* OpenAI, governance structures at
  reinstatement of, 270
Amazon
  corporate ordering and, 160
  efficiency scales for, 28
  information age and, 42
  social considerations for, 20
  social impacts of, 20
  stakeholder constraints and, 36
American Automobile Association (AAA), 168, 169, 171, 172–73
American Bar Association, 186
Amodei, Dario, 271
Anthropic, 271
  as constitutional AI, 275–76
  disclosure mechanisms at, 275
  value alignment in, 275–76
anti-DEI approaches, 50, 51–52
anti-ESG movements, 51–52
  corporate law and, 75
  state pension funds and, 4
antitrust law, ESG practices and, 4–5
Apple, efficiency at scale for, 27, 29
artificial intelligence (AI), governance of. *See also* Anthropic; OpenAI, governance structures at
  AlphaFold, 264–68
    CASP competition, 265, 266
    DeepMind and, 264, 266–68
    developmental risks with, 265–66
    limitations of, 267–68
    mitigation approaches within, 266–68
    transparency principles, 267–68
  California countermodel, 293
  conceptual approach to, 257–58
  constitutional, 275–76
  under corporate law, 79
  corporate ordering and, 8

artificial intelligence (AI) (cont.)
deliberative practices in, 300
in EU, 293–96
under Artificial Intelligence Act, 293–97
fast development of, 260–61
federal approaches to, 290–93
global competition for supremacy, 260
heterogeneity of preferences, 261–64
historical development of, 297–98
hybrid corporate forms, 268–76, 400
adoption of, 269
conceptual approach to, 268–69
implementation of, 272–73
limitations of, 272–73
managers in, 273
need for governance tools in, 276
innovation and, 14, 258–61
internal approaches to, 297–98
jurisdictional requirements for, 155
for large language models, 268–76
National Institute of Standards and Technology and, 291
NGOs and, 258
Office of Science and Technology Policy and, 291
private governance approaches, 264–68
Project Maven, 39
Public Benefit Corporations, 271
safety mechanisms in, 258–61
research for, 14
software engineering and, 14
specialized, 264–68
speed imperative for, 260–61, 290–97
deregulation as tool in, 291
legislative tools in, 290–93
subsidization approaches, 291–93
Winning the Race policy, 292–93
standard-setting for, 258
stewardship imperative for, 258–61, 290–97
at OpenAI, 261–62
under Trump, 290–93
value alignment in, 275–76
Artificial Intelligence Act (AIA), in EU (2021), 293–97
corporate ordering under, 295–97
criticism of, 295
enforcement of, 295
key features of, 294
public law and, 295–97
regulatory mechanisms in, 294–95
Asia, corporate governance in. *See also specific countries*
authoritarian governments and, 22
international stakeholder demands, 22
asset management, asset managers and
ESG-focused, 4
heterogeneous shareholder preferences and, 48–49
ASX. *See* Australian Securities Exchange (ASX)
Atlassian, 253
Auchincloss, Murray, 231
audit committee independence, 9, 164–73
Australian Securities Exchange (ASX), 186
authoritarianism, in Asia, 22
automobile industry, corporate ordering in, 164–73
American Automobile Association and, 168, 169, 171, 172–73
car manufacturing and, 166–67
driving codes and regulatory mechanisms
adoption of, 171–73
ordinance models for, 171–72
public support for, 172
evolution of, 164–65
governance measures for, 169–71
jaywalking offenses, 170–71
Motordom coalition, 169, 170, 171, 172
National Conferences on Street and Highway Safety, 169–70
for parking policies, 171
stakeholder input in, 170
heterogeneity of preferences in, 166–67
stakeholders and, 167
industry cooperation and, 167–69
National Automobile Chamber of Commerce, 168, 171–73
private individuals in, 167–69
public safety campaigns and, 173
Uniform Vehicle Code and, 170, 171
urban transportation and, 165–66
horse-drawn vehicles and, 165
lack of regulatory infrastructure, 165–67
mass transit systems, 166–67
Axon, 288
Azure Custom Neural Voice, 289

Barry, Jordan, 195
Bartley, Tim, 368
Benioff, Marc, 246–47
Bhatia, Pankaj, 235
Biden, Joseph, 75, 237–38
big data, 41
Black Lives Matter (BLM) movement, 45, 105–6, 113. *See also* Floyd, George, murder of
BlackRock, 48–49, 86
BLM. *See* Black Lives Matter movement (BLM)
B&O Railroad, disclosure mechanisms for, 177–79, 182–83
to attract investment and investors, 178

boards of directors, under corporate law, 58–63
decision-making authority, 58
discretion of, 77–78
BP. *See* British Petroleum (BP)
Bradford, Anu, 295
Brehm v. Eisner, 62
British Petroleum (BP), 227–29
Browne, John, 227, 228
Bud Light, 19
business judgment rule, 58–59, 336
business logic, algorithms and, 2
business media, 2–3

California Public Utilities Commission (CPUC), oversight of Uber, 207–9
early demands in, 210–11
in safety report, 209–15
settlement as result of, 213
CalPERS, 4
Cambridge Analytica scandal, 41–42, 310
Canada, international boycott movements in, 22
capital adequacy standards, 136
capitalism
globalization of, 51–52
stakeholder, 21–22
"woke," 87
capped-profit models, 269–71
carbon accounting tools, 249–50
Carbon Disclosure Project, 23, 225, 246
Caremark doctrine, 70–71, 72, 92, 351, 406
Carpenter, Daniel, 139
CASP. *See* Critical Assessment of Structure Prediction (CASP)
CEOs. *See* Chief Executive Officer (CEOs), policy agendas for
Chandler, Chancellor, 60
Chang, Che, 257
Chapek, Bob, 152
Chappelle, Dave, 38
Chevron, sustainability initiatives at, 229–31
Chief Executive Officer (CEOs), policy agendas for, 151–55
for conservative causes, 152
corporate self-regulation and, 153
decision-making in, 153–54
economic boycotts as result of, 152
legitimacy concerns in, 153
for progressive causes, 152
China, efficiency at scale for corporations in, 27–28, 29
Citizens United v. FEC, 139, 188
civil libertarians, Meta and, 1
claims processing protocols, 2–3
classical corporate theory, 321
climate change, climate impact and. *See also* Greenhouse Gas Protocol (GHG); sustainability, corporate frameworks for
analysis of, 255–56
corporate law and, 79
corporate standardization as influence on, 29–31
corporate sustainability and
Carbon Disclosure Project, 225, 246
Greenhouse Gas Protocol, 224–25
intra-corporate divisions on, 227–29
deliberative practices and, 299–300
Environmental Protection Agency and, 249–50
Intergovernmental Panel on Climate Change, 227, 249–50
Kyoto Protocol and, 227, 232
climate resolutions, 4–5
climate sustainability
energy systems and, 14
environmental science and, 14
in global markets, 14
climate-focused investors, 7
climate-skeptical investors, 7
Clinton, Bill, 227
Coase, Ronald, 339
collective action issues, 46–47
complementarity, 144–45
compliance systems
corporate self-regulation mechanisms and, 138–39
corporate surveillance paradox and, 32–33
#MeToo movement, 32–33
monitoring functions for, 119–20
consent, corporate rulemaking and, 103
constitutional AI, 275–76
consultation functions, 302–3
consumer exit options, 34–35
content moderation
algorithms, 2–3
jurisdictional requirements for, 155
at Meta, 1
institutional changes for, 55
moderation strategies, 1
public criticism of, 55
public demands on, 4
contracts, corporate rulemaking and, 103
Cook, Tim, 86
Corporate Accountability International, 39
corporate actions
lobbying compared to, 188–89
managers and, 147
regulatory mechanisms and, 146–48
core business functions in proximity to, 147–48
managers and, 200–1
public interest and, 146–47

corporate activism, through corporate law, 73–80
corporate culture, self-regulation and, 138–39
corporate environmental law, 328–29
corporate governance, 5. *See also* corporate law; ESG movement (environmental, social, and governance movement); Greenhouse Gas Protocol (GGP); securities law, securities disclosure and; *specific topics*
  analysis of, 17–18, 319–20
  for automobile industry, 169–71
    jaywalking offenses, 170–71
    Motordom coalition, 169, 170, 171, 172
    National Conferences on Street and Highway Safety, 169–70
    parking policies and, 171
    stakeholder input, 170
  evaluation of, 16–17
  evolution of, 57
  executive action in, 110–19
    challenges of, 118–19
    disclosure mechanisms and, 114–15
    implementation of, 114–15, 118–19
  foundations of, 19
  gaps in, 55–57
  history of, 8–10
  during information age, 40
  as institutional architecture, 125–28
    design implications of, 126
    legal stalemates in, 127–28
    reconceptualization of corporate legal authority, 127
    scope of institutional work, 125–26
  lobbying and, 189
  long-term implications for, 324–29
    for democracy, 325–26
  methodological approaches to, 330–31
  new frontiers of, 8–10
  paradoxes of, 56–57
  political legitimacy and, 16
  rulemaking and, 107–10
    external inputs and, 108–9
    heterogeneous shareholder preferences and, 107–8
    implementation of rules, 109–10
    legitimacy-building through, 110
    validation mechanism, 108–9
    values-based internal processes, 109–10
  transformation of, 24–25
    from forced transparency, 25
    through systemic frameworks, 24–25
corporate law, 15, 58. *See also* deliberative decision-making, in corporate law; ESG movement (environmental, social, and governance movement); securities law, securities disclosure and; *specific topics*
  artificial intelligence governance and, 79
  authority of, 56
  board of directors under, 58–63
    decision-making authority of, 58
    discretion of, 77–78
  business judgment rule and, 58–59, 336
  corporate activism through, 73–80
  corporate governance gaps and, 55–57
  decision-making authority under
    for board of directors, 58
    corporate hierarchy and, 58
    deliberative, 61–69
    for managers, 58
    process-oriented approach to, 61–62
  in Delaware, 58–63
    corporate hierarchy in, 58
    deliberative decision-making in, 61–63
    gaps in, 90–94
    Supreme Court rulings, 58–59
  democratic deficits of, 325
  discretion architecture in, 91
  evolution of, 93–94
  gaps in, 90–94
    in guidance, 92
  inconsistency of, 92–93
  innovation in, 92–93
  judicial approach in, 60
  judicial review and, 61–62
  managers under, 58–63
    decision-making authority for, 58, 61–63
    discretion of, 59–63
    monitoring of, 61–63
    social conflicts and, 59–63
  oversight duties under, 70–73
    Caremark doctrine, 70–71, 72, 92, 351, 406
    for climate risks, 71
    parameters of mission-critical analysis, 72–73
    for social risks, 71
  without predetermined outcomes, 317–18
  self-regulation mechanisms under, 140–41
  shareholder proposals and, 73–80
    activism through, 78–80
    anti-ESG proposals, 75
    for artificial intelligence, 79
    board discretion, 77–78
    for climate change, 79
    ESG issues, 76–77, 79
    historical transformation of, 74–75, 78–80
    legal frameworks for, 73–74
    limits of democracy for, 77–78
    mechanics of support for, 75–77
    proxy contests, 77–78
  social considerations of, 95–98

corporate ordering. *See also* disclosure mechanisms; driving codes; *specific companies; specific topics*
academic approach to, 184–85
AI and, 8
analysis of, 17–18
architecture of, 9–11
under Artificial Intelligence Act, 295–97
as business response, 7–8
CEO policy agendas, 151–55
for conservative causes, 152
corporate self-regulation and, 153
decision-making and, 153–54
legitimacy concerns, 153
for progressive causes, 152
conceptual approach to, 3–11, 160–62
contemporary accounts of, 329
core mechanisms of, 7
corporate sustainability and, 225
definition of, 3
executive decision-making and, 11
failure of traditional responses to, 5–7
Greenhouse Gas Protocol and, 245
in corporate value chain, 240–41
heterogeneous shareholder preferences in, 4–5
historical evolution of, 160–62
roots of, 190
jurisdictional requirements in conflict with, 155–57
in EU, 155, 156
governance capacity and, 156
regulatory fragmentation and, 155–56
in U.S., 155, 156
limitations of, 148–51
durability as, 149
for rules enforcement, 149–50
time inconsistency issues, 150
methodological approach to, 3, 12–15
analytical strategy in, 14–15
at Microsoft, 276–90
normative arguments about, 329–30
operational costs of, 7, 8
self-regulation mechanisms and, 133–34, 148–51
CEO policy agendas and, 153
implementation of legislative mandates, 136–40
implementation of regulatory mandates, 136–40
lobbying and, 139–40
shareholders and
heterogeneous shareholder preferences, 4–5
primacy doctrine, 5
for social conflicts, 95–98
social responsibility as distinct from, 3
stakeholder theory and, 6
as substitute for regulatory ordering, 141–45
complementarity and, 144–45
deep and narrow in, 142–43
ESG movement and, 144–45
stakeholder concerns in, 143
system feedback and, 9–10
systematization of, 97–98
theoretical approaches to, 3–11, 15–17, 97–98
Uber and, 160, 211–12
corporate social responsibility. *See also* social considerations, of corporations
ordering as distinct from, 3
public focus on, 16–17
corporate surveillance paradox, 32–33
compliance systems and, 32–33
Corporate Sustainability Reporting Directive (CSRD), in EU, 50, 51–52, 84, 237–38
corporations. *See also* corporate governance; corporate ordering; rulemaking, within corporations; *specific corporations; specific topics*
as deliberative institutions, 322–24
private law and, 322–24
public law and, 322–24
tripartite distinction of functions of, 98–101
as analytical tool, 99–100
executive functions, 99, 101
mapping of, 100–1
monitoring functions in, 99–100
review functions, 101
rulemaking functions, 100
Corwin doctrine, 65
CPUC. *See* California Public Utilities Commission (CPUC), oversight of Uber
Critical Assessment of Structure Prediction (CASP), 265, 266
CSRD. *See* Corporate Sustainability Reporting Directive (CSRD), in EU

Dao, David, 38, 45
data privacy, jurisdictional requirements for, 155
data traps, 20, 53–54
debanking, 122–23
decision-making authority, under corporate law. *See also* deliberative decision-making, in corporate law; executive action, decision-making and
for boards of directors, 58
corporate hierarchies and, 58
deliberative, 61–69
for managers, 58
process-oriented approach to, 61–62
Salesforce, 250

DeepMind, 264, 266–68
DEI initiatives. *See* diversity, equity, and inclusion initiatives (DEI initiatives)
DEI washing, 83, 111
Delaware law, 58–63
  corporate hierarchy in, 58
  Delaware Supreme Court rulings, 58–59
  deliberative decision-making under, 65–66
  fiduciary duty obligations under, 307
  gaps in, 90–94
deliberative decision-making, in corporate law, 63–69
  bias in
    lack of, 64
    management, 68
  Corwin doctrine, 65
  in Delaware, 65–66
  evolution of, 63
  expert support in, 64
  governance guidance caps in, 68–69
  information quality in, 64
  infrastructure for, 64
  through institutional mechanisms, 64–65
  Kahn v. M&F Worldwide Corp., 65, 307
  managerial discretion in, 61–63
  Sarbanes-Oxley Act and, 64–65, 66
  social conflicts and, 66–68
  unified governance frameworks for, 66
  Weinberger v. UOP, 65
deliberative practices, in corporate governance. *See also* fiduciary duty obligations
  accuracy in, 303–5
  in AI governance, 300
  benefits of, 306–7
  in climate policies, 299–300
  conceptual approach to, 299–301
  disclosure mechanisms and, 303–5
  discretion compared to, 301–2
  for executive functions, 303–5
  for humanitarian requests, 306
  independent approaches to, 305–6
  investigatory approaches in, 305–6
  at Lyft, 299
  methodological approach to, 301
  for oversight functions, 305–6
  for quality control, 304
  for review functions, 305–6
  for rulemaking, 302–3
    consultation functions, 302–3
    feedback functions, 302–3
    outreach functions, 302–3
    standard-setting, 302–3
  at Uber, 299
democracy, democracies and
  corporate governance and, 325–26
  corporate law and, 78, 325
derivatives markets, corporate self-regulation and, 135–36
DeSantis, Ron, 152
digital platforms, during information age, 46–47
Digital Services Act (DSA), EU (2024), 28
digital technologies, efficiency at scale for
  through monitoring architecture, 31
  through standardization, 27–28
Dimon, Jamie, 86
disclosure frameworks, in securities law, 161, 170
  in EU, 83–84
    Corporate Sustainability Reporting Directive, 84
  in U.S.
    greenwashing, 83
    for social disclosures, 84–85
    vague disclosures, 82
    washing in, 83
disclosure mechanisms, 173–84
  at Anthropic, 275
  B&O Railroad, 177–79, 182–83
    to attract investment and investors, 178
  conceptual approach to, 173–74
  deliberative practices and, 303–5
  development of, 174–75, 176–80
  driving codes and, 162–64
  evolution of, 163, 176–77
  executive decisions and, 114–15
  government conflicts and, 183–84
    during Great Depression, 183–84
  heterogeneity of preferences and, 175–76
  inconsistency in, 180
    lack of standardized reporting and, 181
  investors and investment in, 174–75
    in B&O Railroad, 178
  managerial approaches to, 163–64
  mandatory, 162
  at Meta, 275
  New York Stock Exchange as influence on, 163–64, 180–83
    Committee on Securities, 181
    formalization of templates, 182–83
    listing requirements in, 181–82, 184
    quarterly reporting agreements, 182
    Securities Act of 1933 and, 183–84
  at OpenAI, 275
  Quincy Mining Company, 177
  for railroad industry, 175, 176, 177–79
  requirements for, 126
  road norms and, 161
  under Securities Act of 1933, 163–64, 183–84
    New York Stock Exchange and, 183–84

under Securities Exchange Act of 1934, 184
shareholders and, 163–64
sustainability and, 353
transparency and, 175
Uber and, 202–4, 207–9
U.S. Steel, 179–80
worker movement and, 175–76
discretion, in corporate governance
conceptual approach to, 300
deliberation compared to, 301–2
dispute settlements, Uber and, 213
diversity, equity, and inclusion initiatives (DEI initiatives), 368. *See also* anti-DEI approaches
DEI washing, 111
ESG movement and, 88
globalization of capital and, 51–52
Target and, 19
diversity washing, 83, 111
Dodd-Frank Act, U.S., 24
DoorDash, 193
driving codes
as corporate ordering by automobile industry
adoption of, 171–73
ordinance models for, 171–72
public support for, 172
disclosure mechanisms and, 162–64
evolution of, 163
DSA. *See* Digital Services Act (DSA), EU (2024)
due diligence standards, 136

eBay v. Newmark, 60
economic boycotts
CEO agendas as influence on, 152
of Facebook, 34–35
of Goya Foods, 22
international boycott movements, 22
for LGBTQ+ populations, 46
of Uber, 34–35
efficiency at scale, for corporations, 20, 25–40
Amazon, 28
Apple, 27, 29
in China, 27–28, 29
conceptual approach to, 25
for digital technologies
through monitoring architecture, 31
through standardization, 27–28
in EU
under Digital Services Act, 28
GDPR, 28
Facebook, 27
for gig economy industries, 28, 193
corporate surveillance paradox and, 32
monitoring architecture for, 32
in India, 27–28, 29
monitoring architecture and, 31–33
corporate surveillance paradox, 32–33
of digital technologies, 31
for financial institutions, 31
infrastructure of, 31–32
through renegotiation of standardized practices, 34–39
consumer exit options in, 34–35
employee constraints and, 35–36
industry-set standards as constraints, 36–37
labor market realities as factor in, 35–36
shareholder activism and, 37, 38–39
stakeholder constraints and, 36
with voice mechanisms, 37–39
social impacts of, 39–40
through standardization and uniformity, 26–31
for agriculture industry, 30
climate impact and, 29–31
digital standardization, 27–28
for food production, 30
of global supply chains, 29
internal hierarchies and, 26–27
for petrochemicals and plastics industry, 30–31
of platform power, 27–28
renegotiation of standardized practices, 34–39
of retail industry, 28–29, 30
in seafood industry, 29
for shipping industry, 30
of technology sector, 30
Tesla, 28–29
TikTok, 27–28
at Uber, 28, 193
corporate surveillance paradox, 32
monitoring architecture, 32
in U.S., 28
in Vietnam, 29
energy systems, climate sustainability and, 14
Eno, William Phelps, 168, 373
Enron scandal, 9, 64
environmental, social, and governance movement. *See* ESG movement (environmental, social, and governance movement)
Environmental Protection Agency (EPA), in U.S., 249–50
environmental reporting initiatives, 247–48
environmental science, climate sustainability and, 14
environmental standards, jurisdictional requirements for, 155

EPA. *See* Environmental Protection Agency (EPA), in U.S.
ESG movement (environmental, social, and governance movement). *See also* anti-ESG movements
  antitrust law and, 4–5
  asset managers, 4
  backlash to, 87–88
    DEI initiatives and, 88
    political elements of, 87, 89
  conceptual approach to, 85–86
  corporate law and, 76–77, 79
  corporate ordering and, 144–45
  corporate sustainability and, 224
  evolution of, 86–87
    corporate acceptance in, 86
    corporate retreat from, 88
    criticism in, 85–86
    support during, 85–86
  globalization of capitalism and, 51–52
  institutional capability of, 90
  investors in, 2
  origins of, 86
  as process-focused, 88–89, 90
  as purpose-focused, 88–89
  Securities and Exchange Commission responses to, 87
  social governance challenges in, 89–90
  sustainability reporting and, 87
  as "woke capitalism," 87
ethics policies, at Microsoft, 281–82
ethics washing, 83
European Union (EU)
  AI governance in, 293–96
    under AIA, 293–97
  Artificial Intelligence Act, 293–97
    corporate ordering under, 295–97
    criticism of, 295
    enforcement of, 295
    key features of, 294
    public law and, 295–97
    regulatory mechanisms in, 294–95
  Corporate Sustainability Reporting Directive in, 50, 51–52, 84, 237–38, 239
  Digital Services Act, 28
  General Data Protection Regulation, 28
  globalization of capital in, 51
  international boycott movements in, 22
  Non-Financial Reporting Directive, 83
  securities disclosure frameworks in, 83–84
  social impact investing in, 50
  sustainability reporting in, 5
  Sustainable Finance Disclosure Regulation, 50
  Taxonomy Regulation in, 50
executive action, decision-making and
  calibration of, 113–14
  challenges in, 110–11
  conceptual approach to, 110–11
  in corporate governance, 110–19
  corporate ordering and, 11
  credibility-enhancing mechanisms through, 117–18
  deliberative practices and, 303–5
  governance implications of, 113–14
    challenges of, 118–19
    disclosure mechanisms and, 114–15
    implementation of, 114–15, 118–19
  in Greenhouse Gas Protocol, 233–34
  at Microsoft, 282–85
  nature and scope of, 111–13
  recognition of, 113–14
  shareholder management, 115, 116–17
  social significance of, 113–14
executive compensation systems, 126
executive functions, in corporations, 99, 101
exit costs, for employees, 35–36
exit options, for consumers, 34–35
ExxonMobil, 44
  corporate governance of, 52
  social considerations for, 20
  sustainability initiatives at, 229–31

Facebook
  Cambridge Analytica scandal, 41–42, 310
  corporate ordering and, 160
  economic boycotts of, 34–35
  efficiency at scale for, 27
  employee protests within, 22–23
  social considerations for, 20
facial recognition technology, 287–89
fiduciary duty obligations, 307–17
  adaptability of, 307
  under Delaware law, 307
  evolution of, 308–9
  recalibration of, 317
  remedies, 316–17
  social deliberation requirements, 309–12
    agency costs, 309–10
    competitive dynamics in, 310–11
    coordination problems, 310–11
    for corporate legitimacy, 311
    doctrinal coherence through, 311–12
    harm prevention, 310
    managerial discretion, 309–10
    regulatory pressure through, 311
    risk identification, 310
  standards of review, 313–15
    breaches of standards, 314

deficient processes in, 315
for social risks, 314–15
structural failures with, 314–15
thresholds for, 312–13
financial crisis of 2007, 135–36
Financial Industry Regulatory Authority, 186
Fink, Larry, 86
Floyd, George, murder of, 112
Flynn, Patrick, 249, 251
food production. *See also* seafood industry, corporate standardization of
corporate standardization of, 30

Gary, Elbert, 180
gatekeepers, 336
GCC. *See* Global Climate Coalition (GCC)
General Data Protection Regulation (GDPR), EU (2018), 28
General Motors (GM), 228
GHG. *See* Greenhouse Gas Protocol (GHG)
gig economy industries. *See also* Airbnb; rideshare industry; *specific companies*
corporate rulemaking and, 106–7
efficiency at scale for, 28, 193
corporate surveillance paradox, 32
monitoring architecture and, 32
heterogeneity of preferences and, 200–1
platform-based business models in, 193
progression to public company for, 200–1
quality control issues in, 193
trust in, 192–93
Global Climate Coalition (GCC), 227–28
global corporate conduct, regulation of, 370
Global Impact Investing Network, 49
global markets, climate sustainability in, 14
Global Reporting Initiative (GRI), 234–35
global supply chains, corporate standardization of, 29
globalization of capital, 53
DEI initiatives and, 51–52
ESG principles and, 51–52
in EU, 51
heterogeneous shareholder preferences and, 50–52
in U.S., 50
GM. *See* General Motors (GM)
Google, 19
DeepMind and, 264, 266–68
employee exit costs, 35–36
internal employee conflicts, 22–23
Project Maven, 39
Gordon, Jeffrey, 48
governance triangle, 370
Goya Foods, boycotts of, 22
Great Depression, disclosure mechanisms during, 183–84
Greenhouse Gas Protocol (GHG), 224–25, 232–45
adoption of, 241–45
analysis of, 255–56
corporate ordering, 245
in corporate value chain, 240–41
corporate rulemaking and, 234–36
Corporate Sustainability Reporting Directive, 237–38, 239
corporate value chain in, 236–41
corporate ordering and, 240–41
design philosophy in, 236–37
early success of, 236–37
enforceable standards in, 237–38
global divergences for, 238–39
goals of, 236–37
legislative retrenchment of, 238–39
protocol overhauls, 239–40
Science Based Targets Initiative, 237
creation of, 233
disclosure mechanisms and, 241–42
emissions measures in, 234–36
executive action and, 233–34
global acceptance of, 233
governance of, 243–44
implementation of, 241–45
organizational overextension in, 243–44
organizational retrenchment in, 244–45
sustainability teams, 241–42
materiality of, 239
monitoring of, 241–45
scaling measurements in, 241–42
NGOs and, 235
overhaul of, 239–40
redesign of, 244–45
Salesforce and, 247–48
World Resources Institute and, 233, 234–36
greenwashing, 83, 111
GRI. *See* Global Reporting Initiative (GRI)
growth imperatives
for Lyft, 197
for Uber, 196–97
leadership changes as influence on, 199–200
limitations of, 198–99

heterogeneous shareholder preferences, 4–5, 47–52, 357
for AI governance, 261–64
asset management companies, 48–49
in automobile industry, 166–67
conflict between social good and profit, 47
corporate hierarchies and, 320
corporate rulemaking and, 107–8

heterogeneous shareholder preferences (cont.)
corporate sustainability and, 226–32
evolution of, 232–34
GHG protocol, 232–45
private approaches to, 227–29
disclosure mechanisms and, 175–76
in gig economy corporations, 200–1
globalization of capital and, 50–52
institutional investors, 48–49
Lyft and, 216–17
as practice of reason, 320–22
rideshare industry and, 196–201
social impact and, 20–21
social impact investing, 47–48, 49–50
alternative assets in, 50
in EU, 50
expansion and growth of, 49–50
Global Impact Investing Network, 49
historical development of, 49
UN Sustainable Development Goals, 49
traditional frameworks in, 47–48
Uber and, 196–201
universal owners and, 48
Higgins, Matthew, 265
Hirschman, Albert, 34
Hoffman, Paul, 169
Hoover, Herbert, 169
humanitarian requests, as deliberative practice, 306
hybrid corporate forms, of AI governance, 400, 268–76
adoption of, 269
conceptual approach to, 268–69
implementation of, 272–73
limitations of, 272–73
managers in, 273
need for governance tools in, 276

Iger, Bob, 152
impact funds, 4
incentive structures, in corporations, 326–28
public welfare and, 365
in rideshare industry, 222–23
India
efficiency at scale for corporations in, 27–28, 29
Uber in, 198
information age, corporations during, 40–47
Amazon, 42
collection of information, 41–44
big data, 41
on employee performance, 42–43
legacy of, 44
public hearings on, 41–42
social issues influenced by, 43–44
through social media, 42
collective action problems in, 46–47
conceptual approach to, 40
corporate governance model, 40
digital platforms in, 46–47
ExxonMobil, 44
Internet-of-Things and, 43–44
LGBTQ+ populations and, 46
economic boycotts on behalf of, 46
Meta, 41
retail industry and, 46
social impact of information, 41–44
social media campaigns and, 46–47
stakeholders' access to information, 44–46
Target, 42
Tesla, 43–44
Uber, 42
United Airlines, 45
information collection mechanisms
big data, 41
by corporations, 41–44
big data, 41
on employee performance, 42–43
legacy of, 44
public hearings on, 41–42
social issues influenced by, 43–44
through social media, 42
data traps, 20, 53–54
deliberative decision-making and, 64
General Data Protection Regulation, 28
innovation
AI governance and, 14, 258–61
in corporate law, 92–93
in rideshare industry, 195–96
Instacart, 193
insurance
Lyft and, 216–17
coordination of, 219
heterogeneous preferences and, 216–17
regulatory mechanisms and, 216–17
rulemaking problems with, 216
state legislation for, 220–21
Transportation Charter-Party carriers, 217
in rideshare industry, 192
Uber and, 220
Intergovernmental Panel on Climate Change (IPCC), 227, 249–50
international boycott movements, 22
International Maritime Organization, 30
International Organization for Standardization (ISO), 187
International Swaps and Derivatives Association (ISDA), 135–36
Internet-of-Things (IoT), 43–44

investors, investments and
climate-focused, 7
climate-skeptical, 7
disclosure mechanisms as factor for, 174–75
in B&O Railroad, 178
ESG, 2
institutional investors, 48–49
risk-focused, 2
traditional, 2
in UnitedHealthcare, 2
value-driven, 4
IoT. *See* Internet-of-Things (IoT)
IPCC. *See* Intergovernmental Panel on Climate Change (IPCC)
ISDA. *See* International Swaps and Derivatives Association (ISDA)
ISO. *See* International Organization for Standardization (ISO)

jaywalking offenses, 170–71
judicial review, in corporate law, 61–62
jurisdictional requirements
for AI governance, 155
for content moderation, 155
corporate ordering in conflict with, 155–57
in EU, 155, 156
regulatory fragmentation and, 155–56
in U.S., 155, 156
for data privacy, 155
for environmental standards, 155

Kahn v. M&F Worldwide Corp., 65, 307
Kalanick, Travis, 32, 38, 196–97
Kamel, Fawzi, 38
Kamin v. American Express, 59
Karpathy, Andrej, 263
Khosla, Vinod, 263
Khosrowshahi, Dara, 200, 203
Kovvali, Aneil, 328–29
Kratsios, Michael, 292
Kyoto Protocol, 227, 232

large language models (LLMs), in AI governance, 268–76. *See also* Anthropic; OpenAI, governance structures at
development of, 268–69
law. *See also* corporate environmental law; corporate law; private law, corporations and; public law
legal theory, 329
origins of, 328–29
legal authority, reconceptualization of, 127
legitimacy, political, corporate governance and, 16

LGBTQ+ populations
economic boycotts on behalf of, 46
in information age, 46
Light, Sarah, 328–29
Lindell, Mike, 152
Liu, Sophia, 217
LLMs. *See* large language models (LLMs), in AI governance
lobbying, 188–89
Citizens United v. FEC, 139, 188
corporate action compared to, 188–89
corporate governance and, 189
corporate hypocrisy and, 189
for corporate self-regulation, 139–40, 189
by Political Action Committees, 188
Long-Term Benefit Trust (LTBT), 271
Lund, Dorothy, 48–49
Lyft, 215–23
deliberative practices at, 299
evolution of, 215–16
growth imperative for, 197
heterogeneous preferences and, 216–17
incentive structures within, 222–23
insurance frameworks for, 216–17
coordination of, 219
heterogeneous preferences and, 216–17
regulatory mechanisms and, 216–17
rulemaking problems, 216
state legislation for, 220–21
Transportation Charter-Party carriers, 217
public trust in, 222
regulatory mechanisms
development of, 221–22
rulemaking and, 220–22
rulemaking policies, 218–19
for insurance frameworks, 216
regulatory mechanisms and, 220–22
taxonomic frameworks in, 219
safety frameworks for, 200–1

Macey, Josh, 328–29
Madry, Aleksander, 263
managers
in AI corporate governance, 273
authority of, 96
corporate actions and, 147
under corporate law, 58–63
decision-making authority for, 58, 61–63
discretion of, 59–63
monitoring of, 61–63
social conflicts and, 59–63
disclosure mechanisms, 163–64
fiduciary duty obligations and, 309–10
monitoring functions by, 120–21

mandatory disclosures, 162
Marchand v. Barnhill, 70–71, 72–73
Markoff, John, 278
materiality doctrine, 81–82
  circularity of, 82
  Greenhouse Gas Protocol and, 239
  social accountability issues and, 81
McClintock, Miller, 169, 172
McLane, Louis, 178
media. *See* business media
Meta. *See also* Zuckerberg, Mark
  algorithms for
    engagement optimization, 3
    social impacts of, 20
  civil libertarian funds and, 1
  content moderation at, 1
    institutional changes in, 55
    moderation strategies for, 1
    public criticism of, 55
    public demands on, 4
  disclosure mechanisms at, 275
  during information age, 41
#MeToo movement, 32–33, 45, 105–6
  monitoring in corporations during, 122
Miazad, Amelia, 48–49
Microsoft, AI governance at
  accountability and, 280
  Aether Committee, 277, 281–82, 285, 286–87
  corporate ordering at, 276–90
  corporate rulemaking, 278–82
    Responsible AI Standard, 278–81
  ethics considerations, 281–82
  executive decision-making, 282–85
  fairness in, 280
    in speech-to-text technology, 289–90
  monitoring functions in, 285–90
  Office of Responsible AI, 282
    Fit for Purpose standard, 283–84
    hub-and-spoke governance models, 283
    implementation of, 285
  OpenAI and, 263
  principles-based framework for, 277
  privacy standards, 280
  reliability standards, 280
  review functions in, 285–90
    Azure Custom Neural Voice, 289
    facial recognition technology, 287–89
    Sensitive Uses review process, 286–87
  safety standards, 280
  security issues, 280
  transparency mechanisms, 280
  values as business imperative, 277–78
Miller, Herman, 253
monitoring architecture, in efficiency at scale, 31–33
  corporate surveillance paradox and, 32–33
  for financial institutions, 31
  infrastructure of, 31–32
monitoring functions, of corporations, 99–100. *See also* tripartite distinction of corporate functions
  in corporate governance, 119–24
    adjustments to, 121–23
    compliance mechanisms, 119–20
    managerial discretion in, 120–21
    during #MeToo movement, 122
    performative monitoring, 124
    policy changes in, 121–23
    of workplace inclusion policies, 123
  for corporate sustainability, 245–54
  Greenhouse Gas Protocol and, 241–45
    scaling measurements for, 241–42
  at Microsoft, 285–90
  for technology companies, 123
  for Uber, 205–7
Monsanto
  corporate ordering and, 160
  corporate sustainability and, 228–29
Motordom coalition, 169, 170, 171, 172
Mulvaney, Dylan, 46
Munoz, Oscar, 45
Murati, Mira, 270
Musk, Elon, 151–53, 261–62
Muzaffar, Syed, 217

NACC. *See* National Automobile Chamber of Commerce (NACC)
Nadella, Satya, 263, 277–78
National Association of Manufacturers, 176, 389
National Association of Securities Dealers, 186
National Automobile Chamber of Commerce (NACC), 168, 171–73
National Conferences on Street and Highway Safety (NCSHS), 169–70
National Institute of Standards and Technology (NIST), 291
National Sexual Violence Resource Center (NSVRC), 204
NCSHS. *See* National Conferences on Street and Highway Safety (NCSHS)
necessity of scale, for rideshare industry, 193
Net Zero Cloud, 252
New York Stock Exchange (NYSE)
  disclosure mechanisms and, 163–64, 180–83
    Committee on Securities, 181
    formalization of templates, 182–83
    quarterly reporting agreements, 182
    Securities Act of 1933 and, 183–84
  NYSE Regulation, Inc., 186

NGOs. *See* nongovernmental organizations (NGOs)
NIST. *See* National Institute of Standards and Technology (NIST)
Non-Financial Reporting Directive, EU (2014), 83
nongovernmental organizations (NGOs), 39
  AI governance and, 258
  corporate sustainability and, 235
  Greenhouse Gas Protocols and, 235
Norwegian Sovereign Wealth Fund, 4
NSVRC. *See* National Sexual Violence Resource Center (NSVRC)
NYSE. *See* New York Stock Exchange (NYSE)
NYSE Regulation, Inc., 186

Office of Responsible AI (ORA), 282
  Fit for Purpose standard, 283–84
  hub-and-spoke governance models, 283
  implementation of, 285
Office of Science and Technology Policy (OSTP), 291
Olson, Mancur, 139
OpenAI, governance structures at, 257, 261, 262–64. *See also* Microsoft, AI governance at
  accountability mechanisms, 275
  Anthropic and, 271
  capped-profit model, 269–71
  commercialization of, 262–64
  corporate ordering at, 274–76
    red-teaming in, 274, 276
    system cards in, 275
  crisis management of, 263–64
  disclosure mechanisms at, 275
  founding of, 269–71
  leadership changes at, 263–64, 270
  limitations of, 272–73
  Microsoft and, 263, 276–90
  speed imperatives for, 262–64
  stewardship advocacy, 261–62
ORA. *See* Office of Responsible AI (ORA)
OSTP. *See* Office of Science and Technology Policy (OSTP)
outreach functions, 302–3
Oxfam, 39

Pachocki, Jakub, 263
PACs. *See* Political Action Committees (PACs)
PBCs. *See* Public Benefit Corporations (PBCs)
PCAOB. *See* Public Company Accounting Oversight Board (PCAOB)
Percy, Steven, 235
performance standards, in self-regulation mechanisms, 137–38
performative monitoring, 124
petrochemicals and plastics industry, corporate standardization of, 30–31
Phenix Capital, 50
Pichai, Sundar, 152, 153
platform regulations, rideshare safety and, 14
platform-based business models, 193. *See also* *specific companies; specific topics*
Political Action Committees (PACs), 188
politics, political contexts and
  for corporate self-regulation mechanisms, 132
  for ESG movements, 87, 89
Pollman, Elizabeth, 195
preferences. *See* heterogeneous shareholder preferences
Price Waterhouse & Co. (PWC), 179, 182–83
pricing structures, in rideshare industry, 195
primacy doctrine for shareholders, 5
privacy standards, at Microsoft, 280
private law, corporations and, 322–24
problem-solving, in corporations, 192
profits, corporate social considerations influenced by, 25
Project Maven, 39
proxy contests, 77–78
Public Benefit Corporations (PBCs), AI corporations as, 271
Public Company Accounting Oversight Board (PCAOB), 64
public interest, corporate action and, 146–47
public law
  corporations and, 322–24
  procedural details for, 325
public safety campaigns, by automobile industry, 173
public welfare, private incentives and, 365
PWC. *See* Price Waterhouse & Co. (PWC)

QMC. *See* Quincy Mining Company (QMC)
quality control, 193
  as deliberative practice, 304
Quincy Mining Company (QMC), 177

railroad industry. *See also* B&O Railroad, disclosure mechanisms for
  disclosure mechanisms for, 175, 176, 177–79
RAINN. *See* Rape, Abuse, & Incest National Network (RAINN)
Ranganathan, Janet, 235
Rape, Abuse, & Incest National Network (RAINN), 204, 210, 213, 383
red-teaming, 274, 276

regulatory mechanisms, within corporations. *See also* self-regulation mechanisms, in corporations
academic approach to, 184–85
under Artificial Intelligence Act, 294–95
conceptual approach to, 129–32
corporate action as prelude to, 146–48
core business functions in proximity to, 147–48
managers and, 147
public interest and, 146–47
corporate ordering as substitute for, 141–45
complementarity and, 144–45
deep and narrow focus on, 142–43
ESG movement and, 144–45
stakeholder concerns, 143
fiduciary duty obligations and, 311
for global corporate conduct, 370
Lyft
development of, 221–22
rulemaking and, 220–22
purpose of, 129
in rideshare industry, 191–92
entrepreneurship and, 195–96
political dimension as element in, 195
for rideshare safety, 14
tripartite distinction of corporate functions and, 131
reliability standards, at Microsoft, 280
remedies, in fiduciary duty obligation, 316–17
renewable energy, corporate sustainability and, 231–32
Responsible AI Standard, 278–81
retail industry. *See also specific companies*
corporate standardization of, 28–29, 30
information age for, 46
review functions, for corporations, 101
deliberative practices, 305–6
at Microsoft, 285–90
Azure Custom Neural Voice, 289
facial recognition technology and, 287–89
Sensitive Uses review process, 286–87
rideshare industry. *See also* Lyft; Uber
conceptual approach to, 191–92
corporate problem-solving in, 192
economy challenges for, 193
heterogeneity of preferences in, 196–201
incentive structures in, 222–23
innovation in, 195–96
insurance coverage frameworks, 192
necessity of scale for, 193
as new transportation paradigm, 194
pricing structures for, 195
regulatory mechanisms for, 191–92
entrepreneurship and, 195–96
political dimension of, 195
safety mechanisms in, 201–9
platform regulations for, 14
transportation networks and, 14
sexual harassment monitoring frameworks in, 192
transportation network companies and, 220
state legislation for, 220–21
tripartite distinction of corporate functions in, 191, 221
trust barriers in, 194
worker classification in, 195
risk-focused investors, 2
rulemaking, within corporations, 101–10
application of rules, 104–7
conceptual approach to, 101–2
consent as element of, 103
contractual commitments and, 103
for customer interface, 104–5
definition of rules, 102–4
in deliberative practices, 302–3
consultation functions, 302–3
outreach functions, 302–3
standard-setting, 302–3
disruption as result of, 106–7
functions of, 100
in gig economy, 106–7
governance implications of, 107–10
external input on rules, 108–9
heterogeneous shareholder preferences and, 107–8
implementation of rules, 109–10
legitimacy-building through, 110
validation mechanisms, 108–9
values-based internal processes, 109–10
Greenhouse Gas Protocol and, 234–36
Lyft, 218–19
for insurance frameworks, 216
regulatory mechanisms and, 220–22
taxonomic frameworks for, 219
at Microsoft, 278–82
Responsible AI Standard, 278–81
for production, 104
for quality control, 104
Salesforce, 249–50, 254
standardization and uniformity through, 102–4
for sustainability approaches, 232–33, 245–54
Uber, 204–5
for workplace organization, 105–6
DEI initiatives, 105–6
Russia-Ukraine war, 231

Sacks, David, 292
safety mechanisms, in corporations. *See also* Uber
AI governance and, 258–61
research for, 14

Airbnb, 201
Lyft and, 200–1
at Microsoft, 280
in rideshare companies
platform regulations for, 14
transportation networks and, 14
Salesforce, sustainability frameworks at, 245–54
as business advantage, 246–47
business philosophy for, 246–47
carbon accounting tools, 249–50
Carbon Disclosure Project, 246
commercialization of, 252
Salesforce Sustainability Cloud, 252
environmental reporting initiatives, 247–48
executive decision-making for, 250
exhibits for, 252–54
Greenhouse Gas Protocol and, 247–48
implementation of sustainability, 250
rulemaking in, 249–50, 254
Science Based Targets Initiative and, 253–54
supply chain challenges, 252–54
system design for, 251–52
team-building for, 251–52
Salesforce Accountability Cloud, 252
Sampson, Kate, 218, 219, 221
Sarbanes-Oxley Act (SOX), U.S. (2002), 9, 24, 64–65, 66
Public Company Accounting Oversight Board, 64
Science Based Targets Initiative (SBTi), 237, 253–54
Scott, Kevin, 281
seafood industry, corporate standardization of, 29
SEC. *See* Securities and Exchange Commission (SEC), in U.S.
Securities Act of 1933, U.S., 12, 81
disclosure mechanisms under, 163–64, 183–84
New York Stock Exchange and, 183–84
Securities and Exchange Commission (SEC), in U.S., 87
Securities Exchange Act of 1934, U.S., 81, 184
securities law, securities disclosure and, 80–85
disclosures frameworks in
greenwashing, 83
for social disclosures, 84–85
vague, 82
washing and, 83
in EU, 83–84
flexibility paradox of, 84–85
future approaches and frameworks for, 85
legal regimes for, 81
materiality doctrine in, 81–82
circularity of, 82
social accountability issues and, 81
sustainability reporting under, 84–85
security issues, at Microsoft, 280
self-regulation mechanisms, in corporations, 131–41. *See* self-regulation mechanisms, in corporations
American Bar Association and, 186
analysis of, 157–59
Australian Securities Exchange, 186
under canon law, 133
for compliance systems, 138–39
conceptual approach to, 132–33
constitutional order of, 133–34
federalism and, 133–34
corporate culture and, 138–39
corporate law and, 140–41
corporate ordering and, 133–34, 148–51
CEO policy agendas and, 153
implementation of legislative mandates, 136–40
implementation of regulatory mandates, 136–40
lobbying and, 139–40
for derivatives markets, 135–36
dynamics of, 134–36
financial crisis of 2007 influenced by, 135–36
Financial Industry Regulatory Authority, 186
fragmentation of, 155–56
gaps in, 135
industry bodies for, 185–88
independent, 187
self-regulatory organizations, 186
lobbying and, 139–40, 189
National Association of Securities Dealers, 186
NYSE Regulation, Inc., 186
origins of, 135
political influences on, 132
resource constraints as influence on, 132
standardization and standard-setting in, 185–88
capital adequacy standards, 136
design standards, 137–38
for due diligence standards, 136
independent organizations for, 187
International Organization for Standardization, 187
performance standards, 137–38
by self-regulating organizations, 186
self-regulatory organizations (SROs), 186
Sensitive Uses review process, at Microsoft, 286–87
sexual assault policies
in rideshare industries, 192
Uber and, 203–4
taxonomy of sexual violence, 204–5
Shapiro, Robert, 228–29
shareholder activism, 78–80
shareholder proposals. *See* corporate law

shareholders
corporate ordering
heterogeneous shareholder preferences, 4–5
primacy doctrine for, 5
disclosure mechanisms and, 163–64
executive actions and, 116–17, 126
for Meta, 1
primacy doctrine for, 5
renegotiation of standardized practices by
shareholder activism in, 37, 38–39
shareholder constraints for, 36
for UnitedHealthcare, 2
shipping industry, corporate standardization of, 30
Shlensky v. Wrigley, 59
Simeone v. Disney, 60, 67, 91
Smith, Brad, 281, 285
Smith v. Van Gorkom, 62–63, 307
social considerations, of corporations. *See also* efficiency at scale, for corporations; information age, corporations during
abstention from, 22–24
business strategies as factor in, 23
core business models as factor for, 23
profit maximization as factor in, 25
for Amazon, 20
analysis of, 52–54
in Asia, 22
business decisions linked with, 21–25
conceptual approach to, 19–21
data traps, 20
for ExxonMobil, 20
for Facebook, 20
forced transparency and, 20
heterogeneous shareholder preferences and, 20–21
intensification of, 21
international boycott movements, 22
for Meta, 20
public influence of, 19
stakeholder capitalism and, 21–22
for UnitedHealthcare, 20
social impact investing, 47–48, 49–50
alternative assets in, 50
in EU, 50
expansion and growth of, 49–50
Global Impact Investing Network, 49
historical development of, 49
UN Sustainable Development Goals, 49
social media
corporate information collection through, 42
information age and, 46–47
UnitedHealthcare in, 1–2
social washing, 111
software engineering, artificial intelligence and, 14
SOX. *See* Sarbanes-Oxley Act (SOX), U.S. (2002)
specialized AI, 264–68
speed imperatives
for AI governance, 260–61, 290–97
deregulation as tool in, 291
legislative tools in, 290–93
subsidization approaches, 291–93
Winning the Race policy, 292–93
for OpenAI, 262–64
SROs. *See* self-regulatory organizations (SROs)
stakeholder capitalism, 21–22
stakeholder theory, corporate ordering and, 6
stakeholder washing, 83
stakeholders
access to information for, 44–46
in automobile industry, 170
corporate ordering and, 143
washing, 83
standardization and uniformity. *See also* efficiency at scale, for corporations
in AI governance, 258
in corporate self-regulation mechanisms, 185–88
capital adequacy standards, 136
design standards, 137–38
due diligence standards, 136
by independent bodies, 187
International Organization for Standardization, 187
performance standards, 137–38
by self-regulating organizations, 186
through deliberative practices, 302–3
standards of review, in fiduciary duty obligations, 313–15
breaches of, 314
deficient processes in, 315
for social risks, 314–15
structural failures, 314–15
Starbucks, corporate rules for, 108–9
state pension funds, anti-ESG movements and, 4
State Street, 48–49
stewardship imperative
in AI governance, 258–61, 290–97
at OpenAI, 261–62
systematic stewardship, 48
Stone v. Ritter, 70, 307–8
strategic decision-making. *See* executive action, decision-making and
Su, Shengyuan, 251
supply chain management systems, 2–3
Salesforce, 252–54
sustainability, corporate frameworks for. *See also* Greenhouse Gas Protocol (GGP); Salesforce, sustainability frameworks at

analysis of, 255–56
British Petroleum, 227–29
for climate change
Carbon Disclosure Project, 225, 246
Greenhouse Gas Protocol, 224–25
intra-corporate divisions on, 227–29
conceptual approach to, 224–26
corporate ordering and, 225
Corporate Sustainability Reporting Directive, 50, 51–52, 84, 237–38, 239
disclosure and, 353
ESG movement and, 224
General Motors, 228
Global Climate Coalition and, 227–28
heterogeneity of preferences in, 226–32
evolution of, 232–34
GHG Protocol, 232–45
private approaches to, 227–29
implementation approaches to, 245–54
Intergovernmental Panel on Climate Change, 227
monitoring mechanisms for, 245–54
Monsanto, 228–29
NGOs and, 235
political backlash to, 224–25
with renewable energy, 231–32
rulemaking for, 232–33, 245–54
Salesforce, 245–54
U.S. oil companies and, 229–31
Chevron, 229–31
ExxonMobil, 229–31
volatility of energy landscape, 231–32
World Business Council for Sustainable Development, 235–36
World Resources Institute, 224–25, 233, 234–36
sustainability reporting
ESG movement and, 87
in EU, 5
in securities law, 84–85
sustainability washing, 111
Sustainable Finance Disclosure Regulation, in EU, 50
Sutskever, Ilya, 261–62
Sverchek, Kristin, 218
system cards, OpenAI and, 275
system feedback, corporate ordering and, 9–10
systematic stewardship, 48

Target, 19
information collection by, 42
TaskRabbit, 193, 194
Taxonomy Regulation, in EU, 50
team-building, at Salesforce, 251–52
technology sector. *See also* digital technologies, efficiency at scale for
corporate standardization of, 30
monitoring functions in, 123
Tesla, 19
efficiency at scale for, 28–29
information age and, 43–44
Thomas, Philip, 178
Thompson, Brian, 1–2
TikTok, 27–28
TNCs. *See* transportation network companies (TNCs)
Toner, Helen, 261–62, 276
traditional investors, 2
transgender influencers, 19
transparency, in corporate governance
AlphaFold, 267–68
with disclosure mechanisms, 175
at Microsoft, 280
social considerations and, 20
transformation of corporations through, 25
at Uber, 203–4
transportation network companies (TNCs), 220
state legislation for, 220–21
transportation networks, rideshare safety and, 14
tripartite distinction of corporate functions, 98–101
as analytical tool, 99–100
for executive functions, 99, 101
mapping of, 100–1
for monitoring functions, 99–100
in regulatory regimes, 131
for review functions, 101
in rideshare companies, 191, 221
rideshare industry and, 191
for rulemaking functions, 100
Trump, Donald, 87, 152
AI governance under, 290–93
trust frameworks
in gig economy, 192–93
public trust in Lyft, 222
in rideshare companies, 194
Uber and, 194
TSC Industries v. Northway, 81
Tudorache, Dragoș, 293–94
Twitter. *See* X (Twitter)

Uber, 42. *See also* Kalanick, Travis
consumer boycotts of, 34–35
corporate ordering and, 160, 211–12
CPUC oversight and, 207–9
early demands in, 210–11
in safety report, 209–15
settlements as result of, 213

Uber (cont.)
deliberative practices at, 299
disclosure mechanisms, in safety reports, 202–4, 207–9
growth imperative for, 196–97
leadership changes as influence on, 199–200
limitations of, 198–99
heterogeneity of preferences and, 196–201
incentive structures within, 222–23
in India, 198
insurance and, 220
IPO imperatives and, 199–200
investor preferences, 199
as new transportation paradigm, 194
organizational culture of, 196
safety framework and reports on, 201–15
accuracy in, 205–7
advocacy group support for, 213
CPUC oversight and, 207–15
disclosure mechanisms as part of, 202–4, 207–9
dispute settlements, 213
fines as result of, 212–13
goals of, 202–4
government enforcement of, 211–12
limitations of, 213–15
monitoring foundations in, 205–7
motivation of, 202–4
National Sexual Violence Resource Center, 204
outcomes and lessons from, 213–15
procedural safeguards, 212
Rape, Abuse, & Incest National Network, 204, 210, 213, 383
reliability of, 205–7
rulemaking as part of, 204–5
safety crises, 198–99
scope of, 201–2
on sexual assault, 203–4
suspension threats, 212–13
taxonomy of sexual violence in, 204–5
transparency in, 203–4
trust barriers for, 194
venture capital framework for, 196–97
UN. *See* United Nations (UN), Sustainable Development Goals
Uniform Vehicle Code, 170, 171
Unilever, 52
United Airlines, 45
United Nations (UN), Sustainable Development Goals, 49
United States (U.S.). *See also* New York Stock Exchange (NYSE); *specific topics*
Dodd-Frank Act, 24
economic boycotts in, 22
efficiency at scale for corporations in, 28
Environmental Protection Agency, 249–50
globalization of capital in, 50
international boycott movements against American corporations, 22
National Association of Manufacturers, 176, 389
National Institute of Standards and Technology, 291
Office of Science and Technology Policy, 291
Sarbanes-Oxley Act, 9, 24, 64–65, 66
Public Accounting Oversight Board, 64
Securities Act of 1933, 12, 81
disclosure mechanisms under, 163–64, 183–84
Securities Exchange Act of 1934, 81, 184
sustainability initiatives for oil companies, 229–31
Chevron, 229–31
ExxonMobil, 229–31
UnitedHealthcare, 1–2
algorithms for, 2
healthcare access determinations, 3
social impacts of, 20
shareholders for, 2
universal owners, 48
universal proxy card rule, 78
urban transportation policies, 165–66
horse-drawn vehicles and, 165
lack of regulatory infrastructure in, 165–67
mass transit systems, 166–67
U.S. *See* United States (U.S.)
U.S. Steel, 179–80

value alignment, in AI governance, 275–76
value as business imperative, 277–78
Vanguard, 48–49
venture capital frameworks, for Uber, 196–97
Vietnam, efficiency at scale for corporations in, 29
voice mechanisms, in renegotiation of standardized practices, 37–39

washing
DEI, 83, 111
ethics, 83
greenwashing, 111
social, 111
stakeholder, 83
sustainability, 111
WBCSD. *See* World Business Council for Sustainable Development (WBCSD)
Weinberger v. UOP, 65

West, Tony, 203–4, 211, 212
Winning the Race policy, in AI governance, 292–93
Wirth, Mike, 231
"woke capitalism," 87
Woods, Darren, 78
Woodville, William, 178–79
worker movement, disclosure mechanisms and, 175–76
workplace monitoring technologies, 2–3
World Business Council for Sustainable Development (WBCSD), 235–36
World Economic Forum, 49
World Resources Institute (WRI), 224–36
WorldCom scandal, 9, 64
WRI. *See* World Resources Institute (WRI)

X (Twitter), 151–52

Zuckerberg, Mark, 41, 55, 196

For EU product safety concerns, contact us at Calle de José Abascal, 56–1°,
28003 Madrid, Spain or eugpsr@cambridge.org.

www.ingramcontent.com/pod-product-compliance
Lightning Source LLC
LaVergne TN
LVHW010615190926
848399LV00034B/321
9781009873734